Jefferson the Virginian

JEFFERSON AND HIS TIME

VOLUME ONE

Jefferson
the Virginian

BY DUMAS MALONE

Boston

LITTLE, BROWN AND COMPANY

Fifth Printing

BP

*Published simultaneously
in Canada by McClelland and Stewart Limited*

PRINTED IN THE UNITED STATES OF AMERICA

Introduction

ABOUT twenty years ago I promised myself that I would write a big book about Thomas Jefferson someday. I was teaching history at the University of Virginia, which he founded, and any time that I wanted to I could look up and see Monticello in the dim distance. In the community they continued to repeat a remark of a discerning Ex-President of the United States who had once lectured there. In that place, said William Howard Taft, they still talked of Mr. Jefferson as though he were in the next room. He was there, unquestionably, whether or not any of us really understood what he was saying; and in youthful presumptuousness I flattered myself that sometime I would fully comprehend and encompass him. I do not claim that I have yet done so, and I do not believe that I or any other single person ever can. Nobody can live Jefferson's long and eventful life all over again, and nobody in our age is likely to match his universality.

I have not devoted all these intervening years to him. Until his two hundredth anniversary in 1943, my longest period of concentrated attention was about six months; otherwise I worked on him only as occasion offered, and occasion offered considerably less time than I had expected. My total labors added up to a good many months but they suffered from the fact that they were discontinuous. I wrote a few things about him, but others wrote more, and my small contributions now seem hardly worth mentioning. Since 1943 I have been able to give most of my time to him, under circumstances which call for grateful acknowledgment elsewhere. As a result, here is a volume covering the first major period of his life. Another, covering a second period, is just behind it, and, God willing, there will eventually be two more after these. I have entitled the work as a whole *Jefferson and His Time*, and am venturing to call it a comprehensive biography, hoping that it will seem reasonably commensurate with the achievements and the stature of the man.

There can be no possible question that Jefferson deserves extended and careful treatment. The memorial in Washington which was dedicated on his two hundredth anniversary is tangible evidence of his recognized membership in the trinity of American immortals, along with

George Washington and Abraham Lincoln. Others may deserve to stand beside them, but the supreme eminence of these three is practically unchallenged at the present time. Washington is the major symbol of the independent Republic itself, Lincoln of the preserved Union, but Jefferson surpassed both of them in the rich diversity of his achievements. No historic American, except possibly Benjamin Franklin, played so notable a part in so many important fields of activity and thought: government, law, religion, education, agriculture, architecture, science, philosophy. Jefferson did not have Franklin's spicy wit and does not offer quite such delightful companionship, but it is doubtful if any other public man in all our annals is equally interesting to so many sorts of minds. He was never regarded as the first citizen of the world, as Woodrow Wilson indubitably was for a brief time, but after the passing of Franklin and Washington no American of his period matched him in international reputation; and as a major apostle of individual freedom and human dignity he has long belonged, not merely to his own compatriots, but to the human race.

His fame is probably greater in our generation than it has been at any other time since his death. In this country, it was dimmed toward the middle of the nineteenth century, when slaveholders tended to deride his sayings about human equality and Unionists to deplore his emphasis on State rights. It is ironic that the most extensive account of him appeared at that time. The massive three-volume *Life* by Henry S. Randall was issued shortly before the Civil War. Jefferson's reputation has grown enormously since then, especially in the years since the First World War. In the very recent past, when totalitarianism threatened to engulf the world, men's minds inevitably turned back to this foe of every kind of tyranny. Much has been written about him lately, but no biography has yet matched Randall's in scope and impressiveness.

The explanation is not to be found in lack of interest but, I believe, in the recognized complexity of the subject and the difficulty of exploring the vast materials. Jefferson's public career is inextricably entwined with the history of an entire era, and his diverse interests are bewildering to the minds of our age, which are universal in the aggregate but highly specialized in individuals. The body of materials relating to his life and times is immense. No one has yet exploited the whole of it, and quite obviously no single person ever can. Jefferson's career is still a challenge to the investigator as well as to the interpreter.

Previous research has hardly made the task of the biographer easy, but numerous developments in recent years have made it less difficult. Without going into details at this point I can say, and it would be most unjust and ungrateful in me not to say, that many scholars have surveyed portions of this vast field, and that many writers have illuminated various aspects of Jefferson's genius and particular periods of his long and active life. Some of these studies are classics of their kind. I certainly intend no reflection on them when I say that they leave some gaps, and that they need to be supplemented, assessed, and integrated — in order that a larger synthesis shall result.

In our generation, also, notable progress has been made in organizing the various manuscript collections bearing on Jefferson. His own papers were divided and some of them were widely scattered after Randall's day, and they have never been reassembled in a single place. But new and better guides and indexes have been prepared, and, while film and photostat have not relieved the investigator of the necessity of very great labor, they do enable him to go faster and farther than before.

Thus the times — and the co-operation, conscious or unconscious, of a large number of people — make it possible to write a fuller story about Jefferson than has previously been told. Any biographical or historical work must be described in relative terms. Although I have termed this one comprehensive, I do not make the presumptuous claim that it is final, or the absurd one that it is complete. Others will interpret the same man and the same events differently; this is practically inevitable, since he was a central figure in historic controversies which are still echoing. A great deal more will be said about him after I am done. An edition of his papers is now being prepared under the skillful direction of Julian P. Boyd, and this will be published in upwards of fifty volumes (by the Princeton University Press). This magnificent collection has been a great boon to me, and I take comfort in the thought that anyone who wants to fill the inevitable gaps in my narrative can have recourse to it later on. My biography contains a great many facts (too many, some may think), and I hope it can be consulted with confidence, but my purpose has not been to compile a book of reference.

This first of my four projected volumes, which I am calling *Jefferson the Virginian*, covers almost half of his life by chronological measurement. The forty-one years (1743–1784) ending with his departure for France after the death of his wife and the close of the American Revolution mark a clearly defined period in his private and public life. No other volume will cover so many years, although the second (1784–1801) takes in more territory. In the second period he went on a mission to France, criticized European civilization and enjoyed European culture, returned to America, became Secretary of State, battled against Hamilton, retired to Monticello, became the acknowledged leader of a party, ran second to John Adams and became Vice President, and was finally elected President himself. This time, roughly that of the French Revolution, was the most agitated and on the whole probably the most unhappy of his incessantly active and generally happy life. The third volume (1801–1809) will cover his presidency. The fourth (1809–1826) will carry him through his years of retirement, and in intellectual and spiritual content it should be the richest of them all. I shall refer to Jefferson's more important intellectual, literary, and artistic activities at appropriate points in this story, but I cannot sum them up until the evidence is all in. Since many loose strings must be left dangling, I hope it will be remembered that I intend to tie them up at the end.

My major purposes for the work are that it shall be comprehensive, that it shall relate Jefferson's career to his age, and that it shall be true to his own chronology. As a result it will be long, it will be historical (it can hardly be anything else), and it will be primarily a narrative.

By "comprehensive" I mean something more than the desire to comprehend the labors of other scholars. I have sought to see the whole of a many-sided man. This is no special brand of biography — political or intellectual or anything else. It was chiefly as a public official that Jefferson became eminent, but he was philosophical in spirit, avid in scientific curiosity, deeply concerned with freeing the minds and enriching the lives of men. He was all this before he became publicly conspicuous, and no part of the early story is more important than the development of his mind and personal interests. Although I shall have to postpone final consideration of various intellectual and artistic matters, I have tried to see the man in just proportions at each successive stage.

It is as important to understand the historical circumstances which surrounded and affected Jefferson as it is to ascertain the part he himself played in movements and events. The two tasks are inseparable, but the latter is so exacting in itself that any biographer is likely to neglect the former. I have tried to acquaint myself with Jefferson's major contemporaries, to become aware of the changing climates of opinion in his long age, to be cognizant not only of the shifting states of politics and economics, but also of science, philosophy, and the arts. All this must be regarded as the expression of an ideal, for I do not flatter myself that I can fill this large order.

By keeping this account of Jefferson "true to his own chronology" I mean that I have not viewed him as a static personality like a portrait on the wall, but as a living, growing, changing man — always the same person but never quite the same. Since there was a distinct core of consistency in his thought, many of the changes are more apparent than real and can be largely explained in terms of varying circumstances. One of the advantages of a strict regard for chronology is that the major features of his mind and character can be observed before their outlines were obscured by political controversy. It is easier to reach a confident opinion about the sort of man he was in 1776 than to do so for 1793 or 1800. In my opinion, he did not change fundamentally, but unquestionably there were differences in expression, and these have seemed to some observers to amount to contradictions. If he was notably constant in his pursuit of major ends, he was flexible about minor ones and became more so as he proceeded. To some discerning observers he has seemed an elusive personality. Henry Adams posed the problem better than anybody else has done when he said that "Jefferson could be painted only touch by touch, with a fine pencil, and the perfection of the likeness depended upon the shifting and uncertain flicker of its semi-transparent shadows." [1] It has seemed to me that the only way to catch the real likeness of the man is to watch his picture grow until it assumes its essential outline, and then to watch it change, as time and circumstance employ a fine pencil. He loses none of his fascination but he does lose much of his elusiveness when one follows him through life the way he himself went through it, that is, chronologically.

In this volume we follow him through forty-one years. During more than half of that time he was growing up, going to school, reading law, fitting himself for his inherited station as a leading planter of the Province of Virginia. Then he practised his profession while acquiring further legal learning, performed the public duties which went with his position in society, began to build a famous house, made a happy and advantageous marriage, and started a family. He was at the height of his private fortune and personal happiness in his early thirties when the storm of the American Revolution gathered and broke; and, being a Patriot by conviction, he devoted himself largely though not wholly to public tasks for the next ten years. Disregarding the first thirty years for the moment, I will comment briefly on the nature of the services which really started him on the road to historical immortality.

The American Revolution precipitated his public genius, and the most important external fact to which his early career must be related is the fact of war. This was not a brilliant or swift-moving conflict; it was a slow and tedious struggle, demanding infinite faith and patience from the small group of leaders who carried it through. Jefferson believed that he was sharing in cosmic events in this era, and in the perspective of history he undoubtedly was. Besides starting the Republic on its independent course, the war ushered in an age of revolution which affected the whole of the western world and which did not end until

[1] *History of the United States,* I (1889), 277.

Jefferson himself had grown old. The sort of faith it called for he had in rare measure, and maintained afterwards more persistently than almost any other leader. This in itself is a supremely important historical fact. With a few very conspicuous exceptions, however, his activities did not strike his contemporaries as epoch-making or deeply stirring. During his governorship of Virginia toward the end of the war circumstances could hardly have failed to make him inglorious; and practically all the rest of his services were performed as a legislator — in the House of Burgesses and House of Delegates of Virginia and in the Continental Congress — sitting on endless committees and doing a vast amount of paper work. It was not as a commander like Washington, nor as a fiery orator like Patrick Henry, that he gained his chief title to fame — it was as the draftsman of state papers and legislative bills and legal statutes. He rarely had a continental audience, and only the passage of slow time could reveal the full significance of proposals rejected when he made them, and of words more famous now than they were then.

Jefferson himself thought his authorship of the Declaration of Independence and the Virginia Statute for Religious Freedom more deserving of remembrance than his presidency of the United States. He became much more conspicuous after the American Revolution than he ever was during it, but his services to his fellow men never again squared quite so well with his fundamental principles, and on the whole those principles have fared well at the hands of time. If the essence of his greatness lies in the fact that he applied to the shifting problems of his age an enlightened and humane philosophy, there was no other period when his purposes shone forth with the same purity, or the fundamentals of his philosophy seemed so clear. Other periods of his life may seem more eventful, but only in retirement does he again reveal such a high degree of philosophical detachment. The clue to his purposes must be sought in his own mind; and that developed in no vacuum, but in a particular place at a definite time. If we would genuinely understand him and his career, therefore, we must view him first at home.

Source materials for Jefferson's boyhood, youth, and young manhood are scanty. They begin to be abundant when he became governor of Virginia at the age of thirty-six, and they become progressively richer as the years go by. Though the sources are most meager for the years before he was thirty, I have managed to uncover some fresh details of fact about this difficult period, and I am sorely tempted to list them. However, this would be to exaggerate their significance, and

I rest content with the hope that the early story will seem somewhat fuller and truer as the result of these relatively unrewarding labors. The important task at the beginning is to put the young man properly in his setting of place and time, and to point out his distinctiveness in comparison with his contemporaries. Jefferson's relations with Virginia and Virginians are traced at considerable length in a number of chapters in this book; but, since the treatment is generally chronological and may seem at places to move forward by inches, it seems desirable at this point to summarize some of the general conclusions I have reached.

During the American Revolution, when Jefferson said "my country" he meant Virginia. He was not unique in this respect, and the expression in itself implies no exaggerated emphasis on the state as a unit of government. During this period, actually, he was notable among his countrymen for his devotion to the cause of the feeble Union. But he was a Virginian before he became anything else, and he never ceased to be one. He was deeply rooted in that soil. Ancestors of his had lived in the Colony for at least three generations before him; he received the whole of his formal education there; and until he was forty he had spent scarcely a year outside of the borders of the Province and State. His own "country" was almost the only scene of his activity until he had entered into middle life, and if he did not know more about it than anybody else he described it in his *Notes on Virginia* far more fully than anyone else had ever done.

He was by no means uncritical of Virginia during the American Revolution, however, and at various times he sharply condemned certain aspects of its "aristocracy." These comments and some of his own later actions have led many writers to draw a sharp contrast between the man and his environment. To many people it has seemed paradoxical that a famous advocate of human liberty and a patron saint of democracy should have arisen from a society which was based on slavery and was aristocratic in its tone. In the effort to resolve the seeming paradox some writers have taken the position, in effect, that he was an alien in this society from the time that he began to think. Some have gone back even further, accepting far too readily traditions about his father's origins which must now be modified, and attributing his democracy vaguely to the influence of the frontier, which for some inexplicable reason did not have a similar effect on John Marshall. The chief faults of this school of thinking are the tendency to read back into one period the issues of another, the failure to allow sufficiently for the development of Jefferson's own ideas, and an imperfect understanding, not merely of his personal background, but also of the society of Virginia before the American Revolution.

Certain writers, on the other hand, have gone to such pains to demonstrate the high social position of Jefferson's ancestors, and have so emphasized the refinement of his own tastes, as to imply that, except for his greater intellectual and artistic interests, there was little real difference between him and his "aristocratic" fellows during this early period. In my own opinion, the main personal difference between him and the best of them was one of degree. I am not disposed to elevate him by depressing them; my association in spirit with the leaders of the Province of Virginia before the Revolution has given me too much respect for them for that.[2] But one should not beg the question of his fundamental political attitude, or give the impression that he was primarily a fine gentleman who was incidentally concerned with the advancement of mankind and who in his own person was something of a snob. He never ceased to prefer the companionship of superior minds and to prize good manners, but broad social sympathy was basic in his life. He was born to a privileged position, but from the beginning of his important public career he opposed all the artificialities of aristocracy. Only in the sense that he believed that society should be governed by those who are really the best qualified can he possibly be regarded as a political aristocrat, and it did not take him long to discover that native ability and high character are the sole possession of no class.

In my opinion, however, Jefferson was not violently at war with the dominant forces in his local environment at this or any other time. There was no need for such an optimist to be in a hurry. He was confident that time was fighting for his ideas, and that human progress was certain, if only tyranny and artificial obstructions were removed. In the course of the Revolution he effected certain fundamental reforms in land-tenure, but these long-range proposals were not strongly combatted by the conservatives. He advocated colonial self-government from the beginning, but many other landholders were equally radical in this respect. He was considerably in advance of dominant opinion in his desire to broaden the base of representation, but this in itself did not make him a modern democrat.

If he must be given a single designation, he was a liberal. Liberty was his chief concern, and his major emphasis was on the freedom of the spirit and the mind. Of all his Revolutionary measures in Virginia the ones he cherished most were his statute for religious freedom, which

<hr />

[2] I have summed this matter up in an article entitled "The Great Generation," *Virginia Quarterly Review*, winter 1947, pp. 108–122.

he coupled with entire intellectual freedom, and his unsuccessful bills for the wider diffusion of knowledge by means of public education. This cultivated gentleman, who always indulged his scientific, literary, and esthetic tastes, was a lifelong advocate of liberty for all, and of education for all in proportion to their merit. To call him an enlightened liberal is the best way to sum him up in the first stage of his great career, and to set him in his native society and the thought currents of his time.

His distinctiveness does not lie in the fact that he roundly condemned the society in which he occupied an assured position, for in the early stages of his career he did not do that. He was distinctive because he combined within himself the highest virtues of his native society (excepting the military), while escaping its chief vices. From the beginning he showed the strong sense of public responsibility which was so characteristic of his social order, and he had the largeness of view which was so generally found among the leading Virginians. He gladly emulated the good manners of these gentlemen, but their alleged indolence and their historic love of gaming did not appear in his character or conduct.

Intellectually he exemplified more conspicuously than any of his fellows the liberal and humane spirit, the incessant scientific curiosity and zeal for universal knowledge, and the fundamental belief in the powers of human intelligence which characterized what historians call the Enlightenment. He must be described as a Virginian, and anyone should have been proud to be one, in the greatest age of the Province and State; but he has a further distinction. After Benjamin Franklin he may be regarded as the fullest American embodiment of the ideals of the Enlightenment. Both in his intellectual and his public life he represented them in action. This he did not merely in the years of the American Revolution, when the climate of ideas was favorable, but also in the more conservative period which followed. Then, as we shall see in the second volume of this work, the reaction became so great that he was thrown on the defensive. Perhaps it is even more to his credit that he defended enlightened liberalism when it was derided in high places than that he exemplified it when it was fashionable. His personal opinions were subject to change, and his policies must be described in relative terms. To him, however, freedom of the mind was an absolute.

Throughout his public career he was a statesman as well as a thinker, and, since he may not qualify as a philosopher on technical grounds, he can be most safely described as a philosophical statesman. It is quite common, however, for people who do not like him to refer to him as a "politician" — implying that he was skillful in partisan maneuver, gifted as an organizer, and a master of the art of winning votes. In the Revolutionary era, however, he had no particular reputation for political skill in this modern sense. Until he returned from France and faced Hamilton in Washington's official family he thought of himself, and was regarded by others, as a personally disinterested public man whose prime concern was the promotion of the public good and who made a special point of avoiding factious quarrels. Anyone who doubts this is referred to the story of his unfolding career, based on contemporary records, as told in this and the following volume.

During the period of the American Revolution Jefferson did not have to exert himself much as a candidate for office. His first election, to the Virginia House of Burgesses at the age of twenty-five, was probably engineered by his elders, who had matters well in hand; and his various reëlections to the local legislature were effected as a matter of course, generally if not always without any real contest. Personal influences were doubtless exercised in his behalf before he went to the Continental Congress, but he regarded service in that body more as an obligation than a privilege. Presumably he was elected governor of Virginia by the "progressives" in the Assembly, but the grouping was very loose, and contemporary comments do not show that he was the head or even the lieutenant of what could properly be called an organization. If he ever wanted the office, which is doubtful, he certainly ceased doing so within a very few weeks.

Throughout this entire period Jefferson's political strength lay in his many friendships among the leaders of all shades of opinion, the vigor and definiteness of his ideas, and his reputation as a disinterested and patriotic public servant. Despite the traditional opinion, the disasters which befell him as governor (which are dealt with in considerable detail in this volume) impaired his local standing for only a very short time, and had little or nothing to do with the alleged decline in the spirit of liberalism in the State. Before he had been formally vindicated he received an election to Congress which he duly declined, and it was wholly his own choosing that he did not return to public life sooner than he actually did. His fellows were more than anxious to do him honor. It would be difficult to prove that he ever exerted himself to secure any political office during this period, though he was pleased with his appointment to France; and if he had inordinate personal ambitions, as Hamilton afterwards asserted, he was remarkably successful in concealing them from his Revolutionary contemporaries. He unquestionably valued and probably craved public honors, as he craved human affection, but the sensitiveness of his nature caused him to abhor controversy, and to avoid any that did not center in an important idea. This is not the sort of stuff out of which partisan leaders are generally made.

In his young manhood he was of a type with the greatest Virginians of the era, relatively few of whom were politicians in the narrow sense. He assumed responsibilities by virtue of his position and abilities and thought of himself as engaged in the conduct of public affairs, just as George Washington, George Mason, and George Wythe did. His contemporaries would have been exceedingly surprised to hear the prophecy that he would be heralded in future years as one of the greatest party leaders ever to appear in the United States. They would not have thought of him as an idol of the masses, and this shy and highly intellectual gentleman might never have got started in politics had he begun his career in a more democratic age.

During the Revolution, however, he revealed his unusual power of political expression and gradually became — unconsciously, I believe — a symbol of ideas which inspired hope among the inarticulate as well as the enlightened. Others besides him believed that all men were born free, but it was he who phrased the Declaration of Independence. There were other liberals among the privileged landholders, but it was he who advocated the abolition of entail and primogeniture, who wanted to extend the suffrage and make representation more equitable, and who sought vainly to bring some education within the reach of every child. He was not the only Virginian who had a clear vision of the promise of the vast interior of this continent, but before he left for Paris he drew an ordinance which anticipated the great charter of the West. Before he was widely proclaimed as a great statesman he had showed himself to be a great prophet, and time was fighting for him as he was sure it would for his ideas.

The leaders all knew that he was a devoted and effective public servant. At times he may have seemed remote, but they also knew him as an amiable man and a loyal friend. His sensitiveness to criticism was recognized by some as a weakness, but, since it was accompanied by a sensitiveness to the feelings of others, it was an asset in any private circle and it had certain political uses. It led him to be tolerant of minor differences, and, although it may not have fitted him to be a commander in a crisis, it made him a sympathetic leader of kindred spirits. His industry no one could question. Though he was not personally aggressive and did not become a field soldier, he was a man of notable vigor among the Patriots and there was no reason to doubt his courage. Not until much later did his political foes question that. His Revolutionary contemporaries could hardly have failed to detect some flaws in his character, for he was not impeccable, but they regarded him as a good man — and he now appears a little too good, if anything.

There are gleams of dry humor in some of his communications as governor, but he had not learned to banter as pleasantly as he did after he went to France, and he does not appear to have told many "tall tales" as yet. Even in intimate personal letters he used stilted language — though that bothered nobody then; it was in the manner of the time. If it was almost impossible for him to be familiar, he was exceedingly domestic, concentrating on his little family an intensity of devotion which is unusual among men. In his rural society it was natural to center interests and activities in the home, which was also the heart of the plantation village, but this was specially true of him. He was uniformly generous in financial matters, solicitous of his mother while she lived, and always of his brother and sisters. He had already begun to be a collector of books and a patron of promising young men. He cultivated as best he could the arts and sciences, laid long-range plans for the advancement of society, and, even after he had suffered undeserved disasters as governor and had lost his wife, believed that goodness lay at the heart of things. Part of his inveterate optimism was owing to physical causes. He was strong and, except for periodic headaches, very healthy; his admirable digestion helped him attain the serenity he sought. He had no desire to be the master of others but he applied the most rigorous discipline to himself. That in itself must have made him seem rather formidable as a human being. He was a hard man to know intimately, and still is, but it must have seemed a privilege to know him then, as it does now.

For the privilege of living with him in his age and becoming as well acquainted with him as I have, I am indebted to many persons and institutions. Acknowledgments of special services in connection with this volume are made in a later section, but I cannot fail to say here that it never could have been prepared without the full co-operation of the University of Virginia and the generous financial support of the Rockefeller Foundation.

DUMAS MALONE

New York

Contents

The Heritage of a Virginian

[I]

Jeffersons and Randolphs

1679–1745

THOMAS JEFFERSON was born in a simple wooden house in what is now Albemarle County, Virginia. At that time the district was in the County of Goochland, and Virginia was a province of King George II of Great Britain. By the calendar then in effect the birthday was April 2, 1743, but according to the New Style, which was adopted when Jefferson was still a boy, it was April 13, and thus it has been celebrated through the years. This was a delicious season, for the air of the Virginia Piedmont is soft in April, the dogwood soon opens in the woods, and the wild honeysuckle begins to bloom. The house has long since vanished, but the site is marked and anybody who goes there now can see that it was well chosen. To the southward it overlooks the Rivanna River, often referred to then as the North River or North Branch of the James. This is now a muddy and unimpressive stream but it once was purer. The prospect to the west is finer, for on any clear day the distant Blue Ridge can be seen through a gap in the Southwest Mountains.

The place was called Shadwell. Peter Jefferson, who owned it, had named it for the parish in London where his wife, Jane Randolph, had been christened twenty-three years before. The setting did not suggest the Thames Basin or Hanoverian England, however. This was not a rainy but generally a sunny land, and it had no antiquity or mellowness, for as a seat of settlement it was almost wholly new. The hardwood forests which covered the bottom lands and steep hillsides were broken by only a few clearings where the red soil glowed, and the first wails of this newborn infant could have been echoed by the howling of the wolves. The earliest surroundings of this natural philosopher were beautiful but they were wild. Jefferson was born on the fringe of western settlement, and some will say that he thus became a child of the American frontier.

No influence upon him was more abiding than that of Nature, and throughout life he deeply loved this region of wooded hills and lavender-tinted mountains. But Shadwell was not the home of his earliest memories. When he was two or three years old he was taken from it to Tuckahoe on the James, to an older and better house in a more thickly settled district. At that time no parts of Virginia were thickly settled; with a few exceptions the entire Province was a vast forest. Tobacco plantations and their seats were strung loosely along the rivers, but to all European observers the clearings seemed small and the country looked uninhabited. The vastness of this physical setting was not lost upon Thomas Jefferson; it was reflected in the largeness of his mind. Furthermore, this society as a whole was closer to the frontier than later generations might at first realize. But Jefferson was in Albemarle only intermittently during his boyhood, and he knew the region best after the fringe of settlement had stretched well beyond it. He was used to sparsely settled country, but he did not know the frontier by experience; and though he was always aware of the wilderness, he was not in the physical sense an explorer.

Peter Jefferson, a man of huge stature and legendary strength, was in his mid-thirties in 1743. He performed memorable deeds as a surveyor in uncharted country in later years, but at no time was he a typical frontiersman. He was not yet at the height of his fortunes, though he was a slaveowner and he had other lands below the James thirty miles or so to the southeast, where he had previously lived. He was no landless pioneer but an enterprising young planter who may have ventured a bit too far to the westward in this instance. He had been there several years, however; he had intended to stay; and he may already have planned the extensive group of plantation buildings he eventually erected. He built only a modest unit at first, and it was to this plain house that he had brought his wife and two little daughters the year before his third child and first son was born.[1] Jane Randolph may not have liked the extreme remoteness of Shadwell, and probably was glad that her first stay there was short.

The most important early fact about Thomas Jefferson is not that

[1] Fiske Kimball, "In Search of Jefferson's Birthplace," *Virginia Magazine of History and Biography* (cited hereafter as *Va. Mag.*), LI, 313–325 (Oct. 1943).

NOTE. Explanation of the abbreviations used in the footnotes and further details concerning the works referred to may be found in "Symbols and Short Titles" and "Select Critical Bibliography," following the Appendices.

he appeared on the edge of settlement but that he was born in the Province of Virginia and that, from his first days, he was numbered among its gentry. He was not born to physical hardship as Abraham Lincoln was; he did not know town life from boyhood as Benjamin Franklin did; in the ordinary meaning of the term he was no self-made man. He grew up in the generous society which had been created in a new country and a warm climate by a group of planters, cultivating tobacco and relying on slave labor. From his earliest memories his financial position was assured, and the best educational opportunities which the Colony afforded were later available to him. He gave chief thanks to his father for all this, and he himself would have made Peter Jefferson the dominant character in his early history. But this plantation society centered in families, and Thomas Jefferson's history necessarily begins as the story of a family — or rather of two families, and how they merged.

Jefferson's connections stood him in good stead while he was growing up and he always valued them on personal grounds, but he never spent much of his precious time on the remote subject of genealogy. As a young man he was not wholly indifferent to his ancestry, but in the ripeness of age he made light of it and there are a number of people now living who know more about it than he did. To him the degree of their interest would seem surprising, for he was more interested in the origins of laws and institutions than in the beginnings of any particular family, and he belonged to the school of thought which magnified the influence of environment and minimized heredity — too much, probably. The progenitor in whom he took greatest pride was his father, and this because of what Peter Jefferson did rather than what he inherited.

His father was a man of deeds, not words, but there is indication that this inarticulate squire set considerable store by family traditions. The naming of Shadwell showed that, although Jane Randolph may have made the original suggestion. Furthermore, he afterwards had a place on the Fluvanna River which he called Snowdon after a mountain in Wales near which the Jeffersons were supposed once to have lived.[2] Whether they ever did seems to be beyond the possibility of historical verification and the matter is of no real importance. If they were originally Welsh, they had become predominantly English after they had lived for several generations in Virginia.

Thomas Jefferson's own knowledge of his paternal ancestry went

[2] "Autobiography," in P. L. Ford, ed., *Writings of Thomas Jefferson* (hereafter cited as Ford), I, 1.

back only to his grandfather, after whom he was named. The line can be traced with certainty only one step further — to an obscure man whom we shall call Thomas Jefferson I for the purposes of this story. He was a farmer, naturally enough, and by the year 1679 he was living in Henrico County (which was then much larger than it now is), considerably below the present location of Richmond.[3] He was in the Curls region — so called because of the eccentricities of the James River, which in one stretch of six miles managed to meander through sixteen. This was in the low and level Tidewater country, overspread with heavy forests and flowering shrubs, where practically all of the Virginians then were.

As far to the west as settlers dared go lived an exceedingly enterprising man named William Byrd. From the falls of the James he dispatched traders into the Carolinas to barter with the Indians.[4] In 1682 Thomas Jefferson I, who himself had moved farther westward, had a small business transaction with this magnate. He bought from him a "parcel" of land, consisting of about one hundred and sixty-seven acres. Technically he was then a squatter on this very piece of property, though the presumption is that nobody thought his conduct at all reprehensible. The Governor, finding that the land had escheated to the King, had granted it to another — who had assigned it to the acquisitive Byrd, and the latter at length sold it to the occupant for a "valuable consideration."[5] The real moral of the tale is that neither in financial power nor worldly wisdom were the early Jeffersons a match for the early Byrds. On the other hand, this ancestor of a President must have had some capital, and apparently he was not the sort of farmer who could be easily evicted by a richer man. Presumably this was the place where his son lived afterwards; if so, it was on the south bank of the river some twenty miles below the falls and strategically situated for a landing.

At this time there were land barons in Virginia to whom such hold-

---

[3] In 1679 he was taxed for the first time for "maintenance of the soldiers" being obligated to pay for two tithables. Records, Henrico County Court, in Virginia State Library, Richmond (hereafter cited as Henrico Records, and VSL) 1677–1692, Pt. 1, p. 116; W. G. Stanard, compiler, Extracts from the Records of Henrico County, Va., 1677–1771 (VSL), pp. 38, 46. (Hereafter cited as Stanard, Extracts.) See Appendix I, A.

[4] J. S. Bassett, ed., Writings of "Colonel William Byrd of Westover Esqr," pp. xxix ff.

[5] April, 1682; Henrico Records, 1677–1692, p. 214. Presumably he had not been in possession for two years or he would have been able to take advantage of the law regarding composition of escheats; W. W. Hening, ed., The Statutes at Large, Being a Collection of All the Laws of Virginia, II, 136–137. (Hereafter cited as Hening.)

ings seemed small and such a man inconsequential, but the heyday of the plantation aristocracy had not yet arrived. Though the economic and social structure of the Colony was taking form it had not attained rigidity. Life was dispersed and fluid in this spacious country, and here, for many years yet, vigorous and ambitious men had an excellent chance to rise. This was an unequal society in an age of recognized inequality but, except for the lowest group, the slaves, it was not one of rigid caste. The road to riches and power lay open to those who acquired land while it was still easy to get, and who somehow found labor with which to exploit it.[6] The distinct advantage lay with those who had influence and capital. Labor was always scarcer than land, and slaves rather than acreage came to be the major criterion of prosperity. But no one had many slaves or much ready money in the late seventeenth century, and the status of a small landholder who tilled a virgin soil was far from degraded. His life was undoubtedly crude, but nature was prodigal and the future beckoned.

The first Thomas Jefferson probably had little capital or influence but he went forward on the road to fortune and a genteel station. Besides bearing and transmitting a good name, he increased his holdings and became a man of respectable estate. He acquired no military title but, judging from the number of wolf bounties he collected, he had some prowess as a hunter. He became one of "ye surveyours of ye highways," thus establishing a tradition in the family; he frequently did jury duty, and as a man of recognized integrity he served several times as an executor of wills. His wife, Mary Branch, brought him some property, and when he died in 1697 he had several slaves. Besides his widow, Mary, he left a son Thomas and a daughter Martha.[7] These three names kept reappearing in the family with unfailing regularity; they were all present at Monticello.

It would be easy to make too much of the fact that Mary Branch Jefferson, three years after she became a widow, married a man who could sign the wedding contract only by making his mark, for her second husband, Joseph Mattocks, had property and she herself could write her name.[8] There is no reason to suppose, however, that either she or her first husband was a cultivated person. Probably there was no

[6] J. S. Bassett, in *American Historical Association Report for 1901*, I, 563, states the matter well. The relative fluidity of this society is admirably described in L. B. Wright, *The First Gentlemen of Virginia*.

[7] Henrico Order Book, 1694–1701, p. 169; Henrico Deeds, etc., 1697–1704, pp. 113–119; *Va. Mag.*, I, 208–212. His inheritance on behalf of his wife from Christopher Branch is referred to in Henrico Records, 1677–1692, p. 219; Stanard, Extracts, p. 70.

[8] Henrico Deeds, etc., 1697–1704, p. 213.

time in the history of this Province when it was more difficult to become one. Before the establishment of the College of William and Mary, practically the only educational opportunities were those that England provided a few of the very rich. The result was a generation of men who, if they had the good fortune to read and write, "had no further commerce with the Muses, or learned sciences; but spent their life ignobly at the hoe and spade, and other employments of an uncultivated and unpolished country." [9] Not until the greatest of the name appeared did any of the Jeffersons have much learning, but the lack of it was too general at this time to constitute an insuperable bar to admission into the lesser gentry.

Whether or not the first Thomas Jefferson should be called a yeoman is a question of definition and a matter of no real consequence. The second of the name was officially a gentleman. Before the end of the century Thomas II owned a racing mare, and racing was generally a prerogative of the gentry. More significant than this is the fact that he became one of the "gentlemen justices" of Henrico County before he was thirty, and that he continued to be one for almost twenty years.[10] Among his "honorable" associates were the second William Randolph and an early Francis Eppes. These highly reputable names reappear in the story of his descendants. Besides being a local magistrate he was a captain of the militia. The officers generally dined together after muster, and upon one of these occasions Colonel William Byrd, second of the name and the elegant master of Westover, ate roast beef at Jefferson's house.[11] For at least two years the Captain held the important post of sheriff of Henrico, as a justice might have been expected to do, and he was once recompensed for extraordinary services. He is said to have built a church in Bristol Parish which was called "Jefferson's Church" for half a century. There is no clue to his personality but he must have been vigorous; and there can be no question of his official standing or sense of public responsibility. In this society the two were inseparable.[12]

[9] "Preface to the Statutes of the College," *William and Mary College Quarterly Historical Magazine* (hereafter cited as *W. & M.*), 1 ser., XVI, 242.

[10] He was last on the list in 1706, but was senior justice by 1720 and served at least four years longer; Henrico Records, 1706–1709, p. 8; Henrico County Minute Book, 1719–1724, p. 39; and other references. For the horserace in which he participated on July 1, 1697, see Henrico Order Book, 1694–1701, p. 181.

[11] L. B. Wright and M. Tinling, eds., *Secret Diary of William Byrd of Westover, 1709–1712* (hereafter referred to as Byrd, *Diary, 1709–1712*), entries for Sept. 23, Oct. 21, 1711; see also Feb. 16, 1712.

[12] *Executive Journals of the Council of Colonial Virginia*, III (1928), 470, 500 (hereafter cited as *Council Journals, Colonial Va.*); Henrico Minutes, 1719–1724,

Soon after his father's death and shortly before he attained his majority, he married Mary Field, daughter of Major Peter Field of New Kent County and his wife Judith, who was the widow of Henry Randolph and the daughter of a former speaker of the House of Burgesses. From both the financial and social point of view this was an advantageous alliance.[13] He received grants of land on several occasions for the importation of persons into the Colony; and he engaged in numerous land transactions after the manner of the enterprising planters of his day, though not on the vast scale of the Byrds, the Randolphs, and the Carters. The grant of fifteen hundred acres on Fine Creek, south of the James, and well above the falls, which was made to him and three others by Governor Spotswood in 1718, anticipated the westward movement in which his son took part.[14] He himself had his house at what was repeatedly referred to as Jefferson's Landing, later described as Osborne's.

Here, on the last day of February, 1707/1708, his son Peter was born. There were three children already — Judith, Thomas, and Field — and later there were two more daughters, bearing the inevitable names Mary and Martha. When Peter was eight he lost his mother, and his father appears to have remarried later, though the Captain was again a widower when he died.[15] Long years afterward, writing his autobiography at Monticello, Thomas Jefferson said that his father's mind was naturally strong but that his education had been neglected. In comparison with Thomas's superior opportunities, Peter's were unquestionably limited, as were those of so many others in that dispersed society. He did not grow up in such ignorance as to be seriously handicapped in practical affairs, but the accident of his position within the family may have caused him to be relatively neglected. He lost his mother while he was still a child, and as the youngest of three sons he had only modest expectations in his youth. Attention was probably centered in the heir apparent, the third Thomas, who was born in 1700 and died twenty-three years later on a ship commanded by Captain Isham Randolph. Peter Jefferson himself afterwards married this Captain Randolph's daughter.

Though there can be no question of the honorable standing of Peter's

p. 361; W. Meade, *Old Churches, Ministers and Families of Virginia* (hereafter cited as Meade), I, 125, 137, 440.

[13] *Va. Mag.*, XXIII, 173–175 n. Date of marriage license, Oct. 20, 1697.

[14] Va. State Land Office, Patent No. 10, 1710–1719, p. 378; Henrico Minutes, 1719–1724, p. 342.

[15] Details from *Tyler's Quarterly Historical Magazine* (hereafter cited as *Tyler's Mag.*), VII, 121–122. For these and for the remarriage, see Appendix I, A.

father, the second Thomas Jefferson, there is considerable doubt about the degree of his prosperity in the last decade of his life. He suffered a heavy loss from fire which occasioned him to petition the House of Burgesses for relief; and a few years later, when he failed to contest a suit against him for 6,480 pounds of tobacco, the court ordered an attachment of his property sufficient to satisfy the debt.[16] The will which he drew six years before his death in 1731, and the inventory which ultimately went with it, show that he had considerably more household goods, livestock, and servants than Thomas Jefferson I had had, but they leave many unanswered questions about his land.[17]

Neither Peter nor his elder brother Field lived on the ancestral acres after their father died. As a justice of the peace in Lunenburg, Field maintained the connection of the family with the county gentry. Peter, who was named his father's executor, got the holdings on Fine and "Manikin" Creeks in Goochland County, and if he did not already live on them he soon began to.[18] His inheritance of land was probably fair-sized, though certainly not princely. Besides this he received the bulk of his father's personal possessions, including half of the livestock, a couple of horses, and two slaves, presumably body servants. To a modest extent he was a slaveowner, and by birth and association he was a member of the county gentry. He cannot be described as a completely self-made man, but the enhancement of his fortunes, like the improvement of his mind, must be chiefly attributed to his own exertions.

Soon after he presented his father's will and had it approved in the county court he removed, or returned, to Fine Creek. He was then about twenty-five years old and at the peak of his great physical strength. The County of Goochland, to which he went, had recently been set off from Henrico; it lay above the fall line and straddled the James. Peter's place was on a minor tributary to the south of the river. Here he lived some ten years, until about 1741, developing his plantation, acquiring claims and titles elsewhere, and gaining for himself a recognized standing in the district. The date of his definite establishment as a local leader was 1734, when he followed in his father's footsteps by becoming a justice of the peace; three years later, when he was

---

[16] *Journals of the House of Burgesses of Virginia* (hereafter cited as *Burgesses, Journals*), 1712–1726, Dec. 8, 9, 12, 13, 1720, pp. 293, 295, 298, without a definite indication of the outcome of the petition; Henrico Minutes, 1719–1724, p. 367.

[17] Henrico County, Miscellaneous Court Records, 1650–1807, p. 849. Will dated Mar. 15, 1725, and proved in April. 1731.

[18] Peter's later relations were close with his sister Mary, who married Thomas Turpin; M. Dickore, ed., *Two Unpublished Letters from Thomas Jefferson to His Relatives the Turpins*; A. Brown, *The Cabells and Their Kin*, p. 50.

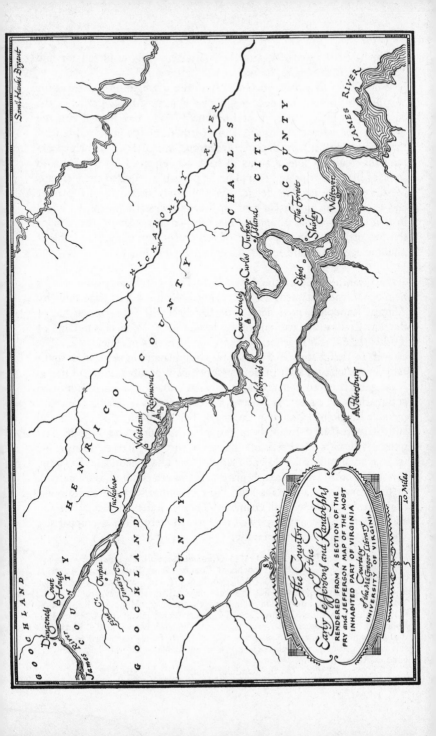

The Country of the Early Jeffersons and Randolphs

thirty, he became sheriff; later still, after he had wandered far and gained laurels elsewhere, he was county surveyor.[19]

When Peter first came to Goochland, the strategic post of surveyor was held by one of his near neighbors, William Mayo, probably the foremost Virginia surveyor of his time.[20] Mayo had helped run the dividing line between Virginia and North Carolina, immortalized by the second William Byrd. Peter Jefferson, who afterwards helped extend this dividing line, appears to have accompanied his neighbor on some of his later trips and from him he probably acquired the elements of surveying. Such knowledge was immensely useful to any planter and it played an important part in Peter's successful career, as it did in that of George Washington. He engaged in surveying throughout the rest of his life and by means of it won for himself an honorable if minor place in the history of American exploration.

On the other side of the James from Fine Creek, and fifteen miles or more to the eastward, was Tuckahoe. The house had been built by Thomas Randolph, now dead, who had been the foremost citizen of the new County. He was one of the seven sons of William Randolph of Turkey Island and is generally known as "Thomas of Tuckahoe." The custom of designating individuals by their plantation seats arose naturally in a society which made a practice of repeating Christian names from generation to generation, and it has proved a boon to confused antiquarians ever since. It became a virtual necessity among the innumerable Randolphs. Not inappropriately have William of Turkey Island and his wife Mary Isham been termed "the Adam and Eve of Virginia." [21] Bearers of the Randolph name sprouted like so many pine trees in an abandoned field and many of them became monarchs of the forest. If descendants through maternal lines are counted, the long roll of this remarkable clan falls little short of comprising the entire body of the gentry. It includes the names of Thomas Jefferson, John Marshall, and Robert E. Lee, and if viewed comprehensively it defies comparison with any other American family.

[19] Justice of the Peace, Nov. 1, 1734 (*Council Journals, Colonial Virginia*, IV, 339); Sheriff, Sept. 20, 1737 (Goochland County Order Book, No. 4, p. 237); County Surveyor, Aug. 20, 1751 (*Ibid.*, No. 7, p. 73). He may have served earlier in both of the latter positions but these are the earliest dates I have found.

[20] There is fresh information in a master's thesis on Mayo by Rosalind S. Parker, Alderman Library, University of Virginia (hereafter cited as UVA). H. S. Randall, *Life of Thomas Jefferson*, I, 6, says that Peter first commended himself to the Randolphs by his usefulness as a surveyor. I have found no record to support this tradition, but it may be correct. (This invaluable work will henceforth be cited as Randall.)

[21] *Va. Mag.*, XLV, 67. On the Randolph family see Appendix, I, B.

Peter Jefferson's first close contact with the Randolphs came through the young master of Tuckahoe, the son of Thomas, who was named William like his grandfather and one of his uncles, thus adding to the genealogical confusion. According to the second William Byrd, this William Randolph was "a pretty young man" who had the misfortune to become his own master too soon. Perhaps he was not sufficiently deferential to the Colonel. That urbane gentleman remarked that he had a strange conceit of his own sufficiency which was accentuated by a small smattering of learning.[22] William of Tuckahoe was five or six years younger than Peter Jefferson, who by all accounts was modest. The friendship of these county neighbors may have been a case of the attraction of opposites, or merely the result of propinquity in a fluid and friendly society. The two young men became magistrates in the same year, and their names were linked from that time forward. They were intimate for more than a decade, and almost a half-century later their lines were joined by the marriage of their grandchildren. There was instability in this branch of the Randolphs and, beginning with Peter, the Jeffersons served to offset it.

On the same side of the river as Tuckahoe and somewhat west of Fine Creek was a place called Dungeness, belonging to Isham Randolph, uncle of young William. The eldest of the many children there was a girl named Jane. She was nineteen and Peter Jefferson was thirty-two when he married her in October, 1739.[23] Perhaps the courtship began a couple of years earlier, for her father and William of Tuckahoe had shared Peter's bond for one thousand pounds sterling when he became sheriff.[24] Isham probably knew and trusted him even before that, but he himself had not yet settled down at Dungeness when Peter first came to Goochland. Isham's daughter had been born in England, and he was no man of the back country. He had had greater opportunities and a more colorful life than Peter's father.

Isham Randolph and five of his brothers attended the College of William and Mary. His grandson observed afterwards that in this family they never hesitated to employ their considerable means for the purposes of education. It is not necessary to add that their social connections were of the best. While Isham was in his twenties, yet unmarried and still living at Turkey Island, he frequently visited West-

[22] Va. Mag., XXXII, 393.

[23] Marriage bond, dated Oct. 3, 1739, in records of Goochland County, reproduced in part in W. & M., 1st ser., VII, 98. The date is wrongly given as 1738 in Randall, I, 7.

[24] Sept. 20, 1737 (Goochland Deed Book No. 3, Pt. I, p. 58). The reference to Peter's taking the oath as sheriff is in Goochland Order Book No. 4, p. 237.

over and was on intimate terms with Captain Jefferson's superior officer in the militia, the second and most famous William Byrd, who was twelve years older than young Randolph. For some weeks in the winter of 1710, after the Colonel had indiscreetly offered to teach him French, Isham was almost continuously at Westover and had lessons from his host, making some progress. But his chief yearning was for the sea, and Byrd helped him satisfy it by recommending him for the command of a ship. By the fall of that year he was referring to Isham as "Captain" and putting tobacco aboard his vessel. Intimate social relations between the two men were maintained during Byrd's later residence in London.[25]

It was probably in 1718 that Captain Randolph found a wife in England. His marriage to Jane, daughter of Charles and Jane Lilburne Rogers, took place in the "parish of White Chapel," London.[26] She appears to have been living with her widowed mother, a distant relative of "Freeborn John" Lilburne. For his times and circumstances Isham had married late, but his wife proved to be as prolific as the other Randolph matrons; they had nine children who survived infancy. The first of these, Jane, was baptized at St. Paul's, Shadwell, on February 20, 1720, when her future husband was about thirteen. Her father was referred to as "Isham Randolph, in Shakespeare's Walk, merchant"; but he was known as "Captain" for almost twenty years longer, and not until the last decade of his life did he wholly abandon the sea. Thus there was a nautical strain in the ancestry of President Jefferson which the critics of his commercial policy quite overlooked; he himself employed nautical terms in figures of speech though he was not a good sailor.

Captain Randolph probably made lengthy sojourns in England after his marriage, and upon at least one important occasion he acted there as agent for his native Province.[27] Sometime before the spring of 1736, he made his last voyage. William Byrd, then back in Virginia, wrote to an agent in England: "Sir John Randolph is dead, and unless his brother Isham return to his own element the sea, I fear he won't survive him many years."[28] Captain Randolph and his family were estab-

---

[25] There are more than forty references to him in Byrd, *Diary, 1709–1712*, beginning Feb. 15, 1709. The references to French begin on Jan. 31, 1710. The more important entries about Isham's ship fall between Mar. 14 and Oct. 20, 1710. Other references begin in April 1712. For later relations, see *Another Secret Diary of William Byrd of Westover*, 1739–1741, ed. by Maude H. Woodfin, p. xxii, citing unpublished diary Apr. 17, 29, 1719, and p. 323 *n*. (Cited hereafter as Byrd, *Diary, 1739–1741*.)

[26] *Va. Mag.*, XXVI, 324.

[27] In 1732 he acted for the Council in opposing two bills then pending in Parliament; *Council Journals, Colonial Va.*, IV, 267, 272.

[28] March 20, 1736; *Va. Mag.*, XXXVI, 215. Isham's brother John, living in Virginia, had been knighted.

lished at Dungeness before this time and had become acquainted with Peter Jefferson.

By inheritance and grant Isham had become a large landholder in Goochland. In the year that Peter Jefferson became a magistrate Randolph got a patent for three thousand acres, and in connection with it he certified to the importation of forty-nine persons into the Colony. Two years later he entered into agreements whereby two bond servants, in return for the time of servitude due him, should make for him respectively one hundred thousand bricks and two hundred and fifty pairs of shoes. He was carrying on extensive building operations and supporting a large establishment. In the year of his daughter's marriage he shared a consignment of three hundred and eighty Negroes. His son-in-law had preceded him as a pioneer but had not been in a position to conduct affairs on such a scale.[29]

His circle of friends was wider than that of the Jeffersons. To Dungeness in 1738 came John Bartram the Pennsylvania botanist, at the suggestion of Peter Collinson, who had become acquainted with Isham in London. The correspondent of Benjamin Franklin had recommended to Friend Bartram that on one leg of his projected journey to Virginia he stop to see Colonel Byrd at Westover and Colonel John Custis, Junior, at Williamsburg, "both curious men," and that he then proceed to Isham's place, where he would receive a warm welcome.[30] Of Bartram's comments on his visit to Dungeness, and on the botanical excursions which he centered there, the following would probably have been of greatest interest to Jane Randolph's plant-loving son. "There grows on the other side of James River," said Bartram to Colonel Custis, "a little above Isham Randolph's, a tree, the kind of which is known in Europe by the name of *Thuyja*, or Arbor Vitae, which if thee could procure some seed thereof, if it growed, would be a curious ornament in thy garden. I doubt not, if thee was to write or speak to Isham, he would procure thee some." His description of his host to Collinson as "a generous, good-natured gentleman, and well-respected by most who are acquainted with him," may sound like faint praise, but at least it reveals that Isham had the characteristic social virtues of his class. This friendly man afterwards regretted that he could not entertain his former guest by sending him the account of some new discovery, and confessed "the want of a penetrating genius in the curious beauties of nature." Perhaps he was unduly modest, but

[29] *Council Journals, Colonial Va.*, IV, lv, 323, 349; see Appendix I, B, 2; *W. & M.*, 1st ser., V, 109–110; Byrd, *Diary, 1739–1741*, p. 14 *n.*
[30] Collinson to Bartram, Feb. 17, 1736, in W. Darlington, *Memorials of John Bartram and Humphrey Marshall*, p. 89.

unquestionably his scientific curiosity fell short of that of his grandson.[31]

Public service was expected of one with Isham Randolph's family connections and landed possessions, and he would probably have been drafted sooner had he settled earlier upon the land. About a year before his daughter's marriage he was elected a burgess for Goochland County, but his entire legislative career actually extended to only a few weeks.[32] His military service was more conspicuous. In the same month that he was chosen a burgess he was appointed adjutant general of the Colony, and he held this office until his death four years later. He was expected to go into the various counties and give instruction in the "form of exercise" that had been prepared for the soldiers. The Council which appointed him described him as a well-known gentleman and universally acceptable in the country.[33] Greater military responsibilities soon fell to his lot. In the year 1740, a contingent of Virginia troops was raised to serve with the British on the expedition against the Spanish at Carthagena. Governor Gooch took charge of these and left the Colony for a year. During his absence Isham Randolph acted as chief officer of the local militia, and for this reason it has sometimes been said that he was designated as lieutenant general of the Colony.[34] There were plenty of military titles in Thomas Jefferson's ancestral record. His maternal grandfather may not have been a conspicuously martial figure, but at least Isham was a link in a highly honorable military tradition. His successor as adjutant general was Lawrence Washington, and when the latter died three years later, the Colony was divided into districts and four adjutants were appointed. Among these was Lawrence's brother George.[35]

It is difficult to recover the personality of a man from his portrait or his epitaph. It may be reported, however, that Isham Randolph appeared in a picture frame as a gentleman in conventional costume, wearing a wig, and with ruffles at his wrists. His full face implied good living, but it was also long, and some people might see in it a resemblance to Thomas Jefferson, even though the latter's nose was rather more uptilted. The epitaph on his tombstone at Turkey Island says that he possessed the distinguishing qualities of a gentleman to an eminent

[31] Bartram to Custis, Nov. 19, 1738, *Ibid.*, p. 312; Bartram to Collinson, Dec. 1738, *Ibid.*, pp. 120–122; Isham Randolph to Bartram, May 24, 1739, *Ibid.*, p. 317.

[32] *Burgesses, Journals,* 1727–1734, 1736–1740, pp. ix, 323, 352. He took his seat by Nov. 25, 1738, and his last session ended on Aug. 28, 1740.

[33] Nov. 9, 1738, *Council Journals, Colonial Va.,* IV, 429; *Va. Mag.,* XIV, 225.

[34] June 14, 1740, *Council Journals, Colonial Va.,* V, 20; Byrd, *Diary, 1739–1741,* June 14, 1740; see also p. 14 *n.* Byrd was a member of the Council. For further details see Appendix I, B, 2.

[35] *Va. Mag.,* XXXI, 272.

degree, and gives further testimony to his good nature. "By an easy compliance and obliging deportment he knew no enemy, but gained many friends, thus in his life meriting an universal esteem." He died at the age of fifty-seven, in November, 1742 – three years after the marriage of his daughter to Peter Jefferson, and only a few months before the birth of their first son.[36]

Peter was older than the average when he married, just as his father-in-law had been. His wife had been promised a dowry of two hundred pounds sterling, but Isham had not paid it by the time he made his will. Jane Randolph probably took a body servant or so with her but she seems to have brought her husband no land. That was generally left to sons if there were any. The rising young planter acquired no fortune by his marriage, but he gained for his unborn children a far more extensive and influential family connection than he himself had enjoyed. It is likely that the couple began their married life comfortably but modestly at Fine Creek and that their first two children were born there.

Four or five years before his marriage Peter had staked out a claim on the Rivanna below the gap in the Southwest Mountains. The date of his earliest known grant in this remote region was June 14, 1734, when his future wife was only fourteen. He may have made his surveys before the leaves fell, and he certainly received a patent for one thousand acres before the passing of another summer. His tract extended southward from Secretary's Ford just above the mountains and included the later site of Monticello and a body of bottom land below the little river.[37] Within a year he began to look for a more suitable homesite than his own lands afforded. His friend William Randolph of Tuckahoe, who had probably interested him in this region in the first place, had acquired lands north of the Rivanna which were still undeveloped. Peter made a deal whereby he acquired two hundred acres of these in return for a bowl of arrack punch concocted by Henry Wetherburn of the Raleigh Tavern in Williamsburg. Not until two years after his marriage, however, did Peter round out the home tract. He then acquired two hundred acres more from his friend and made a cash payment for the whole. Meanwhile, he had patented another small body of land south of the river. It was probably in the year 1741 that he began building on a spot whence he could look downward at

[36] Portrait, *Ibid.*, XXXIV, opp. p. 183; epitaph, *Ibid.*, XIV, 226 *n.* For descendants, see Appendix I, B, 2.

[37] For details about grants, patents, and other land transactions, see Appendix II, A.

a stream or upward toward the mountains; and it was here that Thomas was born two years later.

The domain in this district to which the boy became heir apparent was modest. The acreage to which Peter had title was not extensive by Virginia standards and was not immediately increased. In that era of land-grabbing he received large grants elsewhere but there is no certain way of knowing how many of these he was ever able to perfect; and on one occasion the all-powerful Council administered a distinct rebuff by rejecting one of his petitions as unreasonable.[38] He may have over-reached himself, but in view of the success of others it seems more probable that, despite his connection with the Randolphs, he lacked influence at the seat of power. On the whole, he was a modest specu-lator in land, in comparison with his mighty contemporaries in the Province, and even with certain of his near neighbors.

In the Rivanna region, however, he had the distinction of being one of the first settlers, and this was always a matter of pride to his son.[39] Though unexpected events interrupted his stay, Peter played an impor-tant part in the organization of a County which boasts many distin-guished sons but has been most glorified by the name of Jefferson. In September, 1744, because of the inconvenience attending the upper inhabitants of Goochland, the Assembly provided that after the last day of December the existing County should be divided and a new one bearing the euphonious name of Albemarle be formed. Peter Jefferson, who had been a magistrate in the old County, attended the first meeting for organization in February, 1745, and took oath as a justice of the peace and a judge of the court of chancery, thus becoming one of the first magistrates and first gentlemen of the new one.[40] Associated with him on this occasion was Joshua Fry, a former teacher of mathematics at the College of William and Mary, who was now living on Hardware River, near Carter's Bridge.[41] In March, Fry became county surveyor and county lieutenant — that is, the chief officer — while Peter Jefferson became lieutenant colonel. After a few weeks, however, he practically ceased attending meetings of the county court in Albemarle, and he

[38] May 15, 1741, *Va. Mag.*, XV, 120–121.

[39] Jefferson's statement (Ford, I, 3) that his father was one of the three or four earliest settlers is approximately correct if applied to the Rivanna district; but the date which he gives, about 1737, seems too early.

[40] Hening, V, 266; E. Woods, *Albemarle County in Virginia*, p. 8 (hereafter cited as Woods, *Albemarle*). See also M. Rawlings, *The Albemarle of Other Days*. The Order Book of the County, 1744–1748, is preserved in the clerk's office in Charlottesville, but the records from 1748 to 1783 were lost or destroyed during the Revolution.

[41] On Fry, see P. Slaughter, *Memoir of Joshua Fry.*

soon returned to the Goochland side, taking his young family with him.[42]

His return was at the request of his friend William Randolph, now also referred to as "Colonel," who had suffered other misfortunes than that of becoming his own master too soon. He had married early and well, but by the age of thirty had become a widower. His wife was the daughter of Mann Page, whose house at Rosewell in Gloucester County is said to have contained thirty-five rooms. John Page, the companion of Thomas Jefferson's youth and young manhood, was her nephew. She had borne William Randolph two daughters and a son, who was given the names of his two grandfathers. Thomas Mann Randolph was a couple of years older than Thomas Jefferson, who could say afterwards that he had known him all his life. After his wife died, William of Tuckahoe made a will wherein he named Peter as one of his executors. Three years later, foreseeing his approaching death, he added a codicil in which he included the request that his "dear and loving friend" should move down with his own family to the Tuckahoe house and remain there until Randolph's son was grown.[43]

In the technical sense Peter Jefferson was not the guardian of Thomas Mann Randolph, but the children remained at Tuckahoe with the Jefferson family. Large monetary bequests had been made to the girls and the balance of the estate was to go to the son. As the resident executor Peter was the custodian of the land, and in the practical sense he was far more than a guardian.[44] His economic status was considerably more modest than that of William Randolph, but in view of his standing as magistrate and friend it seems impossible that he could have been asked to assume an undignified position. In general he did such things at Tuckahoe as the master himself would have done had he been there, doubtless doing most of them a good deal better. It is surprising, however, that he should have been willing to leave his own lands in order to care for those of another. Besides being an act of loyal friendship, his move must have seemed advantageous to both families.

[42] He attended on July 25, 1745, but was absent thereafter until July 10, 1746, and was not among the newly commissioned justices who met on Nov. 13, 1746 (Albemarle County Order Book).

[43] Will dated Mar. 2, 1742; codicil, July 20, 1745; recorded Nov. 19, 1745, William Randolph being then dead; proved May 20, 1746 (Goochland County Will & Deed Book, No. 5, p. 73; attested copy UVA; summarized in *Va. Mag.*, XXXII, 394–395).

[44] His Account Book, 1728–1755 in Henry E. Huntington Library, San Marino, California (HEH), photostat UVA, shows transactions on behalf of the estate but does not lend itself to ready summary.

He directed the activities of at least seven overseers at Tuckahoe and reported the production of far more tobacco on Colonel Randolph's quarters than he could have expected from his own fields in Albemarle.[45] His smaller holdings there were still largely forested and he probably thought it desirable to leave the task of pioneering to an overseer and his gang. Planters often did that before moving their families into new lands in the Piedmont.[46] While at Tuckahoe he could keep his eye on his Fine Creek property, which lay near one of the Randolph quarters. Peter Jefferson kept his accounts methodically, as his son did afterwards, but those which remain do not reveal how much he received for his services to the estate. The traditional report that he got only his living expenses is probably correct,[47] but the food and lodging of his growing family constituted a considerable item and he was unquestionably a more prosperous man after this period than he had been before.

Though he did not stay as long as William of Tuckahoe had desired, he guarded the land and the heir for six or seven years altogether.[48] Thus it came about that the home of Thomas Jefferson's earliest remembrance was a Randolph place. The Colonel achieved his reputation as an explorer while they were all living there. Then, during the few years that remained to him after their return to Albemarle, he gained greater local prominence and developed the estate which his son inherited.

[45] In the years 1745–1751 the eight "quarters" produced 629 hhds. and 667,336 lbs. of tobacco.

[46] T. J. Wertenbaker, *Old South*, p. 118, citing the example of the Reverend Robert Rose; T. P. Abernethy, *Three Virginia Frontiers*, p. 46.

[47] Randall, I, 11; S. N. Randolph, *Domestic Life of Thomas Jefferson* (cited hereafter as *Domestic Life*), p. 23.

[48] Various entries in his Account Book show that he maintained a connection with the estate even after he had returned to Albemarle.

[II]

The Services of Peter Jefferson

1745-1757

THE EARLIEST recollection of Thomas Jefferson was of being carried on a pillow by a mounted slave on the journey from Shadwell to Tuckahoe. The circumstances must have been specially impressive, for he was only two or three years old at the time.[1] He had now ceased to be the youngest member of the family but he was still the only boy. At the age of twenty months he had acquired a third sister, and a fourth was born shortly after he turned three. Two more boys were born at Tuckahoe, but one lived only a few weeks and the other did not survive a day. The five young Jeffersons and the three young Randolphs comprised a good-sized group of children, and doubtless a lively one.[2]

If the house was then completed in its historic external form, as seems probable, they could have lived almost as two separate families, thereby diminishing domestic confusion to some degree. It had two distinct wings which were connected by a large room or salon, and thus it assumed the shape of the letter "H." One of the wings had brick ends, but otherwise it was a frame structure, painted white. At that time it may not have contained the fine paneling and rich stairways which were seen in it later, but the rooms had high ceilings and were airy. Jefferson was there as a little boy and he often stopped with Thomas Mann Randolph after he grew up, but he saw no reason to describe such a familiar house in letters. Architecture of this sort did not impress him after he was attracted to classic columns and had

[1] Family tradition as given by Randall, I, 11; *Domestic Life*, p. 6.
[2] Peter Jefferson's records of tobacco at Tuckahoe begin with the year 1745, and the family probably left Shadwell before the birth of Martha on May 29, 1746. They had undoubtedly moved before Sept. 12, 1746, when the Colonel set out on a surveying expedition. On the children, see Appendix I, C.

begun to dream of stateliness; but this home of his first memories, set above a greater stream than the Rivanna, always must have seemed an exceedingly pleasant place.[3]

Colonel Jefferson was directly charged to carry out William Randolph's instructions about the education of his son. The heir was not to be sent to the College of William and Mary or to England on any account whatever, but private tutors were to be employed for his instruction. Thus the credible tradition arose that young Tom Jefferson first studied under young Tom Randolph's teacher in a little house still standing in the yard. This part of his education he afterwards described as "the English school," without giving any details. Presumably, the tutor taught the boys and girls together, as Philip Fithian did in the household of Councillor Robert Carter at Nomini Hall; but even in that case this class, like all the others he was ever a member of, was small.[4] In the absence of authentic information, his boyhood and schooldays at Tuckahoe must be left to the imagination. It is said that once, when desperate with hunger, he fervently repeated the Lord's Prayer in the hope of hastening a meal.[5] The implication is clear that he received conventional religious instruction, but there is certainly no suggestion that there was any shortage of food. In this and in other respects his father was a good provider.

Peter Jefferson was more than that. He was not merely providing a comfortable home for his family while doing a service to a dead friend. He was also venturing far from the tobacco fields upon occasion and carving a reputation for himself out of the wilderness. If his career is at all memorable for its own sake, and not solely as a brief prologue to one that was illustrious, it is because of what he did as a surveyor of boundaries and a maker of maps during the years that he had headquarters at Tuckahoe. This record of exploits and achievements constituted, also, the most distinctive part of the heritage that he transmitted to his descendants.

We have a detailed account of one of the expeditions he went on. His son was not yet four years old when Peter helped mark what was

[3] On the Tuckahoe Randolphs see Appendix I, B, 1. An admirable recent description of the place, with abundant illustrations, is in T. T. Waterman, *The Mansions of Virginia*, pp. 85–92.

[4] Peter Jefferson's Account Book, Aug. 30, 1750, and May 11, 1752, shows payments to John Staples for teaching Thomas Mann Randolph. No mention is made of any other pupil but, since these financial records are incomplete, this need not argue against the credibility of the tradition. Staples appears elsewhere as an assistant surveyor.

[5] Randall, I, 17; *Domestic Life*, p. 8. The story is slightly different in the two versions.

known afterwards as the Fairfax Line. It is a pity that the boy was not old enough to hear the story of this hazardous adventure while the father's memory of it was fresh. The Colonel was never much of a talker, however; he was a man of action.

Between the Potomac and the Rappahannock lay the vast domain of Lord Fairfax known as the Northern Neck. It was a part of the Province of Virginia so far as government was concerned, but title to the soil lay with the Proprietor. The western limits of this princely estate were long the subject of dispute; but finally, by order of the Privy Council, the boundary was drawn for seventy-six miles between the headspring of the Rappahannock, that is, the source of the Conway or Rapidan, across mountain ranges and primeval wilderness to the headspring of the Potomac, which was already marked. This was the Fairfax Line.[6]

The members of the expedition who assembled below the Blue Ridge in September, 1746, comprised some forty men, and at the start they had about that many horses. There were commissioners for the Crown and for Lord Fairfax, the former including Joshua Fry of Albemarle County, and there were surveyors who had been deputed by these gentlemen. Colonel Jefferson and Robert Brooke had been named for the Crown, Captain Benjamin Winslow and Thomas Lewis for the Proprietor. It was Lewis who recorded in crude but graphic language the story of the journey. The journey out, from the head of the Conway (Rapidan) to the headspring of the Potomac, where they drank the King's health and set up the Fairfax stone, required four weeks. The trip back to the starting point, where they drank healths even more lustily and set up another stone, took three.[7]

The preparations had been elaborate but this was no pleasure trip even for the commissioners, who generally went with the baggage by the easiest route. Colonel Jefferson and the other surveyors had to follow the direct line wherever it went, though they always remained mounted as long as they could. It took them over successive ranges of mountains that were "prodigiously full of fallen timber and ivey," up and down precipices where the horses slipped and fell, and through swamps of laurel which appeared impenetrable. One dreadful place they called Purgatory and one stream, dismal enough "to strike terror in any human creature," they named the Styx.[8] Several of the unfor-

---

[6] Fairfax Harrison, "The Northern Neck Maps of 1737–1747," *W. & M.*, 2 ser., IV, 1–15 (Jan. 1924).

[7] *The Fairfax Line: Thomas Lewis's Journal of 1746*, with footnotes and index by J. W. Wayland, a minor classic of American exploration.

[8] *Ibid.*, p. 29, a particularly graphic passage.

tunate horses were killed, and all of them nearly starved. The surveyors suffered repeated falls and were in constant danger. One of them fainted in a swamp, which almost became his tomb. Colonel Jefferson and Captain Winslow were older than the other two and they generally went together when the group worked in pairs. For Peter at thirty-nine the expedition was a feat of endurance, but the only sign of weakness he gave was that once he was "much indisposed."

Thomas Jefferson never stood on the top of the Alleghanies where his father crossed, nor saw the initials "P. J." carved on a beech near the Fairfax Stone. The information about the topography of his native region which he incorporated in his *Notes on Virginia* was gained from several sources, but from his father he could have learned that the mountains are "not solitary and scattered confusedly over the face of the country," but are "disposed in ridges one behind another." [9] He appears not to have referred in writing to his father's connection with the Fairfax Line, but undoubtedly he knew of Peter's victories over the wilderness and was heartened by them, though he himself was an explorer and a pioneer of another sort.

On November 15, 1746, after the senior surveyor for the Crown had carved his initials on a birch tree near the head of Conway, he set out for home. The other surveyors joined him at Tuckahoe early in the new year, and by the last week in February their joint labors were completed. At a greater age Tom would have been deeply interested in their doings. The map of the Northern Neck that was sent to England was described as drawn by Peter Jefferson and Robert Brooke. For the region east of the Blue Ridge they followed the earlier map of Mayo but they incorporated enough new material about the Valley of Virginia to give their own map the value of a source record. Needless to say, this map showed for the first time the Fairfax Line. [10]

The name of Joshua Fry is linked with that of Peter Jefferson in the most important of the latter's activities as a surveyor. In effect if not in fact the two men constituted a partnership. Somewhat more than three years after they helped set up the Fairfax Stone, they surveyed the dividing line between Virginia and North Carolina for ninety miles beyond the point where William Byrd and his fellow commissioners had left it a score of years before. Unfortunately, no chronicler was present to record their exploits, and, except for his "plan," such documents as the junior surveyor left appear to have been destroyed.[11]

The Byrd party had carried the line to Peter's Creek. In the fall of 1749 Colonel Fry and Colonel Jefferson extended it to Steep Rock Creek, in what is now Washington County. The plan itself shows that they crossed New River and many small streams and several ranges of mountains. The hardships and perils that they met must have been talked about in Tom's presence, for they became a tradition in his family. Years later his grandchildren repeated stories which must have come through him: that these men had to defend themselves against wild beasts by day, and to sleep in the trees at night; that their provisions ran low and they had to live on raw flesh; that Peter's courage did not fail when his companions fainted from exhaustion beside him.[12]

He and Fry went further than they had gone when drawing the Fairfax Line and both of them were now older. For their extraordinary trouble and painful service, however, they did not go unrewarded. Before the end of the year they reported their proceedings to the Council, produced an account of their expenses, and presented their maps.[13] Then the members of that body unanimously agreed that each of them was deserving of three hundred pounds sterling beyond all expenses. Nor were their abilities forgotten. Some months later the Acting Governor, following a directive from the Lords of Trade, selected them as the best qualified persons to draw a map of the inhabited part of Virginia. In October, 1751, the Honorable Lewis Burwell, whose daughter was wooed unsuccessfully by the son of Peter Jefferson, asked the opinion of the Council in regard to their compensation. Each was thought deserving of one hundred and fifty pounds sterling for his expense and trouble.[14]

Their map was done by that time, and, unlike the original materials on which it was based, it has withstood the ravages of fire and time for the simple reason that it was printed. It appeared in London in 1751; and a second edition, containing improvements by John Dalrymple, chiefly in the form of wagon roads, was issued four years later.[15] This

[11] The "plan," showing the part of the line drawn in 1728 as well as that drawn in 1749, is at UVA. The expedition appears to have been authorized by the Governor and Council, hence there need have been no legislative act. None has been found, at any rate.

[12] Domestic Life, pp. 19–20.

[13] Dec. 13, 1749; Council Journals, Colonial Va., V, 310.

[14] Oct. 15, 1751; Ibid., V, 354.

[15] Copy of first edition, UVA. In later editions it appears as a map of the "most" inhabited part of Virginia. Some copies have the erroneous date 1775. For comments see E. G. Swem, "Maps relating to Virginia," etc., Bulletin, VSL, VII, Nos. 2, 3, April, July, 1914; P. L. Phillips, "Virginia Cartography," Smithsonian Miscellaneous Collections, XXXVII (Washington, 1896); Va. Mag., XXX, 205. The map

second map was reproduced in successive atlases, and its superiority to all others up to the time that Thomas Jefferson compiled his *Notes on Virginia* was generally recognized. For geographical knowledge of his native country, therefore, he and his contemporaries were deeply indebted to his father. John Henry, father of Patrick, published a map in 1770, but this was not based on original surveys and it has generally been regarded as an inaccurate compilation.[16] Jefferson subscribed for it, but he probably had no more respect for it than he had for the legal training of John Henry's son.[17]

Soon after his map was published, Peter returned to Shadwell from Tuckahoe. His record of the tobacco crops on Colonel Randolph's quarters ends with 1751; thenceforth he farmed his own lands and rounded out his own estate. He drew no more major boundary lines, but he was county surveyor in Goochland that year; he was again a magistrate of Albemarle by the following spring, and a couple of years after that he became county surveyor there in succession to Joshua Fry, who had just died at Fort Cumberland while commanding the Virginia forces on the frontier.[18] George Washington was his lieutenant. Fry has been credited with being the chief constructive influence in the life of Peter Jefferson, and not improperly. His good will continued to manifest itself after he was dead. He named his associate an executor of his will, left him the surveying instruments which they had used together, and in effect bequeathed him his major public offices.[19]

Colonel Jefferson had been made the second military officer of Albemarle when the County was formed. He now succeeded Fry as county lieutenant and also as a member of the House of Burgesses. He served during two sessions of the Assembly in 1754 and 1755 but presumably he did not stand for re-election.[20] His legislative career was

appeared in Thomas Jefferys, *A General Topography of North America and the West Indies* (1768) and *American Atlas* (1775 and 1782); in W. Faden, *North American Atlas* (1777); in Thomas Jefferson's *Notes on Virginia*, and elsewhere.

[16] Phillips, p. 56. For an ironical contemporary comment, see William Rind, *Va. Gazette*, Sept. 27, 1770, communication signed "Geographicus."

[17] Account Book, Apr. 6, 1768.

[18] Peter Jefferson took the oath as county surveyor in Goochland on Aug. 20, 1751 (Goochland Order Book No. 7, p. 73). On the list of justices in Albemarle, in *Council Journals, Colonial Va.*, Apr. 30, 1752, his name was second, being just below that of Fry. Beginning in May, 1754, the surveys in this county were made by him and his assistants (Albemarle Surveyor's Book No. 1, Sect. 2, p. 288). The assistants, Thomas Turpin, John Smith, and John Staples, did most of the work, but surveyor's fees were owing him at the time of his death.

[19] Fairfax Harrison, in *W. & M.*, 2 ser., IV, 15; Slaughter, pp. 35-37.

[20] *Burgesses, Journals*, 1752-1755, 1756-1758, pp. vii, 211, 214, 235, 484. There is an order from him as county lieutenant in *Va. Mag.*, XXIII, 173-175; see also *The Cabells and Their Kin*, p. 77; and, on the functions of a county lieutenant, *Calendar of Virginia State Papers*, I, xxi-xxv. Details of his local activities in these years

approximately as brief and unimportant as that of his father-in-law Isham Randolph, but his service as county lieutenant appears to have lasted until the end of his life. He did nothing in particular in the French and Indian War, but he was the chief officer and the first citizen of the County. During much of this time Tom was away from home, at school in Goochland, but when the boy returned to look at the mountains and flourish in the sunshine of Albemarle there could be no doubt of his established position in the community.

Tom was about nine years old when the family moved back to Shadwell. Not until after his father's death five years later did he observe the full procession of the seasons in Albemarle; but he was here during vacations at least, and henceforth this place was home. It provided the domestic background of his life until he was twenty-seven. No mansion ever stood on this homesite but his father erected a substantial group of plantation buildings before he died.[21] He either enlarged the little house in which the boy had been born or built another wooden structure for the central unit; and he added a dairy, smokehouse, and other outbuildings of the sort until he had a frontage of more than two hundred feet above the river. To the southward the land sloped for several hundred yards to the Rivanna, where he had a water mill. This occupied a good deal of his son's attention, later on. The Three Notched Road passed the place on the north much as the highway does today and, proceeding westward through the gap, crossed the stream at the Secretary's Ford.

The ridge of the Southwest Mountains, which is broken at this gap, enters the present County in the extreme northeast and there it reaches its greatest height, fifteen hundred feet, in a knob which came to be called Peter's Mountain for Colonel Jefferson. As his son said, all the Virginia mountains run in the same direction, from northeast to southwest, but these, being the first discovered, appropriated the latter name to themselves.[22] The range roughly parallels the Blue Ridge, about twenty miles away. On its slopes Tom hunted, and beneath them many of the first plantation houses nestled. There may have been better sites

are scanty because of the gap in the Albemarle County records, but his prominence is unquestionable.

[21] The accounts of Fiske Kimball, *Va. Mag.*, LI, 313–325, and Marie Kimball, *Jefferson: The Road to Glory*, pp. 20–23, replace the hitherto accepted description in Randall, I, 2. On the basis of excavations, Mrs. Kimball believes that the line of buildings ran east and west and that the main house faced south. Extensive building operations were carried on in 1753 and thereafter.

[22] To Chastellux, Sept. 2, 1785, Bixby, p. 13. See also E. C. Mead, *Historic Homes of the South-West Mountains, Virginia.*

on the western side, whence the eye could command the Blue Ridge, but settlers had been attracted first to the eastern, which faced the sunrise. Properties ran in generous strips from the wooded summits to the lowlands. The largest of these dated back to a grant of more than thirteen thousand acres to Nicholas Meriwether which was referred to as "the Grant" because it was so early and so huge. This included the site of Castle Hill, some eight miles from Shadwell, though no plantation house had been erected there as yet. A considerable part of this lordly estate eventually came into the possession of Dr. Thomas Walker.[23] Wherever he may have been living when the Jeffersons came back, he soon served Peter as a friend and his son John afterwards became intimate with Tom. Closer at hand was John Harvie, who had bought lands adjoining the William Randolph property. It is uncertain just when he built Belmont but from an early time he was a near neighbor — as nearness was understood in Albemarle.

The Shadwell tract proper consisted of only four hundred acres but Colonel Jefferson soon purchased the place on the same side of the river that was later known as Pantops. His son always liked this because of its magnificent view. South of the river Peter's lands stretched toward Carter's Mountain and included not only the site of Monticello but also a small tract which he had patented in 1740 and which was known as Portobello. To this he now added another of the same size called Tufton. He also patented a body of woodland which is identified on Thomas Jefferson's land roll as "Pouncey's." Approximately two thousand six hundred and fifty acres that the latter afterwards held in this part of the County were acquired by his father.[24] Peter Jefferson was also increasing his holdings and developing his lands in another part of Albemarle. Three more children joined the family after the removal from Tuckahoe, including the twins, one of whom was a boy named Randolph. Peter built up for his sons two estates of practically the same size, one centering at Shadwell and the other on the South Fork of the James, sometimes called the Fluvanna.

Soon after the County was formed the Assembly had empowered him, Joshua Fry, and others to expend one hundred pounds in clearing the latter stream of rocks, which in several places obstructed navigation.[25] It was broader than the North Branch or Rivanna and, unlike it, served an important function in starting the money crop on the way to market. While the Jeffersons were still at Tuckahoe there had been

[23] Natalie J. Disbrow, "Thomas Walker of Albemarle," in *Papers of Albemarle Historical Society*, I (Charlottesville, 1941), 5–18, with abundant references.

[24] See Appendix II, A, and B, 1.

[25] February, 1745, Hening, V, 377–378.

a notable advance in the use of canoes above the fall line. This was owing to the ingenuity of the Reverend Robert Rose, a large planter, who lashed two of these "tottering vehicles" together and thus enabled them to carry eight or nine hogsheads of tobacco at a time without tipping.[26] Peter's tobacco from the Rivanna district had to go by land, either by wagon or by the crude method of rolling in specially constructed hogsheads, but he was able to employ water transportation on the Fluvanna. His main place there he named Snowdon after the mountain in Wales near the reputed home of his ancestors. In his lifetime the Fluvanna district was the more important part of the County. The courthouse was there, near the present town of Scottsville. He was one of the persons who had determined the location, and he owned houses at the ferry crossing which he leased to the keeper of an ordinary.[27] This was about twenty-five miles from Shadwell.

Not until the region below the Fluvanna had been separated from Albemarle, after Thomas Jefferson went to college, was the town of Charlottesville established by law and the courthouse located there.[28] It was built on its present site, about four miles west of Shadwell. This was too late to do Peter Jefferson any good but it was a convenience to his son as a practising lawyer. Even during the Revolution the county seat contained little besides a courthouse, a tavern, and a dozen houses. A traveler then observed that the region, when viewed from one of its many eminences, appeared as a vast forest, interspersed with plantations four or five miles apart and resembling small villages.[29] This was no land of bustling towns, nor predominantly of small farms. As a rule holdings were larger than in the Shenandoah Valley, though smaller than in Tidewater. When Peter Jefferson knew the region and his son was a boy, this was a silent country of far-flung patriarchal seats, though these were without architectural pretension. Afterwards, plain farmhouses on smaller clearings increased in number.

In the bottoms and on the lower slopes the red soil was rich in its virginal state, before it was exhausted by tobacco or ravaged by ero-

---

[26] T. J. Wertenbaker, *Old South*, p. 129, citing diary of Robert Rose, Mar. 16, June 27, 1749; James Maury, letter of Jan. 10, 1756, in Ann Maury, ed., *Memoirs of a Huguenot Family*, p. 388.

[27] John Harvie's Account Book, HEH., photostat UVA., pp. 12, 49.

[28] November, 1762, Hening, VII, 597. The act dividing the County and forming Buckingham and Amherst was in March, 1761; *Ibid.*, VII, 419. Part of it had been added to Bedford in 1754, *Ibid.*, VI, 441.

[29] Thomas Anburey, *Travels* (1923), II, 184, 187. On the region generally, see Abernethy, *Three Virginia Frontiers*, ch. 2. Charles W. Watts, after careful study of the holdings, concludes that they declined in size in the generation before the Revolution, and that in 1781 they stood approximately halfway between a comparable Tidewater county (James City) and Augusta, in the Valley.

sion. The temperate climate was favorable to Virginia's historic crop, and also to the fruit trees and grains which Peter Jefferson's son afterwards encouraged, while the dogwood, the redbud, and the shadbush made this a sylvan Paradise in spring. By all prevailing standards the district was healthful. The inhabitants often spoke of themselves as mountaineers and congratulated themselves on their freedom from agues and fevers. Before Thomas Jefferson was grown one of them said: "The descent of our lands is so quick, that morasses are scarcely known among us, and the rapidity of our waters so great that none of them has leisure to stagnate." [30] But the very rapidity of these waters increased the difficulties of transportation — which, more than any other single factor, distinguished the Piedmont from the region of the lower James. The large planters had slaves to perform the cruder tasks of pioneering, and they brought with them the agricultural economy and the social traditions of Tidewater; but in this isolated region they could not reproduce precisely the life of Westover or Turkey Island, or even of Tuckahoe. Styles were simpler here, self-sufficiency was more imperative, and one might expect an even more notable spirit of personal independence to be engendered.

For years after Peter Jefferson became a magistrate wolf bounties were listed at sessions of the county court — seventy pounds of tobacco for a young wolf and twice that much for an old one. There were no Indians here when the first settlers came, and during the French and Indian War this was not among the frontier counties but in the tier just before them. Fears of raids were voiced at that time but this had ceased to be a frontier region in the precise sense. Despite its vast body of uncleared lands it had an ordered, if dispersed, society. Nevertheless, residents of Albemarle remembered that Joshua Fry and Peter Jefferson had penetrated uncharted country, and men associated with the County followed their example. Thomas Walker of Castle Hill carried on the dividing line from the point where they had left it; and George Rogers Clark, who was born across the Southwest Mountains from Shadwell just about the time that Peter returned, conquered the Northwest during the Revolution. His younger and equally redheaded brother, William Clark, was born in another county after his family had left this one, but Meriwether Lewis, whose name is linked with his in the history of exploration, was a native. Under the direction of President Jefferson they crossed a continent. The tradition of the wilderness persisted in Albemarle.

[30] James Maury, June 15, 1760, in *Memoirs of a Huguenot Family*, p. 414. Many references to the healthfulness of the region can be found in Jefferson's own writings.

In this congenial locality Peter Jefferson kept on surveying lands and developing his farms until his great strength began to fail. Despite his reputed ability to "head up" two hogsheads of tobacco at the same time, he died when he was still less than fifty.[31] His elder son, then lanky at fourteen, was never to be quite that strong but was destined to live much longer. Perhaps the sire had given too freely of a strength that had seemed so abundant; perhaps he had exposed himself to too many hardships. Or it may be that the unknown malady which assailed him in the summer of 1757 could have been cured at a later stage in the progress of medicine. There were only two physicians in the County at the time and their practice was incidental. Dr. Walker, who attended him, is best known to history as an explorer and land-speculator. His professional visits to his friend were numerous and his services were as skillful as could have been expected.[32] They were unavailing, however, for the patient died on August 17.

He had become a man of substantial property, though it would be an exaggeration to call him a land baron. The Rivanna and Fluvanna tracts together comprised not far from five thousand acres and he had at least half that many more, chiefly in the County as then constituted.[33] He also had certain speculative claims, including an interest in the Loyal Land Company with Dr. Walker and others. For his time he was not much of a speculator, however, and his son was never one at all. The list of his slaves is impressive; he had more than sixty of them, along with twenty-five horses, seventy head of cattle, and two hundred hogs. These and other material details were revealed by the inventory of his considerable estate; and the will which he drew a few months before he died discloses the careful provisions he made for the future welfare of his wife, his two sons, and his six daughters.[34]

He prescribed an eminently fair distribution. He provided for his wife by leaving her for her lifetime the house and plantation at Shadwell, together with a sufficient portion of the slaves, stock, and horses. He left to each of his children a body servant, and to each of his daughters a carefully safeguarded portion of two hundred pounds to be paid within a year of her marriage or twenty-first birthday. He fully maintained the standard of Isham Randolph and he was determined that future husbands should not be kept waiting. He did not

[31] The family traditions are given by Randall, I, 13.

[32] Archibald Henderson, in *Proceedings American Antiquarian Society*, n.s., XLI (1932), 84–85.

[33] See Appendix II, A.

[34] Will dated July 13, 1757; proved Oct. 13, 1757. It and the inventory are in Will Book, No. 2, Albemarle County, pp. 32–34, 41–47; copies at UVA.

weigh the scales heavily in favor of the elder son, and none of the property was entailed. That son did not forget the lesson.

When he became twenty-one Thomas was to have either the lands on the Rivanna or the Fluvanna as he should choose, along with a proper share of the livestock, half of the slaves not otherwise disposed of, and the residue of the estate. The lands that he did not choose were to go ultimately to his brother Randolph, along with a similar portion of the slaves and stock. As the residuary legatee he got the larger share, but the distribution of property between him and his young brother was certainly far more equitable than the distribution of talents. Thomas also got his father's books, mathematical instruments, cherry-tree desk and bookcase; and his designated servant, the "mulatto fellow Sawney," was the most valuable slave.

The estate was a going concern during the remaining years of his minority and provided for the family comfortably. John Harvie was the working executor. There were fewer overseers than there had been at Tuckahoe — generally there were three; and the tobacco crop was only about half of what had come from Colonel Randolph's quarters, though much corn was raised and sold. Food, fuel, and some clothing came from the place, and the actual monetary requirements were slight by any modern standard. Even after his death, Peter Jefferson continued to be a good provider. He had selected men of substance as his executors. Young Thomas Jefferson consulted John Harvie and Colonel Peter Randolph occasionally and he maintained affectionate relations with Thomas Turpin, who was his uncle by marriage; but the one with whom he had most to do in later years was Thomas Walker.[35]

Not until he was grown could Thomas Jefferson do anything about the land and the slaves his father left him. It is uncertain just when he began to use the mathematical instruments that he inherited, but he was interested in surveying throughout his maturity. In spirit at least he could follow the trail across untrodden mountains; and as a draftsman, drawing plats and house plans, he was also his father's son. He probably used the cherry-tree desk in posting early accounts, as he had so often seen the Colonel do. One reason for leaving him the bookcase was that he had gone to it very frequently already. The forty volumes he is known to have inherited constituted an insignificant library in the light of his mature standards, but they formed the nucleus of his first collection.

[35] For details about the executors and later operations, see Appendix, II, A.

One can assume nothing in particular about the first master of Shadwell from the inventory list.[36] Bible and prayer book were there, as in almost every planter's library, along with books useful to a magistrate. There were several volumes of Addison and of English history, a work in astronomy, some books of a geographical nature, and six or eight maps. Thomas Jefferson's statement in old age about his father's neglected education must be coupled with the further comment that he had strong native intelligence and improved himself. This is certainly not to say, however, that this practical and mathematical man ever became an inveterate reader. There were reputable planters who had fewer books than he, but he did not have many. His major acquisitions were of another sort and his achievements were out of doors.

Upon the face of the record, his chief legacy to Thomas was an established position in society and the means to maintain it, but for that alone he would never have been honored in his son's memory as he was. Thomas Jefferson did not set that much store on inherited privilege. He may have imbibed certain democratic attitudes from his father, for the Colonel had associated with crude men on the frontier and in the wilderness and the tradition is that he understood and valued them. This surveyor of boundaries may have been critical of the group within which he had established himself more firmly than any of his ancestors had done. His son, in thoughtful maturity, was not at all displeased by memories of his indifference to social trappings. But Peter Jefferson exemplified the qualities of the ruling group which were really vital. From his career his heir might have observed that the aristocracy of Virginia had not yet grown old, that it was still close to the soil from which it sprang, that it continued to maintain a high sense of public responsibility. This strong and vigorous man may have been deficient in the refinements, but he embodied the fundamental qualities which enabled this society to endure.

For all his lack of book learning he deeply appreciated it, and it was he more than anyone else who caused his son to be well schooled. The tradition is that his dying instruction was that the boy should receive a thorough classical education, and Thomas himself said that he was more grateful for this than for all the other privileges which his father's care had placed within his reach.[37] If he had to choose between his estate and a liberal education he would have taken the latter, but no choice was necessary, for he was given both.

[36] Reproduced in *Va. Mag.*, X, 391. The works of Shakespeare were not included, despite the tradition.

[37] Randall, I, 18; to Joseph Priestley, Jan. 27, 1800 (L. & B., X, 147).

The Road to Enlightenment

⌈ III ⌉

Schooldays in Albemarle

1757–1760

TOM had no masculine companionship within the family after the death of his father. He had been separated from the Colonel much of the time during the past five years and he said relatively little about him afterwards, but undoubtedly he missed him. Late in life he said that from the age of fourteen his whole care and direction were thrown on himself, since he had no relative or friend who was qualified to advise or guide him.[1] This was an overstatement. The loss of his father created a chasm in his life which remained unfilled until his years in Williamsburg, when he found mature counselors whom he honored unreservedly; but in the meantime he consulted the executors occasionally, and he probably did not intend to reflect upon them or upon his mother.

He said much less about Jane Randolph Jefferson, however, than about his father. He acknowledged that she had an ancient pedigree — probably regarding this as a more important fact in his early manhood than he did later on.[2] Various entries in his financial records after he became a man reveal his solicitude for her welfare, and his almost complete failure to mention her name elsewhere may be attributed to his characteristic reticence about the women of his family. Nevertheless, the only remark he is known to have made about her influence was negative, and he probably did not value her counsel very highly. At no time in his life did he turn to women for serious advice, anyway. She may have remembered and sometimes mentioned to him the parish in London for which their place had been named. Perhaps she talked occasionally of her father's friends William Byrd and Peter Collinson, thus serving to link her son with the worlds of polite learning and scientific

---

[1] To T. J. Randolph, Nov. 24, 1808 (Ford, IX, 231).
[2] "Autobiography," Ford, I, 2.

curiosity. As a man of science and learning, however, he gained his chief inspiration elsewhere. He must have inherited some of his diverse talent from his mother, but there is no positive testimony about her personality, and she remains a shadowy figure.

The family tradition was that she was affectionate, cheerful, humorous, and a ready writer.[3] It has also been supposed that she was of more delicate mold than her husband, but almost the only thing about her that we can be sure of is that she had physical endurance beyond the average. She suffered inevitable hardships in connection with successive moves; she bore ten children altogether and brought up eight of them; and she survived her husband. He was considerably older than she, but in those days of incessant childbearing women were often worn out a great deal sooner. She was thirty-seven when Peter died and she lived nineteen years more, remaining a widow longer than she had been a wife. Her death happened to occur in the year that her elder son wrote the Declaration of Independence and the youngest of her children, the twins, attained their majority; but she did not live quite long enough to rejoice in either of these events.

Because of the death of two infant boys at Tuckahoe, daughters predominated in the household and there was a distinct gap between the five older children and the three younger, who were born after the return to Shadwell.[4] Of the younger group, Lucy was less than five when her father died and Anna Scott and Randolph were under two. In his teens Tom probably had little to do with these babies, and he never found real congeniality with Randolph. The five older children, Jane, Mary, Thomas, Elizabeth, and Martha, were born within a period of six years and it is no wonder that their mother did not do so well thereafter. In this group there was one case of obvious inequality. Whether she exhausted herself in bearing Thomas, or there was some mishap in the next delivery, the child she bore just after him was subnormal. The later story of this unfortunate girl can wait, but at least it can be said here that Elizabeth Jefferson afforded little companionship to her well-endowed brother.

Less than three years after her father's death the second daughter, Mary, married and left home, the dowry of two hundred pounds being duly paid to John Bolling. In a history of his family, printed a century later, it is said that he was six feet high and very large, and that he cared little for the ladies until he saw "his lady." Says this quaint record: "After many sighs, &c., he married Miss Jefferson, daughter of that Jefferson who, with Mr. Fry, made a map of Virginia." A footnote

[3] Randall, I, 15-17.
[4] For detailed information see Appendix I. C.

adds that she was a sister of the late President of the United States.[5] At the time of his marriage John Bolling was living in Goochland, which he afterwards represented in the House of Burgesses, and served as sheriff. He had a place called Fairfield, where his young brother-in-law appears to have stopped on his way to and from Williamsburg in student days. The roof was leaky and the young visitor was plagued with rats, but John Bolling was of the gentry and ultimately was called "Colonel," after he had moved to Chesterfield. Mary Jefferson had married well, and bore children profusely. Like her mother, she had ten.[6]

Thomas's sisters Jane and Martha meant more than the others in his life. Jane, nearly three years older than he, was his first favorite. Perhaps it was she who first showed him the Virginia bluebells in the lowlands along the Rivanna, and who wandered with him through the woods when the wild violets were open. It is said that she, more than any other member of the family, stimulated his boyish ambitions and encouraged him in his reading and his cultivation of music. He told his grandchildren of psalm tunes she used to sing to him. By that time he was remembering scenes long past, for he was only twenty-two when she died unmarried and he wrote for her a Latin epitaph.[7]

In the little building in the yard at Tuckahoe the older Jefferson girls probably shared their brother's early schooling. When the family returned to Shadwell, however, there was a separation, for Tom was either left behind in Goochland or was sent back soon thereafter. In 1752, when he was nine, his father placed him in the Latin school of the Reverend William Douglas, minister of St. James Parish, Northam. He boarded at the clergyman's house during the school term and remained under his instruction until the year that Colonel Jefferson died.[8] There were probably other pupils but not many. Because of the dispersed population and the lack of towns in Virginia, education was on an individual rather than a civic basis, and opportunity was largely

[5] *A Memoir of a Portion of the Bolling Family: Wynne's Historical Documents from the Old Dominion, No. IV* (privately printed, Richmond, 1868).

[6] On Bolling, see *Va. Mag.*, XXII, 331; on Fairfield, see *Calendar Va. State Papers*, II, 78. In Jefferson's letter to Page, Dec. 25, 1762, in Ford, I, 341–346, he speaks of the place as being within an easy day's ride of Shadwell.

[7] Randall, I, 40–41; *Domestic Life*, pp. 38–39. This begins: "Ah, Joanna, puellarum optima."

[8] Ford, I, 3. Peter Jefferson's Account Book shows a payment for two years' schooling and board at the rate of £16 a year, presumably for the years 1752–1754. Thomas himself is authority for the statement that he stayed until 1757. On Douglas, see Meade, pp. 457–459; W. S. Perry, ed., *Hist. Colls. Relating to the American Colonial Church*, Vol. I, Virginia (1870), 365, 377, 411–413.

restricted to the gentry. The sons of the greater landowners had all the advantages and disadvantages that go with private instruction. The quality of this instruction was often high, but it naturally varied with the tutors who were available. More often than not they were clergymen.

Some of these teachers of little groups of gentlemen's sons, like Donald Robertson who taught James Madison, have become moderately famous through the grateful comments of their distinguished pupils.[9] In this respect William Douglas was unfortunate, for Jefferson did not speak well of him. He was a Scotchman who had come to Goochland a couple of years before 1752, soon after his ordination. The ecclesiastical authorities preferred graduates of Oxford or Cambridge to men who had been bred in Presbyterianism, and some of the planters, like Robert Carter of Nomini Hall, objected to the Scottish accent in a tutor. James Madison jokingly remarked that the Scottish French he learned from Robertson proved an embarrassment.[10] Thomas Jefferson started out with the same sort of French and may have had the same thought when he first went to Paris, but his surviving comments relate to Latin and Greek, which were his major subjects. In his mature opinion, Douglas knew little of the one and less of the other. Much nearer home a competent classicist was awaiting him, and he probably became aware of the limitations of the Reverend William Douglas after he had begun to study under the Reverend James Maury.

Early in 1758, when he was fourteen, he began to attend Maury's little school. The clergyman was then forty years old and for six years had been officiating in Fredericksville Parish, which now included the part of Albemarle lying north and west of the Rivanna.[11] Maury regarded it as the most extensive and inconvenient parish in the Colony that was regularly served. Even after he established himself strategically on a pleasant plantation beneath the Southwest Mountains, a couple of miles from his wife's uncle, Dr. Thomas Walker, he spoke of himself as leading a postboy's life. He had three churches and a chapel, and was trying to support a family of eight children. Young Thomas Jefferson was soon called upon to be one of the baptismal sponsors for the ninth child, a boy named Abraham. There were to be others later.

It was partly for the instruction of his sons and partly to supplement his income that this man of piety and learning set up a small school in

[9] Irving Brant, *James Madison*, p. 60.

[10] Randall, II, 192 *n.*

[11] Excellent account of Maury by Helen D. Bullock in *Papers Albemarle Historical Society*, II (1942), 36–39, based on the fresh materials in the Maury Deposit, UVA, and citing other sources.

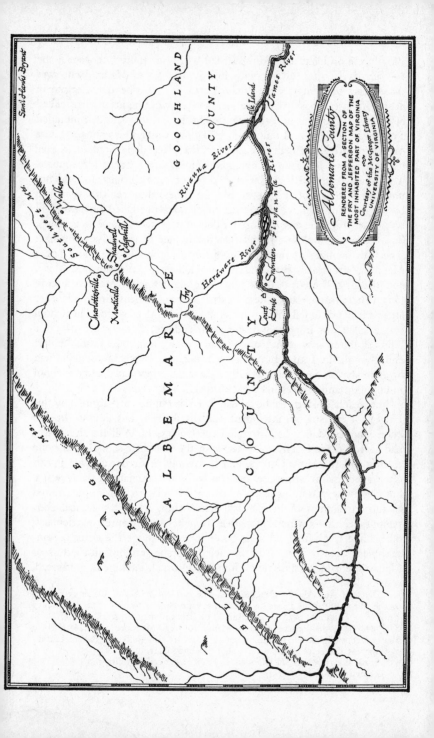

Albemarle County

RENDERED FROM A SECTION OF
THE FRY AND JEFFERSON MAP OF THE
MOST INHABITED PART OF VIRGINIA

Courtesy of the McGregor Library
UNIVERSITY OF VIRGINIA

GOOCHLAND COUNTY

ALBEMARLE COUNTY

BLUE RIDGE Mts.

Sam'l Hawes Bryant

Walker

Shadwell
Edgehill

Charlottesville
Monticello

South West Mts.

Fry

Rivanna River

Hardware River

Carter
Doyle

Elk Island

James River

Fluvanna River

Staunton

a log house on his place. Tom boarded with the family but went home on Saturdays, often taking with him young James Maury, who was three years his junior, rather than Matthew, a prospective clergyman nearer his age. These two were members of what he afterwards called his "class." This was said to have numbered only five, and it included a promising boy from Louisa named Dabney Carr. The younger James Maury pointed out, many years later, the place designated for a race between Tom Jefferson's slow pony and Dabney Carr's swift horse. Tom had suggested that this should occur on February 30, and not until the last day of the month did the others discover that they had been taken in.[12] This early Jeffersonian hoax produced no lasting ill will, however; the disappointed rider of the swift horse was, for a dozen years, the closest friend that the owner of the slow pony had. The fifth member of the class was probably John Walker, and James Madison, afterwards president of the College of William and Mary, and the first Episcopal Bishop of Virginia, came to Maury's before long. Their teacher once described these two as being in good order and well conditioned, like so many hogsheads of tobacco. The school was a small but important fount of friendship. For a score of years Thomas Jefferson was intimate with his county neighbor, John Walker; and, though the future Bishop of Virginia was six years younger than he and may not have been actually a classmate, they had Maury's school in common and always liked each other.

The teacher of these boys had been brought to Virginia by his Huguenot parents, an intelligent and deeply religious couple. In due course James Maury had attended the College of William and Mary, had served there briefly as an usher in the grammar school, had gone to England for Holy Orders, and had come to Fredericksville Parish after a rectorship elsewhere. He was to be unfortunate in many ways, but clearly he was no ordinary schoolmaster. His greatest pupil attested to the correctness of his classical scholarship, while his clerical contemporary, the Reverend Jonathan Boucher, commented particularly on his fine English style.[13] It is easier for us to judge the latter accomplishment than to realize the former, for some sermons and letters of Maury's remain.[14] These reveal him as a spiritual, intelligent, cultivated,

---

[12] Diary of Ann Maury, Oct. 28, 1831. Maury Deposit, UVA. Other references on the "class" are Anne Fontaine Maury, *Intimate Virginiana, A Century of Maury Travels by Land and Sea*, p. 12; Jefferson to James Maury, Apr. 25, 1812 (L. & B. XIII, 144–149); the Reverend James Maury to John Madison, Nov. 24, 1764, in Maury Deposit; Jefferson to Thomas Stone, Mar. 16, 1782, Jefferson Papers, Library of Congress (hereafter LC), 8:1226, about Dabney Carr.

[13] Ford, I, 3; Boucher, *Reminiscences of an American Loyalist*, p. 61.

[14] Maury Deposit.

and observant man, who wrote with vigor generally, with vividness at times, and too often with prolixity.

By the time that Thomas Jefferson began to attend his school Maury was in bad health, worn down by his labors, burdened with the care of his large and growing family. He was already a harassed if not an unhappy man.[15] For boarding and teaching a young gentleman he received twenty pounds a year in 1758 and 1759, when John Harvie paid him on behalf of the Jefferson estate.[16] A decade later, when the price of food had risen and his own children had increased in number, he concluded that this was small compensation for the additional expense to his table, the extraordinary trouble to his family, and his own labor and fatigue from this "toilsome business." Accordingly, he then increased his charge to twenty-five pounds over the protests of certain patrons. Some of the planters, in his opinion, set a higher value on instruction in dancing than on the intellectual and spiritual services that he performed.[17] He had no complaints against the Jeffersons, however, and he was not so embittered when Thomas went to school. He had not yet participated unsuccessfully in the Parsons' Cause.

During the boy's first year in the log schoolhouse, the Assembly passed what was called the Two Penny Act, and against this he heard his teacher inveigh in the household.[18] Like an earlier act, which Maury had accepted as a temporary necessity, it provided that the clergy and certain public officials be paid, not in tobacco, but in money at a specified rate. Owing to the shortness of the crop, this rate was considerably below the market price of the season and the clergy could anticipate a loss. The second act they opposed on legal grounds which seemed unassailable, and upon one important occasion Maury was their standard-bearer. Supported by an Order in Council, he brought suit against his vestry for the balance that appeared to be due him, and but for Patrick Henry he might have been successful. The Hanover County Court had no choice but to rule in his favor, but the jury, under Henry's spell, awarded him damages of only one penny.

This historic controversy culminated after Jefferson had left Maury's and he did not remember much about it afterwards. However, he must

---

[15] His letter of May 31, 1758, to the Reverend William Douglas, Maury Deposit, is particularly depressed; his letters in *Memoirs of a Huguenot Family* speak more of general conditions.

[16] Harvie's Account Book.

[17] Letter to Col. John Bolling, Dec. 1767; to Thomas Bolling, Jan. 23, 1768, in Letter Book, 1763–1768, Maury Deposit.

[18] To William Wirt, Aug. 14, 1814 (Ford, IX, 467). On the Parsons' Cause, see H. J. Eckenrode, *Separation of Church and State in Va.* (1910), ch. 2; G. C. Smith in *Tyler's Mag.*, XXI (1939), 140–171, 193–206.

have regretted the unpopularity with the laity which his teacher gained. Technically, Maury was right, for the Virginia lawmakers had been overruled by the supreme British authorities. On the other hand, he appeared to be opposing the general interest and the judgment of the Assembly, in his own behalf and in the interest of his class. Later issues were thus foreshadowed and on these Jefferson was to take a stand against the clergy. It is obvious that he did not get from Maury his ideas about the relations between church and state. Nor did the future advocate of religious freedom get from this teacher any germinal ideas about the just treatment of dissenters. The boy must have observed that the Rector of Fredericksville was bitterly intolerant.[19] Maury was often critical of the British government, but Jefferson, unlike his friend John Page, never regarded his tutor as the fountainhead of his Whiggish principles.[20]

From his first notable teacher, Jefferson gained none of his characteristic political principles or religious ideas. He was indebted to him, however, more than to any other man, for his training in the classics. After two years in this school he was able to read Greek and Roman authors in the original, and this he continued to do throughout his long life. Gratefully and properly he recognized his inadequately educated father as the first cause, but he also said that the acquisition of ancient languages should be the occupation of only the early years. The "deep and lasting impressions" on his own memory must have come from days at Maury's school.[21]

Years later he told John Adams that the idea occurred to him in early life that the best clues to the proper pronunciation of the ancient languages were to be obtained from modern Greeks and Italians.[22] There is no authority for crediting this idea to Maury, and it is known that Jefferson became acquainted with Italians shortly before the Revolution.[23] As for Greek, which he regarded as the most perfect language, the pursuance of his idea had to be left until he went to Paris. This lifelong student had a natural linguistic gift and he found teachers

---

[19] Maury's intolerance was clearly shown in his posthumous pamphlet, *To Christians of every Denomination among us, especially those of the Established Church* . . . (Annapolis, 1771), directed particularly against the Anabaptists.

[20] John Page on William Price, *Va. Hist. Register*, July 1850, p. 146.

[21] To Joseph Priestley, Jan. 27, 1800, A. A. Lipscomb and A. E. Bergh, *Writings of Thomas Jefferson* (hereafter cited as L. & B.), X, 146–147; to John Brazier, Aug. 24, 1819, *Ibid.*, XV, 207–211. An excellent recent discussion is L. B. Wright, "Thomas Jefferson and the Classics," *Procs. Am. Philos. Soc.*, Vol. 87, No. 3, July 1943, pp. 223–233.

[22] Mar. 21, 1819 (L. & B., XV, 181–182).

[23] *Memoirs of . . . Philip Mazzei*, pp. 186, 193, 203.

everywhere, but Maury was the first important one. In a log house below the Southwest Mountains he received at an impressionable age personal instruction from a sound scholar who was aware of the niceties of language and the beauties of literature.

However rigid James Maury may have been as a churchman, his enthusiasm for the classics was discriminating, just as that of his most famous pupil was. He could hardly have doubted the indispensability of classical training for such a pupil as Thomas Jefferson, who was clearly marked for a profession and the "exalted spheres of life." But he seriously questioned its utility for most of the sons of the gentry, who had tried him no little and whose customary life he had carefully observed. Very few of them prosecuted their studies as long as their twentieth year, he said; they commonly married very young and were soon encumbered with families; they had to give constant attention to the management of their large estates, regardless of inherited fortune. It could not be expected, therefore, that they would have the necessary leisure and repose "for a pleasurable or successful engagement in such parts of literature as the languages, criticism, and curious and deep researches into antiquity." [24]

This was no prophecy of Jefferson's career, but Maury probably encouraged him to delve into modern literature as well as ancient, in the spirit of the Enlightenment, and he probably made a distinctive contribution to the boy's education in his emphasis on the Mother Tongue. The minister described English as "a language as copious and nervous, as significant and expressive, as numerous and musical, nay, to my own ears as enchanting as any that was ever spoken by any of the different families of the earth." [25] For his time and place he had a large library and he must sometimes have given his pupil advice similar to that he gave his own son. "I would recommend it to you to reflect, and remark on, and digest what you read; to enter into the spirit and design of your author; to observe every step he takes to accomplish his end; and to dwell on any remarkable beauties of diction, justness or sublimity of sentiment, or masterly strokes of true wit which may occur in the course of your reading." [26] Jefferson's emphasis was to be more severely practical but he himself afterwards made recommendations not dissimilar to these. Upon occasion he added another

[24] "A Dissertation on Education, in the form of a Letter from James Maury to Robert Jackson, July 17, 1762," ed. by Helen D. Bullock, *Papers Albemarle County Hist. Soc.*, II, 43.

[25] *Ibid.*, II, 47.

[26] To his son James, Feb. 17, 1762 (Maury Deposit). On his library, see *Va. Mag.*, VII, 302.

which he could hardly have got here, namely, that two words should not be used when one will do.

From the story of the projected horse race it must not be assumed that Tom Jefferson was restricted to a slow pony. Perhaps he did not begin riding as soon as his younger kinsman, John Randolph of Roanoke, who is said to have been foaled, not born; but his father doubtless started him early. Thomas regarded George Washington as the best horseman of the age, but he himself was described in later life as an "uncommonly fine rider" and the family remembered him as a fearless one.[27]

In a country without large settlements and where plantation seats were far apart, riding was not a matter of occasional diversion but of daily necessity, and good horsemanship was taken for granted among the gentry. Over the red roads of Albemarle, which wandered so capriciously through the growing trees and the fallen timber, Tom took many a ride, not for purposes of health as in his later life, but simply to go from one place to another. However, he was not one of those Virginians, described by Revolutionary travelers, who would go five miles to catch a horse in order to ride one mile afterwards. On the contrary, he came to believe that the taming of the horse had resulted in the degeneracy of the human body, and he commended walking for exercise from the time that he began to advise the young.[28]

He must have begun his walking early, tramping through the woods and hunting. The family preserved a story about his first adventures as a huntsman. When he was ten he was given a gun by his father and sent into the forest alone in order to develop self-reliance. The inexperienced boy was wholly unsuccessful at first in his quest of quarry; but at length he found a wild turkey caught in a pen, tied it to a tree with his garter, shot it, and brought it home in triumph.[29] This may have been at Tuckahoe, but boyish hunting was in the Albemarle tradition. His grandson, who claims never to have worn hat or shoe until he was ten, used to arise at dawn and tramp barefoot through the snow in quest of wild turkeys;[30] and long years after Jefferson himself shot his first bird, he reported with obvious approval an instance of even greater intrepidity. He had this to say of Meriwether Lewis, who grew up here and whom he sent across a continent:

[27] Comment of his chief overseer, Edmund Bacon, in H. W. Pierson, *Jefferson at Monticello*, p. 74; Randall, I, 68, quoting his grandson, T. J. Randolph.

[28] To Peter Carr, Aug. 19, 1785 (L. & B., V, 85–86). For comments on the Virginians' love of horses, see J. F. D. Smyth, *A Tour in the U. S. of America* (1784), I, 20–23.

[29] Memoirs of T. J. Randolph, p. 3, Edgehill Randolph Papers, UVA.

[30] *Ibid.*, p. 6.

He . . . was remarkable even in his infancy for enterprise, boldness and discretion. When only eight years of age, he habitually went out, in the dead of night, alone with his dogs, into the forest to hunt the raccoon and opossum, which, seeking their food in the night, can then only be taken. In this exercise no season or circumstance could obstruct his purpose, plunging through the winter's snows and frozen streams in pursuit of his object.[31]

He himself may not have showed such zeal as this at any age, but from his youth he was familiar with the habits of the coons and possums. Observation of plants and animals, rather than stalking prey, was characteristic of him in his maturity; and, though he continued to recommend hunting as an admirable form of youthful exercise and appears to have engaged in it himself to some degree, there is no reliable evidence that he was an ardent sportsman.[32] His father had started him in the school of self-reliance, but when he first began to think he may have concluded that nature should be explored and not exploited.

Accomplishments were expected of him as a young gentleman. Dancing, which was proverbially popular, was little short of a social necessity. "Virginians are of genuine blood," said Philip Fithian. "They will dance or die." [33] During his second year at Maury's, his father's executor John Harvie made a payment to Mr. Inglis "for teaching 5 children 6 mo. to dance." [34] This instruction Tom shared with four of his sisters. We do not know whether or not the dancing class went from house to house, as in Westmoreland, thus permitting a better balance of the sexes; but before he entered the Raleigh Tavern he was probably familiar with the minuets, reels, and country dances which were so often mentioned by the pre-Revolutionary diarists. Two years before the Declaration of Independence, one of these said: "Any young gentleman, travelling through the Colony . . . is presumed to be acquainted with dancing, boxing, playing the fiddle, and small sword, and cards." [35] Somewhat less may have been required in the 'sixties, but young Thomas Jefferson had another of these accomplishments besides dancing before he went away to college. It is said that while he was still at Maury's his favorite indoor amusement was playing on the violin, and that he was already proficient for his years.[36]

We have no information about his first music teacher, but it must

[31] L. & B., XVIII, 142.
[32] Comments on his hunting by an old slave may be seen in the ms. Life of Isaac Jefferson, UVA.
[33] Philip Vickers Fithian, *Journal and Letters, 1767–1774*, ed. by J. R. Williams, Aug. 25, 1774 (referred to hereafter as Fithian, by date).
[34] Oct. 24, 1759; Account Book of John Harvie.
[35] Fithian, Aug. 17, 1774.
[36] Randall, I, 18.

have been before he went to Williamsburg and found new opportunities there that he learned to play. In the musical language of his time this was not by "rote or ear," but "by book according to the gamut." [37] On one of his first trips toward the colonial capital he met Patrick Henry, who fiddled by ear. This might be said to sum up the difference between them as statesmen, also, though the younger man's political ear afterwards became sensitive. Jefferson knew the country fiddle tunes, which were played at balls as well as at countless informal rustic gatherings, and he copied them in his music books. Also, at some time he wrote, in a copy of Daniel Purcell's *Psalms set full for the Organ or Harpsichord* (1727), the words of the new version, from the metrical translations of Tate and Brady which were gradually superseding the older psalter. These were the tunes, presumably, that his sister Jane sang so often and that he played with her. He always preferred them to hymns and they always recalled her presence.

What Thomas looked like as he neared seventeen we can only conjecture from the descriptions given of him long afterwards, when observations seemed to be worth recording. He had large hands and feet and by this time must have grown tall; he towered well over six feet eventually and was very strong even though never quite up to his father's standard.[38] His movements are said to have been rather awkward; his hair was reddish in youth, and he freckled quickly. His eyes were hazel, though often described in later years as blue, and, judging by how long he kept them, his teeth must have been magnificent. He had good health throughout most of his life, along with comparable vitality. Nobody ever claimed that he was handsome, but it was often said afterwards that he looked benevolent, and he always prized the quality of good nature.[39] He was thin-skinned, however, and for many years had to overcome his native shyness. He may have been rather indifferent to clothes during his rustic period, as he was when he started to grow old, but he became fastidious enough after he began to notice the girls in Williamsburg. The colonial capital was his finishing school of manners, and he did not become a "compleat gentleman" until after he had begun to go to the Governor's Palace there.

[37] John Playford, *An Introduction to the Skill of Musick* (ed. of 1718), pp. 81–82. He afterwards had this book in his library. For this and other musical items, I am indebted to Mrs. Helen D. Bullock.

[38] On his strength, see Pierson, *Jefferson at Monticello*, p. 70.

[39] Chastellux, whose description of him before he was forty is one of the earliest on record, speaks of his countenance as being "mild and pleasing," while strongly intimating that he lacked "exterior grace"; quoted by Randall, I, 373.

[IV]

At the College
1760–1762

IN the year 1760 Thomas Jefferson emerged from the hills and
entered the College of William and Mary in Williamsburg. His
future friend and rival John Adams was then five years out of Harvard;
but Alexander Hamilton, in the British West Indies, was little beyond
the toddling stage. George Washington, whose advanced schooling
was gained in Indian warfare, had married Martha Custis and was farming at Mount Vernon, hoping that his days of campaigning were over.
Sagacious Benjamin Franklin, who had picked up most of his youthful
learning in a printing shop, was in England, high in scientific favor and
having the time of his life. In this same year King George III ascended
the English throne, unaware that in the village capital of the royal
Province of Virginia there was a stripling who would one day de-
nounce him in immortal language.

Up to this time, so far as we know, the future author of the Declaration of Independence had written nothing suggesting the cadences
of that historic document or anticipating his later grace, but he had
drafted one letter which has survived. This was an eager but stilted
note to John Harvie, proposing that he leave the mountains for the
College. After talking things over with another executor, Colonel
Peter Randolph, he had soberly marshaled his arguments to justify an
important step.[1] He could continue his study of the classics at the
College, he believed; he could learn something of mathematics, and he
could gain "a more universal acquaintance" there. If these reasons were
insufficient, others could have been easily adduced. Having outgrown
Maury's, this promising boy deserved other opportunities and it seemed
highly unlikely that he would waste them. He himself remarked that
the coming of company was causing him to lose a fourth of his time

[1] Jan. 14, 1760 (Ford, I, 340).

at home. He was already impatient with encroachment on his precious hours, and any hindrance to his pursuit of knowledge.

After a while he talked a good deal about going to England, but this possibility seems not to have been considered seriously at first, if it ever was. His advisers were doubtless aware that there was confusion in the College. This was to continue until the Revolution and to cause some of the gentry to question the propriety of sending their sons there for moral improvement and the acquisition of sound learning.[2] On the other hand, there were those who said that education was a good deal worse in England, and with them the mature Jefferson would have heartily agreed. Several Virginians, among them Robert Carter of Nomini Hall (who afterwards fully redeemed himself), had returned "so inconceivably illiterate, and also corrupted and vicious," that Mann Page of Rosewell swore that no son of his should go to school in England. Accordingly, this wealthy planter sent his son John to the grammar school of William and Mary at the age of thirteen and put him to lodge and board with President Thomas Dawson, who was also commissary of the Bishop of London and minister of Bruton Church.[3] Peter Jefferson's son, who entered at a higher level as he was nearing seventeen, likewise escaped foreign contamination, though he gained no high impression of the learning and morals of the clergymen on the faculty during his student days in Williamsburg.

Lodging and eating in the College were not compulsory for "paying scholars," but the surviving records imply that he did not avail himself of the privilege of living in town. He began to pay board on March 25, 1760, and continued to do so for two years and one month. Then, so far as the records show, his college career was over.[4] About this time the faculty were forced to enjoin the housekeeper to serve both fresh and salt meat for dinner, to provide puddings and pies on Sunday and two weekdays, and to see that the suppers were not made up of different sorts of scraps but were the same for every table. The chief complaint came after Jefferson had left the College, but, like the other boys, he probably suffered from the negligence of a housekeeper who was away too often. A year or more after his departure she was away for good.[5]

[2] J. C. Ballagh, ed., *Letters of Richard Henry Lee*, I, 70–71; Fithian, Feb. 12, 1774.

[3] *Va. Hist. Register*, July 1850, p. 146.

[4] "Notes Relating to Some of the Students Who Attended the College of William and Mary," *W. & M.*, 2 ser., I, 27–42; *A Provisional List of Alumni . . . of the College of William and Mary in Virginia, from 1693 to 1888.*

[5] *W. & M.*, 1 ser. III, 196, 262–264. The offending housekeeper, Mrs. Isabella Cocke, was there 1761–1763.

The main building, then more than sixty years old, was generally termed the College, though there was also the Brafferton, where a handful of Indians stayed. Opposite this stood the President's House. Some twenty years after his student days Jefferson described the College and the hospital in Williamsburg as "rude, mis-shapen piles, which, but that they have roofs, would be taken for brick-kilns." [6] This, however, was after he had fallen under the spell of Palladio; his architectural judgment could hardly have been that severe when he was a youth, fresh from the frame buildings of Albemarle. At a later time he also condemned the educational organization of the College and tried to improve it. The statutes had been revised a couple of years before he entered, but in framework the College was essentially unchanged from 1729 until he became governor of Virginia half a century later.[7] It consisted of the grammar school, which was preparatory; the Indian school, which a few redskins still attended; the philosophy school, in which he himself was enrolled; and the divinity school, which he afterwards helped to abolish. Two professors were assigned to each of the two latter; and each of the former had a single master. With the president, the entire faculty consisted of seven men, and there were probably not more than a hundred scholars and students altogether.

With the single but important exception of William Small, professor of natural philosophy, the members of the William and Mary faculty were Anglican clergymen, and for half a dozen years they had been embroiled in controversy with the local political authorities.[8] Two years before Jefferson enrolled there had been an upheaval, and it was as a result of this that Small had come to the College. Because of their activities against the Two Penny Act, which as we have seen affected the pay of the clergy unfavorably, three of the professors had been dismissed by the local governing body, the Board of Visitors. One of these men died but the two others appealed to England for reinstatement and, after Jefferson had left the College, won their fight. This proved bad for Small. When Jefferson arrived on the scene, however, he was there, teaching physics, metaphysics, and mathematics, and through force of circumstances was soon teaching practically everything else.

[6] In his *Notes on Virginia* (Ford, III, 258).

[7] Statutes of 1758, *W. & M.*, 1 ser., XVI, 241–256. See also Jefferson's later bill for amending the constitution, Sect. I (Ford, II, 229–232).

[8] The account of the faculty is based largely on "Journal of the Meetings of the President and Masters of William and Mary College," *W. & M.*, 1 ser., III, 60–64, 128–132, 195–197, 262–265; IV, 43–46, 130–132, 187–192; V, 224–229. See also *Ibid.*, 1 ser., IX, 153–154; XIX, 20; R. Goodwin, *A Brief & True Report concerning Williamsburg in Virginia*, pp. 38–43.

Jefferson's other teacher at first was the Reverend Jacob Rowe, professor of moral philosophy, whose field comprised rhetoric, logic, and ethics. In the August of Jefferson's first year (which had begun in late March and was interrupted by no long summer vacation), Rowe and the Master of the grammar school became far too merry and led the college boys in a row with the boys of the town. Consequently, one of these clergymen was summarily dismissed and the other resigned. The immediate results were favorable to Jefferson. Almost a year passed before a successor to the deposed professor of moral philosophy was installed, and in the interim Small added all or many of Rowe's subjects to his own. He was already giving Jefferson his first views of the "expansion of science," and, according to this eminent pupil, he gave the first lectures ever delivered in the College in ethics, rhetoric, and belles-lettres.[9] Either these subjects had been previously sacrificed to logic, or they had been taught more mechanically by men who lacked Small's happy talent of communication. For nearly half of Jefferson's course Small appears to have been the only regular teacher that he had. Whatever may be thought about the organization, administration, and discipline of the College, here was one of those rare personal influences which prove unforgettable and elicit immortal tribute. He afterwards said that Small probably fixed the destinies of his life.

But for Small, the first year must have been deeply disillusioning to him. In the midst of all the woes created by convivial and riotous members of the faculty, President Dawson himself began to drink notoriously, and, when arraigned before the Board of Visitors on the charge of habitual drunkenness, confessed the fact. His friend, Lieutenant Governor Fauquier, defended him, saying that "he had been teased by contrariety of opinions between him and the clergy into the loss of his spirits, and it was no wonder that he should apply for consolation to spirituous liquors."[10] He was granted a pardon on the promise of future sobriety, but the unfortunate man became quite irresponsible. He died in December. Not until spring did the Reverend William Yates, from whose arid teaching John Page had suffered elsewhere, qualify as his successor. He also became minister of Bruton Church, which Jefferson attended, sitting near the pulpit in the half of the south gallery which was assigned to the College.[11]

The scandals and confusion which the youth observed in his first

[9] "Autobiography," Ford, I, 4; to L. H. Girardin, Jan. 15, 1815 (L. & B., XIV, 231).

[10] W. S. Perry, ed., *Historical Collections Relating to the American Colonial Church* (hereafter cited as Perry, *Hist. Colls.*), I, 517.

[11] W. A. R. Goodwin, *Historical Sketch of Bruton Church,* p. 44.

year must have made a deep impression on so sensitive a mind, but at this immature age he was not deeply interested in the continuing struggle between the clerical faculty and the local governing board.[12] The fundamental question was whether the Bishop of London or the gentlemen of Virginia should have final authority over the College and the Church, and the gentry would have given the same answer to this if Thomas Jefferson had never gone to school in Williamsburg. His later distinction among his fellows was owing to his championship, not merely of local self-government, but of complete religious liberty. The seeds of anticlericalism, however, were probably sown in his mind while he was in college or soon afterwards, when he became intimate with Francis Fauquier. He could hardly have failed to learn that the relations between the brilliant Governor and the local representatives of English ecclesiasticism were far from amicable, and on personal grounds his sympathies may have been enlisted against the clergy.[13] It is a highly significant fact, also, that the early teacher who did most to fix the destinies of his life was the only layman in the faculty of the College.

The surviving record of this influential layman is all too brief.[14] He was a Scotchman, designated as "Mr. William Small" when he was appointed in 1758. He remained in Williamsburg six years, returned to England where he is said to have been the friend of James Watt and Erasmus Darwin, and died at Birmingham in 1775, listed as "William Small, M.D." He had assumed the title after he left Virginia. The circumstances of his going were unpleasant.[15] His predecessor as professor of natural philosophy was successful in his appeal to England and had to be restored. Small had been sent over by the Bishop of London in the first place, but he had less reason than his clerical colleagues to rely on English ecclesiastical authority and during his stay in the Colony he was on more friendly terms than the others with the local political group. It was a sign of the approval of the Board of Visitors that they proceeded to elect him to the chair of moral philosophy, which was again vacant, after he had lost the professorship of natural philosophy. At the same time, however, the Board passed a statute affirming the

[12] J. E. Kirkpatrick, "Constitutional Development of the College of William and Mary," *W. & M.*, 2 ser., VI, 95–108.

[13] Perry, *Hist. Colls.*, I, 464, 470–472, 517.

[14] Besides references to faculty meetings, see *W. & M.*, 1 ser., XVI, 164–168; *Va. Mag.*, XVI, 209–210; *Gentleman's Magazine and Historical Chronicle*, XLV, 151 (London, 1775); Burk, *History of Virginia*, III, 399–400. His salary was paid until Sept. 15, 1764, but he probably left earlier.

[15] The most dependable source is a letter from Stephen to Edward Hawtrey, Mar. 26, 1765 (W. & M. Coll. Papers, Folder 12). This is based on a conversation with Small.

right to remove any member of the faculty at will. Small balked at agreeing to that, went to England to look into the matter further, and declined to return. There were some other matters of disagreement and in the end he aroused the strong displeasure of the presiding officer of the Board, who wrote him a sarcastic letter.[16] At some time Jefferson probably learned about all this and he may have reflected that local authority itself is likely to become tyrannical. What he learned from his favorite teacher was not obedience to authority but delight in the exercise of his mind.

John Page, in the last year of his own life, referred to this same teacher as "illustrious," and credited to him the beginnings of his own abiding interest in all branches of mathematics.[17] Shortly after Small left the College, Jefferson was probably thinking of him when he described the study of mathematics and natural philosophy as "peculiarly engaging and delightful." He certainly was, when he took up mathematics again long afterwards, in order to guide his grandson's course, and endeavored to rub off the dust of fifty years. It was always his favorite subject, he said. "We have no theories there, no uncertainties remain on the mind; all is demonstration and satisfaction. I have forgotten much, and recover it with more difficulty than when in the vigor of my mind I originally acquired it." But, as he soon wrote to another, "thanks to the good foundation laid at college by my old master and friend Small, I am doing it with a delight and success beyond my expectation." [18]

Jefferson observed that Small pursued an "even and dignified line" of conduct, like others whom he particularly emulated in those crucial days.[19] This layman was not one to be involved in student brawls. On the other hand, in an era of disorder, he alone of the faculty denied the arbitrary power of a master to inflict punishment on an offending scholar. John Page called him his "ever to be beloved professor," and Jefferson said that he gave to his studies enlightened and affectionate guidance and was like a father to him. Actually, this unmarried teacher, whose chief complaint about his position was its loneliness, made a daily companion of young Jefferson, and taught him no less through informal talk than by his memorable lectures. As a mature man Jeffer-

---

[16] MS. copy of letter from the Rector of the College, unsigned and without address but obviously to Small, June 25, 1767, Edgehill Randolph Papers, UVA. This copy was doubtless sent to Jefferson, who was thus familiar with the unpleasant episode.

[17] *Va. Hist. Register*, July 1850, pp. 150–151.

[18] To Benjamin Rush, Aug. 17, 1811 (Ford, IX, 328); to the Reverend James Madison, Dec. 29, 1811 (L. & B., XIX, 183). Earlier comment in Randall, I, 53.

[19] To T. J. Randolph, Nov. 24, 1808 (Ford, IX, 231).

son did not forget him. Just when the Revolution was beginning, and public dissension threatened to divide him from his friend as the ocean had already done, he sent him by a reluctant captain what he described as half of a little present that he had laid by. It consisted of three dozen bottles of Madeira which he had kept for eight years in his own cellar, and he promised to dispatch that many more as soon as possible by another ship. He did not know that his old teacher was in the last year of life.[20]

There is some testimony that Small's influence persisted in the College. It has been said that he, more than any other teacher, was responsible for the liberality of spirit which came to characterize William and Mary.[21] Some people called it "skepticism" and thought it dangerous, but Jefferson and his kindred spirits regarded it as the first step towards true knowledge. Historically, William Small was a minor torchbearer of the Enlightenment, and by any reckoning he was one of those rare men who point the way, who show new paths, who open doors before the mind.

To Jefferson he also opened the door of George Wythe's law office, and he and Wythe ushered this inquiring young man into the Governor's Palace. Thus were the benefits of enlightened conversation increased rather than diminished after Jefferson left the College. He was as intimate with Small for two more years as one of his age could be. His life and associations in Williamsburg before he was admitted to the bar cannot be divided into sharply defined segments; but if his college course can be described separately it is best summed up by saying that he continued to be taught privately, and that his tutor was William Small. The same sort of statement can be made about the five years after that, when he studied law under George Wythe. He gained clear title to fame in later years as a prophet and architect of public education, but his own training was pre-eminently personal and private.

Self-imposed, rather than external, discipline shaped his education from his youth onward. In his last decade he wrote: "I was a hard student until I entered on the business of life, the duties of which leave no idle time to those disposed to fulfill them; and now, retired, and at the age of seventy-six, I am again a hard student." [22] The first period of his amazing life differed in many ways from the important and exacting era of public service which followed, but the habit of

[20] To Small, May 7, 1775, LC, 1:140, partly printed in Ford, I, 453–455.
[21] I. A. Coles to Henry St. George Tucker, July 20, 1799 (W. & M., 1 ser., IV, 105–108).
[22] To Dr. Vine Utley, Mar. 21, 1819 (Ford, X, 126).

study persisted. Drafting state papers brought him no such joy as the free pursuit of knowledge, and he could not approach all public problems with the zeal of the explorer; but in all his tasks he could and did manifest the seriousness and the industry of the scholar.

His characteristic habits of study may have been formed even before he went to Williamsburg. Said one of his young admirers who observed him when he was ripe in years and honors:

> His mind must have been by nature one of uncommon capaciousness and retention, of wonderful clearness and as rapid as is consistent with accurate thoughts. His application from very early youth has not only been intense but unremitted. When young he adopted a system, perhaps an entire plan of life from which neither the exigencies of business nor the allurements of pleasure could drive or seduce him. Much of his success is to be ascribed to methodical industry. Even when at school he used to be seen with his Greek Grammar in his hand while his comrades were enjoying relaxation in the interval of school hours.[23]

The family tradition is that during his college days he studied fifteen hours of twenty-four and habitually until long past midnight, only to rise at dawn. This sounds like too severe a program even for him. In vacations he is said to have devoted almost three fourths of his time to his books. Next only to tyranny he hated indolence, which he regarded as the besetting sin of his hospitable Virginia countrymen, and about which he wrote with appalling frequency to his children in later years. "It is while we are young that the habit of industry is formed," he reflected. "If not then, it never is afterwards." If this is true he himself formed the habit early. "Determine never to be idle," he admonished his growing daughter. "No person will have occasion to complain of the want of time who never loses any." Then he made an observation which aptly sums up his own intellectual history: "It is wonderful how much may be done if we are always doing."[24]

Such a regimen and such a philosophy would impose a strain on any but the strongest physique. He learned to guard his unusual natural gifts by physical regularity and systematic exercise, though we cannot be sure just when he became so wise. He ran and walked when in college, and, if the testimony of his grandson can be accepted, he once swam thirteen times across a millpond that was a quarter of a mile

[23] F. W. Gilmer, c. 1816, in R. B. Davis, *Francis Walker Gilmer* (hereafter cited as Davis, *Gilmer*), p. 350; quoted by courtesy of the author and the Dietz Press.
[24] Randall, I, 24; *Domestic Life*, pp. 31, 115, 121. The letters to his daughter Martha were written in 1787.

wide.[25] This seems too much for a boy fresh from the little Rivanna, but the physical endurance of Peter Jefferson's heir was remarkable in his youth and prime. It was probably in Williamsburg that he established the habit of bathing his feet in cold water every morning. This practice he continued for upwards of sixty years and to it he attributed his lifelong freedom from colds. At seventy-six, he reported that only two or three times in his life had he had a fever of more than twenty-four hours; and he then could boast that he had been blessed with "organs of digestion which accept and concoct, without ever murmuring, whatever the palate chooses to consign to them," and that he had not lost a tooth by age.[26]

The severe perfection of this portrait is somewhat relieved by his own statement that during his early years in Williamsburg he was extravagant, by occasional remarks of his about youthful temptations, and by other indications of gaiety and frivolity. The most frivolous period probably coincided with the first years that he studied law, when he grumbled about his law books and indulged in much silly chatter about the girls. He participated in the annual battles between town and gown, but there is no suggestion that he was ever disciplined for his part in student scrapes as was his friend John Walker, who was rusticated in the fall of 1763, along with a couple of other boys who afterwards gained considerable renown.[27] He had left the College then and was living in town, but he reported the episode with some zest. He was a member of a student organization known as the Flat Hat Club, which is notable for its primacy as a secret college society but wholly lacked seriousness of purpose. It is not to be confused with Phi Beta Kappa, of which Jefferson knew nothing. It was primarily convivial and its certificates of membership were couched in humorous Latin phraseology. One of its expressed desires was that each member should be "a great ornament and pillar of things general and particular." John Walker was a fellow member and the fact that there were only six altogether may or may not imply that Jefferson was numbered among the socially elite. He continued to attend meetings after he left college and wrote about one of them in frivolous Latin vein.[28]

[25] Memoirs of Thomas Jefferson Randolph, Edgehill Randolph Papers, UVA., p. 3.

[26] To Dr. Vine Utley, Mar. 21, 1819 (Ford, X, 125); to James Maury, June 16, 1815 (L. & B., XIV, 319).

[27] To John Page, Oct. 7, 1763 (Ford, I, 353); to J. C. Cabell, Jan. 24, 1816 (L. & B., XIV, 413); W. & M., 1 ser., IV, 44–45.

[28] G. P. Coleman, ed., The Flat Hat Club and the Phi Beta Kappa Society, reproducing letters; Jefferson to John Walker, Sept. 3, 1769, UVA photostat from Yale Univ.; printed in Kimball, Road to Glory, p. 141.

John Page said that Jefferson "could tear himself away from his dearest friends, to fly to his studies." [29] It seems likely that he did not cultivate the fine art of friendship consciously and assiduously until after he became somewhat discouraged about the girls. But there is no reason to suppose that he flouted the dominant tradition of sociability or that he failed to avail himself of the great opportunities for friendship which this small academic community afforded. Some of his most enduring associations started there.

One of the distinguishing characteristics of colonial Williamsburg was the seasonal occasion for friendly intercourse which it offered to residents of isolated plantations. In the midst of this sociable village, which teemed periodically, the College was set. Its junior members were drawn from the sons of the gentry and these constituted a close-knit group. There were gradations of rank among them, with the families of the Councillors at the top of the social scale, but there was no such invidious distinction here as John Adams found at Harvard College, where seats in class were assigned according to parental rank or standing. The son of a rugged squire from the Piedmont did not have to take a lower place than John Page of Rosewell. With this particular scion of a highly influential family Jefferson was intimate from the start, and through him became friends with the equally aristocratic Nelsons.

His old schoolmate at Maury's, Dabney Carr, may not have entered until the year after he did. With this single exception, Page was Jefferson's closest college friend. The two were almost exactly the same age and they were to be like brothers for almost half a century. Page had the more impressive economic and social background. Through his grandmother he was a descendant of "King" Carter, and his grandfather, Mann Page, had been a much larger landholder than the second Thomas Jefferson or even Isham Randolph, besides being a member of the Council. It was this Mann Page who had built Rosewell in Gloucester County and left the fabulous house to a son of the same name who spent most of his strength bearing the heavy burden. In this huge, three-storied mansion John had grown up. Jefferson was often to look at its mahogany wainscoting and climb its marble stairways, probably reflecting that his own forebears had been wise in not cultivating magnificence so extravagantly.[30]

To a greater degree than Jefferson's immediate ancestors, the Pages

[29] *Va. Hist. Register*, July 1850, p. 151.

[30] Incomplete autobiography of Page in *Va. Hist. Register*, July 1850, pp. 142–151; Meade, I, 147–148 *n.*, 331–333, especially for Rosewell and churchmanship. The extensive correspondence between him and Jefferson will be cited frequently hereafter.

were devoted to the Church and associated with the College, but John may have been removed from the President's House at the time that poor Dawson got into so much trouble and before the Reverend William Yates came in. He appears to have lodged in the College during the second year that his friend from Albemarle was there, and he may have been with him from the first. He had secured a firm grounding in the classics from his revered tutor, William Price; and, like Jefferson, he enjoyed the special attentions of William Small. Both Small and President Dawson commended him to Governor Fauquier. In religious matters he was more conventional than Jefferson, and, being especially sociable, he was more willing to leave his books. There was no touch of genius on him but he was every inch a gentleman. He was a fellow in philosophical inquiry until his boon companion probed more deeply, and he was an intimate confidant in early matters of the heart.

Since Jefferson remained so long in Williamsburg as a student, it may be safely assumed that he knew practically everybody who attended the College from 1760 to 1767. Among his near contemporaries were these: John Walker, who was destined to be a fellow burgess from Albemarle; William Fleming, to whom some of his earliest known letters were directed; Francis Eppes, to whom he was to be closely bound by marriage; a couple of Harrisons, for one of whom he may later have designed Brandon; John Tyler, with whom he was to be associated as a law student; Austin and Bernard Moore, to one of whom he was to address a memorable letter about the study of law; Jacquelin Ambler, who was to win a girl he dreamed of; and Bathurst Skelton, whose widow he was to marry later on.[31] Some of these names are now remembered chiefly because of their association with his. He overtopped his own college generation, but even among its members he met future leaders of the Colony and State. Thomas Nelson, Junior, who was to succeed him as governor in perilous times, had gone to school abroad but was much in Williamsburg in this period. A more noted group came to the College somewhat later: Edmund Randolph, John Taylor of Caroline, and that James Madison who became a bishop; and early in the next decade appeared John Marshall, briefly, and James Monroe. The James Madison who was to succeed Jefferson as President manifested a degree of unconventionality by attending the College of New Jersey at Princeton, but even without him this is an exceedingly distinguished list.

To those who heard of the recurrent disorders among the students at William and Mary, and of the dissensions within the faculty or between the faculty and the Board, the affairs of this historic college

[31] *Provisional List of Alumni; W. & M.*, 2 ser., I, 27–42.

may well have seemed chaotic during the period that Jefferson knew it best. The successor to President Dawson as commissary of the Bishop of London, the Reverend William Robinson, thought that it had failed to answer the high ends of its institution and doubted if, under existing conditions, learning and religion would strike deep root in the Colony.[32] He proposed that the College be really put under the care of the ecclesiastical authorities in England, and be entirely divorced from local control. There can be no doubt that the situation was anomalous, but the school was more successful than he realized. The secret of its success lay, not in its organization, not in its identification with the English Church, not even in its faculty, but in its intimate association with the community in which it was placed.

The College could be no mere training school for clergymen, though actually it produced better ministers for the Colony than those who were imported directly from abroad. The gentry had no strong desire that it cultivate learning for its own sake, for their ideal was the well-rounded man. It was pre-eminently a school for statesmen and as such, on the North American continent, its product has never been excelled.[33] The extraordinary distinction of its alumni is chiefly owing to the fact that its students were by birth and station the potential leaders of the Colony, and that their college days were spent at the center of provincial life. The most important fact about it was not that it was relatively old, or that it had considerable resources, but that it was located in Williamsburg.

In this distinctive community Jefferson as a young man met the leading gentlemen of the country, and there before he was grown he saw visitors of quite a different sort. The Indians were in the habit of coming to the capital, often in great numbers, and he reports that he was much with them. One historic visit occurred in the spring of 1762, and with brief mention of it we can end the story of his college days. It was that of a Cherokee chief whom he had seen before, as the guest of his father at Shadwell on previous journeys, and he called him "Ontasseté," though there were other names for the same man — Ostenaco, Oconasta, Judd's Friend, and, best of all perhaps, Outacity.[34]

[32] Robinson to Bishop of London, Oct. 16, 1767, in Perry, *Hist. Collections*, I, 529, and other letters there.

[33] For good comments, see H. B. Adams, *College of William and Mary*, pp. 26–29.

[34] Jefferson to John Adams, June 11, 1812 (L. & B., XIII, 160); S. C. Williams, ed., *Lieut. Henry Timberlake's Memoirs* (Johnson City, Tenn., 1927) esp. pp. 129–131, 170; *Burgesses, Journals*, 1761–1765, pp. xvii–xviii; art. on Outacity by K. E. Crane in *Dictionary of Amer. Biography* (hereafter cited as *D.A.B.*).

A party of at least 165 Indians had set out from the Holston country in what is now East Tennessee, and an embarrassingly large number eventually arrived in Williamsburg. The students must have talked about them, and they may have observed Outacity when he was dined at the College. They doubtless heard that he was received by the Governor and Council and granted permission to visit the Great King, his Father, in England. They could hardly have anticipated the sensation which the Cherokee created in London, where he was visited by Oliver Goldsmith and painted by Sir Joshua Reynolds; but before his departure he made a profound impression on a youth who was nearing nineteen and who had not yet crossed the sea. Jefferson was in Outacity's camp when he delivered a farewell oration to his people the evening before he sailed, and as an old man he remembered the splendor of the moon. The college student understood no word of the Chief's prayer for his own safety on the voyage and for that of his people until his return; but Outacity's resounding voice and the solemn silence of his followers around their campfires filled him with awe and veneration.

Years afterward, as governor and President, he was to receive visits from Indians, to address them as a Father, and to smoke with them the pipe of peace. He was to observe this race as a philosopher and to inquire into its languages; as a responsible statesman he was to grapple with the problem of depredations and massacres on the frontier. But he was not soon, if ever, to escape from these early emotions. At this time, unquestionably, he was moved not by fear but by curiosity and compassion. Nonetheless, these warriors must have reminded him that the wilderness was not far away from the college halls he was quitting, from the Capitol where decorous statesmen deliberated, from the Palace ballroom where ladies and gentlemen danced the gay reel and the stately minuet. Of such contrasts was provincial life compounded.

[V]

Williamsburg: Introduction to the Law

1762–1765

WHEN Jefferson first went to Williamsburg as a student it is most unlikely that he had ever seen that large a town. In Virginia both Norfolk and Petersburg were larger, though neither of these was impressive in its size. The major reason for the failure to develop commercial centers in Virginia he himself set forth a good many years after he left college: "Our country being much intersected with navigable waters, and trade brought generally to our doors, instead of our being obliged to go in quest of it, has probably been one of the causes why we have no towns of any consequence." [1] Important business was transacted in Williamsburg but the place would never have become famous because of that.

Legally it was a city and had been laid out on a pleasing plan, but it covered only a square mile and had fewer than two thousand people except during "public times." In the fall and spring, when the courts sat and the Assembly was generally in session, its population was doubled or trebled. Then everybody of political consequence in the Colony was there, and the three hundred houses, with the neighboring plantation seats, were filled to overflowing. Sometimes there were half a dozen guests in a single room.[2]

[1] In *Notes on Virginia;* Ford, III, 213.

[2] Publications of Colonial Williamsburg, Inc., especially Rutherfoord Goodwin, *A Brief & True Report concerning Williamsburg in Virginia*, containing copious extracts from sources; the various handbooks and guides to exhibition buildings, which have been prepared with careful scholarship; and *The Restoration of Colonial Williamsburg in Virginia*, from *Architectural Record*, Dec. 1935. One of the best of contemporary accounts is "Journal of a French Traveller in the Colonies, 1765, I," in *American Historical Review (AHR)*, XXVI (July 1921), 726–747.

From the open space in front of the College, between the President's House and the Brafferton, Jefferson and the other students must often have looked down the "noble great street" to the Capitol, almost a mile away. Before his father was born the width of this central thoroughfare had been fixed at six poles, or to all practical purposes a hundred feet, and afterwards it was named for the Duke of Gloucester. In public times an incessant train of coaches could be seen plowing their way through the powdered oyster shells which looked like sand — or through seas of mud, depending on the weather.

Walking was unpleasant at certain seasons because of the dust or the mud, and Virginians generally preferred to ride, but often in his student days Jefferson must have stretched his long legs on the Duke of Gloucester Street. Before he reached Bruton Church, where at times he listened to the arid preaching of the era, he passed the home of the Honorable John Blair, president of the Council. At an early date two daughters of this prominent family, Anne and Betsey, became his friends. They lived in a pleasant white house, with dormer windows, a high-pitched roof, and outside chimneys at the ends. It was set close to the sidewalk, in conformity with the building laws; and on summer nights the family and their guests used to sit on the steps and sing.[3] On this street, gardens had to be behind the houses, but greens and other open spaces had been left to permit free circulation of the air.

The brick church was almost at the halfway point and stood at the intersection of the Palace Green. Considerably beyond this was the printing office of the *Virginia Gazette*. People often went there to insert notices about runaways, to advertise the sale of "parcels of likely Virginia-born wenches," or to offer to the horse-breeding public the services of stallions in their prime. When Jefferson stopped there, however, it was generally to purchase books and music. Farther down the street was a tavern which had been named for Sir Walter Raleigh and was shaped like the letter "L." It was to gain greatest renown in Revolutionary times, but its famous Apollo Room was already in use. Jefferson danced in it before he ever deliberated at the same place on affairs of state.

Having proceeded so far, one might easily go on a little farther to the Capitol at the end of this broad street. There Peter Jefferson had done brief service as a burgess but his son could not see the chamber where Isham Randolph had taken oath at an earlier time, for this was a fairly new building, erected after a fire. Jefferson later described it as

---

[3] On the singing, *W. & M.*, 1 ser., XVI, 178; on his friendship, letters from and to Elizabeth (Blair) Thompson, Jan. 10, 19, 1787 (Bixby, pp. 19–22); letter to Anne (Blair) Banister, Aug. 6, 1787 (LC, 32:5444).

"a light and airy structure, with a portico in front of two orders." [4] He rather liked the Doric columns, while disapproving of the proportions of the Ionic, and thought this the most pleasing bit of architecture in Virginia, on the whole. It can be seen no longer, for the last part of it burned after Jefferson was dead and it was not restored.

Near the Capitol in the 1760's, as now, was the Public Gaol, and beyond the Capitol he could have come into still another world. Here was an open space known as the Exchange, where planters squared accounts with one another, consigned tobacco to factors and sea captains, and arranged to purchase Negro fellows or some of those likely wenches. Here was the Coffee House, which Jefferson frequented as a young man; here was the second Williamsburg theater, where he, like George Washington, purchased tickets for the play. The gallows, where criminals dangled after each session of the General Court, and the racecourse, where heats of two, three, and four miles were run, were outside the town. He doubtless remembered the gallows afterwards, when he was drafting a bill dealing with crimes and punishments, and the racetrack may have interested him somewhat at first.

He had more freedom to go to that sort of place after he became a law student at the age of nineteen and had lodgings in town. These could have been on either of the two narrower streets that paralleled the Duke of Gloucester, or on some cross street, but nobody knows just where they were. He probably stayed at different places. For a time he studied in the same room with John Tyler and a much less serious young man from Gloucester County named Frank Willis. The latter, who delighted in pranks, sometimes overturned the table when he came in late and found the two others still at work. By the time that Jefferson was grown, he had his servant Jupiter with him in Williamsburg, and during some of his years as a law student he kept horses there, as his gay friend Willis did.[5] But, whether he walked or rode, and whatever point he may have started from, he went more often in the direction of the Governor's Palace than the Capitol at first. Turning from the Duke of Gloucester Street at the Palace Green and passing the yard of Bruton Church, he came to the home of George Wythe. Here he stopped frequently, to be greeted by a middle-sized, hook-nosed gentleman, who was noted for his courtly bow. This dignified brick house became for Jefferson a sort of anteroom to the Palace, though it had meaning in itself.

[4] Ford, III, 257. It has been suggested, though not proved, that the portico was added after his student days and was his idea; Waterman, *Mansions of Virginia*, p. 397.

[5] L. G. Tyler, *Letters and Times of the Tylers*, I, 55; references to Jupiter in Day Books of *Va. Gazette*, in possession of Prof. J. S. Wilson, University of Virginia, such as Feb. 20, 1764; Apr. 3, 1765.

It had been built and was owned by Richard Taliaferro, who has been described as the leading architect or builder of the Colony and whose daughter Elizabeth had married Wythe.[6] Taliaferro had a plantation a few miles out of town, but he probably visited the childless couple and from him Jefferson may have heard something about architecture. Wythe was not interested in that subject; he was to be Jefferson's teacher in the law. For considerable stretches during the next five years the younger man was at Shadwell, but he spent most of the time reading and he got his directions in Williamsburg.

In the year 1762, when Thomas Jefferson finished college and began to study law, George Wythe was about thirty-five years old.[7] If not yet the first at the bar of the General Court he was already one of its most distinguished members. Among those who shared leadership with him were Peyton Randolph, then King's Attorney as his father and grandfather had been before him, and the latter's brother John, who was to succeed him in that family office four years later. Both of these prominent relatives of Jefferson were legal products of the Inner Temple. In Virginia in the eighteenth century, as in Maryland and South Carolina, the quality of the bar had been much improved by the influence of men who had been trained in England.[8]

It was after Jefferson had turned twenty that he wrote with apparent seriousness to John Page about going abroad. He may have thought of accompanying William Small and of making the Grand Tour, but he did not mention the Inns of Court. If he had gone to the Inner Temple he would doubtless have met Charles Carroll of Carrollton, and at the Middle Temple he could have found Charles Cotesworth Pinckney of South Carolina; there would still have been time for him to hear William Pitt in the Commons and David Garrick at the play; at some table he might even have caught snatches of the conversation of Samuel Johnson, though there is little reason to suppose that he would have liked it.[9] He would have formed intercolonial friendships and become a citizen of the world sooner if he had gone to England, but

[6] Will of Taliaferro, *W. & M.*, 1 ser., XII, 124–125. The name is pronounced so as to rhyme with "Oliver." Waterman reproduces his will in *Mansions of Virginia*, p. 217, and refers to him elsewhere, crediting him with considerable architectural influence on Jefferson, pp. 342, 345.

[7] Jefferson gave a statement about Wythe (rhymes with Smith) to John Saunderson, Aug. 31, 1820 (L. & B., I, 165–170) for use in connection with the latter's *Biography of the Signers to the Declaration of Independence* (1822). W. E. Hemphill, George Wythe the Colonial Briton (Doctoral Dissertation UVA, 1937), which I have been privileged to see, covers the period to the Revolution.

[8] Charles Warren, *History of the American Bar*, pp. 18, 46.

[9] Charles Carroll had a low opinion of the educational value of the Inns of Court, but Warren points out the compensating advantages, *Ibid.*, p. 193.

it is doubtful if he would have learned any more law or qualified himself any better for his historical role than he actually did by private study in his own Colony.

There can be no possible question about his mature judgment of foreign education for Americans, for he said that a volume would be necessary to enumerate all its disadvantages. He saw no need whatever for anybody except a student of medicine to go abroad. Among the many advantages of being educated at home was one very practical one, and this he mentioned to one of his young friends. "Cast your eye over America," he said; "who are the men of most learning, of most eloquence, most beloved by their countrymen and most trusted and promoted by them? They are those who have been educated among them, and whose manners, morals, and habits, are perfectly homogeneous with those of the country." [10] He made these patriotic observations more than twenty years after he began to study with Wythe, but if he had had to start all over again it is extremely unlikely that he would have changed his plan.

Other leaders of the growing Virginia bar, like Robert Carter Nicholas, Edmund Pendleton, and Wythe himself, had been educated locally, and the approved method was that of reading in some lawyer's office. [11] Several years before Jefferson entered the College, John Adams, facing a similar problem of legal education in Massachusetts, had made an agreement with James Putnam of Worcester to study for two years "under his inspection," while carrying on his own teaching in the local school. [12] Formal legal instruction was not to begin until after the colonies had become states. Toward the end of the Revolution, under the inspiration of Jefferson himself, Wythe was to assume a chair of law at the College of William and Mary; and a few years later Tapping Reeve was to set up his famous school at Litchfield, Connecticut.

In deciding to study law, Jefferson had no such scruples to overcome as had troubled Adams, for the profession was in better odor in Virginia and he had no craving for the Church. In the narrow sense it was not a profitable calling in this Colony. Because of the jealousy of the dominant planters and their desire to discourage petty practitioners the fees of attorneys had been sharply restricted by statute. [13] But land-

[10] To John Banister, Jr., whose name Jefferson generally misspelled, Oct. 15, 1785 (L. & B., V, 188).

[11] Warren discusses, pp. 164–169, the methods which prevailed in the colonies generally. Some students had to content themselves with studying in a clerk's office and with reading on their own.

[12] Adams, *Works*, I, 32; see also I, 34, 42–44; II, 30–32. The important fact is that he, like Jefferson, kept on studying.

[13] Jefferson could have read about these restrictions in his copy of John Mercer,

holders who followed the law could continue to draw upon their acres for support, and the heir of Peter Jefferson doubtless expected to do just that, realizing that it was one of his many privileges. He was to pursue the law as a learned and useful profession with notable devotion until great public events deflected his course. His choice of Wythe as a guide instead of one of the Randolphs or somebody else, and Wythe's agreement to receive him, were probably owing to their mutual friend, William Small. He was eternally grateful for these good offices and always convinced of the wisdom of his decision, not merely because his mentor was the most learned and possibly the most effective of the local group, but also because of the greater range and liberality of his mind.

Jefferson did not have a high opinion of the apprentice system as such, for he recognized the temptation of a practising lawyer to throw too great a burden of office business on a student. About two years after his admission to the bar he wrote to his uncle by marriage, Thomas Turpin, in regard to the latter's son Philip: "The only help a youth wants is to be directed what books to read and in what order to read them." [14] He himself probably looked up cases for his senior in the law library at the Capitol; he undoubtedly attended sessions of the General Court and may have done some clerical service there; and he probably was set to drawing papers in Wythe's office.[15] From the date of his earliest records Jefferson was a careful draftsman and a good penman, with a clear engrossing hand, and he must have had immediate exercise in paper work. It is unlikely, though, that he was ever an apprentice in any strict sense or that Wythe ever wanted him to be one. There is no existing record that he paid any fee, and it is impossible to say just how long he was physically present in Wythe's office. During his second year he studied for months after Christmas at Shadwell, returning to Williamsburg in the fall of his third; after that he probably read wherever he liked and on his own schedule.

He followed an appallingly rigorous program most of the time, unless the sincerity of his advice to others and the entries in his own notebooks are to be doubted. He had a mild fling as a privileged young gentleman during the first two years, and gave himself some time for

---

An Exact Abridgement of all the Public Acts of Assembly of Va., in force and Use, Jan. 1, 1758 (1759), annotated copy at UVA. The successive acts can now be traced in Hening.

[14] Feb. 5, 1769, in Dickore, *Two Unpublished Letters from Thomas Jefferson.*

[15] The exact location of the office has not been determined, but there is every reason to suppose that it was on the place, where there were plenty of outbuildings.

such frivolities as are common between the ages of nineteen and twenty-one. But though the social gaieties of the provincial capital and of the plantation houses allured him at first, it must have been before he entered upon what he called the "business of life" and while he was still primarily a student that he copied into his literary notebook a sobering extract about the shortage of time.

> Youth is not rich in time; it may be poor;
> Part with it as with money, sparing; pay
> No moment but in purchase of it's worth;
> And what it's worth, ask death-bells; they can tell.
> Part with it as with life, reluctant; big
> With holy hope of nobler time to come.[16]

He never found hours enough to accomplish his intellectual purposes.

In all that he said afterwards about the education of a lawyer, he made it clear that the foundations must be both deep and broad.[17] Knowledge of Latin and French he regarded as absolutely necessary. The first book that he used involved both of these languages, though the French was not such as he was to hear later at the court of Versailles. He thought of mathematics and natural philosophy as studies too useful and delightful for anyone to miss, and regarded them, particularly mathematics, as invaluable in exercising the mind. He continued to make scientific observations with Small until this teacher and friend left for England, and if he needed any guidance in his continued reading of the classics, Wythe was abundantly qualified to supply it.

Wythe's early education had been handicapped by poverty, though he inherited an estate after he became a man. That he was largely self-taught, with his mother's help, and that until the age of thirty he had devoted himself almost exclusively to the law, did not prevent his becoming a noted classical scholar — the best in Virginia, Jefferson said. An English traveler, who had met Wythe even earlier, said that he had a "perfect knowledge" of Greek and of ancient philosophy, particularly the Platonic.[18] He never lured Jefferson into Platonic paths

---

[16] *Literary Bible of Thomas Jefferson* (hereafter cited as *Literary Bible*), ed. by Gilbert Chinard, p. 141, quoting from Young's *Night Thoughts*. On July 13, 1764, he purchased a copy of Young's works, as shown by the Day Books of the *Va. Gazette*.

[17] Throughout life he gave advice on request about the study of law. The letter of Aug. 30, 1814, to John Minor, enclosing copy of a paper written nearly fifty years earlier, is most useful here because of its completeness and also because it reflects his early opinions. See Randall, I, 53–57.

[18] Andrew Burnaby, *Travels Through North America*, p. 53; he met Wythe in 1759. Jefferson's nephew Peter Carr, whose course Wythe directed, studied the

but he led him to improve his Greek, at which he was not so good as at Latin. Wythe later injected classical quotations into his judicial opinions in a way that was little short of pedantic, but early in his career he imbibed the spirit of ancient civilization at its best. The aforesaid traveler, who was generally critical of Virginians, said that to his classical learning he "had joined such a profound reverence for the Supreme Being, such respect for the divine laws, such philanthropy for mankind, such simplicity of manners, and such inflexible rectitude and integrity of principle, as would have dignified a Roman senator, even in the most virtuous times of the republic." Jefferson, to whom the heroes of antiquity were more real than either the Christian saints or modern historical figures, described him as his country's Cato without the Roman's avarice, while someone else called him the American Aristides, thus showing that he was also an Athenian.

Despite his deserved reputation, Wythe's intellectual interests were not so broad as his distinguished pupil's afterwards were, and his apprehension was not so quick. This moderate man may not have been disposed to attack learning on quite so wide a front. Probably he never drew up so long and formidable a list of subjects kindred to the law as Jefferson afterwards commended to the young; probably he did not expect his protégé, along with the law, to study physics, ethics, religion, natural philosophy, belles-lettres, criticism, rhetoric, politics, and history. Jefferson's recommendations suggest that the diet at Wythe's board was generous and well-balanced, but they also show the insatiable appetite of his own omnivorous mind. Wythe was a systematic man and probably encouraged him to work out a regular schedule, without requiring him to fill every moment from dawn to bedtime. If we may judge from Jefferson's own recommendations, the hours from eight to twelve in the morning, when his mental vigor was greatest, were devoted exclusively to the law. The rest of the time, except for a period of afternoon exercise, was given to allied subjects. He relegated literature and oratory to the evening hours, but there is plenty of evidence that he did not neglect them. He would hardly have recommended such a comprehensive and exacting schedule if he had not tried it out himself, and he probably approximated his ideal after a year or two.

The technical study of the law was then "a dreary ramble," as John Adams said, for books that smoothed the student's path did not exist. Textbooks of the modern sort were unknown, and Blackstone's famous

---

classics as well as the law with him; Carr to Jefferson, Mar. 18, 1788, Carr and Cary Papers, UVA.

Commentaries had not yet appeared. All lawbooks had to be imported and there was a sad shortage of them in the colonies generally. There were no American reports of cases, English reports were scarce, and in most colonies collections of their own statutes were hard to get.[19] Few people in Virginia could ever boast a complete set, and the collection which Jefferson eventually amassed was notable in its time.[20] At the beginning an abridgment of the Acts of Assembly was available to him; this extended to January 1, 1758, and by his annotations he brought and kept it up to date. As colonial conditions went, Williamsburg was rich in legal resources, and, like John Adams, he became a systematic purchaser of such books as were obtainable. He never lacked food though it must often have seemed unpalatable.

Wythe started him on *Coke upon Littleton*, which constituted the first of four parts of the *Institutes of the Lawes of England*. He would probably have been directed to the same book if he had gone to one of the Inns of Court, for it had been the lawyers' primer in its homeland for more than a century and a dozen editions of it had appeared.[21] In the course of time this student was to gain a conception of the law, not as an immutable system, but as something that lives and moves. He had no immediate reason to expect that, however, when he began to struggle with the "black letter text and uncouth but cunning learning" of Sir Edward Coke.

Coke had reprinted in the Norman French the classic treatise of Littleton on tenures, which he regarded as "the most perfect and absolute work that was ever written in any humane science," had added an English translation, and had heaped around the text in bewildering mass his own definitions and learned notes. To the beginner this folio must have seemed heavy and formidable, but if he did not wander too far afield he might learn here just how land was held. In Virginia as in the Mother Country this was a matter of the first importance.

This primer of legal learning was more than a book to Jefferson; it was a person. He packed him in a trunk before leaving Williamsburg for a stay at Shadwell, possibly hoping to smother him; he called him an old, dull scoundrel; and he consigned him to the Devil.

[19] Adams, *Works*, III, 50 *n.*; Warren, *Hist. Am. Bar*, ch. VIII; R. S. Morris, "Jefferson as a Lawyer," *Procs. Am. Philos. Soc.*, Vol. 87, No. 3, July 14, 1943, pp. 212–213.

[20] St. George Tucker, in editor's preface to *Blackstone's Commentaries* (Philadelphia, 1803), I, iv. Tucker had been unable to get one for himself.

[21] The edition cited here is the 11th (1719); Jefferson could have used this or the 12th (1738), which was severely criticized. For discussion see art. on Coke in *Dictionary of National Biography;* Sir William Holdsworth, *Hist. of Eng. Law*, V (2 ed., 1937), 466–468.

Other eminent men expressed themselves even more strongly: the old jurist profoundly discouraged John Quincy Adams and Daniel Webster, and he drove Joseph Story actually to tears. But these were younger men not bred in so stern a school. Jefferson learned from Wythe, as John Adams did from Jeremiah Gridley, that there was no choice but to conquer Coke. He gained deep respect for him, as young Story did, and in long retrospect he preferred Coke's crabbed text and uncouth learning to the "honeyed" words of Blackstone, which were so much easier to understand.[22]

Old Coke was not unsympathetic; indeed, he counseled the beginner wisely:

> Mine advice to the Student is, That before he read any part of our Commentaries upon any Section, that first he read again and again our Author himself in that Section, and do his best Endeavours, first of himself, and then by Conference with others, (which is the Life of Study) to understand it, and then to read our Commentary thereupon, and no more at any one Time than he is able with a Delight to bear away, and after to meditate thereon, which is the Life of Reading.[23]

If George Wythe's student followed Coke's excellent advice, this is the passage, in the English translation of the text, which he read first:

> Tenant in Fee-simple is he which hath Lands or Tenements to hold to him and his heirs for ever. And it is called in Latin, *Feodum simplex*, for *Feodum* is the same that Inheritance is, and Simplex is as much as to say, lawful or pure; and so *Feodum simplex* signifies a lawful or pure inheritance.

Then, if his eye happened to stray to the notes in the adjoining column, he could have observed that tenant is derived of the verb *teneo*, "and hath in the law five significations." Coke's definitions, word by word and phrase by phrase, were there for him to read and ponder over.

He probably did not share Coke's reverence for the text very long, and in the end the notes must have seemed minute. They even extended to Littleton's use of an "etc." This was not the best place to discover broad legal principles. But when Jefferson, in the next decade, moved in the Virginia House of Delegates that tenants in fee tail should hold their lands in fee simple and thus acquire a pure inheritance, he could have reflected that he first learned the meaning of these cru-

[22] Warren cites numerous comments, pp. 173–177. The reference to John Adams is from *Works*, II, 46–47, when he was aged 23.
[23] Preface.

cial terms from Littleton and Coke. Even the physical form of this old commentary, unusual in its own day in England, left a lasting impression. The manuscript of one of the best-known bills that he ever drafted for his native Commonwealth reveals Coke's unmistakable influence, in the notes which first accompany and then invade the columned text.[24]

In the course of time he studied the three other parts of the famous *Institutes*. One contained the texts of English statutes from Magna Carta to the time of James I, another dealt with criminal law, and the last was a treatise on jurisdiction. For long years he considered this work the basis of legal study and he commended it again and again. He soon became aware, however, that the law had developed since Coke's day, that new laws had been added by legislatures, and that new developments of old laws had been brought about by judges. He was quite willing to use later digests and treatises, and specifically recommended Matthew Bacon's abridgment, Lord Kames on equity, and other books of the sort. The modernity of his legal training is most striking in the study and the emphasis he gave to the actual cases that were argued and adjudged in the courts of England. John Adams was equally interested in pursuing the law back to its historic fountains, and he also talked of Bracton and other men of ancient learning, but neither he nor any other of Jefferson's contemporaries has left a comparable record of attention to "the Reporters." [25]

It was in connection with these reports of cases that Jefferson began, after a few years, to keep commonplace books. His notes of his reading contain more detailed information about his legal studies than is generally available for the great lawyers of his or any other American generation. These old notes are important documents in the history of the case system. They may now seem wearisome except to legal antiquarians, but there is freshness and timelessness in the advice he gave a young contemporary toward the end of his own training.

> In reading the Reporters, enter in a commonplace book every case of value, condensed into the narrowest compass possible, which will admit of presenting distinctly the principles of the case. This operation is doubly useful, insomuch as it obliges the student to seek out the pith of the case, and habituates him to a condensation of thought, and to an acquisition of the most valu-

---

[24] A Bill for proportioning crimes and punishments, LC 232:42052–42058. These physical qualities do not appear in the published versions.

[25] Jefferson said much about Bracton in his much-quoted letter to Thomas Cooper, Jan. 16, 1814 (L. & B., XIV, 54–59); but in his letter to Bernard Moore, written almost half a century earlier, he minimized the usefulness of *De legibus Angliae*; see Randall, I, 54.

able of all talents, that of never using two words where one will do. It fixes the case, too, more indelibly in the mind.[26]

Under Wythe he started with Coke, whose lore could not be abstracted, and he proceeded step by step until he finally reached maturity from his study of the cases. During his unhurried period of legal tutelage he formed enduring habits of study while, under the influence of men as well as books, ideas germinated within his fertile mind.

His law teacher, besides being a classicist and a courtly gentleman, was a successful practitioner at the bar of the General Court and an esteemed member of the House of Burgesses. Jefferson, soon seeing him in action in both places, noted his easy elocution and chaste language and his urbanity in debate. He himself was to be more precipitate in politics and eventually he took the lead, but there was never a rift between him and his old friend. Always, there was mutual respect and affection.

In Jefferson's early history the name of George Wythe is inseparable from those of William Small and Francis Fauquier. His intimate association with this trio as a trio must have begun before 1764, when Small went back to England and Jefferson himself became twenty-one. It may have dated from his college days, but it probably took form soon after he began to study law. He was not yet grown when, by happy chance, he was regularly admitted as a fourth member of the party which had been dining frequently at the Palace since the Governor's family had returned home. At these dinners, Jefferson said long afterward, he heard "more good sense, more rational and philosophical conversations," than at any other time in his life. His much-quoted statement may reflect the imperfect memory of an old man and the exaggerated emphasis of age on youthful experience, but unquestionably it contains a nugget of important truth.[27]

He was to know Wythe much the longest of the three and to love him most. This learned, temperate, and kindly gentleman, not quick to

---

[26] Randall, I, 55. *The Commonplace Book of Thomas Jefferson,* ed. by Gilbert Chinard (1926) from the ms., LC, includes only the titles of the exclusively legal articles, hence it is most valuable in connection with ideas of government. Enough has been printed, however, to show the scope and carefulness of Jefferson's method. Another commonplace book of his (HEH) deals with equity cases and authorities. Most of the entries in both of these notebooks seem to date from a later time than these years in Williamsburg. Presumably both of them will be published in full in the Papers now being edited at Princeton. A study of Jefferson as a lawyer, including his professional training, is now being made under the auspices of the American Philosophical Society by Edward Dumbauld.

[27] To L. H. Girardin, Jan. 15, 1815; L. & B., XIV, 231.

apprehend but profound in penetration, may have lacked the contagious enthusiasm of the Professor or the sophisticated charm of the Governor, but he was doubtless the wisest counselor and the safest exemplar of the three. Indeed, it is hard to see how a better could have been found.

[VI]

The School of Manners

1762–1765

A SQUARE beyond the Wythe house in Williamsburg stood the Governor's Palace, commanding the green. A generation before Jefferson went there it was described as a magnificent structure, "finished and beautified" with gates and gardens, offices and walks, orchards and a fine canal.[1] The ballroom wing had been added in the meantime but little had been spent on the estate in the last decade. In his maturity Jefferson did not regard the large brick mansion as handsome but, since he had measured it, he spoke advisedly about the spaciousness of its interior. He liked the situation and thought that if the grounds were developed it might be made an "elegant seat."[2] One can only guess what his opinion of it would be in its present restored perfection, but in his student days, when he dined and performed in amateur musicals at the Palace, he undoubtedly found more elegance there than he had ever before observed.

His host was Francis Fauquier, who continued to be the chief resident official of the Province until a year after Jefferson was admitted to the bar. He afterwards described Fauquier as the ablest man who ever filled the chair of government in Williamsburg.[3] Though he may have been thinking of only the colonial period and not of the two first executives of the Commonwealth who sat in the same chair, Patrick Henry and himself, he probably would have made the generaliza-

---

[1] Hugh Jones, *Present State of Virginia* (1724), p. 31. On the Palace, besides the publications of Colonial Williamsburg, Inc., cited in the previous chapter, see Waterman, *Mansions of Virginia*, pp. 30–61.

[2] Ford, III, 258. A detailed floor plan of the Palace, drawn by Jefferson, is in MHS. This is reproduced by Waterman, p. 396, along with another study from the same hand.

[3] To L. H. Girardin, Jan. 15, 1815 (L. & B., XIV, 231).

tion in any case. When he first met this governor, however, his own mind was not yet turned to affairs of state; and he knew his predecessor chiefly as a gentleman, as a patron of learning, and as a friend of the arts.

Fauquier had come to Virginia at the age of fifty-four, two years before Jefferson entered college. He was the son of a Huguenot physician who took refuge in England, found employment at the mint under Sir Isaac Newton, married an Englishwoman, and eventually became a director of the Bank of England. Francis was born in London and until about the time of his marriage into a county family he followed a military career. He then appears to have lived the life of a country gentleman in Hertfordshire. His uncle William, a successful merchant who was addicted to scientific studies, made him his heir; and after the death of this uncle he became like him a director of the South Sea Company and a Fellow of the Royal Society. He is said to have been well regarded in the merchant group and he had many acquaintances in philosophical circles.[4]

The story, long current in Virginia, that his appointment as lieutenant governor was owing to the compassion of Lord Anson, after the latter had won his entire patrimony in a single night's play at cards, emphasizes one aspect of his reputation but cannot be accepted as sober fact.[5] Appointments to colonial offices in the eighteenth century cannot always be fully explained, but this one may be attributed in part to the reputation which Fauquier had gained through a pamphlet published by him the year before the death of Peter Jefferson. Dedicated to Lord Anson, it dealt with the burning question of financial support for the war with France, and it attracted enough attention to warrant two additional editions.[6]

It was of advantage to Fauquier in Virginia that he followed an unpopular governor, and it was to his credit there that he endeavored to maintain harmonious relations between the Colony and the authorities at home.[7] In the ecclesiastical controversy his sympathies were all with the local authorities; and, both in policy and person, he was al-

---

[4] The best account of his early life is Fairfax Harrison, "A Portrait of Governor Fauquier," *Fauquier Hist. Soc. Bulletin*, No. 4 (1924), pp. 343–350.

[5] Burk, *History of Virginia* (hereafter cited as Burk), III (1805), 333–334.

[6] "An Essay on Ways and Means for raising Money for the Support of the Present War Without Increasing the Public Debt," in J. H. Hollander, ed., *A Reprint of Economic Tracts* (1915). The 1st and 2nd eds. were in 1756, the 3rd in 1757. Fauquier first recommended a tax on houses and in the 2nd ed. he substituted for this a graduated capitation tax, but the chief historical significance which has been perceived in this pamphlet by students of economic thought lies in its argument that taxes on necessities will be shifted to employers and ultimately paid by consumers. See editor's introduction, p. 5.

[7] P. S. Flippin, *The Royal Government in Virginia*, pp. 133–136.

most everything that the gentlemen of Virginia could have wished their governor to be. His great personal popularity may be attributed to the fact that he was possessed of all the social virtues, in an eminent degree, and that he found among the people or at least the leaders of the Colony "a character compounded of the same elements as his own." [8] The great landholders, whom he received at the Palace and visited during the recess of the Assembly and the courts, found in his manners a model such as some of them had seen in England and others had read about in books; here was the "compleat gentleman" in living form. He had classical learning of the kind that was associated with the names of the second Richard Lee and the second William Byrd, and was exemplified among his contemporaries by George Wythe. His patronage of science may have chiefly impressed youngsters like Thomas Jefferson and John Page, but the high favor with which William Small was regarded by leading men shows that it was far from unwelcome at the time. In this respect as in others Fauquier was fashionable and modern.

He was a "curious" observer of natural phenomena who discussed current philosophical questions with his appreciative friends. Examples of his own observations survive. During his first year in the Colony he sent to his brother in England an account of a strange hailstorm which descended upon Williamsburg on an unusually hot Sunday afternoon in July. When this was communicated to the Royal Society the savants could have noted with satisfaction that the hailstones were described with scientific precision, both as to their shape and size. The storm broke every pane of glass on the north side of the Palace and destroyed the garden; and the Governor cooled his wine and froze cream with some of the ice next day.[9] Young Jefferson must have heard this story after he came to town and he may have gained from Fauquier his first ideas about the regular recording of the temperature and winds. The latter kept a diary of the weather in Williamsburg for just the years that his young friend was there in college, and afterwards turned this over to an English traveler who published it as an appendix to a book [10] It was precisely the sort of record that Jefferson himself kept so religiously at Monticello and at almost every other place where he stayed for long.

The only serious blot on Fauquier's character was his love for

[8] *W. & M.*, 1 ser., VIII, 173; Burk, III, 333–334.

[9] *Philosophical Transactions of the Royal Society*, Vol. 50, pt. 2 for the year 1758 (1759), pp. 746–747. The storm occurred on July 9, 1758.

[10] Andrew Burnaby, *Travels through North America* (1904 ed.), App. No. 5, pp. 215–251; reprinted from *Travels through the Middle Settlements of North America* (3 ed., 1798), where the author described this as the most valuable part of his collection.

gambling. The later statement that he introduced the "fatal propensity to gaming" into Virginia seems extreme in view of the practices which had been observed there before he came; but he encouraged these by his own example and had a part in making gambling a fashionable form of vice.[11] This was a time of extravagance, and losses are said to have been dangerously high. In his day in Williamsburg a traveler observed that in the taverns at night there was carousing and drinking in one chamber, and a box and dice in the other, and that this sort of thing lasted till morning. He went so far as to say that there was not a public house in Virginia but had its tables all battered with dice-boxes.[12] How deep-rooted such evils were no traveler could really judge; but more sober years were coming. Just prior to the Revolution, a young tutor observed in Westmoreland, that a new spirit of seriousness had entered Virginia life.[13] That seriousness was exemplified by George Washington and by Thomas Jefferson himself. There was more recklessness in the golden decade of Fauquier when there were fewer great things for men to do.

Jefferson said that when he was assailed by moral temptation during his youth and young manhood he used to ask himself how Small, or Wythe, or Peyton Randolph would act; he did not invoke the example of Fauquier.[14] At the Governor's table he heard highly stimulating conversation, and in this court he acquired graces which adorned his life, but he found his moral standards elsewhere. He did not pick up such vices as his elegant host exemplified — unless generosity and love of elegance should be accounted vices. But a certain longing for magnificence, in the spirit of the Renaissance, could be observed among rich Virginia planters and found early expression in the career of Thomas Jefferson. He may have got it from his countrymen or from his reading — but he may have caught it from Francis Fauquier.

It was probably after Jefferson had begun to study law under George Wythe that the musical Governor, who was a good performer himself, associated him with two or three other amateurs in the weekly concerts at the Palace.[15] He may have neglected his instrument for his books while he was at the College, but he afterwards reported that for twelve years before the Revolution he played no fewer than three hours a day.[16] While he was still a student in Williamsburg he

[11] Burk, III, 333.
[12] *Am. Hist. Rev.*, XXVI, 742–743; see also Burk, III, 402.
[13] Fithian, pp. 280–281.
[14] To T. J. Randolph, Nov. 24, 1808 (Ford, IX, 231).
[15] To L. H. Girardin, Jan. 15, 1815 (L. & B., XIV, 232).
[16] Randall, I, 24, 131.

found musical opportunities such as he had never had before, and which as a performer he was not to know again. He had no chance to see sculpture or fine paintings there, but traveling companies brought comic operas from time to time and music was cultivated by amateurs.[17] The professional authority of the place was Peter Pelham, son of a mezzotint artist of Boston and organist of Bruton Church, who supplemented his income by taking pupils, among them Jefferson's friend Anne Blair. At a later time he gained a further supplement by assuming the incongruous position of keeper of the Public Gaol. He then gave condemned criminals a chance to hear music before their execution, taking them to the church in shackles. In later years he often played for Jefferson, who treated him afterwards or paid him for his pains. The auditor filled the role of generous patron; at that time and place the status of the professional was inferior.

Jefferson was hardly proficient enough for the first violin part at the Palace; he probably had the second part and may even have played on the cello, for he was a passable performer on that instrument at a later time. The first violinist was probably John Randolph, brother of Peyton. He was not only a lawyer; he published a book on gardening which Jefferson acquired.[18] Councillor Robert Carter, a close friend of the Governor who played on the harpsichord and the German flute, was probably a member of the group. In his house next door to the Palace he installed an organ which had been built for him in London, and it is likely that Jefferson heard music there. He was unsuccessful in his later attempt to purchase this instrument.[19] It is possible that John Page participated in the concerts. Jefferson bought fiddle-strings regularly before visiting his friend at Rosewell, and undoubtedly he played there. There was a musical accompaniment to many of Jefferson's most intimate associations throughout the first half of his life, and it was probably during these years at Williamsburg that music became the "favorite passion" of his soul. Afterwards he bemoaned the fate which had cast his lot in a country where it was in a deplorable state of barbarism.[20] But this was during the Revolution, some time after Fauquier had gone. In the setting of the Palace ball-

[17] "On Music in Colonial Williamsburg," Report to Dept. Research and Record, Colonial Williamsburg, by Helen D. Bullock, Mar. 21, 1938, made available through their courtesy; unpublished ms. on "Jefferson and Music" by Carleton S. Smith and Helen D. Bullock, made available by their kindness.

[18] *A Treatise on Gardening, by a Citizen of Virginia*, ed. by M. F. Warner (1924); reprinted from 3rd ed. of 1825; 1st ed. *c.* 1765.

[19] L. Morton, *Robert Carter of Nomini Hall*, p. 41.

[20] June 8, 1778 (Ford, II, 158–160), letter without designation, but draft in LC, 3:419, shows it to have been addressed to John Fabroni or Fabbroni.

room, where a little group of enthusiastic amateurs performed when he was young, barbarism seemed remote.

Jefferson's extra-legal activities during his first years as a student under Wythe were not confined to conversations at the Governor's table and musicals in the Palace ballroom; to a degree he played a conventional part elsewhere as a young gentleman. His friendship with older men is one of many signs of the essential seriousness of his nature. They perceived it and reposed more confidence in him than might have been expected at his age, and he in turn valued their companionship because he could learn so much from them. In his relations with his contemporaries he soon became discriminating; he never suffered fools gladly, and it is hard to think of him as ever having been intellectually immature. As a recognized member of the younger gentry, however, he participated in the customary social life, and in the doing showed that in certain important respects he had not yet attained the full stature of a man, even though he now towered a couple of inches beyond six feet.

His social activities were natural and innocent. He danced at the Raleigh Tavern, visited at plantation houses, made wagers with girls, gossiped about courtships, and as time went on served as an attendant at weddings. He was and remained part of a close-knit social group, and he knew well the favored sons and daughters of this fertile land. During the months that he spent away from Williamsburg, which he sometimes called "Devilsburg," he often bemoaned the lack of companionship. To John Page he wrote once from Shadwell: "All things here appear to me to trudge on in one and the same round: we rise in the morning that we may eat breakfast, dinner and supper, and go to bed again that we may get up the next morning and do the same: so that you never saw two peas more alike than our yesterday and today." [21] He was not interested in cultivating this favorite vegetable as yet, and had not observed as he did later that not even two peas are identical. During the same period he wrote to another friend: "I do not like the ups and downs of a country life: today you are frolicking with a fine girl and tomorrow you are moping by yourself." [22] At few times during the course of his long life did he ever seem so bored.

There are many self-conscious passages in the few early letters of his that remain. Had the matter been left to him, he probably would

---

[21] Jan. 20, 1763; Ford, I, 346. Unpublished postscript to this letter, in Franklin Collection, Yale Univ., photostat UVA, reflects equal tedium a few weeks later. (Cited in Kimball, *Road to Glory*, pp. 68–69.)

[22] To William Fleming, 1763 (Ford, I, 352).

have burned those youthful effusions which John Page and William Fleming preserved and which, in the absence of other records, his biographers have worn so bare.[23] They do not reveal half enough but they disclose a great deal which the mature man would not have relished. They are not without charm and cleverness, for he had already learned to turn a happy phrase, but they are filled with learned conceits which are not at all characteristic of one who afterwards wore the mantle of scholarship lightly, as a gentleman was supposed to do. Their humor is often labored, for grace did not yet compensate for the lack of striking wit. Worst of all, they are full of references to girls. These would have horrified him in later years, when he was so reticent about personal affairs and particularly about his relations with womankind. The dignity and restraint of middle age were more characteristic, and also more becoming.

His earliest letters are interspersed with quotations from the classics, with an occasional phrase in French. He referred to friends and acquaintances by using rough Latin equivalents — "Parvus" for William Small, and "Currus" for Dabney Carr. He wrote to William Fleming as "Will," but John Page he addressed as "Dear Page." His use of familiar given names probably declined from the time that he left Maury's school, and it ceased when he and his friends attained maturity; then formality became the rule. While still in the familiar stage he spoke of Alice Corbin, with whom he had bet a pair of garters, of Sukey Potter whom he hoped Will Fleming would marry — though actually he did not; of Nancy Wilton whom Page appears to have courted briefly; of Jenny Taliaferro who played the spinet and sang well. Most of all, he talked of Rebecca Burwell. She provided the only romantic story of his youth, but it is not a particularly good one. He was an indecisive suitor and emerged too rarely from the realm of thought.

This girl, whom he referred to as "R.B.," "Becca," "Belinda," "Campana in die," and "Adnileb," on the pretense that some of these thin disguises would deceive all but his closest friends, was an orphan with the best of connections. Her father became a member of the Council in the year that Thomas Jefferson was born. He was present when Joshua Fry and Peter Jefferson reported that they had extended the dividing line; as acting governor, he consulted the Board about employing them to draw a map of the inhabited part of Virginia, and soon after that he died.[24] The date of the death of Rebecca's mother

[23] Ford, I, 341–360.
[24] *Council Journals, Colonial Va.*, V, 129, 310, 345, 354, 370. He took his seat Aug. 4, 1743, became acting governor on Nov. 21, 1750, and continued until

is uncertain, but when Jefferson met her the orphaned girl was in the charge of her uncle by marriage, William Nelson of York, also a Councillor and afterwards acting governor.[25] He is generally referred to as "President Nelson," while his brother Thomas is known as "Secretary Nelson," and his own son Thomas is usually called "the Signer." It was the latter who succeeded Jefferson as governor of the Commonwealth during the Revolution. Jefferson addressed him as "Dear Nelson" and long maintained intimate relations with this wealthy and influential family, as was natural enough in view of his friendship with John Page. He may have met Rebecca on a visit to York or Rosewell, but he probably saw her first in Williamsburg, when her guardian was there attending to his official duties.

The tradition is that she was beautiful, and according to the scanty record she was also good. Bishop Meade, "gentle annalist" of Virginia churches, ministers, and families, approvingly quotes a passage describing her pious resignation in the early loss of her parents and attributing to her a religious enthusiasm which distinguished her from her giddy companions.[26] William Nelson himself was a zealous churchman, for all his interest in racing horses, and in later life Rebecca appears to have been deeply religious in the conventional sense. The Jefferson of history was not that, but it is possible that an element in her attraction for him in his youth was that she was somewhat more serious than the other girls.

He thought himself deeply in love during the winter before he was twenty and while she was still sixteen. He was at Shadwell that winter, and his struggles with Coke's tough primer of the law were being interrupted by romantic thoughts. Early marriage was the rule rather than the exception in his class, but he had also begun to dream of a trip abroad and he spoke of this as a virtual necessity, though as a matter of fact he never made it. He belabored his puzzled mind, trying to decide what to do, and revealed his tortuous mental processes to his confidant, John Page.

Should he end his suspense by going down to receive his sentence, and at the same time run the risk of being ten times more wretched than before? Would Page join him on his travels in a vessel to be called the *Rebecca*, in which they would sail to many lands, including Italy where a good fiddle could be bought? If so, they might both be

Nov. 1, 1751. The meetings in which Joshua Fry and Peter Jefferson figured were on Dec. 13, 1749, Oct. 15, 1751, and Nov. 1, 1751. See also *Va. Mag.*, II, 232–233, X, 177.

[25] The most important facts about William Nelson are in the *D.A.B.* His laudatory epitaph is in R. A. Brock, *Virginia and Virginians* (1888), I, 59.

[26] Meade, I, 99.

cured of love. If Belinda would not accept his services he would never offer them to another, but she had given him little ground for hope. He wanted to ask her to wait until he had come back, but wondered if this would not seem an unreasonable request. If she consented he would be happy; if not, he would be as contented as he could. Perfect happiness was probably not intended for human creatures, anyway, and one must learn to be resigned. Others of their gay friends would be amused by such sober reflections, he feared, but Page would understand.

All this was in the mood of adolescence, though the language was learned and some of the passages show that his mind had already taken a speculative turn. He was enjoying his reflective sadness, as well as his recurrent hopes. A rival had appeared during his absence but, despite Page's urging, he was not yet willing to approach Rebecca's guardian; he must put the problem before the girl herself. President Nelson would doubtless have chuckled had he heard him.

In the fall, back in Williamsburg, Jefferson wrote hopefully to Will Fleming but soon sent a melancholy note to Page. Before he went to dance with "Belinda" in the Apollo Room he had dressed up his thoughts in the most moving language, but when the time came his actual sentences were few and disordered, while the pauses were frequent and long. It was unfortunate that he did not write to her instead of trusting to his stammering speech. His pen was his strongest weapon and the stilted extravagances of the time would not have seemed artificial to her, as they do to almost any reader now.

Somewhat later he managed to say his piece. He talked about the necessity of his trip to England and deliberately refrained from asking an outright question, though he informed the young lady that such a question would be asked at some later time. To her the remote prospect did not seem alluring and this he must have sensed, for he made no effort to see her again. He explained this inactivity to others on the ground that he had been abominably lazy, but the probability is that he was now deeper in the law than in love. His rival was more aggressive. In the spring, shortly before Jefferson's twenty-first birthday, Rebecca became engaged to Jacquelin Ambler, who was somewhat older than Jefferson and had really made up his mind.[27] Years later, as a member of the Council of State, he was closely associated with Jefferson as governor of Virginia, and later still he served with honor and great personal popularity as treasurer of the Commonwealth. The Revolution seriously affected his fortunes; it also brought him a prize son-in-law whom Jefferson afterwards disliked. At Yorktown in 1779–1780 Mary

[27] On Ambler, *Ibid.*, I, 106–108; *Va. Mag.*, XVIII, 378.

Ambler, daughter of Jacquelin and Rebecca, met Captain John Marshall, and three years later in Richmond she became his wife.[28]

Ambler acted more like an adult than his rival did in 1763 and 1764. Jefferson carried on this rather absurd affair mostly in his imagination. But there was no little wisdom at the base of his uncertainty. Before he encumbered himself with a family he had many important things to do; and, although he did not go to England, he did apply himself to his studies with an intensity which a young wife could hardly have been expected to approve. Such thoughts were doubtless in his mind when he copied into his literary notebook the following strong passage from an eighteenth-century playwright:

> Wed her!
> No! were she all Desire could wish, as fair
> As would the vainest of her sex be thought,
> With Wealth beyond what woman's pride could waste,
> She should not cheat me of my Freedom. Marry!
> When I am old & weary of the World,
> I may grow desperate,
> And take a Wife to mortify withal.[29]

Other entries, even more antifeminist, lead to the supposition that this unhappy experience cured him temporarily of his hankering for girls. From *Paradise Lost* he transcribed this:

> O! why did God,
> Creator wise! that Peopl'd highest Heav'n
> With spirits masculine, create at last
> This Novelty on Earth, this fair Defect
> Of Nature? And not fill the world at once
> With Men, as Angels, without feminine?
> Or find some other Way to generate
> Mankind? [30]

The women of his day in Virginia had few intellectual advantages and, like an English traveler who had recently passed that way, he may have concluded that they were unequal to any "interesting and refined conversation." [31] During the next few years he found satisfaction in friendship with men. When he passed philosophical evenings at Rosewell with John Page, or talked about the law with Dabney Carr on an Albemarle hillside, he was relatively free from disturbing thoughts

---

[28] A. J. Beveridge, *Life of John Marshall*, I, 148–165.
[29] From Otway's *Orphan*, quoted in *Literary Bible*, p. 158.
[30] *Ibid.*, p. 139.
[31] Burnaby, *Travels*, p. 57.

about the "fair defect of nature." Dabney Carr was likewise reading Coke and Matthew Bacon, and he also set high value on "the blessings of science." According to Jefferson, he had "every excellence which good sense, learning, or virtue could give." [32] It was of boon companions such as these that he thought when he copied into his notebook a passage from Euripides:

> Nothing is better than a reliable friend, not riches, not absolute sovereignty. Nay more, the crowd is not to be reckoned with, in exchange for a noble friend. [33]

This saying did more than match a fleeting mood: it voiced a conviction which grew deeper through the years. He was ever afterwards restrained in his comments on individual women, but it was always easy for him to wax sentimental about a friend. It was no accident that his life was extraordinarily rich in friendship, for he cultivated this unceasingly and made of it an art. In a moment of irreparable personal loss, after he had begun to grow old, he wrote John Page: "But friends we have, if we have merited them. Those of our earliest years stand nearest in our affections." With regard to this first group, however, he did not regard himself as wholly fortunate. This was chiefly because of his own longevity, for the companions of his youth vanished from the field before he did. Some of them, also, were eventually parted from him by political differences, though he regarded this as an insufficient cause. It was while he was President that he said to Page: "Of our college friends (and they are the dearest) how few have stood with us in the great political questions which have agitated our country; . . . I did not believe the Lilliputian fetters of that day strong enough to have bound so many." [34]

When he was studying law the period of political strife was remote, but his two best friends soon yielded to the lure of women. He was only twenty-two when John Page married Frances, daughter of Robert Carter Burwell of Isle of Wight County; she was to bear him twelve of his twenty children, thus participating impressively in the divine plan for the generation of mankind. It was in the year 1765, also, that Dabney Carr married Martha Jefferson. The happiness of "Currus" greatly impressed Martha's brother, and before it was cut short by untimely death he himself followed this glowing example. Romance returned to him in maturer and less fleeting form, and within his family he revealed as nowhere else the gentleness and tenderness of his nature. But his own

[32] To Thomas Stone, Mar. 16, 1782, in LC, 8:1226.
[33] *Lit. Bible*, p. 94.
[34] June 25, 1804 (L. & B., XI, 32).

marriage did not occur until eight or nine years after his imaginative quest of Rebecca Burwell.

No picture of Jefferson as a young gentleman survives, but there is a good deal of information about the general social environment in which he lived during his student years. At that time the standards which Fauquier personified and accentuated were already set.[35] The Governor did not introduce them. They had been transplanted from England in the first place, and in the unequal and dispersed society of a sunny agricultural province they had assumed characteristic local form. The polish and elegance of colonial society can be easily exaggerated, and unquestionably there was much crudity behind the façade. Even in the best circles in Virginia there was less smoothness than Jefferson afterwards observed in Paris, where the roughness of the human mind was so rubbed off that one might glide through life without a jostle. Nevertheless, good manners were an essential feature of the prevailing pattern. Even in the relatively fashionable period of Fauquier's governorship the gentleman did not need to be a dandy, and at a later time he was proudly indifferent to the externalities of dress. Ideally, however, the gentleman was hospitable and generous, courteous in his relations with his peers, chivalrous toward women, and kind to inferiors. Not everybody was mannerly; even the Governor was rude under provocation. But there was a high standard of politeness which the gentry recognized and generally observed. Politeness, as Jefferson afterwards remarked, is artificial good humor, and a valuable preservative of peace and tranquillity.[36]

The grandson to whom he made this observation preserved a story of the mollifying effects of the best Virginia manners, and this probably came from Jefferson himself. The sheriff of one of the river counties, who was described as a self-made man though he founded a distinguished family, had strong prejudices against the aristocrats. Approaching the seat of one of the proudest of these, on a business errand, and seeing him before the house, the sheriff resolved not to dismount. But, when he drew near, he was greeted by the gentleman "with such suavity, dignity, and winning grace of manner, that before he became aware of it he found himself standing before him hat in hand." This grandson, struck by the common quality of politeness in the older gentlemen of Virginia who differed in so many other ways, asked his

[35] For an excellent discussion of the ideals and standards of the gentry, see L. B. Wright, *First Gentlemen of Virginia*. The comments of Burnaby in *Travels*, pp. 53-54, are less favorable.

[36] To T. J. Randolph, Nov. 24, 1808 (Ford, IX, 231).

grandfather for an explanation. To this Jefferson replied that they had all been trained in Williamsburg, "the finest school of manners and morals that ever existed in America." [37]

In view of his comments on his own personal difficulties and temptations during his youth, it is surprising that he should have commended the morals as well as the manners of a place where students rioted periodically and drinking and gambling were so rife. He said that he was thrown into the society of cardplayers, horse racers, and fox hunters, and left no doubt that he regarded such company as bad. This statement, however, must be read side by side with other later remarks of his about the grave dangers of dissipation which American students would face in England. In the course of time he came to regard Williamsburg as a relatively moral place.

In this society, pleasure and conviviality were not frowned upon and certain personal vices were condoned. The unpardonable sins were lying and meanness of spirit. Plain speech to one's peers was not expected; insofar as possible the gentleman was supposed to please. The educational ideal was that of the well-rounded man, who was decently familiar with the classics, reasonably current with philosophy, and had at least a bowing acquaintance with the arts. Only in the fields of plantation affairs and government was he expected to be a specialist.

There is no more reason to suppose that Jefferson uncritically accepted the entire social code than that he contented himself with meeting the minimal requirements of education. He conformed outwardly to the prevailing social standards but he escaped the characteristic vices. Well into mature manhood he made small wagers, but in no real sense was he a gambler after he became grown. It is doubtful if he was ever much of a drinker, though he acquired a well-stocked cellar in due course and eventually became a connoisseur of wines. In these early years he dressed as fastidiously as his companions, he enjoyed dancing, and as a matter of course he rode. At no time, probably, was this foe of indolence and lover of books quite conventional, but he responded quickly to refinement and he was rarely if ever coarse. He became a penetrating critic of the society in which he was born and bred, but socially he was in all respects a gentleman. His distinction lies in the fact that he became a great deal more.

[37] Memoirs of T. J. Randolph (Edgehill Randolph Papers), UVA, pp. 9–10.

[VII]

Listening at the Capitol
1765–1766

THE College, the Wythe house, the Palace, the Capitol — these were the focal centers of Jefferson's life in Williamsburg during his student years. The Capitol was last in point of time but it proved the most important in the end, for it became a major scene of his own action. Williamsburg was more than an academic village and a school of manners; it was the seat and school of provincial government. He could see the political institutions of the Colony in actual operation, all the more easily because the place was small, and could become personally acquainted with the able men who made them work.

The Governor, whom Jefferson knew so well and admired so much, was the visible representative of the far-distant King, whose birthday was regularly celebrated in the town and whose name appeared on all public documents of any note. Around Fauquier was gathered a Council of a dozen wealthy and influential men. Jefferson became friends with several of these in the course of social life. He first became familiar with the Council as an official body in its capacity as the highest provincial court of law. In order to learn his future business he went as a listener to the General Court. The Capitol was built in the form of the letter H, and the General Court was held in one wing on the first floor while the burgesses met in the other.[1] There was little occasion for him to climb to the second floor, where committees met and the Council sat in executive session, but he knew the first floor well and there observed the House of Burgesses. Knowledge of it and its members was an important part of the education of future leaders, such as the sons of the gentry were deemed to be.

Through George Wythe, Jefferson soon became personally acquainted with Edmund Pendleton, whose prowess as a debater he afterwards attested. At an early time he marked Pendleton as a leader

---

[1] *AHR*, XXVI, 741.

of the conservatives, but from the beginning he regarded him as a friend. Not until he himself went to the bar did Jefferson become intimate with his mother's cousin, Peyton Randolph, now King's Attorney and soon to be Speaker of the House, but he saw this large man in action. He was always impressed with Peyton Randolph's intelligence but never by his ability as a speaker.[2] Considerably older was another first cousin of Jane Randolph Jefferson, a cousin whom her son regarded as the most learned of the elder group of statesmen. Profound in constitutional lore, Richard Bland looked something like the old parchments which he handled and studied so much.[3] More than any other single man, probably, he laid the philosophical foundations of the resistance to the Mother Country, but Jefferson noted that he, also, was an ungraceful speaker. It was the greatest of the Virginia orators who gave wide currency to these doctrines, and of all the burgesses it was he who most impressed the young man at first. From the time that he heard Patrick Henry as a student he regarded him as pre-eminent in the forensic field.

In his maturity Jefferson was no admirer of mere oratory, but he never questioned the power of eloquence, and even in extreme old age he commended the study of it to youth. He gave it a recognized place in his own program, believing that a law student should read and analyze works of oratory and thus become acquainted with the "elevated style." He copied out examples of English eloquence, some of them now obscure; he found chaste specimens in Livy, Sallust, and Tacitus; and during his evening hours he read Demosthenes and Cicero, whom he continued to regard as the finest models for the forum and the bar.[4] While he was still in college he heard a Cherokee chief deliver an oration which he never forgot; and three years later he stood at the door of the chamber of the burgesses, listening spellbound to Patrick Henry. This memorable experience constituted more than an introduction to vivid local eloquence; it was also a striking example of the sort of political education which as a potential leader he received in Williamsburg.

He had met Patrick Henry in Hanover County more than five years earlier. This was at the hospitable home of Captain Nathaniel West Dandridge, he said, during the Christmas holidays before he entered

[2] To Joseph Delaplaine, July 26, 1816 (Ford, X, 55–56).

[3] Various comments on Bland are quoted in the introduction to his *Inquiry into the Rights of the British Colonies*, ed. by E. G. Swem (1922). See also Jefferson to William Wirt, Aug. 5, 1815 (Ford, IX, 474 *n.*); H. J. Eckenrode, *Revolution in Virginia*, pp. 11, 22.

[4] To Abraham Small, May 20, 1814 (L. & B., XIV, 137); to G. W. Summers and J. B. Garland, Feb. 27, 1822 (L. & B., XV, 353).

college. He was not yet seventeen and Henry was not yet twenty-four. The period of their association was about two weeks, amid the festivities of the season, and the younger of them afterwards reflected that the elder engaged in no conversation which might have given the measure of his information or of his mind. After Jefferson had been exposed to Small, Wythe, and Fauquier, however, it became evident to him that Henry was no man of science and learning. To Jefferson his passion seemed to be for fiddling, dancing, and pleasantry, in the last of which he particularly excelled though he was solemnity itself in public. His manners had something of the coarseness of the poor hunters with whom he loved to pursue deer in the piney woods and to crack jokes around the campfire. He was no fashionable gentleman, though his lineage was reputable; he was one who was instinctively attracted to people of the common sort. Both as a fiddler and as a statesman he played by ear, and Jefferson himself was among the many whom he charmed.[5]

During the spring following their first meeting Henry took his examination for the bar in Williamsburg, when after six weeks of study he was passed by a learned board under circumstances which have led to considerable historical dispute. The severity of Jefferson's later comments on Henry's legal learning, when the latter's biographer asked him about the orator, have been attributed by some writers to the alienation between the two men which occurred toward the end of the Revolution.[6] The most serious of his criticisms, however, can be explained on equally human but less political grounds. He referred a number of times to Henry's laziness and lack of precise information, while recognizing his great public services and his imaginative genius. The contrast between his own painstaking preparation for the bar and Henry's casual knowledge of the law when first examined could hardly have failed to strike him. While he was favored by circumstances at the outset of his career to a much greater degree than Henry, he

[5] See particularly the sketch he sent to Wirt, on request, Apr. 12, 1812, and his letters of Aug. 5, 1815, and Sept. 4, 1816, to Wirt (Ford, IX, 339–45 n., 475–76 n.; X, 59–60). His memory may have been in error about the exact date of his meeting with Henry but there is little doubt that he knew him when he was in college, if not before.

[6] W. W. Henry, *Patrick Henry* (1891), I, 584; II, 144. Wirt, in his *Sketches of the Life and Character of Patrick Henry* (citations from 2 ed., 1818) drew heavily on Jefferson's sketch and letters, but, through modifications and omissions, gave a more favorable impression (see esp. pp. 13–15, 18 n.). M. C. Tyler, *Patrick Henry* (1887), pp. 29–34, though less partisan than W. W. Henry, regards Jefferson's comments on Henry's professional character as inaccurate. So far as Henry's practice is concerned, he proves his point. Jefferson's specific comments may have been too sharp, but his general historical judgment on Henry seems sound.

gained his professional position chiefly by hard work, while his less learned contemporary attained fame as a jury lawyer almost at a bound. Jefferson had the scholar's contempt for shortcuts, and his own talent was of another sort.

He probably thought little about the intellectual limitations of Patrick Henry, however, when the latter called on him in the spring that he became seventeen, or even when as a practising lawyer the orator regularly stopped with him in Williamsburg.[7] If he afterwards questioned the possibility of Henry's ever having read Livy or any other book more than once, at the outset he was probably attracted by the engaging personality and was undoubtedly impressed by the native genius of the man. More than any other prominent leader in the Province, Henry sensed the feelings of the inarticulate and appealed to the unformed West, whence Jefferson himself had sprung. For intellectual stimulus and cultivated conversation the law student went elsewhere, but he gained the most important of his early political impressions from the self-taught lawyer who spoke at the Capitol against the Stamp Act as Jefferson had never heard man speak before. This was on Thursday, May 30, 1765, when he was twenty-two. If "the dull monotony of a colonial subservience," of which he afterwards complained, was not broken at this time, it was sharply punctuated.[8]

The public character of Virginians at this date was hardly one of subservience to the Mother Country. A traveler who had come that way in Fauquier's time remarked: "They are haughty and jealous of their liberties, impatient of restraint, and can scarcely bear the thought of being controlled by any superior power."[9] On the other hand, this visitor also reported that they never refused necessary supplies to the government when called upon, and that they were characteristically a loyal and generous people. Both loyalty and jealous independence of spirit had marked the previous discussion of the stamp tax, and of this young Jefferson had heard.

His teacher George Wythe had played a part in the actions of the Assembly in the previous fall, when an address was dispatched to the King and memorials were sent to the Lords and Commons protesting against the proposed internal tax on both practical and constitutional grounds. Wythe drew a draft of one of these papers, but, as he told Jefferson, it was toned down by his colleagues on the committee, presumably on the advice of Fauquier. The subject matter of these

[7] Randall, I, 40.
[8] To John Adams, Mar. 25, 1826 (L. & B., XVI, 160).
[9] Burnaby, *Travels* (1904 ed.), p. 55. He was in Virginia in 1759–1760.

dignified documents, as the Governor aptly said, was "praying to be permitted to tax themselves." There had been no response to the prayer, however; and in the spring of 1765 the notorious Act had been passed by Parliament and assented to by the King, though it was not to go into effect until the following November.[10]

Neither the Governor nor the local leaders seem to have expected any action on this question at the May session of the Assembly. The business was nearly done and all but a third of the burgesses had gone home when a new member took the veterans by surprise.[11] Jefferson probably heard that his friend from Hanover had presented to the committee of the whole on Wednesday certain resolutions which would be debated next day. He may not have learned that they got into the mails in advance of final action. They aroused heated comment as far away as Boston and sounded the alarm bell of the American Revolution if any single writing did. Jefferson could not fail to hear it, for he was near by.[12]

There was then no gallery in the Capitol, so he took his stand on that Thursday between the lobby and the burgess chamber along with his younger friend John Tyler, who was still studying law with Robert Carter Nicholas.[13] Here they heard Patrick Henry make a speech in which he mentioned Caesar and Brutus, Charles I and Cromwell, and uttered the name of George III. As they remembered it half a century afterwards, he was then stopped with cries of "Treason," and extricated himself from a predicament by adding that this monarch might profit from example. A contemporary account gives a milder version of the famous passage, but a minor lapse of memory on the part of two old men, who had heard the traditional version in the meantime, would be quite forgivable.[14] Jefferson also said that frequently, when listening to Henry, he closed his eyes and afterwards was unable to remember a single word. In the torrent of sublime oratory he could not distinguish waves. Of the indelible emotional

[10] *Burgesses, Journals,* 1761–1765, pp. liv–lviii, 257, 294, 302–304; Jefferson to Wirt,, Aug. 14, 1814, Ford, IX, 469.

[11] Circumstances described by Fauquier in letter of June 5, 1765, to Board of Trade (*Burgesses, Journals,* 1761–1765, pp. lxvii–lxviii).

[12] *Ibid.,* pp. lxvi–lxvii. They appeared in the *Newport Mercury,* June 24, and in the *Boston Gazette,* July 1, inaccurately however, for one that was afterwards passed was omitted; see M. C. Tyler, *Patrick Henry,* p. 67 *n.*

[13] To Wirt, Aug. 14, 1814, Ford, IX, 467 ff.; L. G. Tyler, *Letters and Times of the Tylers,* I, 55.

[14] "Journal of a French Traveller in the Colonies, 1765, I," *AHR,* XXVI (July, 1921), esp. pp. 727–729, 745. The passage is given in its customary form in Wirt, *Patrick Henry,* p. 65, Jefferson being cited as authority. It had previously appeared in Burk's *History of Virginia,* III, 309, however, and Jefferson had probably read it there.

impression that this speech made on him, however, there can be no question.

Whether or not anybody accused Henry of treason, the responsible leaders of the Colony were unwilling to go quite so far in formal action as he desired. Like the Governor, Jefferson reported that the resolutions were opposed by Speaker John Robinson, Peyton Randolph, and George Wythe, and he added the names of Pendleton and Bland.[15] Their ground was that the same principles had been set forth in the still-unanswered address and memorial of the previous session, and that the latter were more likely to be effective because of their more conciliatory tone. In their judgment the question was essentially one of method, if not one of manners. Henry was bolder than they had been, for he attacked the Stamp Act *after* its passage, rather than before, and his audacity had its reward. The members of the ruling group were reluctant to yield any part of their leadership to one whom they regarded as a rash upstart, but it is a measure of their political wisdom that most of them accepted him before long.

Two of the resolutions were either defeated or withheld on the day that Henry made his speech, though both of them got into the papers elsewhere.[16] Another was passed by a single vote. This boldly asserted the exclusive right of the Assembly to lay taxes, and stated that every attempt to vest such power in any other person or persons whatsoever had a manifest tendency to destroy both British and American freedom. Jefferson regarded it as the strongest of them all and said that the debate on it was "most bloody." It was after the passage of this resolution that he heard portly Peyton Randolph say, as he came puffing out of the door: "By God, I would have given one hundred guineas for a single vote." [17] On the next day, before the burgesses met, the young law student stood at the end of the clerk's table and watched Colonel Peter Randolph, then a member of the Council, thumb over the volumes of the journal, trying to find a precedent for the expunging of a vote. He could not recall whether his former guardian found the erasure he was looking for, but he noted that soon afterwards a motion was carried to expunge. According to the Governor, there had happened "a small alteration in the House." The fact was that Patrick

---

[15] To Wirt, Aug. 5, 1815 (Ford, IX, 473 n.).

[16] For a careful analysis of the seven original resolutions and their history, see note in *AHR*, XXVI, 746, citing M. C. Tyler, *Patrick Henry*, p. 67, as giving a correct statement of the form and reckoning of the numbers. Fauquier's letter of June 5, 1765, which was not available to Tyler, gives a slightly different story of events. A copy of five of Henry's resolutions, as reported by the committee of the whole, said to have been taken from the latter's own copy is in LC, vol. 1. Probably it was sent to Jefferson by Wirt.

[17] To Wirt, Aug. 14, 1814 (Ford, IX, 468).

Henry, thinking his work was done, had put on his buckskin breeches, mounted his lean horse, and set out for home.[18]

Jefferson also reported that there was a change of heart on the part of some of the "timid members." By implication he afterwards approved of the expunged resolution and sympathized with the "young hot and giddy members," as Fauquier described them. The four resolutions which were passed said quite enough about the taxation of the people by their own representatives and about the established practice of colonial self-government to put Virginia clearly on record; and his law teacher, who was so intimate with the Governor, thought that even this reiterated statement was unnecessary at the time. We cannot be sure that Jefferson disagreed with Wythe and Fauquier at twenty-two, but his later comments imply that he was no more appalled by the alleged rashness of Henry's course then than he was afterwards. Reviewing the matter in old age, he spoke of the "exact conformity" of their opinions. Also, he noted that the resolutions were supported chiefly by the vote of the middle and upper country. The implications of this observation were later revealed in his own political career.

He may not have witnessed the stirring incident which occurred in the following October, when the stamps arrived in Williamsburg, but he was there that month and could hardly have escaped hearing about it, for the hero was his friend the Governor. Though Fauquier had regretted the action of Patrick Henry in May, he realized that opposition to the Stamp Act had crystallized since that time and obviously regarded the measure as unenforceable. The actual presence of Colonel Mercer with the stamps constituted an embarrassment and placed him in a situation requiring more circumspection, he said, than he had ever before displayed. Going to the Coffee House beyond the Capitol, he was sitting on the porch with the Speaker and several members of the Council when Colonel Mercer came thither, followed by a crowd which Fauquier would have called a mob had he not known the gentlemen of property who composed it. He described the subsequent events in a colorful letter to the Board of Trade.

> I immediately heard a cry, "See the Governor, take care of him." Those who were pushing up the steps, immediately fell back, and left a small space between me and them. If your Lordships will not accuse me of vanity I would say that I believe this to be partly owing to the respect they bore to my character and partly to the love they bore my person.[19]

[18] Tyler, *Henry*, p. 66.
[19] Nov. 3, 1765; *Burgesses, Journals*, 1761–1765, pp. lxviii–lxxi.

Soon afterwards he and Mercer walked "side by side through the thickest of the people." There were "some little murmurs" but they were not molested.

Mercer shortly resigned, and perhaps the honors were no more than even, but Fauquier had maintained public order and his own prestige. There was no such violence here as there had been a few weeks earlier in Boston, where the house of Lieutenant Governor Thomas Hutchinson was destroyed and his valuable books and papers were scattered in the street. Mobs could not be assembled so readily in this agricultural province as in a seaport city, and leadership here was retained by the genteel group. Also, until Lord Dunmore appeared on the eve of the Revolution, the Province of Virginia was fortunate in its governors. Fauquier and his immediate successor, Lord Botetourt, were more tactful and judicious than Sir Francis Bernard and Thomas Hutchinson. It was not from them that young Jefferson gained the low impression that he afterwards held of the manners of British officials.

So far as imperial relations were concerned, from the time of the struggle over the Stamp Act onward, he was more impressed with the agreement of the political leaders of Virginia than by their differences of opinion. He always credited Patrick Henry with giving the first impulse to the ball of revolution there, and in all his later statements he manifested his own sympathy with him and the bolder spirits, including the Lees. He believed that a new political alignment was created as a result of the increased prominence of this group. Factional rivalries probably played a considerable part in these early struggles. The change was symbolized by the discrediting of Speaker John Robinson, who was also treasurer of the Colony and the central figure among the dominant leaders. When he passed from the political scene in 1766, the year before Jefferson was admitted to the bar and three years before he became a burgess, a new period began, though at first the differences from the old one were not startling.[20]

Robinson was involved in dubious financial transactions which Patrick Henry and Richard Henry Lee suspected and which Jefferson afterwards condemned, though he was gentle towards the man himself. In a time of financial difficulty following the French and Indian War, Robinson as treasurer had re-emitted redeemed treasury notes and accepted the paper of various individuals in return, expecting that this

[20] For an illuminating discussion of the political alignment in the pre-Revolutionary years, see T. P. Abernethy, *Western Lands and the American Revolution*, ch. XI. He regards the Stamp Act controversy as significant in drawing Patrick Henry and Richard Henry Lee together, in opposition to the Robinson–Randolph group.

would be redeemed before the time when the notes had to be destroyed
He was also charged with attempting to cover his transactions by setting up a loan office. Henry, without realizing the full implications of
the proposal but scenting scandal, attacked it boldly in the House of
Burgesses and uttered one exclamation which Jefferson never forgot.
"It had been urged," said Jefferson, "that, from certain unhappy
circumstances of the colony, men of substantial property had contracted debts, which, if exacted suddenly, must ruin them and their
families, but with a little indulgence of time might be paid with ease."
Then, as he remembered, Patrick Henry said: "What, Sir, is it proposed,
then, to reclaim the spendthrift from his dissipation and extravagance
by filling his pockets with money?" [21]

The proposal was killed by the Council, not by the burgesses as
Jefferson recalled, and his memory may have been otherwise at fault.
Again he said that Henry was supported by the members from the
upper counties, and that only an aristocratic minority was opposed.
After the death of Robinson in 1766, his private loans from public
funds were discovered, and, insofar as proved necessary, these were
charged against his estate. The names of his beneficiaries were not revealed, though some prominent planters have been strongly suspected.
The fact that Colonel Peter Randolph and Edmund Pendleton were
among the executors of Robinson's will need not imply that they were
personally involved but it does suggest where their political sympathies lay.

The immediate result was the separation of the offices of speaker
and treasurer, as Fauquier had advised, Peyton Randolph assuming the
one and Robert Carter Nicholas the other. Both of these older men
were in office when Jefferson entered public life, and he never questioned their complete integrity. Patrick Henry was now established as
a man of prominence, but he did not dominate the scene. In policy
though not in social intercourse, Jefferson was to be more closely identified with him and with Richard Henry Lee than with the still-powerful
remnants of the old ruling group. Not until afterwards did he speak
disparagingly of the aristocracy, or even condemn extravagance and
debt, but by this early date some seeds of doubt had fallen into his
retentive mind.

In order to complete the story of Fauquier we must anticipate somewhat. The amiable Governor, whose chief fault was his love of gaming
and who may also have erred on the side of magnificence, was still in

[21] *Burgesses, Journals,* 1766–1769, p. xxi; Ford, IX, 339, 466; W. W. Henry, *Patrick Henry,* I, 76.

office when Jefferson began to appear in 1767 before the General Court, but when his young friend entered the House of Burgesses two years later he had passed forever from the scene. After a tedious illness, which he bore with patience and fortitude, Fauquier died at the Palace in March, 1768, at the age of sixty-five. Until the end he continued to be a friend to scientific inquiry, for he prescribed in his will that if he should die from any disease of which the physicians did not know the cause his body might be opened. Also, he strikingly revealed his humanitarian spirit. Regretting that it would be necessary to sell his slaves, he specifically enjoined that the women and children should not be separated, that his former servants should be allowed to choose their own new masters, and that they were then to be sold to those chosen masters at a considerable discount from the market price.[22]

Jefferson was not among the "principal gentlemen" who were present when the unviolated body of Fauquier was laid to rest in Bruton Church, for he was then in Albemarle planting his garden and preparing to start out on a circuit of county courts. But when he got to Williamsburg a little later he undoubtedly heard full details from George Wythe, who was one of the executors of the late Governor's American estate. As a subscriber to the *Virginia Gazette*, also, he could hardly have failed to read and approve the lines which soon appeared there:

> If ever virtue lost a friend sincere,
> If ever sorrow claim'd *Virginia's* tear,
> If ever death a noble conquest made,
> 'Twas when FAUQUIER the debt of nature paid.[23]

Jefferson regarded him as the best of governors, but he owed a greater political debt to Patrick Henry. Fauquier had done most for him in helping him cultivate his tastes and expand the horizons of his mind.

[22] *W. & M.*, 1 ser., VIII, 173–178.
[23] Rind, *Va. Gazette*, communication dated Mar. 10, 1768; see also Dixon & Purdie, *Va. Gazette*, Mar. 3, 10, 1768.

[VIII]

Disciple of Enlightenment

A YEAR after he heard Patrick Henry declaim against the Stamp Act at the Capitol, Jefferson left his Province for the first time and ventured farther from home than he did again until after the American Revolution. Beginning in May, 1766, when he was twenty-three, he made a journey of about three months to Annapolis, Philadelphia, and New York, returning to Virginia by water. This was his nearest approach to a Grand Tour such as young English gentlemen made at the close of their formal schooling. He continued his preparations for the bar for several months longer, and he never ceased to be a student, but this trip, besides being an educational experience in itself, marked with some precision the end of his years of tutelage.

He made the trip alone, though he had not expected to. He had counted on the lively companionship of Frank Willis of Gloucester County.[1] Willis had played disconcerting practical jokes on him and John Tyler when they were reading law in Williamsburg (such as overturning the table or carrying off their lawbooks), but he found Willis entertaining when he himself was not studying. This waggish young man had to start earlier, however, and Jefferson had no company but his own thoughts as he drove to Annapolis in a one-horse chair.[2] On the way he was nearly spilled into a stream when fording it and had other minor misadventures. The account of them which he sent John Page shows that he was not wholly devoid of humor, and his comments on the capital of Maryland show that he was keeping his eyes open.

Observing the lower house of the Assembly in session, he was sharply critical of its procedure, remarking that it was little better than a mob. The members addressed the Speaker without rising from

[1] Jefferson to Willis, July 23, 1766; courtesy of Papers of Thomas Jefferson, Princeton Univ. See also Tyler, *Tylers*, I, 55. According to his Garden Book, he set out from Shadwell on May 11, 1766.

[2] His letter to Page from Annapolis, May 25, 1766, is in *Bulletin N. Y. Pub. Lib.*, II (1898), 176–177.

their seats and he put the question most casually, not bothering to call for a division. The young visitor reflected that there was more decorum in the House of Burgesses. He was struck by the beautiful situation of Annapolis, however, and he must have concluded that the economy of Maryland was much like that of Virginia, tobacco being the chief thing attended to in both of them.[3] He witnessed the celebration of the repeal of the Stamp Act, and to him this was probably the first notable sign of the community of colonial interest.

As he drove onward through Delaware and into Pennsylvania he saw cultivated country which was very different from the Tidewater of Virginia and the heavily forested Piedmont of his youth. The land beyond Newcastle was beautifully laid out in fields of clover, grain, and flax. Crops like these he afterwards encouraged in Albemarle, along with orchards like the luxuriant ones he now saw, and he must have found this part of his journey wholly pleasing.[4] Philadelphia could hardly have failed to arouse his wonderment. There was no such city in Virginia, or anywhere else in the colonies for that matter. It had between eighteen and twenty thousand people, and it stretched for almost two miles along the Delaware. He probably noticed that the people were frugal and industrious, and he may have observed as another did that they were "not remarkably courteous and hospitable to strangers, unless particularly recommended to them."[5] However, he had at least one letter of introduction and he may have had more.

This had been given him by Dr. George Gilmer, nephew of his Albemarle neighbor Dr. Thomas Walker, who had recently returned from the University of Edinburgh and was then living in Williamsburg. It was addressed to Dr. John Morgan, who was already on the road to eminence in Philadelphia. Gilmer had known Morgan in Edinburgh and was confident that his "penetrating genius" would soon discern that Jefferson was a young gentleman eminently worthy of his acquaintance.[6] Nothing was said here about the latter's purpose in coming to the metropolis. This was to receive inoculation against smallpox and it seems more likely that Dr. William Shippen, Junior,

[3] Burnaby, *Travels*, p. 85.

[4] *Ibid.*, p. 88. Burnaby made his journey in 1760. I have drawn freely on his account, particularly for Philadelphia, pp. 88–102.

[5] *Ibid.*, p. 96.

[6] Gilmer to Morgan, May 11, 1766; Hist. Soc. of Pa.; photostat UVA. Presumably Jefferson picked the letter up in Williamsburg several days after it was written or received it on the road. On Gilmer, who will reappear in this story, see R. B. Davis, *Francis Walker Gilmer*, esp. pp. 4–5. F. Kimball in *Procs. Am. Philos. Soc.*, vol. 87 (1943), p. 239, designating Morgan as the inoculator of Jefferson, suggests that by showing the latter some of his collection he may also have contributed to his education in the arts.

gave it.[7] Whoever the officiating physician may have been, the fact that Jefferson was inoculated is noteworthy, for this enables us to place him somewhat more precisely in the history of advancing science and to judge of the progress of his expanding mind.

Agricultural Virginia was relatively free from smallpox but the scourge had appeared there in his time.[8] The method of inoculation sometimes described as "variolation" had been introduced into the Massachusetts Bay Colony in the first quarter of the century, but in Boston it had met with opposition which went to the extremes of mob violence, and it had been officially prohibited in New York. It had been only occasionally resorted to in Virginia up to this time, and the general belief there was that it served to spread rather than to prevent the disease.[9] The mortality from this crude form of inoculation was considerable and a much better method, Jennerian vaccination, was to come; but young Jefferson, who made a point of divesting his mind of prejudice and of forming independent judgments, decided to run the risk. He appears to have suffered no ill effects from taking his stand with the medical pioneers, and in his efforts to prevent this dread disease he remained for a generation in the vanguard.[10]

Another and less significant detail of information about his first trip outside of his own region has been preserved. In New York he chanced to take lodgings at the same place with Elbridge Gerry of Massachusetts, then four years out of Harvard.[11] They were to meet again in the Continental Congress and to be associated in the bitter partisan struggles of still later years against the Federalists. At this time, however, no one would have been likely to think of Jefferson as an embryonic politician, in the sense that we use the term today. It would have been agreed by competent observers that he was admirably prepared to assume the public role which was traditional in his class; but this did not necessarily involve agitation or political

[7] Family tradition in Randall, I, 46. Shippen is known to have administered inoculation before this time (Carl and Jessica Bridenbaugh, *Rebels and Gentlemen*, pp. 278–281, 296). Jefferson had him inoculate one of his servants at a later time.

[8] W. B. Blanton, *Medicine in Virginia in the Eighteenth Century* (1931), pp. 60–62. In the spring of 1763 Jefferson had kept away from Williamsburg partly because of smallpox there; to Page, Jan. 20, 1763 (UVA photostat from Franklin collection, Yale Univ.; postscript, omitted from previous versions, reproduced in M. Kimball, *Road to Glory*, p. 68).

[9] For pertinent contemporary comments see F. N. Mason, ed., *John Norton & Sons*, pp. 31, 38. A stringent law against inoculation was passed in 1770.

[10] *Domestic Life*, p. 67; Jefferson to John Vaughan, Nov. 5, 1801 (letter printed in H. A. Martin, "Jefferson as a Vaccinator," in *N. C. Medical Journal*, of Wilmington, N. C., 1881, p. 32).

[11] Jefferson to Gerry, June 11, 1812; L. & B., XIII, 161. Randall, I, 46, points out that Jefferson was in error about the exact year.

manipulation, and to those who knew him best he must have seemed most distinctive in the diversity of his interests and the universality of his spirit. He had not traveled far as yet but he was already a citizen of the world in his own mind; and he placed his trust, not in temporal powers, but in liberated intelligence.

There is no certain way of knowing just when this apostle of freedom first swore eternal hostility against every form of tyranny over the mind of man, but there can be no doubt that by this time he was bold as well as active in pursuit of knowledge.[12] There is little question that, before he stepped on the public stage, he had arrived at his abiding conviction that human intelligence can unlock not only the treasure house of the past but also the secrets of the universe, thus leading mankind onward to a richer and better life, and that he personally was proceeding on that assumption.

He did not need to express in so many words his belief in the mind until somebody combatted it, or until it appeared that some obstacle to its freedom must be overthrown. This faith was so essential a part of his own spiritual nature and of the framework of ideas within which he operated that he generally took it for granted. It was in the air that his spirit breathed; it was a major element in the intellectual climate in which he chose to dwell. That climate was not Virginian, though many of his countrymen basked in its warmth as he did. It was not American, though it prevailed in important quarters on this continent while he was growing up. So far as he was concerned it was chiefly English in its origins, but it had become international. It was the climate of opinion, or the cluster of ideas, or the pattern of thought, which is commonly described as "the Enlightenment." [13]

If we must date the great intellectual revolution of which he so gladly made himself an heir, it began with Sir Isaac Newton and John Locke, whom he included with Lord Bacon in his trinity of immortals.[14] It had spread through widening circles of select spirits in England and on the Continent, and by the middle of the eighteenth century it was well represented among the colonial intelligentsia — most notably by Benjamin Franklin, to whom he was a successor in more ways than one. Jefferson did not introduce the Enlightenment into the colonies

[12] His famous saying, "I have sworn upon the altar of God, eternal hostility against every form of tyranny over the mind of man," was in a letter to Benjamin Rush, Sept. 23, 1800.

[13] On the Enlightenment in general, see Preserved Smith, *History of Modern Culture*, II, esp. ch. 1; on its earlier American manifestations, see M. Curti, *Growth of American Thought*, ch. 5.

[14] To Benjamin Rush, Jan. 16, 1811; Ford, IX, 296.

but he became its almost perfect embodiment and, after Franklin, its most conspicuous apostle on his side of the Atlantic.

To its major tenets he always clung. Among the most important of these was the belief that the mind of man had emerged from shackles and darkness and had launched itself upon a limitless career of intellectual conquest. By accepting this he by no means severed all links with the past but he did become pre-eminently forward-looking.[15] Like his kindred spirits he adopted certain confident hypotheses about universal natural law and natural rights; and with these an attitude of hostility to arbitrary power of any sort, a belief in the vast improvability if not the perfectibility of man, and an impulse toward humanitarianism. To Jefferson this was not a body of cold doctrine, but of "liberal and expanded thought." It was a warm and moving gospel.

The full implications of this living faith will appear only in the unfolding of his story. But, since he had to become a disciple before he could stand forth as an apostle, a question which may already have been answered in general terms should now be raised specifically. How did the influence of the Enlightenment reach him in the forests of Virginia? The chief personal impact upon his receptive mind came from the Williamsburg trio: Small, Fauquier, and Wythe. They anticipated the greater trinity of Newton, Locke, and Bacon.

William Small acquainted him more familiarly with Sir Isaac Newton and opened before his eyes the vistas of an ordered universe. This mathematician and natural philosopher may not have talked often with his eager pupil about the dignity of human nature, since he doubtless assumed it, but first among Jefferson's teachers he showed him what the mind can do. Francis Fauquier, who kept charts of the temperature, discussed philosophical matters at his generous table, and provided so solicitously for the future of his slaves, represented the Enlightenment in its humanitarian as well as its scientific aspects. George Wythe, as a classicist, belonged more to the past than either of the others. But the study of the Greek and Latin masters had served to enrich and liberalize his mind, not to enslave it, and throughout life he was notably humane. It may be assumed that he and both the other men were familiar with John Locke, whose general ideas were so well known at this time and in this place that they might almost be taken for granted, along with those of Newton.[16] Young Jefferson, however,

[15] For ties between the philosophers and the past, see Carl Becker, *Heavenly City of the Eighteenth-Century Philosophers*, pp. 29–31, and elsewhere.
[16] Further reference to Jefferson's own familiarity with Locke is made in ch. XIII.

was now less interested in political theory than he was in general learn-ing, and he appears, not inappropriately, to have made obeisance to Bacon first. Before he set out for Annapolis he had in his possession at least one of Bacon's books.[17]

Jefferson eventually followed the path of free inquiry further than any of his local contemporaries and he gathered richer fruits as he went along, but the general spirit of the leaders among his countrymen was not uncongenial with his own. At a later time he found some of the large planters conservative in political and economic questions, as guardians of their own interests; but the greatest of them were men of large affairs, in touch with the European world and affected by its major currents of thought. The Anglican clergy may have lacked spirituality, as the Evangelicals claimed, and unquestionably they struggled to maintain their special privileges, but they were not other-worldly and there were strong traces of rationalism among them. If his contemporaries wondered about young Jefferson in these and the next few years it was not so much because of the way he was going as because they questioned the wisdom of anybody's going so far.

The zest with which he embarked on intellectual pursuits was similar to that shown by other enlightened spirits, but it was manifested by him to such a marked degree as to be characteristically individual. The habits of unremitting study which he had formed by his college days and which he ever afterwards maintained are not to be thought of pri-marily as the expression of a stern sense of duty. No Calvinist in New England could have been more rigorous in self-discipline than he was, but the supremely significant fact about his lifelong quest of knowledge is that he found in it "infinite delight." He always loved to study, for by this means he expanded the horizons of his mind and gained the power of knowledge, which was the only power he really craved.

Jefferson had begun to visit the office of the *Virginia Gazette* in Williamsburg and to buy books there during his years as a law student.[18] At a later time not even he could have read all the volumes in his library; but he probably read everything he bought in these years.

[17] On Oct. 28, 1765, he had a copy of Bacon's philosophy bound, as shown by the Day Books of the *Va. Gazette*, in the possession of Prof. J. S. Wilson of the University of Virginia.

[18] Entries from the Day Books, 1764–1766, show numerous purchases by Jeffer-son. These are reproduced in William Peden, Thomas Jefferson: Book-Collector (ms. dissertation, UVA, app. H). This valuable study is briefly summarized in "Some Notes concerning Thomas Jefferson's Libraries," *W. & M.*, 3 ser., I, 265–274 (July, 1944).

Accordingly, his fugitive early book lists assume disproportionate importance. Still more can be learned about his early tastes from the notebooks he kept. Into these he copied extracts from the authors he read and, together with a few surviving letters from his young manhood and scattered references in later writings, they provide the best available clues to his early thought. The notebook which has been termed his "Literary Bible," and which he began to keep when he was about twenty-one, is particularly valuable.[19]

The classical writers engaged him most at first, despite the impulse toward natural philosophy which William Small gave him. They constituted a "rich source of delight" to him throughout life and were the chosen companions of his old age. From his days in Maury's school, Latin was a ready instrument, and he found this language most useful in making himself a scholar in the law. As for Greek, he read Homer in Pope's translation to begin with; then, under the inspiration of Wythe, he turned to the original, which he ever afterwards preferred. He read Euripides at this time but apparently not Aeschylus; he never cared for Plato, and with Aristotle he seems not to have concerned himself at all. He was acquainted with the Latin poets, especially Virgil, and he valued the maxims of Seneca and the republican moralities of Cicero.

Like most other people he was more imaginative in his early years than he was afterwards. He was sensitive to the niceties of words as well as to natural beauty, and at this stage he was fond of English poetry.[20] He read a great deal of it, but in this field he appears to have been relatively conventional and easily pleased. He bought the works of Milton before he was twenty-one, and he copied numerous extracts from him in his notebook, including diatribes against women from *Paradise Lost*. He afterwards recommended to the young that they read the best of the poets, and he himself was familiar with the older masters and almost the whole of the eighteenth-century group. For a time he kept up with literary fashion, and his knowledge of English verse was more than superficial, but he never regarded himself as a man of "happy imagination" and poetic fancy.[21] He read more for profit than pleasure and he sought no avenue of escape from life.

He was familiar with Shakespeare from an early time, valuing him

[19] Gilbert Chinard edited this as *The Literary Bible of Thomas Jefferson. His Commonplace Book of Philosophers and Poets*. I have drawn heavily on both the text and comments in this important work.

[20] To John D. Burk, June 21, 1801 (Ford, VIII, 65).

[21] To William Short, May 15, 1815; *MHS Collections*, 7 ser., I, 232. For his knowledge of poetry as shown later, see his "Thoughts on English Prosody," in L. & B., XVIII, 415-451.

not only for his observation of human nature, but also because he best displayed the "full powers of the English language." [22] He was acquainted with current English drama and rarely missed a chance to attend the theater in Williamsburg. For nondramatic fiction he cared little. His earliest favorite among the writers in this field was Laurence Sterne, whom he long chuckled over. In Jefferson himself, however, little humor had appeared as yet except in the form of elaborate exaggeration. He was particularly fond of history, but his interest in this subject was probably greatest after he became a public man.

Like other disciples of the Enlightenment, he was aware of the value of modern languages. He had employed French from the beginning of his study of the law and he soon took up Italian.[23] Perhaps he was attracted to Italian in the first place because it was the source of musical terms; before long he also found that it had contributed richly to the language of architecture. He had not yet tackled Spanish and he said regretfully, late in life, that he never learned German.[24] He had a distinct flair for languages but modern literature meant little to him except in English. Shortly before the Revolution, when he discovered Ossian, he showed interest in Celtic. This was akin to his enduring interest in Anglo-Saxon, which began when he was struggling with legal terms as a law student.[25] He liked to trace words, as well as legal and political institutions, to their sources; and even in his early manhood his spirit was that of a scholar rather than a literary man.

It is far more important to consider the predominant purposes of this omnivorous young man than it is to draw up a full menu of his reading, for he only tasted some things, while others he devoured. His appetite never ceased to be Gargantuan but even he had to make some selection; and he did this, not in the fastidious spirit of a *gourmet*, but in the mood of an ambitious workman who wanted to build up his strength. He greatly desired to make of himself a cultivated person, he did not scorn the traditional embellishments of genteel life, and he loved learning and the arts for their own sake. But, as one who lived in a new and undeveloped country, he was most anxious to acquire

[22] Randall, I, 56.

[23] *Va. Gazette*, Day Books, entry of Feb. 4, 1764, showed the purchase of Italian books, including a dictionary.

[24] To Peter Birkman, May 30, 1823 (LC, 223:40,050). A German song, with interlined English translation, in his writing, at UVA is printed in M. Kimball, *Road to Glory*, p. 108, and in part in Randall, I, 25. He may have worked this out with a dictionary in young manhood and have forgotten about it, but in itself it does not prove that he ever learned German.

[25] To Herbert Croft, Oct. 30, 1798 (L. & B., XVIII, 363). His well-known essay on Anglo-Saxon follows, pp. 365-411.

knowledge that was useful to man. He regarded the human mind, not as a toy to be played with, but as an instrument to be used in the cause of progress.

By the time that he assumed a full share of the business of life, his own mind was unusually well equipped for the accomplishment of practical purposes as broadly conceived. Also, it was thoroughly emancipated — as he properly believed it had to be before it could be fully employed. We might be tempted to believe that this lifelong champion of liberty was born into intellectual freedom in some ideal state of nature. No one was more aware than he, however, that customs, traditions, and imperfect human institutions impose shackles on the mind; and he himself must have had to throw off some of these. The records of his inner life in this important period are distressingly incomplete, but they bear traces of struggle and strongly suggest that this struggle was primarily in the sphere of religion and morals. It is a fair assumption that the first major obstacle to the freedom of the mind which he clearly perceived was the doctrine of supernatural revelation; and that, after he had rid himself of this, the major intellectual problem of his young manhood was that of finding adequate moral sanction elsewhere.

His general manner in regard to religious questions throughout life was one of reticence, since he regarded these as a private concern. He wrote and talked about them very little, as he did about intimate personal matters of other sorts. He has left no diaries comparable with those of the Adamses wherein he revealed his secret and sacred reflections. But he did keep notebooks of his reading, and his "Literary Bible" is specially valuable in providing clues to his nonpolitical thought.

One cannot be sure, of course, that he accepted all the sentiments of Homer, Euripides, and Cicero, of Shakespeare, Milton, and Bolingbroke, that he copied; or that a unified philosophy could be fabricated from all these fragments. In certain cases, however, later comments and actions show the quotations to have been extraordinarily apt. Thus he copied this sentence from Lord Bolingbroke: "No hypothesis ought to be maintained if a single phenomenon stands in direct opposition to it." [26] Whether or not, under the inspiration of Fauquier, he learned from this English writer to apply to the Bible and theology the same tests as to secular history and scientific hypotheses, the acceptability of this dictum to him is obvious in the light of what he said later. Urging his nephew, Peter Carr, to apply critical tests to the New Testament,

[26] *Literary Bible*, p. 41. See penetrating comments of Chinard, *Ibid.*, pp. 19–20, 34–35, and ch. 2 in the valuable study of Adrienne Koch, *Philosophy of Thomas Jefferson*.

he wrote: "Your own reason is the only oracle given to you by Heaven; and you are answerable, not for the rightness, but uprightness, of the decision." [27] He certainly did not regard the intelligence of any single human being as infallible, but he saw no escape from the obligation to employ the mind fearlessly in every field.

He concerned himself much, in his twenties, with the mysteries of death and immortality. In the year that he became President of the United States, replying to a communication about the transmigration of souls, he had this to say about the "country of spirits":

> . . . When I was young I was fond of the speculations which seemed to promise some insight into that hidden country, but observing at length that they left me in the same ignorance in which they had found me, I have for very many years ceased to read or to think concerning them, and have reposed my head on that pillow of ignorance which a benevolent Creator has made so soft for us, knowing how much we should be forced to use it.[28]

During his inquiring youth and young manhood he did not find the answers; and, characteristically, he addressed himself to the problems of this world which reason can better understand. On the other hand, he did find noble and inspiring maxims and examples, not in the Christian Scriptures, which he undervalued at this stage, but primarily in the writings of classical antiquity, and out of these he evolved a working philosophy. He attached himself to no school of shallow optimism. In extract after extract one can perceive the mood of disenchantment, as in this one from Pope's *Iliad*:

> To labour is the lot of man below;
> And when Jove gave us life, he gave us woe.[29]

He learned from the Greek poets "not to expect too much from life; not to dream of a chimerical bliss, . . . but to do his duty, without expecting to be rewarded . . . , to cultivate his friends and love his country even to the point of self sacrifice." [30] From ancient writers he learned the possibility of courageous resignation, and under their inspiration he worked out for himself a program which was little short of the heroic.

Allowance must be made for the period in his life when he recorded these somber reflections. Melancholy was not characteristic of Jefferson

[27] Aug. 10, 1787 (L. & B., VI, 261).
[28] To Rev. Isaac Story, Dec. 5, 1801 (Ford, VIII, 107).
[29] *Literary Bible*, p. 128.
[30] Chinard, *Ibid.*, p. 12.

in his ripe maturity; his temperament was then notably sanguine. The extracts which he copied marked an early and passing phase. He had a disappointing love affair in his early twenties, and soon afterwards lost a favorite sister; he was not wholly at ease in social relationships as a young man; and not until after his own marriage did he find himself as a domestic being. It was at the beginning of this period of imperfect personal adjustment that he wrote to John Page about bearing up "with a tolerable degree of patience under this burden of life," of proceeding "with a pious and unshaken resignation," and of arriving at such a philosophy that few things could disturb him at all and nothing could disturb him much.[31]

Before he attained domestic happiness he had probably worked out his enduring philosophy of life; it was marked by cheerfulness not gloom, and he afterwards described it as Epicurean, though he hastened to say that the term was much misunderstood. He came to believe that happiness was the end of life, but, as has been said, he was engaged by "the peculiar conjunction of duty with happiness"; and his working philosophy was a sort of blend of Epicureanism and Stoicism, in which the goal of happiness was attained by self-discipline.[32] At no time after he became mature did he emphasize mere amusement, or pleasure for its own sake. This was true in the arts as well as in literature.

Thus he appears as an exceedingly serious young man, who had worked things out in his own mind just about as far as he thought they could be worked out by him, and who had freed himself entirely from the need of a churchly sanction. He was not wholly a rationalist, however, and he did feel the need for some sort of authority which he was unwilling to concede to church or priest. This he found within an individual's own breast in the conscience, which he regarded as a special moral sense, as truly a part of man's nature as his sense of sight or hearing, his arm or his leg.[33] How early he reached this opinion it is difficult to say. He may have groped for a time in a dim borderland of ethical uncertainty, but he had definitely emerged from it before he wrote the earliest of his notable public papers, for these are marked by a burning consciousness of moral values. Addressing King George III in 1774, he said: "The great principles of right and wrong are legible to every reader; to pursue them requires not the aid of many counsellors."[34] The issues of his time do not now seem that simple, but it is highly significant that he saw them not merely as political and eco-

---

[31] July 15, 1763 (Ford, I, 349–350).

[32] Koch, p. 6, and ch. 1 *passim*, taking issue with Chinard in *Literary Bible*, pp. 16–17; Jefferson to William Short, Oct. 31, 1819 (Ford, X, 143).

[33] To Peter Carr, Aug. 10, 1787 (Ford, IV, 429); good discussion in Koch, ch. 3.

[34] In his "Summary View" (Ford, I, 446).

nomic but as moral issues, and that they aroused his righteous indignation.

He was certainly not immoral, though some lapses might have been expected when he was young; and, after the period of youthful doubt, it would be improper to term him irreligious. As has been well said, "He was a pious man, if the religion of a humane morality is recognized as a kind of natural piety." [35] But unquestionably he was secular in these years and he probably would not have called himself a Christian.

At some time before the American Revolution he copied the dictum of Bolingbroke that the teachings of Christ comprise an incomplete body of ethics; and that a system collected from the writings of the ancient "heathen" moralists would be "more full, more entire, more coherent, and more clearly deduced from unquestionable principles of knowledge." [36] Young Jefferson may not have wholly agreed with the English writer at this stage; and in the ripeness of years he found in the teachings of Jesus "the purest system of morals ever before preached to man." [37] Eventually he regarded the "heathen" moralists as insufficient. Even in his old age, however, he was fully convinced that the "priests" (Protestant as well as Catholic) had "adulterated and sophisticated" the teachings of Jesus for their own selfish purposes; and from his twenties until his death he was anticlerical in varying degrees of bitterness. He served for a time as a vestryman in his parish, as a leading planter was supposed to do; he continued throughout life to have warm personal friends among the "enlightened" clergy; and he always contributed generously to local churches. But before he attacked the special privileges of the Establishment in Virginia, ecclesiastical authority and traditional theology had wholly ceased to have validity for him. The right to complete intellectual and religious freedom which he afterwards championed so conspicuously for all men he had already claimed for himself.

[35] Koch, p. 39.
[36] *Literary Bible*, p. 50.
[37] To S. Kercheval, Jan. 19, 1810 (L. & B., XII, 345).

The Business of Life

$\lceil$ IX $\rceil$

The Young Lawyer
1767–1771

JEFFERSON began to practise law before he reached the age of twenty-four, and he continued to do so for seven years. The five years since he finished college had not been employed solely in preparation for his profession; he was deliberately fitting himself for the whole of life as he expected to live it. But he had studied law with the utmost seriousness, and, considering the time he had spent, his professional career was short. In the light of the generation of conspicuous public service which followed, his legal career itself may be regarded as a period of further preparation, and an exceedingly important one. At the time, however, the impressive facts were that he threw himself into his profession with characteristic vigor and quickly achieved an honored position in it.

From the beginning he was probably more interested in the study of law than in practice, but if he rebelled against the drudgery incident to his calling he did not do so because of any repugnance for details. The main reason for his early abandonment of law was not that he disliked it, nor that he preferred the political arena. He never hated anything connected with it quite as much as he loathed the controversies and recriminations which afterwards befell him as a public man. His practice of law was a constituent part of the business of life until the courts were closed shortly before the outbreak of the American Revolution, and it was the central part up to the time of his marriage. He never disliked practical affairs in themselves. He always attended to them industriously and systematically, and he complained about them only when they interfered unduly with more delightful things — such as the enrichment of the mind and the enjoyment of domestic life. He had little reason to complain of undue interference before his marriage. Thus he appeared in his first years at the bar as a man of business. Apart from the interest which inheres in most of his activities, small or large and private as well as public, this period is of particular significance in revealing his habits as a man of affairs and the degree of his practical effectiveness.

Before he mounted his horse to ride to court he had already entered upon the business of life to some extent. The year that he attained his majority and came into his inheritance he had ceased charging the expenses of his education against his father's estate and had nominally assumed the headship of the family.[1] Also, he had had to choose between the Rivanna and the Fluvanna lands which Peter Jefferson had left to him and his young brother. On this subject there was probably no question in his mind at any time. He succeeded to the lands on which his father had lived and immediately assumed a position of dignity and responsibility in that part of the County.

The Rivanna estate comprised about half and much the more important part of his total inheritance of somewhat more than five thousand acres.[2] The family seat at Shadwell, with its four hundred acres, did not actually belong to him until after his mother's death in the year of the Declaration of Independence. Considerably before that time he built for himself a house on the forested hill across the way, but until 1770 he continued to live at Shadwell. From the age of twenty-two, also, he rented from his mother the farm there, with the slaves who were on it. He had twenty slaves or more in his own right, but these were otherwise employed. The gristmill which his father had built was already his. It stood on the north bank of the little river, and the water which turned its wheels was brought by a canal from a dam half a mile above it. It was a profitable piece of property until it was swept away, with its house and dam, in the "great fresh" of 1771.

He was not yet devoting himself much to agriculture, though he had assumed the necessary financial responsibilities and had begun to keep his Garden Book. The first entry in this, made in clear hand on March 30, 1766, has a more poetic flavor than he probably realized when he recorded the simple fact that the purple hyacinth had begun to bloom.[3] All the observations of that year had to do with flowers — with the narcissus and puckoon in the family garden, with bluebells in the low-

[1] Account with estate in Fee Book; HEH, UVA photostat.

[2] See Appendix II, B, 1.

[3] References will generally be by date only and, unless otherwise indicated, all will be to E. M. Betts, *Thomas Jefferson's Garden Book* (Am. Philosophical Soc., Philadelphia, 1944), cited as *Garden Book*.

ground and wild honeysuckle in the woods. Thus he appears first as an observer of the pleasant phenomena of nature. By the time that he became a lawyer, however, he had become more utilitarian; that year he sowed peas. Henceforth he continued to record plantings of flowers and vegetables, shrubs and trees, but he had not started his Farm Book as yet. It is impossible to believe that he was ever indifferent to the crops of tobacco and corn on his red fields, but during his years as a bachelor he left his farms pretty much as they were, probably committing the details of management to a single steward or overseer.

With one matter which directly affected him as an Albemarle planter, however, and which was also of considerable public interest, he actively concerned himself from the time that he was grown. His efforts to improve the navigation of the stream which flowed through his lands antedated his services in the House of Burgesses and even his practice of law.

To the best of his knowledge, no hogsheads of tobacco had ever been transported on the North Branch of the James to its junction with the larger stream. About the time that he came of age, however, he learned that a canoe had recently been used on its lower waters. Taking a canoe himself, he explored the only seriously obstructed section and concluded that this could be made navigable to loaded boats merely by the removal of loose rock. He then set on foot a subscription, obtained two hundred pounds, and interested his neighbor, Dr. Thomas Walker, who was a member of the House of Burgesses.

It was in October, 1765, that an act of Assembly was passed "for clearing the great falls of James river, the river Chickahominy, and the north branch of James river." The legislative act merely authorized a "laudable and useful" undertaking which was to be effected by private means. Three groups of trustees were set up to receive subscriptions and to make the necessary contracts. In the group assigned to the North Branch (Rivanna) was young Jefferson, along with other prominent gentlemen of the County. With almost every person named on the other lists he was afterwards associated in public or private life. This appointment, therefore, constituted the first official sign of his identification with the leaders of the County and Province. Locally he was the initiator of the project and probably the most active member of the group.

The work of clearing away the obstructions appears to have been finished by the time of his marriage; and for a generation afterwards the stream was used "completely and fully," he said, for the carrying-down of produce. Throughout the eighteenth century the navigable section began at Milton falls, a mile or two below Shadwell, so boats did not actually go past his mill, but the short land haul was not much of an inconvenience to him. Years after he initiated this undertaking he took great pride in it. Shortly before he was elected President he asked himself whether his country was the better for his having lived at all. Then, rather dubiously, he drew up a list of things in which he had been the instrument, beginning with this youthful effort to further the flow of agricultural commerce and following with the Declaration of Independence, which was clearly second to it in point of time. Whether or not this was his most memorable action before the Revolution, as he himself believed, it was his first piece of constructive public service.[4]

In the year 1767 the family at Shadwell, besides Thomas, consisted of his mother and four other children. Jane Randolph Jefferson was now forty-seven, several times a grandmother, and an old lady by the standards of the time. His younger sister Elizabeth, unmarried at twenty-three, was undoubtedly regarded as an old maid. Lucy, now fifteen, remained at home a couple of years longer; then she married Charles Lilburne Lewis, who was also descended from Isham Randolph. Besides her there were the twins, Anna Scott and Randolph, who were twelve.[5]

Peter Jefferson's thoughtful provisions for the maintenance of the younger children and for the portions of the girls had been rigorously carried out and continued to be. Enough of the financial records of the family have survived to show that a good deal of bookkeeping was required and that the elder son assumed much of the burden of this after he grew up. A decade before he became important as a draftsman of state papers he showed that he was particularly good at keeping accounts, and at any sort of paper work in which diligence, accuracy, and neatness were required. He not only made a record of the agreement with his mother whereby he hired five of her Shadwell hands at six pounds each per annum; he also kept vouchers for the sides of pork, the quarters of beef, and the bushels of corn that he furnished her. For his unmarried and not wholly responsible sister Elizabeth he began to keep a special account as soon as she was grown, though his inability

[4] His list of services, drawn about Sept. 1800, is in LC, 219:39161; printed without precise date, Ford, VII, 475-477. Other important references on this matter are LC, 211:37587, notes on the several acts of Assembly for clearing the Rivanna River, 1764-1806; memo. in LC, 1:68, on making the Rivanna navigable; and Hening, VIII, 148-150, giving Act of 1765.

[5] For details, see Appendix I, C. It will be recalled that one of his sisters had died and two had married.

to prevent her from mixing her charges with his own at a store in Richmond caused it to become sadly confused.[6] There are no surviving letters from this period to illustrate the generosity and affection which he so consistently manifested towards all of his close relations, but his scrupulous exactitude in keeping the financial records of the family was manifested from the first. Life in the plantation village of Shadwell was doubtless hospitable, generous, and friendly, as it so generally was in that clime and region, and as it always was afterwards at Monticello; and Jefferson himself was far from parsimonious; but he did like to put everything down in black and white.

The major personal records (as distinguished from letters) which remain and which serve to illuminate so many of the details of his own life had their beginning in this period. They are wholly objective in form but they are fascinating documents of their kind and are of great importance to anyone who would understand him.

The Garden Book, which he started in 1766 and kept more or less continuously for upwards of half a century, contains a much greater variety of items than its title would imply and reveals from the outset the utilitarian cast of his ingenious mind. In it he noted that it would take 2500 peas of the sort he was planting to fill a pint measure; that a horse would generally eat 8 or 10 bundles of fodder in a night and 1170 during an Albemarle winter; that 50 hills would yield 2000 cucumbers in a season. Some random bits of horticultural lore he copied out of books, but he gained more from his own observations or from friends or neighbors, who told him something of interest which he promptly put down. To these he added, after he became a builder, all sorts of miscellaneous calculations about bricks, mortar, wheelbarrows, and the like. This is no diary of esthetic rapture; it is a systematic, though fragmentary, factual record which served a useful purpose to a practical man.

The Account Books, as they are commonly called, which he kept in unending series until the week before he died, are distinctly informal.[7] During his years as a practitioner he listed law cases here as in a day book, and when he had finished with them or transferred them to a more permanent record he scratched them off. He recorded here the most trivial items of cash expenditure. The first entries, made in the summer of 1767, show him attending court across the mountains in

[6] These accounts are in his Fee Book, Huntington Lib., UVA photostat. In their present form they may date from 1770, after the fire at Shadwell.

[7] These invaluable records are in several repositories, as is shown in the Bibliography attached to this work. A complete set in photostat is at UVA. Reference to them hereafter will be by date only.

Staunton. He paid a shilling to a washing woman, and gave a blacksmith five shillings for shoeing his horse. Thenceforth, wherever he went, he carried the memorandum book for that year with him, jotting down at night all the expenditures that he remembered and adding other items of interesting information which he had recently acquired. Considering the circumstances, the entries are remarkably clear and understandable; they rarely record impressions, but they have made it possible to chart his daily movements to a degree which is rarely possible in the lives of even the most notable of men.

In another book he began to keep a formal record of his important cases, and he also had a fee book which served as a ledger and contained various accounts.[8] These records, made with more careful hand than the daily memoranda were, would delight the most critical of eyes. He listed his cases by dates and number, separating them by neatly drawn lines and leaving space for filling in the story of later developments. After the lapse of more than a century and a half the writing is clear as crystal. Had he been so disposed, he could have easily prepared a copybook for his sisters' children.

From this beautifully kept record we learn that on February 12, 1767, he got a client in the person of Gabriel Jones of Augusta County, and entered caveat in his behalf for one hundred acres of land near Warm Spring. About six weeks later he received three pounds from Jones, though the case continued into another year. He was long to know this eccentric lawyer of the Shenandoah Valley, at first as a friend and later as a political foe, and he had much early business from this County, just beyond the Blue Ridge. That was where the West began; later he said with only slight inaccuracy that Staunton was the farthest he ever went in that direction.

This outlying county seat was then small and crude. That summer he took a case there for John Madison, father of his young friend James of Maury's school and for long years the county clerk. The tradition is that John Madison did him the honors of the place at the beginning of his legal career, taking him at length to a loft where a party were playing cards by torchlight. Madison, who had a powder horn beneath his coat, dropped powder behind each man and trailed it out the door. Then, just as an unlucky player was invoking the devil, he fired the train and caused the gamesters to rush headlong from the accursed place. This is probably the first story that Jefferson ever told

[8] Huntington Lib., photostats at UVA, referred to hereafter as Case Book and Fee Book.

about riding the circuit.[9] It is a pity that he did not tell more, but he was no Abraham Lincoln.

His business in the county courts was extensive; he had cases in forty or more of them before he got through. Unlike Patrick Henry, however, he did not lay the foundations of his legal reputation in this country practice. No stories survive about his participation in dramatic trials, such as the Parsons' Cause, and he gained no particular reputation as a jury lawyer. In that field Patrick Henry was the greatest of his generation in Virginia, and after his death many doubted if he would ever be excelled.[10] Even in Henry's case much of the country practice was routine business, such as bringing actions of debt; and his systematic young friend from Albemarle was unquestionably his superior as a draftsman of legal papers and was more diligent in matters of detail.

The county courts were informal and the more important trials did not occur in them; "family tribunals" they have been called. At a later time Jefferson spoke of the procedure in Albemarle as slovenly, and his careful study of English cases could have availed him little there. The few surviving comments from his contemporaries about his abilities as a speaker give the impression that during his young manhood these were greater than has been commonly supposed. Edmund Randolph said that he spoke with "ease, perspicuity and elegance," though his style was less impassioned than in his writing.[11] It was impossible for him to bellow; if he raised his voice it soon grew husky. No gathering that he attended in those years was ever very large, but even in a small, informal courtroom he could not hope to match Patrick Henry by appealing to the emotions of jurymen.

The county court was a notable institution in Virginia, both in its judicial and executive aspects.[12] Its magistrates were not jurists; as in his father's and grandfather's day they were the leading citizens of the various districts. Personal acquaintance with such men was of great importance to anyone who would play an important part in provincial affairs, and making a round of the counties constituted a political education in itself. Jefferson went regularly to those that were near his own and he came to know somebody in practically every one of them, he said. It is doubtful if ever during his entire career he had such a wide personal acquaintance in Virginia as he did before the Revolution when

[9] Memoirs of T. J. Randolph, pp. 12–13, Edgehill Randolph Papers, UVA. On Madison, see W. & M., 2 ser., II, 185.

[10] Henry, Patrick Henry, I, 24–26, and elsewhere.

[11] Va. Mag., XLIII, 123; traditional account in Randall, I, 50.

[12] See note of B. W. Leigh in Revised Code of the Laws of Virginia (1819), I, 244; Mercer, Abridgement, pp. 62–64.

he was actively engaged in the practice of law. It was on court days that the farmers flocked to the various seats, that slaves and lands were sold, that auctions of all sorts were held.[13] On such occasions the studious young lawyer rubbed elbows with ordinary citizens to a greater extent than he ever did afterwards. He gained for himself no such personal following as Patrick Henry did, but he made innumerable acquaintances and gained an insight into the thoughts of common men which could not be got from books.

Both by training and temperament he was better fitted for practice before the General Court, to which George Wythe introduced him early in this first year.[14] Not even this tribunal was composed of judges who were learned in the law. It was made up of the members of the Council, chosen for wealth and standing without regard to legal knowledge. As he himself said, "their decisions could never be quoted, either as adding to or detracting from, the weight of those of the English courts on the same points." [15] During his last years as a law student and his early years as a practitioner, accordingly, he had made careful study of cases in the courts of King's Bench and Common Pleas.[16]

The domestic judgments of the General Court were authoritative, whether formed on sound legal principles or not. Such cases of domestic character as had been reported, therefore, he studied and abstracted with care. These he found in certain manuscript volumes that were in the possession of his violin-playing friend John Randolph, the attorney general. The record covered only the decade from 1730 to 1740; and there were no more reports thereafter until 1768, when he himself began to commit to writing some of the leading cases of the day. In the midst of his own practice he served as a self-appointed reporter and as such was a pioneer.

Whatever may be said about the prominent gentlemen who served as lay judges, the Virginia bar at this time contained men of high professional competence. Wythe was probably the most learned member — almost too learned, some people thought. He had dwelt so long with the ancient writers that it was hard for him to keep from giving a line from Horace the force of an act of Assembly.[17] Edmund Pendleton had had less time for literature, but he was probably more effective as a lawyer. Though a most amiable man in personal relationships he was

---

[13] Numerous items about court days can be found in Purdie & Dixon, *Va. Gazette*, for 1767 and other years of Jefferson's practice.

[14] "Autobiography" in Ford, I, 4. The circumstances have not been disclosed.

[15] Preface to his *Reports of Cases determined in the General Court of Va.* (1829).

[16] For his abstracts, see Chinard, *Commonplace Book*.

[17] H. B. Grigsby, *Va. Convention of 1776*, p. 129; for an excellent comparison with Pendleton, see pp. 125–130.

not above baiting Jefferson's guileless teacher, upsetting his equanimity, and thus robbing him of his strength.[18] The star of Thomson Mason, who was comparable with George Wythe in legal erudition, had risen; and John Randolph, who had succeeded his brother as King's Attorney, was an uncommonly able man. He suffered by comparison with the relative newcomer, Patrick Henry, however, when they locked horns in criminal cases, which were the latter's special forte. During this period the orator is reported to have worn a black suit and tie-wig when he appeared in the General Court, to the considerable improvement of his appearance.[19] Jefferson acted with him on certain occasions, proving himself to be no master of overwhelming eloquence but an impressive speaker as long as his voice held out. When they appeared together each of the men characterized himself, so Edmund Randolph said: "Mr. Jefferson drew copiously from the depths of the law, Mr. Henry from the recesses of the human heart." [20]

Two of the arguments which Jefferson used in actual cases have been preserved in the reports which he made and which were published after his death.[21] He may have selected these chiefly because of the questions they dealt with, for one had to do with slavery and the other with the clergy.

About two years after he began to practise he took without fee the case of one Samuel Howell. The latter's grandmother was a mulatto, begotten of a white woman by a Negro man and bound by the law to serve until the age of thirty-one. During her servitude she was delivered of Howell's mother, and the latter, during her own servitude, was delivered of Howell. This third mulatto was suing for freedom from the master to whom he had been sold and who claimed his services until he was thirty-one. Jefferson's scholarly argument was doomed from the outset and the Court did not even wait to hear that of the equally humane Wythe on the other side. Jefferson's contention was that one act had made a servant of the first mulatto, and that a later one had extended it to her children, but that it remained for some future legislature, *if any should be found wicked enough,* to extend it to grandchildren and other issue more remote.[22] The language of his peroration must have been startling, especially when coupled with an

---

[18] Wirt, *Patrick Henry*, p. 48.
[19] Henry, *Patrick Henry*, I, 126.
[20] *Va. Mag.*, XLIII, 123.
[21] *Howell* vs. *Netherland*, Apr. 1770; *Godwin et al.* vs. *Lunan*, Oct. 1771. These can be conveniently consulted in Ford, I, 373–381; 399–412. In his *Reports*, Jefferson subjoined an opinion about the relations between Christianity and the common law which is not germane here.
[22] Ford, I, 381. Italics mine and mood changed.

earlier reference of his to the law of nature: "under that law," he said, "we are all born free." [23] That he had come to such a philosophical position by the time this case was adjudged in 1770 is a significant item in the history of his thought, but such an assertion carried no weight with a practical-minded court in a slave-owning society.

In the other reported case he represented the churchwardens and vestrymen of a parish in Nansemond County in an action whereby they sought to oust an unworthy clergyman named Patrick Lunan. The latter was accused of profane swearing, drunkenness, and adultery; he was said to have declared that he cared not what religion he professed so long as he got his pay in tobacco, and also to have exposed his private parts to public view. The main question was whether or not the right of visitation and deprivation resided in the Court; and by means of an elaborate historical treatise Jefferson undertook to prove that it did reside in the Court, as representing the King. His contention was upheld in October, 1771, and he got a five-pound fee, but the case was still awaiting adjudication three years later when he retired from practice. He had upheld the power of the provincial Court over the clergy, but at a later time he would not have conceded so much to the prerogative of the King.

Judging from the number of his cases Jefferson had a substantial legal business. In the seven years of his practice he listed nearly a thousand in his formal record.[24] The fact that Robert Carter Nicholas wanted to turn over his business to him in 1771 is indicative of his standing; while the further fact that he declined to take it, except for a very few cases which he finished, shows that he already had just about as much as he could do.[25] His clients, at one time or another, included members of most of the leading families of the Province: Randolphs and Pages, Carys and Harrisons, Nelsons and Lees, Carters and Byrds. In the second year of his practice he recorded in his Case Book, apparently with pride: "The Honble Wm. Byrd retains me generally." [26]

His cases dealt with land ownership, debts, the recovery of slaves, slander, assault and battery. He rendered opinions, for which he generally charged twenty shillings; he drew some deeds and advised about wills; he instituted suits in chancery. Even though his jury trials may

[23] Ford, I, 380.

[24] In his Case Book, 941 cases are listed by name. His legal business is discussed by Randall, I, 47–48. It is now being analyzed by Edward Dumbauld, who has given me the benefit of valuable informal comments.

[25] Case Book, No. 612. First of these cases finished Apr. 16, 1771.

[26] Case Book, June 14, 1768. This item and those in the following paragraph are quoted through the courtesy of the Huntington Library.

not have been colorful, there is human interest in many of his dry entries; and they show clearly that the serious young lawyer, whose arguments tended to be so elaborate, had abundant opportunity to observe the seamy side of life. In the first year of his practice, for example, there were such as these:

1767, *June* 9.
    Gordon (a seafaring man) v. George Wythe (my friend).
    Defend him totis viribus. Take no fee.

1767, *Aug.* 18.
    John Thompson (Augusta) v. Moses Collier . . . [et al].
    Bring action of trespass for taking pl's son and keeping him 2 or 3 days. Also for entering his house and taking forcibly a bottle of whiskey and shirt.

1767, *Nov.* 17.
    David Frame (Augusta) v. James Burnside (Augusta).
    Bring action of slander for saying he saw the pl who is a married man in bed with Elizabeth Burkin, etc. [Dismissed at plaintiff's request.]

Whether or not this business was profitable depends on the criteria that are applied. The statement of Jefferson's executor that his average profits as expressed in dollars were about $3000 a year has often been quoted.[27] For those days that sum would have represented a handsome addition to the living and income that he got from his landed estate. In this generous estimate, however, the word "profits" is loosely used to designate the sums that were due him. Never did the fees that he charged aggregate much more than £500 a year, and they generally amounted to less; furthermore, he never succeeded in collecting as much as 50 per cent. His legal business reached its greatest volume in 1770, and in that year he managed to collect £213 of the amount that was due him.[28]

It is doubtful if he had any more trouble with collections than other lawyers did. Difficulties of this sort were general and notorious. The year that he was admitted to the bar another lawyer announced that the backwardness of his clients in paying him would have obliged him to quit his practice had he been impelled by no other reason. John Mercer had appointed a receiver, but the latter, out of £10,000, had not yet been able to collect enough to cover his own wage and Mercer's

[27] Randall, I, 48.
[28] A summary of his receipts, fees due, and total business for the years 1767–1772 is in Account Book for 1773. From other records it appears that his business declined somewhat thereafter.

taxes. Accordingly, the unfortunate lawyer now felt compelled to sue.[29] The situation was so serious that, in May, 1773, Jefferson, Pendleton, John Randolph, Patrick Henry, and two other lawyers inserted a notice in the *Gazette*.[30] They announced that it would not be possible for them to continue their practice in the General Court on the same terms as heretofore. Even if the fees allowed by law were regularly paid, they said, these would barely compensate them for their incessant labors or reimburse their expenses and the losses incurred by the neglect of their private affairs. Yet even these confessedly moderate rewards were withheld in large proportion by the "unworthy part" of their clients. Accordingly, they announced that after a specified date in the fall they would require full payment before rendering an opinion, and would not prosecute or defend a case unless they received the tax in advance and half the fee. By that time Jefferson had already found it necessary to give more of his time to his personal affairs, and in the year following this announcement he wholly retired from practice.

In his years as a bachelor, that is, until he was nearing twenty-nine and had been almost five years at the bar, absence from home disturbed him much less than it did after he had a family of his own, and unquestionably his journeys imparted increased interest to his life. On his way to the county courts and to Williamsburg he generally went on horseback or in a one-horse chair. His servant Jupiter, who was just his age, as a rule went with him or followed close behind, possibly carrying his luggage in a cart. The name of this trusted companion of the road, who had been going with him since his days as a law student, recurs in his Account Books with regularity. Jefferson was always giving money to Jupiter — to pay a saddler in Staunton, to pay for ferriages to Williamsburg, and for bread and candles there. He even borrowed small coin from Jupiter at times when he himself ran out.[31]

He and his slave did not keep house; both in the county seats and in the provincial capital he stayed generally in such lodgings as the times afforded, though *en route* he frequently stopped with relatives or friends, such as the Carrs and Thomas Mann Randolph, whom the slaves called "Tuckahoe Tom." His visits to Williamsburg coincided with the court sessions and thus fell in the most crowded times, when the regular residents had too many guests. In the second year of his practice, if we may judge by the size of his various bills, he lodged at Charlton's on the broad Duke of Gloucester Street and took many

[29] Rind, *Va. Gazette*, Feb. 19, 1767.
[30] May 20, 1773; reproduced in Ford, I, 416.
[31] Details from Account Books, 1767–1771.

meals at the Raleigh Tavern across the way, going to the Coffee House beyond the Capitol frequently for food and liquid entertainment, and occasionally to Ayscough's and Mrs. Vobe's.

If the gaming in these places was as constant as has been reported, the clatter of the dice-boxes must have been trying to one who prized tranquillity so much. He made many visits to John Page at Rosewell, riding or driving to York, then ferrying to Gloucester. At the home of this friend he fiddled and talked in company which was often if not always mixed. It was a pleasant life, and as a young gentleman who bought for himself not only books and fiddlestrings but also broadcloth, silk hose, and buckskin gloves, he played his conventional part in it. He continued to indulge in idle social chatter when he wrote to Page but it was not in his nature to be silly for very long.

The playhouse in Williamsburg had several good seasons during his early years as a lawyer. The Virginia Company of Comedians which came there in 1768 may not have been the equal of the London Company of the elder Lewis Hallam which had visited the capital in his boyhood, or of the American Company of David Douglas which had appeared there when he was in college, but it put on a considerable number of plays that spring and when he was there he rarely missed one.[32] Among these were Addison's *The Drummer*, *The Merchant of Venice*, Otway's *Venice Preserved* and *The Orphan*, and *The Beggar's Opera*, with Peter Pelham conducting the orchestra. Farces were often added to the main attraction and the spirit of the company was as comic as its name implied. There were no other regular theatrical performances until the spring of 1770; and before the gaieties of that season were in swing a disturbing event had occurred on the banks of the Rivanna and had been reported in Williamsburg.

On February 22, 1770, this item appeared in the *Virginia Gazette*:

We hear from Albemarle that about a fortnight ago the house of Thomas Jefferson, Esq., in that county, was burnt to the ground, together with all his furniture, books, papers, &c., by which that Gentleman sustains a very great loss. He was from home when the Accident occurred.[33]

To be exact, the conflagration occurred on February 1. Jefferson had dined with the family, probably about two o'clock, and had then gone to Charlottesville on business.[34] He had his first news from a

[32] Purdie & Dixon, *Va. Gazette*, Mar. 31; Apr. 7, 14; May 12, 19, 26, 1768.
[33] Purdie & Dixon.
[34] Memoirs of T. J. Randolph, UVA, p. 2.

servant who was dispatched after him and who undoubtedly reported that no lives were lost. The tradition is that he immediately asked if they had saved his books, and that the slave replied, "No, Master, all lost, but we save your fiddle." Presumably this was the instrument he had bought for five pounds in Williamsburg the year before. Actually, a few books were saved, along with two or three beds, but little else. For two or three years he had been planning to leave Shadwell as soon as his building operations on the mountain would permit, and work was sufficiently advanced at Monticello for him to move there late in the following November, to endure the rigors of winter in a single room.[35] The other members of the family continued to live at Shadwell until after his mother's death, probably making the best they could of the remaining buildings.[36]

Jefferson estimated at two hundred pounds sterling the value of his books that were burned, but it was not the monetary loss that evoked his groans. These were mainly law books which he could not immediately replace, and with them were destroyed the notes which he had carefully prepared for his cases in the approaching General Court. "These are gone," he wrote Page, "and like the baseless fabric of a vision, leave not a trace behind." [37] Unlike John Marshall, he did not learn through the ear but through the eye; he was not one who could speak on the spur of the moment; he put all important things down on paper and without notes he was lost. He wondered, therefore, if it would not be possible for him to get a postponement of his cases, believing that an exception might justly be made in such singular circumstances. He managed to maintain a light tone of youthful banter in writing to this good friend, but he could not conceal his deep concern.

His friends hastened to console and help him, though Page at the time had troubles of his own.[38] His wife had just lost her mother, so he penned only a few hasty lines at York, which the younger Thomas Nelson enclosed. The latter promised to speed Jefferson's order to the booksellers and assured him that his cases would be postponed. The elder Thomas Nelson offered to make him a loan from his own collection, and in the meantime sent hinges, locks, and pulleys, doubtless thinking that these would be needed at Monticello sooner than had been expected. By sending him nectarines, apricot grafts, and grapevines for the orchard he was planting on the hillside there, George Wythe

[35] To James Ogilvie, Feb. 20, 1771 (Ford I, 390–391).
[36] F. Kimball in Va. Mag., LI, 315.
[37] Feb. 21, 1770 (Ford, I, 370).
[38] Thomas Nelson, Jr., John Page, and Thomas Nelson, Sr., to Jefferson, Mar. 6, 1770, MHS.

showed that he maintained his classic calm.[39] Like Page, he congratulated his young friend on his philosophic spirit, predicting that he
would not only surmount his difficulties but be the richer for his
unfortunate experience. Soon thereafter Page, now more at leisure,
wrote him in sentimental vein.[40]

It is probable that he did get a continuance of his cases, or most of
them; at all events, he managed to get through the busiest of his legal
years. He restored his books at the earliest possible time, borrowing
for this purpose one hundred pounds which Dabney Carr had lying idle,
though this sum alone was not enough. Within three years he had more
volumes than he had lost.[41] His personal papers, however, were not
replaceable, and it is largely for this reason that the story of his life
up to 1770 can never be told with such fullness as can that of his later
years. He himself said: "The letters of a person, especially of one whose
business has been chiefly transacted by letters, form the only full and
genuine journal of his life." [42] During his young manhood, when he
was fresh in the world of affairs, he probably did not make copies of
his letters so carefully as he did afterward; but we would know considerably more about him before he reached the age of twenty-seven
if the house at Shadwell had not burned.

Fortunately, the loss was not so complete as he implied. He said that
he was destitute of papers of every kind, whether public or private,
of business or amusement. But he had preserved his memorandum
Account Books and was thus enabled to draw up new records.[43] His
Garden Book almost certainly was at Monticello. Probably he had
continued his boyish habit of reading on his hilltop and for that reason
also kept his commonplace books there. He has left a fairly full, though
largely an external, story of his young manhood; but it was not until
after the fire that he became *par excellence* a keeper of records and
began to accumulate documentary treasures such as have rarely been
amassed by any man. This was a part of the business of life which he
took seriously and attended to with care.

[39] Wythe's letter of Mar. 9, 1770, from MHS, is reproduced in *Garden Book*,
p. 20.
[40] April 1770, MHS.
[41] In his Account Book for 1773, he noted that he had 1256 volumes.
[42] To Robert Walsh, Apr. 5, 1823, UVA.
[43] Account Book, 1770, *c.* June 1.

[x]

Among the Burgesses

1769–1771

THE coming of a new royal governor to Virginia about six months after Fauquier died was an event of great interest in the Province, and it had important effects on the career of Jefferson, who was twenty-five years old at the time. He was in Williamsburg in late October, 1768, when the Right Honorable Norborne Berkeley, Baron de Botetourt, arrived. He was not among those who extended an official welcome to his Lordship about sunset or who had supper with him afterwards at the Raleigh Tavern, but he could hardly have failed to view the festive illumination of the "city" that night. Then it was that people of all ranks "vied with each other in testifying their gratitude and joy that a nobleman of such distinguished merit and abilities" had come to dwell among them.[1] Though Jefferson preferred Fauquier, who was not a lord and was technically only a deputy governor, he was not yet suspicious of noblemen as such, and, like most other people, he probably thought it a compliment that the British authorities had sent to the Colony a resident governor general.

There were some people in Virginia and more in England who questioned the wisdom of appointing this Lord of the Bedchamber, who had suffered serious if not discreditable financial reverses; but the description of Botetourt by Junius as "a cringing, bowing, fawning, sword-bearing courtier" was extreme.[2] Now about fifty, he had been

[1] Purdie & Dixon, *Va. Gazette*, Oct. 27, 1768. Botetourt (whose name is pronounced in Virginia so as to rhyme with "Hottentot") took the oath at the Capitol immediately after his arrival; Council Journals, Colonial Va., Oct. 26, 1768, UVA photostats. For reception and comment, see Goodwin, *Williamsburg*, pp. 55–57. Entries in Jefferson's Account Book leave no doubt that he was there, though there is no entry for this day.

[2] For comments on the appointment see *Sir Henry Cavendish's Debates of the House of Commons*, II, 21 *n.*, 24, 25 *n.*; E. Channing, *Hist. U. S.*, III, 103; C. W. Coleman, in *W. & M.*, 1 ser., V, 165–170; Rowland, *Mason*, I, 133.

a diligent Tory member of the House of Commons, and had come into his title four years before he sailed to America. Nobody could question his loyalty to his King, and everybody agreed that he was a good companion. He wore a smile upon his face, and the Virginians were disposed to take him at his face value. In the end they loved him more than they had Fauquier or any other of their viceroys. Jefferson regarded him as both an honorable and an amiable man, but he never became intimate with him.

Botetourt provided the occasion for Jefferson's early entrance into political life. On the day after his arrival the new Governor properly dissolved the old Assembly, which was not then in session, and soon after that he issued writs for the election of a new one. As a result of this action the freeholders of Albemarle met in the courthouse in Charlottesville before the middle of December and elected Thomas Jefferson as one of their two burgesses; and in the month of May, 1769, he took his seat for the first time as a member of a legislative body.[3] During the next fifteen years he performed his public service primarily as a legislator.

The electors who chose him on this occasion were men possessing at least fifty unsettled acres, or twenty-five if they had a plantation and small house.[4] For the times the suffrage was liberal, since that much land could be rather easily acquired. The freeholders voted openly, however, and the opinions and preferences of the recognized leaders were generally determinative. Jefferson's friend Dr. Thomas Walker, who had just returned from an important Indian conference at Fort Stanwix, was re-elected.[5] The other burgess in the previous Assembly had been Edward Carter, whose holdings in the County considerably exceeded Jefferson's and included Carter's Mountain, towering over Monticello. Carter had failed to attend during the last session, however, and this fact probably was to his disadvantage.[6]

It is impossible to determine now just how sharp the contest was, but presumably there were no public issues. The campaigning of that era, which they called "burgessing," was wholly personal and consisted primarily of providing drinks and other refreshments at or before elections — "swilling the planters with bumbo," as one observer put it.[7]

[3] Council Journals, Colonial Va., UVA photostats, Oct. 27, Nov. 1, 1768; Purdie & Dixon, *Va. Gazette* Dec. 15, 1768, reporting Jefferson's election.
[4] Act of 1762 (Hening, VII, 517–530).
[5] Purdie & Dixon, *Va. Gazette*, Dec. 1, 1768, reported that he and his two sons had passed through Philadelphia before Nov. 21; and Jefferson's Account Book, Nov. 26, 1768, shows that they were back by then.
[6] Woods, *Albemarle*, pp. 163–164.
[7] Letter of Theodorick Bland, Sr., June 27, 1765 (*Bland Papers*, I, 27).

Jefferson and Carter may have provided rum jointly, and the former recorded other expenditures for drinks and cakes.[8] All this was modest, however, and it had the flavor of gentlemanly hospitality. By nature Jefferson was not good at electioneering or at mingling with a crowd. "His manners could never be harsh," one of his friends observed, "but they were reserved towards the world at large." [9] It was fortunate for this future hero of the plain people that his career began in a period when influential gentlemen were at the helm. The meeting at the courthouse was for him a sort of prelude to politics, but it can be more aptly described as a genial introduction to public life.

At that time and place a man of his estate and training was expected to share the burden of public affairs, and his ultimate election to the Assembly might have been confidently expected without any special effort on his part. Normally he would have served first as a local magistrate and possibly he did. A couple of years later he was a justice of the peace and member of the county court, as his father had been, and he may have begun this service before he attained the more responsible post of burgess.[10] At all events, he quickly telescoped his father's public career.

Early initiation into public affairs was not uncommon in the Province but his election at the age of twenty-five to a position which his father had attained only in the ripeness of years was a tribute to him, nevertheless. The leaders among the local gentry had undoubtedly perceived that Peter Jefferson's son was a young man of unusual talent and diligence, and they must have been impressed with the enterprise and public spirit which he had shown in his vigorous efforts to improve the navigation of the Rivanna. In later years his fellow citizens of Albemarle congratulated themselves on their foresight in giving him this early appointment, and with it the opportunity to become more widely known. The freeholders of his County elected him as soon as they very well could, they retained him as their representative until he proceeded to larger tasks, and they never let him be a prophet without honor at home. Both they and he had reason to be proud of this unfailing loyalty.[11]

He afterwards claimed that he always disliked public life, but there is no more evidence that he avoided it at the outset than there is that he made vigorous efforts to enter it. Participation in matters of local

[8] Account Book, Dec. 5, 9, 1768.

[9] Edmund Randolph, in *Va. Mag.*, XLIII, 122.

[10] On June 12, 1771, it was reported that he and others had declined to serve longer; Council Journals, Colonial Va., UVA photostats.

[11] Address of the Citizens of the County of Albemarle [Dec. 1789]; LC, 53:9021-9022.

government was as much a part of the normal business of life as practising law or cultivating his farms. Service in the House of Burgesses was not continuous but periodical, and he was still a bachelor who could easily take the road. He was not personally aggressive and did not crave power, but he always set high value on the esteem of his fellows and at this stage he craved honor. In that sense but probably in no other he had more than the "little spice of ambition" which he acknowledged.[12]

He could not have failed to see that in this region the only real promise of distinction lay in the field of public affairs. As has been well said, "to live and act *like gentlemen* was a thing once so common in Virginia, that nobody thought of noticing it."[13] Lawyers achieved little prominence merely as lawyers. Patrick Henry first attracted attention in a public case, and all of the able practitioners in the General Court whom history remembers were statesmen as well. Science and philosophy were not professions here; they were merely the avocations of gentlemen who must obtain support and gain prominence by other means. Years after Jefferson entered the House of Burgesses an eminent jurist sagely remarked: "The truth is, that Socrates himself would pass unnoticed and forgotten in Virginia, if he were not a *public* character."[14] Jefferson was not yet a public character but he had taken a necessary step if he would ever become one.

He did not wait until the eve of the Assembly to go to Williamsburg with his trusty Jupiter. He was there during most of the month of April, 1769, attending to legal business and diverting himself at odd times.[15] Early in May, along with the other burgesses, he took the oath in the Council chamber at the Capitol. Since this was his first session, the procedure probably impressed him more than it ever did afterwards. The formalities required a good deal of walking to and fro but fortunately the distances were short. After being sworn, the burgesses returned to their own chamber, whence they were summoned again to the Council room to attend the Governor; he then instructed them to go back and choose a speaker. They unanimously elected Peyton Randolph, the mace was laid on the table, and Lord Botetourt was informed.[16] This was by no means the end of it, however, for they then attended His Excellency again and learned with-

[12] To James Madison, June 9, 1793, Apr. 27, 1795 (Ford, VI, 291; VII, 10).

[13] St. George Tucker, Apr. 4, 1813, in *Memoirs of the Life of William Wirt* (1850), I, 316.

[14] *Ibid.*, I, 317.

[15] Account Book entries, Apr. 6–May 5, 1769.

[16] *Burgesses, Journals*, 1766–1769, pp. 187–189. The session began on May 8.

out surprise that he had approved their choice. His Lordship was wearing a light red coat. The Speaker, now formally recognized, laid claim to the ancient rights and privileges of the House — particularly freedom of speech and debate, exemption from arrest, and the protection of their estates. These the Governor solemnly promised to defend. Then, slowly and with long pauses, he made them a little speech. The members finally returned to their own places and resolved that an address be presented to His Excellency in response to his "very affectionate" words. These resolutions were drawn by the young Burgess from Albemarle.

All this was traditional procedure, embroidered by deliberate design. In this provincial setting the visible representative of a distant monarch was putting on as best he could a royal show. He had ridden from the Palace to the Capitol in a superbly furnished coach of state, which had been presented to him by the Duke of Cumberland, uncle of the King, and now bore the Virginia arms. Jefferson and the other burgesses had no doubt watched it as six white horses drew it up the broad Duke of Gloucester Street.[17]

If the later foe of kings regarded this parade and all these reflections of regal splendor as unbecoming to a representative body which was jealous of its own prerogatives, he gave no such suggestion in the first of his public papers. The brief resolutions which he drew at the request of Edmund Pendleton were in the courtly style.[18] We need not be surprised to find in them such standardized expressions as "a most humble and dutiful address," "his Majesty's sacred person and government," and "a lively sense of his royal favor." More honeyed words than these appeared in the petition which the House of Burgesses had sent to George III the year before, when as a matter of fact it was asserting its own rights. The iron hand was covered, almost concealed, by its velvet glove.[19]

If Jefferson's early draftsmanship is to be judged at all from these stereotyped resolutions it must be from the last of them. In this he effected a felicitous juncture of loyalty with firmness, thus aptly expressing the spirit of this polite but self-reliant group. If any questions affecting Great Britain should arise he hoped they would be discussed on this ruling principle: "her interests, and ours, are inseparably the same." And, finally, he prayed that "Providence, and the royal pleasure, may long continue his Lordship the happy ruler of a free and happy people."

[17] Goodwin, *Williamsburg*, pp. 57, 240.
[18] May 8, 1769 (Ford, I, 369).
[19] Apr. 14, 1768 (*Burgesses, Journals*, 1766–1769, pp. 165–171).

He had to content himself with this slight production, for the address which he drew soon thereafter was thought by the committee to follow the diction of the resolutions too strictly, and not to amplify the subjects sufficiently. The chief objector, Robert Carter Nicholas, was then asked to draft the paper, and in Jefferson's opinion he did this "with amplification enough." [20] Some of the phrases of the younger man reappeared in less rhythmical form in the address which was adopted, but this was a less distinguished piece of writing than his original resolutions, whatever may be thought of them. Time showed much more convincingly that he was a better writer than the veteran Nicholas or any other of the distinguished committeemen, but this experience at the beginning of his legislative career left an unpleasant memory of chagrin. Time also showed that sensitiveness was characteristic of his nature and constituted his chief personal weakness as a public man.

Pendleton was undoubtedly aware of his diligence and of his skill in all sorts of paper work, and probably anticipated that he would prove a useful committeeman, as in the next few years he did. Jefferson was appointed to two other committees in his first session but it is unlikely that he was immediately introduced into the inner circle of the legislators, as has been claimed.[21] In formal sessions he was a silent member even after he had become much more mature. He was always at his best in a small group, and he did not like to raise his voice.

He never sat in a larger legislative body than the House of Burgesses. The members must have crowded the small chamber and have had little elbow room, if ever they were all there. Each of the fifty-seven counties was entitled to two of them, and three boroughs and the College of William and Mary each had one. Nearly all of the leaders whom Jefferson had seen in action during his student days were still in evidence, for the principle of continuity in office prevailed. Peyton Randolph was even more dignified and stately, since he had become a permanent presiding officer, but Jefferson found him affable and kind. Richard Bland looked more than ever like a piece of parchment. Robert Carter Nicholas was weighted with care, being the treasurer of the Colony, but he was not yet at the point of offering his law practice to the young committeeman whom he had chagrined. Patrick Henry was dressing better but he was never anything but plain, nor was he at all remarkable until he began to speak. He generally remained inactive until a crisis arose, bothering little with routine or

[20] Ford, I, 369; *Burgesses, Journals,* 1766–1769, pp. 199–200.

[21] Hilldrup, *Pendleton,* p. 75. His committees were Privileges and Elections and Propositions and Grievances.

detail. Richard Henry Lee was a more even speaker, though he never attained such heights; and adroit Pendleton was the best director of parliamentary affairs.[22]

From Charles City County, where Jefferson afterwards found a wife, had come big Benjamin Harrison. Archibald Cary, whose daughter married Thomas Mann Randolph of Tuckahoe, was there from Chesterfield; he was one of the smaller men. Jefferson's early client Gabriel Jones had crossed the mountains from Augusta; and his friend Thomas Nelson, Junior, had come up from York. More important than any of these in history and in Jefferson's future career, however, was a splendid figure of a man from Fairfax. Ordinarily, George Washington did not have much to say but he had come to the meeting with something in his pocket. It was probably at this session that Jefferson met him for the first time, but a decade passed before they knew each other very well.

Though the new burgess from Albemarle was one of the taller among many tall members, he did not yet tower in this company and at his age he could hardly have been expected to. He learned far more from their deliberations than he contributed to them. These able Virginians constituted an experienced, vigorous, and self-confident group, banded together by common interests and infused with a common spirit. They did not need the spur of Patrick Henry's passionate oratory at this meeting. In closed sessions there was some dissent, but on questions which affected their liberties as legislators and their rights as colonists they stood practically as one.

Jefferson had an opportunity to observe this united front somewhat sooner than Lord Botetourt did. On May 16, 1769, by unanimous vote the burgesses passed certain resolves; and on the next day the genial representative of the King who had sought to avoid just this eventuality found it necessary to dissolve them. Despite all the lengthy ceremonial at the beginning they remained in session for only ten days.

Much turbulent water had gone over the dam since Jefferson had heard Patrick Henry inveigh against the Stamp Act in this same chamber, and had witnessed in Annapolis the rejoicings at the repeal of that obnoxious measure. His relative Richard Bland had written a pamphlet, entitled *An Inquiry into the Rights of the British Colonies*, which he read and from which he profited. He himself never bothered, however, to follow Bland in denying the virtual representation of the colonies in Parliament, which certain Britishers had alleged as a

[22] Good descriptions and characterizations of most of these leaders are in H. B. Grigsby, *Va. Convention of 1776* (1855).

justification for taxation. That question was closed in his mind by the time that he began to speak of the "connected chain of parliamentary usurpation." Of all the acts of "usurpation" which had followed the imposition of the stamp taxes, the temporary suspension of the legislature of the Colony of New York left the deepest impress on his mind.[23] The previous Assembly had addressed itself to this question, and Jefferson himself retained the conviction that never, until they had surrendered their common sense, would Americans admit that they held their political existence at the will of Parliament. This issue arose again and became dominant in the end.

A more burning issue in this session was provided by the Townshend duties, voted by Parliament two years earlier and still on the statute books. These had been imposed at the instance of a showy and cynical British minister who derided the distinction between internal and external taxes. Since the obstreperous colonists had objected to the one, he would accomplish a similar purpose by giving them the other. By this time Jefferson may already have reached the conclusion he afterwards proclaimed: that the controversy over internal and external taxes was a sham battle. But, in direct opposition to Townshend, he believed that Parliament had authority to impose neither, rather than a right to impose both. The burgesses were not yet ready to say that. They were opposed to laws designed to raise revenue under the guise of regulating external trade, but they were willing to acquiesce in measures for "preserving a necessary dependence."

At this juncture they were particularly concerned about what had happened in Massachusetts. The Bay Colony continued to be a seat of trouble. Jefferson himself said that the struggle which led to the American Revolution began in each colony "whenever the encroachment was presented to it," and that there was opposition in Massachusetts earlier than in Virginia.[24] Also, for various local reasons, the internal struggle was more acute and the violence much greater there. A board of customs commissioners was now seated in Boston and thus the duties on glass, paper, colors, and tea constituted a more visible "encroachment." As in a more famous instance several years later, the Massachusetts patriots appealed to the other colonies, and Jefferson's countrymen did not fail them. If the Virginians and the New Englanders were not the chief actors in the Revolution, he thought they were.[25]

In February, 1768, the House of Representatives of Massachusetts

---

[23] Judging from his comments in his "Summary View," Ford, I, 435–436.
[24] To Benjamin Waterhouse, Mar. 3, 1818 (Ford, X, 103).
[25] Ibid., X, 329 n.

Bay had sent to the other colonial legislatures a circular letter, urging united action against the Townshend duties. At their next meeting the Virginia Assembly had petitioned the King and addressed the Lords and Commons; and by direction the Speaker of the Burgesses wrote to the Speaker of the Massachusetts House that the Virginia representatives "could not but applaud them for their attention to American liberty." [26] Furthermore, he spoke of their own "fixed resolution to concur with the other colonies in their application for redress." Judging from what had happened already, Botetourt had little reason to hope that his conciliatory manner would suffice to detach the Virginians from their concert with their brethren to the North.

Unfortunately, the British authorities had chosen to make an issue of the Massachusetts circular. They had ordered it to be rescinded and the House of Representatives had refused. The secretary of state for the colonies, Lord Hillsborough, instructed hapless Botetourt and the other provincial governors to dissolve any assembly which approved the circular. Furthermore, some months before Jefferson attended his first session, Parliament approved this policy and recommended the revival of an old statute which allowed the government to call to England for trial persons accused of treason outside of the Kingdom. The threat was specifically directed against the "traitors" in Massachusetts, but the law could have been applied to Patrick Henry and Peyton Randolph just as well, had it been seriously intended.

On the ninth day of their session the burgesses accepted the challenge without flinching. They declared again that they, not Parliament, had the right to levy taxes on the Colony. They also asserted the right of petition to the King, and the lawfulness of procuring the concurrence of the other colonies. As usual, they assured the King of their loyalty, but in the same breath they asked him to avert the "dangers and miseries" which would ensue from the transportation of anyone to England to be tried.[27]

Botetourt had hoped to conciliate them and keep them silent, but under his instructions he had now no choice. He was dressed in scarlet when he summoned them into his presence and said: "I have heard of your resolves, and augur ill of their effect. You have made it my duty to dissolve you; and you are dissolved accordingly." [28] This was about noon on a Wednesday. With the greatest order and decorum the "late representatives of the people" went immediately to the Apollo Room of the Raleigh Tavern; they elected Peyton Randolph

[26] Apr. 15, 1768 (*Burgesses, Journals*, 1766–1769, p. 174).
[27] *Burgesses, Journals*, 1766–1769, p. 214, and frontispiece.
[28] *Ibid.*, p. 218.

moderator and proceeded to transact highly important business in the best of form. Jefferson needed to do nothing but go along with this powerful current. On the next day he put his name to the first significant public paper that he ever signed.[29]

This was what was known as an "Association," and because of the great prestige of the Colony and the historic eminence of the signers it became one of the more famous of its kind. It was a nonimportation, nonconsumption agreement, based on part of a draft of George Mason's which Washington had brought with him from Fairfax County.[30] Scholarly and patriotic Mason, who avoided legislative duties all he could, was not there. He had favored nonexportation also, but the others were not yet prepared to go that far. Jefferson was among the great number of "principal gentlemen" of the Colony, including eighty-nine of the "late representatives," who signed the final report of a special committee after it was approved on Thursday and then drank toasts to the King, the Governor, and others. He still regarded himself as a loyal subject, but from this beginning he was wholly resolute in his defense of colonial "rights."

He and the others promised that they would not import, and that after September 1 they would not buy, any goods taxed by Parliament for the purpose of raising revenue. A similar agreement about a long list of other articles was to remain binding until the Townshend Act had been repealed. At designated dates they also promised to cease to import wines and slaves. They set up no machinery of enforcement, however, and this proved to be an ineffective measure.[31] It was an important gesture and threat, nevertheless, and Jefferson took it more seriously than most.

Unless Lord Botetourt intended to dispense with the Assembly altogether and thus leave routine business unattended to, he had to issue writs for a new election. This he did in August and the elections were held in September. As Jefferson remembered, the only casualties were among the very few burgesses who had dared dissent from the opinions of the dominating group. In the courthouse at Charlottesville he himself was returned by the voice of the freeholders of Albemarle. His legislative career had lasted only ten days so far; but, having survived an election, he was now a veteran of sorts.[32]

His second session, in November and December of this year, was

[29] May 18, 1769; *Ibid.*, pp. xxxix–xlii.
[30] Rowland, *Mason*, I, 136–140.
[31] Lingley, *Transition in Va.*, pp. 57–58.
[32] Purdie & Dixon, *Va. Gazette*, Aug. 10, Sept. 7–28 1769; Ford, I, 7.

interrupted by no crisis and lasted about six weeks. He served on more committees this time, but like the others he was largely occupied with routine affairs, such as individual petitions and bills for the docking of entails on land.[33] So far as imperial relations were concerned this meeting was serene, and Lord Botetourt basked in the sunshine of popularity. No penalties had been imposed on the burgesses because of the actions of last May. This was one of many instances of the inconsistent and vacillating policy of the unstable ministry in England. After having uttered unnecessary threats, as Edmund Burke pointed out, the ministers now knelt to be kicked.[34] In Virginia it was courtly Lord Botetourt who did the kneeling, and the burgesses proceeded to bestow on him, not a kick, but the nearest thing to a caress that they could put in words.

In his opening address the Governor made a most conciliatory announcement. The British administration, far from wanting to impose further taxes on America for purposes of revenue, intended to propose at the next session of Parliament that the duties on glass, paper, and colors be taken off. He wisely failed to speak of tea, and, humorously conceding that the present ministers were not immortal, he admitted that their successors might attempt to undo their works. But he did not believe the plan would fail. As for himself, he was willing to be declared infamous if he did not at all times, in all places, and upon all occasions exert every power to obtain satisfaction for the colonies. The burgesses were enchanted, and Jefferson himself believed that the Governor meant everything he said.[35]

The response to such an important announcement was not entrusted to a young burgess who might possibly have claimed something more; it was left to the sage veterans, Pendleton and Nicholas. They expressed gratitude and loyalty to the King, and they undoubtedly voiced the prevailing sentiment about the Governor himself. "Your Lordship's great regard and attention to the welfare and true interest of this colony has before endeared you to us all; but your generous and noble declarations, upon this occasion, demand our warmest and most grateful acknowledgments." [36] The Governor had made himself the hero of the hour and could hardly have been denied generous applause.

It seemed to Thomas Jefferson afterwards that this sort of thing smacked too much of humility, and that, while Botetourt said all he

[33] *Burgesses, Journals,* 1766–1769, pp. 262, 296, 298, 310, 316.
[34] Cavendish, *Debates,* II, 21.
[35] *Burgesses, Journals,* 1766–1769, p. 227; Ford, X, 330.
[36] *Burgesses, Journals,* 1766–1769, p. 234.

could, he could not say enough. To certain critics of the ministry in the House of Commons, on the other hand, and among them men who had opposed the Townshend duties in the first place, the speech and conduct of the Lord of the Bedchamber seemed absurd. In the opinion of Burke and others he had said far too much: he had laid on Parliament the odium for imposing burdens, and had given all the credit for removing them to his King.[37] Even Lord North recognized the issue. Said he: "The language of America is, We are the subjects of the King; with parliament we have nothing to do. That is the point at which the factions have been aiming: upon that they have been shaking hands."[38] Jefferson would have approved, for he afterwards claimed that he held this position from the first. But there is no record that he said so, publicly, until four years later and he believed that he was in advance of public opinions when he did. Meanwhile, it was recognized in England as in Virginia that Botetourt was amiable and much beloved.

He was a man around whom pleasant stories gathered. From his friend Anne Blair, Jefferson could have heard one which ought to have appealed to his musician's heart, whether or not he loved a lord. One summer evening as the Blairs and their guests sat singing on their steps, they saw a lantern and candle coming up the street. The pedestrians soon stopped as though to listen, and the music abruptly ceased. Whereupon a voice called out: "Charming, charming! proceed for God's sake, or I go home directly." Then all sprang up and the air echoed with "Pray, walk in, my Lord." No, he would not do that, but he would sit on the steps beside them. This he did till the party broke up and the guests went home.[39] In December the Speaker and the burgesses gave a party at the illuminated Capitol to Botetourt which Jefferson was entitled to attend. It was noted that the patriotic spirit which had given rise to the Association of gentlemen in Raleigh Tavern was now manifested by the ladies at the Capitol. Nearly a hundred of them came in homespun gowns. They undoubtedly fluttered about His Lordship, who had no lady of his own at the Palace but managed, nevertheless, to give splendid entertainment there.[40]

Jefferson was one of those who regarded the struggle with the British authorities as far from over. The duty on tea remained and was supported by the ministry in Parliament on the ground that the

---

[37] Jan. 9, 1770, *Parl. Hist.*, XVI, 670, 675; May 9, 1770, Cavendish, *Debates*, II, 14–36, esp. 20–22, 26, 31. In *Parl. Hist.*, XVI, 1001–1010, the latter debate is dated May 8, and is reported in much less detail.
[38] Cavendish, *Debates*, II, 31.
[39] Anne Blair to Martha Braxton, Aug. 21, 1769 (*W. & M.*, 1 ser., XVI, 178).
[40] Purdie & Dixon, *Va. Gazette*, Dec. 14, 1769.

Mother Country must retain the right to tax. The practical inconvenience to the colonies might now be slight, as Lord North said, but the principle for which the more aggressive patriots had contended had been denied.[41] Throughout the preliminaries of the Revolution Jefferson kept principles clearly in mind and the action which he took in June, 1770, illustrates the point. He then signed another Association agreement which was to be binding until the offensive act of Parliament had been *totally* repealed or a meeting of one hundred Associators had provided otherwise. This agreement, which was made by a large group of burgesses and local merchants during the spring session of the Assembly, went further than that of the previous year by setting up county committees of enforcement. It soon appeared, however, that these could not be genuinely effective, since the spirit of Association had everywhere declined.[42]

It was during this session that Lord Botetourt signed Jefferson's commission as lieutenant of Albemarle and chief commander of the militia there.[43] Thus, at the age of twenty-seven, he became the ranking official of his County and could be called Colonel. His service in this important post may not have been continuous, but he was occupying it when war actually broke out and Colonel Jefferson then concerned himself diligently with military affairs. He did not see much more of Botetourt, for in October the genial Baron was gathered to his fathers. Jefferson was then in Williamsburg attending the General Court and no doubt was present at the funeral services in Bruton Church and in the College chapel, where the remains were interred.[44] The ceremonies were the most elaborate that had ever been seen in Virginia and are reputed to have cost seven hundred pounds sterling. Also, he was a member of the Assembly which afterwards voted that an "elegant" statue of this much-mourned gentleman be erected in marble at public expense. This statue later became a landmark and caused the memory of His Lordship to remain green in Williamsburg.[45]

Jefferson afterwards viewed the death of Botetourt, which had seemed so tragically untimely, as a fortunate event for the cause of the Revolution. He believed that if this conciliatory courtier had lived on he would have been able to embarrass the measures of the patriots greatly. It seemed to him that his Virginia countrymen had

[41] Mar. 5, 1770; *Parl. Hist.*, XVI, 853–855.

[42] *Burgesses, Journals*, 1770–1772, pp. xxvii–xxxi.

[43] June 9, 1770; LC, 1:52. This is followed by a similar commission, signed on Dec. 15, 1770, by William Nelson, acting governor.

[44] Goodwin, *Williamsburg*, pp. 61–62, with citations. Jefferson noted in his Account Book on Oct. 15, 1770, that Botetourt had died the day before.

[45] *Burgesses, Journals*, 1770–1772, p. 138.

fallen into a sad state of insensibility to their actual situation.[46] Not only was the tea tax unrepealed; the Declaratory Act, by which Parliament had asserted the right to bind the colonists by their laws in all cases whatsoever, still hung suspended over them like the sword of Damocles. Others than he had noted the cooling of the spirit of Association — because of the defection of the northern provinces, some people said. A meeting of Associators was called for December 14, 1770, but so few met that they could do nothing but adjourn until summer.[47] Jefferson was in Williamsburg that day and was probably numbered among these few. He continued longer than most people to be scrupulous about the agreement into which he had entered. In the year 1771, as a prospective bridegroom, he particularly wanted building materials and furnishings and fine clothes. Not until June, however, did he feel free to authorize his agent in England to purchase certain articles which had been previously prohibited.[48]

As a public man he had now come into a barren period. Of all the sessions of the House of Burgesses that he attended before his marriage, his first was much the most exciting. Following the Boston Massacre there was a reaction against patriotic activities even in Boston, and the Virginians had no other burning grievances for several years. The time for him to appear as a rebel had not yet arrived. But it was as inevitable as anything can be that he would take his stand against what he regarded as tyranny, for the spirit of liberty was the essence of his mind.

During his early legislative career, he said, he made an effort for the emancipation of slaves which came to nothing. Whether he made or seconded an abortive motion which was not entered on the record, or his memory was at fault in regard to the form of his proposal, undoubtedly he already had a strong desire to mitigate the evils of slavery. But, as he reflected, nothing liberal could then expect success.[49] He was still living in the "dull monotony of a colonial subservience" and, both as a local patriot and a humanitarian, he had to wait for a more propitious hour.

Momentarily, he had to combat ills created by the forces of nature.

[46] Ford, X, 330 n.; I, 7.
[47] Burgesses, Journals, 1770–1772, p. xxxi.
[48] To Thos. Adams, June 1, 1771 (Ford, I, 394–395).
[49] "Autobiography," in Ford, I, 4. Randall, I, 58, says that in his first session he introduced a bill giving to owners the right to manumit their slaves. In a letter to Edward Coles, Aug. 25, 1814 (Ford, IX, 477), he speaks of a bill moderately extending to slaves the protection of the laws which was introduced by Richard Bland and seconded by him. The surest indication of his attitude at this time is to be found in his argument in Howell v. Netherland, April, 1770 (Ford, I, 373–381).

The "great fresh" of 1771 destroyed many other things besides his mill; that summer he attended a special session of the Assembly which President William Nelson had called on account of the general devastation.[50] He was again in Williamsburg in October when still another governor arrived. Lord Dunmore was fated to arouse controversy, not to compose it. There could be no valid objection, however, when he dissolved the Assembly. In late November, Jefferson was re-elected by the freeholders, while his contemporary John Walker was chosen in place of his father.[51] During this same year, however, Jefferson declined to serve longer on the county court, and when the new Assembly finally met in February, 1772, he was not there. By that date he had married, and for several years he had been building a house. Colonial rights might still be in jeopardy but supremely important personal matters had to be attended to. The time had come for him to settle down.

[50] July 11–20, 1771; *Burgesses, Journals,* 1770–1772.
[51] Purdie & Dixon, *Va. Gazette,* Dec. 5, 1771. The election was on Nov. 29.

[XI]

Beginning at Monticello
1769–1772

BY the year that he began to practise law Jefferson had given a name to the little mountain across the Rivanna from Shadwell and had started to graft cherry trees there.[1] He had translated "little mountain" into Italian, a language he was now familiar with, and undoubtedly he pronounced the word in the Italian manner. A month after his twenty-fifth birthday he made an agreement for leveling the top of this elevated place and by this time, if not earlier, he had decided to build a house there.[2] Not yet, however, did he know who was going to live in it besides himself.

In the year he entered the House of Burgesses laborers of his began to dig a cellar in the stiff mountain clay.[3] The work which he thus inaugurated he continued for ten or twelve years; he returned to it as a new task a decade after that; and the building of the mansion at Monticello in its historic form proved to be little short of a lifetime's work. Nothing else that he ever did was more characteristic of him as a person and a mind. In spirit he was pre-eminently constructive, and he could not think of himself or of his house or of human society as finished. But he was not merely creating an architectural or intellectual monument; he was a deeply domestic being, making a home. Throughout his maturity his spirit ceaselessly roamed the universe, searching out the good things in it, but his heart was on his mountaintop, and if his ghost now walks it is surely there.

Few activities interested him more than building, and it is unfortunate that the scanty early records do not reveal just when this in-

[1] First known reference, *Garden Book*, Aug. 3, 1767.
[2] *Ibid.*, p. 12, quoting Account Book, May 15, 1768.
[3] *Ibid.*, p. 16.

terest was manifested first. The natural supposition is that, as an enthusiastic boy at home from school, he watched the building operations that his father was carrying on at Shadwell and observed Peter Jefferson at the drawing-board. It is said that while he was in college he got his first work on architecture from an old cabinetmaker; and as a law student he may have picked up ideas and books from Richard Taliaferro, father-in-law of George Wythe, who was called an architect at the time and was certainly a builder.[4] The study of architecture for purposes of personal improvement was quite in accord with the tradition of the Renaissance as perpetuated in England, and in that country this was pre-eminently the age of the gentleman amateur.[5] In his own developing region Jefferson became notable for his knowledge of the arts, but his consuming interest in architecture began, not with his concern for culture, but with his desire to engage in actual construction, or to help his friends do so. He had to be his own designer and builder, but he considerably surpassed amateur standards before he was through and he soon came to be regarded by his local contemporaries as an authority. It is possible that he designed other houses before he did his own, though the first full chapter of his architectural story was written in the bricks and mortar of Monticello.

To many at the time it must have seemed that his personal project was impracticable. In deciding to establish a plantation seat on such a height he was following no precedent that could be found in Virginia, or in England for that matter, and he appeared to be flying in the face of common sense. The difficulties in carrying on construction in such a place were immense. The woods were thick, much grading had to be done in stubborn soil, and, besides the building materials themselves, water had to be brought to the hilltop at first. He had to figure with exactitude just how much of it was required. His choice of a site does not show that he was an impractical theorist, for in the course of time he actually worked out his problems. It does show, however, that he had not disciplined his mind to the loss of imagination; and events proved that in matters connected with his home he was least disposed to count the labor and the cost.

His choice also revealed a sensitiveness to natural beauty which he did not often express in words. His eye, like his mind, sought an extended view. From this spot he could see to the eastward an expanse of forested country, rolling like the sea; and to the westward he could

[4] M. Kimball, *Road to Glory*, p. 147, citing letter of William Short, July 8, 1828; Waterman, *Mansions of Virginia*, pp. 342, 345, about Taliaferro.
[5] B. S. Allen, *Tides in English Taste* (1937), I, ch. 2; II, 125–126.

look across the treetops to a mountain wall of lavender and blue. The lesser and scattered intervening hills flattened out somewhat when viewed from this eminence, but the country was little marred by the hand of man as yet and the prospect was majestic, though not quite stupendous. The eye could ask for nothing better, except for the presence of a body of shimmering water. Despite what he had done for it the Rivanna was not that.

According to the agreement, a plot on the northeast end of the mountain was to be leveled by Christmas, 1768, and be paid for in wheat and corn. In the spring Jefferson was planting fruit trees on the southeast hillside, spacing them properly in an almost ideal spot. The excavations of 1769 were for the foundations of the first outbuilding. By summer he had arranged for the molding and burning of brick and had set a man digging a well; by early fall he had laid out on the north side of the mountain a park more than a mile in circumference, had ordered 8,000 chestnut rails to be mawled, and had arranged for a friend who was sailing for England to buy articles for the house there.[6]

His house plans were still tentative. The first thing he had done was to get a few drawings of other dwellings, crudely executed by other hands.[7] He could not hope to find satisfactory models in his immediate locality, and even when he surveyed the entire Province most of the private houses seemed to him ugly and uncomfortable. He thought it fortunate that they were perishable. They were generally of wood, and in reaching his own early decision to use brick he had to combat a strong contemporary prejudice against it, because of the belief that rain could less easily penetrate wooden walls. He wanted to employ durable materials and to contribute to permanent improvement. There were expensive mansions in Virginia at that time. Rosewell, which he visited so often, was fabulously so; and Westover and Carter's Grove, which he must have known, were places of note. But, after he had informed himself about what had been done in other lands, he was convinced that the first principles of the art of building were unknown in the Colony, and that scarcely a model existed "sufficiently chaste to give an idea of them."[8] To the twentieth-century observer of mellow river mansions and restored Williamsburg his strictures seem much

[6] *Garden Book*, p. 17; Account Book, July 25, Sept. 20, Sept. 23, Oct. 22, 1769.

[7] On his successive plans, see F. Kimball, *Thomas Jefferson, Architect*, pp. 22–29, and plates at the end of the volume, reproduced from MHS. This invaluable work is supplemented for this period by M. Kimball, *Road to Glory*, ch. 8, incorporating additional items which the former reviewed. See also the drawings in Waterman, *Mansions of Virginia*, pp. 388–390.

[8] Comment in *Notes on Virginia*; Ford, III, 258.

too severe and his standards rather arbitrary. All the domestic architecture of Virginia prior to the building of Monticello cannot be thus dismissed with a wave of the hand. He probably did not have quite such strong feelings about local houses in 1769 as he did when he definitely expressed them a dozen years later, but at the very beginning his tastes and ambitions caused him to search for better examples elsewhere.

It is not at all surprising, therefore, that he turned to books. That was a common practice when anyone wanted to build better than the average, and he could not have been expected to blossom forth spontaneously as a creative designer in his middle twenties. His distinction lay in the fact that he referred to more books than others did, that he went beyond British works to more remote sources, that he attained results which accorded with his own superior tastes and special needs. His first collection of architectural works was notable in his locality, and it was representative of more than one of the trends and fashions of his times.[9] He was most influenced, however, by English architects who had imitated Palladio, and by the great Italian himself, who had gone back to Roman antiquity for his models and his rules. Thus did a freedom-loving and forward-looking American attach himself to a school which found its inspiration in the distant past and which now impresses one as dogmatic. It may seem that some explanation is called for.

The facts themselves, as they appeared in the last third of the eighteenth century, can be left to speak for themselves, but something may be said here in regard to the developing architectural philosophy of Jefferson. Like most other men he was not all of a piece, but in this instance the alleged inconsistency is more apparent than real. Liberty was never anarchy to him, but freedom to seek the truth. It seemed proper enough that there should be rules in architecture as there were laws in nature, and rules were exceedingly useful to a young gentleman amateur on the edge of civilization who wanted to build a house. If that structure had not been harmonious within itself, restrained, and symmetrically proportioned it would not have been a fitting habitation for him, or at least for the sort of man he aspired to be. What he valued most in classical antiquity he prized in architecture: simplicity, serenity, and reserve — coupled with the sort of dignity which seemed

[9] F. Kimball, *Jefferson, Architect*, pp. 34–35, 90–101, listing his architectural books with probable dates of acquisition. As an indication of the catholicity of his collection, it may be noted that by 1783 and probably by 1771 he had a copy of Chambers, *Designs of Chinese Buildings, Furniture . . .* (1757).

appropriate to his majestic site. For what he wanted he now turned, not to the more monumental works of Palladio, but to the country style of his lesser villas.[10]

He probably introduced himself to certain English disciples of Palladio, such as James Gibbs and Robert Morris, before he made the acquaintance of the master himself. One of the books by Gibbs which he acquired among the first gave rules for architectural drawing and measurement which were better than those generally available to American builders, and he followed these until he found others that seemed superior.[11] As his father's son he took to mechanical drawing. His procedure was that of the draftsman, not the freehand artist; and at this stage he drew, not with pencil, but wholly with ink.[12] His mind was mathematical and he had a penchant for precision. This was one reason, though not the only one, why he was so greatly attracted to Andrea Palladio from the time that he discovered him.[13]

A person of Jefferson's classical training must have been impressed by the information that the Italian had examined the stately monuments of old Rome with unparalleled diligence and attention, thus making himself the master of the noblest ideas of the ancients. It was claimed that Palladio, walking through the rubbish, had discovered "the true rules of an art, which till his time were unknown." [14] He probably seemed to his disciples the Newton of architecture, though Jefferson never placed him quite that high. In the works of this master, however, Jefferson found rules for the proportions of the five orders, along with various other measurements, and as time went on he refigured the proportions of his own house accordingly. Nor could he fail to perceive the kinship of spirit between the distinguished son of Vicenza and himself. In his first chapter Palladio quoted Vitruvius in regard to the chief desiderata in a building: conveniency, solidity, and beauty. Then he said: "As for the beauty of an edifice, it consists of an exact proportion of the parts within themselves, and of each part with the whole: for a fine building ought to appear as an entire and perfect body,

---

[10] For a general characterization, see Waterman, pp. 341–342. He credits Jefferson with the 'authorship" of a whole group of Virginia houses in this style, admittedly on the basis of circumstantial evidence, however (p. 345).

[11] James Gibbs, *Rules for Drawing in Architecture* (London, 1753). He also had a copy of Gibbs, *A Book of Architecture containing Designs of Buildings and Ornaments* (London, 1728).

[12] *Jefferson, Architect*, p. 26.

[13] Of the various eds. of *The Architecture of A. Palladio* which he eventually owned, he appears to have had that of Leoni (London, 1742) by or before 1770. My own references are to the ed. of Leoni of 1721.

[14] Prefatory note, Leoni, *Palladio* (1721).

wherein every member agrees with its fellow, and each so well with the whole, that it may seem absolutely necessary to the being of the same." [15] There is here no denial of the freedom of the mind to reach its own conclusions, but the strong hope is held out that the order and harmony which Jefferson was seeking might be found.

The design of the main house which Jefferson decided on about 1770 shows distinct traces of Palladian influence, but it went back to his own earlier, more conventional, and more practical plan of a central mass with wings.[16] To this he afterwards added octagonal bays or projections, which may have been inspired by the *Select Architecture* of Robert Morris. If he did draw plans for other dwellings before his own the best case can be made for the Harrison place, Brandon, which bears a striking resemblance to one of Morris's plates.[17] There can be little doubt that he used some of the designs of this English architect as starting points, at this and other times, and from him he could also have received counsels of moderation in ornament. "I think a building, well proportioned, without dress, will ever please," said Morris; "as a plain coat may sit as graceful and easy on a well-proportioned man: . . . But if you will be lavish in ornament, your structure will look rather like a fop, with a superfluity of gaudy tinsel, than a real decoration." [18]

Fundamentally, Jefferson was austere. He preferred chaste architectural models and he worked out his proportions mathematically before he drew his plans in ink. He was not an unbridled genius in this or any other field; there was nothing lawless about him, despite his pioneering bent. He was unusually scholarly and painstaking, and at the same time receptive; and he had a rare gift of adaptation which constituted a form of originality. He provided for his personal needs with ingenuity, and at Monticello he did not slavishly follow any single guide. The elevation which he drew before 1772 showed a central portico of two orders, the stronger Doric capitals supporting the Ionic columns, as Palladio had prescribed.[19] This drawing is impressive but it has an unfamiliar look to modern visitors, for the upper columns were never placed. By the year of his marriage he had also worked out a general plan, including the dependencies.[20] Almost anyone who has

[15] *Ibid.*, p. 1.

[16] *Jefferson, Architect*, Fig. 18 and notes. This should be compared with Fig. 11, which appears to have been directly inspired by Palladio, and also with Fig. 24.

[17] Waterman, pp. 366-367.

[18] Robert Morris, *Select Architecture: Being Regular Designs of Plans and Elevations* (London, 1755), Preface.

[19] *Jefferson, Architect*, Fig. 23; Waterman, p. 391; Leoni, *Palladio*, Bk. I, ch. 12.

[20] *Jefferson, Architect*, Fig. 32 and notes. Reproduced in this volume.

been to Monticello can recognize this, for it was largely carried out in the course of time. It was a country scheme, such as had great vogue in eighteenth-century England, and was strongly reminiscent of Palladio.[21]

The idea was to connect the supporting buildings, keeping them under one roof for the convenience of the owner. Jefferson once flirted with the idea of having "offices" run all around the mountaintop, but abandoned it as grandiose. He now planned a succession of rooms in two L-shaped blocks, connecting with the main house and each terminating in a square outbuilding. After studying the lay of his land, he decided to take advantage of the slope by sinking the service rooms below the level of the main structure, covering them with terraces and having them open outwards rather than upon the inner court. His adaptation of the scheme was individual, but in putting the meanest rooms out of sight he was following the counsel of the master. Palladio drew an analogy from the human body, which contains some noble and beautiful members and others which, though useful, are ugly and disagreeable. Then he reverently said: "But as our blessed Lord has ordered our members so as to make the finest of them to be the most exposed to sight, and concealing them that are not seemingly so: just so we must contrive a building in such a manner that the finest and most noble parts of it be the most exposed to publick view, and the less agreeable disposed in byplaces, and removed from sight as much as possible." [22]

The major danger was that comfort and convenience would be sacrificed to stateliness by putting kitchen, pantries, woodhouses, laundries, servants' quarters, and the like too far away. There was reason to put them at a distance in those days, for there were no screens, and Jefferson had plenty of domestic servants to carry things to and fro. Accordingly, the housewife's objection to his placing the basement kitchen on the opposite side of the house from the dining room would not have been so quickly raised then as now. On the other hand, it would have been unfortunate if he had placed his stables under the northwest wing as he once planned; actually, he kept them at a greater distance and eventually used that wing chiefly for coaches and an icehouse.[23] He did not get around to building his terraces until after the Revolution. Nor did he put up at the turns the Chinese temples he once considered, or the octagons with domes like those at Lord Burlington's

[21] Allen, *Tides in English Taste*, I, 64. See Jefferson's favorable comment on Moor Park, seen by him during his tour of 1786 (L. & B., XVII, 243).

[22] Leoni, *Palladio*, Bk. II, ch. 2, p. 58.

[23] *Jefferson, Architect*, Fig. 31; *Garden Book*, Plate XVIII.

famous house at Chiswick which he afterwards preferred.[24] He was not without romantic impulses, but prudence and practical necessities imposed restraint.

The first structure that he erected was one of the outbuildings, often referred to as "the southeast pavilion." He moved to this simple brick building in the November after the house at Shadwell burned. Here he had parlor, kitchen, hall, bedchamber, and study all in one. Hither, as tradition has it, he brought his bride. Probably no part of the main house was completed at the time of his marriage.[25] They were still making and laying bricks after the Declaration of Independence, and as late as 1778 Jefferson contracted for stone columns. The house was not wholly done in 1781 when the British rode up the mountain, and it was remodeled extensively fifteen years after that. He had only begun to create an architectural monument when he became a husband. What Mrs. Jefferson came to was only a mansion in the making. On paper the house proper had five rooms on the first floor, after the octagonal projections were added.[26] These consisted of a central parlor or saloon, with a dining room and bowroom on one side and a bedroom and dressing room on the other. The precise form of the second floor is uncertain, but presumably the large library over the parlor was flanked with bedrooms.

According to Palladio, the "conveniency" of a house consisted in its suitability to the quality of its master.[27] In the common meaning of the term, the house at Monticello was not for some time a convenient one, if it ever was really, and amid all the clatter of construction it must have lacked the tranquillity which its owner so greatly prized. Those who knew the workings of his mind, however, must have observed as a contemporary did that in his locality he took pride in running before his times, and that he purposed to assume a style of living more refined than had been handed down to him by his own ancestors or was practised by his contemporaries in the Province.[28] In polite learning the second William Byrd may have been his equal, and as a man of the world his superior, but as a man of both taste and learning he had no contemporary or historic rival in Virginia. In more senses than one he had set himself upon a mountain.

[24] Kimball, p. 126.

[25] Account Book, Nov. 26, 1770; *Garden Book*, p. 70; to James Ogilvie, Feb. 20, 1771 (Ford, I, 391); Randall, I, 65. Mrs. Kimball believes that the northwest wing of the main house may have been habitable (*Jefferson, the Road to Glory*, p. 156).

[26] *Jefferson, Architect*, Fig. 24. There is some question about the exact date when Jefferson added the octagonal projections, but they were in the completed house before he remodeled it.

[27] Leoni, *Palladio*, Bk. II, ch. 1, p. 57.

[28] Edmund Randolph in *Va. Mag.*, XLIII, 122.

Yet he was never one who desired to be gazed at. He sought privacy as well as elevation and he had good reason to expect it in this inaccessible place. His joy was in a new creation. America itself was that, as he said later; at least, in comparison with Europe, it was built on a better plan.[29] The time for effective political planning was not yet come, but he could create an appropriate setting for the sort of life he aspired to live. Whether he was in any strict sense original does not matter. He was trying to bring to this new Country the best wisdom of his age; and, in the attempt to solve his own problems, he figured things out in advance with a diligence and exactitude which were unparalleled in his native society.

Nothing was too small to excite his interest and homely matters concerned him along with the artistic. He had planted an orchard on the hillside below the southeastern outbuilding before he established bachelor quarters there. He had set out ingrafted pears and apples, cherry trees still to be "inoculated," peachstocks on which he intended to graft almonds, and quinces and nectarines besides. In the hollow he had planted pomegranates, figs, and walnuts, along with peachstocks to be inoculated with apricots.[30] He was picking up bits of horticultural lore from his neighbors, reading in a garden dictionary, and planting bushels of clover seed, but he had not worked out a full garden plan as yet.[31]

His mind also turned to questions of landscaping, but he never did have his retainers dig the rectangular flower beds behind the house which he showed on his general plan.[32] The open ground on the west seemed to him to call for a shrubbery, and for this he drew up an impressive list. At this stage there was more immediate need for thinning trees, removing undergrowth, and domesticating the place generally. Nonetheless, he wanted it to remain an asylum for wild animals except beasts of prey, and he was already thinking of procuring a buck-elk to be monarch of the wood. Somewhat later he did stock his park with deer but he was not able to do much with landscaping for many years. The suggestions which he wrote down in his Account Book are of chief interest here because they show that, for all his classicism, he was eclectic in his tastes.[33] He thought of Chinese ornaments as well as Grecian and was not even averse to Gothic.

---

[29] To Angelica Church, Feb. 17, 1788; quoted in *Garden Book*, p. xv.
[30] Mar. 14, 1769 (*Garden Book*, p. 15).
[31] He did this about 1774 (*Ibid.*, Plate V; see also Plate VI).
[32] *Ibid.*, Plate III and comments.
[33] *Garden Book*, pp. 25–27; also in Randall, I, 60–62. In *Jefferson, the Road to Glory*, p. 161, Mrs. Kimball attributes them to the influence of Thomas Whately's *Observations on Modern Gardening* which Jefferson had acquired by the summer of 1771.

Most striking and startling of all were the alternative plans which he set down for a burying place. The one that he established later was a great deal simpler than either of these. He now recorded in his Account Book the Latin epitaph which he had written for his sister Jane, along with mournful poetic bits from both Latin and English. As a literary being he was not untouched by the sentimental melancholy of his time. But the sad reveries of this highly intellectual young planter could have been more easily explained by almost any observant person who had attained maturity. The simplest statement of his case, though not necessarily a complete one, is that he was in love and needed a wife. It was fortunate that he did not have to wait for one much longer.

[XII]

Attaining Domestic Felicity

1772-1774

ABOUT the time that he moved to Monticello and set up bachelor quarters in the first outbuilding there, Jefferson began to make regular visits to a place in Charles City County called the Forest, where there was an attractive young widow. To say that he paid court to her is to be quite precise, for he lived in a courtly age and this shy and reserved man tended to be formalistic in social matters as in architecture. His attitude toward love and marriage was strictly conventional, and his early manner toward women was stilted. This was a real romance, nevertheless, and his marriage to Martha Wayles Skelton on New Year's Day, 1772, ushered in the happiest period of his life. External circumstances cast some shadows on the domestic scene during the next ten years, but the atmosphere was one of unusual spiritual serenity. He never had the slightest doubt that he was well mated.

This genuine love match was preceded by an uncertain affair which Jefferson himself described afterwards as improper. His relations with his neighbor Mrs. John Walker were unknown or unnoticed at the time, but they were widely advertised years later, when he was a conspicuous target of scurrilous attacks. As a notorious episode this story really belongs to his history as President, when he was several times a grandfather, but the events themselves fell within a period when he was young and only locally prominent. The known facts should be stated here though their importance must not be exaggerated.[1]

He had served as an attendant at the wedding of John Walker and Elizabeth [Betsey] Moore at the age of twenty-one. Jack Walker was not quite the same sort of friend as John Page and Dabney Carr, but

[1] For the history of the whole affair, extending to the year 1809, see Appendix III.

he had been intimate with Jefferson from their days at Maury's school. They had been at college together and they loved each other, Jack said. Dr. Thomas Walker of Castle Hill, his father, was one of Peter Jefferson's executors; he advanced some of his own money to his ward when the latter went to William and Mary, though there is no reason to suppose that this was not repaid. Betsey was the daughter of Colonel Bernard Moore, and two of her brothers were at the College in Jefferson's time. The young couple eventually settled down at Belvoir, on the old Nicholas Meriwether estate, five or six miles from Shadwell.[2] Jefferson not only continued to be intimate with Walker; he gave elaborate advice to one of Betsey's brothers about the study of law, and became good friends with Colonel Moore, from whom he got garden items and at whose home, Chelsea in King William County, he visited.[3]

It was in the year he was twenty-five that Jefferson made a mistake. He was then unmarried, full of physical strength and vigor, and for four months his friend was away from home. John Walker was attending a conference with the Indians at Fort Stanwix and acting as a clerk of the Virginia delegation of which his father was a member. Before he left he made his will, naming Jefferson first among his executors, and he entrusted his wife and baby daughter to this friend's special care. It was just after his return that Jefferson was elected to the House of Burgesses with Dr. Thomas Walker. A generation afterwards John said that during his absence Jefferson's conduct towards Mrs. Walker was improper; and the President of the United States candidly admitted to certain particular friends that at one time it was. Singling it out from the other accusations which his enemies had hurled against him, he said this privately: "I plead guilty to one of their charges, that when young and single I offered love to a handsome lady. I acknowledge its incorrectness."[4] Also, when he was in his sixties, he did what he could in private to make amends to his alienated friend, and to relieve Walker's mind in a time of embarrassing publicity by exculpating the lady from all blame. Such action was in full accord with his strict code of manners and morals.

Jefferson's incorrect conduct was not reported to the injured husband in 1768, however, or soon afterwards, and the natural supposition is that the lady did not regard the offense as grave. Jefferson continued to be intimate with Walker and with various close relatives of his; and

[2] Slaughter, *Memorial of Joshua Fry*, p. 63. The exact date of the coming of the Walkers to Belvoir is uncertain, but unquestionably they were near neighbors of Jefferson by or before 1768. On the place see E. C. Mead, *Historic Homes of the South-West Mountains*, pp. 159–162.

[3] Randall, I, 53–57; *Garden Book*, 1767, 1768, pp. 6, 10, 12.

[4] To Robert Smith, July 1, 1805 (Bixby, p. 115); see Appendix III.

only two or three years after this, as one of five trustees, he offered for sale certain lands belonging to Betsey's father in order to pay the Colonel's debts.[5] For a decade and half longer his standing in this circle was of the best. It was not until after he had gone to France in 1784 that Mrs. Walker told her husband about Jefferson's designs on her. When he was at a safe distance she unfolded a lurid story of "base transactions" — in 1769 and 1770, when he was still a bachelor, and extending into 1779, when he had been for some years a married man. As Walker wrote it all down fifteen or twenty years after he got the report, it was a disgusting tale which bore the marks of gross and will-ful exaggeration, whatever may have been the cause.[6]

In the absence of other testimony, such an incredible story cannot be accepted in detail. All we can be sure of is that Jefferson made ad-vances of some sort to his friend's wife while he himself was single, that he deeply regretted his actions afterwards, and that he accepted all the blame. He may possibly have erred more than once in his youth-ful ardor, but this sensitive man was not bold toward women and the awkward maneuvers which Mrs. Walker reported suggest none of the accomplishments of a rake. He was much more in character as a de-voted husband and kind father than as an aggressive lover, and it is hard to believe that he would have persisted in the face of rebuffs at any age. He generally observed the proprieties almost to the point of stiffness; he was notably loyal to his friends; and there is no reason whatever to question his complete fidelity to his own wife. He would have been in a safer position, however, if he had got her sooner than he did, when he was nearly twenty-nine.

In Virginia as a rule people did not wait as long as Jefferson did to marry. His delay had distinct advantages, besides some dangers, for it enabled him to devote himself to his studies and to his profession to a degree which would have been difficult in wedded life. By the year that the house at Shadwell burned, however, he was aware that as a bachelor he had missed many joys. His friend and brother-in-law Dabney Carr had not yet proceeded as far along the road to profes-sional success and public prominence as he had, and may have had a harder time making ends meet. Yet Jefferson believed that the husband of his sister Martha, "in a very small house, with a table, half a dozen chairs, and one or two servants," was "the happiest man in the uni-verse."[7] Utterly neglecting "the costly apparatus of life," Carr spoke,

[5] Rind, *Va. Gazette*, Jan. 10, 1771.
[6] LC, 155:27117–27121; see Appendix III.
[7] To John Page, Feb. 21, 1770 (Ford, I, 373).

thought, and dreamed of nothing but his young son. This was a boy named Peter, who was born that year and of whom we shall hear again.[8] Jefferson did not then know that he himself would never have a son for long. On the contrary, he soon had reason to believe that he would acquire one ready-made, for Martha Wayles Skelton had one.

She was five and a half years younger than he and at eighteen had married Bathurst Skelton, who had followed him in college. Her son John was born when she was nineteen, and less than a year after that she became a widow and went back to her father's place in Charles City County, west of Williamsburg.[9] After a decent interval she was doubtless in the provincial capital for part of the social season, and by the autumn of 1770 Jefferson had probably met her there. At all events, he gave Jupiter money to buy hair powder and buckles for him that fall and he bought many tickets for the play.

Perhaps he visited the Forest before December. Beyond a doubt he was there then, as he was regularly during the next year, tipping the servants with unfailing regularity and conducting himself generally in a handsome manner.[10] Early in 1771 he made inquiries about the coat of arms of his own family, though he did so with private display of wit. He asked a merchant friend, who oscillated between Virginia and England, to search the Herald's office for him. "I have what I have been told were the family arms," he said, "but on what authority I know not. It is possible there may be none. If so, I would with your assistance become a purchaser, having Sterne's word for it that a coat of arms may be purchased as cheap as any other coat." [11] He was in no parsimonious mood, however; and he did not scorn "the costly apparatus of life." He purposed to carry on his line in a distinguished manner, and he was aware of the fact that Martha belonged to a wealthy family.

She was the eldest daughter of John Wayles, who was born in Lancaster, England, and had acquired a large legal practice in Virginia — more because of his industry and practicality than his learning, Jeffer-

---

[8] Born Jan. 2, 1770; *W. & M.*, 1 ser., XV, 117.

[9] Death notice of Bathurst Skelton in Purdie & Dixon, *Va. Gazette*, Oct. 6, 1768.

[10] Various items in Account Book.

[11] To Thomas Adams, Feb. 20, 1771 (Ford, I, 388–389). Attempts to trace this inquiry have been unsuccessful up to the present, though there is evidence that Jefferson used a coat of arms to some degree, whether or not he was technically entitled to do so. The best documentary evidence is a wax seal on a letter to Jan Ingenhousz, July 9, 1787 (original in Am. Philos. Soc.). This agrees essentially with the coats of arms reproduced on the cover of *Domestic Life* and by Curtis in *The True Thomas Jefferson* (1901), p. 18. It should also be noted that he later used a seal bearing the motto, "Rebellion to Tyrants is Obedience to God," though this had no connection with any coat of arms.

son thought.[12] More important still, he had acquired a large landed estate, along with debts which were considerable but seemed to be amply covered. Jefferson and others found him a most agreeable man, and he conducted his extensive affairs in a generous and optimistic spirit.

Her mother had died soon after Martha was born, leaving no other children. She was of the prominent Eppes family, which had been associated to some degree with the early Jeffersons, and by her marriage settlement she had assured her descendants of certain inherited lands and slaves. There were three other girls in the family, the daughters of another of John Wayles's wives. One of these girls, Elizabeth, who played an important part in the family life of Jefferson later on, may already have married Francis Eppes, first cousin of Martha, and another was engaged. John Wayles had three wives and lost all of them. The third one was the widow of Reuben Skelton. Martha had added to the genealogical confusion by marrying his brother Bathurst.[13]

That alliance had proved short-lived, and by the early months of 1771 Jefferson wanted to offer her another. He found her responsive but he was discouraged at first by his failure to solve the housing problem.[14] In June his prospect of becoming "more regularly a paterfamilias" were much brighter, and he then made an important change in the order he had previously given to his merchant friend. By that time he had seen a "forte-piano" and he now wanted that sort of instrument instead of a clavichord. Purposing to give this to Martha, he desired the case to be of fine mahogany, solid not veneered, and the workmanship very handsome. Also, he ordered for himself some stockings of the best quality, along with "a large umbrella with brass ribs, covered with green silk, and neatly finished." He was impatient for these articles, particularly the piano, and predicted rather humorously that his orders would be somewhat enlarged thereafter. It was at this date, also, that he sought a builder to help him at Monticello; things were moving on the mountain but not as fast as he liked and he himself could not be there all the time.[15]

He may not yet have set up in his books his account with the estate of Bathurst Skelton; but about this time he opened another one prematurely. This was for John Skelton, son of Bathurst, with himself as guardian in behalf of Martha his wife. He made an entry on account

[12] Autobiography, Ford, I, 6.
[13] See Appendix I, D, for genealogical details.
[14] To James Ogilvie, Feb. 20, 1771 (Ford, I, 390–391).
[15] To Thomas Adams, June 1, 1771 (Ford, I, 395). He said "an architect," but was probably using the term loosely.

of the boy but attached no figures. He was not to acquire a stepson, after all, for John Skelton died in the summer before the marriage, not yet having reached the age of four.[16] John was only a fleeting memory to Jefferson, though possibly a poignant one since he was exceedingly fond of children. Martha was a present reality and a future hope. Writing to his prospective brother-in-law late that summer, he avowed his sentiments for her in language of formal extravagance which sounds artificial to the modern ear: "Offer prayers for me too at that shrine to which tho' absent I pray continual devotions. In every scheme of happiness she is placed in the foreground of the picture, as the principal figure. Take that away, and it is no picture for me." [17] Somewhat later, within the Wayles family circle, he referred to her as Patty but he closely guarded that intimate name.

The surviving descriptions of her are meager, and there is none contemporary with these events. In comparison with him, she certainly was not tall; as an old slave put it, she was "low." The tradition is that her figure was slight, though well-formed, that she had large hazel eyes and luxuriant auburn hair. Within the family much was said afterwards about her beauty, and this can be accepted in essence though not in full detail.[18] Jefferson himself was straight and strong and his countenance was not unpleasing, but he was not a handsome man; beyond a doubt he prided himself on winning a pretty wife. There is considerable evidence of her amiability and her sprightliness of manner.[19] Her gaiety of spirit offset the characteristic seriousness of her lover; in her presence he could unbend. Gentle and sympathetic people always attracted him most, and clearly she was that sort, though she may have had her fiery moments before childbearing wore her out.

She was not only a "pretty lady" but an accomplished one in the customary ways, and her love for music was a special bond with him. She played on the harpsichord and the pianoforte, as he did on the violin and the cello. The tradition is that music provided the accompaniment for his successful suit: his rivals are said to have departed in admitted defeat after hearing him play and sing with her.[20] In later years he had the cheerful habit of singing and humming to himself as he went about his plantation. This is not proof in itself that he was a pleasing vocal performer, but with Martha in the parlor it was probably

[16] The date given in his copied memorandum is June 10, 1771. The account is in his Fee Book.

[17] To Robert Skipwith, Aug. 3, 1771 (Ford, I, 399).

[18] The flattering account in Randall, I, 63–64, was based on the tradition.

[19] Robert Skipwith to Jefferson, Sept. 20, 1771; MHS. Comments from later years will be given hereafter.

[20] Randall, I, 64.

easier for him to sing than it ever was afterwards.[21] By this time he had found opportunity to take violin lessons in Williamsburg from Francis Alberti, who had come to the capital as a player and had remained as a teacher.[22] Martha is said to have taken lessons on the harpsichord from the same man. No doubt she shared Jefferson's enthusiasm when he induced the Italian to come to Monticello at some time after the wedding, and to continue to give instruction there.

Jefferson tried to get a better violin for himself, as well as the handsome pianoforte for his future wife. He is said to have carried with him on his early travels a "kit" or small fiddle, on which he played at odd moments with a minimum of annoyance to his hosts; and he had purchased an instrument for five pounds in Williamsburg.[23] He now had his eye on the fine violin which John Randolph had imported; and during the spring that he went most often to the Forest he made an agreement with the Attorney General which George Wythe and Patrick Henry witnessed, among others.[24] He was to get this prized instrument if he survived his friend, and Randolph was to get books of his to a high value if things went the other way. The bargain was somewhat jocular and it seems one-sided, unless Jefferson felt pretty confident that he would be the survivor. Actually, he did get Randolph's violin four years later under circumstances which he had no reason to predict. He was not now thinking of revolution and his wishes were well expressed by another. "May business and play, music and the merriment of your family lighten your hearts," said his prospective brother-in-law.[25]

During the fall of 1771 he had to do something besides visit Martha. He had to go to court in Williamsburg and to get himself re-elected to the House of Burgesses, among other things. By this time he had decided that the legal business of Robert Carter Nicholas was an additional burden which he could not assume. His declination was not wholly because of the demands of his own practice; there were other important matters to be attended to.[26] On Christmas Eve he set out with Jupiter from Monticello on his way to be married, but he did not arrive until after Christmas Day. Francis Eppes signed the wedding bond with him and he paid forty shillings for the license on the last day of the old year; the wedding was on the first day of the new. Two

[21] H. W. Pierson, *Jefferson at Monticello*, p. 86; ms. Life of Isaac Jefferson, UVA.
[22] First reference in Account Book, Jan. 31, 1768. See Randall, I, 131–132, for the tradition; here, however, Alberti is wrongly named Dominico.
[23] Account Book, May 25, 1768.
[24] Apr. 11, 1771 (Ford, I, 392).
[25] Robert Skipwith to Jefferson, Sept. 20, 1771; MHS.
[26] Oct. 31, 1771, Case Book, No. 612; Randall, I, 49.

clergymen were present and there was at least one fiddler. The atmosphere must have been gay, and in due course the servants were well tipped.[27]

The homeward trip was delayed by a stay of more than two weeks at the Forest — in whatever seclusion the couple could find. In mid-January they set out in a phaeton, which had already been mended at Shirley and had to be mended again at Tuckahoe. Not until they left the hospitable seat of the Randolphs where the bridegroom had lived as a boy did silence fall. He then ceased keeping his accounts. Before the end of the month they were at Monticello, where the ground was covered with three feet of snow. The story is that they arrived late at night, having left the phaeton at Colonel Carter's Blenheim, and proceeded eight miles over a mountain road on horseback, only to find that the fires were out and the servants were all in bed.[28] Martha's introduction to her unfinished home may have been discouraging, but she had her husband's company for a couple of uninterrupted months. The House of Burgesses met without him in February and he did not go to Williamsburg on legal business until the mountainside was green.

The leaves had only begun to turn in late September when their first child was born, an hour after midnight. Like so many others on both sides of the family she was named Martha. For six months they wondered if she would survive; then she "was recovered almost instantaneously by a good breast of milk" — supplied by a Negro wet-nurse no doubt. This experience convinced her father, who already had little confidence in medicine as then practised, that it was better to rely on nature than doctors, especially in the case of infants.[29] After this early fright it fortunately turned out that Patsy — as she was called in the family — had inherited her father's robust constitution as well as his sanguine temperament, and she was a comfort to him to the end of his life.

Not until eighteen months after the birth of Patsy was there another baby; meanwhile, the health of the mother excited no comment and presumably was satisfactory. During the early part of Jefferson's second year as a married man he was often away from home, and by the spring of 1773 the political pot had begun to simmer. But these were pleasant months on the mountain — that is, until tragic events occurred in May.

The first of these and the more shocking was the death of Dabney Carr, who was not yet thirty. Jefferson's friend had made marked

---

[27] Account Book, Dec. 1771, Jan. 1772.
[28] Family story, told by Martha Jefferson Randolph, in Randall, I, 64; *Garden Book*, Jan. 26, 1772.
[29] To T. M. Randolph, Oct. 19, 1792, recounting the experience (LC, 78:13465).

progress at the bar; practising in the same courts as Patrick Henry, he had become the most serious forensic rival of that orator who had yet appeared. He had recently made an impressive debut in the House of Burgesses, which Jefferson had partly contrived and of which he was always proud. He was more prosperous now than he had been soon after Peter Carr was born. He was in Charlottesville when he died of bilious fever; Dr. George Gilmer, who now lived near by at Pen Park and attended all the Jeffersons, was unable to combat it.

The family tradition is that the burial was at Shadwell, before Jefferson could return to Albemarle from Williamsburg. Within a week, however, he set two men grubbing a graveyard on his mountain, beneath an oak tree where he and Dabney are reputed to have read and talked together and to have agreed that they should both lie someday. Soon he had the remains of his friend interred at this spot. This was not the fanciful burying ground which he had conjured out of his earlier romantic melancholy; it was a plot of only eighty square feet. But from that time it was a hallowed place.[30]

He believed that of all men living he loved Dabney Carr the most, and he was performing a deeply sentimental act. Yet he noted with cool precision how many hours were required for the grubbing and calculated that one laborer could do an acre in four days at that rate. Also, he recorded the fact that the first peas had come to the table and calmly observed that it had been a remarkably forward spring. He was never one to give free expression to his emotions; and he was quite in character in turning for relief to figures, to garden peas and the weather, to the prosaic affairs of every day. This strong, strange man did not wear his heart upon his sleeve.

His eagerness to perform friendly service was shown in his efforts to provide for the legal business of Dabney Carr. He never lost touch with the affairs of his widowed sister, and her six children found in him a second father. She stood beside him some years later in his own hour of greatest sorrow, and by that time her family had joined his; he himself was then teaching little Peter as he would have his own son.[31]

Soon after the grubbers vanished from the graveyard word came of the death of John Wayles.[32] This was less tragic, for he was a widower

---

[30] *Garden Book*, May 22, 1773, and p. 44; Plate XXI shows the location. See also *Domestic Life*, p. 47.

[31] To William Fleming, May 19, 1773; Ford, I, 415. See Appendix I, C, note 3, for his relations with the Carrs; and Wirt, *Patrick Henry*, p. 89, for a good comment on Dabney.

[32] May 28, 1773, recorded in Account Book on May 31.

of fifty-eight and his children were all grown or nearly so. Jefferson liked him and undoubtedly mourned his loss but from the practical point of view there were compensations; the result was the doubling of his own estate. He became involved in a maze of financial transactions as one of the executors, along with his brothers-in-law, Francis Eppes and Henry Skipwith. When he went to the Forest in July and acquired from a servant there at an odd moment a couple of mockingbirds, he could hardly have anticipated how vexing and protracted these affairs would be. The immediate prospect was distinctly favorable.[33]

The division of the property was made in 1774, two years after his marriage. Jefferson then acquired, on behalf of Martha, more than eleven thousand acres of land. His father-in-law had left a heavy debt to an English mercantile firm, however, and he promptly sold some six thousand acres in order to meet his proportionate share of this. The net effect of the inheritance was to add to his own possessions Poplar Forest in Bedford County, and Elk Island and Elkhill in Goochland. The latter place played a part in his history through the Revolution, but only Poplar Forest was permanently retained. Early in the fall after John Wayles died he made his first recorded visit to this favorite seat of his later years.[34]

There was one difficulty but it seemed small at the time. He did not get cash for the lands he sold; rarely could anybody get that in Virginia. He received from the purchasers what he called bonds and we should call notes; and the English creditors of John Wayles would not accept these in settlement, preferring Jefferson's bond. Accordingly, though his share of the debt was covered it was not paid. As things turned out, he was not able to collect from his own creditors until after the currency had depreciated and was compelled to provide for his inherited debt all over again. In the year 1774, however, he had no reason to anticipate this misfortune, and he was fully warranted in thinking of himself as a wealthy man.

So far as his own patrimony was concerned, his operations from this date through the Revolution consisted primarily in disposing of outlying lands and acquiring others nearer home. Outside of the County he acquired by patent one bit of property which greatly interested him. It contained Natural Bridge, which he afterwards described as the most sublime of the works of nature.[35] In round figures he had some

[33] Ford, I, 6; Account Book, July 9, 1773. For details of transactions and the later history of the Wayles inheritance, see Appendix II, B, 3.
[34] Sept. 8, 1773; Garden Book, p. 42.
[35] It was in this period that he acquired Lego, north of the Rivanna. For details of transactions see Appendix II, B, 2. Comment on Natural Bridge in Ford, III, 109.

five thousand acres from his own patrimony, concentrated in Albemarle; and about that many outside the County from the Wayles estate. The immediate effect of his wife's inheritance, however, was more than the doubling of his ease of circumstances, for his slaves were increased at a higher rate. By this time he had somewhat more than 50 in his own right, and he listed 135 whom he held on behalf of his wife. At Monticello, domestic servants were abundant and a number of the favorites came into his possession through her. Ursula, the fat woman who nursed Patsy and later children, and her husband "King" George, had been acquired for Mrs. Jefferson, while the noted Hemings family, who were mostly "bright" mulattoes, came through the Wayles estate. Jefferson was kind to his servants to the point of indulgence, and within the framework of an institution he disliked he saw that they were well provided for. His "people" were devoted to him; and they made his home life comfortable and jolly.

Now that he had so many slaves, or as he said "servants," and so much land, he had to expand his records. In the year 1774 he began his Farm Book.[36] Through force of circumstances, however, his personal interest in agriculture was not fully manifested for a score of years.[37] Public affairs had not yet disrupted his life but he was still a busy lawyer, and he gave less personal attention to his farms than to his home. The plantation seat was the center of life in Virginia, and particularly so with him. Bricks were still being molded and burned at Monticello and building was going on. By this time he had had at least one of the "roundabouts" made; four of these ultimately encircled the mountain, being connected by oblique roads.[38] He had kept on planting fruit trees, and in the spring of 1774, soon after the peaches had come into full bloom, he laid out a permanent vegetable garden on the southeastern slope between the orchard and the first roundabout. It was to have at each end a rectangular isosceles triangle, and he gave specific measurements for the hypotenuse and legs.[39]

During his wife's second confinement he stayed close by, diverting himself and making himself useful by planting vegetables. In the beds he put numbered sticks and in his record he rendered homely names in Italian. Thus garlic appeared as *Aglio di Toscania*, but, although this variety came originally from Tuscany, it was only garlic by any name. Succory or wild endive was put down as *Radicchio di Pistoia;* a white onion was *Cipolle bianche di Tuckahoe;* and beans given him

---

[36] Original at MHS, photostat UVA. Now being edited by E. M. Betts.
[37] See Appendix II, B, 2.
[38] *Garden Book*, Nov. 12, 1772, and p. 38.
[39] *Ibid.*, Mar. 31, 1774, and Plates IV, V.

by somebody across the mountains were *Fagiuoli d'Augusta*.[40] The Italian names reflect the influence of a new neighbor. Philip Mazzei was a friend of his in two Revolutions, and figured in a historic controversy relating to George Washington into which Jefferson fell a score of years after he met the enthusiastic Florentine on the little mountain in Albemarle.[41] Their early association provides the first striking example of Jefferson's penchant for international friendship and illustrates other ways of his.

Mazzei was something of a Benvenuto Cellini in his youth, according to his own report, and as such would hardly have appealed to Jefferson; but he had come to Virginia with the useful purpose of planting vineyards and was under the patronage of the very merchant, Thomas Adams, from whom Jefferson had ordered a pianoforte. Immediately upon his arrival in the Province, he and his laborers had gone temporarily to the home of Francis Eppes. Then, with Adams, he had set out for the Shenandoah Valley, where the latter had property and hoped Mazzei would settle. It was unfortunate for these plans that they stopped for an evening at Monticello. This was in November, 1773.[42]

Early the next morning, Mazzei and his host got up before the others, thus revealing one of the latter's habits. Jefferson took him for a considerable walk, showed him a tract of land which he could buy, and offered to give, or more probably to lend, him some of his own land. On their return, Adams, on looking at Jefferson, said: "I see by your expression that you've taken him away from me. I knew you would do that." [43] The host smiled and suggested that they have breakfast. He was never backward when given the opportunity to acquire and keep an interesting acquaintance. He got Mazzei established near by at Colle, keeping him as a guest until his house was built. Soon a dozen Italian workmen arrived, and to their delight the tall, friendly Virginian, who cultivated the linguistic arts as he did his garden, talked with them in Tuscan, which he had picked up unaided.

Thus did Jefferson help introduce Italian wines and vegetables into the red-clay country, and with them new varieties of spades and bill-hooks and a novel sort of hunting coat. The vineyards, though cultivated diligently for several years, did not prove permanent; but some

---

[40] *Ibid.*, pp. 47, 51.

[41] His famous letter to Mazzei, Apr. 24, 1796, is in Ford, VII, 72–78.

[42] *Memoirs of ... Philip Mazzei*, pp. 165–166, 192–193; R. C. Garlick, Jr., *Philip Mazzei, Friend of Jefferson*, pp. 40–47.

[43] *Memoirs*, p. 192.

of the vignerons merged with the population.[44] Jefferson, who had subscribed to the wine company, added to his own cellar, which had previously contained chiefly rum, Madeira, port, and small beer. From Mazzei he got certain delicacies of food, such as anchovies, but he paid generously; in this, as in most of his friendships, he gave more than he received.[45] An exception should be made in the matter of talk, for he finally admitted that Mazzei wore him out.

Other events in his domestic life before he entered more actively upon his public career can be described from his Account Book for 1774.

March 1. My sister Elizabeth was found last Thursday being Feb. 24.

4. Sent my mother a quarter of stalled beef 118 lbs. weighed by Mr. Bryan for which charge @ 20/ comes to 23/8.

6. A flood in the rivanna 18f. higher than the one which carried N. Lewis's bridge away and that was the highest ever known except the great flood of May 1771.

7. Sold my two old book cases to Mr. [Charles] Clay for £5 of which credit him 40/ for performing the funeral service this day on burying my sister, Elizabeth, & 40/ more for preaching Mr. Carr's funeral sermon, which last sum charge to D. Carr's estate. The other 20/ is a gratuity.

10. Took admn. of E. Jefferson's estate.[46]

These prosaic entries mark the end of one of Peter Jefferson's children, who had wandered both in body and in mind. The details of the sad story were buried with the victim, and at Monticello itself the balance was soon redressed. At about eleven o'clock on the morning of April 3, Martha Wayles Jefferson gave birth to another daughter, who was named Jane Randolph for her grandmother. At least she survived long enough to acquire a name. She lived about eighteen months, to be exact. The personal prosperity of her father was now at its height and his domestic tranquillity was relatively unmarred. Until he took the turn of the road which led straight to political revolution, joys had predominated over cares and sorrows and he was an enviably happy man.

[44] Jefferson to Gallatin, Jan. 25, 1793 (L. & B., IX, 14–15).
[45] Account Book, Sept. 13, 1772; Dec. 3, 1773.
[46] *Ibid.*, 1774. The first four items are successive.

Revolting Against an Empire

[XIII]

The Growth of a Political Mind

FOR more than two years after his marriage Jefferson's activities were largely personal and professional. This was not merely because of domestic circumstances and his own inclination; it was owing even more to the conditions of the times. The longstanding but intermittent quarrel with the Mother Country did not become acute until the spring of 1774, when the teapot really began to boil. He had not attained "a marked grade in politics" by then, and he did not become a public character in the full sense until some months afterwards.[1] But he had already identified himself with the most aggressive group of the local patriots, and upon occasion he had been exceedingly active behind the scenes. What was more important, he had given much thought to fundamental political questions while the imperial controversialists appeared to be marking time.

He absented himself from the meeting of the House of Burgesses just after his marriage, for personal reasons his colleagues could easily understand; and after that the Governor saved the young husband trouble by keeping the Assembly prorogued for another year. His Excellency John Murray, Earl of Dunmore, Viscount Fincastle, Baron of Blair, of Moulin, and of Tillymont, undoubtedly believed that he was sparing himself difficulty as well. This Scottish peer, who had come to the governorship of the Province of Virginia from that of New York, had been received with the honors befitting one who was so many times a lord, but it soon appeared that he was a man of different temper from his courtly predecessor. The spirited Virginians did not like his haughty airs. Jefferson himself disliked arrogance as he did few other qualities, and Dunmore was probably the first high British official in whom he observed it. He had no particular personal contacts with the Governor, unless it was at Dunmore's instance that he drew plans for

[1] Edmund Randolph in *Va. Mag.*, XLIII, 122.

the enlargement of the College of William and Mary and the alteration of the Palace.[2] But he was on hand in the spring of 1773 when Dunmore ran into his first serious political difficulties, and he then played a characteristically patriotic part.

The Governor would have preferred to get along without the Assembly, but he had to call it because of forgeries of paper currency which the Treasurer had detected. The burgesses, including Jefferson, attended to this special business when they met in the month of March. While complimenting the Governor on his energy in bringing the counterfeiters to justice, however, they rebuked him politely for the summary methods he had used. His Excellency replied to them tartly, and he wrote to his superior in England: they "seem at least obliquely in some degree to censure my conduct." There did not really seem to be much doubt about it.[3] He also said: "There are some resolves which show a little ill humour in the House of Burgesses, but I thought them so insignificant that I took no notice of them." He showed thereby either a deplorable lack of foresight or an unusual spirit of restraint. These resolves created a standing Committee of Correspondence, and constituted one of the more fateful acts in the preliminaries of the Revolution.[4] The Governor could still prorogue the Assembly but such action on his part was now rendered relatively ineffectual, for the Committee could continue to meet.

There had been an incident in Rhode Island, where a revenue vessel called the *Gaspee* had been burned, and the question of sending offenders to England for trial had come up again. Along with Patrick Henry, Richard Henry Lee, Francis Lightfoot Lee, Dabney Carr, and possibly some others, Jefferson had concluded that the old and leading members lacked the zeal which the times required. Accordingly, this little group met privately in the evenings at the Raleigh Tavern for consultation. They were all convinced, he said, that the greatest need was for unity of colonial action. This could hardly have been attained during the next few years without the Committees of Correspondence. There had previously been local committees in Massachusetts but Jefferson himself never had any doubt that the one in Virginia was the first that was set up to represent a colony as a whole.[5] He never claimed that the original idea was his, and credit for it seems to belong

[2] Waterman, *Mansions of Virginia*, pp. 394–398. He speaks more confidently about the College than he does about the Palace.

[3] *Burgesses, Journals*, 1773–1776, pp. ix–xi.

[4] Mar. 12, 1773 (*Ibid.*, p. 28); Dunmore's comment, p. x.

[5] "Autobiography," in Ford, I, 7–9; to S. A. Wells, May 12, 1819, *Ibid.*, X, 128. On the general subject see E. D. Collins, in *Annual Report Am. Hist. Asso., 1901,* I (1902), 345–371.

to Richard Henry Lee. He did say that his group drafted the resolutions, that he was asked to introduce them, and that he gained that privilege for Dabney Carr, who thus made his political debut in connection with an important action. Both of them attended the first meeting of the committee of eleven, but neither was appointed to the select committee of three, which was distinctly more conservative in temper. Nonetheless, he and his brother-in-law helped create an agency which was designed to tie the colonial patriots together and which undoubtedly served to promote the revolt against the Empire.[6]

But the time for open revolt was still not ripe, and Dunmore continued to save him trouble by proroguing the Assembly. It did not meet again until May, 1774, and it was in this interim of a year that Dabney Carr and John Wayles died, that he had to take care of his wife's large inheritance, that he induced Philip Mazzei and his vignerons to settle near Monticello. Not until after the birth of his second daughter did he have much freedom or occasion to engage in important public business.

There had been grave developments in the sphere of imperial relations in the meantime. Dunmore was probably wise, from his restricted point of view, in putting off the Assembly as long as he could; but his timing proved to be bad, for news of fresh woes in Boston reached Williamsburg during the session. The British officials had blundered into a major crisis. They had caused the hated tea tax to become a highly visible reality and had united colonial opposition by permitting the East India Company to import tea direct, to the injury of American merchants.[7] The cargoes of some of the ships had met a spectacular fate in Boston, and the Virginians now learned that Parliament had passed the Port Act. According to Jefferson, this involved the "utter ruin" of a prosperous commercial city. The tinder had been laid for some time and a spark had now ignited it. The question was whether the fire would rage only in the vicinity of Boston or would sweep down the seaboard. He was one of those who helped it spread.

A neighbor of George Washington's, whose mind was more like Thomas Jefferson's, was in Williamsburg on private business during that fateful month of May. George Mason commented informally on the situation, saying much in praise of Patrick Henry. "Whatever resolves or measures are intended for the preservation of our rights and liberties, will be reserved for the conclusion of the session," he pre-

[6] Eckenrode, *Revolution in Va.*, p. 33; Henry, *Patrick Henry*, I, 162; *Burgesses, Journals*, 1773–1776, pp. 41–43.

[7] A. M. Schlesinger, *Colonial Merchants and the American Revolution* (1918), pp. 262–264.

dicted. "Matters of that sort here are conducted and prepared with a great deal of privacy, and by very few members; of whom Patrick Henry is the principal. At the request of the gentlemen concerned, I have spent an evening with them upon the subject." [8] Jefferson was probably one of these "very few members," and he certainly belonged to a little group who were now plotting privately about means of taking "an unequivocal stand in the line with Massachusetts."

He and his fellows had "cooked up" something by the time that Mason wrote. He himself has been given the major credit for the idea of a general day of fasting and prayer to signalize the closing of the port of Boston, and as the most scholarly member of the party he probably did most of the rummaging for precedents and Puritan forms. He did not introduce the pious resolutions, however. He and the others wisely induced Robert Carter Nicholas, whose character was more grave and religious, to do that. Nobody in the House of Burgesses dissented. Lord Dunmore did not stop with the prorogation of the Assembly this time; he dissolved it. He claimed that this paper reflected highly upon the King and Parliament, but the most significant of its phrases was the one that spoke of "our sister colony of Massachusetts Bay." [9]

Jefferson was among the great body of burgesses who proceeded to the Raleigh Tavern and signed another Association, and he soon attended a meeting of the Committee of Correspondence which ordered that letters be sent to similar committees elsewhere, about the calling of a general congress. [10] If he did not march to Bruton Church with other former burgesses on June 1, in solemn defiance of Lord Dunmore, it was only because he was not in town; and he and John Walker called for a patriotic service of prayer in his parish in Albemarle, without bothering to consult the Governor. [11] The purpose of this, as proclaimed in words which he no doubt wrote, was "devoutly to implore the divine interposition in behalf of an injured and oppressed people." The people met generally throughout the Province, he said,

[8] Mason to Martin Cockburn, May 26, 1774; Rowland, I, 169.

[9] Ford, I, 9–10; Burgesses, Journals, 1773–1776, p. 124.

[10] Burgesses, Journals, 1773–1776, p. 138. In connection with the Association it is said that Mason, Henry, R. H. Lee, and Nicholas were "for paying no debts to Britain"; James Parker to Charles Steuart, June 17, 1774, in Mag. of History, III (March, 1906), 153. I have found no evidence that Jefferson made this proposal, as stated in Brant, Madison, p. 141.

[11] Purdie & Dixon, Va. Gazette, June 2, 1774; Ford, I, 418. The Account Book implies that Jefferson was not in Williamsburg on June 1. The sermon in St. Anne's parish was to be preached by the Reverend Charles Clay, with whom he had had numerous personal contacts. He himself had been elected a vestryman but it is uncertain whether he ever served; see Meade, II, 49.

with anxiety and alarm in their faces, and the effect was "like a shock of electricity, arousing every man and placing him erect and solidly on his centre." [12] He had helped translate the local grievance of Boston into a common cause, and unquestionably he himself was among the first to be electrified.

His distinguished contemporary John Adams, writing to him long afterwards, said that the real revolution in America was "in the minds of the people" and was effected between 1760 and 1775, before a drop of blood was shed at Lexington. [13] The observation can be readily applied to Jefferson with only minor changes in words and dates. He had strongly armed his mind before critical events occurred, and was more than ready for them when they came. He never did set forth his political philosophy in full and systematic form, but he gave valuable clues to its development. He went through an evolutionary rather than a revolutionary process, and with him thought long preceded action and determined its direction in advance.

His early study had not been concentrated on problems of government. It was naturally centered on the law until he was admitted to the bar and it probably continued to be for a good many months after that. But he left place in his rigorous schedule of reading for what he called "politics," and he laid great emphasis on the history of legal doctrines and institutions. By no means the least of his services to his own Commonwealth during the Revolution were in the technical field of law, and these were made possible only by the knowledge which he had laboriously acquired as a student and a practitioner and to which he made additions after he ceased attending court.

The step from the study of law to that of government was so short that he could easily have taken it without any special deliberation. It would have been strange indeed if he had not given some thought to political theory and done some reading on the subject while he was inquiring so diligently into legal origins. It is reasonable to suppose, however, that his interest in general political questions was stimulated by his entrance into the House of Burgesses, when he assumed his traditional responsibilities as a public man; and unquestionably it was accentuated thereafter by his growing awareness of the fundamental problems which must be solved. [14]

[12] Ford, I, 12. He had forgotten that the meetings were not all held on the same day.

[13] Adams to Jefferson, Aug. 24, 1815 (*Works*, X, 172).

[14] Chinard, *Commonplace Book*, pp. 4–14, gives invaluable clues to the chronology of Jefferson's early reading. In *Jefferson, the Road to Glory*, pp. 209–210. Mrs. Kimball cites a bill of books, including works of Locke and Montesquieu,

Throughout life he was deeply interested in the application of knowledge to human affairs, and with him human affairs came to include a great deal of government. In old age he spoke of the "enormities" of the times in which he had happened to live, and lamented that they had deflected him from the delightful pursuit of knowledge. They did not really deflect him, for he continued to study assiduously and to deal in applied scholarship throughout his long generation in public life. The real effect of circumstance was to direct his reading and thinking into political channels to a greater degree than he had expected, and thus to restrict somewhat the scope of his intellectual activities, though most people would regard these as quite broad enough.

The dates of the various entries in his notebooks cannot be determined with entire confidence; and, even if they could be, the works that he cited cannot be assumed to have been the source of his ideas. These ideas he shared to greater or less degree with his contemporaries and he could have plucked many of them from the air. In numerous instances the printed page served him chiefly by providing confirmation or clarification of beliefs and opinions that he already held. Beyond any question, however, he prepared himself with extraordinary care to meet the issues of his time. He gave a positive answer to the challenge of one of the ancient writers whom he had made a companion of in his youth:

> . . . For with slight efforts how should one obtain great results? It is foolish even to desire it.[15]

It is a more important fact that he read widely and stored his mind with riches than that he abstracted particular writings. More important still was the spirit of fearless inquiry in which he pursued knowledge. Years after he made his extracts from the history of the common law, he described them in words which can be applied just as well to his notes on the subject of government:

> They were written at a time of life when I was bold in the pursuit of knowledge, never fearing to follow truth and reason to whatever results they led, and bearding every authority which stood in their way.[16]

---

which he ordered in 1769, as indicating a sharp change in his interest at that time. (Bill dated Sept. 19, 1769; VHS.) In view of the scarcity of his early book lists this is an important item, but I shall not attempt to date the history of his thought so precisely.

[15] From Euripides (*Literary Bible*, p. 92).

[16] To Thomas Cooper, Feb. 10, 1814; L. & B., XIV, 85.

Before he seriously thought of independence from Great Britain he himself had attained full intellectual freedom and had let his mind take him where it would, regardless of authority. There were, however, two significant exceptions: he found moral sanctions in the monitor within every human breast, and he found them in the laws of nature. In each case he was performing an act of faith, but the results were by no means unfavorable to the cause of liberty.

Before the imperial crisis became acute in 1774–1775 and he first had occasion to present his political ideas in an important way, the doctrine of natural rights was one of his postulates. Just where he got it is a fascinating question, but one to which it seems impossible to give a specific answer. If he did not draw on John Locke in the first place but got the ideas of that noted writer secondhand, he certainly had his very phraseology by heart in 1776.[17] The simplest explanation of his failure to copy much from Locke in his student notebooks is that he was familiar with his most important ideas already. For the same reason, probably, he did not bother to copy extracts about natural rights from the writings of other prominent exponents of the theory.[18] Having accepted the doctrine as a disciple of the Enlightenment, he took it for granted ever thereafter, just as he did the freedom of the mind.

Like so many of his "enlightened" contemporaries, Jefferson believed that men had originally been in a state of nature; that they had then been free to order their own actions and to dispose of their own persons and property as they saw fit; that government was instituted among them in the first place by consent. In the Declaration of Independence he summarized the current doctrine in its classic American form. Two years before that, describing colonial grievances and ostensibly addressing the King, he spoke "with that freedom of language and sentiment which becomes a free people claiming their rights, as derived from the laws of nature, and not as the gift of their chief magistrate." Even as early as 1770, he had said publicly that under the law of nature all men are born free.[19]

Jefferson said relatively little at any time about the social contract which was supposed to have preceded the formation of society; when

[17] Admirable discussion in Becker, *Declaration of Independence*, ch. 2; valuable specific comments in Chinard, *Commonplace Book*, pp. 41–44, 54; learned discussion of alleged differences from Locke in R. B. Perry, *Puritanism and Democracy*, pp. 184–187.

[18] Such as Lord Kames; see Chinard, *Commonplace Book*, pp. 16–19, and arts. 557–568.

[19] Ford, I, 380, 445.

he referred to contracts or compacts he generally meant charters, constitutions, or other formal agreements of the historical sort. Even if the hypothetical prehistoric contract had been successfully challenged in his day, as it was afterwards, it is practically inconceivable that he would have surrendered his conviction that men were born to freedom and not to slavery, for with him this was a profound moral conviction.[20] He did not use his terms with the precision of an academic philosopher and in papers directed to particular occasions he did not bother to define them; but in the early stage of his political career he employed the term "right" primarily in a moral sense. He was confident that force could not give it, and that it could derive from no king. He found its source in the universal law of nature; it arose from the nature of things. "The God who gave us life gave us liberty at the same time," he said.[21] Nothing less could have been expected of God, for liberty was right, just as force was wrong. He was far from being a cynic. He never ceased to believe that good, not evil, lay at the heart of the universe; and it was this faith that kept him from being a mere intellectual and gave him his rare quality of spiritual leadership.

He clearly recognized the radical implications of the doctrine of natural rights when he applied it in 1770, prematurely, to the institution of slavery. Accepting the doctrine as wholeheartedly as he did, he could not have failed to judge other time-honored but unjust institutions by its universal standard. Besides being an honest thinker, however, he was practical; and during the years that he was formulating his own ideal he considered the characteristics and merits of various forms of government. This he did, presumably, when reading Montesquieu's *Esprit des Lois*. At a later time he turned against this noted writer, especially because of his predilection for things British and his assertion that a republic could be effective only if its territory was small. Before he himself revolted against the British monarchy, however, he had copied into his notebook in the French numerous quotations from Montesquieu, with summaries and reflections of his own. Thus he commented:

> He [Montesquieu] considers political virtue or the Amor Patriae, as the energetic principle of a democratic republic; moderation, that of an aristocratic republic; honor, that of a limited monarchy; and fear, that of a despotism; and shews that every government should provide that it's energetic principle should be the object of the education of it's youth.

[20] Excellent discussion in Koch, *Philosophy of Thomas Jefferson*, ch. 15
[21] Ford, I, 447.

That it's laws also should be relative to the same principle. In a democracy, equality and frugality should be promoted by the laws, as they nurse the amor patriae. . . .[22]

The order in which these four forms of government were listed — democratic republic, aristocratic republic, limited monarchy, and despotism — was precisely that of his own preference in the ripeness of his political maturity. But the only one of them which we can be absolutely sure that he strongly opposed before the imperial crisis became acute was the last. From the moment that he embraced the cause of intellectual liberty and human progress it had been utterly impossible for him to favor a despotism; from his early manhood the beacon by which he steered his bark was hope, not fear. On the other hand, if he had regarded the existing English government as really a limited monarchy, in which honor ruled, he probably could have lived under it happily for a good many years. It was in 1774 that he made a direct though wholly unsuccessful appeal to the King. Not until two years had passed and blood had actually been shed did he become an avowed republican. Within that brief period, however, his mind became fully prepared, not only for the Commonwealth of Virginia, but also for the Republic of federated states. He went to the pains of surveying with scholarly thoroughness the history of the various federative systems of Europe which might serve as models for the American experiment.[23]

In the light of the thinking he had already done, the avowal of republicanism which he made in 1776 at the age of thirty-three might easily have been anticipated. But there is a real question about his early attitude toward aristocracy and democracy, for he did not immediately challenge, and he never wholly repudiated, the tradition in which he himself had been bred. The society of Virginia was threatened with loss of fluidity now that the British policy had restricted its westward movement, but it was still characterized by a high sense of honor and a general spirit of moderation, as Montesquieu had said that a limited monarchy and an aristocratic republic ought to be. Jefferson himself was not only a fine gentleman whose fortunes had improved; he was also a recognized member of a ruling group which ruled well on the whole. He afterwards spoke of the "ciphers" of the aristocracy and undoubtedly there were such; but the contemporary record shows that he admired Peyton Randolph and Edmund Pendleton, as he afterwards did George Washington, and that he greatly valued the services which such intelligent and responsible leaders performed.

[22] Chinard, *Commonplace Book*, arts. 777–778, and pp. 31–38.
[23] *Ibid.*, pp. 24–28, and arts. 749–757, probably dating from 1774–1776.

It would have been surprising if he had wanted to substitute for leadership of this sort the rule of the uneducated crowd about whom so many grave doubts had been expressed by the ancient writers. The fact is that never in his life did he believe it necessary to choose between such alternatives. By the time of the Declaration of Independence he was convinced that aristocracies of birth and wealth were artificial and unjust, but what he sought to liberate and promote was a "natural" aristocracy of talent and virtue. He himself first appeared in the forum as one who had inherited a noble tradition of responsibility along with great privileges. It is exceedingly doubtful that he harbored any dreams of popular leadership at the outset, but there is abundant evidence that he was motivated from the first by the spirit of *noblesse oblige*.

The following quotation which he copied from Euripides reflects the mood of his student days rather than that of his maturity, but this sort of pride lingered in him for many years.

> To be of the noble born gives a peculiar distinction clearly marked among men, and the noble name increases in lustre in those who are worthy.[24]

His interest in a coat of arms had been expressed somewhat humorously, but he was fully aware of his own superior status and his first concern was to prove himself worthy of his privileges. Afterwards, the lamp by which he guided his feet was that of a reasoned and humane philosophy.

As a reasoning human being he weighed the merits of a democratic republic. He had read in Montesquieu that the right of suffrage is fundamental in such a government, because, as he himself observed, the people exercise their sovereignty by their votes.[25] The idea of popular sovereignty probably seemed to him a reasonable one when it first dawned upon him — much more reasonable, certainly, than the divine right of kings. Not until 1776, however, did he make any serious effort to extend the suffrage, and in practice his advocacy of a more democratic government was always conditioned by circumstances. This is another way of saying that his working philosophy was by no means devoid of common sense.

In the year 1774 his later actions could not have been predicted in detail, but there could be no possible doubt of the temper of his mind or of the trend which his thought had taken. He was essentially of the intellectual type, veering toward the utilitarian; he formed his maturing

---

[24] *Literary Bible*, pp. 10, 84.
[25] *Commonplace Book*, art. 776.

convictions in the light of the fullest information that he could obtain; and while freeing himself from the tyranny of ancient dogma he had revealed himself also as a man of faith. He embraced natural law while denying revelation, and he recognized in human reason and in the moral sense of the individual an authority which he would not grant to priests and kings. His chief concern was for the attainment and maintenance of liberty, and this provides the best single clue, not only to his motives in the Revolution but also to his entire career. It was not yet inevitable that he should revolt against the Empire, but it was little short of certain that he would be content with no external control which was more than nominal. Also, it could have been confidently predicted that he would assess local political institutions in the light of reason, and when the opportunity came would try to improve them. He regarded tyranny as wrong in theory and generally stupid in practice. There was no question in his mind that self-government was right in theory, and that in practice it was more likely than despotism to be intelligent. Being a believer in the educability of mankind, he might have been expected to favor the gradual but steady extension of self-government. His immediate concern, however, was to preserve it in the degree that it already existed in the American colonies.

[XIV]

Championing Colonial Rights
1774–1775

JEFFERSON'S chief literary contribution to the patriotic cause before the Declaration of Independence was made in the summer of 1774, somewhat by accident and under circumstances that were disappointing to him at the time. For quite different reasons the situation was discouraging to Lord Dunmore. Having dissolved one Assembly because of the solemn mischief which Jefferson and his little group of zealots had started, the Governor hopefully ordered the election of another one. He soon learned, however, that he was going to be confronted with the same determined faces, and hastened to prorogue the new body before all the returns were in. He did not permit the Assembly to convene, actually, until nearly a year had passed.

There was another meeting which he could not stop — a convention which was called for August in Williamsburg and consisted of the selfsame burgesses. He had no troops wherewith to disperse these resourceful gentlemen; they were unable to assemble officially with his consent but were quite able to do so unofficially without it. That is, most of them were; but unluckily Jefferson could not get there.

The freeholders of Albemarle, meeting in Charlottesville toward the end of July, 1774, conformed with the general pattern of procedure. They left their delegation exactly as it had been before by re-electing Jefferson and John Walker as their representatives.[1] Also, they adopted resolutions which the former had drawn. He elaborated these ideas, expecting to present them to the convention, but after he had set out for Williamsburg he was stricken with dysentery on the hot road and

---

[1] Reported, Purdie & Dixon, *Va. Gazette*, Aug. 4, 1774. See also June 16, 1774, supplement; and July 14, 1774.

forced to turn back.[2] Besides being unheroic in itself, this necessary retreat occurred at a most unfortunate time, for the crisis had incited him to put his thoughts in order and had emboldened him to essay a more conspicuous public role.

Perhaps he would not have moved any faster toward a position of commanding leadership if he had continued his journey to the provincial capital. He might have received more votes for delegate to the general Congress in Philadelphia if he had been present at the convention, but the seven who were actually chosen would probably have been elected in any case.[3] All the members of the delegation, which was headed inevitably by Peyton Randolph, were Jefferson's seniors in public life and better known than he; and they were generally regarded as "glowing patriots." George Washington stood third on the list, and Patrick Henry was fourth. Later in Virginia, Jefferson was described as the penman of the Revolution, as Washington was its sword and Henry its tongue; but no one of the three was pre-eminent as yet, and Jefferson least of all.

He foreshadowed his fame, however, by now appearing, not as a soldier or speaker, but as a writer. He had presented his ideas in the form of resolutions, which were to be moved as instructions to the Virginia delegates to Congress and then be embodied by Congress, he hoped, in an address to the King. Unable to be the bearer of his own paper, he sent it on in two copies, one of these he addressed to Peyton Randolph, whom he expected to preside, and the other to Patrick Henry. He never knew what happened to Henry's copy; probably that careless orator mislaid it somewhere. The other one was laid on the table for inspection and was read in the presence of a large number at Randolph's house, where it was applauded though not wholly approved. It was never acted on officially, but, without his knowledge, it was printed in Williamsburg as *A Summary View of the Rights of British America.* He did not supply the title and did not appear by name. Before the year was out it was reprinted in Philadelphia and appeared twice in England.[4] This accidental pamphlet of twenty-three

[2] Ford, I, 13, 418–420.

[3] Observation of Edmund Randolph, *Va. Mag.,* XLIII, 216–217. In order the delegates were: Peyton Randolph, Richard Henry Lee, George Washington, Patrick Henry, Richard Bland, Benjamin Harrison, and Edmund Pendleton. See also James Madison to William Bradford, Aug. 23, 1774 (Brant, *Madison,* p. 142). There was some unwarranted suspicion of Bland at the time.

[4] Ford, I, 421–447, with historical and bibliographical note and Jefferson's own corrections. It has been reproduced in facsimile from the 1st ed., with an excellent introduction and bibliographical note by T. P. Abernethy (New York, 1943), the note showing the location of copies. The text of all the editions is the same. The preface to the English editions has been attributed to Arthur Lee.

pages gained wider currency than any other writing of his that was published during the Revolution except the Declaration, and it clearly anticipated that more famous and more polished document. It contributed to his contemporary reputation, and until this day it has commanded the deeply respectful attention of historians.

Jefferson had not had time to perfect his paper and realized that there were inaccuracies in it. The pamphlet reveals very considerable learning and contains glowing sentences, but it is more noteworthy for boldness and fervor than for historical precision or literary grace. Written in the white heat of indignation against the coercive acts of the British government, the *Summary View* has a distinct place in the controversial literature of the period. But it was more than a tract for the times; it embodied a reasoned theory of imperial relations which, actually, was better adapted to a later era. As a contemporary indictment of British policy it bordered on recklessness, but it was distinctive in its emphasis on philosophical fundamentals and its prophetic quality. When the circumstances of its writing are remembered, "a range of inquiry not then very frequent, and marching far beyond the politics of the day" will surely be granted it, as Edmund Randolph said.[5]

The intemperance of Jefferson's language would have made his resolutions unacceptable as the official statement of a responsible group desiring to accommodate a dispute, and he himself recognized that his paper was too strong for the Virginia convention. He was modest about it after his passions had cooled. When twice as old as when he wrote it he said: "If it had any merit, it was that of first taking our true ground, and that which was afterwards assumed and maintained." [6] One thing he meant by the expression "true ground" was the complete denial of the authority of Parliament over the colonies. Inseparable from his position was a theory of imperial organization which he afterwards claimed that he had held from the beginning of the controversy. This was that the relation between the colonies and the Mother Country was the same as that between Scotland and England from the accession of James I to the Act of Union, and between Hanover and England in his own time, "having the same executive chief but no other necessary political connection." [7] In Virginia up to August, 1774, nobody but George Wythe had agreed with him in these matters, as he remembered. Edmund Randolph, also relying on memory, afterwards

[5] *Va. Mag.*, XLIII, 216.
[6] Jefferson to John W. Campbell, Sept. 3, 1809; Ford, IX, 258.
[7] Ford, I, 12.

said that the principle of bowing to external taxation by Parliament, "as resulting from our migration, and a necessary dependence on the mother country," was generally conceded in Virginia until Jefferson shook it.[8] But ideas like his had occurred to some other American minds.

The logic of the situation was quite clear to Benjamin Franklin, for one, before Jefferson had even entered the House of Burgesses. As early as 1768 that sage observer had concluded that, in logic, there was really no middle ground between the power of Parliament to make all laws for the colonies and that of making none; and he had drawn an analogy between the colonies and Scotland that was practically identical with the one Jefferson afterwards employed.[9] In earlier stages of the growing controversy, colonial opposition had unquestionably been directed against particular measures which could be termed unconstitutional; but the readiness of certain Americans to take the next step and repudiate Parliament altogether, while avowing loyalty to the King, had been observed by Lord North four years before Jefferson put himself definitely on record.[10] Jefferson's concept was essentially that of "imperial partnership" or a "commonwealth of nations," and he was one of the Americans who anticipated the British empire of self-governing states, even if he was not the only one.[11]

Undoubtedly, he put himself in the vanguard of the Patriots in Virginia and in the colonies as a whole by publicly advocating the repudiation of Parliament at this juncture. Events were moving rapidly and ideas were crystallizing with them, but not even at the Continental

[8] Randolph, in *Va. Mag.*, XLIII, 216. Before Jefferson sent his paper, however, James Madison had privately referred to the denial of parliamentary authority as orthodox doctrine; to William Bradford, July 1, 1774 (Brant, *Madison*, p. 145).

[9] Discussed by Becker, *Declaration of Independence*, pp. 101–104. Verner W. Crane, who is making a study of Franklin in England, has called my attention to the importance of a comment in *Monthly Review*, 1 ser., LI (London, 1774), 391. The reviewer [Edward Bancroft] points to the action of the Assembly of Massachusetts Bay in 1773, in claiming independence of Parliament, and connects this with earlier proposals of an American advocate [Franklin]. It appears that previously Franklin had counseled against pressing this issue, and that in 1774 he again sought to evade the question of sovereignty for practical reasons.

[10] May 9, 1770; Cavendish, *Debates*, II, 31.

[11] Mention should be made of James Wilson, who expressed similar ideas about this time. On the general question see R. G. Adams, *Political Ideas of the American Revolution*, ch. 3; R. L. Schuyler, in *Pol. Science Quart.*, XXXVIII (1923), 104–114; and *Parliament and the British Empire*, chs. 1, 2; C. H. McIlwain, *The American Revolution: A Constitutional Interpretation*; Becker, *Declaration of Independence*, ch. 3. An excellent article by A. M. Lewis, "Jefferson's *Summary View* as a Chart of Political Union," is scheduled for publication in the *William & Mary Quarterly*.

Congress, which met in the early fall, was it possible to go as far as he desired. Congress then claimed for the provincial assemblies the exclusive power of legislation in all matters of taxation and internal policy, subject only to the negative of the King, but they cheerfully consented to the operation of parliamentary acts that were limited to the regulation of external commerce.[12] Throughout his paper Jefferson's emphasis was on what Parliament could *not* do. He minimized necessary concessions and practical limitations, and proclaimed colonial "rights" in a sweeping and dogmatic way. "The young ascended with Mr. Jefferson to the source of those rights," said a later commentator; "the old required time for consideration, before they could tread this lofty ground, which, if it had not been abandoned, at least had not been fully occupied throughout America."[13]

At the moment it did not seem the part of political wisdom to assume such a lofty position, and Jefferson would have been lonely in it if the controversy with the Mother Country had been soon resolved. By attempting to ascend to the source of authority in a time of crisis he laid himself open to the charge of being an impractical theorist. Nevertheless, he located ultimate authority in precisely the same place that he did two years later when he was drafting a much more important document. Fortunately for him, general opinion had caught up with him by then. Or, to be more precise, the uncompromising Patriots were then in control of Congress, and they were ready to square action with theory.

Jefferson gave no general statement of the doctrine of natural rights in his *Summary View*, but he based his whole argument on it. Even on practical grounds he might have come to the same conclusion about Parliament. He might have contented himself with saying that the British Americans had once been essentially self-governing, and that because of their present stature and circumstances they *ought* to be. But he grounded his argument on the nature of things — as they were in the beginning and evermore should be. His presuppositions may be questioned, and there were flaws in his historical presentation, but morally his case was strong.

He took the position that originally, in England, the ancestors of these British Americans had been free, just as their more remote Saxon forefathers had been in their native wilds; and that they had a natural

---

[12] *Journals Continental Congress*, I, 42, 68–69; John Adams, *Works*, II, 374–375. Adams said that the resolutions represented a compromise which nobody really liked. Also, it should be remembered that Jefferson was not in Congress until 1775.
[13] Edmund Randolph, in *Va. Mag.*, XLIII, 216.

right to emigrate and establish laws and regulations of their own, just as the Saxons did. His cousin Richard Bland had said much the same thing a decade earlier. In his own studies, however, Jefferson had given particular attention to the Saxons, especially in connection with land tenure, and he believed that they exemplified English liberty in its purest form. The important consideration is not that he idealized them, though he did; it is that his mind craved historical as well as philosophical authority, and that he could not be content without finding precedent somewhere for the freedom he was so sure was right.

He also followed Bland in asserting dogmatically that the conquest and settlement of the American wilds had been made wholly at the expense of individual colonists: "for themselves they fought, for themselves they conquered, and for themselves alone they have right to hold." [14] No aid from the British treasury was given them until after they had become valuable for commercial purposes, he said. In his opinion, this later help gave no title to the authority of Parliament; it was wholly a commercial matter and could be repaid by trade privileges. He greatly overstated the case for the individual settlers, who could not have survived without British protection prior to the time that he himself became grown. But he was not writing history; he was trying to play a part in making it by passionately pleading what seemed to him a sacred cause.

These settlers, having emigrated by right and established themselves by their own exertions, "thought proper to adopt that system of laws under which they had hitherto lived in the mother country, and to continue their union with her by submitting themselves to the same common Sovereign, who was thereby made the central link connecting the several parts of the empire thus newly multiplied." [15] He claimed that there was a compact between the colonists and the King which was embodied, partly at least, in the early charters. He by no means regarded these charters as royal gifts; on the contrary, he emphasized the restrictions that they imposed on royal power. For example, he perceived tyranny in the Stuart practice of parceling out lands to favorites and in erecting new governments. To his mind, this family of princes had no more right to dismember the province of Virginia when once established by charter than they had to divide England itself. The Stuarts had met their deserved reward, however, and he found more pertinent examples of arbitrary power in later acts of Parliament.

By the time that he drafted this paper Jefferson had arrived at a conclusion which would have caused any English mercantilist to raise

---

[14] Ford, I, 430.   [15] *Ibid.*, 431.

his eyebrows; namely, that the exercise of free trade with all parts of the world was a natural right of the colonists. No law of their own had taken away or abridged this right. Indeed, he found confirmation of it in the "solemn treaty" of March 12, 1651, between the Commonwealth and the House of Burgesses. Some of the later acts for the regulation of commerce seemed to him indefensible on practical grounds, but his most important assertion was this: "The true ground on which we declare these acts void is, that the British parliament has no right to exercise its authority over us." [16]

His historical arguments were one-sided, and in the scholar's sense they are no more than half-truths. His grounds were not historical after all; they were moral. He lived in an age when philosophers as well as statesmen quoted history for their purposes; and it is from his purposes, primarily, that he must be judged. These were clear and, as human hearts go, they were pure. His chief aim was to overthrow parliamentary authority which had been unwise in practice and was wrong in principle, and at the same time to safeguard self-government.

Like other patriotic pamphleteers he was most disturbed, not by restrictions on trade, but by parliamentary meddling with the internal affairs of the colonies. Violations of right were less alarming during the reigns immediately before that of George III, he said, "because repeated at more distant intervals than that rapid and bold succession of injuries which is likely to distinguish the present from all other periods of American story." He continued:

> Scarcely have our minds been able to emerge from the astonishment into which one stroke of parliamentary thunder had involved us, before another more heavy, and more alarming, is fallen on us. Single acts of tyranny may be ascribed to the accidental opinion of a day; but a series of oppressions, begun at a distinguished period, and pursued, unalterably through every change of ministers, too plainly prove a deliberate and systematical plan of reducing us to slavery.[17]

He used strikingly similar language two years later, then laying the onus not on Parliament but on the King and thus becoming an open secessionist.

He cited the specific acts prior to 1774 which formed a "connected chain of parliamentary usurpation," speaking at considerable length and with great emotion about the suspension of the legislature of New York which had occurred even before he became a burgess. "One free and independent legislature hereby takes upon itself to suspend the

---

[16] *Ibid.*, 434.　　　　　[17] *Ibid.*, 435.

powers of another, free and independent as itself; this exhibiting a phenomenon unknown in nature," he said.[18] The measures against Boston, which had precipitated the present conflict and provided the occasion for his own pamphlet, he regarded as "acts of power, assumed by a body of men, foreign to our constitutions, and unacknowledged by our laws." [19] He admitted that the actions of the exasperated participants in the Boston Tea Party were not strictly regular, that these men did wrong in destroying the "obnoxious commodity," and that they were properly amenable to the laws of the land, that is, to the laws of Massachusetts Bay. But the coercive acts of Parliament which followed this famous event were wholly intolerable to him. He entered solemn and determined protest against them, addressing this to the King, "as yet the only mediatory power between the several states of the British empire." At the same time he boldly pointed out the King's own deviations from the line of duty.

Several of these charges reappeared in his draft of the Declaration of Independence, and one of them was too strong for the stomachs of the patriots even when they were ready to renounce allegiance to the King. Jefferson erred on the side of optimism when he asserted in his *Summary View* that the abolition of domestic slavery was the great object of desire in the colonies. Speaking for Virginia, he was correct in saying that previous attempts to prevent importations of slaves from Africa had been defeated by the royal negative. No doubt he caused his more temperate colleagues to shake their heads, however, when he termed this a shameful abuse of royal power, which showed that His Majesty preferred the immediate advantage of a few British corsairs to "the lasting interests of the American states, and to the rights of human nature." [20]

He really need not have bothered to address the King at this time, for his language was so unconciliatory as to doom his appeal to failure. One of his more positive proposals would have aroused the fears of the English Whigs immediately, if they had been disposed to pay any attention to this rash young man. He suggested that the King resume the exercise of his negative upon parliamentary legislation, in order to prevent the passage of laws injurious to other parts of the empire. This was one way of saying that the colonies had just the same rights as England, and he hedged the King about with restrictions, but it would have seemed to many that he was advocating an increase of royal power. He said that fortune had placed the King in a post where he held the balance in an empire; and that this empire would be great if it were well-poised. The latter reflection was prophetic.

[18] *Ibid.*, 436.   [19] *Ibid.*, 439.   [20] *Ibid.*, 440.

More important than his specific appeal to the King was the philosophy which underlay it. This left no place for royal tyranny, or for tyranny of any sort. He regarded himself as the spokesman of a free people who had derived their rights from God and the laws. "Let those flatter who fear," he said, "it is not an American art. To give praise which is not due . . . would ill beseem those who are asserting the rights of human nature. They know, and will therefore say, that kings are the servants, not the proprietors of the people. Open your breast, sire, to liberal and expanded thought. Let not the name of George the third be a blot in the page of history." [21] He revealed his own moral emphasis but underrated the practical difficulties when he said: "The whole art of government consists in the art of being honest." It is doubtful if his chiding admonition ever reached the royal ear, but some of his own countrymen remembered that he had subordinated the King himself to natural law and had boldly charged him with specific offenses, and within two years they gave him opportunity to base on this philosophy a convincing justification of revolution.

He talked little of colonial concessions, but at the moment he claimed that he did not seek independence of the Mother Country:

> . . . It is neither our wish nor our interest to separate from her. We are willing, on our part, to sacrifice everything which reason can ask to the restoration of that tranquillity for which all must wish. On their part, let them be ready to establish union on a generous plan. Let them name their terms, but let them be just. Accept of every commercial preference it is in our power to give for such things as we can raise for their use, or they make for ours. But let them not think to exclude us from going to other markets to dispose of those commodities which they cannot use, or to supply those wants which they cannot supply. Still less let it be proposed that our properties within our own territories shall be taxed or regulated by any power on earth but our own.

Then he uttered a saying which of itself entitles this bold pamphlet to immortality. It belongs, not to the American colonies, but to mankind; not to the year 1774 merely, but to all the years thereafter.

> . . . The God who gave us life gave us liberty at the same time; the hand of force may destroy, but cannot disjoin them.[22]

From the beginnings of his conspicuous public career the blessings of liberty were much dearer to Jefferson than those of empire. He

[21] *Ibid.*, 446.   [22] *Ibid.*, 447.

may be properly charged with failure to appreciate the practical problems which the generally incompetent British officials of his time were facing, and with insistence upon a degree of local self-rule which not even the English friends of American liberties could have been expected to concede in theory. The sort of empire he advocated, and the only sort he would have been content with, was one composed of self-governing units, bound together only by mutual benefits. In recognizing the King as the formal tie he had no thought of substituting an omnipotent monarch for an omnipotent Parliament. To his mind, ultimate authority lay in the laws of nature and the human beings whom God had made free; day-to-day authority lay in the various local legislatures, those of America and England itself. The King was the mediator but he was subject to natural law. The ability of such a loose-jointed empire to survive any serious crisis might have been gravely doubted on both sides of the Atlantic.

Never in his life did Jefferson value political organization or governmental power for their own sakes; his major concern was for the ends they served. The net result might have been much the same if the legislative authority of Parliament in external matters had been conceded by the colonists, and that body in turn had sharply restricted itself in practice. Even if the alternative had been clearly presented, however, Jefferson would have thought that this would be to start at the wrong end. He placed his faith supremely in individuals and in local units of a manageable size, and he believed that the power to grant necessary practical concessions should be left with them.

There is no evidence that this pamphlet led to the threat of the author's proscription in England, as he believed, or that it was utilized by the opponents of the ministry.[23] If it had any immediate effect there it was to play into the hands of the ministry, who were seeking

[23] Jefferson's statement in old age (*Ibid.*, 13–14) contains several errors. Since the text of the two English editions is identical with the American, it could not have been "interpolated a little" by Burke. In the incomplete record of parliamentary proceedings in the period I have been unable to find a bill of attainder bearing Jefferson's name which was commenced in either house. The pamphlet did not create a great stir in England but it was talked about; see London *Public Advertiser*, no. 14089, Nov. 25, 1774, communication signed "Coriolanus," who does not mention Jefferson by name. There was a brief review of it in November, 1774, in the *Monthly Review; or Literary Journal* (London), LI, 393; this is partially quoted in Ford, I, 423. The pamphlet was attributed to Jefferson in the index, but the boldness of the anonymous preface seems to have attracted greater attention. There is a much longer notice of a new essay by John Dickinson by the same reviewer, who has been identified as Edward Bancroft; B. C. Nangle, *The Monthly Review, First Series, 1749–1789; Indexes of contributors and articles* (Oxford, 1934). For much of the above information I am indebted to Verner W. Crane.

to justify their repressive policy by claiming that the Americans were going to extremes. It was no service to the opposition for Jefferson to press his theoretical claims, and he had definitely parted company with the handful of English leaders who were still championing colonial liberties. Edmund Burke had a liberal concept of empire and regarded the American love of freedom as an inescapable fact, but that eminent conciliator begged the philosophical question and sought a solution based on common sense. He avoided a "refined policy," eschewed abstract ideas of right, and in this crisis regarded the resort to "mere general theories of government" as "arrant trifling." [24] Jefferson's line of argument would not have appealed to him. And certainly the young Virginian did not at this time see eye to eye with Chatham, though in many ways he admired him, for that great imperialist viewed the distinction between external and internal control as sacred. He conceded to the colonies the right of taxation, but the supreme power of Parliament to regulate commerce he would yield to the insistence of no man.[25]

Jefferson's first important political paper caused him to appear as a champion of freedom and self-government who would yield little or nothing to the exigencies of the moment. That is, he would yield practically nothing to the far-distant Mother Country. To his brethren on the American continent, on the other hand, he was quite prepared to make concessions. Individual rights and local self-government came first in his thinking, but he fully realized the necessity for concerted action on a continental scale and had a clear vision of colonial union. In this sphere he was no impractical theorist, nor merely a long-range prophet, but a realistic statesman.

He had played an important part in the creation of the Virginia Committee of Correspondence, and at successive stages of the imperial controversy he had consistently made common cause with the Patriots of other provinces. It would be improper to employ the term "nationalist" this early, but he was a strong unionist from the start. No saying of his is as vivid as Patrick Henry's at the first Continental Congress: "I am not a Virginian, but an American." Neither he nor the fervid orator had any real thought of ceasing to be a Virginian. But if his interests were not imperial they were far more than provincial; they had assumed a continental scope.

In the year 1774 he gave a sign of this which could not have been expected from Patrick Henry. Not long after the adjournment of the

---

[24] Mar. 22, 1775; *Parl. Hist.*, XVIII, 484.
[25] Jan. 20, 1775: *Ibid.*, XVIII. 154 *n.*

Virginia convention, he received from another province a printed proposal for a complete collection of American state papers. The man who sent it, Ebenezer Hazard, then living in New York, became a pioneer editor of historical records; while the patriotic gentleman who received it in Albemarle County afterwards performed distinctive service as a collector of Americana. The episode was prophetic. Jefferson proceeded to get an impressive list of subscribers from his friends and neighbors and left Hazard in no possible doubt of his enthusiastic patronage.[26]

These actions had to do with the past — with "curious monuments of the infancy of our country," as he afterwards described them. They illustrate at this early date the lifelong Americanism which accompanied his loyalty to Virginia and which, to his mind, conflicted with it in no way. Of more immediate importance, as reflecting his unionism, was a private comment which he made on the limited sovereignty of the Continental Congress. A score of years later, when he sought to limit the centralizing tendencies which Alexander Hamilton personified, his undiscriminating political foes might have found this early observation of his surprising.

> We are to conform to such resolutions only of the Congress as our deputies assent to: which totally destroys that union of conduct in the several colonies which was the very purpose of calling a Congress.[27]

This illuminating comment on the dangerous limitations of congressional power was coupled with others of a critical nature on the Association which Congress adopted in October. He did not wholly approve of that famous nonimportation, nonconsumption agreement — not because it went too far, though he disliked certain of its details, but because it did not go far enough. He duly signed his printed copy, notwithstanding, and he had others attach their names to it. Among these were his young brother Randolph, who was now nineteen, his brother-in-law Francis Eppes, and his violin teacher Francis Alberti.[28]

He intended to be "a conscientious observer of the measures generally thought requisite for a preservation of our independent rights," he said; and he was much embarrassed in December by one of his own orders which turned out to be in violation of them. The restrictions

[26] Printed letter, Aug. 23, 1774, with list of subscribers; LC, 1:109–110. See also Hazard to Jefferson, June 30, 1775 (LC, 1:144); Jefferson to Hazard, Feb. 18, 1791 (L. & B., VIII, 127).

[27] Ford, I, 448.

[28] Printed copy of Association with six signatures (LC, 1:126).

came at an unfortunate time for him, since he was engaged in building operations. Some months earlier he had ordered for use at Monticello fourteen pairs of sash windows, and these were now *en route* despite his countermand. He fully expected his glazed windows to be condemned when they reached the Virginia shore, however, and he acquiesced in this infringement on his liberty as an individual.[29]

He bowed to virtual necessity beyond a doubt, for in Virginia the provisions for the enforcement of the Association were rigorously carried out. Congress had enjoined that every county, town, and city should choose a committee to observe the conduct of all persons respecting the agreement, to publish the names of offenders, and thus to cause the "enemies of American liberty" to be condemned and outlawed.[30] This was high-handed action which a theoretical advocate of personal freedom might have been expected to condemn. But there is no indication that Jefferson questioned its essential wisdom, and there is evidence that he played a patriotic part in carrying the restrictions into effect. The Albemarle committee was not among the first to be elected; the earliest work of organization in Virginia was done in the eastern counties. When a committee was selected, however, his name was the first upon the list, followed by that of his friend and fellow burgess John Walker. In late 1774 and early 1775, he was not only the first citizen of his County but its first Patriot as well.[31] Meanwhile, in the neighboring County of Orange, young James Madison had been elected as a member of a similar committee, and service on it constituted his introduction to public life.[32]

No less a person than Lord Dunmore is authority for the statement that the county committees now constituted virtually the only government in the Province. "There is not a Justice of the Peace in Virginia that acts, except as a committee-man," he said.[33] Thus he testified to the suspension of the county courts, as he also did to the great unwillingness of lawyers to attend the General Court, which was now

[29] Jefferson to Archibald Cary and Benjamin Harrison, Dec. 9, 1774 (Ford, I, 449–451).

[30] *Journals Cont. Congress*, I, 79.

[31] List with vote in Account Book, 1775, without precise date. The election probably took place before Dec. 8, 1774, when he recorded in his Account Book the names of captains in Albemarle to whom Association papers were to be sent. On the general subject, see Eckenrode, *Revolution in Va.*, ch. 4; C. W. Coleman, in *W. & M.*, 1 ser., V, 245–255. There is no reference to the Albemarle committee in either case. It should also be noted that Jefferson's wife and children were at Elkhill in another county for several months that winter and that he was generally with them there (Account Book, Dec. 11, 1774; Apr. 7, 1775).

[32] Brant, *Madison*, p. 155.

[33] To Dartmouth, Dec. 24, 1774 (Force, 4 ser., I, 1062). This letter was made available to Parliament and was afterwards printed in Dixon & Hunter, *Va. Gazette*.

largely restricted to criminal cases. This was what Jefferson meant when he said that the Revolution shut up the courts of justice and ended his own career as a practising lawyer. The last case that he listed in his formal record was dated Nov. 9, 1774, and was numbered 939. This referred only to an opinion on a will, anyway; so to all practical purposes his legal career ended before that. He turned over his unfinished cases to young Edmund Randolph, son of the Attorney General, apparently expecting to abandon practice for good. He would have been fully warranted in doing so even if times had been more peaceful, for the Wayles inheritance had greatly increased his burdens as a man of business, while relieving him of any need to supplement his income.

There is no reason to suppose, however, that he welcomed the closing of the courts in order to escape his own debts to British merchants, as Dunmore and some of his partisans asserted that many of the planters did.[34] He had provided for his debts, or so at least he thought. Nor did he have the desire or occasion to apply tar and feathers as a local committeeman. There was little violence or disorder among these people who were so accustomed to self-government.

In the middle of March, 1775, Jefferson set out for Richmond to attend a provincial convention as the first delegate from his County. He had no reason whatever to suppose that his appeal to the King, or any other, had been heeded. His knowledge of occurrences in England was at least two months behind the events themselves; but, by the month of February, he could have read in the *Virginia Gazette* a speech of George III at the opening of Parliament and the addresses of the Lords and Commons which strongly supported it. He undoubtedly knew that the opposition to the policy of coercion had been ruthlessly beaten down.[35] The King had complained bitterly of "violences of a very criminal nature" in Massachusetts and of "unwarrantable attempts" to obstruct commerce, and had assured Parliament of his determination to withstand every attempt to weaken or impair its "supreme authority." Such attitudes were irreconcilable with the

[34] *Ibid.* See also James Parker to Charles Steuart, Feb. 11, 1775, in *Mag. of History*, III, 158 (March, 1906). The reason commonly assigned by the Patriots was that the Fee Bill had expired, that Dunmore would not let the Assembly meet, and that no other power could establish fees. Jefferson may have shared the earlier opinion of Pendleton that, in the temporary absence of legislation, the General Court could determine fees or at least continue the old schedule. Documents bearing on the matter are in LC, 1:95–97. Presumably he himself rendered an opinion but I have not found it. See Hilldrup, *Pendleton*, pp. 99–100.

[35] Dixon & Hunter, *Va. Gazette*, Feb. 4, 1775; *Parl. Hist.*, XVIII, 33–47.

views Jefferson had expressed, and thus he must have reflected as he took the Richmond road.

Before the convention assembled, however, a later item appeared in the *Virginia Gazette*. This reported that the petition of Congress to the King had been received in London the day before Christmas and had been duly communicated to Lord Dartmouth.[36] The petition led to no change in policy but the Virginians did not know that yet. Some of them seized upon what appeared to be a fresh hope of conciliation, as Patrick Henry and Thomas Jefferson soon found out.

The Virginia convention of March, 1775, amounted to a meeting of the burgesses without the authorization of the Governor, and it was held at a place where they were wholly free from his control. Richmond was a central point, though by no means a city, and the sessions were held in the structure known to history as Old Saint John's Church. It was a simple white building, and its atmosphere befitted the solemnity of the occasion. Here Patrick Henry uttered his most famous words: "Give me liberty, or give me death." The clash of resounding arms had not yet been heard at Lexington and Concord, but he believed war inevitable unless the colonists should become abject. He said, "let it come." So far as is known, Jefferson did not say that, but he strongly supported Henry's resolutions, even going so far as to make a speech.[37]

The just fame of Patrick Henry as a Revolutionary statesman is attributable to his insistence upon decisive action in successive crises. No one else did so much as he to give impetus to the ball of Revolution in the Province. Jefferson said that several times but, unlike Henry's biographers, he did not magnify the importance of this particular occasion; he did not regard it as the beginning of the Revolution. Henry's audacity in urging defense measures at this time, and Jefferson's in backing him, should not be exaggerated. There had already been considerable military preparation in Virginia and the citizens generally were in a resolute state of mind. Three months before this, Lord Dunmore had reported that independent companies of militia were being formed in the counties — to protect the committees, he said. Dissatisfied with the colorless resolutions which had been presented to the convention, Henry introduced more vigorous ones.

---

[36] Dixon & Hunter, *Va. Gazette*, Mar. 18, 1775.

[37] The proceedings of the convention of Mar. 20–27 were published in Dixon & Hunter, *Va. Gazette*, Apr. 1, 1775, and afterwards in pamphlet form. The traditional story is in Henry, *Patrick Henry*, I, 254–272, with the orator's famous speech as reported long afterwards.

He moved that steps be taken by the Colony as a whole and that a committee be chosen to prepare a plan for embodying, arming, and disciplining a sufficient number of men. Since such action gave promise of greater unity and effectiveness it was naturally favored by a realist like George Washington. The support of this man of solid worth was invaluable but he was characteristically silent. The more philosophical Jefferson was not. "He argued closely, profoundly and warmly" on the side of the redoubtable Patrick Henry and eloquent Richard Henry Lee (otherwise designated as Demosthenes and Cicero), his post in the debate being "that at which the theories of republicanism were deposited." [38] They managed to carry the resolutions — but the vote was dangerously close.

The opposing "conservatives" could hardly have been against arming the Colony at a time when the citizens were already arming themselves; and most if not all of these delegates were active in connection with the county committees. Ostensibly, they objected to the timing of the action. Men like Robert Carter Nicholas, Edmund Pendleton, Benjamin Harrison, and Richard Bland still had hopes of conciliation and clung to the proprieties. Beneath the surface of the resolutions, furthermore, they suspected deeper designs on the part of Henry. Apparently he purposed that the committee should assume the full powers of government, many of which had already slipped from the Governor's hands. However, his scheme was scotched, and thus it came about that this was not a revolutionary gathering, after all.[39]

Jefferson was a member of the committee of twelve that was set up to prepare a plan for the militia, though his name was next to the last while Henry's was first. The plan which was adopted was innocuous enough. In general the convention regularized and provided for the enlargement of the county organizations which had already sprung up independently. More picturesquely, it recognized the tomahawk as standard equipment along with the rifle, and prescribed as uniform the hunting shirt. The militiamen were already good shots, and some of them afterwards printed "Liberty or Death" on their hunting shirts, but they did not become an effective military body under centralized control because an orator made an immortal speech.

Jefferson may have wanted the Patriots to assume the full form of governmental authority at this time, since they had already assumed so much of the substance. Yet, despite his radicalism on the imperial

[38] Edmund Randolph, in *Va. Mag.*, XLIII, 223.
[39] Eckenrode, *Revolution in Va.*, pp. 47–49; James Parker to Charles Steuart, Apr. 6, 1775 (*Mag. of History*, III, 158), reporting Henry's "scheme" in a hostile spirit.

question and the uncompromising spirit he had manifested in his pamphlet of the previous summer, the presumption is that he did not. His later silence about the meeting suggests that there was something about it that he did not like; and, even if he had favored taking this revolutionary step in advance of actual bloodshed, he was willing to modify his natural pace in the interest of unity.

A motion of his own in the convention reveals his continuing concern for unity in the colonies. This merely called upon the Committee of Correspondence to inquire about the state of sentiment in the Province of New York, where, as the newspapers reported, there had been a defection of the House of Representatives from the Association. It is the language not the substance of Jefferson's resolution that is significant. To his mind, a defection from the compact of Association was an atrocious perfidy, a desertion of "the Union with the other American Colonies formed in General congress for the preservation of their just rights." He was unwilling to condemn the New Yorkers on the basis of hearsay, but he left no possible doubt of his own determination that the Union should be preserved.[40]

One late action at this meeting turned out to be important to him, personally. The convention re-elected its delegation to Congress, leaving Peyton Randolph at its head. Next after the perennial presiding officer came Washington and Henry, but until the last day of the session the name of Jefferson was still absent from the list. Then he was appointed a deputy to serve in case of Randolph's nonattendance. If he had cared to be mathematical, he might have regarded himself as one of the first eight or ten leaders of Virginia. Despite his abilities and zeal he could hardly have expected to stand higher than that as yet, for he was only thirty-two. He went to Philadelphia in the summer after Peyton Randolph was called home, and by that time the appeal to reason had given place to the appeal to arms.

[40] Ford, I, 451–452.

[XV]

A Patriot Goes to Philadelphia

1775

IN 1775 news did not travel with the speed of sound. Jefferson heard the report of the shots at Lexington and Concord about two weeks after the embattled farmers fired them. This was in early May, more than a month after the adjournment of the convention in Richmond. Meanwhile, he had brought his little family from Elkhill on the James, where they had been staying, back to Monticello, and there had observed with sorrow the damage a late frost had done to his hillside orchard.[1] Soon, however, he was gratified by events in his stable. Before he was plunged again into public affairs he made this entry in his faithful Account Book: "Allycroker's colt by Young Fearnought was foaled May 7." He named the colt Caractacus and recorded his lineage with pride. On the paternal side it was particularly distinguished, for Old Fearnought, sire of Young Fearnought, was the most famous stallion of his time in the Province and he and his sons were treated with royal deference. Caractacus was not only the latest of the blooded horses at Monticello; he indisputably belonged to the first equine family of Virginia.[2]

On the same day in May that he acquired a future mount, Jefferson sat down to write a letter to Dr. William Small in England. His ostensible purpose was to tell his old teacher he was sending him three dozen bottles of Madeira, but inevitably he spoke of the action between the King's troops and his own "brethren" of the Bay Colony. He had learned of it just that week and spoke of it as an accident, but he

---

[1] *Garden Book*, p. 66.

[2] Account Book, May 7, 1775; genealogy inside cover of Farm Book; Fairfax Harrison, "The Equine F F Vs," *Va. Mag.*, XXXV, 329–370, esp. pp. 355–361 on Old Fearnought.

reported that a "phrensy of revenge" had seized upon all ranks of the people.[3] The "phrensy of revenge" in Virginia was not wholly due to news from the North. According to one of Lord Dunmore's few partisans the brush at Lexington and Concord was only a Yankee trick, designed to alarm and involve the other colonies.[4] Jefferson would have vigorously disputed that assertion, but before he learned of events near Boston his own Governor had aroused fierce local indignation. On the night of April 20–21 Dunmore removed from the magazine in Williamsburg the powder belonging to the Colony that was stored there and placed it on a British schooner in the James River. This high-handed action provided the oratorical Patrick Henry with an opportunity to become a man of stirring deeds. He led an independent company from Hanover toward the capital and, although he did not restore the powder, he managed to secure its value in money. Dunmore in turn fortified the Palace, put his wife and children on a man-of-war, and declared Henry an outlaw, thus making him more than ever the hero of the populace.[5]

Jefferson was not that sort of man on horseback, even after Caractacus had grown up, but he soon went to Williamsburg for important public reasons. Lord Dunmore had called the Assembly to meet, ironical as that action seemed.[6] The Governor gained some comfort from the thought that Patrick Henry, whom he regarded as a man of "desperate circumstances," would be at a safe distance — in Congress, along with other leading Whig characters of the Colony. Also, he had certain conciliatory proposals of Lord North's to present.

Jefferson said that these constituted the major reason for calling the Assembly, and that his own desire to answer them was the main reason why he attended. Otherwise, he would have gone straight to Philadelphia to replace Peyton Randolph, for that massive statesman had hastened back to preside over the burgesses, being succeeded in the chair of the Continental Congress by John Hancock.

Jefferson spent only ten days in the Assembly but these were busy

[3] May 7, 1775, Ford, I, 453–454; entire letter LC, 1:140. He wanted Small to know the real temper of the colonists.

[4] James Parker to Charles Steuart, May 6, 1775 (*Mag. of History*, III, 158–159).

[5] Most of the documents about the powder episode and the independent companies are in Force, 4 ser., II. A company from Albemarle, of which Jefferson's friend George Gilmer was a lieutenant, also set out for Williamsburg but it turned back after learning of Henry's action; see Gilmer Papers, *Colls. Va. Hist. Soc.*, n.s., VI (1887), pp. 75–85. In his *Memoirs*, pp. 209–212, Mazzei gives further details but many of these are inaccurate. He says that Jefferson was enlisted as a private. The latter's name appears on no list, but his brother Randolph was a member.

[6] Call dated May 12, 1775.

and exciting. The burgesses pressed the question of the gunpowder and soon threw Dunmore into utter panic. On the eighth day of the session he became so fearful of his personal security that he joined his family on the man-of-war *Fowey* and transacted business thereafter on shipboard. To the Virginians he was chiefly a nuisance after that.

Before the lord took flight Jefferson served on a committee which drafted an address and confronted the short, dark man in person. The Governor had called the Assembly to consider the "alarming situation" of the country, but the committee flung the words back in his teeth by blaming this situation wholly on the British ministry.[7] The most interesting passage in this address dealt with the courts, which Dunmore wished to reopen to civil cases. By this time the debts to British merchants had become a major consideration on both sides. Jefferson agreed with his fellows that debtors should not be sued by their British creditors, since the cessation of commerce had now made it impossible for them to sell their tobacco. "Money, my Lord, is not a plant of the native growth of this country," the committee said.

Jefferson drafted the reply to Lord North's motion, though this was not adopted in final form until after he had left for Philadelphia.[8] The proposal, in brief, was that any colony which should make such a contribution to the defense of the Empire and such fixed provision for the support of its own civil government as met the approval of Parliament should be exempted henceforth from imperial taxation for revenue. Lord Dunmore was not notably acute but he was sufficiently so to expect little enthusiasm for this plan in the Virginia Assembly, whose "violence of temper" had already been manifested. The newspapers had prejudiced the people against the proposal, he said; they called it a device to divide the colonies, and insisted that no negotiations whatever be begun until all the objectionable acts of Parliament had been repealed.[9] In England, Lord Chatham had urged just such a repeal and Jefferson believed that the rejected resolutions of that statesman would have offered real hope of conciliation.[10] This he said despite the fact that they also called for the express recognition of parliamentary authority, which he himself had explicitly denied. The strong supposition was that this authority would be exercised primarily if not solely in the field of external relations, and as a practical man he concluded that these terms might have been accommodated with those offered by Congress.

[7] June 5, 1775; *Burgesses, Journals*, 1773–1776, pp. 187–188.
[8] North's and Chatham's proposals were reported about the same time. Purdie, *Va. Gazette*, Apr. 28, 1775, supplement; Dixon & Hunter, *Va. Gazette*, Apr. 29, 1775.
[9] To Dartmouth, May 15, 1775 (*Burgesses, Journals*, 1773–1776, p. xxiii).
[10] To Small, May 7, 1775 (Ford, I, 454).

The burgesses would have rejected Lord North's terms, even if Jefferson had not been there, though he may have had to overcome the scruples of Robert Carter Nicholas and others, as he said.[11] The admirable address which was adopted was considerably more moderate in tone than the *Summary View*, and it is possible that he was not responsible for the whole of it. On the other hand, he had learned something about practical statesmanship since the summer of 1774, as his comment on Chatham showed, and the fact that this was an official pronouncement imposed inevitable restraint.

Polite as the reply was, it was wholly firm and entirely without comfort to Lords North and Dunmore. The proposal only changed the form of oppression without lightening the burden, the committee said, and for half a dozen reasons they would not accept it. The first one was that Parliament had no right to meddle with the support of civil government in the colonies. The language of this objection showed clearly the Jeffersonian touch: "For us, not for them, has government been instituted here." The Colony of Virginia was unwilling to saddle itself with a perpetual contribution that was expendable by Parliament. Not merely was the mode of raising money objected to; the freedom of granting it was also contended for. Furthermore, the objectionable acts of Parliament were unrepealed, and while asking for a gift the British were making dispositions to invade America. This sort of procedure could not be reconciled with American freedom. There was inconsistency, also, in asking for a proportionate payment for imperial defence, without granting to the colonies a free trade with all the world. This objection sounds just like Jefferson. So does the last and most important one. "We consider ourselves as bound in honour, as well as interest, to share one general fate with our sister Colonies; and would hold ourselves base deserters of that union to which we have acceded, were we to agree on any measures distinct and apart from them." These

[11] The account in his "Autobiography" (Ford, I, 15) differs in detail from his much earlier statement of September 13, 1786, to François Soulés (*Ibid.*, IV, 309), but in each instance he claimed the authorship of the reply. Also he wrote "drawn by T. Jefferson" beside a quotation from this paper in his copy of Marshall's *Life of George Washington*, II, 211. His memory was somewhat confused about the events, however. The resolution of June 10, which differed from the final address only in trivial details, was presented by Archibald Cary for the committee (*Burgesses, Journals*, 1773–1776, pp. 212–214). Presumably this was the same committee which was appointed on June 2 to draw an address on the Governor's speech and of which Jefferson was a member. A committee of eight was appointed on June 10 to draw an address on the resolution, and this was adopted after Jefferson had left for Philadelphia. (*Ibid.*, pp. 219–221.) All the important work of drafting had been done by June 10, and Jefferson may have taken to Philadelphia a copy of the address in its final form, but this could not have been an authenticated copy, as he claimed.

were unionist words, quite in line with Jefferson's convictions, and they were also the language of common sense.

Before this strong, calm paper was finally approved Jefferson had set out in his phaeton for Philadelphia. Nine years earlier he had gone to the colonial metropolis to be inoculated against smallpox, but this was the first time he ever left his native Province on a public mission. He made many other trips to Philadelphia in later months and years, and the immediate results of some of them were of much greater historical importance, but this one was more memorable than any other in that it marked his entrance on the continental stage as a public man. But for the challenge of political crisis he would have continued to be a prosperous planter, a responsible local leader, a humane and enlightened Virginian who operated of necessity within a restricted sphere and spent most of his time at home.

When he ferried across the Potomac on his way to the Continental Congress, he crossed his Rubicon. He did not at that time abandon local responsibilities but he appeared unmistakably as an American, as a champion of rights which were confined by no boundary line. The merger of his private life with public pursuits was still incomplete, but there could be no turning back, and from this date onward his story becomes an integral part of the history of the Republic.

Not until another year did he and his fellow Patriots become open revolutionaries, but he was determined to secure a redress of the colonial grievances which he had already described so sweepingly. He afterwards said that the Virginia planters were "a species of property annexed to certain mercantile houses in London," but primarily his motives were neither economic nor personal.[12] Actually, he was more prosperous now than he ever was afterwards, and his happiness as a husband and father had just come into flower. On purely personal grounds he ought to have been a conservative. But, as he said, he was drawn into public affairs "by emergencies which threatened our country with slavery, but ended by establishing it free." [13] This he said after he had paid the price of liberty and knew how great it was. From the beginning to the end he regarded the issues of these years as momentous. To him this was no mere local struggle, but one of those great crises which come but once in a millennium; or at least he thought that, until the vaster cataclysm in France showed him that such things could happen twice in a single lifetime. Such an emergency warranted the

---

[12] Ford, IV, 155.
[13] To D'Ivernois, Feb. 6, 1795 (Ford, VII, 2); to Maria Cosway, Sept. 8, 1795, reproduced in Helen D. Bullock, *My Head and My Heart*, p. 142.

neglect of his extensive private affairs, separation from his family, and any other sacrifices which might be demanded.

The details of his important journey to Philadelphia are interesting and informing.[14] On the day before he left Williamsburg he received from the treasurer of the Colony £315 for the use of the Virginia delegates. The expenses of the various delegations were borne locally, and continued to be until the Constitution of 1787 went into effect. As paymasters the individual colonies, not Congress, called the tune. In Virginia these funds were raised by subscription, and Jefferson himself had made a contribution. He could well afford to do so, and he was in a generous frame of mind. The future champion of democracy traveled impressively. By the time he reached Philadelphia he had four horses. One of these, an animal named General, sired by the noted Janus and six years old, he purchased for £50 in Fredericksburg, where he remained three days and also bought harness, a postilion's whip, and swingletrees. He had at least two servants: Jesse, who rode postilion, and Richard, apparently a body servant.

After he crossed the Potomac and came into another "country," he began to keep his records in Maryland currency, the exchange fortunately being favorable to Virginia. He may have been struck by the difficulties and annoyances arising from the lack of a uniform intercolonial medium but the problem was not serious the rest of the way, since the currency of Pennsylvania and Delaware was on a par with that of Maryland. This sort of information he invariably jotted down. In Annapolis he stopped long enough to have the pole of his phaeton mended; he visited the seat of government, as he had done nine years before; also, he availed himself of the opportunity to purchase books. Beyond Wilmington, not being sure of his way, he hired a guide and horse at no small cost. The total distance from Williamsburg to Philadelphia by the common route was approximately 325 miles, but because of his stops he took ten days to cover it. That was a slow-moving age, and he never lived to see a fast one.

Soon he had to say good-by to one prominent delegate from his "country." Two days after he arrived, grave news came from Bunker Hill, and on the day after that George Washington, recently elected commander of the Continental forces, set out for the camp before Boston. A troop of light horse in uniform, numerous militia officers, all of the delegates from Massachusetts, and many other delegates accompanied the General for a little way. Jefferson was probably

14 Details from Account Book. He started on June 11, 1775.

among them, as John Adams was, hearing the martial music and viewing the pomp of war.[15]

Congress had been in session for about six weeks, and it sat for almost as many more before recessing. During this period Jefferson and one or both of his servants lodged with a cabinetmaker named Benjamin Randolph. The cost of his lodgings, however, was only about half of that of keeping his four horses. He had an account at the City Tavern and generally took dinner and supper there. Probably he fell heir to the place of Peyton Randolph or George Washington at the daily table which had been formed earlier by them, along with Richard Henry Lee, Benjamin Harrison, and four other delegates.[16] He bought all sorts of things in this enticing market, including books and music, and he paid a barber for shaving him by the week. The times were perilous but he faced them as a fine gentleman.

Congressional duties left him little opportunity for pleasure, however. The sessions in the State House, later known as Independence Hall, began at nine and continued till four or five and sometimes until six, and committees often met in the evening. As the hot summer wore on, attention to business became more and more painful to all, and, as many remarked, the results of the lengthy deliberations were small.[17] The sixty-odd delegates did not comprise a numerous body — actually the House of Burgesses was larger — but this was an unwieldy body. "Its progress must be slow," wrote John Adams to his wife. "It is like a large fleet sailing under convoy. The fleetest sailors must wait for the dullest and slowest. Like a coach and six, the swiftest horses must be slackened, and the slowest quickened, that all may keep an even pace." [18] Unanimity among the delegations was necessary for the passing of any motion or resolution, and even Samuel Adams realized how hard it was to arrive at that.

Jefferson was constant in attendance, though he was a silent member in debate. He felt no chagrin for that, saying later that Washington and Franklin also disliked the disputation of the legislative floor. On committees and in conversation, however, he was "prompt, frank, explicit, and decisive." John Adams believed that not even Samuel Adams was more so, and said that the young Virginian soon seized upon his heart. Thus he dated the beginning of an historic friendship.[19] John

---

[15] June 23, 1775, John Adams to Mrs. Adams (E. C. Burnett, ed., *Letters of Members of the Continental Congress*, I, 142). See also *Ibid.*, 139.

[16] George Reade to Mrs. Reade, May 18, 1775 (*Ibid.*, 92).

[17] *Ibid.*, 96, 107, 118, 148, and elsewhere.

[18] June 17, 1775 (*Ibid.*, 132).

[19] To Timothy Pickering, Aug. 6, 1822 (*Works*, II, 514 *n.*). See also comment of C. F. Adams (*Ibid.*, I, 616–617).

Adams remembered that Jefferson brought with him to Congress "a reputation for literature, science, and a happy talent for composition," and recorded, a few months after he first met him, the earliest known tribute to his linguistic attainments and ambitions. He reported James Duane of New York as saying that Jefferson was "the greatest rubber off of dust" that he had met with, that he had learned French, Italian, Spanish, and wanted to learn German.[20]

The familiar statement that writings of his were passed around, remarkable for their "peculiar felicity of expression" was not contemporary; but if the reputation of his "masterly pen" was not firmly established in June, 1775, he was clearly predestined to paper work from the beginning of his congressional career. No other Virginian in attendance, except possibly Pendleton, had like diligence or skill in it. Both Patrick Henry and Richard Henry Lee were primarily speakers, and in the previous Congress they had proved disappointing as draftsmen.[21] Benjamin Harrison was a large, cheerful gentleman and something of a wit; but he had gained no laurels as a writer. Obviously, the most populous Colony must be represented on committees which drew important papers; and the youngest and most literary member of the delegation was inevitably called on.

Only a few days after he had taken his seat, a committee reported a Declaration on the Necessity of Taking Up Arms which Congress deemed unsatisfactory. The original committee consisted of John Rutledge of South Carolina, who is supposed to have done the drafting, William Livingston of New Jersey, John Jay, Benjamin Franklin, and Thomas Johnson of Maryland. To their number John Dickinson, the writer of the well-known *Letters from a Farmer of Pennsylvania*, and Jefferson were now added.[22]

It is a pity that no photographer was present when he and Franklin first bowed to each other, and that no stenographer recorded the first words they spoke. The eminent Doctor had recently returned from England and his conduct at this time was grave and modest, though he was bold in counsel whenever his opinion was sought.[23] Jefferson, who liked the conjunction of intellectual boldness with learning and modest manners, probably took to him from the start. This was the beginning of Jefferson's important association with John Jay, who was even younger than he was, and of his long friendship with Rutledge.

[20] Oct. 25, 1775 (*Works*, II, 422). It seems unlikely that Jefferson had learned Spanish that early.
[21] E. C. Burnett, *Continental Congress*, p. 51.
[22] June 26, 1775 (*Journals Cont. Cong.*, II, 107–108). See also *Ibid.*, 106–107.
[23] John Adams to Mrs. Adams, July 23, 1775 (Burnett, *Letters*, I, 175).

His first clash appears to have been with John Dickinson, whom he always regarded as an honest man, though he did not like the way his mind worked.

Jefferson was asked to draft a new paper but, as he remembered, Dickinson objected to this as too harsh. Committeeman Livingston commented on it at the time. "We are now [July 4, 1775] working on a Manifesto on arming," he wrote. "The first was not liked by the Congress and was recommitted. The second was not liked by the committee. Both had the faults common to our Southern gentlemen. Much fault-finding and declamation, with little sense or dignity. They seem to think a reiteration of tyranny, despotism, bloody, &c. all that is needed to unite us at home and to convince the bribed voters of the North of the justice of our cause." [24]

Like all of Jefferson's writings about the imperial controversy, this paper burns with a sense of injustice; but it was much less impetuous than his *Summary View* and cannot properly be described as declamatory. He made two drafts, and when set side by side they show that he weighed his words.[25] He used alternative expressions, as he did when drawing the Declaration of Independence, and afterwards struck out the ones that seemed less desirable. He had now entered upon his most fastidious stage as a literary craftsman. His arguments, however, were largely those he had used previously, and the real objection of Dickinson was not so much to the harshness of his phrases as to his basic theory of empire. The older man was asked to draw another paper, and with minor amendments it was adopted. He incorporated part of Jefferson's draft and used expressions of his own which were almost if not quite as severe. He did not achieve as logical a sequence of ideas or as smooth a literary effect, however, and he begged the question of the precise authority of Parliament within the empire, thus leaving a wider door to conciliation.[26]

As Jefferson said and Dickinson repeated, the actions of the British government had compelled the Americans to change the ground of opposition and to accept the appeal from reason to arms. But Jefferson sought approval "before supreme reason," spoke of charters of compact that had been freely made, and again termed the King the link between the several parts of the empire. He did not explicitly deny all parliamentary authority as he had done previously, but he did so by implica-

[24] Ford, I, 464 *n.*

[25] *Journals*, II, 128–139.

[26] *Ibid.*, 140–157. The claim of G. H. Moore, in C. J. Stillé, *Life and Times of John Dickinson* (1891), p. 363, that Dickinson drew the whole paper seems untenable now that the drafts have been published.

tion. This was still too strong a dose for the Farmer of Pennsylvania. Some of Jefferson's more striking expressions were retained in the final draft, and can still serve as mottoes:

> Our forefathers, inhabitants of the island of Great Britain, left their native land to seek on these shores a residence for civil and religious freedom.[27]

> . . . our attachment to no nation upon earth should supplant our attachment to liberty.[28]

Other passages of his, which were omitted, contained strong and vivid phrases:

> To ward these deadly injuries from the tender plant of liberty which we have brought over, and with so much affection fostered on these our own shores, we have pursued every temperate, every respectful measure.
> We have supplicated our king at various times, in terms almost disgraceful to freedom; . . .
> . . . to preserve that liberty which he [our Creator] committed to us in sacred deposit.[29]

Jefferson avowed the hope that civil war might be averted, but his more conciliatory colleague was also more boastful. It was Dickinson, not he, who said:

> Our cause is just. Our union is perfect. Our preparations are nearly completed. Our internal resources are great; and our Assurance of foreign Assistance is certain.[30]

Despite the fact that Dickinson watered down Jefferson's draft of the Declaration upon Taking up Arms, the more resolute Patriots regarded it as a spirited manifesto and it proved to be generally popular.[31] A second humble petition to the King which that delegate drew, and which was adopted practically without amendment out of deference to him, was viewed differently by Jefferson. In connection with this he reported a sally of wit from his corpulent colleague Harrison which was less than just to Dickinson. The latter expressed his delight by saying: "There is but one word in the paper, Mr. President, of which I

[27] *Journals*, II, 129, 142.
[28] *Ibid.*, 134, 147.
[29] *Ibid.*, 134, 138.
[30] *Ibid.*, 154; slightly modified in final version.
[31] John Adams to James Warren, July 6, 1775 (Burnett, *Letters*, I, 152); Stillé, *Dickinson*, p. 358.

disapprove, and that is the word *Congress*." Then Harrison ponderously arose and said: "There is but one word in the paper, Mr. President, of which I approve, and that is the word *Congress*." It should be noted that this word appeared only once, but it may be added that George III did not deign to reply to the petition, despite its tone.[32]

The reply to Lord North's conciliatory motion, which Jefferson drew soon thereafter, was more vigorous. The committee itself was strong, consisting of Franklin, John Adams, and Richard Henry Lee, along with Jefferson, and, because of his association with the reply of the House of Burgesses to the same proposal, he was the natural draftsman. One paragraph was inserted at the suggestion of the sagacious Franklin, but the paper as a whole followed the line of argument that had already been used in the more polite paper of the Burgesses. It was an *ad hoc* document without the quality of immortality, but there was power in its phrases.[33]

> A proposition to give our money, accompanied with large fleets and armies, seems addressed to our fears rather than to our freedom.
>
> We do not mean that our people shall be burthened with oppressive taxes, to provide sinecures for the idle or the wicked, under colour of providing for a civil list.
>
> While parliament pursue their plan of civil government within their own jurisdiction, we also hope to pursue ours without molestation.
>
> We are of opinion that the proposition is altogether unsatisfactory, because it imports only a suspension of the mode, not a renunciation of the pretended right to tax us: . . .

He spoke of "indiscriminate legislation" and a "high breach" of colonial privilege, described the proposition as "unreasonable and insidious," and stated boldly that "nothing but our own exertions may defeat the ministerial sentence of death or abject submission."

He labored under no illusions about the probable effect of these various congressional papers on the British government. Soon after he arrived in Philadelphia he wrote his brother-in-law, Francis Eppes, that war was now "heartily entered into, without a prospect of accommodation but through the effectual interposition of arms." [34] To forthright John Adams these petitions and addresses seemed like children's

---

[32] "Autobiography," in Ford, I, 17–18. The petition was signed July 8, 1775 (*Journals*, II, 158–162). For other comments, see Burnett, *Letters*, I, 158–159 n.

[33] *Journals*, II, 202, 224–234.

[34] June 26, 1775; Ford, I, 459.

play at marbles or push-pin, though he afterwards confessed that he had underestimated their value. "I was in great error, no doubt, . . . for these things were necessary to give popularity to our cause, both at home and abroad; and, to show my stupidity in a stronger light, the reputation of any one of those compositions has been a more splendid distinction than any aristocratical star or garter in the escutcheon of every man who has enjoyed it." [35]

Jefferson hoped that a vigorous military campaign would force the enemy to negotiate, but it was in connection with the war of words that he rendered his chief contribution and gained his chief renown. He was not yet the penman laureate of the Revolution; indeed, he was not crowned by public opinion until these fateful years were viewed retrospectively; but by the summer of 1775 he had clearly demonstrated his rare skill in what came to be known generations later as "psychological warfare." He had relatively little to do with the military proceedings of Congress, which led to the actions of greatest immediate importance, though he followed the course of external events with deep interest. It was the necessity of putting military affairs in "good train" which caused the delegates to remain in tedious session when some of them believed that they had been too long together and all were possessed with "an impatience for home." [36]

Jefferson's stay in the hot city was relatively brief but, like everybody else, he welcomed the recess. He started south on August 1, though he was unable to go straight to his mountaintop; first he had to attend another Virginia convention in Richmond.[37] It had assembled two weeks earlier, and Charles Lewis of Albemarle was sitting in his place. To all practical purposes this body ruled the Province. In addition it passed certain military measures to which Dunmore would not have consented. It elected officers to command three regiments of militia. Patrick Henry, who had become a symbol of bold action, was chosen first and was designated as commander in chief. Peyton Randolph was again available for Congress but Henry, like Washington, was regarded as ineligible and Pendleton asked to be excused on grounds of health. The vote was as follows: [38]

[35] To Jefferson, Nov. 12, 1813 (*Works*, X, 78–80).
[36] Burnett, *Letters*, I, 151, 171, etc.
[37] The proceedings of the convention of July 17–Aug. 26, 1775, can be conveniently seen in Force, 4 ser. III, 365–397. See also Lingley, *Transition in Va.*, ch. 6, *passim*.
[38] Force, 4 ser., III, 379.

Peyton Randolph	89	Benjamin Harrison	83
Richard Henry Lee	88	Thomas Nelson, Jr.	66
Thomas Jefferson	85	Richard Bland	61
	George Wythe	58	

When Bland asked to be relieved on account of the infirmities of age, Patrick Henry, with Jefferson and Colonel Carrington, headed a "strong party" to elect George Mason, but for personal reasons that learned man begged off, recommending Francis Lightfoot Lee, who was elected.[39] The dominant attitude toward public service at the time was reflected in the argument which Jefferson and others advanced to him: namely, that one could not refuse to obey the orders of his "country," whatever these might be. Election to office in Virginia was regarded more as a call to duty than as a political reward, and the prevailing practice was to re-elect men whose labors had been acceptable. It would not be proper to rank the leaders in the Colony by the vote for delegates in which Jefferson stood third. From other evidence it is clear that half a dozen others were more prominent than he. Unquestionably, however, he was now regarded as a proved public servant.

He spent only a week at the convention, but he found time to attend to one bit of unfinished personal business before he set out for home. He delivered to Carter Braxton an order for £13 in favor of the Attorney General, John Randolph. This constituted the purchase price for the latter's fine violin, and by paying it Jefferson dissolved the bargain they had made more than four years before.[40] Unlike his brother Peyton and his own son Edmund, John Randolph could not go along with the Patriots, and, now that the line had been sharply drawn, he purposed to remove to England, leaving behind him the instrument he had expected to keep till death. The first fruits of victory were Jefferson's, but it is doubtful if he felt triumphant. Soon after his return to Monticello he wrote to his old friend:

> . . . I now send the bearer for the violin & such music appertaining to her as may be of no use to the young ladies. I believe you had no case for her. If so, be so good as to direct Watt Lenox to get from Prentis's some bags or other coarse woolen to wrap her in and then pack her securely in a wooden box.[41]

[39] Mason to Cockburn, Aug. 22, 1775; Rowland, I, 206. He was practically forced to accept appointment to the committee of safety, however. Pendleton's experience was similar; see letter to Jefferson, Nov. 16, 1775, LC, 2:184.

[40] Account Book, Aug. 17, 1775; earlier agreement April 11, 1771, Ford I, 392.

[41] Aug. 25, 1775; LC, 1:162. This passage is omitted from the printed version of the letter in Ford, I, 482–485. Randolph replied Aug. 31, 1775; LC, 1:165.

Randolph delivered over the cherished instrument, thus completing a highly interesting transaction. Meanwhile, the younger violinist had clearly revealed his personal attitude toward the public issue in his private letter.

> I hope [said Jefferson] the returning wisdom of Great Britain will, ere long, put an end to this unnatural contest. There may be people to whose tempers and dispositions contention is pleasing, and who, therefore, wish a continuance of confusion, but to me it is of all states but one, the most horrid. My first wish is a restoration of our just rights; my second, a return to the happy period, when, consistently with duty, I may withdraw myself totally from the public stage, and pass the rest of my days in domestic ease and tranquillity, banishing every desire of ever hearing what passes in the world.

He urged Randolph to inform the British ministry of the true state of colonial opinion, and, while claiming that he still favored conciliation, expressed the belief that the Americans would demand better terms, now that blood had been spent.

> . . . I wish no false sense of honor, no ignorance of our real intentions, no vain hope that partial concessions of right will be accepted, may induce the Ministry to trifle with accommodation, till it shall be out of their power ever to accommodate. . . . I am sincerely one of those [who wish for reunion] and would rather be in dependence on Great Britain, properly limited, than on any other nation on earth, or than on no nation. But I am one of those, too, who, rather than submit to the rights of legislating for us, assumed by the British Parliament, and which late experience has shown they will so cruelly exercise, would lend my hand to sink the whole Island in the ocean. . . . Whether Britain shall continue the head of the greatest empire on earth, or shall return to her original station in the political scale of Europe, depends, perhaps, on the resolutions of the succeeding winter. God send they may be wise and salutary for us all. . . .

John Randolph contented himself with expressing a strong desire for the continuation of personal friendship. "We both of us seem to be steering opposite courses," he said; "the success of either lies in the womb of Time."

Jefferson had a respite of about a month from public duties. During that time occurred the death of his second daughter, Jane Randolph, who had lived less than a year and a half altogether, but he has left only a bare record of the event. He picked up some of the threads of plantation life at Monticello, and in late September he was commissioned by the Committee of Safety as county lieutenant and commander of the militia of Albemarle, but the Colonel was unable to do much service at home just then.[42] He had to set out again for Philadelphia.

He went by Orange Courthouse and Culpeper this time, remaining longer within sight of the mountains, and he made a quicker trip than his previous one from Williamsburg. He took at least one slave along, a boy named Bob, whom he had Dr. Shippen inoculate before he returned. He returned to his old lodgings with Benjamin Randolph but now shared the place with other delegates and engaged with them in common-stock housekeeping. These included Peyton Randolph, whose wife was with him, and Jefferson's old friend Thomas Nelson, Junior, another fat man, though alert and lively for his weight; and there may have been others.[43] The old Speaker had not displaced John Hancock as presiding officer in the State House and he did not linger long. Jefferson was with him in the October evening when he died of apoplexy at a house outside of the city whither he had gone to dine. The remains were removed to Christ Church from Benjamin Randolph's, and Jefferson undoubtedly attended the elaborate funeral services with the other members of Congress, wearing crape around his arm.[44]

He was kept busy attending the sessions in the State House, which lasted all day, though they did not accomplish much. The expeditions of Montgomery and Arnold to Canada provided the most exciting news. When he learned of the capture of Montreal he jubilantly declared that the success of American arms corresponded with the justice of the colonial cause, and he added an optimistic prophecy: "In a short time, we have reason to hope, the delegates of Canada will join us in Congress, and complete the American union, as far as we wish to have it completed." [45] It will be recalled that they did not.

The delegates as a rule were too optimistic, but in the fall of 1775 they generally recognized that the prospects of a peaceful settlement were remote. In the second week after Jefferson's arrival one of them wrote: "In one word all hopes of speedy reconciliation are given over, and we unanimously determine to push the war with the greatest vigour." [46]

Soon thereafter, they learned that the King had proclaimed the

[42] Sept. 26, 1775, LC, 1:168; other details from Account Book.
[43] Various references in Account Book; Jefferson to Nelson, May 16, 1776 (Ford, II, 2; John Adams, *Works*, II, 422).
[44] Account Book, Oct. 22, 1775; Jefferson to Joseph Delaplaine, July 26, 1816 (Ford, X, 55); *Journals Cont. Cong.*, Oct. 23, 1775, III, 302-303.
[45] To John Randolph, Nov. 29, 1775 (Ford, I, 492).
[46] Samuel Ward to Henry Ward, Oct. 11, 1775; Burnett, *Letters*, I, 226.

colonies in a state of rebellion and had threatened dire punishment to traitors.[47] This proclamation called for a strong answer, and Jefferson might well have been asked to draft it, but actually he was not. Virginia was represented on the committee by Richard Henry Lee, who spoke much better than he wrote, but with him were two men who were regarded as good penmen, James Wilson and William Livingston.[48]

As Jefferson read their report he must have noted that Congress as a body had caught up with his thinking in some respects — but not in all. "What allegiance is it that we forget? Allegiance to Parliament? We never owed — we never owned it." He had said that more than a year before. Unquestionably he approved of this statement: "To support our laws, and our liberties established by our laws, we have prepared, ordered, and levied war." But he would not have contented himself with invoking the British Constitution; he would have mentioned the higher law of nature. Also, if left to his own devices, he would have spoken more sharply about George III.

He did just that on the very day that this report was laid open to the members. Ostensibly, he set out to inform his Loyalist friend, John Randolph, of the death of the latter's brother Peyton which had occurred six weeks before; but he seized the occasion to speak his mind about the King, whom he now described as an immense misfortune to the entire Empire.[49]

> . . . We are told [he said], and everything proves it true, that he is the bitterest enemy we have. . . . To undo his empire, he has but one truth more to learn; that, after colonies have drawn the sword, there is but one step more they can take. That step is now pressed upon us, by the measures adopted, as if they were afraid we would not take it.

He himself would hate to take it but he left no doubt of his resolution.

> Believe me, dear Sir, there is not in the British empire a man who more cordially loves a union with Great Britain, than I do. But by the God that made me, I will cease to exist before I yield to a connection on such terms as the British Parliament propose; and in this, I think I speak the sentiments of America.

[47] Burnett, *Continental Congress*, pp. 115–116; *Journals*, Nov. 9, 13, 1775, III, 343, 353. A copy of the proclamation of Aug. 23, taken from a newspaper dated Nov. 13, was preserved by Jefferson; LC, 2:182–183.

[48] Committee appointed Nov. 13; report presented Nov. 29; adopted Dec. 6 (*Journals*, III, 353, 392, 409–412).

[49] Nov. 29, 1775; Ford, I, 491–493.

He did not say that secession from the Empire was inevitable, but unquestionably he thought that it was becoming so.

> We want neither inducement nor power, to declare and assert a separation. It is will, alone, that is wanting, and that is growing apace under the fostering hand of our King. One bloody campaign will probably decide, everlastingly, our future course; and I am sorry to find a bloody campaign is decided on.

In the meantime, there was little that he could do except perform routine tasks on committees. He served on half a dozen in one period of two weeks in December; but no single assignment of his in the entire session turned out to be important, and several of his reports were left languishing on the table. The most spirited of his proposals came to nothing. Having been informed that Ethan Allen, the hero of Ticonderoga, had been captured near Montreal, Jefferson drafted an impassioned protest against his being taken in irons to England, to be punished for pretended treason. He threatened retaliation to stop the progress of butchery and to compel the enemy to respect the "rights of nations," but milder counsels prevailed among the delegates, who merely instructed Washington to seek an exchange.[50] Jefferson's opinions about British unscrupulousness were now deep-seated, but the important thing to note here is that his own normal mildness of manner completely vanished when he was speaking or writing — especially when he was writing — about cruelty and what he regarded as injustice. When aroused, this man who loathed contention could become passionate indeed.

Toward the end of December, he left Congress for Monticello. No recess had been ordered but the free movement of the members was characteristic of this body. Since a colony had only one vote regardless of the number of its delegates, not all of them needed always to be there. Jefferson had ample reason to believe that Virginia would be adequately represented in his absence. Throughout the fall he had been in an anxious state of mind about his family. He had set aside one day in each week, or the larger part of it, for writing letters, but he did not receive the ones he wanted. In the middle of the session he still had no word whatever about his wife and daughter. "The suspense under which I am is too terrible to be endured," he wrote his brother-in-law.

---

[50] *Journals*, Dec. 2, 1775; III, 402; Ford, I, 494–495. Allen was exchanged after two or three years' imprisonment.

"If anything has happened for God's sake let me know." [51] Patty and little Patsy were not then at Monticello but were visiting Francis and Elizabeth Eppes at the Forest. They were in the best of hands; but his fears about his wife's health had started. Also, there were many things he wanted to do at Monticello. It was high time that he went home.

Fortune was with him when he returned to Congress. Then there was something of real importance for him to do.

[51] To Francis Eppes, Nov. 7, 1775 (Randall, III, 570). See also letters of Oct. 10, 24, and Nov. 21 to Eppes, and letter of Oct. 31 to Page in *Ibid.*, III, 568–570; Ford, I, 488–489. Unfortunately, his correspondence with his wife has not been preserved.

[XVI]

Herald of Freedom

1776

IN Virginia, Lord Dunmore ushered in the year 1776 by bombarding Norfolk. Jefferson was on the homeward road by that time but before he left Philadelphia he knew that war had actually begun in his own Province, and, like practically everybody else, he placed the responsibility squarely on the shoulders of the Governor. That dour Scot, after flitting from one ship to another, had issued an emancipation proclamation from the *William* early in November.[1] It was not destined to rank with Lincoln's. Despite the fact that he retained only the shadow of authority he had declared martial law; and he had summoned the slaves to revolt and join his banner. There was some fighting in the coastal country but he did not have enough troops to make much of a showing. He attracted some runaway slaves and encouraged a few Loyalists, but he served chiefly to infuriate the Virginians and to drive them along the road to independence.

Luckily, Jefferson and his family were remote from the scene of Dunmore's activities, and he reflected that only such places as lay on the water's edge were actually endangered. John Page was much concerned about his house in the Tidewater county of Gloucester, but Monticello was still a haven of peace and the contemporary records of its master reflect little consciousness of a state of war. As county lieutenant he had duties to perform, and it may have been at this time that he carefully listed the volunteers from Albemarle; but he also broached a pipe of Madeira of the vintage of 1770, began to stock his park with deer, and welcomed to his stable another foal of the proud line of

[1] Nov. 7, 1775. See *Dunmore's Proclamation of Emancipation*, with an account by Francis Berkeley (McGregor Library, Univ. of Va., 1941).

Fearnought. For four months he lived as a country gentleman in virtual retirement.[2]

He was quite prepared to resume his public duties as soon as he was really needed, but he welcomed the opportunity to put his thoughts in order and to remain with his wife, about whom he continued to be troubled. He was urged by his friend Nelson, who had his own lady with him in Philadelphia, to bring her with him but she was in no condition to go. It would have been unlike him to give any further explanation, but the chances are that she carried other children than those who finally appeared upon the record and that there were mishaps which went unmentioned.

Jefferson had no special reason to be alarmed about his mother, then living at Shadwell, but on the last day of March she suffered what was supposed to be an apoplectic stroke, lingered for an hour, and died in her fifty-seventh year. He left only a bald and unemotional record of the event, partly through accident it may be, but also because of his consistent reticence in all personal matters.[3] This was just about the date that he had expected to return to Congress, but in the meantime he himself fell ill and was incapacitated for some five weeks longer. The report got around that he was suffering from an inveterate headache which had a hard name; probably it was what we now call migraine. By early May he was over it, and in the fullness of time he descended from the mountain. He would have preferred to go to Williamsburg, where the last and most noted of the Revolutionary conventions of Virginia was assembling, but duty called him to Philadelphia and he was ready.

Accompanied by his servant Bob he went again by the upland route, carrying with him funds he had collected for the purchase of powder for Virginia and for the relief of the poor in Boston, and after a week's journey he arrived at his old lodgings.[4] Eight days later he removed to a new brick house, three stories high, on the southwest corner of Market and Seventh Streets. This belonged to a bricklayer by the name of Graff (spelled "Graaf" by him), then newly married. Jefferson's quarters on the second floor consisted of a bedroom and parlor, which had the stairs between them. He did his writing in the parlor and commonly used a folding writing-box which his former landlord, the cabinetmaker Benjamin Randolph, had made from Jefferson's own drawing.

---

[2] Page to Jefferson, Nov. 11, [1775], LC, 2:178–181; list of volunteers, LC, 6:1063; Account Book, Jan. 28, Feb. 8, Mar. 26, 1776.
[3] Account Book, Mar. 31, 1776; Jefferson to —— Randolph, Aug.–Sept. 1776, MHS, UVA photostat.
[4] Details in Account Book, beginning May 7, 1776.

He still had it half a century later. "It claims no merit of particular beauty," he then said. "It is plain, neat, convenient, and, taking no more room on the writing table than a moderate quarto volume, it yet displays itself sufficiently for any writing." On this box and in this brick house he drafted the Declaration of Independence.[5]

The period of debate was over, as Thomas Paine had said. While Jefferson was still at Monticello he received from Nelson in Philadelphia "a present of 2/ worth of Common Sense," and thus became acquainted with Paine's catalytic pamphlet. Furthermore, he went to great pains to sound out local sentiment before he left home and became convinced that nine tenths of the people in the upper counties favored independence. In Philadelphia he found awaiting him a month-old letter from John Page in which this friend exhorted him: "For God's sake declare the colonies independent and save us from ruin." Also, he had one of the same date from another old college-mate who said: "The notion of independency seems to spread fast in this colony, and will be adopted, I dare say, by a majority of the next convention." But Jefferson was only a delegate to Congress, and he had to await specific instructions from his "country."[6]

On May 15, 1776, the gentlemen in Williamsburg instructed their delegates to propose to Congress that the united colonies be declared free and independent states. Twelve days later these delegates presented their instructions. While the resolution lay on the table in the State House in Philadelphia, the people in Williamsburg generally assumed that Virginia had already declared her independence. Ardent patriots hoisted a new flag, that of the Continental Union, over the Capitol, and the convention proceeded to create a new government. On June 28 it adopted a constitution and there could then be no possible doubt that the Virginians had severed their imperial bonds and embarked on an independent course. Whether the states preceded the Union or the Union preceded the states is as futile a question as that about the hen and the egg, but the historic primacy of the oldest and strongest of the colonies in the cause of freedom was generally and generously recognized. Thus, within a few weeks, this apostrophe appeared in print:

[5] On the box, see his letter to Ellen Coolidge, Nov. 14, 1825, *Papers, M.H.S.*, p. 361; on the house, the thoroughly documented account in J. H. Hazelton, *Declaration of Independence* (1906), pp. 149–154.

[6] From Thomas Nelson, Jr., Feb. 4, 1776, *N.-Eng. Hist. & Geneal. Register*, LVI, 54; from Page, Apr. 6, 1776, *Ibid.*, LVI, 55; from James McClurg, Apr. 6, 1776, LC, 2:216; to Nelson, May 16, 1776, Ford, II, 3.

And now, when Britain's mercenary bands
Bombard our cities, desolate our lands,
(Our pray'rs unanswer'd, and our tears in vain,)
While foreign cut-throats crowd th' ensanguin'd plain;
Thy glowing virtue caught the glorious flame,
And first renounc'd the cruel tyrant's name!
With just disdain, and most becoming pride,
Further dependence on the crown deny'd.
Whilst freedom's voice can in these wilds be heard,
Virginia's patriots shall be still rever'd.[7]

During the months of May and June, 1776, one of "Virginia's patriots" was feeling a little sorry for himself in Philadelphia. Jefferson had begun immediately to serve on committees, and these filled up a good deal of time. During this period he dealt particularly with the affairs of Canada, drafting several reports and referring frequently in letters to the misfortunes the American expedition had suffered.[8] He was much more interested in the affairs of Virginia, however, and he made more important use of his new writing-box in drafting a constitution for his own Commonwealth. This document, which he sent to the convention by George Wythe about the middle of June, will be considered later. The main thing to be said here is that Jefferson sent with it a list of charges against King George III, which the convention attached to its new constitution as a preamble. His fellow planters did not follow the precise wording in which he declared the King "deposed," but they did declare that, because of the acts of misrule enumerated by Jefferson, the government of their "country" as formerly exercised under the Crown of Great Britain was totally dissolved. Thus they joined with him in setting the backdrop for a more famous action.

One of his specific recommendations to his own countrymen ought also to be mentioned here. He proposed that such colonies as should be established in Virginia's domain west of the mountains should be "free and independent of this colony and of all the world." [9] He did not intend them to be subordinate. At this early date he advocated the policy which was afterwards embodied in legislative acts of original states and in ordinances of Congress, and which permitted the historic expansion of the American Republic through the creation of new

[7] July 27, 1776; Frank Moore, *Diary of the Revolution* (1876), quoting *Freeman's Journal*.

[8] See particularly reports of May 21, June 17, 1776 (Ford, II, 4-6, 30-39); letters to Nelson, May 19, to Fleming, July 1, and to Eppes, July 15 (*Ibid.*, II, 3, 39-40, 63-64).

[9] Ford, II, 26.

states, equal in all respects to the old. His prophetic finger pointed to the enlarged Union of the future.

In Philadelphia the pace was slower than in Williamsburg, but the tempo was quickening. With customary care the denouncer of George III and the prophet of an expanding confederation made certain notes on proceedings; these he incorporated long years later in his autobiography with a glow of satisfaction.

> In Congress, *Friday, June 7*, 1776. The delegates from Virginia moved in obedience to instructions from their constituents that the Congress should declare that these United colonies are & of right ought to be free & independent states, that they are absolved from all allegiance to the British crown, and that all political connection between them & the state of Great Britain is, & ought to be, totally dissolved; . . .[10]

This was the first of the famous resolutions presented for the delegation by Richard Henry Lee.

Jefferson did not participate in the debate on the floor that took place a couple of days later, though he noted the arguments. In the course of this debate it appeared to him and others that the middle colonies and South Carolina "were not yet matured for falling from the parent stem, but that they were fast advancing to that state." [11] Accordingly, it was decided to postpone the final decision until July 1, and to appoint a committee in the meantime to prepare a declaration. This consisted of Jefferson, John Adams, Franklin, Roger Sherman, and Robert R. Livingston.[12]

Since Richard Henry Lee had presented the resolution for independence in the first place, there has been much speculation about his failure to be appointed to the committee instead of Jefferson. If this was because of his unpopularity within the Virginia delegation and the desire to build Jefferson up against him, as John Adams said, there was no sign of any alienation of the two men at the time. Two or three days after the committee was named, Lee set out for Virginia to see his ailing wife and to attend the convention in Williamsburg, as apparently he had intended doing all along. There is more reason to suppose that Jefferson envied Lee this opportunity than that Lee envied Jefferson. To both of them the proceedings in Williamsburg seemed more vital at the moment than the drafting of a document in Philadelphia. This

---

[10] Ford, I, 18. Other resolutions related to foreign alliances and a confederation.
[11] *Ibid.*, 24; see also 19–24.
[12] June 11, 1776, *Journals*, V. 429.

particular document they undoubtedly regarded as important, but nobody then knew it would turn out to be immortal. It might not have been if Lee had drawn it.

At all events, it was inevitable that a Virginian should be appointed to the committee and, despite his youth, Jefferson was a natural choice. His voice was uncertain but his pen was known to be potent and there could be no doubt that his mind was prepared. Presumably, the five members met at the house on the Bristol pike where Franklin was confined with the gout, and discussed the general form of the Declaration. Then Jefferson was asked to draft it. Whether or not he and Adams were appointed to a subcommittee, as the latter said and he himself denied, is unimportant; and even if the conversation between the two men did not occur precisely as Adams reported it long afterwards, the reasons which he then assigned were valid. It was the part of wisdom to assign the lead to a Virginian, for the middle colonies were lukewarm and the New Englanders were deliberately keeping themselves in the background at this stage. Also, Jefferson bore no such odium of mistrust and unpopularity as Adams attributed to himself and he was doubtless regarded as the better writer. However, he appears to have submitted his draft first to Adams and then to the ailing Franklin, and an early copy of it in the handwriting of the forthright delegate from Massachusetts survives as a priceless document.[13]

In the seventeen days between June 11, when the committee was appointed, and June 28, when they reported to Congress, Jefferson made his draft. He consulted no book or pamphlet, though he felt entirely free to do so and had no desire to be original. The purposes which he had in mind he afterwards stated with unexcelled frankness and clarity:

> . . . Not to find out new principles, or new arguments, never before thought of, not merely to say things which had never been said before; but to place before mankind the common sense of the subject, in terms so plain and firm as to command their assent, and to justify ourselves in the independent stand we are compelled to take. Neither aiming at originality of principle or sentiment, nor yet copied from any particular and previous writing,

[13] See the admirable study of J. P. Boyd, *The Declaration of Independence;* pp. 9–12, 40, Document IV, etc. Later discoveries are incorporated in an article by the same editor in *N. Y. Times Mag.,* Apr. 13, 1947. These include a letter from Franklin to Benj. Rush, June 26, 1776, discovered by Lyman H. Butterfield, implying that Franklin was confined to the house of Edward Duffield on the Bristol Pike, during June. The partially conflicting accounts of Jefferson and Adams are in Ford, I, 24–27 n., and J. H. Hazelton, *Declaration of Independence,* pp. 141–146. See also Carl Becker's brilliant work, *The Declaration of Independence,* ch. IV.

it was intended to be an expression of the American mind, and to give to that expression the proper tone and spirit called for by the occasion.[14]

He did copy a good deal from a particular and previous writing of his own. Beside his writing-box he spread out the charges against the King which he had sent to Virginia. These constituted the substantial foundation of the longest section in the Declaration. Another paper, which his fellow Virginians adopted before their constitution, was also available to him: the Declaration of Rights, largely drafted by George Mason and afterwards renowned. The phraseology of the even more famous philosophical paragraph in the intercolonial Declaration is similar to parts of this and may reflect its direct influence. Jefferson could have drawn on George Mason for his own statement of fundamental human rights, and he would have thought this not amiss, but the ideas were in his mind already. They belonged to no single man but, in his opinion, were the property of mankind. Certainly they were the property of the American Patriots, whose mind he was trying to express, and it really made no difference where they came from.

Jefferson's task was to impart the proper tone and spirit, and to do this he labored long. He was a ready writer but he could also be a fastidious one, and he never weighed his phrases more carefully than now. He even corrected the paper after it was formally adopted, in order to get a better word. He regarded capitalization and spelling with considerable indifference in letters, but here he went to unusual pains to regularize them.

The history of the evolving text of the Declaration has been studied by scholars with great care, in the effort to determine the authorship of every phrase and to distribute credit with impartial hand. Certain minor changes can be credited to Adams and Franklin; the authorship of others which Jefferson inserted at a later time in his Rough Draft will probably remain forever doubtful. In the first place he wrote: "We hold these truths to be sacred and undeniable." We cannot be sure whether it was he or Franklin who substituted "self-evident." [15] It is possible that the expression "unalienable rights" was owing to a printer's error, for Jefferson himself wrote "inalienable." The changes have been counted and recounted, but the ones made by his colleagues on the committee appear to have been few, and the document they approved and reported on June 28 was undeniably Jefferson's. Then it

---

[14] To Henry Lee, May 8, 1825; Ford, X, 343.
[15] Boyd, p. 22; Document V, p. 1. Since the discovery of a still earlier draft, he thinks the "Rough Draft" should really be called the "Committee Draft."

ran the gamut of Congress — to his own deep chagrin but with results that were generally beneficial.

Congress properly kept it on the table for a few days, for they still had to reach a decision on the question of independence itself. It was on July 2 that this question, which John Adams described as the greatest that ever was debated in America, was decided.[16] The resolution originally presented by Richard Henry Lee was then adopted and the delegates as a group were free to consider the precise form of the Declaration. They examined it during the three days, July 2–4. Jefferson dutifully observed the proprieties by listening in silence while less partial judges commented on the merits and demerits of his work. John Adams loyally supported every word of it, however, and Benjamin Franklin told him a comforting story while he writhed. This was about a hatter, whose inscription for a handsome signboard was subjected to such criticism that it was finally reduced to his name and the figure of a hat.[17]

Jefferson and some of his Virginia friends believed that Congress weakened the Declaration, but there can now be little doubt that the critics strengthened it. This they did primarily by deletion. The most important single omission was the perfervid charge against the King about the slave trade. In simpler form this had been accepted by Jefferson's fellow Virginians, who had included it in the preamble to their constitution just as he wrote it, even though they did not then outlaw the slave trade as he desired. In Congress, the South Carolinians and Georgians favored the continuance of the traffic; and certain of the Northern brethren were dubious about such sweeping condemnation, being aware that some of their people had engaged in the dirty business. Others besides George III were blameable. From the literary point of view this omission was no loss, for the charge was really out of character with the rest of the document. It was one of those rare Jeffersonian passages which are consciously rhetorical and betray a striving for effect.[18]

Also, Congress rewrote and greatly reduced the final paragraph, attaching to it, not Jefferson's assertion of independence, but the original resolution of Lee. These changes contributed to directness and thus constituted an improvement, but from Jefferson's Rough Draft certain touching expressions may be resurrected and allowed to speak for themselves — such, for example, as these: "We must endeavor to forget our former love for them, . . . We might have been a free and

[16] To Mrs. Adams, July 3, 1776; *Works*, IX, 418.
[17] Ford, X, 119–120 *n.*, 268.
[18] Becker, *Declaration of Independence*, pp. 212–216.

a great people together; . . ." Plenty of felicitous phrases were left —
more, probably, than in any other of Jefferson's compositions and quite
enough for any single document. In the last sentence Congress inserted
the phrase, "with a firm reliance on the protection of divine providence," but left his final words in their original form except for capitalization: "we mutually pledge to each other our lives, our Fortunes,
and our sacred Honour." They could not improve on these.

The literary excellence of the Declaration is best attested by the
fact that it has stood the test of time. It became the most popular state
paper of the American Republic not merely because it was the first,
but also because to most people it has seemed the best. No other American document has been read so often or listened to by so many weary
and perspiring audiences. Yet, despite interminable repetition, those
well-worn phrases have never lost their potency and charm.[19] So far
as form is concerned, the continuing appeal of the Declaration lies in
the fact that it is clear and simple and that, for all its careful craftsmanship and consummate grace, it was not so highly polished as to lose
its edge. Only in its reiterated charges against the King does it even
approach the declamatory. It may lack the stark grandeur of certain
passages from Lincoln, it may be almost too felicitous; but it has notable elevation of spirit and solemnity of tone. Intended as an expression of the American mind, it was also Jefferson at his literary best.[20]

Its immediate purpose was to justify the secession of the colonies
from the Mother Country. Thus, as every American should know, the
great document begins:

> When in the Course of human events, it becomes necessary for
> one people to dissolve the political bands, which have connected
> them with another, and to assume among the powers of the earth,
> the separate and equal station to which the Laws of Nature and
> of Nature's God entitle them, a decent respect to the opinions of
> mankind requires that they should declare the causes which impel
> them to the separation.

It is hard to see how Jefferson could have combined in such compass a larger number of important ideas or could have better imparted
the tone of dignity, solemnity, respectful firmness, and injured virtue
which the circumstances required. It was *necessary* to dissolve these old
political bands. The American people were *entitled* to an independent

[19] See M. C. Tyler, in *Lit. Hist. of the Amer. Revolution* (1897), I, 520–521.
[20] The best discussion of the literary qualities I know of is that of Carl Becker,
Declaration of Independence, ch. 5.

station under the laws of God and Nature, but they had a *decent respect* to the opinions of mankind and were thus impelled to give reasons for their course.

Before stating the specific reasons he took the whole controversy out of the realm of petty and selfish squabbling by setting it on a high background of philosophy. The philosophical passage in the Declaration, which he wrote as a single brief paragraph, became the most famous part of the document; and, as a summary of human rights and a justification of revolution in behalf of them, it is doubtful if it has ever been excelled. Actually he outlined a whole system of philosophy in a few sentences.[21] To this epitome of current wisdom, which he himself regarded as a creed, we must turn again as men have done through the generations. At the time, however, attention was focused on the specific rather than on the general grounds of revolution, for these were familiar to others besides enlightened gentlemen and the statement of them awakened echoes in more minds.

The charges in the Declaration were directed, not against the British people or the British Parliament, but against the King. There was definite purpose in this. Jefferson, and the great body of the Patriots with him, had already repudiated the authority of Parliament, and in his *Summary View* he had made a futile appeal to the Monarch. Now, this last tie was to be cut and the onus must be put on George III himself. Such a personification of grievances was unwarranted on strict historical grounds. This was the language of political controversy, not that of dispassionate scholarship. Nevertheless, in these charges Jefferson gave an extraordinarily full summary of the whole controversy with the Mother Country. He included the major grievances against Parliament by a clever literary device which avoided even the mention of that name.

> . . . He [the King] has combined with others to subject us to a jurisdiction foreign to our constitution, and unacknowledged by our laws; giving his Assent to their Acts of pretended Legislation.

Certain acts of "pretended" legislation were then specified.

At the bar of history these charges now seem extreme. Almost any modern historian can make a better case for the British authorities than Jefferson did, for he really granted them no case at all. This is not to say that he made any charge which could not have been backed by facts. These grievances were actual not imaginary; they recalled in every instance specific policies and events. They constituted a "long

[21] Well summarized in R. B. Perry, *Puritanism and Democracy*, p. 125.

train of abuses" and certain of them could properly be termed "usurpations," but historians of a later generation, who have been in position to study this controversy calmly, assign most of them to official stupidity or to helplessness in the face of the larger imperial problem, rather than to a deliberate design to reduce the colonies "under absolute despotism." By implication, certain of these charges were manifestly unjust. The causes of the American Revolution cannot be adduced from the Declaration alone, and Jefferson may be charged with over-simplifying an exceedingly complicated situation. This would have been a fault in an historian but under the circumstances it may be regarded as a virtue in a statesman.

He carried this over-simplification even further in another paper, which was written five years later and has remained obscure. In an address to an Indian chief, toward the end of his governorship of Virginia, he described the causes of the Revolution as a teacher might to a child.

> . . . You find us, brother, engaged in war with a powerful nation. Our forefathers were Englishmen, inhabitants of a little island beyond the great water, and, being distressed for land, they came and settled here. As long as we were young and weak, the English whom we had left behind, made us carry all our wealth to their country, to enrich them; and, not satisfied with this, they at length began to say we were their slaves, and should do whatever they ordered us. We were now grown up and felt ourselves strong; we knew we were free as they were, that we came here of our own accord and not at their biddance, and were determined to be free as long as we should exist. For this reason they made war on us.[22]

This sounds much *too* simple. But Jefferson's failure to allow for the complexities of the imperial problem and to grant any credit to British good will cannot be attributed to the fact that he had a simple mind or conspicuously lacked a sense of historical justice. The relativity of circumstances must always be remembered. On the verge of revolution Jefferson and his colleagues could not be expected to be dispassionate; he had long since weighed the conflicting arguments, and the preponderance on the Patriots' side seemed so great that he saw no need for apothecary's scales. He was wandering in no mist of doubt, seeking the totality of truth. His task as a statesman was to grasp the essence of the controversy, and as the penman of independence to set it forth — not in neutral shades but in bold contrasts of black and white.

[22] Address to Brother John Baptist de Coigne, June 1781 (L. & B., XVI, 372).

To his mind the fundamental issue was simple: British policy constituted a perilous threat to liberties that were dearer to him than life itself. Furthermore, he was convinced that British policy centered in the personality and was inseparable from the determination of a stubborn King. To him George III was not merely a symbol but a powerful personal obstacle to the sort of self-government he and his fellows were claiming as a natural human right. In his own mind he coupled the monarch with ill-fated Charles I. That year Jefferson heard from Benjamin Franklin a motto which he attributed to one of the regicides: "Rebellion to tyrants is obedience to God." He seized upon this immediately, put it on his own seal later, and made it a personal slogan throughout life.[23] In 1776 especially this was a stirring call to action, for the historical circumstances seemed to him strikingly analogous to those that had led to the successful revolt against the Stuart King. Jefferson was not a complete historian; and if a philosopher is one who can never quite make up his mind, he was no philosopher. If passionate devotion to causes one deems fundamental is partisanship, he was very generally a partisan, and certainly was one at this stage. But at no time afterwards did he ever doubt that his general estimate of this situation was correct.

He did not change his opinion about George III when he met him ten years later; but, considering the Declaration toward the end of his own life, he himself valued the "principles of the instrument" more than his wholesale indictment of British policy at the age of thirty-three.[24] Such, also, has been the judgment of history. It is not for the charges against the King but for the brief philosophical paragraph that posterity has been most grateful to him. Said Abraham Lincoln when the author of the Declaration had been dead for a generation: "All honor to Jefferson — to the man, who in the concrete pressure of a struggle for national independence by a single people, had the coolness, forecaste [sic], and sagacity to introduce into a merely revolutionary document an abstract truth, applicable to all men and all times, and so to embalm it there that to-day and in all coming days it shall be a rebuke and a stumbling-block to the very harbingers of reappearing tyranny and oppression." [25] These words from Lincoln could have been echoed with eminent appropriateness during the latest and greatest of wars, for the doctrines of the

[23] Franklin suggested the motto for the seal of the United States in the summer of 1776; see references to this and to Jefferson's own seal in the following chapter. For Jefferson's crediting the motto to a regicide, see his letter to Edward Everett, Feb. 24, 1823 (L. & B., XV, 415).

[24] To Madison, Aug. 30, 1823; Ford, X, 269.

[25] Apr. 6, 1859, to H. L. Pierce and others, responding to an invitation to attend a celebration in honor of Jefferson's birthday in Boston (L. & B., I, xvii).

Declaration stand in complete antithesis to those which the totalitarians of the twentieth century proclaimed. Jefferson's words should make tyranny tremble in any age.

They have alarmed conservative minds in his own land in every generation, and some compatriots of his have regretted that the new Republic was dedicated to such radical doctrines at its birth. Whether it would have been thus dedicated, amid such incense of universalism, if Jefferson had not officiated at the altar, no man can say. At the dawn of American independence Congress made his words official and held "these truths to be self-evident; that all men are created equal; that they are endowed by their Creator with certain unalienable rights; that among these are life, liberty, and the pursuit of happiness; that to secure these rights, governments are instituted among men, deriving their just powers from the consent of the governed."

The immediate deduction was the right of revolution against a government which was destructive of these ends. Another deduction was inescapable: the governments to be established here must aim first of all to secure these rights. American democracy might have developed as the resultant of other forces, geographical and economic, but the fact is that this passage became its major charter. "The history of American democracy," as has been wisely said, "is a gradual realization, too slow for some and too rapid for others, of the implications of the Declaration of Independence." [26]

It will require a long book to show in convincing detail what Jefferson himself sought to realize, how he tried to do it, how he both succeeded and failed; but two important questions of implication should be raised here. One is about property, which he did not mention in this famous passage; the other is about the natural equality of men, which he proclaimed.

Was there any significance in his omission of the word "property," which had been used by John Locke, and his substitution for it of the phrase "pursuit of happiness"? It is exceedingly doubtful that his contemporaries thought there was. Locke presupposed the pursuit of happiness, and Jefferson always assumed as basic the right of an individual to hold property. He did not anticipate communism. Nevertheless, his use here of a more inclusive phrase than the word "property" was probably deliberate, and if it does not clearly indicate a philosophical distinction between different sorts of rights it does suggest the characteristic shading of his thought. From his later statements and actions there can be no doubt that such rights as freedom of mind, conscience, and person were the ones he cherished most. These unquestionably

[26] Ralph Barton Perry, in *Puritanism and Democracy*, p. 133.

were inalienable, and also desirable in themselves; property was indispensable, just as government was, but, like it, was a means to human happiness and not an end.[27]

Other expressions then seemed much more significant. At the Virginia convention shortly before this, during the discussion of George Mason's Declaration of Rights, certain "aristocrats" objected to the statement that men are by nature equally free and independent, "as being the forerunner or pretext of civil convulsion." The revolutionary character of the doctrine was recognized. The objectors were calmed down, however, by the observation that this was mostly talk and that the generalization did not apply to slaves, at any rate.[28] If Jefferson had been present and had been questioned on this point he would have said that the general statement did apply to slaves, and that these unfortunate creatures had lost their freedom and all semblance of equality through the operation of human law, which in this respect was in conflict with the higher law of Nature. His own recommendations to that convention do not reveal him as an impatient reformer, and in reality he never became one, but they leave no doubt that he took his own philosophy seriously. Slavery in his native region was one of the contradictions he always had to face; it was one of the tyrannical forms he was unable to abolish. The natural equality he talked about was not that of intellectual endowment, but, as Lincoln so clearly perceived, he proclaimed for all time the dignity of human nature.

At a crucial moment in 1776, Congress was under the control of men who were willing to adopt, under the pressure of imperial circumstances, what amounted to a charter of individual liberty and human rights, and to inscribe it indelibly on the page of history. This was translated into democratic terms as soon as men began to employ them widely. Thus a sensitive and fastidious gentleman, who prized privacy

[27] This question is ably summarized and discussed by Perry, *Ibid.*, pp. 184–186, with citations. Gilbert Chinard holds to the position that Jefferson made a definite distinction between inalienable rights and rights of a second class, though he sees in him no hostility to property; *Thomas Jefferson* (2 ed., revised, 1939), pp. 80–85. Adrienne Koch finds ample proof for Jefferson's recognition of the right to property as a basic natural right; *Philosophy of Thomas Jefferson*, p. 175. The claim made by Parrington that Jefferson's action marked a complete breach with the Whiggish doctrine of property rights is extreme; *Main Currents in American Thought*, I, 344. A good statement of Jefferson's later attitude toward different sorts of rights is in his letter to Noah Webster, Dec. 4, 1790, in Ford, V, 254–255.

[28] Hilldrup, *Pendleton*, pp. 169–170, citing Rowland, *Mason*, I, 240. The original authority for the observation, however, is Edmund Randolph; see *Va. Mag.*, XLIV, 45. The inapplicability of the Declaration of Rights to slaves and free Negroes was affirmed by the Virginia courts at a later time, in disagreement with Jefferson's friend George Wythe; Margaret V. Nelson, *A Study of Judicial Review in Virginia, 1789–1928* (New York, 1947), p. 184.

and disliked the rabble, became a major prophet not only of freedom but also of democracy. He himself was slower to use the latter term than to realize the implications of his doctrine, and his actions at this time were not motivated by personal political ambition. Nor had he proceeded in a mood of sentimentality. He felt with his mind and his mind left him in no doubt that what he had said was right.

On July 4 this thoughtful and observant man arose at dawn according to his custom, noting in the back of his Account Book that the temperature was 68° Fahrenheit at 6 A.M. On his way to or from the State House that very day he paid for a thermometer, but undoubtedly he had used this or another one already. His record of the temperature from this time forward, wherever he happened to be, was practically unbroken. He never ceased being interested in climate, though he believed that likes and dislikes in this respect were largely a matter of habit. To one of his upbringing this day must have been quite comfortable. His highest reading of the thermometer, 76°, was at one o'clock. His thoughts were not wholly of the place and season, however, for on that day he also paid for seven pairs of women's gloves, destined for Monticello.

On July 4, 1776, at Oxford, where Lord North was chancellor, honorary degrees were conferred by that ancient and honorable university on Thomas Hutchinson, late Governor of Massachusetts Bay, and Peter Oliver, late Deputy Governor.[29] In England they could not be expected to know just what was happening in Congress, and not even the delegates in Philadelphia thought of this as the birthday of the American Republic.

The great decision was made on July 2, when the resolution of independence was adopted. What actually happened on July 4 was that twelve states agreed to the written Declaration embodying this resolution, while the delegates from New York refrained from voting. The action did not become unanimous until July 15, when the resolutions of the New York convention were laid before Congress. In the meantime, the Declaration was authenticated by the bold signature of President John Hancock, and by that of Secretary Charles Thomson; it was printed and transmitted to the various assemblies, conventions, committees, and commanding officers; and on July 8 in Philadelphia it was first proclaimed by the local Committee of Safety. John Adams has left a brief account of this event, which occurred in the State House yard in the presence of a great crowd of people.[30]

[29] *Annual Register, 1776* (4 ed., London, 1788), p. 159.
[30] To Samuel Chase, July 9, 1776; *Works*, IX, 420. For an admirable summary of chronology, see Burnett, *Continental Congress*, pp. 188–197.

Jefferson must have been present but he was not in the spotlight; nobody announced that he was the author of this paper or led him forward upon the stage to take a bow. Cheers mounted to the sky; battalions paraded on the Common; and the bells rang all day and most of the night. This was in celebration not of a document but of an event. The tie with the Mother Country had been cut and Congress as a body was responsible for that dangerous and fateful action. Not until July 19 did Congress order that the Declaration be engrossed on parchment and signed by the members. Jefferson himself could not have affixed his own name until August 2. The names of the delegates were well known, but the signatures themselves were not made public until the following January and Jefferson's was one of many, even then.

This is another way of saying that his chief fame from the Declaration lay in the future. As he poked around the shops of Philadelphia bystanders may have pointed him out as an influential delegate, but they did not hail him as the author and he probably would not have wanted them to. At the moment, in fact, his pride in authorship was slight, for he believed that Congress had manhandled his composition and marred its strength. He cared little for general applause but he wanted to guard his own literary reputation among the select. He made copies of his own draft as it had emerged from the committee, and sent these to some of his friends; they could compare it with the final version and judge whether it was better or worse for the critics.[31]

Richard Henry Lee, who was entitled to a copy on other grounds, believed that the critics had "mangled" the paper, and most of Jefferson's friends in Virginia sent comments which were gratifying to him personally. Pendleton thought the charges against the King an improvement over those in the preamble to the Virginia constitution, and John Page was highly pleased with the Declaration as a whole. But these friends did not differentiate sharply between the act of asserting independence and the document in the case. Thus Lee said that the "Thing itself" — that is, independence — was so good that no cookery could spoil the dish for the palates of freemen. Nobody regarded the paper as in any sense a private affair and Page's prayer was the natural and proper one: "God preserve the United States." [32]

[31] To R. H. Lee, July 8, 1776; Ford, II, 259. In *The Declaration of Independence*, Boyd reproduces all the known drafts and copies in Jefferson's hand. These include the copies made for Lee and Wythe and an unidentified copy which may have been sent to Pendleton or John Page.

[32] To William Fleming, July 1, 1776, Ford, II, 41; from R. H. Lee, July 21, 1776, *Letters*, I, 210; from Page, July 20, 1776 (*N.-Eng. Hist. & Genealog. Reg.*, LVI, 152); from Pendleton, July 22, 1776 (LC, II, 277). For general comments on contemporary indifference to the Declaration as a document, see J. C. Fitzpatrick, *Spirit of the Revolution*, esp. ch. 2.

Nobody except Jefferson himself took his wounded pride as an author very seriously and he proceeded to dismiss the paper from his mind. He kept his contemporary record of events, but not until later did he put them in their present form and by that time his memory was confused. Because of an ambiguous statement in what passed for the official record, he, like nearly everybody else, forgot the exact date at which he affixed his signature. As an old man he talked much about such antiquarian matters, because they were so often referred to him, but in July, 1776, the most important fact was that independence had been proclaimed in the name of the officers of the Continental Congress. This was political revolution and it brought grave dangers in its train. Jefferson did not forget, however, that in a moment of high faith he had formulated a creed for himself and the Republic. His dominant concern henceforth was to translate this into legal institutions and to make it a living reality. During the next three years in Virginia he devoted himself more impressively to this task than to the more immediate one of winning the war and the equally imperative one of establishing a more perfect Union.

Liberalizing a Commonwealth

[XVII]

Framing a Government

1776

JEFFERSON remained in Congress from the middle of May, 1776, until the beginning of September, and his devotion to the general American cause did not slacken, but his heart was always in Virginia. He had hardly arrived in Philadelphia before he expressed the hope that he might be recalled for a time to attend the convention in Williamsburg. This was not primarily because the fateful question of independence would be raised there. He could anticipate what the answer to that would be, and as things turned out his presence would not have affected the decision. What he wanted was a share in framing the new government of his Commonwealth. "It is a work of the most interesting nature and such as every individual would wish to have his voice in," he wrote to his friend Nelson, who was back in Virginia at the time. "*In truth it is the whole object of the present controversy;* for should a bad government be instituted for us, in future it had been as well to have accepted at first the bad one offered us from beyond the water without the risk and expense of contest." [1]

Obviously he was not one of those who would rest content with freeing the Province from external control. He regarded political independence not as an end but as a means, and was more deeply concerned about what should follow the formal separation than about the action itself. Furthermore, what he said and did about the constitution of Virginia made it abundantly clear that he was no mere purveyor of philosophical generalities, but a man of practical purpose who was formulating a definite program.

At the outset he questioned the right of the convention to create a

[1] To Thomas Nelson, Jr., May 16, 1776 (Ford, II, 1–2). Italics mine, as well as a minor change in punctuation.

permanent constitution, believing that such a document should be the work of deputies specially elected for that purpose and thus be based more indubitably on the popular will.[2] His objections, which were presented by Edmund Randolph in his absence, were overborne on practical as well as theoretical grounds, and there would have been no point in his pressing them further at this juncture. But the fact that he raised them again afterwards showed that he was very serious about them; and anyone who looked behind the scenes could see that he was already a more thoroughgoing champion of popular government than Edmund Pendleton or George Mason or Patrick Henry.

The draft of a constitution that Jefferson made before the middle of June and sent to the convention by George Wythe was not considered as a whole, for the ostensible reason that it arrived too late. To Wythe himself this seemed a sufficient explanation. The weather in Willamsburg was hot, the delegates were tired, and a draft for which George Mason was chiefly responsible had been accepted by the committee and presented on the floor. The only feasible procedure with regard to Jefferson's draft seemed to be to draw upon it for purposes of amendment.[3] That the delegates were willing to do this and to adopt his preamble (containing charges against the King) practically as he had written it, was all he could have reasonably expected. What the result would have been if he had been able to throw his plan into the hopper at the beginning and to urge it in person is a matter of sheer speculation. The fact is that George Mason, not he, became the major architect of the new government and that he was not satisfied with the results. The differences between his draft and that of the committee did not seem great at first glance, and a first glance was all that most of the delegates gave to Jefferson's document, but some of these differences were important.

The convention adopted a Declaration of Rights before it did a constitution, thus establishing a theoretical foundation in advance. Jefferson himself soon did much the same thing by placing the philosophical section at the beginning of the Declaration of Independence. His countrymen, who had expressed the rights of men as human beings and not merely as Englishmen, had made history. The Virginia Declaration of Rights, often incorrectly called the Bill of Rights, exercised great influence both at home and abroad and was regarded in later years as an epoch-making document. Said Lafayette: "The era of the American Revolution, which one can regard as the beginning of a new

[2] Edmund Randolph, in *Va. Mag.*, XLIV, 43.
[3] Wythe to Jefferson, July 27, 1776 (LC, 2:284).

social order for the entire world, is, properly speaking, the era of declarations of rights." [4]

Jefferson was always proud that the first notable American paper of the sort emanated from his own Commonwealth. Certain of its articles did not go quite as far as he desired. For example, freedom of religion was only vaguely described in it, whereas in his proposed constitution he included freedom from the requirement to frequent or maintain *any* religious institution. He already favored the disestablishment of the Church and he soon drew a better statement of the ideal of religious freedom. As far as it went, however, he thought the Declaration of Rights admirable and he regarded its chief author, George Mason, as a sincere republican and a man of the first order of wisdom.

In Jefferson's opinion the new Commonwealth had the first requirement of a good government: it was based on a sound doctrine of human rights. The next question was just how the Declaration of Rights was to be interpreted and applied. The immediate answer was given in the constitution that was adopted and the machinery that was actually set up. The convention was dominated by moderate men, not radicals, and they had no desire to usher in a political and social revolution. The plantation aristocrats had led the revolt against Great Britain, with some dissent on the part of extreme conservatives; and, having brought about this break, they sought to maintain their own political and economic position. They were willing to do lip service to human rights and as a group they were humane men, but most of them would probably have been content to restore local conditions as they had existed before 1763, when the British government changed its policy. Jefferson himself was no wild radical in practice, but he looked forward, not backward, and was more determined than the other leaders to carry his ideas about human rights to their logical conclusion.

This determination was not strikingly manifest in the proposals about the *structure* of the state government that he included in his draft of a constitution, for these were almost if not quite as conservative as the ones actually adopted. Referring to the entire era of the American Revolution, he afterwards said: "In truth, the abuses of monarchy had so much filled all the space of political contemplation, that we imagined everything republican which was not monarchy. We had not yet penetrated to the mother principle, that 'governments are republican only in proportion as they embody the will of the people and execute it.' Hence, our first constitutions had really no leading principles in them." [5] The course of development was natural enough and really called for

[4] *Mémoires* (1837), II, 305.
[5] To Samuel Kercheval, July 12, 1816 (Ford, X, 37).

no apology. Like the other state governments established in this period, that of Virginia grew directly from the one that already existed, and he himself had no strong inclination to fly in the face of experience at the time.

What his countrymen actually did was to substitute for the royal governor one who was elected by the Assembly and, in the reaction against executive authority, largely to shear him of power. The same sort of thing soon happened in other provinces, and Jefferson may have been adjudged conservative in wanting to grant to the governor a larger share of the appointive power. The other major existing agencies were continued in slightly different form. The old Governor's Council had served in both an executive and legislative capacity. The convention accordingly provided for an executive Council of State, chosen by the Assembly, and an upper legislative house elected by the people, which, following Jefferson's suggestion, they called the Senate. He himself had no objection to a long term for senators. The Assembly selected the judges as well as the governor, and the net result was that it dominated the government. Jefferson did not intend to go quite that far, for he wanted the governor, whom he called "the administrator," to appoint many of the judges, and he favored a higher degree of executive and judicial independence. In his plan the legislative control centered less in the Assembly as a whole than in the more representative lower house, to which he assigned the election of both the governor and the Senate.[6]

The degree in which the new government was democratic or representative depended less on its external form than on the provisions for the election of the members of the legislature. It was in connection with the *basis* rather than the structure of the government that Jefferson showed himself to be more forward-looking than any of the other contemporary leaders, and an outstanding advocate of popular rule on the basis of just representation. He did not advocate the abandonment of property qualifications for voting, but he favored extending the suffrage to freeholders possessing a quarter of an acre in town or twenty-five acres in the country, and coupled with this the proposal that fifty acres of land be granted to every person of full age who did not already have that many. Under existing conditions the result would have been practically universal white male suffrage. Also, he would have forbidden the granting of free land to others. Thus he sought to extend economic opportunity and to lessen special privilege. Furthermore, he

[6] Drafts of Jefferson's proposed constitution in Ford, II, 7-30; admirable discussion by D. R. Anderson, *Am. Hist. Rev.*, XXI, 750-754, replying to W. C. Ford in *Nation*, LI, 107-109; excellent account of general alignment in Abernethy, *Western Lands*, ch. 11, esp. pp. 158-161.

recommended that representation be based on the distribution of voters, that is, practically on the population, and not on the county-unit system which was continued. His desire to bring about a more equitable system of representation may be explained in part by his residence in the growing Piedmont region, which was discriminated against, but it was rooted in the conviction that the overrepresented Tidewater was the seat of privilege and unjust power.

Jefferson took little pride in his proposals to this convention, for these afterwards seemed conservative and he doubted if he himself had penetrated to the true republican principle at the time. But no other leader in Virginia then went so far as he in the advocacy of popular representative government. Until the eve of the Civil War the constitutional struggles in the Commonwealth centered in the questions of the suffrage and the basis of representation, and at the very outset he ranged himself on the democratic side. Also, he proposed that the importation of slaves should cease, and he saw no place for an Established Church in a free society.

George Wythe said the system that was set up in Jefferson's absence required reformation and that he was the man who must effect it.[7] What was established was in reality an aristocratic republic, bottomed on inheritance. It is true that Patrick Henry, the popular idol who was still regarded as an upstart by some of the wealthiest planters, was elected governor, but the ruling group as a whole viewed him without alarm.[8] To say that he had been a radical in imperial relations would be to beg the question. His personal power lay chiefly in the realm of the emotions and, although he had a keen sense of public opinion, he had no domestic program worthy of the name. Furthermore, he was indolent by nature and during the year 1776 his health was bad. His physical incapacity threw an added burden on John Page, who received the highest vote for the Council of State and became its president. The latter could be counted on to remain an agreeable gentleman while dealing with vexatious routine, but unlike his friend Jefferson he had not wholly emancipated his mind from his inherited privilege. In domestic matters he must be characterized as a conservative.

The supremely important legislative department had not been organized as yet, but anyone could have predicted that Edmund Pendleton, who had fallen heir to the position formerly occupied by Peyton Randolph, would be elected speaker of the new House of Delegates when it assembled in the fall. No one symbolized better than he the

[7] To Jefferson, July 27, 1776 (LC, 2:284).

[8] His election has been attributed to a tacit alliance with the conservatives; Abernethy, *Western Lands*, p. 158.

ruling group, for this delightful man and highly effective leader clung to old ways and feared drastic change. There were others of more liberal temper, like George Mason, who had been very prominent of late and might be induced to share the public councils again, but if there was to be a reformer's role Jefferson was much the likeliest candidate for it. Both by inheritance and association he belonged to the ruling group, but he already envisaged a more rational and progressive society and was eager to move toward it.

During the summer of 1776 he was deeply concerned lest his influence in Virginia would be weakened by his absence in Congress. He had been elected for a term of one year which would expire in August, and by the middle of June he had concluded that he did not care to be re-elected. He was already a strong believer in the principle of rotation in office, anyway. He expressed his personal wishes to his neighbor Dr. George Gilmer, who was acting in his stead in Williamsburg, and also wrote to Pendleton, the president of the convention. The second letter had not been received when the ballot for delegates in Congress took place, and Gilmer was absent on that day. Jefferson's plea for relief was presented by Edmund Randolph but the convention re-elected him, nevertheless.

He might have viewed this disregard of his wishes as a compliment, but as a matter of fact he was greatly disturbed by the bald report of the vote which he got in Philadelphia about July 1. He learned that the delegation had been reduced from seven to five; that Benjamin Harrison and Carter Braxton, who were in Congress with him, had been dropped entirely, and that his own name stood next to last on the list. He naturally presumed that the existing delegation had been discredited. "It is a painful situation to be 300 miles from one's country, and thereby opened to secret assassination without a possibility of self-defence," he wrote to his friend William Fleming. "I am willing to hope nothing of this kind has been done in my case, but yet I cannot be easy." [9]

Afterwards he learned that the reduction in the size of the delegation was owing chiefly to Patrick Henry and that the political maneuvers were not directed against him. His friend Fleming assured him that the decline in his vote was attributable solely to the report of his letter to Gilmer, that otherwise scarcely anybody would have voted against him, and that he was as high in the estimation of his countrymen as ever. [10]

[9] Force, 4 ser., VI, 1582, giving vote; E. Randolph to Jefferson, June 23, 1776 (LC, 2:260); Jefferson to Fleming, July 1, 1776 (Ford, II, 41).
[10] Fleming to Jefferson, July 27, 1776 (LC, 2:283).

Numerous stories had been circulated about Braxton and Harrison, and some may also have been told about Jefferson, but Fleming's statement in regard to his standing is convincing. There was considerable intrigue at the convention but he was definitely aligned with no faction. He dwelt in the lofty realm of ideas and was on the best of personal terms with leaders of every complexion. The election of delegates to Congress took place before his proposed constitution for Virginia had been presented, but that document was probably not regarded by many people as dangerously radical. He had not aroused the serious disquietude of the conservatives.

He did not want his vote reduced if he was voted for at all; nobody would have, and he was more sensitive than most men. His chief immediate concern, however, was to get out of Congress. The reasons which he gave to Edmund Pendleton were personal, not political, and they were generally regarded as sufficient though no formal action was taken on them until the Assembly met in the fall. This is what he said:

> . . . I am sorry the situation of my domestic affairs, renders it indispensably necessary that I should solicit the substitution of some other person here, in my room. The delicacy of the House will not require me to enter minutely into the private causes which render this necessary. I trust they will be satisfied. I would not urge it again, were it not unavoidable. I shall with cheerfulness continue my duty here till the expiration of our year — by which time I hope it will be convenient for my successor to attend.[11]

His friends were in no doubt about the "private causes." His wife was staying with Francis and Elizabeth Eppes at the Forest until he could return home. He did not get as many letters from that quarter as he wanted, but every one he did get brought him such an account of her health that he found it painful to remain in Philadelphia. He had promised to stay until August 11, and he actually stayed about three weeks longer. The reason was that neither Braxton nor Harrison had the legal right to start another term, as he had; and they did not hesitate to go home when they wanted to. He had to wait until Richard Henry Lee arrived, for otherwise Virginia would have been without a quorum.[12]

[11] Burk, *Hist. of Va.*, Vol. IV, App. 13; thence taken by Ford and published with minor changes, II, 61. Both Girardin, who prepared this volume of Burk, and Ford date it July 1776, and it may have been a second letter. If so, the reasons were almost certainly the same as in the one read to the convention after the election of June 20, 1776.
[12] To Page, July 20, 1776; to Eppes, July 23, 1776 (Ford, II, 71–73).

Meanwhile, he was busy enough. Throughout his service as a delegate he gave close attention to queries and commissions which came from his "country." These included such diverse matters as the supply of salt, about which he could do little or nothing; the new state seal, for which he sent suggestions; and the disputed boundary with Pennsylvania, on which the Virginia delegates vainly invited conference. For Congress he helped draw up rules of procedure, anticipating in some degree his important service as a parliamentarian twenty years later; he received and recorded numerous depositions dealing with the sad course of events in Canada; and he shared with his congenial colleague John Adams the thankless task of proposing a revision of the articles of war. Most of this was tedious business but it was conscientiously attended to.[13]

The collaboration of the famous trio of the Declaration of Independence was continued in another matter which had no immediate public results but is of considerable interest in itself. On July 4, 1776, Franklin, Jefferson, and Adams were appointed as a committee to bring in a device for the seal of the United States, and from their deliberations that summer two historic mottoes emerged. The design recommended by them in August was by Pierre Eugène Du Simitière, a Swiss artist living in Philadelphia from whom Jefferson also procured a design for Virginia; but all three of the committeemen made suggestions and they approved a modified version of Franklin's for the "other side" of the seal of all the states. The motto, "Rebellion to tyrants is obedience to God," was in Franklin's proposals. Jefferson liked it so much that he added it to Du Simitière's design for Virginia and, as has already been said, adopted it at some time himself, stamping it on the wax with which he sealed his own letters. He had no doubt of the appropriateness of the saying at that hour.[14]

The over-elaborate design of Du Simitière, which fortunately was not accepted by Congress, contained an even more famous motto,

[13] Report of committee to draw up rules for Congress, July 10, 1776, Papers Cont. Cong., 23:19–22; comment of Adams on revision of articles of war in "Autobiography," Aug. 19, 1776, *Works*, III, 68; on Pennsylvania boundary question, Ford, II, 64–66.

[14] *Jour. Cont. Cong.*, V, 517–518 (July 4, 1776) and 689–691 (Aug. 20, 1776), the latter containing lengthy editorial note with quotations; suggestions of Franklin and Jefferson, LC, 2:291; Coat of Arms of the States of America designed by Du Simitière, LC, 2:230. The coat of arms for Virginia is in LC, 2:291. Into this Jefferson wrote "Rebellion to tyrants is obedience to God," with an alternative, "*Rex est qui regem non habet.*" His own seal is well reproduced in B. J. Lossing, *Pictorial Field-Book of the Revolution* (N. Y., 1852), II, 548. The motto is attributed to Franklin by Randall, III, 585–586, but see Jefferson's letter to Edward Everett, Feb. 24, 1823. L. & B., XV, 415. For the latest full discussion see J. P. Boyd, ed., *Papers of Thomas Jefferson*, I (1950), 677–679.

"E Pluribus Unum," and this was adopted at a later time. It was taken, presumably by the artist, from the motto of the *Gentleman's Magazine*. As used by the London periodical during the generation before the Revolution it meant that one magazine was made up from many newspapers, and the thought of applying it to the American federation of states was an inspiration. As a member of the committee Jefferson shares the credit of sponsorship, and both mottoes reflected his sentiments, but at this time and place he and his colleagues were stressing "Rebellion to Tyrants" more.

This was a period of unpropitious military events but Jefferson expected a brief war. Shortly before the adoption of the Declaration he said that the opinion was universal that the trial would be severe only during the next three months.[15] From George Wythe and others he learned of the movements of Lord Dunmore, who was still hovering off the Virginia coast; but he had nothing but contempt for the Governor and was confident that the Americans could never be conquered, though they probably would have to give up places lying on the water's edge.[16]

He was less hopeful about the working-out of an acceptable framework of government for the federation, which was a far more difficult undertaking than framing the constitution of a single state. He kept notes on part of the debate on the Articles of Confederation.[17] These dealt particularly with the crucial questions of quotas of contribution and the manner of voting in Congress. It was proposed that state contributions should be based on population, and the question arose whether or not slaves should be counted. On this issue Northern delegates voted in the affirmative and Southern in the negative, the latter being outvoted. Jefferson did not enter into the debate.

On the other question the clash was between the large and small states, the former favoring a vote based on population, and the latter an equal voice for every state. In this dilemma Jefferson proposed a plan privately to John Adams, and he recalled it to the latter several months later when the Confederation was again on the carpet and the situation seemed desperate. It was "that any proposition might be negatived by the representatives of a majority of the people of America, or by a majority of the colonies of America;" and he believed that this plan would safeguard the interests of both large states and small. At the time, however, his contribution to the cause of union seemed to be

[15] To William Fleming, July 1, 1776; Ford, II, 41.
[16] From Wythe, July 27, 1776, LC, 2:284; to —— Randolph (Aug.–Sept. 1776), MHS, 1:49.
[17] Ford, I, 38–47.

negative, for as a spokesman of Virginia he made it perfectly clear that his State would not now agree that the Confederation should dispose of lands that Virginia claimed.[18]

It was this question of western lands, more than anything else, which afterwards delayed the ratification of the Articles of Confederation; and Jefferson himself manifested no spirit of narrow provincialism in later years when he formulated policies of western expansion. For both of these reasons the attitude he took in 1776 is a matter of considerable historical interest. The best clue to it is probably to be found, not in his local patriotism, nor in any abstract doctrines of state rights, but in the actualities of the land question itself. In his mind this was not primarily a question of rivalry between one state and another, for he claimed that he was indifferent to that and at a later time the vast extent of Virginia's domain made it relatively easy for him to be generous in spirit. His major concern was not for the land but for the people who settled on it; and at this time he believed that the interests of the pioneers could be better safeguarded by states than by Congress, which seemed more susceptible to the pressure of speculative land companies. He was deeply sympathetic with squatters, but had little patience with absentee groups who came seeking special favors. What he most relied on for the protection of individuals was local self-government, and he was already on record as favoring the early development of it in Virginia's outlying lands; but until he could be reassured about the attitude of Congress toward the small landholders he preferred to depend on the states to protect them — particularly on his own State, for he had good reason to believe that he could be influential there.

At this stage he did not stand out as specially local or particularistic; almost all his colleagues were that, to a considerable degree. He was willing to concede much to the cause of union, and if he minimized the military dangers so did practically everybody else. But it was characteristic of him to lay major stress on human values and to think in long-range terms. He had no doubt that in the states, not in Congress, one could do most for men as men. This was the most important public reason why he himself was so anxious to go home.

While he waited impatiently for Richard Henry Lee to arrive, he discussed with Wythe and Pendleton the problem of developing the legal institutions of his Commonwealth. The latter suggested that he

[18] On his plan, see letter to Adams, May 16, 1777 (Ford, II, 130). For his statement of Virginia's position about lands, see *Jour. Continental Cong.*, VI, 1083, and VI, 1077. See also Jefferson to Pendleton, Aug. 13, 1776 (Ford, II, 80). His general attitude is well discussed by A. M. Lewis, in "Jefferson and the Kentucky Pioneers," an article scheduled for early publication in the *Miss. Valley Hist. Rev.*, to which I am especially indebted.

become a judge, and was unwilling to accept all the reasons Jefferson assigned for declining. Pendleton could not assent to his being considered unqualified, but, as he added, "I readily do to your usefulness in the representative body, where, having the pleasure of Mrs. Jefferson's company, I hope you'll get cured of your wish to retire so early in life from the memory of man, and exercise your talents for the nurture of our new constitution." [19] This was precisely what Jefferson purposed to do. He would not withdraw from the public service but he would enjoy his wife's company; he would enter the House of Delegates, and he would nurture the new constitution. His ideas on the latter subject, however, were more advanced and more constructive than those of Pendleton or anybody else.

In late August he wound up his affairs in the Quaker City. He reimbursed Mrs. Nelson, wife of his fellow delegate, for sundry articles bought by her for Mrs. Jefferson; he settled accounts for his two horses and bought guitar strings; he purchased a hat for himself and another for Colonel Thomas Mann Randolph; he paid Mrs. Graff in full for his lodgings.[20] On September 3 he left Philadelphia and, proceeding by Lancaster, Frederick, and Leesburg, he arrived six days later at Monticello.

About a month after that he received notice from John Hancock that he had been appointed a commissioner to the Court of France, to serve with Benjamin Franklin and Silas Deane. Under other circumstances he would have been strongly tempted to accept this confidential appointment. He had previously told Franklin he would like to go with him, and Franklin afterwards very much wished he had had Jefferson's companionship instead of that of his colleague Arthur Lee. But, as Jefferson wrote to the President of Congress, circumstances peculiar to the situation of his family compelled him to decline an alluring mission. The trouble was that he could neither leave them behind nor take them with him.[21] Europe would have to wait.

Public service could be adjusted to the exigencies of domestic life far more easily in Virginia than in France or Pennsylvania. When the Assembly met in October, George Wythe, who was now attending Congress and had his own wife with him, made available to the Jeffersons his house in Williamsburg. Accordingly, the senior delegate from Albemarle took his lady with him to the place which he had so often

[19] From Pendleton, Aug. 10, 1776; LC, 2:289.
[20] Account Book, esp. Aug. 27–Sept. 3, 1776.
[21] Resolutions of Congress, Sept. 26, 1776, and letter of Hancock, Sept. 30, 1776, MHS; Jefferson's reply, Oct. 11, 1776 (Ford, II, 91–92); Franklin to Jefferson, Dec. 21, 1777, Yale Univ., courtesy J. P.

visited in student days.[22] Judging by the doctor's bills he paid for her that fall she was not wholly recovered, but at least she was near him. Never again during her lifetime did he go so far away as Philadelphia. He was not sacrificing his career on the altar of domestic necessity, however. The local role he had chosen was admirably suited to his talents, and in playing it he performed some of the most significant of all his public services.

[22] From Wythe, Nov. 18, 1776; LC, 2:313–314.

[XVIII]

The Way of a Legislator: Freeing the Land
1776–1779

THE years during which Jefferson was a legislator in his own Commonwealth comprised his most creative period as a statesman during the American Revolution, and there was no part of his entire career that he afterwards looked back upon with greater satisfaction. The incomplete autobiography he wrote in old age is a generally modest and unpretentious document, but deep pride shines through his account of his services to Virginia during the critical early years of independence, when, as he reflected, he was striving to eradicate every fiber of aristocracy and to lay the foundation for a truly republican government.[1] Never were his purposes clearer nor his motives purer, and at no other time, perhaps, was the essence of his philosophy and statesmanship so unmistakably revealed. No wonder he looked back on this period with the emotions of nostalgia.

His own pride was in his program as a whole rather than his immediate accomplishments, but some distinction must be made between them. Strictly speaking, his period of legislative activity in the State of Virginia lasted less than three years — from the time that he took his seat in the House of Delegates in October, 1776, until he became governor at the beginning of June, 1779. Most of his most important proposals were still pending at the latter date; some of them were afterwards adopted through the agency of other men when he himself was viewing other scenes; and some of them were never adopted at all. He was pre-eminently a political architect, looking to the future, not a short-range reformer; and the plans that were still in the blueprint

---

[1] Ford, I, 48–69, especially 68–69. Owing to the careful records he kept, he made few serious errors of fact in this later account, but greater reliance must be placed on contemporary records.

stage when he left the House of Delegates have contributed far more to his immortal renown than the specific measures of his that were adopted in the triennium.

This is certainly not to say that in the years 1776–1779 the deputy from Albemarle was a prophet without honor in his own Commonwealth. A mere list of the motions he made, the bills he drafted, and the committees he served on in his first session is an index of his prominence. It would be too much to claim, as often has been claimed by his later admirers, that he dominated the legislative scene; but unquestionably he assumed a position of great influence at the outset and largely maintained it during the sessions that followed. This he was able to do because he had effected in his own person a rare blend of the qualities of a prophet and those of a practical statesman. The prophetic role appears the greater in the perspective of history, and his contemporaries could hardly have failed to glimpse it. To them, however, he also appeared, and appeared much more frequently, as one who was engaged in the humdrum tasks of legislation.

To the outward eye he was far from being an impractical visionary. He was ceaselessly industrious and bore his full share of legislative routine. The details of such activities as drawing bills for the raising of additional battalions of infantry and for changing the value of copper coin, and of such services as reviewing the action of a county committee which had fined an unintentional violator of the continental Association, need not concern us here.[2] It is important, however, to note his prominence in these day-to-day affairs and his recognized leadership in matters of legislative prerogative and procedure.[3]

He generally managed to steer clear of factional quarrels in which issues were chiefly personal. The line between progressives and conservatives in the Virginia government frequently shifted and often was indistinct. He was more consistently on the progressive side than any other prominent leader, and in fundamental thinking he stood farthest to the left. To a notable degree, nonetheless, he continued to maintain cordial personal relations with all groups and to retain their confidence. Thus in 1777, when it was alleged that the conservative Harrison faction was trying to legislate the more pro-

[2] Illustrations drawn from first session; Ford, II, 109–116, 118–119.

[3] The latter may be illustrated by the part he played during his second year in a disagreement between the two houses about the course to be followed in making appropriations. Two reports of the conference committee which he presented are given in Ford, II, 135–142; see *Journal of the House of Delegates of Virginia* (hereafter cited as *Delegates, Journal*) Dec. 4, 1777; Jan. 8, 1778; Jan. 23, 1778. This matter was still pending at the end of the session.

gressive Richard Henry Lee out of the Continental Congress by limiting length of service there, it was Jefferson who was asked to draw the bill. In doing so he followed his own previously expressed convictions about the desirability of rotation in office, and he appears not to have offended Lee.[4] An even better illustration of his amiability can be drawn from the continuing cordiality of his personal relations with Pendleton, whom he sharply opposed on important questions of policy. Pendleton himself deserves much of the credit for this, however; he never ceased to be a gentleman.

The strength of Jefferson's position at this stage did not lie in political organization. It lay in his personal effectiveness, his conciliatory manners, his enduring friendships, his disinterested patriotism, and the intrinsic forcefulness of his ideas. He carried with him to the House of Delegates a more definite and comprehensive program of reform than anyone else had formulated, but he realized that certain desirable ends could not be immediately attained and was willing to be patient. It seems unlikely that he was as deeply disturbed about the defects of the constitution while a member of the dominating legislative department as he was during and after his governorship; but even if he had been, he was convinced that a specially chosen convention was necessary for a revision of the frame of government. The prospect of such a convention became more not less remote as the war went on.[5] Accordingly, he had to content himself with operating within the existing framework.

He judged, however, that the general spirit of the times was more favorable to political change than it was likely to be after the military conflict was over, and he tried to take full advantage of every opportunity to translate human rights into legal forms. He was a long-range optimist and had a high degree of general confidence in human nature, but he was never disposed to leave human rights to chance. In regard to political rulers he was a consistent pessimist, for he was convinced that if left to themselves they would become tyrannical and corrupt. Also, he was convinced that rebellions and convulsions were inevitable if crying abuses were not corrected. This was not pessimism precisely, but it reflected a more acute consciousness of wrong and injustice than is common among men, particularly among men who themselves are privileged.

[4] For Jefferson's draft of May 12, 1777, see Ford, II, 128–129. He would have limited continuous service to two years. In the bill that was adopted the limitation was made three years; Hening, IX, 299. In the October session, 1777, the bill was amended, so that no person should be eligible to serve more than three years in any term of six; Hening, IX, 388.

[5] See his comment in *Notes on Virginia* (Ford, III, 229).

Most of his local contemporaries were more complacent and, unlike him, some of them were greedy; but it was not because of conspicuous lack of integrity or patriotism on their part that he raised and bore forward the standard of enlightened liberalism during these years. In general he thought well of his colleagues, but he was acutely aware of the dangers of apathy and he believed in striking while the iron is hot.

Somewhat later, in his *Notes on Virginia*, he said:

> . . . It can never be too often repeated, that the time for fixing every essential right on a legal basis is while our rulers are honest, and ourselves united. From the conclusion of this war we shall be going down hill. It will not then be necessary to resort every moment to the people for support. They will be forgotten therefore, and their rights disregarded. They will forget themselves, but in the sole faculty of making money, and will never think of uniting to effect a due respect for their rights. The shackles, therefore, which shall not be knocked off at the conclusion of this war, will remain on us long, will be made heavier and heavier, till our rights shall revive or expire in convulsion.[6]

As a political strategist Jefferson sought to take advantage of the general spirit of a time when conservatives had not become deeply alarmed, and when lip service at least was rendered the liberal and humane ideas of the Enlightenment. Also, as a legislative tactician he recognized the importance of seizing the initiative. This is one reason why his first session was such a busy one.

His earliest recorded action could hardly have been termed radical, though it was typical of him in its emphasis on legal regularity: he asked leave to bring in a bill for the establishment of courts of justice.[7] A measure of this sort might have been expected to appeal to men of conservative temper, concerned to restore orderly processes, but the immediate opening of all the courts was opposed by landed gentlemen on other grounds. Numerous planters were included among the debtors who feared legal action at a time when tobacco was almost valueless as a commodity. Jefferson himself was aware of the difficulty and became reconciled to the enforced delay. He had to wait for the opening of most of the courts.[8] He also had to wait for

[6] Ford, III, 266, in the section on religion.
[7] *Delegates, Journal*, Oct. 11, 1776; Ford, I, 48.
[8] As Ford notes, Jefferson's statement in his Autobiography about later events is erroneous. It amounts to a telescoping of the developments of at least two years. He was the first-named of a committee of ten to draw the bill, but on Nov. 1, 1776, as shown by the *Journal*, the committee was instructed to divide the subject into five different bills. In this session certain acts were passed that dealt with the

the removal of the seat of government from Williamsburg to a more central place. His bill calling for this was ostensibly designed for the convenience of the members and citizens. But it bore a progressive stamp, for it was primarily a move against Tidewater dominance. Interest combined with inertia to defeat it, a month after he introduced it.[9]

During the first week of his first session, however, the stage was set for the most important of his immediate activities as a legislator and reformer. The date, October 12, 1776, was significant in his history, for on that day the House of Delegates gave leave for the preparation of two bills. One of these was to enable tenants in fee tail to convey their lands in fee simple, while the other called for the general revision of the laws. Of the two actions the latter was the more important. As a result of it he was enabled to set forth in due course a long-range program emphasizing humane criminal laws, complete religious freedom, and the diffusion of education, and thus to appear on the page of history as a major prophet of intellectual liberty and human enlightenment. But it was his bill against entails, introduced on October 14, that he afterwards described as the first blow against the entrenched aristocracy. He regarded it as a radical action and always prided himself on being the wielder of the ax.[10]

His primary objection to the continuance of the old ruling group in power was not that it had ruled badly, for, as contemporary governments went, it had not. What he most disliked about the existing system was its essential irrationality and injustice. In the light of history the Virginia aristocracy was notable for its sense of responsibility, but Jefferson believed that it could not long maintain its high

---

places of holding county courts, and a court of admiralty was set up; Hening, IX, 202–206, 227–233, 242–243. On Nov. 25 he presented for the committee bills for establishing a court of appeals and a high court of chancery, but on Dec. 13 both were referred to the next session. The major actions in regard to the courts were taken at the October session, 1777, except for the court of appeals which was not established until still another year; Hening, IX, 368–369, 388–399, 401–419, 522–525.

[9] *Delegates, Journal,* Oct. 14, Nov. 11, 1776; Ford, II, 106–109.

[10] To John Adams, Oct. 28, 1813; Ford, IX, 427. From the bare record in the *Journal,* Oct. 12, one cannot be sure that Jefferson in person asked leave to prepare this bill, as he afterwards claimed; Ford, I, 49. The committee consisted of Bland, Jefferson, Starke, and Bullitt, and from the order it might be supposed that Bland was the mover. The bill was presented by Jefferson on Oct. 14, however, and he was undoubtedly the leader from that time on. He was also the second-named member of the committee to prepare a bill for the revision of the laws, and it was Bland, not he, who introduced it on Oct. 15. It would have been like Jefferson to get somebody else to make the original motion, but his later prominence in the matter leads to the strong supposition that he stimulated the action in this case.

sense of public obligation on its existing foundation. The trouble was that it was based, not on merit, but on inherited privilege. It was this basic privilege that he sought to undermine for the benefit of the future. He had no desire to reduce government to the dull level of mediocrity, but he did try to restore what he called the natural order of freedom and to give talent and virtue, which were scattered through all ranks of society, a chance to rise. His purposes may now be regarded as democratic, and he himself described them in current terms of natural philosophy, but they may also be thought of as the purposes of a man who joined faith in human beings with common sense.

He had already manifested deep interest in the fundamental question of the distribution and tenure of land. He was thoroughly aware that the granting of large tracts· to influential men during colonial times had furthered the development of great estates, and that the power of the ruling group was based on these. He was opposed to the granting of more acres to persons who already had them in abundance; he wanted land for the landless. He had proposed to the convention of 1776 that men who did not own fifty acres should receive grants enabling them to attain that acreage, and that nobody else be entitled to a free grant. He had shown great sympathy for the squatters in outlying districts. He was sure they would settle the land in spite of everybody; he favored making grants to them in small quantities, rather than sales; he wanted them to hold their lands without having to make even a token payment to the State like the old quitrent to the King. He had already recommended the prevention of irresponsible purchases from the Indians, such as had been made by western land companies.[11] He himself was not appreciably involved in western speculation. He had inherited from his father a share in the Loyal Company, in which his neighbor Dr. Thomas Walker was the moving spirit, but nothing came of it. He afterwards said that, with trivial exceptions, he never was interested in a foot of land off the waters of the James River.[12] Many of his contemporaries saw in the vast unallotted domain of the Commonwealth an opportunity to build up and perpetuate individual fortunes, but he saw in it the opportunity to create a stronger society of small farmers.

In the course of his legislative career he concerned himself with the land question in all its more important phases, and he viewed all phases with the same eyes; but the victories over landed privilege

[11] See especially his proposals to the convention (Ford, II, 25) and his letter to Pendleton, Aug. 13, 1776 (Ford, II, 78–81), replying to Pendleton's of Aug. 3 (LC, 2:286). See also letter from Pendleton, Aug. 26, 1776 (LC, 2:296).
[12] To Madison, Nov 11, 1784 (Ford, IV, 3).

that he remembered most vividly in other years were the abolition of entails and primogeniture. The two reforms were widely separated in time, since one of them was effected immediately and the other was not finally brought about until nearly ten years later, but he coupled them in his own mind. The terms themselves are relatively unfamiliar in the twentieth century, and Jefferson thought them already archaic in the last quarter of the eighteenth. They signified artificial methods of restricting inheritance, and were objectionable to him on rational no less than social grounds.

It must not be assumed that all Virginia estates were entailed: Peter Jefferson's was not, and even in Tidewater the practice was by no means universal. Nor should it be supposed that they descended necessarily to the eldest son, for this they did only in the absence of a will, and it was unusual for a man of large property to die intestate. Randolph Jefferson had been provided for, as well as Thomas. However, the entailing of land was permitted by the English law which was extended to the Colony, and by Virginia law it was further extended to the slaves annexed to the land. Thus a wealthy planter could bequeath all or any part of his estate to his son and the heirs of the latter's body begotten, or to the heirs begotten by a particular marriage, or he could restrict its transmission in some other special way. Such an entail, once made, was protected by law and could be defeated only by an Act of Assembly.[18] Numerous petitions for the docking of entails were presented at sessions of the House of Burgesses before the Revolution. Jefferson himself presented one on behalf of his wife, asking permission to sell certain entailed lands and to entail others instead. Such petitions were commonly granted, but the procedure was troublesome, and wealthy planters had frequent occasion to regret the restrictions on the disposition of property which dead hands had imposed.

This was probably one of the reasons why Jefferson's bill for the abolition of entails was passed so promptly. Only those who clung most tenaciously to ancient establishments strongly objected to the removal of this relic of mediaevalism after it was seriously proposed by a forward-looking man. Among these traditionalists he named Pendleton as his chief opponent. According to his later account this

[18] See comments on the Virginia situation by St. George Tucker in his edition of *Blackstone's Commentaries* (Philadelphia, 1803), III, 119 *n*. Most writers on the subject until recently have laid too much emphasis on the legal forms and too little on actual practice. Clarence R. Keim, "Influence of Primogeniture and Entail in the Development of Virginia," University of Chicago *Abstracts of Theses, Humanistic Series*, V (1928), 289–292, concludes that their importance has been overestimated.

adroit parliamentarian, finding that he could not maintain the general principle of entails, proposed and almost carried an amendment which would have left to the landholder himself the choice whether he should convey his lands in fee simple or fee tail. The important clash was probably between him and Pendleton on this issue, as he remembered, but the contemporary record shows that he himself introduced a moderate proposal, much like the one he afterwards attributed to Pendleton. Then, apparently growing bolder as he felt out the opposition, he proposed and carried amendments which abolished entails altogether. Thus Jefferson not only simplified an exceedingly complicated situation; by the same stroke he facilitated economic change and furthered social mobility.[14]

He made his successful attack on primogeniture later in connection with the general revision of the laws, when he drew a bill directing the course of descents.[15] He was elsewhere when this was finally adopted, so his struggle can only have been in the committee. He said that Pendleton again opposed him, yielding ground amiably when forced to, and finally urging that at least a double portion be allowed the eldest son.[16] Even after the passage of Jefferson's bill there was nothing to prevent anyone from making just that provision by will; and he may have exaggerated the effects of this particular reform. A famous foreign commentator on American democracy, Alexis de Tocqueville, afterwards pointed out that the very existence of a law of partible inheritance deprived fathers of the inclination to discriminate unfairly between children.[17] Even in this region of plantation seats, however, such inclination had been far from general. Jefferson did not destroy the country gentry as a group with the blows of his mighty ax, and there is insufficient reason to believe that he wanted to, but he did remove legal vestiges of Old World aristocracy.

The abolition of entails, unlike that of primogeniture, occurred immediately, but it appears to have aroused relatively little resentment.[18] One arch-conservative, Landon Carter, expressed himself about it violently in a contemporary letter to George Washington which is

[14] Later account in Autobiography, Ford, I, 49–50; drafts of his bill of Oct. 14 and amendments of Oct. 18, 1776, *Ibid.*, II, 103–105; bill as passed by the Delegates on Oct. 23 and accepted by the Senate on Nov. 1, in Hening, IX, 226–227. It should be noted that Pendleton was not on the committee.

[15] The *Report* of the revisors will be discussed in the following chapter. This bill comprised chapter 20 of it; as adopted in the October session, 1785, it is in Hening, XII, 138–140.

[16] Ford, I, 60.

[17] P. Bradley, ed., *Democracy in America*, I, 49–50, and ch. 3, *passim.*

[18] Lingley, *Transition in Virginia*, p. 181, following Randall, I, 200–202, overestimates this, in my opinion, as most other writers on the subject have done.

noteworthy in another respect — in the course of it the Westmoreland planter addressed the General as "my dear George." Few people
were ever that familiar with the stately commander, and few people
then were equally alarmed.[19] This embittered proprietor interpreted
the movement against entails as an attack on the "right to do as we
please with our own property," which he regarded as the "very basis
of the American contest." That was to reduce the causes of the
revolt to a narrow compass indeed. The bill was then pending in
the Senate, after having passed the House, and Carter's prayer that
at least ten persons could be found to reprobate and detest such a crying injustice shows that he regarded the continuing opposition to it
as slight. Then he vehemently exclaimed:

> . . . It is called docking all entails; but is it not entailing one
> they cannot dock? The curses of posterity on them who must in
> that very contest for liberty entail a load of debts upon those who
> are to come, after they have robbed them of their very estates to
> pay that debt from, by overturning the very principles of justice
> on which they built their very claim of freedom. This is what I
> call sowing the seeds of contention, which must spring up sooner
> or later, and all from the poisoned soil of popularity.[20]

As this observer saw it, the greatest danger lay in the craving of
political leaders for popularity, and he heaped his most unflattering
comments on Patrick Henry, speaking of him ironically as "this great
man." In connection with the "cursed bill," however, he specifically
mentioned Jefferson, and obviously he found that propertied gentleman quite incomprehensible, except on the ground that he was a
"midday drunkard." Thus he wrote to Washington:

> . . . Was any man in your camp to say who is the greatest
> drunkard and most pernicious to society, he who only drinks at
> night and is perhaps ashamed of it in the morning, or he who gets
> drunk (sub die) at mid-day, as old Bacchus used to say, I dare
> say the midnight drunkard would be the most to be respected.
> . . . It is not usual for those who are against a bill to be the
> bearers of it, and this bill (as cursed in its nature as the removal
> of a neighbor's landmark, his will and pleasure in giving his own
> property away) borne about by the famous T. J——n!

The bearer of the bill against entails was no sort of drunkard, and
he doubtless included Landon Carter among the "half-dozen aristocratical gentlemen, agonizing under the loss of pre-eminence," who

[19] Oct. 31, 1776, Force, 5 ser., II, 1304–1307.
[20] *Ibid.*, p. 1307.

had ventured sarcasms on the otherwise peaceful transition from a monarchy to a republic. In the summer of 1777 it seemed to Jefferson that the people in general had simply taken off an old suit of clothes and put on a new one. He wrote Benjamin Franklin: "Not a single throe has attended this important transformation." [21] Long afterwards one of his implacable foes said that the bill for cutting off entails "was of obvious necessity from the form of our new institutions, and the prevailing temper of the people, and had only to be proposed by any member, in order to be adopted by a large majority, as it was in others of the States." [22] This was an understatement, designed to belittle Jefferson, just as his own contemporary remark to Franklin was too sanguine. He had aroused some fears, and eventually he raised up a host of bitter enemies, but he does not appear to have angered many people before his governorship of Virginia. This was partly because of the temper of the times. It was also because his own program had not yet fully unfolded. Never during this period did it become a clear issue in itself.

His land reforms were part and parcel of a movement which swept through the other states and resulted in the abolition of primogeniture and entail in practically all of them within ten years of the Declaration of Independence. [23] It would be too much to claim that he was the initiator of a general movement which was actually the resultant of many forces, but he undoubtedly took the lead in the large and influential Commonwealth of Virginia. There he attempted to set an aristocratic society in the current of democracy by broadening its economic base. In the next decade no less a person than George Washington observed that the distinction of classes had begun to disappear in the Old Dominion, and there were later laments because historic plantation seats had passed into alien hands. [24] The decline in the fortunes and power of the prerevolutionary land barons may be attributed to deeper causes than formal legislation, however, and the blame that was laid on Jefferson by disgruntled aristocrats was considerably greater at a later time than during the early years of the Revolution. It is doubtful if many then viewed this landed gentleman as a traitor to his class because he had effected the abolition of entails. The danger really lay in his implacable hostility to artificial privilege of every sort. That was sure to cause him trouble sooner or later.

[21] Aug. 13, 1777; Ford, II, 131–132.
[22] Henry Lee, Jr., *Observations on the Writings of Thomas Jefferson* (1832), p. 115.
[23] Allan Nevins, *American States during and after the Revolution*, pp. 441–445.
[24] Citations, *Ibid.*, p. 442.

because he was certain to tread on the toes of many sorts of men.

The whole record of his thought until this time shows that his policies were motivated by philosophical rather than narrowly political considerations, and there is no evidence that he was ambitiously courting favor with the multitude. Nevertheless, in actions like these he laid the firm foundation of his great popularity in later days. He was not one to crack jokes around a campfire like Patrick Henry, but he had ideas that were sure to appeal to common men. His conception of the free movement of property was quite in accord with the philosophy which was fated to become dominant among ordinary Americans. The expression "three generations from shirtsleeves to shirtsleeves" sums it up roughly. Jefferson did not say this, so far as is known, but in any age he would have disliked any and all schemes designed to perpetuate wealth without regard to the capabilities of the possessor. He believed in freedom to acquire property, which to him was largely identified with land; and, for all his generosity, he was tenacious of his own; but he also believed in the freedom to lose it. The way must be left open for the fit to rise, and, by unavoidable implication, for the unfit to fall. In such a philosophy there is relatively little comfort for the sentimentalist or the paternalist, but to Americans of enterprise it has sounded like fair play and common sense.

Jefferson contributed directly to the development of representative government in Virginia's western country during his first session as a delegate, thus aiding the small settlers in the way he regarded as most fundamental. He strongly supported the movement to set up Kentucky as a new county which succeeded late in 1776. Also, he played a characteristic part in the continuing conflict over the granting of western lands, though he did not afterwards mention this among the important services that he rendered his State. His silence on this subject may have been partly protective, for the implementation of his progressive ideas was faulty and the results of the policy he finally approved were disappointing.[25] In the perspective of history, however, his concern for the squatters and his hostility to the speculators is probably more significant than his attitude toward outmoded primogeniture and entail. This was a more controversial question and, being also more confused, it required greater vision.

[25] On the new counties see Abernethy, *Western Lands*, pp. 165–166, and references cited; on the whole question of policy, *Ibid.*, ch. 17. A. M. Lewis, "Jefferson and the Kentucky Pioneers," is specially valuable for relations with George Rogers Clark.

The complex problem was in essence twofold: settlers had filtered into the unoccupied lands and remained there without title; and various land companies were making vast claims in the region beyond the mountains. Jefferson's fear that the latter would be supported by Congress was a major reason for his insistence at this stage that Virginia maintain her western claims. In his own legislature he and George Mason tried to bring order out of chaos, to safeguard the small holders, and to defeat the excessive claims of the speculative companies. They may have differed somewhat in emphasis, but they collaborated in bills which were presented in January, 1778, and were the undisputed leaders of the liberal faction.[26] By this time they were forced to regard the western lands not merely as a seat of settlement but also as a source of revenue, for the currency was rapidly depreciating and there was need to support the credit of the State by proceeds from sales. As we have seen, Jefferson preferred to give lands in small portions. They were specially anxious to defeat the purposes of outside speculators, though Jefferson's policy was not dictated primarily by motives of local self-interest nor even by theories of state rights. It was based fundamentally on human grounds.

In 1778 Mason and Jefferson were defeated by the conservatives, whom Pendleton and Benjamin Harrison led.[27] The latter were not disposed to expedite the influx of small settlers into the West, for they feared that the value of eastern property would be thereby reduced. George Washington agreed with them that soldiers or prospective soldiers would be drawn off, and for this reason opposed the measure. The conservative leaders also had a tender feeling for the land companies, in which they were personally interested in varying degree. To use modern terms, they upheld private business interests — for business with them centered in land. On the other hand, Mason and Jefferson — especially Jefferson — stood primarily for the public interest, sought to further actual settlement, and supported unprivileged common men.

In consultation with Jefferson, Mason redrew the bills establishing a land office and settling the western claims; these were passed in June, 1779, after Jefferson became Governor.[28] They took care of persons who had actually moved in before January 1, 1778, by granting them four hundred acres at a nominal price, along with a pre-emption

[26] Mason to Jefferson, Apr. 3, 1779 (LC, 3:460). Because of his relations with the Ohio Company, Mason's disinterestedness is less certain that that of Jefferson.

[27] Abernethy, pp. 218–219. The position of Governor Patrick Henry was uncertain, though he supported the bills of 1779.

[28] Hening, X, 35–65.

of one thousand more at the regular price of forty pounds per hundred acres. Provision was made for those who had moved in since that date, by granting them pre-emption to four hundred acres at the regular price; but, unhappily, nothing was done for future settlers. What amounted to a compromise was worked out with the most Virginian of the land companies, and provision was made for the future sale of the remaining lands at the regular price without limit of acreage.

Some degree of order was thus brought out of chaos, but events proved that the solution as a whole was more favorable to men of means than to small settlers, and that the opportunity to establish a genuinely democratic land policy for Virginia had been lost. Absentee owners gobbled up huge tracts, paying for them in depreciated currency, and poorer farmers soon began to complain.[29] Certain of Jefferson's long-range purposes had been sacrificed to the attainment of immediate results, but to him, doubtless, the future prospects did not seem unpromising. At the time it looked as though there was plenty of land for everybody; poor men as well as rich could take advantage of the depreciation of the currency; and if large estates were not buttressed by artificial laws of inheritance, nature might be expected to set centrifugal forces to work. Such forces were actually operating among the aristocrats of Virginia already, for other than legislative reasons. War and debt threatened to exact a toll which Jefferson himself did not regard as just or desirable.

His efforts to solve the problem of the outstanding obligations of Virginians to British merchants proved as futile as any human attempt to stay a storm, and in his own case they were positively harmful, but there can be no doubt of his honorable intentions. In his first session, when his plans for the immediate reopening of the courts were blocked by fears of executions for debt, he had drafted a compromise proposal which would have suspended such executions whenever suitable security should be given for the eventual payment of the money.[30] Even this was too much for the debtors. The matter was deferred, and not until January, 1778, did Jefferson return to it. The bill he then presented was regarded as part of the liberal program, just as the land-office bill of that session was, but it would have been better for him if it had been defeated.[31]

[29] Abernethy, *Western Lands*, pp. 228–229.
[30] Dec. 6, 1776; Ford, II, 122–223.
[31] *Delegates, Journal*, Jan. 13, 1778; Hening, IX, 377; Ford, II, 199–201, giving the bill that was incorporated in the report of the revisors; Abernethy, p. 219; Randall, I, 215–216.

His bill provided for the sequestration of the property of British subjects in Virginia, which was proper enough in principle. It also provided that suits between British subjects and citizens of Virginia should be continued in the same condition as they were before the courts were closed, and to this no valid objection could have been raised during the war. The unfortunate provision was for the discharge of debts to British subjects through deposits in the loan office which was set up. A debtor could make payment in the lawful money of the Commonwealth, the supposition being that the State would assume responsibility from that point and settle accounts with the British after the war. The trouble was that eventually the depreciated currency of Virginia, as Jefferson said, had no more value than oak leaves.[32]

Without going into the tangled story of the postwar period, when these obligations were adjudged to be still binding, it is sufficient to say that Jefferson availed himself of this law. He had received bonds (notes, we should say) from the purchasers of the Wayles lands he had sold, and his own British creditors had declined to take these. If they had accepted them, events proved that they would have been protected by the treaty of peace, but at the time they preferred to have Jefferson continue in their debt. He was afterwards paid for these bonds in Virginia currency and he says that he took this very currency to the loan office.[33] He had what satisfaction there was in the thought that it was used by the State in the conduct of the war, but he had to pay his own debts all over again. The full effects of this error of judgment on his part, both as a statesman and as the manager of his own affairs, did not burst upon him until after the war was over; he then bore them like the philosopher he was.[34]

His other important activities in this legislative period can be discussed best in connection with the general revision of the laws, which occupied a large part of his attention during nearly the whole of it. In that great task he showed himself to be a statesman in the best sense of the term, but he was freed from the necessity of adjusting himself to the exigencies of the day in the House of Delegates. This notable work of legal draftsmanship provides a surer index of his intelligence and prophetic vision than any he gave as a leader on the floor. Also, by means of it he commended himself far more to distant generations.

---

[32] In the May session, 1780, the part of the act allowing the payment of debts into the treasury was repealed; Hening, X, 227.

[33] He made a large payment into the treasury as late as Feb. 2, 1780; Account Book.

[34] See Appendix II, B, 3.

[XIX]

Architect of Laws: Slavery and Crime

IT IS doubtful if many of Jefferson's colleagues in the Virginia Assembly, when they passed the bill calling for a revision of the laws, had any such far-reaching and philosophical purposes in mind as he did. Now that the King and his minions no longer stood in the way, he believed that the code should be corrected "with a single eye to reason, and the good of those for whose government it was framed." [1] The legislators were prompt, however, and they showed their willingness to give him the lead by naming him first on the committee of five to make recommendations. [2] It was a distinguished list. After him came Pendleton and Wythe, the learned George Mason, and the liberal-minded Thomas Ludwell Lee. George Wythe resigned from Congress in order to accept what he regarded as a more important appointment.

They met for a preliminary conference in Fredericksburg in January, 1777, and the final report was submitted two and a half years later, after both Pendleton and Wythe had become judges and Jefferson had begun his term as governor. The best account of the procedure has been given by him himself, and it shows that he intended to be practical in action despite his larger philosophical purposes.

> . . . At the first and only meeting of the whole committee, (of five persons), the question was discussed whether we would attempt to reduce the whole body of the law into a code, the text of which should become the law of the land? We decided against that, because every word and phrase in that text would become a new subject of criticism and litigation, until its sense should have been settled by numerous decisions, and that, in the meantime, the rights of property would be in the air. We concluded not to meddle with the common law, *i.e.*, the law preced-

[1] Ford, I, 57–58.
[2] *Delegates, Journal*, Oct. 26, Nov. 4, 1776.

ing the existence of the statutes, further than to accommodate it to our new principles and circumstances; but to take up the whole body of statutes and Virginia laws, to leave out everything obsolete or improper, insert what was wanting, and reduce the whole within as moderate a compass as it would bear, and to the plain language of common sense, divested of the verbiage, the barbarous tautologies and redundancies which render the British statutes unintelligible. From this, however, were excepted the ancient statutes, particularly those commented on by Lord Coke, the language of which is simple, and the meaning of every word so well settled by decisions, as to make it safest not to change words where the sense was to be retained.[3]

Oddly enough, Pendleton, who generally supported ancient things, favored the preparation of a new and complete Institute on the model of Blackstone. He was backed by Lee but the other three members opposed, for the reason already mentioned and the further reason that such an undertaking would have been too arduous and bold. Even the more limited task which was agreed upon seemed too arduous for Mason, who claimed that he was not well enough read in the law and asked to be relieved. Soon thereafter Lee died, so the work was distributed among the remaining three.[4] Jefferson's assignment consisted of the common law, insofar as they thought of altering it, and the statutes to the legal beginning of the Colony; the remainder of the English statutes were committed to Wythe, and the Virginia laws to Pendleton. The division threw into Jefferson's part the laws concerning crimes and punishments, descents, and religion. He also considered the question of public education, and ventured far into the domain of the Virginia laws, though these were specifically assigned to Pendleton.

One reason for this was that he did a good deal of editing in connection with Pendleton's portion. The revisors worked separately but in the spring of 1779 they met in Williamsburg and went over the first two sections, "weighing and correcting every word, and reducing them to the form in which they were afterwards reported." When they got to the third part, however, they found that Pendleton, instead of simplifying the language of the Virginia laws, had copied the acts *verbatim*, only omitting what was disapproved. Being called home by a family matter, he asked the two others to put his draft in the form they desired and authorized them to report him as concurring.[5]

[3] To Skelton Jones, July 28, 1809 (L. & B., XII, 298-299).
[4] Ford, I, 58-59.
[5] Jefferson to Skelton Jones, July 28, 1809 (L. & B., XII, 300). In his later accounts Jefferson may have exaggerated the differences between him and Pendleton. During the final stages of the revision this conservative friend accepted him

The report finally submitted to the General Assembly included one hundred and twenty-six bills. A few of these which were of immediate importance were translated into law at that very session, but amid the exigencies of war the report as a whole was deferred. It languished for five years longer. Then, when Jefferson was back in the Continental Congress for a spell, it was printed, at the instance of James Madison. Certain conservatives at that time opposed the code on general principles, but Madison found it more popular in the Assembly than he had expected, and during the next two years, as the result of persistent pressure on his part, approximately half the bills became law without serious amendment. The remainder were referred to a new committee, and in the course of time approximately as many more were enacted in substance. Jefferson himself was in France while his friend Madison was struggling so valiantly; he was Secretary of State in George Washington's first administration before the last of the British laws had been repealed and the legal transition from Colony to Commonwealth had been completed.[6]

After he went to Europe and began to circulate in philosophical circles there, Jefferson remarked to a friend that only three or four bills in the Revisal would strike the attention of foreigners.[7] The bulk of it was indeed local in its nature. He could hardly expect European savants and illuminati to be interested in measures dealing with the organization of the militia, the prevention of the infection of horned cattle, the improvement of the breed of horses, and the apprehension of horse stealers. Insofar as Jefferson himself dealt with such matters, he was the philosopher come to earth and performing a useful mundane function. The three or four bills that he deemed generally interesting, however, were broadly philosophical in concept and still command attention after a century and a half. They can be easily singled out as the ones dealing with citizenship, crime and punishment, religion, and education; and the credit for all of these belongs to him. Before considering them, however, we must first mention the important question of slavery.

---

as the final arbiter in minor matters of disagreement with Wythe. The implication is that there was now no disagreement between him and Jefferson. See Pendleton to Jefferson, May 11, 1779 (LC, 3:484, partly quoted in Ford, II, 195).

[6] *Report of the Committee of Revisors Appointed by the General Assembly of Virginia in 1776* (Richmond, Nov. 1784); *Delegates, Journal,* chiefly October session, 1785; Hening, chiefly vol. XII; Jefferson to Madison, Feb. 20, Apr. 25, 1784 (Ford, III, 396, 473); Madison to Jefferson, July 3, 1784, Jan. 9, 1785, Jan. 22, 1786, Dec. 4, 1786, Feb. 15, 1787 (*Writings,* Hunt ed., II, 60, 118–119, 215–216, 291, 308–309); Ford, II, 196; Lingley, *Transition in Va.,* pp. 184–188.

[7] To Hogendorp, Oct. 13, 1785 (Ford, IV, 102–103).

Jefferson would not have placed on any select list the bill on this subject, for it was merely a digest of existing laws. By the time that the revisors submitted their formal report they did not need to recommend that the importation of slaves be prohibited. The Assembly had already seen to that, and, according to Jefferson's later account, the action was taken on his motion. In this instance he seems to have fallen into the not unnatural error of confusing the general with the particular. He favored the discontinuance of the slave trade before the Revolution and definitely proposed it as early as 1776, but the successful measure of 1778 was introduced by another at a time when he was not present in the House.[8] However, there can be no possible question that he favored the bill; and his general attitude was so well known that even a bitter enemy attributed this salutary reform to him in later years.[9]

Also, he strongly favored emancipation. The revisors had a plan, he said, and had embodied it in an amendment which was to be presented whenever the bill on slaves was taken up. It was not taken up until after he had gone away, and those who were then on the ground concluded that the public mind would not bear the proposition.[10] He himself was acutely aware of the difficulties of the situation, but he abundantly revealed the depth of his own feeling on this dark subject in certain passages in his *Notes on Virginia*. He wrote these before the revisors' report had been printed, and without knowing that they would ever meet the public eye.

He had perceived an encouraging change in attitude since the beginning of the Revolution, he said. The harshness of masters was abating, the spirit of the slaves was rising from the dust, and the condition of the latter was being mollified. But no one could find in his words any ground whatsoever for the opinion that slavery in eighteenth-century Virginia was or would ever become a beneficent institution. He regarded it as fundamentally cruel, and was in no possible doubt that it undermined the morals and destroyed the industry of the masters while degrading the victims. Worst of all, it sapped the

[8] Ford, I, 51–52; Hening, IX, 471–472. As given in the *Delegates, Journal*, the legislative history is as follows: On Oct. 14, 1778, it was ordered that leave be given to bring in a bill to prevent the future importation of slaves, and that the committee of trade prepare and bring in the same. On Oct. 15, Richard Kello of Southampton presented a bill. This passed the House of Delegates on Oct. 22, under a slightly different title. On Oct. 27, as amended by the Senate, it was agreed to. Jefferson did not appear in the House until Nov. 30. I have found no evidence of his intimacy with any member of the committee of trade.

[9] Henry Lee, Jr., *Observations*, pp. 122–124. His own claim was made as early as 1800; Ford, VII, 476.

[10] Ford, III, 243; much later comment, *Ibid.*, I, 67.

foundation of all liberties by denying that freedom was the gift of God and the birthright of all men, regardless of their color or condition.

All this he said, much better than anyone can paraphrase it, in a passage which became deservedly famous.

> . . . There must doubtless be an unhappy influence on the manners of our people produced by the existence of slavery among us. The whole commerce between master and slave is a perpetual exercise of the most boisterous passions, the most unremitting despotism on the one part, and degrading submissions on the other. Our children see this, and learn to imitate it; for man is an imitative animal. . . . If a parent could find no motive either in his philanthropy or his self-love, for restraining the intemperance of passion towards his slave, it should always be a sufficient one that his child is present. But generally it is not sufficient. The parent storms, the child looks on, catches the lineaments of wrath, puts on the same airs in the circle of smaller slaves, gives a loose to the worst of passions, and thus nursed, educated, and daily exercised in tyranny, cannot but be stamped by it with odious peculiarities. The man must be a prodigy who can retain his manners and morals undepraved by such circumstances. And with what execrations should the statesman be loaded, who permitting one half the citizens thus to trample on the rights of the other, transforms those into despots, and these into enemies, destroys the morals of the one part, and the amor patriae of the other. . . . With the morals of the people, their industry also is destroyed. For in a warm climate, no man will labour for himself who can make another labour for him. This is so true, that of the proprietors of slaves a very small proportion indeed are ever seen to labour. And can the liberties of a nation be thought secure when we have removed their only firm basis, a conviction in the minds of the people that these liberties are of the gift of God? That they are not to be violated but with his wrath? Indeed I tremble for my country when I reflect that God is just: that his justice cannot sleep forever; that considering numbers, nature and natural means only, a revolution of the wheel of fortune, an exchange of situation, is among possible events: that it may become probable by supernatural interference! The Almighty has no attribute which can take side with us in such a contest.[11]

The accuracy of his startling picture of the actual operations of slavery was afterwards questioned by reputable observers; he must have witnessed such scenes of fury as he described, but passionate

[11] *Notes on Virginia*, from answer to Query XVIII; Ford, III, 266–267.

despots were probably less common than he implied, especially in the household. John Taylor of Caroline, for one, thought that slaves called forth feelings of benevolence far more often than angry violence.[12] But Jefferson's opposition to slavery was primarily on moral grounds; and he combined compassion for the victims with an even deeper concern for the character of the masters and the dignity of human nature.

In his *Notes on Virginia* he also gave currency to the plan of gradual emancipation which was drawn by the revisors to remedy the highly undesirable situation.[13] This provided that all slaves born after the passing of the act should be freed, that they should remain with their parents for a time, that they should be trained at public expense for useful employment, and that they should be colonized as soon as they reached maturity. He purposed to send them somewhere, probably into the vast interior of the continent, and to aid them in the establishment of a free and independent society. They were to remain in alliance with the white man's state, however, until they should be strong enough to stand alone. Meanwhile, an equal number of white settlers should be brought from Europe to replace them. It was a humane plan and he regarded it as realistic.

According to his own estimate there were considerably more than two hundred thousand slaves in Virginia at this time, comprising almost half of the total population.[14] The immediate removal of that many inhabitants, comprising the bulk of the laborers, would have disrupted the economy, and Jefferson himself did not regard it as either feasible or desirable. Even the colonization of an annual crop and the bringing of white replacements from abroad was an undertaking which would have staggered a more timid mind. It was much simpler to leave well enough alone and to retain the laborers Virginia already had. He did not want them kept as slaves, however, so he had to face the alternative of incorporating them into the state after they had been freed. This he rejected for reasons which to him seemed sufficient: "Deep rooted prejudices entertained by the whites; ten thousand recollections, by the blacks, of the injuries they have sustained; new provocations; the real distinction which nature has made; and many other circumstances will divide us into parties, and produce convulsions, which will probably never end but in the extermination of one or the other race." [15] His humane mind could not contem-

---

[12] U. B. Phillips, *Life and Labor in the Old South* (1929), p. 362, citing John Taylor's comments on this very passage from Jefferson.

[13] Ford, III, 243-244.

[14] Ford, III, 187-192.

[15] Ford, III, 244.

plate such a prospect with composure, and he never ceased to favor a policy of colonization.

Because of the vividness of his contemporary comments on the Negroes, and even more because of his historic eminence, they have been frequently drawn upon for quotation. Detached from their context, however, they can easily give a false impression. In comparing the blacks and whites to the great disadvantage of the former, as he did in his *Notes on Virginia*, he was not endeavoring to sum up the common talk of the countryside.[16] He provided, unquestionably, a valuable index to local opinion and to this opinion in its most enlightened form. If his judgment on the Negroes was unfavorable, that of his local contemporaries generally was probably far more so. His observations were less notable in themselves, however, than in the spirit in which he made them.

His comments on the race were those of a scientific mind, softened by humanitarianism. Or, to put it more precisely, they represented the tentative judgment of a kindly and scientifically minded man who deplored the absence of sufficient data and adequate criteria. There were more distinct traces of sentimentalism in his attitude toward the Indians, whose native eloquence he extolled extravagantly, but he felt the need of a more scientific procedure in both cases. Thus he commented: "To our reproach it must be said that, though for a century and a half we have had under our eyes the races of black and red men, they have never yet been viewed by us as subjects of natural history." Furthermore, he thought it "a circumstance of great tenderness" that an unfavorable conclusion about the Negroes might "degrade a whole race of men from the rank in the scale of beings which their Creator may perhaps have given them." Though he expressed his own judgment frankly he did so with great diffidence.

> . . . I advance it, therefore, as a suspicion only, that the blacks, whether originally a distinct race, or made distinct by time and circumstances, are inferior to the whites in the endowments both of mind and body. It is not against experience to suppose that different species of the same genus, or varieties of the same species, may possess different qualifications. Will not a lover of natural history then, one who views the gradations in all the races of animals with the eye of philosophy, excuse an effort to keep those in the department of man as distinct as nature has formed them? This unfortunate difference of colour, and perhaps of faculty, is a powerful obstacle to the emancipation of these people. Many of their advocates, while they wish to vindicate the liberty of

16 Ford, III, 244–250.

human nature, are anxious also to preserve its dignity and beauty. Some of these, embarrassed by the question, 'What further is to be done with them?' join themselves in opposition with those who are actuated by sordid avarice only. Among the Romans emancipation required but one effort. The slave, when made free, might mix with, without staining the blood of his master. But with us a second is necessary, unknown to history. When freed, he is to be removed beyond the reach of mixture.[17]

He was not talking to the unlettered and inarticulate slaves, nor to their distant descendants, thousands of whom now bear the marks of physical mixture. It would have been truly "a circumstance of great tenderness" if he had been. He was not even addressing his country-men, who were obviously not ready for the dose of emancipation and personal restraint he would have prescribed. He was thinking aloud in the invisible presence of the world's humane philosophers, propounding the gravest of social questions and giving his own an-swers with tentativeness and becoming modesty. He did not want the problem to go by default but there was little he could do then and there except think about it.

As an observer he maintained an open mind about the abilities and potentialities of the subject race. Years later he learned with great pleasure that there was in the United States a "very respectable" Negro mathematician. On receipt of some of his work Jefferson wrote: "No-body wishes more than I do to see such proofs as you exhibit that nature has given to our black brethren talents equal to those of the other colors of men, and that the appearance of a want of them is owing merely to the degraded condition of their existence, both in Africa and America. I can add with truth that nobody wishes more ardently to see a good system commenced for raising the condition both of their body and mind to what it ought to be, as fast as the imbecility of their present existence, and other circumstances which cannot be neglected, will admit." The Negro mathematician found him deeply sympathetic with his aspirations, but Jefferson as a phi-losopher and statesman never veered from his pessimism with respect to the fundamental problem. He was nearing eighty when he wrote these words: "Nothing is more certainly written in the book of fate than that these people are to be free. Nor is it less certain that the two races, equally free, cannot live in the same government." In the next decade after that the judgment was echoed by Alexis de Tocque-ville.[18] A volume would be required to assess it in the light of later

[17] Ford, III, 250.
[18] *Democracy in America*, I, 373. He cites the very words of Jefferson in his

history, hence all that can be said here is that Jefferson intended his judgment to be both kindly and realistic.

Jefferson's bill declaring who should be deemed citizens was a part of the Revisal. This was passed soon after he became governor, and it did not include freed slaves. However, it did include all white persons who should afterwards migrate into the State and give proof of intent to reside there. It contained a strong assertion of the "natural right which all men have of relinquishing the country in which birth or other accident may have thrown them, and seeking subsistence and happiness wheresoever they may be able, or may hope to find them." He thought it important, and when he was combatting both the Federalist party and the British on the question of expatriation, he listed this act among his more signal achievements. Liberal provision for naturalization was quite in character with his later policy, and his pride in this measure was wholly justifiable.[19]

The bill for proportioning crimes and punishments is better known, and it turned out to be much more controversial. It was not considered until the whole report was brought up, and it then encountered such fierce opposition that the whole Revisal was endangered. The hostility to it had not subsided a year later, when despite mollifying amendments it was defeated by a single vote. "Our old bloody code is by this event fully restored," wrote Madison to him in France.[20]

Jefferson had reason to be disappointed, for, during the years 1776–1779, he gave more time to this bill than to all the rest together. It required him to go through the Saxon period of the law, consulting authorities like Bracton, and to study the chief writers on criminal law, such as Beccaria. The bill he drew after all this labor is notable for its studied simplicity, and the draft he submitted in advance to George Wythe represents, probably, the highest point he had yet attained in craftsmanship. This is certainly true of its physical form, for it is an extraordinarily beautiful document.[21] For the benefit of his own memory, he attached notes in Anglo-Saxon characters, in Latin, old French, and English, attesting the meticulous carefulness of his procedure. In printed versions these are naturally put at the bottom

Autobiography, begun in 1821; Ford, I, 68. Jefferson's letters to the Negro mathematician, Benjamin Banneker, and to Condorcet about him, Aug. 30, 1791, are in Ford, V, 377–379.

[19] *Report of Revisors*, ch. 55; Hening, X, 129–130; Ford, VII, 476.

[20] Madison to Jefferson, Jan. 22, 1786, Feb. 15, 1787, *Writings*, II, 215, 308.

[21] It may have escaped attention because it is filed in one of the last volumes of his papers; LC, 232:42,052–058.

of the pages, but Jefferson himself placed them in columns, parallel with the text, after the manner of his old lawbook, *Coke upon Littleton;* and, as in the work of the old master, they frequently encroach upon the text. The penmanship is beautifully clear, and no other document that Jefferson ever drew better exhibits his artistry as a literary draftsman.

The main significance of Jefferson's proposals lay in his attempt to relax the severity of punishments, and to make them at the same time more humane and more rational. This was quite in the spirit of the enlightened liberalism of the age which he so well embodied. His purpose had been formed before the beginning of his official labors as a revisor and had aroused some forebodings in the mind of Pendleton. In the late summer of 1776 that realistic observer wrote him: "I don't know how far you may extend your reformation as to our criminal system of laws. That it has hitherto been too sanguinary, punishing too many crimes with death, I confess and could wish to see that changed for some other mode of punishment in most cases; but if you mean to relax all punishments, and rely on virtue and the public good as sufficient to prompt obedience to the laws, you must find a new race of men to be the subjects of it, but this I dare say was not your meaning." [22]

This was not Jefferson's meaning, and when the time came all of the revisors agreed with him that capital punishment should extend only to treason and murder.[23] As reasonable men they had been satisfied by the writings of Beccaria and others that extreme punishments were neither rightful nor effective. Jefferson's summary of this humane and rational philosophy in Section I of his bill was masterly, and much of it could be appropriately quoted in the twentieth century in a textbook of penology. It is no longer necessary, as it was then, to point out that a member of society, "committing an inferior injury, does not wholly forfeit the protection of his fellow citizens, but after suffering a punishment in proportion to his offense, is entitled to their protection from all greater pain." Jefferson aptly described capital punishment as "the last melancholy resource against those whose existence is become inconsistent with the safety of their fellow citizens"; and he called attention to the social desirability of reforming offenders instead of exterminating them. It was not on grounds of sentimental humanitarianism, however, that he objected to extreme severity. He believed the experience of all ages and countries had shown that cruel and sanguinary laws defeated their own

[22] Aug. 10, 1776; LC, 2:289, modernized for punctuation.
[23] Ford, I, 60, 62; bills as presented, *Ibid.*, II, 203–220.

purpose. Long before William S. Gilbert had conceived the comic operatic figure of the Mikado he sought in deep seriousness to make the punishment fit the crime. He proposed that the death penalty be no longer exacted except in cases of treason and murder; and, with the advice of the committee, he tried to set up a scale of just punishment in other cases.

He was notably successful in attaining his purpose to frame a bill that would be comprehensible to laymen. He wrote George Wythe about it:

> . . . In it's style I have aimed at accuracy, brevity & simplicity, preserving however the very words of the established law, wherever their meaning has been sanctioned by judicial decisions, or rendered technical by usage. . . . Indeed I wished to exhibit a sample of reformation in the barbarous style into which modern statutes have degenerated from their antient simplicity. And I must pray you to be as watchful over what I have not said as what is said; for the omissions of this bill have all their positive meaning. I have thought it better to drop in silence the laws we mean to discontinue, and let them be swept away by the general negative words of this, than to detail them in clauses of express repeal.[24]

His bill was finally rejected in his own country, largely because it mitigated penalties in advance of general public opinion — as, for example, in the case of horse stealing. From the point of view of contemporary philosophers and from that of enlightened opinion today, its chief weakness lay in the particular penalties he substituted for death. He had recourse to the *lex talionis* in certain cases. Afterwards he said that he could not remember just why this was; but contemporary records show that it was partly because of his own general policy of going back to simple ancient precedents, and partly because of the judgment of his fellow revisors. Thus, when speaking of his draft to Wythe, he said:

> I have strictly observed the scale of punishments settled by the Committee, without being entirely satisfied with it. The lex talionis, altho' a restitution of the Common law to the simplicity of which we have generally found it so advantageous to return will be revolting to the humanised feelings of modern times. An eye for an eye, and a hand for a hand will exhibit spectacles in execution whose moral effect will be questionable; and even the membrum pro membro of Bracton, or the punishment of the of-

[24] Nov. 1, 1778, LC, 3: 440; printed with some verbal changes, Ford, II, 203 *n*.

fending member, altho' long authorised by our law, for the same offense in a slave, has you know been not long since repealed in conformity with public sentiment. This needs reconsideration.

The matter may have been reconsidered but the scale appears to have been left without material change. At all events, the following section appeared ultimately in cold print:

SECT. XIV. Whosoever shall be guilty of rape, or sodomy with man or woman, shall be punished; if a man, by castration, if a woman, by boring through the cartilage of her nose a hole of one half inch in diameter at the least.

Within ten years, when he was in Paris and copies of the Revisal had been circulated among the intelligentsia, he reported that the principle of retaliation was much criticized, and that in the case of rape, particularly, the punishment was regarded as indecent and unjustifiable. He himself was then in favor of altering this section of the bill, though for another reason: "the temptation women would be under to make it the instrument of vengeance against an inconstant lord, and of disappointment to a rival." [25] He was willing to leave the more unnatural sex crimes largely to public opinion. Thus, in his own mind he divided the genus "buggery" into the species sodomy and bestiality. He provided a severe penalty for the former but of the latter he said in a note: "Bestiality can never make any progress; it cannot therefore be injurious to society in any great degree, which is the true measure of criminality in foro civili, and will ever be properly and severely punished, by universal derision. It may, therefore, be omitted. It was anciently punished with death, as it has been latterly." [26] This was one of those offenses which, in Jefferson's opinion, should be pitied rather than formally punished. He felt much the same way about excusable homicide and suicide.

In the effort to find a substitute for the death penalty, he and the other revisors had chief recourse, not to retaliation — which actually was invoked in relatively few cases — but to public labor.[27] This was to be performed on roads, canals, and other public works; and he afterwards concluded that it would not have reformed the offenders. When tried elsewhere the experiment proved unsuccessful. The exhibition of criminals as a public spectacle on the highroads with shaved heads and mean clothing produced in them an abandonment of self-respect which plunged them into the most desperate and hardened

[25] To Madison, Dec. 15, 1786; Ford, IV, 334.
[26] Ford, II, 211 n.
[27] See his own summary in Notes on Virginia, Ford, III, 250–251.

depravity.[28] Before the Virginia Assembly got around to passing a law, he had become convinced that the methods of confined labor being tried out in Europe, as they were later in Philadelphia, constituted an improvement, and he himself aided his countrymen in their plans for a prison. The penitentiary afterwards built in Virginia was hardly an ideal institution by modern standards, but at least it was preferable to the chain gang. Jefferson expressed only mild dissatisfaction with the fresh bill that was adopted by the Assembly in 1796. By then the legislators were willing to limit capital punishment to treason and murder, as he had advocated almost twenty years earlier. Instead of the distinctions of murder and manslaughter, which he had preserved in his bill, they introduced the new terms of murder in the first and second degree, and he did not regard himself as competent to judge whether or not this constituted an improvement.[29] He continued to be convinced that the general principles he had enunciated were right, but he was dubious about the specific penalties he had prescribed and he never regarded the bill on which he labored most as his greatest contribution to the Revisal. At last, he gave that honor to his bill for establishing religious freedom.

[28] Ford, I, 63.
[29] Ford, I, 65; VII, 476–477; to Skelton Jones, July 28, 1909, L. & B., XII, 301; Lingley, *Transition*, p. 189.

[XX]

Church and School

OF all the contests in which Jefferson engaged as a member of the Assembly of Virginia the one on the subject of religion was the most bitter. He himself said it was the severest of his entire life.[1] Much more detailed information is available about other struggles of his career, such as his political duel with Alexander Hamilton, and he may have overestimated the rancor that persisted in his own State after the disestablishment of the Church. By championing the cause of freedom he probably gained more friends at home than he lost, for the dissenting sects were grateful. Most of the attacks from which he suffered in later years, when he was a more conspicuous target, originated elsewhere. He regarded these later attacks as clerical rather than religious, claiming that they emanated from church groups closely associated with state governments (as in New England) or otherwise moved by political considerations. At all events, the religious controversy persisted in some form to the end of his life and even pursued him beyond the grave. Viewing it in the large, he exaggerated neither its intensity nor its duration.

As a member of the committee on religion he was in the thick of the local fight from the outset, and he framed his famous bill for religious freedom early in his work as a revisor. It was not actually introduced until after he had become governor, however, and was not enacted until seven more years had passed.[2] This was at the end of a full

---

[1] Comment in old age, in Ford, I, 53. My opinion that this was the most controversial subject before the Assembly is based on the petitions presented on both sides, and the communications in the papers. During the period, October–December, 1776, for example, there were far more communications on the subject of religion in Purdie, *Va. Gazette*, and Dixon and Hunter, *Va. Gazette*, than on any other that was under legislative consideration. These show that public opinion was sharply divided. I found no reference to entails.

[2] Bill in Ford, II, 237–239; he afterwards said he drafted it in 1777. Admirable

decade of legislative conflict in which many men were engaged, and important victories had already been won for freedom. The credit was not wholly his, but in 1776 he probably was the foremost advocate of the entire separation of Church and State in Virginia, and unquestionably he became the major symbol of complete religious liberty in connection with his own measure. Such he remained during the years that he played on a larger stage. Then he was properly acclaimed as a prophet, correctly judged to be a free thinker, and unjustly charged with impiety.

He always regarded religion as a strictly private affair, like marriage and domestic life. He said little about it in his early letters and he undoubtedly thought in 1776, as he did in 1800, that his personal views had no bearing on any public conflict. While retaining a profound belief in the moral foundation of the universe, he had long since freed his mind from the shackles of man-made ecclesiasticism and doctrine, and he viewed departures from orthodoxy and the rise of dissenting groups with complete equanimity. Indeed, his respect for the honest opinions of all men caused him to look with entire tolerance on other forms of religion than Christianity itself. When asserting that the legitimate powers of government extend to only such acts as are injurious, he said: "But it does me no injury for my neighbor to say that there are twenty gods, or no god. It neither picks my pocket nor breaks my leg." [3] He made no parade of his own free thinking; he neither flouted nor derided conventional observances; and he was a scrupulously moral man. It was not on questions of private morals and personal beliefs that his thought centered during the Revolution, however; it was on religious freedom and the relations between particular groups and the State.

He read Locke and Shaftesbury among others, and transcribed notes which leave no doubt about the trend of his thinking, even though these have been transmitted to us in scraps. [4] He was convinced that complete religious freedom should be recognized by human law because of the very nature of religion. The care of every man's soul belongs to himself; no one can prescribe the faith of another; God himself cannot save a man against his will; and any form of spiritual compulsion is doomed to inevitable failure. State religion, therefore, was to him a contradiction in terms. The State should neither support nor oppose any particular

summary of the whole controversy to the end of the century in Lingley, *Transition in Virginia*, pp. 190–211.

[3] *Notes on Virginia*, in Ford, III, 263.

[4] "Notes on Religion," in Ford, II, 92–103; and in LC, 2:323–327, in a different order. See Ford's comments on uncertainties about these notes.

form of church but should leave all of them strictly alone. In the course of time this became the official American position.

Despite the musings of a philosophical statesman, the position of the Established Church in Virginia would not have been seriously challenged but for the rise of the dissenting sects.[5] The first of these to flourish consisted of the Presbyterians. They were followed by the Baptists, who were the most severe critics of the Establishment, and by the Methodists, who had a low opinion of the spiritual state of the Anglicans but still regarded themselves as part of the Mother Church and had little to do with politics. The complaint that the parsons of the Establishment were cold and formal, which was made by the fiery Evangelicals, did not impress Jefferson, for he made a point of keeping his own emotions under strict control. He had long ago observed that some of the official clergymen were immoral and slothful, and he did not condone any of their carnal lapses. They were probably as good as most of the clergymen in England, however, and their alleged "infidelity" was not alarming to a disciple of the Enlightenment who did not even admit the validity of the term.[6]

Jefferson expressed far greater bitterness in later life against the Presbyterians of his own State and against the clergy of New England than he ever did against the colonial Anglicans as a group; and he found out that the alliance between Church and State was stricter in Connecticut and Massachusetts. He wrote John Adams: "Our clergy, before the Revolution, having been secured against rivalship by fixed salaries, did not give themselves the trouble of acquiring influence over the people." [7] What he objected to, on rational grounds, was the preferred status and special privileges which had caused them to become an artificial aristocracy and enabled them to exercise an unwarranted degree of authority. He believed in a free society.

Furthermore, he noted that the dissenters now outnumbered the Anglicans. He had seen plenty of them in Albemarle, and they were specially strong in the Piedmont country generally. He did not assert that they were persecuted. On the contrary, he observed that after a century of dominance the spirit of the Anglicans had subsided into moderation. The laws remained oppressive, however, and the spirit of the dissenters "had risen to a degree of determination which commanded respect." [8] This observation suggests, at the same time, his own attitude. His friendships continued to be chiefly among the An-

[5] Eckenrode, *Separation of Church and State in Virginia*, ch. 3.

[6] Good discussion of character of clergy in E. L. Goodwin, *Colonial Church in Virginia*, pp. 92–94.

[7] Oct. 28, 1813 (Ford, IX, 426).

[8] *Notes on Virginia*, in Ford, III, 262.

glicans, who were moderate on the whole, and he had respect rather than regard for the dissenters; but he was unalterably opposed to oppressive laws. He regarded uniformity of religious opinion as no more desirable than that of face and stature. On the other hand, he saw distinct advantages in differences of opinion, for the various sects would act as censors of one another. He rightly concluded that in this matter there was safety in numbers.[9]

The Assembly of 1776 did much to relieve the dissenters.[10] As Jefferson himself said, it got rid of statutory oppressions insofar as these were contained in acts of Parliament. Furthermore, it exempted dissenters from taxes in support of the Established Church. The act providing a fixed salary for ministers was suspended at this time, and three years later it was definitely repealed.[11] The latter action was taken after Jefferson had framed his famous bill, however. There were unsolved problems relating to the power of vestries, and some questions about the disposition of church buildings and glebe lands were not finally answered for a generation, but the most important political question that remained was one of policy. Should there be a general assessment for the support of religion or should the churches be supported wholly by voluntary contributions? For a time some of the dissenters favored this degree of connection with the State; but Jefferson believed that even forcing a man to support a minister of his own persuasion was a deprivation of liberty, and it was in reaction against the movement for assessment that his bill was finally passed.

At the common law, he said, heresy was still a capital offense; and by act of Assembly denial of the Trinity or the divine authority of the Scriptures was punishable by disabilities and even by imprisonment. He believed that the public was still secured against this residue of "tyrannical laws" by the spirit of the times; and he doubted whether the people would suffer an execution for heresy or a sentence of imprisonment "for not comprehending the mysteries of the Trinity." [12] Being himself unwilling, however, to rely on a temper of tolerance which might prove temporary, he sought to sweep away all such laws. The method he employed was not one of detailed specification but of inclusive statement. He summed up everything in a single comprehensive section of his bill.

[9] Ibid., 264–265. This same idea reappears in fuller form in one of Madison's papers in the Federalist, where it is extended to civil rights (P. L. Ford, ed., 1898, no. 51, p. 347).

[10] Act of Dec. 9, 1776 (Hening, IX, 164–167); well summarized by Lingley, pp. 200–201.

[11] Session of Oct., 1779 (Hening, X, 197–198).

[12] Notes on Virginia, in Ford, III, 265.

Sect. II. We the General Assembly of Virginia do enact that no man shall be compelled to frequent or support any religious worship, place, or ministry whatsoever, nor shall be enforced, restrained, molested, or burthened in his body or goods, or shall otherwise suffer, on account of his religious opinions or belief; but that all men shall be free to profess, and by argument to maintain, their opinions in matters of religion, and that the same shall in no wise diminish, enlarge, or affect their civil capacities.[13]

He went the whole way. He did not limit liberty to Protestant sects or to Christian groups, but extended it to all without any qualification whatsoever. Also, he sought to give to this act the quality of eternity. In the third and final section, after admitting that no Assembly could pass an irrevocable law, he included a declaration that the rights which had been asserted were "of the natural rights of mankind."

In the philosophical preamble he expressed the same sort of thoughts that he had already jotted down in the course of his reading. His sharp condemnation of past rulers, civil and ecclesiastical, who in "impious presumption" had "assumed dominion over the faith of others," and thus had established and maintained "false religions" throughout all time over most of the world, represented his historical judgment; and his objections to enforced contributions to any church were directed particularly against the assessment bill. To him, however, it seemed that practically everything he said was timeless. He was not merely expressing thoughts or even convictions, but what he regarded as eternal truths. Nor were these limited to the subject of religion; they constituted an assertion of complete intellectual liberty. The mind is by nature free and altogether insusceptible of coercion; the opinions of men are not under the jurisdiction of civil government; truth will prevail if left to herself; errors cease to be dangerous when one is permitted freely to contradict them.

Some of these maxims of his own faith did not appear in the final act. His bill was first introduced soon after he became governor, and enough people then regarded it as a "diabolical scheme" to prevent its passage.[14] Sentiment had changed by the end of the year 1785, after he had crossed the Atlantic and James Madison had persuaded the legislators to give belated attention to the recommendations of the revisors. They were then ready to go as far as Jefferson desired in statutory enactment, but a considerable number of them demurred at his philosophical preamble. It was then proposed that a brief statement

[13] Ford, II, 239.
[14] Ibid., 237 n.

from the Declaration of Rights be substituted for it. This amendment was defeated by a large majority in the House of Delegates, but it bobbed up again in the Senate and would not down. In the end Madison agreed to the deletion of some of the more sweeping statements about the supremacy and illimitability of reason; and, as a result, the statute did not rest on quite so broad a base as the one its author had designed. Nevertheless, Madison dared believe that in Virginia "the ambitious hope of making laws for the human mind" had been forever extinguished.[15]

The Assembly did not weaken the bill enough to mar Jefferson's pride in authorship; and, before a year was out, he was rejoicing over the favorable notice of it in the Old World. He naturally wrote to Madison, who had presided as midwife at its legislative birth.

> The Virginia act for religious freedom has been received with infinite approbation in Europe & propagated with enthusiasm. I do not mean by the governments, but by the individuals which compose them. It has been translated into French & Italian, has been sent to most of the courts of Europe, & has been the best evidence of the falsehood of those reports which stated us to be in anarchy. It is inserted in the new Encyclopedie, & is appearing in most of the publications respecting America. In fact it is comfortable to see the standard of reason at length erected, after so many ages during which the human mind has been held in vassalage by kings, priests & nobles: and it is honorable for us to have produced the first legislature who had the courage to declare that the reason of man may be trusted with the formation of his own opinions.[16]

The immediate attention this statute received abroad may be attributed partly to Jefferson's own activities, for he promptly had it printed and he circulated it as widely as he could. Its importance in his own history is owing partly to the emphasis he himself always gave it. He rated it as second in importance only to the Declaration of Independ-

[15] To Jefferson, Jan. 22, 1786; *Writings*, II, 216. The amendment to strike out the preamble, made on Dec. 16, 1785, was defeated 66 to 38. This is one of the rare cases in which the ayes and noes on one of Jefferson's bills were inserted in the record. Among those favoring the amendment were Benjamin Harrison, John Tyler, Joseph Jones, and Jefferson's old friend John Page; among those opposing it were Madison, John Taylor, and W. C. Nicholas. It was defeated a second time on Dec. 29, 1785; Jefferson's old playmate and friend, Thomas Mann Randolph, then appeared on the conservative side. The two houses finally agreed on Jan. 16, 1786, and the bill was signed three days later. All the above is from *Delegates, Journal;* the act is in Hening, XII, 84–86.

[16] Dec. 16, 1786 (Ford, IV, 334).

ence in such lists of his own achievements as he afterwards drew up.[17] As an official pronouncement it emanated from a single Commonwealth, not from the federal Union, but he undoubtedly believed that he had spoken for the human race. Despite the deletions made by the Assembly it was a proclamation of both the intellectual and the religious independence of the individual, and as such it deserves to be ranked with the declaration of the political independence of a group of states. Its fame was not fortuitous. After more than a century and a half it remains an ineffaceable landmark of human liberty; and men in any land would do well to turn to it at any time that persecution for opinion may raise its ugly head.

Before he knew what the fate of his bill for the more general diffusion of knowledge would be, Jefferson went so far as to say that it was the most important one in the entire report of the revisors.[18] He did not quite mean that, but if it had been enacted as he drew it and proved effectual in practice it probably would have been listed with the statute for religious freedom among his greatest achievements. Unfortunately, however, it was not passed until almost the end of the century, and he could take little pride in the truncated statute which then emerged from the legislative mill. The most constructive part of his program of reform remained in the blue-print stage, and for long years it looked as though his efforts to illuminate the minds of the people generally had been crowned with futility. In the light of history, however, nothing else that he did or proposed during his entire career showed him more clearly to be a major American prophet. By the time that the report of the revisors was submitted, when he was thirty-six, he had ceased to be a mere disciple of enlightenment; he had become an apostle, even though his full stature was not yet perceived everywhere.[19]

In long retrospect, Americans have come to regard him as the chief prophet of public education in the first half-century of the Union;

[17] In the summary which he drew in September 1800, the earliest I have found, he lists first his services in rendering the Rivanna River navigable, possibly because he started out with the idea of following a chronological order, as in general he continued to do. This summary is in LC, 219:39,161. It is printed, with approximate date, in Ford, VII, 475–477. The brief description on his tombstone is generally known.

[18] To George Wythe, Aug. 13, 1786; Ford, IV, 268.

[19] Bill in Ford, II, 220–229. Jefferson's comments in his *Notes on Va., Ibid.*, III, 251–256, are contemporary; his brief comments in his Autobiography, *Ibid.*, I, 66–67, were made much later. The documents on the subject are reprinted as appendices in the excellent monograph of R. J. Honeywell, *Educational Work of Thomas Jefferson* (Cambridge, Mass., 1931).

and it is doubtful if any other American name has been so often cited in popular addresses and writings on this perennially interesting subject. This is owing in part to the political eminence he attained, and partly to the apt sayings that are scattered through his collected writings. Some of the most famous of these quotations are from private letters, such as one to George Wythe from Paris in which he said: "Preach, my dear Sir, a crusade against ignorance; establish and improve the law for educating the common people." [20] Not until after his death could such sayings as these gain wide currency, and they might have remained forever unknown if he had been politically obscure.

The most important reason for the recognition of his importance as an educational prophet, however, is that his fundamental ideas have withstood the test of time. Some of them became so generally accepted that they can almost be taken for granted, and one is tempted to believe that they were indigenous to the American soil. They found fertile ground on the new continent, beyond a doubt, but before they took root they had to be seminated. Jefferson started sowing his seed in the early morning of the Republic. There have been other conspicuous crusaders against ignorance, but he anticipated the great American doctrine in the bills he drew in Virginia. Also, he added refinements and qualifications that were distinctive of his own discriminating philosophy, and even now the larger public is not fully aware of these.

His greatest services were rendered to posterity, but his immediate activities stand out in sharp relief against their specific background of place and time. In colonial and Revolutionary Virginia formal education was largely a private matter and its benefits were almost wholly restricted to the gentry. Judging from its fruits, including Jefferson himself, the system was better than he thought it. Its chief merit was that it produced capable leaders, and he was concerned that it should continue to do this, on the basis of a more rational plan. He was unquestionably correct in concluding that the existing system rested on a dangerously narrow base.

The preamble to his historic bill does not lend itself to detached quotation, as the sayings in his letters do, but it contains a clear statement of purposes he continued to cherish throughout his life.

His emphasis was on public purposes. The most important of these was to guard the freedom and happiness of individual members of society, but he did not describe education here in terms of personal refinement and culture. Fear of tyranny, even though this was only incipient tyranny, was prominent if not predominant in his thought.

[20] Aug. 13, 1786 (Ford, IV, 269).

He saw the most effective preventive in the illumination of the minds of the people at large. He was particularly anxious to give them knowledge of the facts of history, in order that they would recognize dangerous political ambition in any shape.

Second only to his purpose to prevent tyranny and safeguard freedom was the desire to assure wise and honest government. This necessitated the training of leaders. Nothing in his plans called for the diminution of the educational opportunities of those whose parents were able to pay for them. However, he expected that some of these fortunate persons would prove unworthy to receive and unable to guard "the sacred deposit of the rights and liberties of their fellow citizens"; and he was convinced that it was folly to leave the public welfare dependent on the accidental circumstances of wealth or birth. Accordingly, he sought to make higher schooling available without charge to selected youths of marked native ability who would emerge from the unprivileged groups.

From our point of view Jefferson's specific proposals represented a modest compromise between public and private education, but in contemporary Virginia they seemed both comprehensive and revolutionary. By means of this bill for the diffusion of knowledge he sought to establish, throughout the State, schools of two levels. The "hundred" schools, which we should call primary, were to serve relatively small districts or "hundreds," and were designed to effect his purposes of general public enlightenment. Three years of education were to be given gratis to all white children, male and female. However, these schools were not to be wholly public, for any child whose parents could pay for him might stay longer if he liked.

On the next level there were to be "grammar" schools, set up in districts including several counties. Provision was made for the lodging and boarding of the students. The State was to own the grounds and buildings, but most of the running expenses were to be met by the parents, and to a much greater extent than the "hundred" schools these were to be private. Only the youths of great native ability "raked from the rubbish annually," and subjected thereafter to specified processes of elimination, were to be supported by the State. A final survivor of the competition was to be sent annually to the College of William and Mary, at the charge of the Commonwealth.

Not very long after he drew the bill, Jefferson summarized his own expectations from it:

> . . . The ultimate result of the whole scheme of education would be the teaching all the children of the State reading, writing, and common arithmetic; turning out ten annually of superior

genius, well taught in Greek, Latin, geography, and the higher branches of arithmetic; turning out ten others annually, of still superior parts, who, to those branches of learning, shall have added such of the sciences as their genius shall have led them to; the furnishing to the wealthier part of the people convenient schools at which their children may be educated at their own expence.[21]

These proposals reveal him as a realistic and discriminating democrat, or as an informed and critical aristocrat — whichever term may be preferred. His concern was to broaden the educational base of society and, at the same time, to search out and utilize for the public good the aristocracy of worth and genius which he afterwards described as "the most precious gift of nature."[22] He tried to frame a comprehensive program. "The general objects of this law," he said, "are to provide an education adapted to the years, to the capacity, and the condition of every one, and directed to their freedom and happiness."[23] He expected no Utopia overnight but he was convinced that he was on the right track. In later years his American countrymen had no doubt he was, though they were more disposed than he to emphasize quantity for its own sake and more reluctant to apply selective standards at any stage of the educational process.

According to Madison, the Assembly gave Jefferson's bill indulgent consideration when they took it up in 1786, but they deferred it because they regarded the financial requirements as beyond the powers of the State.[24] The author himself believed that the necessary tax would be only the "thousandth part" of what would be paid to the kings, priests, and nobles who would rise up if the people were left in ignorance. He afterwards said that wealthy men were reluctant to assume the burden of educating the children of the poor, but other practical difficulties may be recognized which reflect less on human nature.[25]

The geographical problem was particularly difficult. Naturally and properly, Jefferson devised a system for the entire State, but this was really an imperial domain, including a vast and sparsely settled region beyond the mountains. Virginia was not like Massachusetts, and the setting up of primary schools which would be within walking distance of every house would have been difficult and costly even in Tide-

[21] *Notes on Virginia*, Ford, III, 252.
[22] To John Adams, Oct. 28, 1813 (Ford, IX, 425).
[23] Ford, III, 252.
[24] To Jefferson, Dec. 4, 1786 (*Writings*, II, 292). See also *Delegates, Journal*, Dec. 21, 1785.
[25] To Wythe, Aug. 13, 1786 (Ford, IV, 269); reference to the later history of the act of 1796 (*Ibid.*, I, 67).

water.[26] Jefferson himself stated that it would not have been proper for him to specify details of organization, but actually he did devise and incorporate a rather complicated general plan. Certain features of this came in for valid criticism, and amendments of some sort were necessary. After he had finally emerged from the shackles of public life he amended his own plan, but that is another story. The only part of his bill that became law in the eighteenth century was the portion dealing with the primary schools, and the establishment of these was left to the will of the localities. As things turned out, the will proved lacking. All he was able to do, therefore, was to set up a guidepost for the future.

He already envisaged a system of public education which had as its apex an institution of the highest learning, but his legislative efforts to transform the College of William and Mary were unavailing. In the bill he drew he was sharply critical of his alma mater, baldly asserting that it had not answered expectations.[27] He regarded it as subject to public direction, however, and believed that its charters could and should be so altered and amended as to render the institution publicly advantageous, in proportion as it was publicly expensive. Furthermore, he thought it the peculiar duty of the legislature at this crucial time to aid the seminary where the future guardians of the rights and liberties of their country might be "endowed with science and virtue, to watch and preserve the sacred deposit." The specific amendments proposed by him looked toward the much closer identification of the College with the State and the enlargement of its services until it should deal with all the "useful sciences." Without saying so precisely, what he really anticipated at this early date was a state university.

The tie with the State was to be tightened by causing the reduced governing board to be elected annually by the Assembly and by providing for more stable support from public funds. A unique administrative provision was for three chancellors, to be chosen from the judges of the High Court of Chancery or of the General Court, who were to constitute a judiciary in all disputes relating to faculty or students. In view of Jefferson's later role as the founder of a university, however, none of his recommendations are quite so interesting as those relating to the enlargement of the faculty and the designation of fields of service. He wanted to increase the professors from six to eight, to get rid of the two chairs of divinity and the Indian school, and to introduce the study of law, medicine, history, and modern languages. There being no longer real need for an Indian school, he thought that a missionary to the

[26] Difficulties summarized in Honeywell, p. 14, ch. 3.
[27] Bill in Ford, II, 229–235.

Indians might be appointed instead, but this missionary was also to perform a scholarly service: he was to investigate their laws, customs, and, most of all, their languages.

On half a dozen counts Jefferson showed himself in this bill to be an American prophet in the field of higher education. He himself believed that it was defeated by the dissenting sects; they still looked with disfavor upon an institution which had been historically Anglican, and their fears were not allayed by his amendments. He was not permitted to transform the College into a genuinely public institution or to enlarge its faculty. During his governorship, however, when he served as a member of the board of visitors, he was able to change the professorships to some degree and thus to become a pioneer as well as a prophet. He did introduce professorships of law, medicine, and modern languages, and if these were not the first of the sort in the United States the people in Williamsburg have been many years in error. Law and medicine were committed to his old friends George Wythe and James McClurg, while modern languages were entrusted to an Italian, Charles Bellini. The gratitude and affection of the latter for Jefferson were excessive. He is perhaps the only man in history known to have addressed the philosopher as "My dearest Thomas." [28]

Jefferson took special pride in the work of Wythe, and before he went to France he was ambitious to add other professorships: on the ancient languages and literature of the North, for example. Also, he still wanted to find somebody to deal with the customs and languages of the Indians.[29] Not for long years did he return to a detailed consideration of the needs of higher education, but in one fundamental respect he showed himself in his late thirties to be qualified to found a university: his scholarly interest was universal.

This learned and extraordinarily farseeing architect of laws and institutions also sought to further a high educational purpose by establishing a public library in Richmond.[30] His bill for this was not enacted, but by his personal activities as a collector of books during these Revolutionary years he amply demonstrated his own conviction that they were of supreme importance. No American of his generation did more by precept and example, if anybody did so much, to emphasize the sacred freedom of the human spirit and the necessary nourishment of the mind.

[28] *W. & M.*, 2 ser., V, 1–29.
[29] Comments in *Notes on Virginia*, in Ford, III, 252, 255–257.
[30] Ford, II, 236–237.

⌈XXI⌋

The Amenities of War

1777–1779

AS a member of the House of Delegates, Jefferson did not have a full-time position. It is true that the sessions were longer than they had been in the old House of Burgesses; once he was seventy-nine days in unbroken attendance.[1] But even in these war years this was unusual, and despite his being an important public character he could spend most of his time at home.

His work as a revisor of the laws he did almost entirely at Monticello, since that was much the best place to do it. His library there was growing by leaps and bounds. After the deaths of Peyton Randolph and Richard Bland he had purchased the books these distinguished kinsmen had left, including some rare volumes of Virginia manuscripts. The books he got from the Reverend Samuel Henley, after that philosophical professor left the College of William and Mary, were of a somewhat different character, but everything was grist for his mill.[2] He was also collecting old Virginia newspapers and laws. Finding that many of the latter had disappeared, he set out to assemble all that remained — in manuscript, in fugitive printed sheets, or in any other form.[3] While acquiring and preserving these perishable materials of local history, he was thinking of posterity, but he was also facilitating his own immediate task.

He had other public responsibilities besides those of a delegate and revisor, but most of these were local in their setting. As county lieu-

---

[1] Payment for 79 days, Oct. 20, 1777–Jan. 24, 1778, noted in his Fee Book.

[2] To H. P. Taylor, Oct. 4, 1823 (L. & B., XV, 472); to Henley, June 9, 1778 (Ford, II, 160–161); Mar. 3, 1785 (MHS); from Henley, Nov. 16, 1785 (*Papers, MHS*, p. 15).

[3] Details given in letters to George Wythe, Jan. 16, 1796 (L. & B., IX, 319–323); to W. W. Hening, Jan. 14, 1807 (*Ibid.*, XI, 138–139); and elsewhere.

tenant, Colonel Jefferson had to do much paper work in connection with the militia, and in the spring of 1777 his name was added to the list of Albemarle magistrates as a justice of the peace. He kept in intimate touch with the affairs of the Commonwealth, whose future he was seeking to chart, and through letters from members of Congress he was informed of the affairs of the Continent. He showed no such diligence in correspondence, however, as he did later. Much of his time was given to the public councils and most of it to public matters, but he could continue to be a diligent legal scholar, an enthusiastic observer of nature, a generous country gentleman, and a solicitous pater familias. This was a combination of roles he greatly liked.

He had his wife with him briefly in George Wythe's house on the Palace Green during his first session in the Assembly, but she was not in Williamsburg when the delegates next met in May, 1777. That was the major reason why he himself was there for only sixteen days in a session of eight weeks. He was given a leave of absence because of impending domestic events. At ten in the evening on May 28, after he got back to Monticello, their first and only son was born. This short-lived infant appears in the record merely as "our son." For a time they probably thought of him as another Thomas but presumably he was never christened, and in his third week, soon after ten in the evening, he died.[4]

For more than a year longer little Patsy remained the only child. She was nearing six when her precise father made another entry in his notebook. "Our third daughter born," he recorded on August 1, 1778, giving the hour as 1:30 A.M.[5] Undoubtedly he was disappointed not to get a boy — but he loved children, even girls. This one was named Mary. It may not have been wholly on her account that he remained in Albemarle until the fall session of the Assembly had almost run its course, but by that time the persistence of this young life seemed relatively sure. She did not live as long as he did but she grew up, being afterwards known as Maria and, more familiarly, as Polly. She became a pretty lady like her mother, as the servants said.

The year of Polly's birth, 1778, was one of much building and planting at Monticello. In February the Master contracted for three stone columns and recorded that 90,000 good bricks had been made. In one month in midsummer he said that 14,120 were laid. In the spring, among other acts of husbandry, he added numerous grafted trees to his orchard: cherries, apples, pears, quinces, plums, apricots, and bitter almonds. In the fall he got from Philip Mazzei's neighboring place,

[4] Account Book, June 14, 1777.
[5] Ibid., Aug. 1, 1778. It will be recalled that his second daughter had died.

Colle, the shoot of an olive tree sprung from Italian stock, reflecting as he planted it that it would take ten years to bear. He measured with exactitude the circumference of the roundabout walk encompassing his mountaintop, and the distance to the place where his millhouse should stand. Now as always his activities were unceasing — but they had the domestic flavor and the constructive quality that he most liked.[6]

He was not unaware that a war was going on, and not uninformed about its dirty side. His friend Thomas Nelson, Junior, who was closer to the scene of military action, wrote him luridly about the conduct of the "damned invaders," who played the very devil with the girls to satisfy their lewd appetites and left few virgins behind them.[7] This correspondent and others repeated the sad story of the general apathy and selfishness of the people. "Rely on it, our confederacy is not founded on brotherly love," wrote his friend John Harvie, who was briefly a congressman. When Washington was at "Forge Valley" and Congress was at York, Pennsylvania, Harvie said in great discouragement: "The avarice of individuals will be more fatal to the liberties of America than the sword of the enemy." He was sure his fellow Virginians would execrate the states of Pennsylvania and Delaware if he were there. However, he reported Burgoyne's surrender; and news of the French alliance came after that.[8]

This turn of events reassured the naturally optimistic Jefferson. By the summer of 1778 he was saying that all doubt of the favorable outcome of the war was removed by the interposition of France. Accordingly, he thought it not improper to employ what leisure he had from public duties in the philosophical pursuits of which he was so fond.[9] He used the term "philosophy" in no technical, academic sense, but gave it the generalized meaning that was current in his age. Its closest modern analogy is science but there was a sweeping universality about it, for by observing the diverse manifestations of nature he and his contemporaries hoped also to discover the divine plan for man. Philosophy included many things, among them the study of climate and temperature he was then carrying on at Monticello and continued all his

[6] *Garden Book*, pp. 76–80, and notes.
[7] Jan. 2, 1777, from Baltimore, in LC, 2:354.
[8] Sept. 10, Sept. 20, Dec. 29, 1777, in LC, 3:390–391, 392, 404–405.
[9] To Giovanni Fabbroni, June 8, 1778. This highly interesting letter, on which this and the following paragraph are largely based, was published without name in Ford, II, 156–160, from a draft now in LC, 3:419; autograph letter at Clements Library, Ann Arbor, Mich., photostat UVA. Jefferson was probably replying to Fabbroni's letter of Sept. 15, 1776, in LC, 2:301, giving the date 1777 in error. If this surmise is correct, that letter was 21 months in reaching Jefferson. Fabbroni may have made a brief visit to America, but the implication is that he had not. He was a friend of Mazzei's.

life. "I make my daily observations as early as possible in the morning and again about 4 o'clock in the afternoon," he said. The theodolite he had bought at the first of the year he regarded as a philosophical instrument; by means of it he calculated the angle of intersection of distant mountains with the horizon.[10]

His mind was also much on music, which was not philosophy precisely but was one of the good things to be found in the vast harmony of nature. He wrote to a young Italian friend of Mazzei's, then in Paris, that music was the favorite passion of his soul, though unhappily it was in a barbaric state in America. He was now longing for a band of domestic musicians but his fortune was not equal to that. He had a gardener, a weaver, and a stonecutter, however, and hoped to secure a vigneron. He believed that in cultivated Italy or France his correspondent might find for him men of these useful trades who could also perform on the French horn, the clarinet, the hautboy, or the bassoon. This letter was actually captured by the British, and he did not get musical workmen from Europe, but it is noteworthy that he wanted an orchestra of this homely and useful sort.

Meanwhile, he was giving thought to celestial mechanics. In June, 1778, there was an eclipse of the sun which John Page and the Reverend James Madison observed at Williamsburg with indifferent success because of atmospheric conditions. These were somewhat better at Monticello where Jefferson stood watch, but he was at a disadvantage because he lacked a thoroughly dependable timepiece. Accordingly, he wrote the ingenious David Rittenhouse in Philadelphia, reminding him of the promise to make him an accurate clock, solely for astronomical purposes.[11] He spoke admiringly of that mathematician's noted representation of the solar system known as an "orrery." Also, he expressed the personal opinion that the governing of a commonwealth did not require the first order of ability and that higher and better things were expected of a philosopher.

Rittenhouse had been principally employed of late in the civil government of Pennsylvania, and Jefferson, with the zeal of "a true Whig in science," was mildly upbraiding him. As he put it, "nobody can conceive that nature ever intended to throw away a Newton upon the occupations of a crown." The geniuses of men, he believed, should be employed according to their orders and degrees. "I doubt not," he said, "there are in your country many persons equal to the task of conducting government: but you should consider that the world has but one

10 *Garden Book*, p. 80.

11 July 19, 1778, Ford, II, 162–163. He probably did not know how successful Rittenhouse had been in observing the same eclipse.

Ryttenhouse [*sic*], and that it never had one before. . . . Are those powers then, which . . . are, like air and light, the world's common property, to be taken from their proper pursuit to do the common-place drudgery of governing a single state, a work which may be executed by men of an ordinary stature, such as are always and everywhere to be found?"

He had made no scientific contributions that would have warranted his comparing himself with Rittenhouse and Franklin, and he made no such comparison. Nor did he claim for himself the exemption from ordinary civil obligations that he believed they were entitled to. He could hardly have failed to see that his major public employment in the Commonwealth of Virginia had closely accorded with his special talents and his training. In the spring of 1779, nevertheless, he talked to his friend Edmund Pendleton about retiring. This collaborator of his, who knew so well where his demonstrated talent lay, answered him with neat finality: "You are too young to ask that happy quietus from the public, and should at least postpone it till you have taught the rising generation the forms as well as the substantial principles of legislation." [12]

If George Washington had been consulted at this juncture, he would have been less sympathetic and would have laid the emphasis elsewhere than on the rising generation and local legislation. He was forced to think of immediate necessities and to view the whole Continental stage. In the winter of 1778–1779 it seemed to him that the common interests of America were moldering, and would sink into "irretrievable ruin" if better men were not soon sent to Congress. Writing to Benjamin Harrison, then speaker of the House of Delegates, he asked: "Where is Mason, Wythe, Jefferson, Nicholas, Pendleton, Nelson, and another I could name? The harassed Commander expressed the same idea a few months later to George Mason, when he again inquired where the men of ability were. "Let this voice . . . call upon you, Jefferson and others," he said.[13] In his opinion these patriotic leaders were much too absorbed in their own affairs and those of their Commonwealth.[14]

[12] To Jefferson, May 11, 1779 (LC, 3:484).

[13] Washington to Harrison, Dec. 18–30, 1778 (Fitzpatrick, XIII, 467); to Mason, Mar. 27, 1779 (*Ibid.*, XIV, 301).

[14] Beveridge in *Marshall*, I, 125–130, misses the point of Washington's complaint against the Virginia leaders. His surmise that the question, "Where is Jefferson?" was echoed among the "shivering soldiers and officers" is fanciful. The prominence of Jefferson in their minds may not be assumed, and if the beginnings of John Marshall's personal estimate of his later political foe "may be found in their relative situation and conduct" during this period, it is hard to explain why James Monroe, who went through the same sort of hardships as Marshall, arrived at an entirely different personal estimate of Jefferson.

The county lieutenant and first citizen of Albemarle was not resting under his own vine and fig tree, but he was considerably engaged in long-range tasks with little direct bearing on the winning of the war. Furthermore, to some people he appeared to be indulging his personal tastes too complacently in these perilous times. There was more than a joke in the remark of Edward Rutledge of South Carolina about his condescending to come down from above and interesting himself in human affairs.[15] But his contemporaries did not blame him for not being in the Continental Army. Entirely apart from his family obligations, his greater usefulness in the public councils was obvious.

How good a soldier he would have been, if circumstances had caused him to become one, is a matter of sheer speculation. Being a skillful horseman and a ready writer, he could have been an effective military aide, especially if he had been as young as Alexander Hamilton or James Monroe, but he was somewhat too old and rather too prominent for that sort of post. He had had no experience commanding troops in the field. He always preferred persuasion to command, anyway, and he had no ambitions whatever for military glory. There is significance in the fact that he was rarely called "Colonel," though many of his fellows often were designated thus, without having any better claim to the title than he had. Quite clearly, his contemporaries thought of him as a civilian type.

No one who did as much as he to bring about this war could be termed a pacifist. Nor was he unique in being too sanguine at this stage about the larger military situation; most people underestimated the difficulties, as Washington often lamented. But unquestionably his temperament and philosophy tended to make him err on the side of optimism. He not only thought the war more nearly won than it actually was; he also kept on regarding it as more civilized than it turned out to be. He overestimated both the reasonableness and the politeness of men; and he believed that, even in the midst of conflict, the amenities should and could be generally observed.

While still in Congress he wrote these words:

> When necessity compelled us to take up arms against Great Britain in defense of our just rights, we thought it a circumstance of comfort that our enemy was brave and civilized. It is the happiness of modern times that the evils of necessary war are softened by the refinement of manners & sentiments and that an enemy is an object of vengeance, in arms, & in the field only.[16]

15 To Jefferson, Feb. 12, 1779 (LC, 3:450).
16 Declaration concerning Ethan Allen (Ford, I, 494).

This was preliminary to his burning indictment of the British for violating the "rights of nations" in the case of Ethan Allen, who had been captured in Canada and, as he thought, badly treated. The measure of his indignation was also the measure of his sense of propriety. At no time had his resolution wavered but he assumed that men would generally wage war like gentlemen. He even invested a letter of introduction of a young soldier with a sort of idyllic charm. In these words he commended a recruit to the patronage of a high officer "in the school of honor":

> The bearer hereof, Mr. Strother Jones, son of a friend of mine [Gabriel Jones], is now setting out for the American army to share in the defense of his country. He is from nature well principled, for war bold, honorable & modest: but he is young also & will need the fatherly hand of some one to lead him thro' the mazes of military delicacy & duty on so large a scale. . . .[17]

Even before he became governor, the aura of honor and humanitarianism with which Jefferson had surrounded war was occasionally dispelled. The very fact that he was so humanitarian in spirit made him the more relentless whenever he believed that the rights of humanity had been violated. This was shown not only in his threats of reprisal against the British for their reported treatment of Ethan Allen. It was also shown in a case of treason, when one Josiah Phillips was spreading terror through the southeastern counties of Virginia and, in Patrick Henry's words, was warring against the human race. For a good many months this murderous insurrectionist was Public Enemy Number One. Treason was subject to the penalty of death in Jefferson's generally humane bill for proportioning crimes and punishments; and in this instance treason was countered by a bill of attainder which he introduced precipitately in the House of Delegates.[18]

The later description of this action by Edmund Randolph as a "striking and shocking" violation of the Declaration of Rights was not technically correct. Randolph was attorney general at the time and should have remembered that the bill of attainder was not actually employed; the outlawed Phillips was tried and condemned by regular legal process, probably on the suggestion of the judges, and there seems no doubt that he richly deserved his fate.[19] Nor can there be any doubt that

[17] Apr. 18, 1777, to an unnamed officer (LC, 2:203); punctuation slightly modified.

[18] May 28, 1778 (Ford, II, 149-154, with detailed editorial note).

[19] *Va. Mag.*, XLIV, 223. W. P. Trent gave a history of the case in *A.H.R.*, I, 444-454 (Apr. 1896). He definitely discredited Randolph's credibility as a witness. He discredited Jefferson's to no considerable degree but described his attitude as inconsistent with his professed ideals.

Jefferson was normally a stickler for legality and dreaded any sort of arbitrary power. He expressed no regret about his attitude in this extreme case, however. In the pursuit of such objects as winning the war and preventing the suffering of the innocent he could be ruthless. Before he became governor, however, he was relatively free to indulge his fondness not only for philosophical inquiry but also for the amenities. His relation with the Convention prisoners, which is interesting in itself, is a case in point.

In January, 1779, some four thousand of the troops, English and Hessian, who were surrendered by Burgoyne at Saratoga marched nearly seven hundred miles from Boston to Albemarle County. According to the Convention they were to be sent to England, and when Congress demurred Burgoyne said, "The public faith is broke." They were known as the "Convention troops," notwithstanding. Conditions for which Jefferson was in no way responsible were bad when they arrived in his neighborhood. The barracks on a high hill a few miles northwest of Charlottesville were unfinished, the weather was unspeakable, and the meat provided for them was largely spoiled because of slovenly butchering and lack of salt. Within a few weeks the rumor spread that the prisoners would be moved elsewhere; and Jefferson, soon after he had brought his family back from a visit to the Forest, took the matter up.

He discussed it at length with Governor Patrick Henry, addressing some arguments to the self-interest of the County and the State but concerning himself to a notable degree with the interests of the troops themselves.[20] They were now living in completed barracks with gardens and poultry of their own; they were in excellent health; and in his opinion they had rendered captivity comfortable.

> . . . I would not endeavor to show that their lives are valuable to us [he said], because it would suppose a possibility that humanity was kicked out of doors in America, and interest only attended to. . . . But is an enemy so execrable, that, though in captivity, his wishes and comforts are to be disregarded and even crossed? I think not. It is for the benefit of mankind to mitigate the horrors of war as much as possible. The practice, therefore, of modern nations, of treating captive enemies with politeness and generosity, is not only delightful in contemplation, but really interesting to all the world, friends, foes, and neutrals.[21]

[20] To Patrick Henry, Mar. 27, 1779 (Ford, II, 167–180).
[21] *Ibid.*, II, 175–176.

For humane reasons, no less than for local pride, he wanted the Convention prisoners to stay; and probably he would have argued thus in any case. The fact was, however, that he also had a deep personal interest and liked to have them near by — chiefly because of the officers, who added greatly to the joy and charm of life. The highest ones had become near neighbors of his.

The ranking British officer, Major General William Phillips, formerly second in command to Burgoyne, rented Colonel Carter's place, Blenheim. The ranking Hessian, Major General Baron de Riedesel, took Philip Mazzei's place, Colle; and about the middle of February his vivacious wife and three young daughters joined him there. The Italian was going to Europe on a financial mission for the State of Virginia which Jefferson and others had contrived. Jefferson had hastened to rent Colle to four young officers, one of them a German who played the violin, but the necessities of the Riedesels seemed greater and they got the place. Mazzei with his wife and stepdaughter remained about three weeks, under circumstances of vast confusion. The General had his revenge, however. Within a week his horses destroyed Mazzei's vineyard and brought the latter's experiment in vine culture in Virginia to a decisive end.[22]

Jefferson regretted this and probably would have preferred the young officers as neighbors, but the Riedesels were a good exchange for the Mazzeis. The exuberant Florentine had worn Jefferson down, and his wife was a person of unpleasing manners, though the stepdaughter was a favorite of Mrs. Jefferson's. The Baron made numerous and expensive improvements at Colle and his family settled down in relative comfort, though the Baroness complained a good deal. She was fearful of rattlesnakes and terrified by thunderstorms, and as the season wore on she loathed the heat. The Baron himself suffered a sunstroke before they left. They could hardly have been expected to like this country, but things were made easier for them by their kind and cultivated neighbor and his amiable wife.[23]

Jefferson sedulously avoided discussion of public matters with the officers, but he recognized no bar to the exchange of hospitalities. Preserved in his papers are invitations to and from the chief Britisher, one of which we shall cite.

[22] Mazzei, Memoirs, pp. 224–226; Garlick, Mazzei, pp. 51–53; Letters and Journals relating to . . . the American Revolution, by Mrs. General Riedesel, trans. by W. L. Stone (1867), p. 154; Memoirs, and Letters and Journals, of Major General Riedesel, trans. from the original German of Max von Eelking by W. L. Stone (1868), II, 65.

[23] The Baroness made colorful comments on Colle and Virginia in her Letters and Journals, esp. pp. 155–157, but oddly enough she did not mention Jefferson.

Major General Phillips sends his Compliments to Mr. and Mrs. Jefferson, requests the favour of their company at dinner on Thursday next at Two oclock to meet General and Madame de Riedesel. Major General Phillips hopes Miss Jefferson will be permitted to be of the party to meet the young Ladies from Colle.[24]

The Baron afterwards said that Jefferson showed him marks of friendship from the first moment of their acquaintance.[25] The Virginian's relations with General Phillips were friendly upon the surface, and he impressed that proud officer with the liberality of his sentiments; but he preferred the Hessians to the British as a group and it was they, chiefly, who enriched his life. The Baroness, who was stout and handsome, created consternation in Albemarle by wearing riding boots, but according to her own account she charmed the rustics with her singing. Jefferson could hardly have failed to hear her. He showed generous hospitality to the Riedesels at Monticello, the two ladies became real friends, and the little German girls became particularly attached to Mrs. Jefferson.[26]

The circle was wider than the two families. It included other German officers, among them Captain Baron de Geismar who played the violin. There were special reasons why he wanted to be exchanged and Jefferson exercised his good offices for him almost immediately.[27] Geismar left all his music for his former host when he finally went away; the two men corresponded afterwards; and they met again in Europe.[28]

Jefferson lightened the heavy hours of another young Hessian, who was deeply interested in philosophy. John Lewis de Unger wrote Jefferson that his greatest loss in leaving Virginia was "the satisfaction of conversing with a person in whom I find all the qualities which can arouse esteem and affection," and that he hoped he might find another such benefactor elsewhere.[29] The lord of Monticello was not a recognized sage as yet, but already he had begun to exert the lure upon the

[24] Apr. 11, 1779 (LC, 3:462). See also 3:463, Apr. 12, 1779. There is a note on Phillips in *Official Letters of the Governors of Va.*, II, 210, note 165; and one on him and Riedesel in Henry Belcher, *The First American Civil War, First Period*, II (London, 1911), 298–299.

[25] To Jefferson, Dec. 4, 1779 (LC, 6:652). They may have met before Jefferson got the invitation from Phillips.

[26] Riedesel to Jefferson, June 13, 1780; LC, 5:735.

[27] To R. H. Lee, Apr. 21, 1779 (Ford, II, 180–181); from R. H. Lee, May 22, 1779 (Ballagh, *Letters*, II, 56–57).

[28] Among the earlier letters of Geismar may be cited one of Feb. 26, 1780, and a fragment, probably from the same year, in LC, 5:706; 6:1037.

[29] Nov. 13, 1780 (LC, 6:975, in French). Jefferson's reply of Nov. 30, 1780, is in Ford, II, 373–374.

young which gained him so many disciples in later years. No small part of this attraction was owing to his sincere interest in them and in their future course. In reply to this young man he said:

> . . . When the course of events shall have removed you to distant scenes of action where laurels not tarnished with the blood of my country may be gathered, I shall urge sincere prayers for your obtaining every honor & preferment which may gladden the heart of a souldier. On the other hand should your fondness for philosophy resume it's merited ascendancy, is it impossible to hope that this unexplored country may tempt your residence by holding out materials wherewith to build a fame founded on the happiness & not the calamities of human nature?

Another German officer, writing to someone else after Jefferson became governor, gave a bit of description that is worthy of special note because comments of this early date on Monticello and its residents are so rare.

> . . . My only Occupation at present [said the unnamed officer], is to learn the English language. It is the easier for me, as I have free Access to a copious & well chosen Library of Colo. Jefferson's, Governor of Virginia. . . . The Governor possesses a Noble Spirit of Building. He is now finishing an elegant building, projected according to his own fancy. In his parlour he is creating on the Cieling [sic] a Compass of his own invention by wich [sic] he can know the Strength as well as Direction of the Winds. I have promised to paint the Compass for it. He was much pleased with a fancy Painting of mine . . . As all Virginians are fond of Music, he is particularly so. You will find in his House an elegant Harpsichord, Pianoforte & some Violins. The latter he performs well upon himself, the former his Lady touches very skilfully & who, is in all respects a very agreeable, sensible & accomplished Lady.[30]

In the midst of war Jefferson conversed with former enemies in the international language of art, music, and philosophy, as well as the universal speech of human kindness. One of his regrets about becoming governor was that his friendly intercourse with these cultivated prisoners was interrupted. He was distinctly helpful to them, however, as an executive. When Riedesel, still suffering from his sunstroke, wanted to take advantage of certain medicinal springs in the summer, the Governor provided the necessary passports and granted him all possible

---

[30] Extract from a Hamburg paper enclosed in a letter from Jacob Rubsamer to Jefferson, Jan. 1, 1780 (LC, 6:994), and presumably translated by the former.

freedom of movement.[31] He lent his aid to the efforts of Riedesel and others to secure exchange, and carried on with the Baron a correspondence marked by mutual affection and touched with humor. Madame at length had another child and Jefferson sent condolences on the birth of another *daughter*.[32] Also, when the Baron congratulated him on his election as governor, he said that condolences were really in order. This time he was speaking in grim seriousness.

His new office was no bar to continued friendliness toward the Hessians, but the Convention troops eventually became one of his serious problems, and the later course of events was not favorable to amicable relations with General Phillips. Jefferson soon had a more notorious British prisoner to deal with than any he had known in Albemarle. General Hamilton, recently of Detroit, did not wage civilized warfare, and toward him Jefferson was relentless. If he did not know it already, he learned in the next two years that this war involved exceedingly bitter business.

[31] LC, 2:200, draft of a letter presumably addressed to Riedesel; Jefferson to Riedesel, July 4, 1779 (L. & B., IV, 300–301); to Phillips, June 25, 1779 (LC, 3:518).
[32] May 13, 1780 (Ford, II, 302).

The Ordeal of a War Governor

[XXII]

The Limitations of Executive Power

JEFFERSON was thirty-six years old and a member of the Assembly on June 1, 1779, when the two houses on joint ballot elected him Governor of Virginia. He was gratified that his public conduct was thus approved, but he soon remarked that the appointment was unlikely to add to his personal happiness. Replying to one letter of congratulation, he said: "In a virtuous government, and more especially in times like these, public offices are, what they should be, burdens to those appointed to them, which it would be wrong to decline, though foreseen to bring with them intense labour, and great private loss." [1] He had not been in office a month when he said: "The hour of private retirement to which I am drawn by my nature with a propensity almost irresistible, will be the most welcome of my life." [2] That hour did not come until two painful years had passed.

At the time of his election his wife and two daughters were not with him. They were at the Forest, making one of their frequent visits to the hospitable Eppes family, and the lady did not intend to come to Williamsburg soon. [3] He himself was compelled to spend most of his time at the seat of government, however, and he found it necessary to put a steward in full charge at Monticello. [4] Williamsburg was still the capital and the governor was expected to reside at the Palace, where Patrick Henry had followed truculent Dunmore, gracious Botetourt, and brilliant Fauquier. Jefferson had well known this former seat of royal prerogative since his student days, and at some time before he occupied it he drew plans for alterations which appear to have been

[1] To Richard Henry Lee, June 17, 1779 (Ford, II, 192).
[2] To Maj. Gen. William Phillips, June 25, 1779 (LC, 3:518).
[3] Jefferson to John Page, June, 1779 (Ford, II, 188).
[4] *Garden Book*, pp. 88–89. This was Thomas Garth, the first of a well-known family in Albemarle. Other references to him are on pp. 71, 74. He had also served as steward in 1778.

partially carried out.[5] Probably his family did not move in until fall, and he managed to spend most of August and September in Albemarle, but during nearly all the rest of his governorship he was chained to his post. He established a home in a rented house in Richmond when the government moved there in the spring of 1780, and took a considerable retinue of domestics with him. The house belonged to his uncle by marriage, Thomas Turpin, and it had a garden.[6] He was more fortunate than some of the other war governors of the era in being able to keep his family near him, and no doubt he was physically comfortable; but neither in the old capital nor the new one could he reproduce the free and elevated life of Monticello, and he soon came to regard himself not as a public servant but as a public slave. His fellow executives in other states felt much the same, for they were all engaged in an onerous and thankless task, but it is doubtful if any of them regretted so much the loss of liberty, on personal as well as on philosophical grounds.

The political implications of his election are not wholly clear. The bare facts are that on the first ballot he had a plurality but not a majority, the other votes being divided between two intimate friends of his youth and young manhood, John Page and Thomas Nelson, Junior. On the second ballot Page got most of Nelson's votes but Jefferson got enough of them to be elected, the final tally being 67 to 61.[7]

This unnatural competition of persons caused momentary embarrassment on both sides. Page, who was already president of the Council of State and lieutenant governor, could not see the new Governor at once and soon had to leave town. Therefore, he wrote a little note which called for a reply and thus left a pleasant record.[8] He wanted to leave no shadow of suspicion that he had "low dirty feelings" and was avoiding his old friend in order to hide embarrassment. Jefferson was not to be outdone in politeness or expressions of affection. "It had given me much pain," he wrote, "that the zeal of our respective friends should ever have placed you and me in the situation of competitors. I was comforted, however, with the reflection that it was their competition,

[5] Waterman, *Mansions of Virginia*, p. 394; drawings themselves, MHS. An inventory of the household furniture in the Palace, dated June 16, 1779, also found lodgment in his papers (LC, 3:508–509).

[6] He took possession on Apr. 17, 1780 (Account Book). The state paid the rent; see Gov. Benjamin Harrison to Jefferson, Oct. 3, 1782 (*Official Letters of the Governors of Virginia*, hereafter cited as O. L., III, 336). For other details see Dumbauld, pp. 45–46, and Appendix II in that work.

[7] *Delegates, Journal*, June 1, 1779. On the first ballot the vote was Jefferson 55, Page 38, Nelson 32.

[8] Page to Jefferson, June 2, 1779 (LC, 3:493); Jefferson to Page, June, 1779, (Ford, II, 187–188).

not ours, and that the difference of the numbers which decided between us, was too insignificant to give you a pain, or me a pleasure, had our dispositions toward each other been such as to admit those sensations." As for the constructions of the world, the world might go to the devil!

The rivalry caused no rift in ancient friendship. Page remained in office for almost a year, and when he did leave the government he regretted that he had to do so in Jefferson's administration. The political differences between them soon ceased to seem important, but in June, 1779, their respective friends divided roughly into the progressive and conservative groups which have been described already. The former were more expansionist in Western policy, less associated with mercantile interests, and more liberal on questions of human rights.[9]

Having served three successive terms of a year, Patrick Henry was no longer eligible. Jefferson was chairman of the committee of the House of Delegates which had notified him of his unopposed re-election the year before. He himself was generally regarded as being with Henry rather than against him, and his own political support came chiefly from the back counties, while Page and Nelson were favored by Tidewater.[10] But Jefferson had not created anything deserving the name of an organization. If anybody had a personal organization Patrick Henry did, and it was probably a relief to his successor when Demosthenes retired to his place Leatherwood in the forests of Henry County. There, as he wrote Jefferson, he heard scarcely a word of public matters; and he believed that his health would never again permit him to apply himself closely to sedentary business. He took a seat in the Assembly, however, before a year had passed, and he followed a legislative course which did not meet the Governor's full approval. By the summer of 1780 at least, Jefferson became aware that the influence of his predecessor was something of a hindrance; and at the session of the Assembly in the following fall, so another observer said, the majority party was headed by Henry, who carried everything in the House of Delegates as he pleased. He, not Jefferson, was the most popular political leader of the Commonwealth.[11]

The new Governor's disinterested devotion to the State and the revolutionary cause, not his political skill, had most impressed his associates.

[9] Abernethy, *Western Lands*, pp. 217–218, 219, 222–223.

[10] J. J. Pringle to Arthur Lee, Aug. 19, 1779; UVA photostat of original in Harvard Coll. Lib.

[11] Henry to Jefferson, Feb. 15, 1780; in Henry, *Patrick Henry*, II, 48–49; Theodorick Bland, Sr., to Theodorick Bland, Jr., Jan. 8, 1781, in *Bland Papers*, II, 51; Maude H. Woodfin, in *Essays in Honor of William E. Dodd* ed. by A. O. Craven, pp. 35–36. The particular issue in the May session of 1780 was that of the currency, which will be referred to hereafter.

Richard Henry Lee, who was often involved in intrigue, wrote him: "Every good Whig will wish success to a governor whose principles of action are not the incentives of whim, or the suggestions of partiality; but who is influenced by motives of sound whiggism, which I take to be those of genuine philanthropy." [12] Another contemporary said privately: "I wish [his] excellency's activity may be equal to the abilities he possesses in so eminent a degree. In that case we may boast of having the greatest man on the continent at the helm. But if he should tread in the footsteps of his predecessor, there is not much to be expected from the brightest talents." [13] The reference was not to a program of domestic reform, for Patrick Henry had none. Jefferson's own long-range program, as embodied in the report of the revisors, was presented soon after this; and the spirit and needs of the hour were such that it was left lying on the legislative table. The immediate question was the prosecution of the war on Virginia's part and, as this observer saw it, "never was a country in a more shabby situation." It was practically defenseless, he said. At such a time oratory and personal politics promised little. Unfortunately, the same might have been said of high intellectual attainments and prophetic insight into the distant prospects of a republican society.

Jefferson's own statement, when accepting the election, that he was fearful lest his poor endeavors should fall short of the kind expectations of his country, was something more than a polite expression.[14] Fundamentally he was modest, and his major services up to this point had been rendered in the legislative rather than the executive department. However, there was no reason for anybody to suppose that he lacked administrative qualifications, in the narrow sense in which they were then understood. This industrious and systematic man who had shown such diligence in details might have been expected to be more efficient than his predecessor in daily business. But Jefferson could not have been a high-powered modern executive even if he had wanted to be one. The constitution of the State and the spirit of the times made that quite impossible.

His scrupulous observance of the constitutional limitations upon the executive might have been anticipated by anyone familiar with the workings of his mind. To him fundamental law was not so sacred that it could not be changed. Quite the contrary. But until it was changed it stood as an expression of the public will and could not be challenged by a particular official. Fear of governmental authority and its tendency to aggrandizement was thoroughly characteristic of him. Most of the Patriots believed in what he called a free and mild government, but no one did so more firmly than he, and few were more reluctant to yield it to the exigencies of immediate circumstances. It may have been his weakness but unquestionably it was his genius to take a long-range view of things.

He did not fully share the jealousy of executive power, as compared with legislative, which was so rampant in that period and which had left its negative impress on the constitution of his State. He never approved of legislative omnipotence, and became bitter about it before the Revolution was over; but he was even more bitter about the alleged proposals to establish a dictatorship in Virginia in 1776 and again, at the close of his administration, in 1781.[15] He was passionately hostile to autocracy at the end of his own executive experience, just as he was before it began. He was determined that the outcome of this war should not be the loss of the freedom men were fighting for. He was no advocate of anarchy or irresponsibility, but both as an executive and a legislator he was a champion of liberty under law.

At the beginning of his governorship he had no choice, or at least he saw no choice, but to be an executive in the restricted sense and carry out the expressed will of the Assembly. That body had elected him for a term of one year, and he could not lawfully serve more than three. He was directly responsible to it, and he had no veto with which to check it. His contemporary, Governor George Clinton of New York, occupied a much stronger constitutional position, and it would have been surprising if Clinton had not been considerably the more effective of the two.[16] The major formulation of public policy was not

[15] *Notes on Virginia* (Ford, III, 231). Only the proposals of 1776 need concern us here, and these are far from clear. On Dec. 21, 1776, just before adjournment, the House of Delegates passed a resolution which said in the preamble that the present imminent danger made it necessary that "the usual forms of government should be suspended during a limited time." By a Senate amendment which the House accepted this passage was stricken out, and for it was substituted the statement that "additional powers be given the Governor and Council." This was really a more accurate description of the action taken, for this strengthened the executive by granting specific powers during the recess. (*Journal of the House of Delegates . . . 1776*, pp. 107–108.) Something more drastic may have been talked about privately, but, on the other hand, the comment Jefferson made five or six years later may have been exaggerated because of the undoubted resentment he felt toward Patrick Henry by that time. It has been vigorously combatted by the partisans of Henry, who was governor in 1776; see Henry, *Henry*, I, 505–509. Jefferson's name does not appear on the record on Dec. 21, and it is possible he was not in the House that day.

[16] The theoretical powers of the executives in the various states are described in the useful monograph by Margaret B. Macmillan, *War Governors in the American Revolution*, ch. 4. The executive was strongest in New York and weakest in Penn-

expected of the governor of Virginia in 1779. During the administration of Patrick Henry some leaders had questioned the ability of a popular assembly to carry on the business of war.[17] But such opinions were not general, and Jefferson, like George Washington, had to make the best of legislative dilatoriness and incompetence. The only real question is whether he did all that he could have done to correct this weak situation. He undoubtedly exerted influence through reports, recommendations, and private representations, but he did not do so to the same degree as Governor William Livingston of New Jersey, who remained in office longer but whose constitutional position was only a little stronger than his own.[18] In part the difference lay in the relative aggressiveness of the two men. As danger drew nearer the Assembly made temporary grants of considerable authority to the executive, but these were belated.[19] Whether they would have been wielded more effectively by a Clinton or a Livingston is a matter of sheer speculation.

Jefferson as governor was not only the creature of the Assembly; supposedly he was guided by the Council of State, a body of eight men elected periodically by the legislature. On the few occasions when he used the pronoun "I" instead of "we" in official papers, he said he was acting by and with the advice of the Council. He did not believe that the governor should merely act "as the clerk and authenticator" of the votes of the councilors; but he did believe that their advice should control whenever it was unmistakable. Only in the case of a divided vote, or in an emergency when there was no vote at all, was the governor to act on his own responsibility.[20] Jefferson's first formal statement should not be taken literally, but he expressed confidence only in his own impartiality, assiduous attention to duty, and sincere devotion to the great American cause. Beyond that, he said, he must rely on the wise counsels of the Assembly and of those who had been appointed to aid him.[21] One gains no impression of irresolution or personal weakness from his official utterances, but quite clearly he was more concerned to be reasonable than to dominate the Council or anybody else.

His group of special advisers during the first months of his governorship included John Page, James Madison, and John Walker — his still

sylvania and New Hampshire. Virginia stood somewhat below the middle in this respect, but the distinction was merely between "varying degrees of weakness" (*Ibid.*, pp. 68–69).

[17] John Banister to Theodorick Bland, Jr., June 10, 1777, in *Bland Papers*, I, 58.
[18] Macmillan, ch. 11, esp. pp. 221 ff.
[19] See especially acts of sessions of October, 1780, and May, 1781, in Hening, X, 383–386, 413–416.
[20] To Governor James Barbour, Jan. 22, 1812 (Ford, IX, 335–337).
[21] Answer to the Assembly (*O. L.*, II, 3).

affectionate friend from Albemarle. He worked harmoniously with these men and had their full confidence. This association marks the beginning of his intimate friendship with Madison, whom he had previously served with in the House of Delegates but had not known well. This serious little man was another enlightened liberal and scholar in politics. In the time of greatest emergency, unfortunately, these particular friends of Jefferson were off the Council. During his second year, ironically enough, one of his constitutional advisers was his former rival, Jacquelin Ambler, husband of the Belinda of his romantic youth and afterwards the father-in-law of John Marshall. It is also ironical that the records of the Council during three fourths of his governorship were lost at the time of Benedict Arnold's raid on Richmond, which some people thought he should have prevented. From those which remain, it appears that he was diligence itself in official business. He and his Board met practically every day at ten o'clock, and even when the exigencies of war prevented a quorum he himself went through the forms and left records that he had attempted to hold a meeting.[22]

The rest of the executive machinery was cumbersome. The Assembly had accepted the recommendation of the revisors by establishing a board of war and a board of trade. These were subject to the direction and control of the Governor and Council, but neither was effective and both were abolished within a year.[23] Jefferson had played an important part in creating these boards, but his relations with them were not wholly harmonious and he shed no tears when they were dissolved.

Throughout his administration he gave the impression of unfailing zeal and incessant labor. He had clerks to copy official papers, but from the outset he was enmeshed in details and swamped by paper work, as the war governors generally were. Even during his first year there were vexations enough, and serious difficulties were to be expected unless the war should end. Jefferson could not have avoided trouble if he had had far greater power and wisdom, and it is hard to see how anyone could have been genuinely effective in the larger sense with the instruments which were available to his hand. Also, this was a

[22] *Journals of the Executive Council of the State of Virginia*, II (1932), ed. by H. R. McIlwaine. This volume covers the period Oct. 6, 1777–Nov. 30, 1781. Madison and Walker retired on Dec. 25, 1779, and John Page on May 24, 1780. Dudley Digges was lieutenant governor thereafter. Ambler, who had previously been on the board of trade, was appointed on May 24, 1780. Beginning Dec. 25, 1779, William Fleming was a member, but owing to the confusion between two persons of the name, I am not absolutely sure that he was Jefferson's old college friend.

[23] Hening, X, 15–18, 291–292.

period of growing public apathy and discouragement, and at times there was actual disaffection. Opinion about the war was more uniform in Virginia than in most of the states, but the work of the Revolution was done by a relatively small group. Jefferson had come down from the rarefied atmosphere of thought and legal scholarship in order to participate continuously in the conflict. This action gratified George Washington, who needed help from civilian officials, but before the war was over it caused Thomas Jefferson to suffer far beyond his just deserts. Deep disappointment did not come immediately — but this polite and thoughtful man found out, all too soon, that war played havoc with philosophy and the amenities.

The reception of Henry Hamilton, former Lieutenant Governor of Detroit and notorious on the frontier as the "scalp-buyer," was definitely an executive matter, and, although not the greatest of Jefferson's problems, it was almost the first. In the February before his accession Hamilton had been captured at Vincennes in Virginia's northwestern county of Illinois. The captor was another native of Albemarle, George Rogers Clark; and his letter announcing the capitulation, though addressed to Patrick Henry, was actually received by Jefferson.[24] The news was specially pleasing to the new governor because he had been associated in spirit with the exploits of this hardy frontier soldier from the inception of his bold and brilliantly successful plan to conquer the Northwest.

Jefferson was probably one of the gentlemen in Williamsburg to whom, late in 1777, Clark set forth his plan to carry the war from Kentucky into the Indians' own country, and who communicated this plan to Governor Patrick Henry. He was a member of the Assembly which granted the Governor the necessary power in general terms; and Patrick Henry consulted him, Wythe, and Mason, about future rewards to the members of the expedition. As a result, Clark not only received secret instructions from Henry; he also got a private letter from these three gentlemen, assuring him that if he and his associates were successful they might rely on the Assembly for grants from the conquered lands.[25]

[24] Dated Apr. 29, 1779. Printed in Jefferson's *Works*, Washington ed., I, 222–224, and reprinted in various places, including "George Rogers Clark Papers," *Colls. Ill. State Hist. Lib.*, VIII (1912), 169–174 (referred to hereafter as *Ill. Colls.*).
[25] Jan. 3, 1778, *Ill. Colls.*, VIII, 37–38. See also Clark to Mason, Nov. 19, 1779, *Ibid.*, VIII, 115–116; Henry, *Patrick Henry*, I, 583; and Abernethy, *Western Lands*, ch. 15, where the whole story of the enterprise is freshly summarized. In "Jefferson and the Kentucky Pioneers," A. M. Lewis makes the nice point that this promise of lands was in accord with Jefferson's policy of making small grants to actual settlers.

THE LIMITATIONS OF EXECUTIVE POWER 309

Heartened by this extralegal act, Lieutenant Colonel Clark proceeded to capture Kaskaskia and overrun the Illinois country, thereby writing a dramatic and heroic chapter in the history of the American Revolution. Also, he greatly strengthened the claim of Virginia to the region beyond the Ohio, which was soon designated a county by legislative act. It was largely because of him that Jefferson as governor was the civil chief of this vast domain. The recapture of Vincennes by Hamilton, who sallied forth from Detroit, was a serious annoyance, but Clark retaliated with another brilliant exploit. Marching across the drowned lands, he surprised the fort and captured the commandant himself. Not knowing what else to do with this troublesome officer, he sent him to Kentucky, to be conducted thence to Virginia. News of Clark's triumph reached Jefferson before the prisoner did, and Hamilton constituted, as it were, the dregs in the cup of victory.

The Governor of Virginia was convinced that the conduct of the Lieutenant Governor of Detroit had been barbarous; and he was no little embarrassed when General Phillips, the high British officer with whom he had exchanged hospitalities, interested himself in Hamilton's fate. The scalp-buyer was not brought to Williamsburg until after the Assembly had voted George Rogers Clark a sword. In the middle of June Hamilton and Captain William Lamothe arrived from Chesterfield County in handcuffs. According to his own story, which must be accepted with considerable reservation, they were conducted to the Palace and stood at the Governor's door half an hour, weary, wet, and hungry; they were then carried off to jail, accompanied by a mob.[26] There they found Philip Dejean, Justice of Peace for Detroit. Two days later — on the very day that the report of the revisors, including Jefferson's bill for the proportioning of crimes and punishments, was presented to the Assembly — the Governor and Council decided on the fate of these three, whom they linked in common barbarity and regarded as war criminals.

These were men of another stripe from the British and Hessian officers with whom Jefferson had consorted so pleasantly in recent months, and the Council had no thought of honoring them with gracious treatment. On the contrary, they advised that they be put in irons and confined in the dungeon of the public jail, that they be debarred the use of pen, ink, and paper and be excluded from all conversation except with the keeper. The latter was Jefferson's organ-playing friend, Peter Pelham. The specific reasons assigned were Hamilton's incitation of the Indians to perpetrate their "accustomed cruelties" on United States

26 Hamilton's Report, July 6, 1781; *Ill. Colls.*, VIII, 197.

citizens, without distinction of age, sex, or condition, and his inhuman treatment of American captives. Dejean and Lamothe were regarded as his willing accomplices. A more general reason which was assigned for the action of the executive was the savage and uncivilized conduct of British officers in the war and their foul treatment of prisoners. Whether or not these general charges were too sweeping, Jefferson had facts about the sufferings of Virginians, and from personal observation he knew that British prisoners in American hands had been treated with humanity and consideration. General Phillips himself could testify to that.

Jefferson could hardly have been a passive auditor during the session of the Council, and there is no reason to suppose that he hesitated to issue the official order putting these severe penalties into effect. That very day, in a letter about Hamilton, he said: "It is impossible for any generous man to disapprove his sentence." On the next day he reported that the justice of the action was confirmed by "the general sense" of the people.[27] The latter observation was contained in a letter to the President of Congress, which he dispatched with scrupulous correctness; and his confidence that the approval of the members might be expected was borne out by the event. Thus Richard Henry Lee wrote him: "The reasons assigned for Hamilton's treatment are strongly and pointedly set forth. His fate is well merited." Another correspondent said that the proceedings were received by Congress "with the utmost applause," that the whole matter was "beautifully stated," and that the sentence was "judicious and spirited." [28]

Unquestionably the sentence was spirited, but the best person to judge whether or not it was judicious was George Washington. Jefferson sent him a copy of the executive order while reporting Clark's success. "It will add much to our satisfaction to know it meets with your approbation," he said. He was much pleased, therefore, to learn that Washington had no doubt of the propriety of the proceedings against these cruel men.[29] On the American side there was little or no protest against the severity of the treatment; but General Phillips, speaking for the British, raised a troublesome question, which Jefferson passed on to Washington and Congress. Did not Hamilton's formal capitulation forbid confinement of this sort? Jefferson did not think it did, being legalistic in his turn. Hamilton had signed an

---

[27] Minutes of Council, June 18, 1779, *O. L.*, II, 9–11; Jefferson to Theodorick Bland, June 18, 1779, *Ibid.*, p. 13; to John Jay, June 19, 1779, *Ibid.*, p. 14.

[28] R. H. Lee to Jefferson (Ballagh, II, 86); A. B. to Jefferson, July 13, 1779 (LC, 4:547; on the basis of handwriting, assigned by JP to Cyrus Griffin).

[29] Jefferson to Washington, June 19, 1779 (Ford, II, 240–241); Washington to Jefferson, July 10, 1779 (Fitzpatrick, XV, 401).

agreement but it contained no stipulation about the treatment of prisoners. He had said that he relied on the generosity of his enemies, but Jefferson had an answer for that. "Generosity, on a large and comprehensive scale, seems to dictate the making a signal example of this gentleman," he wrote to Washington.[30] He also replied to the British talk about the possibility of reprisals: "When . . . we are desired to advert to the possible consequences of treating prisoners with rigour, I need only ask when did these rigours begin? Not with us assuredly." [31] In his opinion it was high time to teach respect for the "dictates of humanity," and in such a case retaliation became "an act of benevolence." The murdering of innocent women and children and the unjustifiable severities on American captives must stop.

He was sensitive about the charge of violation of faith, however, and sought Washington's advice. On sober second thought the General concluded that, according to the usage of war, Hamilton was on a different footing from a mere prisoner at discretion, though he certainly merited discrimination and might be confined to a room.[32] Congress did not intervene, holding this to be a question for the executive power of Virginia.[33] Jefferson and the Council, however, accepted Washington's counsel as decisive. It was received in Williamsburg during the Governor's absence in Albemarle, but his advisers assumed authority for taking off the irons. After he returned it was agreed that the three prisoners should be at large within certain limits, taking the parole in the usual form. Unfortunately, however, the prisoners objected to that part of the parole which restricted them from saying anything to the prejudice of the United States. As Jefferson informed Washington, they were then remanded to confinement in jail, which he considered as voluntary, until they could determine to be "inoffensive in word as well as deed." [34] Washington agreed that the objection of the prisoners to the customary parole was unreasonable, but he was pressed by the British, who had already begun to retaliate. Pressure was also brought to bear on the Governor in behalf of prisoners from Virginia. The threat of further reprisals, he said, was shocking beyond expression, and he prayed that these might be averted. Nevertheless, though perfectly willing to extend the privileges of the prisoners as soon as they signed the parole, he refused to be bullied. "In every event I shall resign myself to the hard neces-

[30] July 17, 1779 (Ford, II, 247).

[31] July 22, 1779 (O. L., II, 30). Letter now believed by JP to have been to Gen. William Phillips.

[32] Aug. 6, 1779 (Fitzpatrick, XVI, 68–69).

[33] Aug. 21, 1775 (Journals, XIV, 985).

[34] Oct. 1, 1779 (Ford, II, 258–259).

sity under which I shall act," he said. There was no trace of senti-mental weakness here; in this matter he was hard as iron.[85]

Not until after another year was the matter settled, following a discreet suggestion from Washington that the prisoners be exchanged. Jefferson was adamant about Hamilton at first, because of fear of his influence over the Indians, but in late October, 1780, hoping that the action would have a happy effect on the situation of the Virginia prisoners on Long Island, he allowed Hamilton to go to New York. Under these circumstances the recalcitrant Britisher was willing to sign the parole. Thus he passed out of Jefferson's hands; and a few months later he was formally exchanged and went back to England.[86] By that time the Governor was involved in far greater difficulties, and the troublesome Hamilton affair had receded into the background of his mind. It involved a normally humane man in embarrassing con-tradictions while it lasted, and it sharply illustrated the hard necessi-ties of war.

As part of his executive duty Jefferson kept in touch with the mili-tary situation in the region whence this notorious prisoner had come. He continued to support George Rogers Clark as fully as he could. With respect to Kentucky and Illinois, however, he was subject to the same limitations as at home, namely, the shortage of men and money, espe-cially money. The depreciated currency of Virginia could not be circulated in the Illinois country, and he had to advise Clark to with-draw to the Kentucky side of the Ohio. He interested himself mi-nutely in the building of a fort below the junction of that river with the Mississippi; work on it was begun during his first year as gover-nor, and it was named for him. So was one of the three new counties which were set up in Kentucky that year.[37] He wanted the people of the Illinois country also to share, insofar as possible, the benefits of the "free and mild" laws and government of Virginia, and cordially ap-proved Clark's "mild conduct towards the inhabitants of the French villages." [38] During his first year as governor, however, he concerned himself more with the American pioneers south of the Ohio, as was natural from the political point of view and probably inevitable from

[85] To Washington, Oct. 8, 1779 (Ford, II, 261).

[86] To Washington, Oct. 25, 1780 (Ford, II, 354); Hamilton's Report, *Ill. Colls.*, VIII, 204–207.

[37] See, in particular, Jefferson to Clark, Jan. 29, Apr. 19, 1780, in *Ill. Colls.*, VIII, 386–391, 414–416; Hening, X, 315–317 (Session of May 1780); Abernethy, *Western Lands*, pp. 247–249.

[38] To County Lieutenant John Todd, Jan. 28, 1780 (*Ill. Colls.*, V, 143); to Clark, Jan. 29, 1780 (*O. L.*, II, 93).

the military. He was fully aware of the desirability of a successful attack on the focal center of British power at Detroit, and was willing to support Clark in such an expedition if this commander of the Virginia forces should think it feasible; but at this stage he talked more about building the fort below the Ohio and about attacking the Indians who were immediately menacing.[39] Not until his second year (in the fall of 1780) did he definitely plan a movement against Detroit in co-operation with the Continental forces, and even then the plan proved abortive. He did not render his greatest services to the Northwest as the chief executive of Virginia, but as a member of Congress a few years later. He made a signal contribution to the political development of the region after his State had formally ceded it to the Union, and his governorship was then only an unpleasant memory.

[39] Besides the letters of Jefferson to Clark already cited, see Jan. 1, 1780 (UVA), and Jefferson to Washington, Feb. 10, 1780 (Ford, II, 298–299). In "Jefferson and the Kentucky Pioneers," A. M. Lewis strongly emphasizes the Governor's reluctance to co-operate with the Continental forces until after the attitude of Congress toward the land question was clarified.

[XXIII]

The Frustrations of a War Governor

1779–1780

DURING nearly a year and a half of Jefferson's governorship, his State was spared the shock of actual invasion. Until late October, 1780, he was physically safe in the executive chair in Williamsburg or Richmond, generally engaged in unspectacular paper work. Virginians had met defeat and death on the battlefields of South Carolina before then, but the enemy had not yet ascended the tidal rivers and brought terror to the heart of his own country. For him this was predominantly a time of frustration. His humor was not robust enough to laugh away all the vexations, and the period was deeply colored at last by sorrow. The major difficulties proved to be beyond his control; and, feeling unequal to the burden that had been imposed upon him, he tried to get rid of it, only to find that escape was impossible. This was not an acutely perilous time, but it was an increasingly disappointing one, and danger kept drawing nearer.

Before the military invasion, the chief problems of the Commonwealth were the important but unexciting ones of procuring money, supplies, and soldiers. In his first days as an executive Jefferson had some hope that the crucial financial question could be answered.[1] While he was in the House of Delegates he had introduced a bill for the forfeiture and sale of the property of British subjects. With minor amendments this was passed, and one of his early official acts was to issue a proclamation carrying it into effect.[2] In a few months, however, he had to inform the Speaker of the House of Delegates

[1] To William Fleming, June 8, 1779 (Ford, II, 189–190).
[2] Bill reported May 27, 1779 (Ford, II, 182–186); act in Hening, X, 66–71; proclamation of July 1, 1779 (Ford, II, 243–244).

that the proceeds from sales could not be immediately relied upon.[8] The chief trouble was delay in the courts. He said drily that the matter had been thrown into "a course of legal contestation . . . which may not be terminated in the present age." Following his suggestion that something be done to expedite procedure, the Assembly amended the law; and in anticipation of returns they made a large appropriation to meet the requisitions of Congress. The delegates and senators were more hopeful than Jefferson, but they were doomed to disappointment. The returns from this source were not only delayed and insufficient upon their face; worse still, they were rendered practically valueless by the depreciation of the currency.[4]

At the very beginning Jefferson foresaw the same difficulty in connection with taxes, for he correctly predicted that they would not catch up with depreciation. According to his own reckoning, the ratio of Virginia currency to specie about the time of his inauguration was 12½ to 1. The Assembly struggled with the tax question in the fall, but by the first of the year the ratio was 40 to 1. At the end of his administration it was 250 to 1. Then he paid £27 for nine chickens and £2400 for 160 pounds of brown sugar.[5] The inflationary process was reflected in his own salary. He was first paid at the rate of £4500 per year, which was certainly much less than it sounded; in the following fall the figure was raised to £7500; and in May, 1780, in order to put matters on "a more permanent footing," the Assembly changed his salary to 60,000 pounds of tobacco.[6]

He was opposed to the financing of the war by the reckless use of the printing press, though he never could do much to stop it. In his first month as governor he wrote Richard Henry Lee: "It is a cruel thought, that, when we feel ourselves standing on the firmest ground, in every respect, the cursed arts of our secret enemies, combining with other causes, should effect by depreciating our money, what the open arms of a powerful enemy could not do." Some of the "secret enemies" must have been in the current Assembly, for that body provided for an emission of £1,000,000.[7] Jefferson hoped that Virginia could co-operate with other states in reducing the vast amount of paper money in circulation, and he thought every other

[8] Oct. 22, 1779 (Ford, II, 264–265).

[4] Hening, X, 153–156, 168; I. S. Harrell, *Loyalism in Virginia*, pp. 92–98, 111. The criticism of Jefferson in Eckenrode, *Revolution in Va.*, p. 202, for passing this question on to the Assembly, seems unwarranted in the light of the full circumstances.

[5] Summary given in Account Book, 1781; particular items on May 17, June 11. His figures coincide closely with those given in L. G. Tyler, *Letters and Times of the Tylers*, I, 72–75, where the history of the depreciation is sketched.

[6] Hening, X, 118, 219, 278–279.

[7] To Lee, June 17, 1779 (Ford, II, 193); Hening, X, 31.

remedy "nonsensical quackery." Soon, however, he saw no sure hope except in an early peace or a large loan of hard money.

The best prospect of co-operation appeared within a year. Congress proposed that the old currency, both state and continental, be withdrawn, that new notes be substituted at the rate of 1 to 40, and that these be pledged by the faith of the United States as a whole. This eleventh-hour proposal was conspicuously championed in the House of Delegates by George Mason and Richard Henry Lee, with Jefferson's full sympathy. Patrick Henry, emerging from retirement at Leatherwood, opposed the measure with temporary success; it was agreed to after the orator had departed.[8] But execution was suspended until the majority of the states should approve, and in the meantime a further emission of paper money was authorized. This was followed during the next year by others in a dizzily ascending scale.[9]

The initiative in fiscal matters was not with the executive, and if Jefferson had had it he could have done little to check the roaring torrent of inflation that engulfed the continent. It is easy enough to say that the taxing power should have been employed more rigorously and that the executive should have done more to expedite collections; but many people thought the war was being fought against taxation, and there had long been a serious scarcity of specie in Virginia. As Jefferson's committee had told Lord Dunmore before the Declaration of Independence, money was not a plant of the native growth of this agricultural country.

The normal way in which the State would have procured hard money, or its equivalent in credits, was by shipping tobacco abroad. But, soon after his accession, Jefferson said that the trade of Virginia had not been so distressed since Lord Dunmore ravaged the coasts. A "parcel of trifling privateers," supported by two or three larger British vessels, had completely nullified the small naval force of the Commonwealth. He was annoyed that the Continental Navy had done nothing in the Chesapeake Bay region, but he had not lost his dry humor. He observed that the same bad luck had attended the disposition of prizes; even though they were taken by the Virginia Navy

[8] Act of May session, 1780, in Hening, X, 241–254; Jefferson to Madison, July 26, 1780, in Ford, II, 319–320; Rowland, *Mason*, I, 350–356; Henry, *Patrick Henry*, II, 51–53, giving favorable view of substitute proposed.

[9] Session of May, 1780, authorizing £2,000,000, Hening, X, 279–286; Oct., 1780, £6,000,000, *Ibid.*, X, 347–350; March, 1781, £10,000,000, *Ibid.*, X, 399; May, 1781, £20,000,000, *Ibid.*, X, 430–431. Not even these figures tell the whole story, for authority was often granted the executive to make further emissions if necesssary. Between the sessions of Oct. 1780 and March 1781, emissions totaled more than £11,000,000; see *O. L.*, II, 377.

off their own capes it always seemed expedient to carry them elsewhere. "A British prize would be a more rare phenomenon here than
a comet," he said, "because the one has been seen, but the other never
was." [10]

Occasionally, supplies did slip through. In the autumn of his first
year he reported that three vessels had arrived, loaded with ordnance
and other necessities; and the Frenchman who had procured these
invaluable articles was rewarded with a generous grant of land and
the commission of lieutenant colonel.[11] In his second summer as governor, however, he wrote to the French minister: "Our own efforts
to establish a force on the water have been very unsuccessful; and
our trade has been almost annihilated by the most contemptible part
of the enemy's force on that element." By that time, for reasons of
economy, the Assembly had reduced the navy to even more trivial
proportions, and a French fleet was in American waters. Jefferson
asked no special favors from it. "The interest of this State," he said,
"is intimately blended, so perfectly the same with that of the others
of the confederacy that the most effectual aid it can at any time receive, is where the general cause most needs it." Nevertheless, he
hoped something might be done to free Chesapeake Bay, the channel
of Virginia's commerce.[12]

From the beginning he realized that the State could not depend
on arms carried across the ocean, for the enemy still reigned there.
After five years of war the supply remained inadequate. Because of
the lack of arms the Council, during his temporary absence in Albemarle in August, 1779, acted in a way which caused him considerable embarrassment. At a time when the magazines of the State had
been reduced to about three thousand stands of arms, Lieutenant Governor John Page and his associates detained five thousand that were
intended for the use of the United States and had providentially come
into a Virginia harbor. The action gave offense to Congress, and Jefferson, who was not responsible, was called upon to explain it. This
he did on the ground that the arms were justly due the State because
of previous gifts to "the Continent." [13]

There was a confusion of accounts, to be sure, and he described
this with genial irony:

[10] To John Jay, June 19, 1779; Ford, II, 243.
[11] Jefferson to the Speaker of the House of Delegates, Oct. 29, 1779, O. L., II, 50
and note.
[12] To Chevalier de la Luzerne, Aug. 31, 1780; O. L., II, 176.
[13] Page to the President of the Board of War in Philadelphia, Aug. 28, 1779;
O. L., II, 37. Jefferson to the President of Congress, Dec. 16, 1779; Ford, II, 282–
288, quotation on p. 283.

. . . It is a fact, which we are to lament, that, in the earlier part of our struggles, we were so wholly occupied by the great object of establishing our rights, that we attended not at all to those little circumstances of taking receipts, and vouchers, keeping regular accounts, and preparing subjects for future disputes with our friends. If we could have supported the whole Continent, I believe we should have done it, and never dishonored our exertions by producing accounts; . . .

The case he made was all the more appealing because generosity of spirit toward the common cause breathed through his entire letter.

The Governor urged the development of local manufacturing, saying that the making of war implements in Virginia was as necessary as that of bread. The State had established a foundry near Westham and had made a special contract with one John Ballendine for the erection of a furnace in Buckingham, but he proved less a help than a hindrance. The most promising prospect during Jefferson's administration was that of a factory and foundry on the James, to be built by a French company, Messrs. Penet, Windel & Co. Following a legislative resolution, Jefferson drew a contract with them.[14] This company was also to have the right to construct a canal from Westham to Richmond, thus avoiding the falls, and the whole matter became entangled with the claims of the same John Ballendine, who had begun a canal four years before and completed about one twentieth of it. Jefferson became a lawyer again when he discussed the latter's rights in detail, and he showed that he had not lost his youthful interest in the navigation of the James. His summary of the situation was amusing and far from legalistic.

A very simple calculation then will inform us, that, in his hands the completion of this Work will require near a century, and then a question arises whether Mr. Ballendine will live so long. . . . It is right that in cases of such general importance, the interests of a few individuals should give way to the general good, full compensation being made them . . .[15]

In this matter, as in that of the estates of British subjects, he tried to cut the cords of legal procedure and urged prompt legislative action. It was the chairman of the legislative committee who declared that the Assembly could not assume judicial powers; and it was General Nelson, afterwards regarded as a more forthright man than his learned

---

[14] Articles of agreement, signed July 22, 1779; *O. L.*, II, 23–28.
[15] To the Speaker of House of Delegates, Oct. 30, 1779; *O. L.*, II, 51–54; quotation on p. 54.

friend Jefferson, who recommended in December, 1779, that the contract with the French company be referred to the next Assembly. The postponement defeated the purpose of the contract, and in the end nothing came of the plan on which Jefferson had spent so much labor.[16] This was another case of frustration.

Even though too little was done about the manufacture of arms, even though foreign trade was almost annihilated and the value of the currency was approaching that of oak leaves, he could have reasonably expected that an agricultural province like Virginia would be blessed with an abundance of foodstuffs. Ordinarily the State sold flour to Maryland and Pennsylvania; but crops failed disastrously in 1779, and by fall Virginia had to purchase from her neighbors.[17] Salt, which was so necessary in preserving beef and pork, had long been wanting, and there was little more wheat than was needed for the next year's sowing. The result was an embarrassing situation with respect to the Convention prisoners. Jefferson had assured Patrick Henry that they could be more easily fed in Albemarle County than anywhere else; but he now had to write the President of Congress that these troops could not be supplied with flour, according to the agreement, and that it must be sent from some other place. The Congressional Board of War, chuckling over the difficulty, said that the prisoners might be given Indian corn, though the British were at liberty to send them flour if they wanted to.[18] Unfortunately, not even corn was plentiful. Jefferson included it in the embargo of six months that he declared on the last day of November, 1779, by advice of the Council and under authority of an act of Assembly. This extended to all the chief provisions, both meat and grain, none of which might be exported from the State to any other.[19]

In his days as a legislator, Jefferson may have devoted more time to the affairs of his Commonwealth than Washington thought advisable; but he always viewed the conflict between the States and Great Britain with the eye of a unionist, not a localist, and he was anxious that Virginia should contribute her proper share to the common cause. Under the existing organization the major responsibility lay with the Assembly. He believed that the legislature made the task of meeting the requisitions of Congress its chief business until there was actual

[16] O. L., II, 23 n, citing letter of Penet to Governor and Council, May 20, 1780, Calendar State Papers, I, 352.

[17] Jefferson to the Governor of Louisiana, Nov. 8, 1779; O. L., II, 59–61.

[18] Jefferson to President of Congress, Sept. 25, 1779, O. L., II, 38–39; report of board of war, Oct. 18, 1779, Ibid., 39 n.

[19] Nov. 30, 1779; O. L., II, 72.

invasion, and that it strained the resources of the State in trying to supply the men, money, and provisions that were asked for.[20] The legislators did attack the problem in a commendable spirit of devotion to the "glorious cause," though they were open to criticism for the tardiness of their successive actions.[21] The trouble was not so much that they did too little as that they did it too late. They were not in continuous session and, as Jefferson said, the physical problem of getting them together was greater than in more compact communities. If he himself was blamable, it was for his failure to call them more frequently. Not until his governorship neared its end did he exercise his authority to advance the time of meeting. Even for this, however, he had to get the consent of the Council.

He cannot be justly charged with complacency during this period, but he was convinced that Virginia had done well, everything considered. He summarized the whole matter in a letter to the President of Congress in the summer of 1780. "It would have given me great pleasure," he said, "to have been able to show Congress that their requisitions had been complied with in this state accurately in time, quantity and every other circumstance." He did not have that pleasure, but he did claim that up to this date Virginia had paid practically the whole of the requisition of money.[22] He made no comparisons with other states at that time, but he afterwards asserted that his Commonwealth was always above par in what was actually furnished.

His emphasis on the general cause was even more notable in the matter of troops than in that of money. He was never so shortsighted as to believe that the defense of the State should be made within or on its borders. A year and a half before he became governor he drafted a bill authorizing the executive to order the militia to the defense of sister states when they were invaded.[28] However, the militia were supposed to serve local needs primarily, and he, like all other competent observers, had a low opinion of their prowess. More effective and more lasting aid to the larger cause could be given by troops incorporated in the Continental Army. He was concerned to fill Vir-

[20] To Skelton Jones, July 28, 1809; L. & B., XII, 302.
[21] See particularly the act for raising a supply of money for the services of the United States, session of Oct. 1779; Hening, X, 165–171.
[22] July 27, 1780; see Ford, II, 322–328, quotation on p. 328. He said that about $13,381,000 had been paid, and that only a little more than $500,000 was still due. On the general subject, see C. J. Bullock, *Finances of the United States, 1775–1789*, esp. pp. 153–158.
[28] Jan. 13, 1778; Ford, II, 143. As was customary, this act was limited in its duration. He himself as governor acted under larger grants of authority which were made later.

ginia's quota and was sympathetic with Washington's desire to lengthen terms of enlistment. In temper he was no soldier, but he viewed military requirements with high intelligence, and he gained Washington's full approval by his loyal co-operation.

He had to admit that the quota of Virginia in the Continental Army was not filled during his first year as governor.[24] He did not quite say so, but it was in this connection that the infrequent meetings of the legislators and their lack of long-range planning were most unfortunate. The Assembly did the customary things. Just before Jefferson became governor it offered bounties to soldiers and premiums to recruiting officers, but, as he stated afterwards, these encouragements did not have the expected results. To what extent the failure may be attributed to him as an administrator is now almost impossible to decide, but there can be no question of his spirit or of his diligence.

Supplementary measures in the fall again failed to fill the quota. At that time, however, when British activity had shifted to the South, and South Carolina was in grave danger, greater discretionary power was given the Governor. He was empowered to order to her aid such state troops as could be sent under the terms of their enlistment, and as many as fifteen hundred of the militia.[25] Jefferson ordered certain new levies to go southward. There were rumors of the invasion of Virginia toward the end of the year, but he never took these as seriously as his own Board of War did.[26] To meet this particular menace he depended on the militia. His confidence may have been unwarranted, but, in terms of the larger strategy of the war, he did well in sticking to his original purpose to add strength where it was most needed on the continent as a whole.

Late in November he wrote to Washington: "No inclination is wanting in either the Legislature or Executive, to aid them [in the South] or strengthen you; but we find it very difficult to procure

[24] According to the resolution of Congress, March 9, 1779, *Journals*, XIII, 298, this quota was 11 out of a total of 80 battalions, the same as that of Pennsylvania but smaller than that of Massachusetts. By the resolution of Feb. 9, 1780, *Ibid.*, XVI, 150, it was set at 6070 men, the same as that of Massachusetts and above that of Pennsylvania. The question, just how many troops were in the Continental service, was partially one of definition. Returns were faulty. From Washington's correspondence with Jefferson, 1779–1780 (Fitzpatrick, XVII, 75–76, 321–324, etc.), it appears that even he was uncertain about the exact number. From these sources and from the returns now preserved in Jefferson's papers (especially Oct. 1, 1779, in LC, 5:727), it appears that there were between 3000 and 4000 on that date.

[25] Hening, X, 214.

[26] Formal actions of the Board of War, Nov. 8, 1779–Mar. 25, 1780, are in a manuscript volume at the William L. Clements Library, Ann Arbor, Mich., entitled Board of War, List of Warrants. A communication of Nov. 16, 1779, and the reply of the Council on Nov. 18 bear on this point.

men." [27] It was even more difficult to procure supplies for the new levies. The Governor had trouble with his Board of War and Board of Trade on that account in the late winter and spring. The price of shirts was too high, and the cost of rum, without which it was supposed the troops could not move southward, was exorbitant. Jefferson and the Council took the position that the necessary commodities would have to be bought, regardless. The two Boards acquiesced reluctantly, and one of them said that the paying of such prices "must go near to ruin the state." [28] The decisions of the executive were in line with the urgent request of Washington, who said "there never was greater occasion for the states to exert themselves in procuring clothing for their respective troops." [29] In this sort of situation Jefferson was one of the governors he most relied on.

Before these levies were in full motion southward, disaster befell Charleston and the flower of the Virginia troops in the Continental service. At the request of Congress, Washington had detached the Virginia line from his own forces and sent it to General Lincoln in South Carolina. On the last day of May the Governor had to make a sad report about these men.[30] They had been shut up in the beleaguered city and had been surrendered there. The wisdom of sending Virginians into other states was questioned more after that, but Jefferson did not change his mind about the supreme importance of supporting the general cause, and he retained the confidence of the Assembly. A few months earlier a wise Virginian in Congress had said: "The governor need not fear the favor of the community as to his future appointment, while he continues to make the common good his study. I have no intimate acquaintance with Mr. Jefferson, but from the knowledge I have of him, he is in my opinion as proper a man as can be put into office, having the requisites of ability, firmness, and diligence." The legislators must have believed that, for they re-elected him, leaving no record of such votes as may have been cast against him.[31]

The summer of 1780 fell between the surrender of Charleston to General Clinton (May 12) and the distressing battle of Camden, where Gates was overwhelmed by Cornwallis (August 16). After the former event and before he knew of Clinton's return to New York by sea, Jefferson wrote to Washington: "There is really nothing to oppose

[27] Nov. 28, 1779 (O. L., II, 70–71).
[28] Mar. 17, 1780 (O. L., II, 107); see also Feb. 4, 16, 1780 (Ibid., 96, 101–102).
[29] Apr. 15, 1780 (Fitzpatrick, XVIII, 263).
[30] May 30, 1780 (O. L., II, 124).
[31] Joseph Jones to James Monroe, Mar. 7, 1780, in D. C. Gilman, James Monroe, pp. 13–14; Boyd, Papers of Thomas Jefferson, III, 410, on the election of June 2, 1780.

the progress of the enemy northward but the cautious principles of the military art." He politely intimated that Continental assistance would be welcome. "Your Excellency will readily conceive," he said, "that after the loss of one army our eyes are turned towards the other, and that we comfort ourselves if any aids can be furnished by you without defeating operations more beneficial to the general union, they will be furnished. At the same time I am happy to find that the wishes of the people go no further, as far as I have had an opportunity of learning their sentiments." The lack of money cramped every effort and he was painfully aware of the shortage of arms. "As far as they will go," he wrote the President of Congress, "they have been, and will be, cheerfully submitted to the common use." [82]

Washington was sympathetic but helpless. He said that he himself was compelled "to see the honor and dignity of the States daily insulted without the power either to prevent it or retaliate." He could give only one answer: "To oppose our Southern misfortunes and surmount our difficulties our principal dependence must be the means we have left us in your quarter." The Commander could not consider his native Commonwealth alone or the Southern department merely; he must reserve his strength to oppose Clinton in the Northern theater. By aiding General Gates the Governor of Virginia must do the best he could to meet the reduced but continuing menace from below. [83]

His vigorous actions during the summer were directed almost wholly against this Southern danger. Jefferson reported that twenty-five hundred of the militia would soon set out, and that some state troops would also be put in motion. Meanwhile, in a region which had always depended primarily on transportation by water, they were furnishing all the wagons they could collect. Furthermore, the Assembly ordered the raising, not of more militia as requested by Congress, but of three thousand regulars enlisted for eighteen months. Jefferson asked Washington to arrange for the officering of these men, cheerfully transferring to him every power the executive might exercise in this connection. [84] There was some division of opinion as to the proper destination of these newly recruited regulars. Jefferson favored sending them to Gates, when raised, as Congress finally requested. He now regarded South Carolina as prostrate and did not

<hr>

[82] To President of Congress, June 9, 1780 (Ford, II, 306); to Washington, June 11, 1780 (Ibid., II, 309).

[83] Washington to Jefferson, June 29, 1780 (Fitzpatrick, XIX, 98).

[84] To Washington, June 11, July 2, 1780 (Ford, II, 309–310, 315); Hening, X, 257–262.

think it right for the whole burden of the southern war to fall on North Carolina.[35]

As the fall of Charleston and the loss of the Virginia line spurred him and his State to reinforce the army of General Gates, it convinced him of the need to improve the service of information. Nearly a month after the surrender he wrote Washington that the intelligence from the southward was lamentably defective.[36] To remedy this defect he established a line of riders, forty miles apart, from Richmond to the neighborhood of the hostile army, hoping that news would be conveyed at the rate of 120 miles in 24 hours. To the other end of the line he sent a gentleman whom he described as sensible and judicious. This commissioner, who was to watch and listen for him and whose character he thus assessed, was James Monroe, then aged twenty-two, a tall and athletic young man who rode well but did not laugh easily. The arrangement was desirable in itself, but in history it has far more than military significance. This sign of official confidence was highly gratifying to Monroe, and it played an important part in establishing him as Jefferson's disciple. The Governor would have denied the term "master," but there was a difference of fifteen years in age between the two men and at this stage their deepening friendship was unequal.[37]

Monroe's solemn face had lighted up more frequently since he had formed a connection with Jefferson and begun to chart his future course under his elder's guidance. For some months he had been at loose ends. He had been a brave and effective officer in the Continental Army, but had left it in confused circumstances. He had come to Williamsburg armed with a commendatory letter from Washington, but he was unable to find a suitable opportunity to serve in the forces of his own State. Jefferson's kind offer to guide him in legal studies rescued a bewildered young man from deep discouragement and fixed his ultimate course. The removal of the capital to Richmond confronted him with an immediate problem, however. Should he remain in Williamsburg and attend the lectures of George Wythe, or should he accompany the busy Governor to Richmond? He got

[35] To Madison, July 26, 1780 (Ford, II, 320); to John Mathews of Com. of Congress at Headquarters, Sept. 2, 1780 (O. L., II, 181).
[36] June 11, 1780 (Ford, II, 308).
[37] Jefferson gave instructions to Monroe in a letter of June 16, 1780, now in the ms. book belonging to the W. L. Clements Library, Ann Arbor, Mich., and previously cited. On the same date he wrote Gov. Nash of North Carolina about the plan; O. L., II, 130–131. See also the document of June 10, quoted in W. P. Cresson, *James Monroe*, p. 55. Monroe's lengthy report of June 26, 1780, is available; see *Writings*, Hamilton ed. (1898), I, 3–8.

good advice from his sagacious uncle, Joseph Jones, then a member of Congress:

> . . . You do well to cultivate his [Jefferson's] friendship, . . . and while you continue to deserve his esteem he will not with-draw his countenance. If, therefore, . . . he wishes or shows a desire that you go with him, I would gratify him. Should you remain to attend Mr. Wythe, I would do it with his approbation, and under the expectation that when you come to Richmond you shall hope for the continuance of his friendship and assistance.[88]

Jefferson did not assume personal command of the militia and take Monroe into the field as his aide, as Jones had hoped he would, but he soon solved his young friend's military difficulties by sending him to the South as commissioner, to collect and forward information. This delighted Colonel Monroe's heart, and in the fall, when Jefferson himself needed encouragement, his protégé thanked him effusively in his awkward and almost illegible writing.[89] Though his private fortune was small, he declined to accept any compensation for his work in the Carolinas; he announced that he was now determined to stick to his legal studies unless his mentor thought he should play a further public part; and he said that he owed everything to Jefferson's friendship. Actually, he did further military service before the war was over, but the most important fact is that he had formed a personal tie which was never severed.

His new disciple gave the Governor useful information, but nobody prepared his mind for the defeat of Gates at Camden. On the day before it occurred he wrote the General, saying that he would send him five hundred regulars in a few days and congratulating him on his "successful advances on the enemy." Also, he set out on a little recess from public business, after a "long and laborious confinement." When he got back he received from Governor Rutledge of South Carolina a copy of an intercepted letter from no less a person than Cornwallis. Viewing events from the other side, the letter said, "There never was a more complete victory." [40]

Jefferson did not have to get the news itself from British sources, and the worst of it was that the raw Virginia militia had behaved

---

[88] Mar. 7, 1780; D. C. Gilman, *James Monroe* (1911), p. 15. Monroe's immediate action is uncertain.

[89] Monroe to Jefferson, Sept. 9, 1780; *Writings*, I, 8–11.

[40] To Gates, Aug. 15, 1780, in L. & B., IV, 96–97; *O. L.*, II, 167–168; Cornwallis to Lt. Col. Balfour, Aug. 16, 1780; letter sent by Jefferson to Washington on Sept. 26, in L. & B., IV, 108–109 *n*.

badly. State pride did not dispose him to excuse them; he sent condolences to General Stevens, their commander.[41] There were some compensations in misfortune. He wrote to General Stevens a little later: "The subsequent desertions of your militia have taken away the necessity of answering the question how they shall be armed." More philosophical reflections were contained in a letter to the President of Congress. "The scene of military operations," he said, "has been hitherto so distant from these states, that their militia are strangers to the actual presence of danger. Habit alone will enable them to view this with familiarity, to face it without dismay; a habit which must be purchased by calamity, but cannot be purchased too dear. In the acquisition of this, other misfortunes may be incurred, for which we should be prepared." [42]

It did not fall to his own lot to go to the battlefield, to learn how to fight by fighting, but he realized after Camden that he must make immediate and even greater efforts to stop the progress of the enemy.[43] As later reports trickled in the losses loomed larger, not smaller. These included not only the slain, the captured, and the deserters from the militia, but all the cannon on the field, four hundred wagons (including one of his own that had been impressed, and two horses with it), all the tents which had been so hard to come by, and vast numbers of small arms which would be sorely missed. A large part of these supplies had been contributed by his Commonwealth.[44] The disaster practically nullified the incessant labors of the summer, and forced him to start again.

To Washington he reported promptly that a new army was forming to serve in North Carolina. For the times this sounded impressive on paper. Virginia was providing the three thousand newly-levied regulars and a thousand or more militiamen, including some from the Piedmont and western counties whom he regarded as really good.[45] It is difficult to determine how many actually got to the southern theater before late October, when attention was distracted by a threat from the seacoast; but some militiamen did reach Gates, for he com-

[41] Sept. 3, 1780 (Ford, II, 333). See also letter of same date to Gov. Nash of North Carolina, in O. L., II, 186, and partial defense of the militia by the editor (Ibid., II, 184 n).
[42] To Stevens, Sept. 12, 1780 (Ford, II, 338); to President of Congress, Sept. 3, 1780 (Ibid., II, 335).
[43] To the Council, Aug. 28, 1780, in O. L., II, 170.
[44] Details from various letters, chiefly that of Cornwallis and one from Jefferson himself to an unknown person, Sept. 13, 1780 (VHS); see note 49 below.
[45] Sept. 3, 23, 1780 (Ford, II, 331–333, 343–344).

plained of their lack of equipment. Jefferson countered with the flat assertion that to wait until they were fully equipped would be to put an entire end to the sending of reinforcements. He sent them on, hoping they would be supplied by Congress.[46]

Quite clearly, the major problem was that of equipment, not men. He reported to Washington that the troops who were being collected were unarmed. Virginia had no tents; now there were provisions in abundance and he was busily ordering the impressment of them, but wagons were practically unavailable. The treasury was drained dry and there was no prospect of getting any more paper money until the Assembly should meet in October. Also, a dangerous spirit of disaffection was discovered in several of the southern counties. Hundreds had gone so far as to take oaths of allegiance to the British King and a time had been set for insurrection. This was in September. Next month the fire broke out in another county; a dangerous revolt in Pittsylvania was prevented by the seizure of the ringleaders in their beds. Disaffection was not general, but Jefferson correctly concluded that something brilliant in the military line was needed to restore the spirits of the people.[47]

He could not contribute that sort of brilliance, and nobody else did in this deeply depressing period of the war. His time was chiefly spent in issuing orders for mobilization and impressment and in begging arms and tents of Congress. The details of his manifold activities are too wearisome to go into.[48] He was still convinced that the supremely important thing for Virginia to do was to support the Southern Army; he assumed a resolute tone in official communications; and he indulged in relatively few recriminations. He made no spectacular efforts to inspirit his people, but he set a high example of personal devotion to a cause which he had not ceased to regard as sacred. At the same time he revealed in private that he was unutterably weary, that he did not regard himself as effective, and that he definitely wanted to get out of office before the end of his term.

Early in September he wrote: "The application requisite to the duties of the office I hold is so excessive, and the execution of them after all so imperfect, that I have determined to retire from it at the

[46] To President of Congress, Oct. 14, 1780 (Ford, II, 348).

[47] To President of Congress, Sept. 4, 14, 1780 (Ford, II, 334, 340–342); to Va. delegates in Congress, Oct. 27, 1780 (*Ibid.*, II, 356–357); to John Mathews, Sept. 2, 1780 (*O. L.*, II, 181).

[48] Details of his routine activity during late August and early September are in *O. L.*, II, 170–174, 187–195.

close of the present campaign. I wish a successor to be thought of in time who to sound whiggism can join perseverance in business and an extensive knowledge of the various subjects he must superintend. Such a one may keep us above water even in our present moneyless situation." [49] Presumably he intended to get out before spring, when there would be another general election, for George Mason, who had heard the report, urged him to stay at least until after that. The enlightened master of Gunston Hall dreaded the choice of a successor by the existing Assembly. [50] It was dominated by Patrick Henry.

A more violent protestor than Mason was John Page. Jefferson tried to persuade this old friend to become his successor, though he left no information as to the methods whereby this succession was to be brought about. Page strongly rejected the suggestion, saying that Jefferson's resignation would give him great uneasiness and the country much distress. [51] When the Governor repeated the proposal Page again rejected it, saying that he had quitted the ship (that is, had resigned as lieutenant governor), worn down and fatigued, in calm weather; while Jefferson was proposing to leave the helm when the utmost skill was needed to steer through the storm. [52] By the time this letter came another squall was threatening, and Jefferson had let the Assembly meet without offering to resign. Page then encouraged him to make the best of the situation and urged him not only to serve out this term but to accept another, as the law allowed.

> . . . I know your Love of Study & Retirement must strongly solicit you to leave the Hurry, Bustle, & Nonsense your Station daily exposes you to [he said]. I know too the many Mortifications you must meet with, but 18 Months will soon pass away. Deny yourself your darling Pleasures for that Space of Time, & despise not only now, but forever, the Impertinence of the silly World All who know you know how eminently qualified you are to hold the [station] you hold, & that Circumstances may happen within the Compass of the Time above alluded to, which may require the Exertion of greater Abilities than can be found in any other Person within this State. [53]

Except for Richard Henry Lee, who was too unpopular to be thought of, Page knew of no one else who could possibly manage the

[49] Sept. 13, 1780, to an unnamed person [probably R. H. Lee]; VHS, courtesy of JP. This letter is in O. L., II, 205, with the erroneous date Sept. 3.

[50] To Jefferson, Oct. 6, 1780 (LC, 6:932–933).

[51] To Jefferson, Sept. 22, 1780 (LC, 6:905–906).

[52] To Jefferson, Oct. 20, 1780 (LC, 6:942–943).

[53] To Jefferson, Dec. 9, 1780 (LC, 6:996).

important affairs which might come up, and he assured his weary and homesick friend that others held this opinion as well as he. Whether encouragement like this, or consciousness of the difficulties of the hour, swayed Jefferson the more, there was really nothing for him to do but endure the hurry, the bustle, the nonsense, and the mortifications, while hoping that nothing worse impended.

[XXIV]

The Menace of Invasion

1780–1781

THE CHARACTER of Jefferson's last eight months as governor, and particularly the last six, was determined by military events over which he had little or no control. He adjusted himself to these with the best of spirit but with increasing difficulty, and at last he was overpowered by them. The defeat at Camden had dangerously weakened the defenses to the south and he properly directed his efforts toward repairing them. The penultimate period opened, however, with a threat from the east, where a British detachment under General Leslie landed. This proved to be only a landing party, but at the very beginning of the new year a slashing raid by Benedict Arnold from the coast spread consternation in the interior and deeply embarrassed the Governor. The traitor's forces were soon contained at Portsmouth, and for a time high hopes were entertained of Lafayette's projected expedition against him. These were dashed, however, when hostile reinforcements came under General Phillips. Even then, Jefferson's own interest continued to be chiefly in the Southern theater, but through force of circumstances, if not because of bad judgment, the dwindling resources of the State were considerably dissipated. Richmond was again imperiled from the east but the speedy return of Lafayette saved it temporarily from the invader. The final phase began only when Lord Cornwallis unexpectedly drove into the State from North Carolina and linked the British forces. Then the fates pursued Jefferson into the depths of the forest, and the feeble government collapsed under the blows of the enemy. But it was brought low by attrition and inanition before that time, and Jefferson himself, though still struggling valiantly, had already appeared as the sport of circumstance.

The fact that Virginia had hitherto escaped invasion from the east can be best explained on grounds of the ignorance, caution, or indifference of the enemy. It was not owing to the military strength of the State, which was so largely spent elsewhere, and certainly not to the inaccessibility of the region. Few other commonwealths were equally vulnerable on the side of the water. This sparsely settled country was penetrated by broad arms of the sea on which any fleet could ride, and by long, navigable rivers which were so many avenues into the interior. There was no real obstacle below the fall-line — that is, roughly, the longitude of Richmond. This was well understood by the generally unmilitary James Madison, who was in Congress, and it was by no means unknown to Jefferson, whose father had mapped this country, and who himself had a liking for geography.[1] On the other hand, Jefferson knew there was little to attract the invader, for there were still no important centers.

In the early fall of 1780 he admitted that if the enemy should attack Virginia from the coast in force, the State would be incapable of effective resistance. But, although he had heard that the British were thinking of taking Portsmouth near the mouth of the James, he regarded this event as unlikely for two reasons: Clinton would hardly dare send the necessary force from New York; and if he did dispatch it the French could send a superior fleet and bottle up the enemy.[2] Events proved that he underestimated the military audacity of the British and overestimated the likelihood of naval aid in Chesapeake Bay throughout this period. On grounds of the balance of sea power alone he was probably not justified in turning his eyes away from the coast and fixing them on the army of Cornwallis. But he was correct in judging the Southern danger to be much the greater; and if, in terms of local defense, there was risk in largely disregarding the seaboard, major strategy and the general interest of the Continent seemed to require it.

In late October the unexpected happened. Then, as Jefferson reported in some alarm to Washington, a hostile fleet was sighted in the bay.

"We are endeavoring to collect as large a body to oppose them as we can arm," he said; "this will be lamentably inadequate, if the enemy be in any force. It is mortifying to suppose that a people, able

---

[1] Madison to Pendleton, Jan. 16, 1781, in Hunt, I, 122–123. The raid on Chesapeake Bay in May, 1779, shortly before Jefferson became governor, was hardly an "invasion," though he used that term in describing it to John Jay (June 19, 1779; O. L., II, 14).

[2] To President of Congress, Sept. 14, 1780 (Ford, II, 340).

and zealous to contend with the enemy, should be reduced to fold their arms for want of the means of defence. Yet no resources, that we know of, insure us against this event. It has become necessary to divert to this new object, a considerable part of the aids we had intended for General Gates." He added a depressing afterthought: "Of the troops we shall raise, there is not a single man who ever saw the face of an enemy." [3]

Soon it became known that Commodore Rodney, son of the Admiral, was the ranking naval officer and that General Alexander Leslie was in command of the military force. Early reports were that the soldiers numbered from four to five thousand, but these were afterwards found to have been exaggerated. Enemy landings were made on both sides of the James, but the cavalry at Newport News were soon removed and the whole force was concentrated at and near Portsmouth. The militia, which had been assembled on both sides of the river, were in a chaotic state, but except for fortifying their position and seizing cattle the enemy were quiescent. Jefferson commented on the slightness of their naval support and was quite correct in his early opinion that this was not a real invasion. [4]

He soon reported to Gates and Washington an interesting bit of intelligence confirming this supposition. Early in November a British emissary was taken who was trying to get to Carolina. When about to be searched he was observed to put something into his mouth that looked like a quid of tobacco. As described by Jefferson, this was a letter, "written on silk paper, rolled up in gold beater's skin, and nicely tied at each end, the whole not larger than a goose quill." It showed that Leslie was now awaiting orders. These came on a ship which got through to the Carolinas and returned. Then, almost exactly a month after their sail had first been sighted, the enemy vessels put out to sea. There had been little wanton destruction. Luck was with Jefferson and with Virginia. [5]

Now, said he to Gates, we can again give attention to the reinforcement of the Southern Army. Gates had been relieved, however, and in mid-November General Nathanael Greene, the new commander of the Southern department, visited Richmond, where he was greatly disturbed to find strong sentiment against the sending of further mili-

[3] To Washington, Oct. 22, 1780 (L. & B., IV, 120–121).
[4] To President of Congress, Oct. 25, Nov. 3, 1780 (Ford, II, 353, 358); to Gates, Oct. 28, 1780 (L. & B., IV, 125–126); to Gen. Stevens, Nov. 10, 1780 (O. L., II, 230).
[5] Jefferson to Gates, Nov. 10, 1780 (Ford, II, 361–362); to Washington, Nov. 10, 1780 (L. & B., IV, 129) giving Leslie's letter to Cornwallis; to Speaker of House of Delegates, Nov. 24, 1780 (Ford, II, 369).

tary resources to the Carolinas.⁶ The Governor did not fail him, but spoke strongly to the Assembly, now in lengthy session. Rejoiced though he was at Leslie's departure, Jefferson called for an increase rather than an abatement of preparations. Leslie's troops might have gone to reinforce Cornwallis (actually they had) and there might be a new embarkation from New York for the same purpose. South Carolina and Georgia now weighed nothing in the scale, he said, and North Carolina had been lately ravaged. Therefore, the weight of responsibility rested on his own State. He thought it infinitely important to keep the war outside of Virginia's borders and to lose no time about it.⁷ This was good advice, based on sound strategy. He underestimated the likelihood of future enemy landings on the Virginia coast; but, on the other hand, he may have been taking what we should now call a calculated risk — one that seemed minor in view of the situation to the southward.

General Greene was no little encouraged by the response of the Assembly to the strong appeal of the Governor; and Jefferson himself, after Leslie withdrew, believed that he could meet Greene's requisitions. The latter had brought General von Steuben with him to Virginia, and when Greene proceeded to North Carolina he left the noted drillmaster behind, as temporary commander of the Continental forces in the State and his personal representative. Steuben was popular at first, and he provided much-needed leadership in matters of organization and military training. For one thing, he appointed Colonel William Davies to command the base at Chesterfield Courthouse and charged him with the organization and equipment of the Continentals. By the middle of December he sent reinforcements to Greene which enabled the latter to open his campaign to reconquer South Carolina.⁸ Outwardly, things were going well, and if Jefferson had resigned at this time he could have retired with honor. But, most unfortunately, on the last day of the year a new menace appeared in the east. He had not counted on having to cope with Benedict Arnold, and that hated foe upset several of his calculations.

While the British were still at Portsmouth he had concluded that he must get rid of the Convention prisoners who had been so long in Albemarle and who now invited trouble. Late in November the British, of whom he was more fearful than of the Germans, were

⁶ To Gates, Nov. 19, 1780 (Ford, II, 368); J. M. Palmer, *General von Steuben*, pp. 239–240.
⁷ To Speaker of House of Delegates, Nov. 24, 1780 (Ford, II, 369–370).
⁸ Palmer, *Steuben*, pp. 240–242.

marched across the Blue Ridge and down the Shenandoah Valley toward Frederick, Maryland. The Hessians remained in the State some months longer, but he finally got them as far as Winchester.[9]

These were actions of prudence, looking toward a reduction of military responsibilities. More surprising was his revival of the project of an expedition against Detroit, for an offensive in that distant quarter seemed to involve an unwise dispersal of limited forces and resources. He thought it necessary at this time, however, and he was not one to let immediate local considerations blind him to the requirements of a larger strategy. He had long contemplated a movement against the British post where the attacks of the Indians on the western settlements were instigated, but he had been deterred from it because of the excessive burden it would have laid on the state treasury. Whether he could have secured co-operation from the Continental forces at an earlier time is doubtful, and he had preferred independent action, being reluctant to weaken the claims of Virginia to western lands until reassured about the probable attitude of Congress. Between the battle of Camden and Leslie's raid, however, he broached to Washington the question of Continental aid for an expedition which promised such great general advantages, and before Arnold swooped down he definitely planned one under the command of George Rogers Clark.[10] He was now convinced that satisfactory terms could be worked out between Virginia and Congress for the cession of the Northwest territory. He had wanted to guard this against speculators for the benefit of small settlers but had not wanted to keep it for any other reason.

He was sure that Clark's popularity would rally a sufficient body of militia, and under other circumstances it probably would have. He asked for powder and money, and Washington was not encouraging, though he thought there might be enough of the former. The Governor would not be rebuffed. By the middle of December he informed

---

[9] To the President of Congress, Oct. 26, 1780 (Ford, II, 355); to Washington, Nov. 26, 1780 (*Ibid.*, II, 370–371).

[10] The most important specific references for the episode as a whole are the following: To Washington, Sept. 26, 1780 (Ford, II, 346–347), which should be compared with the letter of Feb. 10, 1780, to Washington (Ford, II, 298–299); to Clark, Sept. 29, 1780 (*O. L.*, II, 213); from Washington, Oct. 10, 1780 (Fitzpatrick, XX, 148–149); to Washington, Dec. 15, 1780, saying that Clark was in Richmond (Ford, II, 375–378); to Clark, Dec. 25, 1780, giving instructions (*O. L.*, II, 250–253); from Washington, Dec. 28, 1780 (Fitzpatrick, XXI, 23–24); to Clark, Jan. 13, 1781 (*O. L.*, II, 273); to Clark, Feb. 19, 1781 (*O. L.*, II, 362–363); to Clark, Apr. 20, 1781 (*O. L.*, II, 488). Abernethy, *Western Lands*, pp. 251–255, is particularly good for Clark's troubles in Pittsburg, and gives many references. A. M. Lewis, "Jefferson and the Kentucky Pioneers," supports the thesis that Jefferson's delay in seeking co-operation with the Continental forces was chiefly due to his earlier uncertainties about the attitude of Congress toward western lands. For the ultimate outcome, see *Ill. Colls.*, VIII, cxlii–clxvii.

the Commander in Chief that immediate action on Virginia's part was imperative, regardless of all other calls and dangers. He had learned of the situation from Clark himself, who had come to Richmond, and he issued detailed instructions to the latter on Christmas Day before he got another reply from Washington.

The reasons for his bold decision were chiefly two. A serious secession movement had arisen in Kentucky, and he feared that if successful this would mean not only the separation of these counties from Virginia but also that of the entire West from the Union. Furthermore, he had learned from Clark that a confederacy of British and Indians was then being formed to devastate the Virginia frontier in the spring, and he believed that, besides imperiling the western country, this would draw off the most valuable part of the militia. He wanted to anticipate this by sending Clark against Detroit with his regular force, along with militia from beyond the Alleghanies and a few of the most northern counties. Thus the dispersal of forces would be more apparent than real. All he now asked from Washington was the loan of certain military necessities from the store at Fort Pitt. The question who should bear the expense would have to be left to the justice of Congress. There would be immense long-range benefits from this enterprise, he believed. Future quiet on the frontier would be assured, and an extensive and fertile country would be added to the "empire of liberty." The case was convincingly presented and the provisions seemed adequate. If his plan could have been carried out it would undoubtedly have brought great benefits to the general cause and have prevented a vast amount of future trouble — whatever the effect might have been on the immediate military situation of Virginia. But, as things turned out, the timing was bad and the obstacles were insuperable.

Not until after Benedict Arnold had raided Virginia did he learn from Washington that Colonel Daniel Brodhead at Pittsburg had been instructed to co-operate, though he did not let the intervening events upset his larger strategy. He detached Clark from the local military service he had been doing in this emergency, and, late in January, started him off to Pittsburg with a brigadier general's commission. But to all practical purposes the western expedition then passed wholly from Jefferson's hands. His urgent request that Brodhead allow Colonel Gibson's regiment to go with Clark was denied by the unco-operative officer at Pittsburg; and when he learned from Clark of the unwillingness of the militia of Berkeley and Frederick counties to go west he had to admit that any attempt to force them would result in open disobedience. Like him, they were now more deeply concerned about dangers much closer home, and they did not share his vision. He was encouraged by Clark's persistence in the face of the unexpected difficulties the General ran into in Pittsburg, and he continued to believe that victory in the West was supremely important to the East, but at this stage there was little he could do but hope. When Clark finally dropped down the Ohio in the summer — much later and with a much smaller body of men than had been intended — his friend the Governor was no longer in office, and when he arrived in Kentucky he found that Fort Jefferson had been abandoned. The abandonment of the expedition against Detroit became inevitable. It had been well conceived and perhaps it could not have been planned earlier, but unquestionably it had been planned too late. Events revealed more petty selfishness in the hearts of men than was allowed for in Jefferson's humane philosophy, and the affairs of the West remained in a parlous state. His immediate successors in the governorship were much less interested in those affairs than he was, and this was one of many reasons why George Rogers Clark continued to be his friend. His vision of possibilities in the West is also one of the many important reasons why later generations have remembered him; but after the last day of the year 1780 he was swamped with local military problems.

Almost before Jefferson knew what had happened Arnold made a brilliant foray into Virginia. This was damaging enough in itself, but it assumed an importance in his history far in excess of its military significance — for political reasons. This brief period in his career need not be subjected to such microscopic examination as it received afterwards from his foes and partisans, but his activities should be described and his movements charted in some detail. Besides being intrinsically interesting, the episode throws light on his character as a man of action in a serious emergency.

Soon after Leslie's departure, Washington informed the Governor that there was talk of another embarkation in New York. He neither scouted nor encouraged the hope of naval aid from the French off the southern coast, but he emphasized the advantages the enemy would enjoy if they should again come to the lower parts of Virginia and remain there. They could move up and down the rivers in small parties, he said, while the defenders on the land would not have the means to transport themselves across these same waterways quickly enough to get at them. A month later he reported that a British force had actually sailed and that it was supposed to be destined southward.[11]

[11] To Jefferson, Nov. 8, Dec. 9, 1780; Fitzpatrick, XX, 326–327, 447–448. His letters of Dec. 27, 1780, and Jan. 2, 1781 (Ibid., XXI, 21, 51–52), in the latter of which he said that Arnold was in command, were too late to be of any help to Jefferson.

Jefferson should not have been surprised when he heard on the last day of the year that another fleet had been sighted in the bay. However, the report sent him by his friend General Thomas Nelson, Junior, of the militia was not full; and he understood that it was to be followed shortly by a more precise one. He promptly submitted such news as he had to General Steuben, the ranking Continental officer, saying that, until further information was received, he could only dispatch General Nelson into the lower country to take such steps as the exigencies of the moment might require.[12]

The day happened to be Sunday, and he did not think it necessary to call the Council. Before it met in regular session on Monday morning, however, he had written several other letters to officers and officials, "requiring several necessary measures to be taken," and had given orders for stationing couriers. Unfortunately, the line of post riders which he had previously established had been discontinued for reasons of economy. In the minutes of the Council the fleet was described as British, but when transmitting the news to the House of Delegates, then on the point of adjournment, Jefferson only said that he suspected it of being hostile — because of its size and also because of the information from Washington.[13]

He may have still cherished vain illusions about immediate French support, and he appears to have maintained his unruffled manner. About this time a Virginia officer, who had foot in stirrup to go elsewhere, heard the news, hastened to the Governor's house, and met him walking on the hill by the side of his garden. Jefferson then said that unless he had other information to justify the measure he would not disturb the country by calling out the militia.[14] Presumably the Council shared his scruples; they approved his prompt but limited actions, at any rate. Precise information of the sort that Jefferson required did not come until fifty hours after the first intelligence, and in the meantime this

[12] The events of these days can be sufficiently recovered from contemporary records, especially the *Journals of the Council of the State of Virginia*, II (*Va. Council Journals, State*), 268–272, and O. L., II, 254–270, giving the letters. The extracts from Jefferson's own diary, which are reproduced in O. L., II, 270–271 *n.*, are not contemporary in that exact form, but they were undoubtedly based on contemporary records and they check well with these, including his Account Book. Valuable information of a descriptive nature is also contained in numerous affidavits collected by his partisans at a later time and now preserved in his papers. Some of these appeared in print in Richmond *Enquirer*, as on Aug. 23, 1805. Specific reference will be made hereafter to certain of these later documents.

[13] O. L., II, 254, 256.

[14] Col. William Tatham to W. A. Burwell, June 13, 1805 (LC, 150:26215–26216); an extract from this or a similar letter in Jefferson's own hand is in LC, 6:1017. Late testimony like this need not be accepted in detail, but Tatham's rather vivid statement accords with impressions gained from more sober contemporary sources.

first report became "totally disbelieved," he said. If this disbelief was somewhat less than total, he and his advisers probably thought that if a hostile force was approaching it was only a raiding party.[15] The period was one of rumors; but in this instance optimism did him disservice. On Tuesday the report of an enemy invasion was definitely confirmed, and Jefferson and his Board took action they should have taken two days earlier.

He called part of the militia: one half, from counties near Richmond and Petersburg, to assemble at those places; one fourth, from another group, including his own Albemarle; and a specified number of men from the more distant Shenandoah Valley. He had already given General Nelson blanket authority, but he now definitely empowered him to draw out the militia of the lower counties in any way that he thought proper. He wrote Nelson direct, telling him that he intended to put 4600 militia in the field. He sent the orders to the various county lieutenants by members of the Assembly, who were returning home after adjournment. If not the best of messengers they were probably as good as were available; they might have moved faster had they known they had Benedict Arnold to contend with. Jefferson also wrote to other persons, apparently missing nobody who was important. Plans were also made for the removal of stores, if this should prove necessary. All this was on Tuesday; it was a busy day.

On Wednesday night he learned that the enemy were at anchor opposite Jamestown, but they did not land and proceed against Williamsburg as expected. (It was afterwards reported that Chancellor Wythe and one or two other old gentlemen were shooting partridges near the riverbank and "took a shot" at the enemy.) [16] Favored by wind and tide, Arnold decided to go farther by water. Jefferson did not know how far as yet, but on Thursday, after he had received a report at 5 A.M., and had been advised by the Council, he called *all* militia from the counties centering in Richmond and Petersburg, both of which were threatened. The need was so pressing that he asked them to come in small detachments without waiting to form companies.

It was already obvious, however, that they were not going to arrive in sufficient number to form an effective defense for the capital. Accordingly, he gave orders to withdraw arms, military stores, and important records to the foundry, five or six miles up the river near Westham. He did not yet know that this was Arnold's chief physical objective. About sunset he learned that the British had landed at Westover, north of the James, and he then properly concluded that they were making

15 This was Tatham's memory of Jefferson's statement.
16 William Tatham, in the letter cited.

for Richmond. He promptly ordered the stores which were still there and those that were being carried up the river to be taken across it. At 7:30, having remained in the capital quite as long as was prudent, he set out for Westham to supervise the operations there in person. Until eleven or twelve the erstwhile philosopher of Monticello gave his attention and direction to the safeguarding of the public property. Then, saying that he would cross the river in the morning and make the necessary arrangements for transportation on the other side, he went on to Tuckahoe for the night. His family had gone ahead, and on Friday he sent them on to Fine Creek, where he had inherited a place from his father.

On that day at 1 P.M. the enemy entered Richmond in triumph. A detachment went on to the foundry, destroyed it and did other damage, and then returned to the capital. Jefferson was at Westham for a time that day but the British did not see him. He saw them in Richmond, however, from Manchester across the river. His horse failing him after all this riding, he borrowed another and tried vainly to see General Steuben, under whose command he placed all the militia. This can hardly be dismissed as a case of "passing the buck," for it was a wise action, if belated.[17] He missed the Baron at several places, though he rode over much the same ground for two days. He spent Saturday night with his family at Fine Creek, but otherwise was wholly occupied with public matters — at Westham, Manchester, and elsewhere — riding incessantly through snow and rain.

On Sunday, when he was again in Manchester, the enemy retired from the capital. This was one week after he had heard of an approaching fleet. Early Monday morning he was back in his official seat. On Wednesday the enemy fell down the river toward Portsmouth, where for some weeks they stayed. Catching his breath after this startlingly rapid affair, he reported events to Washington and the President of Congress with customary conscientiousness. The troops commanded by the "parricide" Arnold amounted to some 1,500 infantrymen and from 50 to 120 horsemen, he said. Opposed to them in the neighborhood of Richmond had been only about 200 militiamen, though these were now much more numerous, especially on the south side of the James. General Steuben, a zealous friend, "descended from the dignity of his proper command to direct our smallest movements," he said; his vigilance prevented the enemy from crossing the river, which might have been fatal.[18]

[17] Palmer, *Steuben*, p. 246.
[18] To President of Congress and Washington, Jan. 10, 1781 (*O. L.*, II, 266–268, quotation, p. 268).

As he summed up the losses afterwards, he comforted himself that they had been less than might have been expected. In Richmond there were no permanent public buildings to be destroyed, since none had yet been built. The invaders overlooked the frame structure at the corner of Fourteenth and Cary Streets where the Assembly met. The legislators were not there and the streets were not filled with the saddled horses which made the place look like an Arabian village in times of session.[19] Apparently the invaders harmed neither the Governor's rented house nor the single-story brick building on the hill behind it where the Council sat. Nearly everything else in the straggling town was built of wood. Most of the public stores that were movable had been transported, in considerable confusion undoubtedly but with celerity. The chief damage was up the river, where the boring mill and magazine were destroyed and the roof of the foundry was burned, though the chimney stacks and furnaces of the latter were uninjured. Some stores were lost, chiefly leather, but most of the firearms were afterwards recovered from the water and Jefferson believed that much of the gunpowder which had been thrown into the canal could be saved by remanufacturing.[20]

The loss which Jefferson's friends felt most called upon to explain in later years was that of important public records, including those of the Council. A sad mistake was made by some wagoners, who lodged these papers in the magazine instead of placing them at the landing on the river; they could not be moved again before the enemy swooped down.[21] The British did not know how effectively they were destroying the Governor's record. He went to great pains afterwards to procure copies of letters from the recipients, and there can be no question of his unremitting personal efforts to preserve the public property.

Years later a supporter explained why he went into day-by-day details of the Governor's movements during Arnold's raid: "For we wish any man, who can discover the slightest remissness in these movements, to lay his finger upon the point and say *when* and *where* it was." [22] It would be difficult indeed to find any remissness in Jefferson's movements or actions from the moment that the report of the invasion was confirmed. The only real question is that of his delay in recognizing

[19] J. D. Schoepf, *Travels in the Confederation* (1911), II, 65; various valuable details from Mrs. Louise T. Catterall, Valentine Museum, Richmond.
[20] The best summaries are in the letter to Washington, Jan. 10, 1781, already cited, and a letter to the Speaker of the House of Delegates, Mar. 1, 1781, in *O. L.*, II, 378–379.
[21] Deposition of Daniel L. Hylton, Oct. 12, 1796, in LC, 100:17,225.
[22] Thomas Ritchie in Richmond *Enquirer*, Aug. 23, 1805.

the seriousness of the situation. He himself was of the opinion, soon after the event, that if the militia had been called two days earlier Arnold might never have got to Richmond; and he blamed the loss of those two days on faulty intelligence.[23] This defect he immediately tried to correct, but he never explained satisfactorily his failure to interpret more realistically the intelligence he did receive.

His later references to his original doubts about the status of the fleet in the bay were not emphatic, nor were they to any considerable degree recriminatory. But at this distance they seem disingenuous; they do not quite ring true; they are a little less, though not much less, than candid. It would have been better if he had admitted the unvarnished truth: Arnold had caught him off his guard. It would have been better if he had erred on the side of self-reproach and had assumed more than his proportionate share of blame, just as he had shouldered more than his share of labor. Neither civil nor military officials often do that, but such an attitude would have been in character with the high-minded and personally disinterested public official that he was. He could have stood on his record as a whole, without attempting to excuse himself even by implication. Or, as so many lesser men would have done, he might have burst forth in fierce indignation against others who were more at fault than he and then have stopped thinking about the matter. Actually he did neither. There is no doubt that he had vengeful feelings toward Benedict Arnold, whom he regarded as "the greatest of all traitors," and would have liked to see captured and exhibited as "a public spectacle of infamy." [23a] But when dealing with colleagues whose good will he had no reason to suspect he was rarely denunciatory. He was characteristically polite, regardful of others, and slow to anger. On the other hand, he was too proud and sensitive to endure criticism and reproach in self-forgetful silence.

He received censure in unmerited degree later on. Meanwhile, he had words of comfort from the person who was best able to view the situation as a whole. Washington agreed that the experience had been mortifying, but, considering the geography of Virginia, wondered that

[23] To Jacob Wray, Jan. 15, 1781, in *O. L.*, II, 276–277.

[23a] Phrases quoted from this letter of Jan. 31, 1781, to an unknown person, authorizing an attempt to capture Arnold and offering a reward. This included a passage (seen by me through courtesy JP), stricken out by him, in which he approved taking Arnold dead if he could not be taken alive. Without this passage the letter is in Ford, II, 441–443, with a note saying it was probably to G. R. Clark; and in *O. L.*, II, 312–313, where it is given as addressed to Gen. Muhlenberg. There is no address on the original, and it may never have been sent. It is better regarded as a revelation of Jefferson's state of mind than as an illustration of punitive action.

the State had been molested so little. He feared similar experiences in the future, but regarded the evils to be apprehended from these predatory expeditions as relatively small. They were not to be compared with the injury to the common cause and to Virginia itself that would result from the conquest of the region to the south. There was no doubt whatever in his mind that the policy of this highly vulnerable State should be to keep the weight of the war at a distance. The principal object of Arnold's operations had been to make a diversion in favor of Cornwallis, and the surest way to get rid of him was to show him, by the continued reinforcement of General Greene, that he had failed of his intention. In other words, Jefferson's own major policies were right, and should be continued. If he had committed a military sin — and the wise and magnanimous General did not even imply that he had — this was a venial sin, not mortal.[24]

A much more severe military critic whom Jefferson had to cope with at this stage was General von Steuben, who had been greatly annoyed by the delay and confusion of the mobilization, who regarded the war commissioner, Colonel George Muter, as incompetent, and who believed that things were done better in New Jersey under Governor William Livingston than in Virginia under Governor Thomas Jefferson.[25] The former Prussian staff officer was determined that the shame and disgrace of Arnold's virtually unopposed raid should not be repeated, and in trying to carry out one of his cherished plans he soon became engaged in altercation with the champion of self-government. In important respects the episode was revealing.

Before Arnold came Steuben had recommended the fortification of a bend of the river below Richmond at a place called Hood's, and he believed that this would have been a considerable obstacle to the invader. Jefferson had punctiliously referred the matter to the Assembly but that body had found no time to consider it before adjournment. After both the legislators and raiders had gone Steuben brought up the matter again, whereupon the Governor and Council assumed the authority to approve the proposal. Steuben quite naturally thought they might have done this in the first place.

Even now they were much too dilatory from the point of view of Frederick the Great's disciple, and a sharp exchange of letters ensued. There had been a serious misunderstanding between the General and the civilian officials about the methods of procuring the necessary labor. Steuben wanted to summon in neighboring militiamen, regarding them

24 To Jefferson, Feb. 6, 1781; Fitzpatrick, XXI, 191–192.
25 Palmer, Steuben, pp. 248–249.

as soldiers under orders, or he wanted Negroes as substitutes. To his brusque demand the Governor raised firm legal objections. "The executives have not by the laws of this state any power to call a freeman to labor even for the public without his consent, nor a slave without that of his master," he said. Therefore, voluntary labor must be hired, quickly if possible but slowly if necessary. In supreme disgust Steuben wrote to Washington: "The executive power is so confined that the Governor has it not in his power to procure me 40 negroes to work at Hood's." In military terms this was a *reductio ad absurdum*. Indeed, in military terms this unprofessional war, waged in fits and starts by temporary soldiers, was little less than that. Jefferson himself never succeeded in resolving the contradiction. His ingenious mind finally figured out a way to get around the legal limitations upon the employment of the militia in fatigue duty, but he did not get the fortifications erected soon enough to delay the next invasion, and in his last message to the Assembly he posed the vexing question of employing freemen and slaves in necessary military works at a time when the currency was worthless.[26]

It was the militia, he said, who "environed" Arnold at Portsmouth and prevented that bold soldier from making any other raids for upwards of two months. Not until late March did British reinforcements come and create new dangers. Meanwhile, the situation was disturbing enough to cause the Governor to advance the date of the Assembly to March 1, despite the inconvenience to the members. His explanation was entirely adequate: "One army of our enemies lodged within our country, another pointing towards it, . . . without a shilling in the public coffers, was a situation in which it was impossible to rest the safety of the State." [27] The emissions of paper money, ordered or permitted by the last Assembly, and amounting to more than £11,000,000, had been dispensed as fast as they came off the printing press, and many urgent calls had not yet been answered. These facts may be cited against later allegations that Jefferson as governor was foolishly economical.

Despite dangers and difficulties, reinforcements had gone to General Greene. These consisted chiefly of militia from the western counties, whom Jefferson always considered as Virginia's best. Those counties had been drawn on as little as possible for the operations

[26] Jefferson to Steuben, Feb. 12, 1781, in *O. L.*, II, 333–334; to Col. William Call, Apr. 18, 1781 (*Ibid.*, II, 484); to Speaker of House of Delegates, May 10, 1781 (*Ibid.*, II, 512). The excellent account of this episode in Palmer, *Steuben*, pp. 251–253, is marred by an inadequate appreciation of the real legal difficulties that Jefferson faced.

[27] To Speaker of House of Delegates, Mar. 1, 1781 (*O. L.*, II, 377).

around Portsmouth.[28] The Governor was still wondering about the best way to raise troops to meet all the calls on him. He would have preferred to rely on regulars, and he deeply regretted the interference with drafting operations which had resulted from calling the militia in such numbers from so many counties. In any case where the manpower had been drained from a county and the filling of a levy seemed impracticable, he was forced to exercise his authority to suspend drafting. This was one reason why he waited as long as he could before calling out the militia.

He did not like the existing system — or lack of system. He told the Assembly: "Whether it be practicable to raise and maintain a sufficient number of regulars to carry on the war is a question: that it would be burdensome is undoubted. Yet it is perhaps as certain that no possible mode of carrying it on can be so expensive to the public and so distressing and disgusting to individuals as by militia." [29] His concern for individuals did not go to the point of condoning avoidance of militia duty, or resistance to drafting or impressment. Whenever the spirit of disobedience appeared he favored subduing it immediately. "Laws made by common consent must not be trampled on by individuals," he said.[30] But he regarded militiamen as civilians who had been drawn from their farms and homes to do temporary service in local emergencies. They should not be sent to a distance; they should not — they could not — be kept in armies very long. Perhaps he was too solicitous, but he had to be realistic. The men who were serving around Portsmouth were being kept beyond their time for a purpose. Although he did not speak of it publicly there was a definite plan to catch the traitor. If it could have been carried out his governorship would have been regarded, then and thereafter, as definitely successful.

At last French naval support in the Chesapeake Bay region promised to be something more than a figment of Jefferson's imagination. Heeding the request of the Virginia delegation in Congress, the French minister, La Luzerne, urged Admiral Destouches to send a few ships from Newport to check Arnold. By late February a man-of-war and some smaller vessels actually arrived, though they did not stay long.[31] Meanwhile, Washington had formed a plan for Lafayette to operate

[28] Jefferson to Steuben, Feb. 15, 18, 1781 (O. L., II, 346, 357); to President of Congress, Feb. 17, 1781 (Ibid., II, 350–352); Palmer, Steuben, p. 253.

[29] O. L., II, 378.

[30] To Col. Vanmeter, Apr. 27, 1781 (O. L., II, 499).

[31] Jefferson to Steuben, Feb. 19, 1781 (Ford, II, 459); Louis Gottschalk, Lafayette and the Close of the American Revolution, p. 191. I have not given space to the special mission of Benjamin Harrison to Congress; see Madison to Pendleton, Jan. 16, 1781 (Writings, I, 124).

in conjunction with a larger naval force. Before the middle of March the Marquis got his detachment as far south as Annapolis, and he himself went on to Yorktown and Williamsburg to consult the military authorities in Virginia. He and the Governor did not see each other this time, but the letters they exchanged marked the beginning of a lifelong correspondence and heralded an historic friendship.[32]

Certain sentences in Jefferson's welcoming letter are particularly revealing. Modestly and realistically he wrote:

> I trust that your future Acquaintance with the Executive of the State will evince to you that among their faults is not to be counted a want of disposition to second the Views of the Commander against our common Enemy. We are too much interested in the present scene and have too much at Stake to leave a doubt on that Head. Mild Laws, a People not used to war and prompt obedience, a want of the provisions of War & means of procuring them render our efforts often ineffectual, oblige us to temporise and when we cannot accomplish an object in one way to attempt it in another. . . .[33]

These limiting circumstances he wanted Lafayette to know. A couple of days later he understated the case by saying that he had to reduce his own expectations at times. "I know," he added, "that you will be satisfied to make the most of an unprepared [people] who have the war now for the first time seriously fixed in their country, and have therefore all those habits to acquire which their northern brethren had in the year 1776 and which they have purchased at so great an expence."[34] Fortunately, Lafayette was already used to the inconveniences arising from popular government, and believed that these were compensated by numberless blessings. He was reluctant to sign impressing warrants for horses, much as he needed them, and he wanted to be informed of the exact state of the militia laws. Delighted to find a foreign officer who appreciated conditions in civilian America, Jefferson hastened to say that under existing conditions impressment of property was indispensable, and that he had no fear of Lafayette's exercise of these powers. Washington's letter of introduction, forwarded at this late date, was not really needed. Quite obviously, these two men were going to like each other.[35]

[32] Well discussed by Gilbert Chinard in his ed. of *Letters of Lafayette and Jefferson*, pp. 5–13.

[33] Mar. 10, 1781 (*O. L.*, II, 401). He had written on Mar. 2, 8 (*Ibid.*, II, 382–383, 393).

[34] Mar. 12, 1781 (*O. L.*, II, 405).

[35] Lafayette to Jefferson, Mar. 17, 20, 1781 (Chinard, *Letters*, pp. 26–27, 30–31); Jefferson to Lafayette, Mar. 19, 1781 (*O. L.*, II, 416–417).

To Steuben the Governor spoke much to the same effect but in a quite different tone. The Baron, angered because of the failure to obtain the expected men, supplies, and horses for Lafayette's expedition, complained bitterly to Jefferson, asking that his letter be laid before the Assembly. In reply, after summarizing his orders to the county authorities about the militia, the Governor said: "We can only be answerable for the orders we give, and not for the execution. If they are disobeyed [in the counties] from obstinacy of spirit or want of coercion in the laws it is not our fault; we have done what alone remained for us to do in such case, we have ordered other militia from other counties." [36] In the matter of horses, the quartermaster applied for militia to aid him in executing his powers of impressment. This request Jefferson denied. "We did not think proper to resign ourselves and our country implicitly to the demands of a quartermaster," he said, "but thought we had some right of judgment left to us. We know that an armed force to impress horses was as unnecessary as it was new." Nothing caused quite so much irritation as the seizure of horses, and Jefferson soon was directed by the Assembly to authorize county lieutenants to restrain this form of impressment. He wrote to General Greene: "As tedious as is the operation of reasoning with every individual on whom we are obliged to exercise disagreeable powers, yet free people think they have a right to an explanation of the circumstances which give rise to the necessity under which they suffer." [37]

So far as Lafayette's expedition was concerned, all this turned out to be much ado about nothing, for the expected naval aid did not come. The fleet that sailed into the bay in late March was not French but British. The event, which was so fateful to Governor Jefferson, hung by a hair. Not knowing that there had been a naval battle, he tried hard to inform his allies of the presence of the foe, only to learn afterwards that Destouches, though claiming a victory, had gone back to Newport. [38] Reinforcements soon came to Arnold under General William Phillips, Jefferson's former neighbor, who as an exchanged prisoner had returned to the fight. Lafayette, forced to abandon the expedition, went back to Annapolis and then to Head of Elk. Jefferson would have shared the glory if the Marquis had caught Arnold, but he could claim none when Cornwallis surrendered at Yorktown after he himself had retired.

* * *

[36] Mar. 10, 1781 (*O. L.*, II, 399).

[37] Apr. 5, 1781 (*O. L.*, II, 456).

[38] Several letters of Mar. 21, 1781 (*O. L.*, II, 421–423); excellent account of whole affair in Gottschalk, ch. 9.

He might have shared the credit of another enterprise, which Steuben conceived and Lafayette approved before he left. The Baron boldly proposed that he march immediately with two thousand picked militia to join Greene, the supposition being that with this reinforcement the latter would be able to defeat Cornwallis decisively. Richard Henry Lee regarded this as a master stroke; General Weedon of the militia thought it would practically terminate the war; and no less an authority than George Washington believed that, if carried out, it would probably have ruined Cornwallis.[39]

From what Jefferson himself said about the strategy of the war he might have been expected to approve the proposal. Almost a month later, when the local situation was still precarious, he wrote Lafayette that so long as Greene was kept superior to Cornwallis Virginia really had little to fear. What he was most afraid of was what the British themselves hoped, namely, that they would be able to rally Loyalists and other disaffected elements in the South. "The British force may harass and distress us greatly," he said, "but the Carolinas alone can subdue us. . . . We therefore think it our first interest to keep them under in that quarter, considering the war in our own country but as a secondary object." [40] He regarded the militia left in the State as only a defensive force, frankly recognizing the probability that they could do little more than impede the enemy.

It is possible that the Governor was overborne by his Council when they considered Steuben's proposal, but, just as he would have been condemned if it had been accepted and then followed by local disaster, so he must bear the blame for its unfortunate rejection. He and his advisers recognized that the plan was founded on "very probable principles," but, now that the enemy had been reinforced at Portsmouth, they were unwilling to weaken local defenses further. The detachment which Steuben wanted would take so large a proportion of the available arms that the remaining militia in the east would be practically powerless. The best they could offer, therefore, was the speediest possible reinforcement of Greene from the Piedmont and southwestern counties, where there was reason to suppose the militia could supply arms.[41]

Jefferson also wanted to expedite the raising of the Continental levies of regulars, and the sending of these to Greene. He was in-

[39] Lee to Jefferson, Mar. 27, 1781, in Ballagh, II, 217; other letters quoted in Palmer, *Steuben*, p. 260.

[40] To Lafayette, Apr. 23, 1781 (*O. L.*, II, 494). At this time the British had actually advanced up the river and were again threatening the capital.

[41] Mar. 21, 1781 (*Va. Council Journals, State*, II, 322).

volved in several contradictions. Not only had this work of enlistment been interfered with by the embodiment of the militia; he was also acutely aware that both the militia in the east and those now with Greene in the Carolinas had already served a longer tour of duty than was customary and must be shortly relieved. "Thus pushed for men," he wrote one of his high officers, "the Baron's proposition was not acceded to as exposing the country too much." [42] The issue was not merely between local and general strategy, nor even between the military and civilian points of view in this amateurish war. Considerations of war weariness, of disaffection, and of local psychology also entered in.

The calls of the militia specified no precise term of service, and Jefferson's attempt hereafter to limit this to two months was not legally necessary. On practical grounds it probably was, if he did not want to be faced with wholesale desertions. It is curiously ironical, however, that at this critical time he ordered an extensive shifting of the militia. This was not a case of fiddling while Rome burned, for the Governor's violin was quite neglected, but it was a case of applying principles of human justice in a period of grave emergency. Such a time called for a less scrupulous and more ruthless man.

Steuben, now more contemptuous than ever of the feeble and, to his mind, indecisive government of Virginia, wanted more support against Phillips and Arnold in Portsmouth if he could not go to the aid of Greene. At this juncture, however, Jefferson was very unwilling to "harass" the militia any more than was absolutely necessary. Accordingly, while urging Steuben and others to explain things to them and to express appreciation of their long and arduous services, he called upon the county lieutenants to round up their delinquents. The penalty of six months' service on these men he thought entirely proper. Burdens must be equitably distributed between counties and within them.[43] Unquestionably he had a keener sense of justice than of military efficiency. It was not because of pressure from him and the Council that Colonel George Muter, the commissioner of war, finally resigned. They had declined his offer to submit himself to a formal investigation and denied having had complaints against him. In place of this official, Jefferson named Colonel William Davies, a Continental officer whom Steuben regarded as thoroughly competent,

[42] To Gen. Weedon, Mar. 31, 1781 (O. L., II, 446). See also letter to Greene, Mar. 30, 1781 (Ibid., II, 443–444).

[43] To County Lieutenants, Apr. 11, 1781 (O. L., II, 465); to Steuben, Weedon, and Muhlenberg, Apr. 3, 1781 (Ibid., II, 451–453).

but Davies, viewing the administrative confusion with the eye of a professional, thought it now little short of irremediable. Also, when Lafayette came back, this friendly officer said that more militia seemed to be going off than coming in. To a military man this was another *reductio ad absurdum*.[44]

By the spring of 1781, when the Governor was thirty-eight years old, his official troubles had become so great that even reading about them is painful. To these personal sorrow was now added. On April 15, he made another mournful entry in his Account Book: "Our daughter Lucy Elizabeth died about 10 o'clock A.M. this day," he wrote. The infant was in only her second year. On the next day, which was so inclement that he doubted the presence of a quorum at the Council meetings, he begged to be excused from attending. His wife was in a situation in which he did not wish to leave her, he said.[45]

Three days after that he received intelligence that the enemy were in motion up the James in eleven square-rigged vessels. It looked as though the interior would be penetrated again, but he was not caught napping this time. He did all he was supposed to do, did it promptly, and remained in his appointed place throughout the ten-day period that the immediate danger lasted. Certain members of the Council were out of town at the most perilous time, doubtless for quite sufficient reasons, but he was always there and he gave no sign that he was particularly perturbed. He did not think there was much in Richmond now that the enemy could damage, and he soon learned that Lafayette was coming back.

Lafayette came in time to save the capital. Phillips and Arnold got no closer than Manchester, across the James to the south, and they caused chief damage by burning tobacco warehouses there and at Petersburg. Lafayette, advancing by forced marches, reached Richmond on the evening of Sunday, April 29, and very shortly after his arrival he and Jefferson first met. The militia joined the Continental regulars of the Marquis, and the "cowardly plunderers" (as Jefferson described them) were soon sailing down the river. There was no reason to suppose that the enemy would soon come back. It seemed to the Governor that the new Continental levies within the State could be sent to Greene as they were raised, and that Richmond was a safe

---

[44] Jefferson to Muter, Mar. 2, 1781 (*O. L.*, II, 383); to Davies, Mar. 22, 1781 (*Ibid.*, II, 424); Palmer, *Steuben*, p. 261; Gottschalk, *Lafayette*, p. 228.

[45] To David Jamieson, Apr. 16, 1781; Ford, III, 13. Four members appeared but they transacted only the single item of business which Jefferson had written them about; *Journals*, II, 335.

enough place for the Assembly to meet at the scheduled time in early May.[46]

The legislators themselves did not think so, for no quorum came; and on May 10 those who had braved the dangers determined to meet two weeks later in Charlottesville.[47] Jefferson had no choice but to follow them, and the position of the government in the capital soon became quite untenable, anyway. The tide of war turned swiftly and unexpectedly. Phillips and Arnold reversed their course and came back up the river for a more important purpose than a predatory raid. They were going to join Cornwallis, who had adopted a new plan.[48] His Lordship, leaving behind him a smaller force to cope with Greene, made straight for Petersburg; and there, on May 20, the armies of the enemy were linked. Jefferson had certainly not anticipated this. General Greene, though continuing to serve the Continental cause bravely and effectively, was no longer Virginia's shield; and, so far as local defense was concerned, the troops and supplies sent to him were wasted. The military hopes of the Commonwealth now centered necessarily in Lafayette.

The Governor was still going through the customary motions, but he had to admit to the Marquis that the machinery of enforcement in the counties had largely broken down. If his calls did not produce the necessary reinforcements, he wrote, "I shall candidly acknowledge that it is not in my power to do anything more than to represent to the General Assembly that unless they can provide more effectually for the execution of the laws it will be vain to call on militia." [49] After a last conference with Lafayette, and what proved to be his last official meeting with the Council on May 15, he left Richmond. Apparently his family were already at Tuckahoe; he himself remained in that familiar seat several days before riding homeward. This was not a precipitate flight but a dignified, if discouraged, retirement before a new alignment of superior forces.

[46] Jefferson to various county lieutenants, Apr. 19, 1781 (O. L., II, 485–486); to Col. William Preston, Apr. 21, 1781 (Ibid., II, 489); to Lafayette, Apr. 23, 1781 (Ibid., II, 494); to President of Congress and Washington, Apr. 23, 1781 (Ibid., II, 495); to Members of the General Assembly from certain counties, May 1, 1781 (Ibid., II, 500); to President of Congress and Washington, May 9, 1781 (Ibid., II, 509–510); Gottschalk, Lafayette, pp. 221–223. No quorum of the Council was present Apr. 26–May 5, but Jefferson was there every day at the appointed time; see Journals, II, 341–342.

[47] Delegates, Journal, May 7–10. Jefferson addressed his customary letter to the Speaker on May 10 (O. L., II, 510–512).

[48] The whole matter is illuminated by the correspondence in Cornwallis's Answer to Clinton's Narrative (London, 1783), pp. 55–73.

[49] To Lafayette, May 14, 1781 (O. L., II, 515). See also letter to the Speaker, May 28, 1781 (O. L., II, 523).

One question of formalities was now wholly pointless. From the former commander at Portsmouth he had received a letter addressed to "Thomas Jefferson, Esq., American Governor of Virginia"; and, not to be outdone, he had addressed his reply to "William Phillips, Esq., commanding the British forces in the Commonwealth of Virginia." [50] But on May 13, Phillips, whom his recent neighbor described as "the proudest man of the proudest nation on earth," lay dead in Petersburg; and Jefferson, retiring to supposed safety with what remained of Virginia's officialdom, was now only the shadow of a governor. In his native County he soon ceased being even that.

[50] Jefferson, to Va. Delegates in Congress, May 10, 1781 (*O. L.*, II, 513).

[XXV]

Exit His Excellency

RETIRING before the enemy under the inexorable pressure of events, the government of the proud Commonwealth of Virginia not only lost all semblance of impressiveness. In the process of transferring its seat from Richmond to Charlottesville it practically dissolved. The constituent parts were incompletely reassembled during Jefferson's few remaining days as chief magistrate. He had called the Council to meet on the day appointed for the convening of the adjourned legislature, May 24, but only one of his advisers joined him by then. Another showed up six days later, but there never was a quorum, and, though he himself was always on hand, there were no further official transactions of the Board. So far as he was concerned it had ceased to exist.[1]

In his last days as the head of a moribund executive department he held a council of another and more colorful sort. A delegation of Illinois Indians, from the George Rogers Clark country in which he was so deeply interested, visited him and thus served as a reminder of that imperial domain. He smoked the pipe of peace with Brother John Baptist de Coigne, though otherwise he never used tobacco. Also, as the Great Father, he addressed the Chief in words of simple eloquence which he charged not only with sympathy but also with confidence and hope.[2]

To him in June, 1781, as in July, 1776, this was a struggle against tyranny in the name of freedom; and he spoke of its prospects

[1] *Va. Council Journals, State*, II, 345–346.

[2] To Brother John Baptist de Coigne, June, 1781 (L. & B., XVI, 371–377). A passage from this speech has already been quoted in connection with the Declaration of Independence and Jefferson's interpretation of the meaning of the war. One of the few references to this council by a contemporary is in a letter from John Taylor, a member of the Assembly, to D. C. Brent, Oct. 7, 1796 (LC, 100:17217–17218).

with an optimism which seems absurd in view of British successes and the immediacy of his own peril. After six years of attempted conquest, he said, the enemy had won no more land than would serve for the burial of their slain warriors. Upon the face of it this was merely an idle boast, designed for psychological effect. The Governor, it seems, was whistling loudly to keep up courage. Other words of his, however, show that his optimism was not wholly feigned. This was the same sort of struggle that it had been at the beginning, and, in the larger view, he saw victory as inevitable. "But peace is not far off," he said. "The English cannot hold out long, because all the world is against them." [3] The logic seemed unescapable if one argued deductively after viewing the international scene, and before many months it was borne out by events. Despite the deep darkness of the hour Jefferson had retained both his philosophy and his faith.

His view of the local situation was another matter. He saw clearly and stated frankly that Virginia was nearing the end of her resources and that he himself could do practically nothing more. Before he addressed the Indian Chief with such show of confidence he appealed as a last resort to Washington to come to the rescue of a sinking State. His last letter to the Commander in Chief in this period of suspended animation was not a pretentious communication nor was it querulous, but it was touching and he himself regarded it as final. [4]

If Washington was not already aware of the rapid deterioration of the military situation, the Governor left him in no possible doubt of it. The forces of Cornwallis and Arnold, united at Petersburg, had moved northward, and they had been joined by fresh reinforcements, brought by water from New York. Jefferson did not know that Virginia was to be freed of Benedict Arnold, who was granted leave to return to the North; but it was an occasion of grave concern to him that there were now some seven thousand enemy troops within the Commonwealth. Lafayette, not yet reinforced by Wayne from Pennsylvania, stood between the British and Fredericksburg, but, with his regulars and such militia as could be armed, he had less than half that number. Cornwallis might not be able to annihilate the Marquis; actually, the Earl soon found the "boy" dangerously elusive. But Jefferson foresaw that the enemy, restraining him with part of their much larger force, could use the rest to waste an unarmed country. What he most feared was the acquiescence of a weary people, un-

[3] L. & B., XVI, 375.
[4] To Washington, May 28, 1781 (O. L., II, 524–525). He wrote the President of Congress more briefly on the same date, and also issued certain orders to county lieutenants (Ibid., II, 522–524).

der events which they could see no human power prepared to ward off. He issued more orders to the militia to join Lafayette but he had no assurance that these would be heeded. What his exhausted and discouraged country needed was the aid and presence of the greatest of its sons. Washington's judgment must be formed on a view of the whole Continental scene, not a single part; but Jefferson believed that his appearance among his countrymen would restore full confidence. "Should the dangers of this State and its consequences to the union be such as to render it best for the whole that you should repair to its assistance," he said, "the difficulty would be to keep men out of the field." To Washington this painfully consistent unionist turned, because there was now no use appealing to anybody else.

It was only as a private citizen, however, that he himself could hope to feel the comforting effects of the Commander in Chief's presence. He was speaking his valedictory as a war governor. "A few days will bring to me that period of relief which the constitution has prepared for those oppressed with the labours of my office," he said, "and a long declared resolution of relinquishing it to abler hands has prepared my way for retirement to a private station." Washington could not yet promise to come to the rescue of Virginia, but he could say this:

> Give me leave before I take leave of your Excellency in your public capacity to Express the obligations I am under for the readiness and zeal with which you have always forwarded and supported every measure which I have had occasion to recommend thro' you, and to assure you that I shall esteem myself honored by a continuance of your friendship and correspondence shou'd your Country permit you to remain in the private walk of life.[5]

On the very day that Jefferson wrote Washington the Assembly held its first formal session in Charlottesville.[6] The month of May had almost run its flowery course before the legislators managed to organize. The two speakers, Benjamin Harrison of the House of Delegates and Archibald Cary of the Senate, with some other members, were guests at Monticello. They could not have been left in much doubt about the state of their host's mind, but Jefferson would have guarded himself better against later controversy if he had made to the Assembly at this time a formal statement of his unwillingness to serve longer. Perhaps he thought this unnecessary because his sentiments were well known; perhaps he believed that anything he said publicly

[5] To Jefferson, June 8, 1781 (Fitzpatrick, XXII, 190).
[6] There was no quorum until May 28.

at this critical juncture would be liable to misinterpretation; perhaps, with characteristic deference to the legislators, he wanted to leave the ultimate responsibility with them. Unfortunately, however, they did not immediately provide the relief he undoubtedly longed for and almost certainly expected. They resolved to ballot for governor on June 2, the precise date on which his second term of one year ended. This happened to fall on Saturday and when the day came they postponed action till Monday, not anticipating that action would then be impossible.

On Sunday, June 3, Jefferson stretched legalities sufficiently to write several official letters which are of some interest in themselves and of more in that they were his last. He accepted the proposal of the President of Pennsylvania that the final settlement of the boundary between that State and Virginia be postponed. He agreed that it was impracticable to determine this by astronomical observations during the present season, and that in the meantime the line of Mason and Dixon should be extended for twenty-three miles by surveyor's compass. This was a good note for Peter Jefferson's son to end on.[7]

But the fates were not content that his administration should expire so calmly. Before sunrise on Monday a gigantic horseman rode up the mountain to tell him the British dragoons were coming. He and his guests ate a normal breakfast, traditionally a large one, and the legislators afterwards gathered momentarily in Charlottesville. They did not take time to elect a governor, however; they merely adjourned to Staunton, beyond the Blue Ridge, after the House of Delegates had agreed that forty members should constitute a quorum.[8] The villain of the piece (though not a really vile one) was Lieutenant Colonel Tarleton; the hero was towering Jack Jouett; the victims were the scampering legislators and a stranded gentleman who presumed himself to be a private citizen and had a family to look after.

In Hanover County, several days earlier, Cornwallis had planned to distress the Virginians by breaking up the Assembly. Also, the Earl had learned that Steuben, with recent levies intended for General Greene, was at Point of Fork on the upper James to the southwest of Charlottesville, covering Continental stores there. Detaching Tarleton with one hundred and eighty dragoons and seventy mounted infantry, Cornwallis sent him to disrupt the government; he despatched a slower-moving force under Lieutenant Colonel Simcoe against Point

[7] To the Virginia commissioners, to the President of Pennsylvania, and to the Surveyor of Monongalia County, June 3, 1781 (*O. L.*, II, 531–552).

[8] *Delegates, Journal*, June 4, 1781.

of Fork and Steuben. After completing his mission Tarleton was to join Simcoe. Meanwhile, the main body was to proceed westward through Goochland County to unite later with the two detachments.[9] Simcoe put Steuben to flight, bringing that already unpopular officer into considerable discredit, and the main body of the enemy, making headquarters shortly at Elkhill, destroyed much of Jefferson's property. But it was Tarleton who did most damage to his reputation.

The dragoons and mounted infantry, starting from Hanover on that Sunday when Jefferson wrote his last official letters, covered seventy miles in twenty-four hours. Riding chiefly in the night, they counted on surprise and but for accident would have achieved it. At a tavern bearing the incredible name of Cuckoo, some forty miles from Charlottesville, Captain John Jouett, Junior, known in local story as "Jack," observed them. The son and namesake of the keeper of the Swan Tavern in Charlottesville, who was himself something of legendary figure, he was even taller than Jefferson and weighed more than two hundred pounds. Also an expert horseman, he knew the back trails and bypaths, and through the night he followed them. It is said that the scars made on his face by the lashing branches of the undergrowth remained with him all his life. Legend also has it that when he arrived at Monticello before sunrise, he was regaled by Jefferson with old Madeira; he then rode on to arouse the sleeping legislators in Charlottesville.[10]

Jouett was well ahead of Tarleton. The latter rested his men for three hours during the night, paused to capture and burn a baggage train, stopped to pluck several of the "principal gentlemen of Virginia" from their beds, and gathered in a visiting congressman from North Carolina. The legend is, also, that he partook of a generous breakfast at Dr. Thomas Walker's.[11] Tarleton's delay, however, was relatively slight and should detract nothing from the glory of Jack Jouett's ride, which, as an isolated feat, was obviously more difficult than the far more famous one of Paul Revere. It came toward the end of the Revolution, rather than at the beginning, and the ensuing events were less heroic, but the chief difference between the two rides lies in the fact that no poet immortalized Jouett. In passing him

[9] Banastre Tarleton, *History of the Campaigns of 1781 and 1782* (Dublin, 1787), pp. 302–303.

[10] The best account is Virginius Dabney, "Jouett Outrides Tarleton," *Scribner's Mag.*, vol. 83, pp. 690–698 (June, 1928).

[11] The safest account is Tarleton's *History*, pp. 303–305. Randall, I, 335–336, makes only slight reference to Jouett but tells a good story. He designates the prisoners as the two Walkers, William and Robert Nelson, Colonel Simms — a senator — and Francis Kinlock of North Carolina.

by writers have missed an opportunity, for he might have been de-
picted in scarlet coat, with military plume and hat, and was in other
respects a highly dramatic figure. He rendered great service to Thomas
Jefferson, for if the British had captured him they would probably not
have released him so quickly on parole as they did the other Patriots.
They would hardly have caught such an early riser in bed, however,
and made him suffer the indignity of being dragged forth in his
nightshirt.

By the time Tarleton's men got to the ford of the Rivanna below
Charlottesville, this was guarded. They stormed through, nevertheless, destroyed stores of firelocks and gunpowder, and despite Jack
Jouett captured seven dilatory members of the Assembly. "The attempt to secure Mr. Jefferson was ineffectual," reported the Colonel;
"he discovered the British dragoons from his house, . . . before they
could approach him, and he provided for his personal safety with a
precipitate retreat." In this case discretion was undoubtedly the better part of valor, but Tarleton did not have firsthand knowledge of
Jefferson's movements. He sent somebody else (Captain McLeod) up
the mountain and he himself hastened on toward Simcoe, though that
officer really did not need him. It is difficult to sift truth from legend,
but the former Governor was by no means the first to flee, and there
was no sign of terror in his almost too deliberate movements. If no
Don Quixote, neither was he a Falstaff.

The indisputable facts are that he first sent off his guests, that he
dispatched his family in a carriage a couple of hours later, and that
he himself did not leave Monticello until practically every other man
was gone and the enemy were actually approaching. Family tradition
has embroidered the story. It is said that his delay was partly occasioned
by the necessity of having his horse shod; that he started off once, dis-
mounted to look through a telescope, saw no soldiers, and turned back;
then noting that he had dropped his small sword at the observation
point, he returned to that place, took another look through the telescope, and saw redcoats filling the streets of Charlottesville.[12]

A late but credible account is that he was warned of immediate
danger by a young officer who found him "perfectly tranquil and undisturbed."[13] The subsequent emphasis of his partisans on his composure seemed necessary to them because of the charges of personal
cowardice which were hurled at him by political enemies long after
the events. He himself termed these too ridiculous to be taken seri-

[12] These traditions enter into the account given by Randall, I, 337–339. For
Jefferson's own story, see Ford, VIII, 368–369 n.
[13] Deposition of Capt. Christopher Hudson, dated July 26, 1805 (LC, 151:26426).

ously, as they were, but one of them rankled in his mind. Thinking it unsafe to go by road, he went past the gap and through the woods to the next eminence. This was afterwards referred to hilariously as the affair of Carter's Mountain. The impression is unescapable that he remained at home too long for comfort, not that he left precipitately; and charges based on the circumstances of his flight would have been ridiculous when so many others were fleeing, and generally more hastily.

He sent his family to Colonel Carter's Blenheim, where he joined them for dinner, and somewhat later to the Coles place, Enniscorthy, also in Albemarle. By the middle of the month he took them to his own Poplar Forest in Bedford County. The British came nowhere near them, but in this safe place he was so unlucky as to fall from his horse (said to have been Caractacus) while riding over his farm. Though not seriously injured, he was largely confined to the house for six weeks or more thereafter. At a much later time certain domestic enemies asserted that his accident occurred while he was fleeing in terror.[14] He took it quite casually during the summer that it happened, but any spiteful commentator might have pointed to it as a symbol of his precipitate descent into a state of helplessness.

His whole procedure was as dignified as that of any wartime fugitive but the circumstances did not lend themselves to heroic legend. Tarleton did him greatest disservice in the timing of his raid. He would have been kinder if he had waited until the Assembly had chosen another governor. No responsible person at the time seems to have questioned Jefferson's own judgment that his term had expired, or to have blamed him for the interregnum that followed. He could hardly have been expected to follow the fleeing legislators to Staunton without a formal request from the Assembly, or at least an informal one from the speakers, that he continue to serve in the unexpected interim. Lacking that, he saw no alternative but to interpret the law strictly, according to his custom. Assuming that his term had expired, resignation was technically impossible, but the report reached Richard Henry Lee as far away as Westmoreland County that he had "resigned." [15] It would be nearer the truth to say that the government abandoned him than that he abandoned the government, but there must have been some people then, as there were more thereafter, who believed that he had abdicated in utter impotence.

During late May and early June consternation had spread among a proud people. "Such terror and confusion you have no idea of," wrote

---

[14] Letter of Thomas Turner, quoted in Richmond *Enquirer*, Aug. 23, 1805.
[15] Lee to Washington, June 12, 1781; Ballagh, II, 234.

Miss Betsy Ambler. "Governor, Council, everybody scampering." [16]
It was the daughter of Jefferson's old flame, Rebecca Burwell, now
an invalid, and of Jacquelin Ambler, an honored member of his
Council, who was speaking. An amusing story of somebody's flight
before the enemy had been told. "But this is not more laughable,"
said Betsy, "than the accounts we have of our illustrious Governor,
who, they say, took neither rest nor food for man or horse till he
reached C——r's Mountain." There was much merriment in the Ambler family over the troubles of Mr. Jefferson, and John Marshall
heard of this in later years. [17]

They were having serious troubles of their own, also, and the
Councilor, whom Betsy referred to as her "best beloved father,"
though less conspicuous than his former rival, was certainly no more
heroic. He was one of those who never did succeed in getting from
Richmond to Charlottesville for meetings of the Council, being
forced to remain in a well-hidden place in Louisa County. Said his
daughter: "The public office which he holds makes it absolutely
necessary for him to run no risk of falling into the hands of the
enemy. We therefore see him safely lodged in the old coach every
night, with faithful old Sam as his guard, while we endeavor to make
ourselves as comfortable as we can in the overseer's tiny dwelling,
which will scarcely hold us all." Soon after this Ambler tried to go
on to Charlottesville, but the enemy got there before him and he
had to turn back. Nor was he able to follow the itinerant legislators
to Staunton; not until the Council was back in Richmond, more than
a month after Tarleton's raid, did John Marshall's future father-in-
law return to his official seat. [18]

An anecdote survives about Patrick Henry, Speaker Benjamin Harrison, and John Tyler, who went together from Charlottesville to
Staunton. Stopping at a rude hut in the hills and introducing themselves as fugitive legislators, they were greeted as cowardly knaves
by an old woman and told to ride on. Explanations were met with
derision and unbelief, until it was finally revealed that Patrick Henry
was among them. Then the old woman concluded that everything
must be all right. The story has been told as a tribute to the orator's
popularity; it also serves as a reminder that the tribune of the people,
no less than the philosopher of Monticello, was forced to take flight
and that his situation was by no means without embarrassment. [19]

[16] Betsy Ambler to Mildred Smith, 1781, presumably in June; *Atlantic Monthly*,
vol. 84, p. 538.
[17] A. J. Beveridge, *Life of John Marshall*, I, 144, quotes this passage.
[18] July 10, 1781; *Va. Council Journals, State*, II, 354. Quotation is from his daughter's letter.
[19] Tyler, *Tylers*, I, 81-83.

Patrick Henry was exceedingly active in the Assembly which met beyond the Blue Ridge in safety but amid continuing rumors. Since only forty were necessary for a quorum the House of Delegates was able to convene on June 7, the appointed day; but they got along without a governor for nearly a week. Not until June 12 was an election held and the choice then fell on Thomas Nelson, Junior, who besides being a prominent citizen, a devoted Patriot, and an old friend of his predecessor, was then the ranking officer of the militia. There is no record of the ballot but the probability is that some votes were cast for Jefferson.[20]

Owing to the scarcity of records it is almost impossible to determine the precise circumstances and the order of events. About a half-century later Jefferson said that he approved of this combination of the civil and military authority in one person, and that he himself "resigned" in order that it might be effected. He was using his terms loosely, and after all those years his remembrance of his own state of mind had doubtless become hazy. Some of his partisans have asserted that his name was not formally withdrawn until after a "plot" to establish a dictatorship had been foiled, and that Nelson was then proposed by Jefferson's supporters in the Assembly.[21] Not long after this session he himself wrote, and within a few years said in cold print, that a move was made to set up a dictator, "invested with every power legislative, executive, and judiciary, civil and military, of life and death" over persons and property, and that this was defeated by only a few votes.[22]

Since there is nothing in the brief official *Journal* to indicate the formal presentation of such a proposal, he may be charged with relying on hearsay evidence and letting his fear of despotism run away with his imagination. On the other hand, there must have been

[20] The outcome of the election is given in *Delegates, Journal,* June 12, 1781. Eckenrode, *Revolution in Va.,* p. 227, says some votes were given Jefferson in the Senate, but gives no reference. The Senate journals have not been preserved, but Henry, *Patrick Henry,* II, 143, citing a manuscript note, says that he was nominated there. John Taylor of Caroline in a rather confusing letter to D. C. Brent, Oct. 7, 1796, based on his own recollections as a delegate, speaks of Jefferson as failing in the election (LC, 100:17217–17218).

[21] Jefferson's statement is in his "Autobiography," in Ford, I, 70. The classic partisan interpretation is that of Randall, I, 346–352, based in part on Girardin's account in Burk, *Hist. of Va.,* vol. IV, which Jefferson approved — in his extreme old age, however. As the term "resignation" was technically incorrect, the same can be said of the term "impeachment."

[22] *Notes on Va.,* in Ford, III, 231–232, and note quoting letter from Archibald Stuart, Sept. 8, 1818. Stuart, who lived in Staunton but was not a member of the Assembly, said that he communicated the facts to Jefferson at the time. The evidence of formal action, however, is insufficient; see Edmund Randolph, in *Va. Mag.,* XLIV, 315.

a good deal of informal talk at Staunton about a dictatorship, and the two persons whose names were reported to him probably participated prominently in this. One of them was George Nicholas, a young man of considerable military experience who was making his political debut as a representative from Hanover County, and the other was the veteran Patrick Henry. The man most talked about as a possible dictator, however, was not the latter, as Jefferson's partisans claimed, but George Washington, and after him General Greene.[23] At this very time Richard Henry Lee, who was not there and did not believe that the Assembly could organize, was proposing that Washington go immediately to Virginia, that he be entrusted by Congress with dictatorial powers, and that when the legislature did convene it be strongly urged to continue these powers in him from six to ten months.[24] To many people the situation seemed to require unprecedented action, and the Assembly actually went a considerable distance toward military dictatorship by vesting Nelson with powers which Jefferson never had and would not have wanted. Furthermore, the new Governor, under the pressure of circumstances, so far overstepped the bounds in the next few months that another legislature legalized certain of his actions after the event.[25]

Jefferson showed no bitterness about either the election or the conduct of his successor, and he was careful not to criticize Patrick Henry in public, but from this time on he was deeply distrustful of him. The chief reason, though not the only one, lay in an action of the House of Delegates, which he attributed primarily to the influence and animus of that wordy statesmen, even though George Nicholas initiated it. After the election of Nelson as governor and before the House authorized the presentation of a pair of pistols and a sword to gallant Jack Jouett, the following resolution was adopted:

> *Resolved*, That at the next session of Assembly an inquiry be made into the conduct of the Executive of this State for the last twelve months.[26]

This event marked the nadir of the entire public career of Thomas Jefferson.

News, whether good or bad, traveled slowly in those days and the former Governor, disabled at Poplar Forest, was off the beaten track.

[23] Henry, *Patrick Henry*, II, 145–148.
[24] Lee to James Lovell, June 12, 1781 (Ballagh, II, 237).
[25] In November, 1781 (Hening, X, 478).
[26] *Delegates, Journal*, June 12, 1781. On Henry's connection with this, see Edmund Randolph, *Va. Mag.*, XLIV, 321.

To that place a letter was brought him by private hands from his recent guest and old friend, Speaker Archibald Cary of the Senate, a more conservative man than he but reputedly as firm a foe of dictatorship. Cary told him that General Nelson had just arrived in Staunton to succeed him, that the legislature at length would give ample powers to the executive, and that a bill had passed the two houses for establishing martial law twenty miles around both armies. He hoped that Jefferson's personal losses from the British had not been as great as reported. Continuing, he said:

> . . . I must give you one more piece of News respecting yourself. An address was ready to be offered the Senate to you [that is, in commendation of him]. What can you think stopt it. George Nicholas [Cary's nephew] made a Motion in the Delegates House for an inquiry in your Conduct, a Catalogue of omissions and other misconduct. I have not seen the Particulars. Your friends Confident an inquire would do you Honor second the Motion. I presume you will be serv'd with the order, as this step Taken I persuaded Winston not to make Motion; I heard something of this kind was to be brought on the Carpit, and if I know you it will give you no pain.[27]

He knew Jefferson well but was very much mistaken about his attitude. Few things that ever happened to him as a public man gave him greater pain. He reflected afterwards that only forty had been necessary to make a quorum and that this particular House was not a genuinely representative body, but there was more bitterness than comfort in the thought.[28]

Not until late July did he do anything about the matter. Though not riding Caractacus by then, he was sufficiently recovered to be back at Monticello, looking things over. The damages there were slight. Tarleton turned out to be a genteel raider; he gave strict orders that nothing was to be harmed, and during the eighteen hours that Captain McLeod was on the mountain he guarded everything with sacred care.[29] It is likely that Jefferson got the actual resolution from the House of Delegates about this time. Three members of the Council who had served with him, including Jacquelin Ambler, did not know about it until the middle of the month, and were then very much surprised. They naturally assumed that it implied censure of them as well as the Governor, and in all fairness it should have. Under these embarrassing

[27] To Jefferson from Staunton, June 19, 1781 (LC, 7:1138). Edmund Winston was senator from the district including Bedford, Henry, and Pittsylvania counties.
[28] *Notes on Va.*, in Ford, III, 229–231.
[29] Jefferson to Dr. William Gordon, July 16, 1788, in Ford, V, 38.

circumstances they wondered if they ought to continue to attend meetings, but, since their absence would deprive the Council of a quorum, they decided to stay.[30] It was after this that Jefferson wrote to Nicholas in pained dignity, asking him to specify the "unfortunate passages" in his conduct which would be adduced against him when the Assembly met.[31]

George Nicholas, a short and ungainly man of about twenty-seven, was not only the nephew of Speaker Archibald Cary; he was the eldest son of Robert Carter Nicholas, the late treasurer, whom Jefferson had known and honored.[32] Before long he moved from Hanover County to Albemarle, and the later history of his family was closely entwined with that of the man whose conduct he now wanted to investigate. He himself, besides becoming so grotesquely fat that he was caricatured as a plum pudding with legs, attained considerable weight as a public man; and in the next decade, after he had removed to Kentucky, he was aligned with Jefferson while Patrick Henry was flirting with the Federalists. There were both personal and political reasons why Jefferson's resentment against the mover of the resolution did not last. At first, however, his pain was not greatly alleviated by the discovery that the intrepid delegate from Hanover was suffering some embarrassment of his own.

Replying to Jefferson's letter in sprawling and rather childish writing, the young man said that no particular instances of misconduct had been specified. However, as a freeman and a representative of freemen he stood on his right to ask the executive to account for the many miscarriages and losses the State had suffered, so far as they were concerned in them or might have prevented them. He was distinctly on the defensive, however, and he spoke of the executive in the plural, obviously meaning to include the Council. He had acted in no spirit of personal pique, he said, and was quite willing to change any opinion he might have formed if it should prove groundless. Since Jefferson had requested it, he mentioned certain things which seemed to require explanation. These began with the lack of opposition to Arnold's raid and included alleged failures to issue timely orders to the militia, along with a few other minor matters of the sort. There was no mention whatever of Tarleton's raid, which ought to have been fresh in a legislator's mind, nor was there reference to the absence of the Governor from the scene of danger at any other time.[33]

[30] *Va. Council Journals, State*, June 16, 1781; II, 356.

[31] To Nicholas, July 28, 1781 (LC, 7:1145).

[32] See H. B. Grigsby, *Hist. of Va. Federal Convention of 1788*, I (1890), 78–79, and II (1891), 281–298, for comments on Nicholas.

[33] Nicholas to Jefferson, July 31, 1781 (LC, 7:1146–1147).

Apparently Nicholas soon withdrew some of these specifications and substituted others. The accusations to which Jefferson drew up detailed answers for the benefit of the Assembly dealt wholly with Arnold's raid. He afterwards said that Nicholas, unlike many other legislators, was not in Richmond in that troubled time and did not realize just what the conditions were and just what was done to meet them. At all events, the accuser appears never to have reflected on the Governor's personal courage, nor to have charged him with general incompetence. Before the Assembly met he must have undergone a complete change of heart, for he then presented no charges of any sort.[84]

The accused said nothing in public and little in private during the interval, but what he did say showed that he was deeply wounded. Early in August he received through Lafayette a belated letter from the President of Congress asking him to go abroad as a peace commissioner. He may have overstated his disappointment that he was unable to accept the post. He wrote Lafayette that he was losing the only opportunity he ever had, and perhaps ever would have, to combine public service with private gratification. But he must remain in Virginia until the legislature met. His immediate task was to show that public poverty and private disobedience, not the misconduct of public officials, had produced misfortunes, and he hoped to find in private life a happiness which was as impossible to the minister of a commonwealth as to any slave.[85] The Marquis was more optimistic. He correctly predicted to the French Minister that Jefferson would accept a foreign appointment some day. Also, while recognizing that the machinery of Virginia government was too rusty for any governor to make it function effectively, he made another wise forecast. To Washington he said: "Time will prove that Jefferson has been too severely charged." [36]

The argument about re-entering public life went on intermittently between Jefferson and his friends for many months. Edmund Randolph pressed him about the appointment as peace commissioner. He still found this attractive, but he had taken final leave of everything of the sort, he said. "I have retired to my farm, my family and books from which I think nothing will evermore separate me. A desire to leave public office with a reputation not more blotted than it deserves will

---

[84] Undated paper published in Ford, VIII, 363–369 n., esp. pp. 366–368 n. The form of this memorandum and of others of the sort (LC, 6:1011–1014) is such that one cannot be sure of completeness. There can be no doubt, however, that the contemporary charges dealt primarily with Arnold's raid. Jefferson himself said that several years later Nicholas made an honorable retraction.

[85] Jefferson to Lafayette, Aug. 4, 1781 (Ford, III, 48–49); Pres. of Cong. to Jefferson, June 15, 1781, and other related documents, MHS.

[36] To Luzerne, Aug. 14, 1781 (A.H.R., XX, 605); to Washington, Sept. 8, 1781, in Gottschalk, Letters of Lafayette to Washington, p. 135.

oblige me to emerge at the next session of our assembly and perhaps to accept of a seat in it, but as I go with but a single object, I shall withdraw when that shall be accomplished." These words distressed Randolph. "If you can justify this resolution to yourself, I am confident that you cannot to the world," he said. George Mason, entirely oblivious of the scheduled investigation, noted only the report that Jefferson was going back into legislative harness and hastened to discuss with him things which must be done and which he alone could do.[37]

He was not present when the Assembly met in the autumn. The Albemarle delegation was then complete, and not until late in November was there a vacancy which permitted his election. The House of Delegates paid no attention to the resolution for an inquiry until about that time, which was after the surrender of Cornwallis at Yorktown and the freeing of Virginia from the dread invaders. Jefferson congratulated Washington on the return to his native State, which he himself had urged so plaintively, and upon the glorious victory which resulted from the co-operation with French naval power that he had long anticipated.[38] These events did not occur soon enough to save his administration from disaster, but they created a state of mind which made an investigation of it seem superfluous.

The House of Delegates had to go through the forms. On November 26 they named a committee to receive and state charges against the former executive. This consisted of John Banister, John Tyler, Turner Southall, Haynes Morgan, and George Nicholas, the original mover — whose fire had quite subsided.[39] The news was transmitted to Jefferson by his friend John Harvie, who gave this encouraging report from Richmond: "I have the satisfaction to find that in the opinions of all men I have converse with, that the administration before the last, is now viewed as having been honorable to the chief magistrate, and preservative of the rights of the people, and the constitution of the land. In short I think, Sir, in no period of your life has your character shone with a superior lustre, to what it will do on your appearance in the Assembly, to which place may your own inclination and the voice of the people speedily send you." [40]

The gubernatorial career of his successor had not been marked by an equally scrupulous legality; but, the crisis now being over, there was no more need to cavil at the conduct of that gallant Patriot and soldier

[37] Jefferson to Randolph, Sept. 16, 1781 (Ford, III, 49–50); Randolph to Jefferson, Oct. 9, 1781 (LC, 7:1162); Mason to Jefferson, Sept. 27, 1781 (LC, 7:1157–1158).

[38] Oct. 28, 1781 (Ford, III, 51).

[39] *Delegates, Journal,* Nov. 26, 1781.

[40] To Jefferson, Nov. 27, 1781 (LC, 7:1181).

than there was at Jefferson's. Thomas Nelson, who had wasted his health and spent his fortune in the "sacred cause," found it necessary to retire, and Benjamin Harrison succeeded him. The committee of investigation had not yet reported and Jefferson had not made his appearance, but on the day that Harrison was chosen he was unwittingly elected a delegate to Congress.[41]

He was on the floor of the House of Delegates on December 10, and within the next two days he voluntarily read aloud the charges he had got from Nicholas during the previous summer and his answers to them.[42] That young man absented himself on this occasion, and nobody else had presented any charges. On December 12, John Banister reported for the committee that no information had been offered on the subject matter of the inquiry, and that in their opinion it had been ordered in the first place because of groundless rumors. Accordingly, they moved a resolution which was unanimously adopted. This was a complete vindication, but it contained an extended reference to popular rumors which the Senate preferred to leave out, along with a few minor bits. The House agreed, and the Senate in turn voted unanimously. As amended, the resolution reads as follows:

> *Resolved*, That the sincere thanks of the General Assembly be given to our former Governor, Thomas Jefferson, Esq. for his impartial, upright, and attentive administration whilst in office. The Assembly wish, in the strongest manner, to declare the high opinion which they entertain of Mr. Jefferson's ability, rectitude and integrity, as Chief Magistrate of this Commonwealth; and mean by thus publicly avowing their opinion, to obviate and remove all unmerited censure.[43]

This was not so profuse an apology as the original resolution of the House of Delegates, and it did not so definitely stamp the censure of the former Governor as undeserved, but it reduced to a minimum the references to rumors and hostile criticism. If the legislators hoped to banish these to oblivion, as presumably they did, they were unsuccessful; they could not control the partisan tongues and pens of the future. But they did attain their immediate purpose. At that place and time they gave Jefferson sufficient vindication.

* * *

[41] *Delegates, Journal*, Nov. 30, 1781. The vacancy in the Albemarle delegation to the Assembly occurred on Nov. 21, when Isaac Davis accepted a position as deputy commissioner of provisions and thus became disqualified as delegate. Jefferson's election to replace him followed shortly.

[42] Ford, VIII, 366–368 n.

[43] Hening, X, 568–569, showing resolution adopted by the House of Delegates and the parts stricken out by the Senate. See also *Delegates, Journal*, Dec. 12, 17, 19, 1781.

The discredit which he suffered among his own countrymen as the result of his governorship has often been exaggerated by later writers. His prestige was certainly not injured to such a degree that he was denied early opportunity to perform important public service. On the very day that he was formally exonerated he declined the appointment as delegate to Congress, and from that time forward it was office that was seeking him, not he who was seeking office. He was persistently reproached by his friends for his successive refusals, and forced to do a great deal of explaining. There is no reason to suppose that he had lost to any considerable degree the good will and the deep respect of the responsible leaders of the Commonwealth.

The effects of his misfortunes on his popular leadership are more difficult to determine. It has often been said that after his term the government of the State passed into the hands of the conservatives, such as Nelson and Harrison, and, since Patrick Henry and Richard Henry Lee had now swung to the conservative side, that liberalism went into eclipse after the "fall" of Jefferson, and, presumptively, because of it.[44] The applicability of these vague though convenient terms to the situation is questionable, and if liberalism was eclipsed in Virginia in this period the primary cause was the war itself. The Report of the revisors had been shelved in the first months of Jefferson's governorship, when his prestige was high; and during the next two years his own attention was concentrated on the conduct of the war, not on any program of reform. This is certainly not to say that he forgot the principles of freedom which had caused him to embark upon the struggle in the first place. But, so far as persons were concerned, the distinction between progressives and conservatives became blurred in his mind as in those of most other people.

It has already been pointed out that his influence was not that of the head of a political faction. Contemporary comments emphasized his impartiality. Toward the end of his governorship his intimate friend George Gilmer, commenting on the election of inferior men as delegates from Albemarle County, bemoaned the rise of party spirit, by which he meant petty factionalism. Speaking of Jefferson himself he said: "The envious only hate the excellence they cannot reach. Heaven inspire every one with that laudable ambition of serving their country as you have done without one self interested motive."[45] Jefferson's influence at this time was owing primarily to his example of patriotic devotion and his many personal friendships, which continued to cut

[44] Eckenrode, *Revolution in Va.*, pp. 228–229. Like many others, I myself long accepted this interpretation without serious question.
[45] Gilmer to Jefferson, Apr. 13, 1781 (LC, 7:1120).

across factional lines. Previously, as a long-range reformer, he had been influential for these reasons and because of the intrinsic forcefulness of his ideas. Such opposition as those ideas (religious freedom, for example) met later, when thrown into the arena by James Madison, was probably not a whit stronger than it would have been if Jefferson had never been governor of the State.

The chief political significance of his troubles as an executive and the investigation of his conduct was not contemporary. Others besides Madison took his vindication for granted, once the danger of invasion was past, and regarded the investigation as inconsequential, except in what it did to his own spirits.[46] But when he became a national political figure, and aroused opposition on other grounds in other places, the old charges were unearthed, wildly exaggerated, and used for partisan purposes. From the political point of view, they were far more important in 1796 than they were in 1782, and they were displayed periodically thereafter. As late as 1805, when he had been four years President, a friendly Virginia editor said: "Among the various charges which have been urged against Mr. Jefferson, the most important are those which relate to his conduct during our revolution. From these insinuations it has been inferred that Mr. J. has neither the spirit nor the talents to conduct the administration of our government. The man, who was unable to discharge the duties of a governor of Virginia, is declared unfit to be the president of the Union." [47]

The degree of Jefferson's success or failure as governor must be adjudged from the facts themselves, as already presented in these pages in what may have seemed wearisome detail. They speak more convincingly than any summary any biographer may make. At the conclusion of the account of this highly controversial period, however, it may be said without much doubt that the most conspicuous failure was that of the government rather than the Governor. The agencies which had been created in 1776 were ill-suited to the conduct of a war, or to the meeting of serious crises of any sort. This was a major lesson of the entire American Revolution.

Jefferson's position on the important question of the organization of the state government will appear hereafter in the discussion of the specific proposals he made during the next two years. He undoubtedly believed that the executive department should be considerably stronger than it was in his own administration, but he was notable in his genera-

[46] Madison to Jefferson, Jan. 15, 1782 (Hunt, *Writings*, I, 170).
[47] Thomas Ritchie in Richmond *Enquirer*, Aug. 23, 1805. In this number, he reviews the whole history of these charges; and in this and succeeding numbers he considers them seriatim, under the title, "Vindication of Mr. Jefferson."

tion for his devotion to the sovereign law. His scruples were something of an embarrassment in such an abnormal period, and his legalistic temper would have been a handicap at any time if he had not coupled with it a genuinely progressive concept of the necessary mutability of man-made instruments. Though characteristically an efficient man, he had little chance here and possibly little inclination to be an effective organizer of administration; and he was made for much higher things than the details he attended to so faithfully in his own person. To say that he was a misfit as an executive would be to say too much. But there were other tasks which he liked to do, and did, a great deal better. For a variety of reasons he was not the most effective of the war governors, but of all the war governors he was incomparably the greatest mind and the greatest man.

Starting Again

[XXVI]

A Philosopher Surveys His Country

JEFFERSON'S unequaled knowledge of his native region was no accident. It was due to the incessant curiosity and the habits of methodical study and observation which he combined with his ardent patriotism. Being the sort of man he was, he might have been expected to learn more about his State than anybody else. There was much that was fortuitous, however, in the circumstances that occasioned him to make his accumulated information widely available to others. Because of the inquiries of a Frenchman he cast this in systematic form and added to it, and he afterwards made it into a book. Never again did this incidental author publish anything which can be properly termed a book. Long before he died, his *Notes on the State of Virginia*, commonly referred to as *Notes on Virginia*, became famous — partly because he wrote them, no doubt, but also because the work was distinctive in itself.

It did not appear in print until after he went to France and entered upon another phase of his career. By that time he had supplemented his materials in order to combat more effectively the erroneous opinions of French naturalists about America — particularly their theories about the degeneracy of animal life in the New World. Our concern here is not with the whole of the long history of a noted book, and least of all with the parts of it which were chiefly designed to correct European scientific ideas. Our interest is in the main circumstances of its preparation, and, what is more important, the major ideas about the Commonwealth and the Republic which were in Jefferson's mind toward the close of the Revolution. He did more than describe his country; he revealed his own thought.[1]

---

[1] The first printing was finished on May 10, 1785, in Paris, when he was minister there. An account of the publication and foreign reception of the book will be given in the following volume of this work, where it can be fitted more read-

He began to assemble the Notes some months before he ceased being governor. He was still exulting over the departure of General Leslie and did not yet know that Benedict Arnold was coming when he said that the Secretary of the French Legation had unknowingly done him a good turn by causing him to become much better acquainted with Virginia. The Marquis de Barbé-Marbois (generally referred to by his American contemporaries as Marbois) was seeking information about the various states of the American Union for the benefit of his own government, and had drawn up a set of queries. These got into the hands of James Monroe's wise uncle, Joseph Jones, then in Congress, and he turned them over to the person in the State who could best reply to them and who also happened to be governor. At the first chance, late in 1780, Jefferson occupied himself busily with the questions, but he was in Richmond and needed his materials at Monticello. He had long been making memoranda about Virginia on loose sheets of paper, which he had bundled together without bothering to put them in order, but he was not able to get at these for some time. When Marbois wrote him direct, and he replied in March, the British had again deprived him of most of his leisure but he hoped to have more before long. This was another way of saying that he expected to retire at the end of his second year as governor.[2]

He got even greater leisure than he anticipated. Besides ceasing to be governor in June, 1781, he was confined to the house after his fall from his horse. He must have taken with him to Poplar Forest his old memoranda and all that he had afterwards been able to collect, and have brought all these papers back to Monticello in the late summer.[3] He did

---

ily into the chronology and can be directly related to Jefferson's numerous other efforts to give correct information about America. The chief study of publishing details is Alice H. Lerch, "Who was the Printer of Jefferson's Notes," in *Bookmen's Holiday* (1943), pp. 44–56. Two studies of the *Notes* appeared after the present volume had gone to the printers. Marie Kimball, *Jefferson, War and Peace, 1776 to 1784* (New York, Coward-McCann, 1947), ch. XI, drawing extensively on manuscript sources, gives the whole history of the work. Ruth Henline, "A Study of *Notes on the State of Virginia* as an Evidence of Jefferson's Reaction against the Theories of the French Naturalists," *Va. Mag.*, LV, 233–246 (July, 1947), is based primarily on the book itself and deals suggestively with matters I speak of only briefly here.

[2] To Chevalier D'Anmours, French vice-consul in Virginia, Nov. 30, 1780, LC, 6:993; "Autobiography," Ford, I, 85; to Marbois, Mar. 4, 1781, Ford, III, 68, replying to a letter of Feb. 5, 1781. Presumably, Jones handed the questions to Jefferson in late October, 1780, when he arrived in Richmond from Philadelphia; *Letters of Joseph Jones*, p. 33.

[3] One reason for his lingering at Monticello when the British were approaching may have been his desire to get these papers, or he may have sent somebody back for them before he left for Poplar Forest. They could hardly have been among the books and papers of his which were removed at some time to Augusta County

the actual writing quickly and could have dispatched his replies to Marbois before fall. However, he hoped to pick up some odds and ends of information at the meeting of the Assembly, much as he dreaded that meeting on other grounds. Soon after his vindication by the legislature he was ready to send his answers, conscious as he was of their imperfection, but, no safe conveyance being available, he committed them to Councillor Jacquelin Ambler. Rebecca Burwell's husband did not find a suitable messenger for an embarrassingly long time, but in late March or early April, 1782, the manuscript was in the Frenchman's hands.[4]

Presumably he received from Jefferson a more elaborate reply to his queries than from anybody else, and certainly he got far more than he had any reason to expect.[5] He had sent out what in modern parlance would be called a questionnaire. Jefferson did not stick to the precise order, but the form of his response and of the resulting book was largely determined by the questions, twenty-three all told. He had no secretarial assistance but he sent copies to various people for comments. Others who learned about the work wanted to see copies, and it was for this reason that he finally decided to print. During the next two years he somewhat enlarged and revised his manuscript, and he thought the lengthy comments from his friend Charles Thomson, secretary of Congress, so important that he added them as an appendix in the first printing.[6] He was eager to get corrections and supplementary information, especially in scientific matters.

In the book as finally published the longest section is the one reply-

---

for safety; the latter had not come back by Mar. 24, 1782, when the replies had already been sent to Marbois; see letter to Madison, Ford, III, 53.

[4] Charles Thomson to Jefferson, Mar. 9, 1782, LC, 8:1220, replying to a letter of Dec. 20, 1781, and saying that the answers to Marbois had not yet been received; Jacquelin Ambler to Jefferson, Mar. 16, 1782, LC, 8:1225, explaining his delay; Jefferson to Marbois, Mar. 24, 1782, LC, 8:1227, describing the full circumstances.

[5] Two sets of queries have been located (courtesy JP). One was sent Thomas McKean of Delaware (Pa. Hist. Soc.). The other, from the papers of Joseph Jones, is now in LC, 235:42226. However, the latter omits the final query, no. 23. Jefferson gave 23 answers, though not in the same order as in these documents. The only other reply to Marbois that I know of is in *Letters and Papers of Maj.-Gen. John Sullivan*, III (New Hampshire Hist. Soc., 1939), 229–239; original HEH. See Marie Kimball, Jefferson, *War and Peace*, p. 383, note 34. Sullivan's relatively brief reply was dated Dec. 10, 1780.

[6] He said that he made the revision in the winter of 1782, but he undoubtedly made corrections and insertions as late as 1784. For convenience of reference my citations are to the text as given by Ford, III, 85–295. This follows the original edn. (which bears 1782 on the title page and is wrongly dated by Ford as 1784), and gives in footnotes the important variations in other edns. The appendix of Charles Thomson is scattered in the form of notes. Jefferson's manuscript draft of the work is well discussed by Marie Kimball, p. 382, note 30.

ing to the question about mineral, vegetable, and animal productions, comprising about one fourth of the whole. This is the natural history section *par excellence*, and it speaks specifically of the theories of the French naturalists, especially Buffon. The strong presumption that Jefferson did most of his enlarging and correcting in this section is borne out by the letters of inquiry he wrote during the next two years and the answers he received. He had considerable doubt whether some of his political comments in other parts of the work would be received charitably by his countrymen, but he was quite willing to make these on his own authority. In matters of natural history, on the other hand, he sought support from observers whom he regarded as better qualified than himself. He wanted to verify his descriptions of "curiosities" and, most of all, to buttress his contention that there had been no degeneracy of animal life in America.

His objects are nowhere better expressed than in a letter to his friend and neighbor Thomas Walker, to whom he sent in the fall of 1783 the portion of his manuscript which he was most anxious to make accurate. "That part particularly which relates to the position of Monsr. de Buffon I would wish to have very correct in matters of fact," he said. Calling attention to the table of animals he had made, he asked this explorer to send him the heaviest weights of American animals that he knew, "from the mouse to the mammoth." Being specially anxious to set his mind straight about the large beasts, he sent to half a dozen qualified observers what amounted to a questionnaire about the moose. At this stage, the bigger the animals the better he liked them, but he wanted precise information or reasonable conjectures. Also, he sought comments on the Indians, and his method of procedure is shown by the free use he made of an answer to Buffon which Archibald Cary sent him.[7]

In spite of his doubts about the adequacy of his information he probably enjoyed writing the natural history section most, and as an index of his position in the history of advancing science many people will find it the most interesting portion of his book. But this was not a book as yet; and that portion was the slowest in completion. Most of what turned out to be his *magnum opus* was tossed off in a few

[7] To Thomas Walker, Sept. 25, 1783, W. C. Rives Coll., LC, kind permission of Mrs. Philip M. Rhinelander, Washington; loose memoranda for the Notes preserved at MHS, microfilm UVA (quotations from a number of these given by Marie Kimball, pp. 270–273); from George Rogers Clark, Feb. 20, 1782, MHS, and to Clark, Nov. 9, 1782, LC, 9:1376, chiefly about big bones and "curious shells." Still later inquiries are shown by such letters as the following: from Charles Carter, Feb. 9, 1784, LC, 10:1638, about a "white negro"; from Gen. John Sullivan, Mar. 12, 1784, LC, 10:1646; from Gen. William Whipple, Mar. 14, 1784, MHS; from John Sullivan, June 22, 1784, LC, 11:1751–1752 — the three last about the moose.

summer weeks and based on materials he had already collected and already understood. It was an *ad hoc* work, like practically everything else he ever wrote; it was unpretentious and unlabored, and at no time was he much concerned about its literary form. But he did more than throw together an extraordinary mass of materials descriptive of his own Commonwealth. He also interjected reflections which gave the work as a whole a philosophical tone, related it to a far larger region than Virginia, and imparted to it a quality of timelessness, if not of immortality. If he was not thereby revealed as a man of genius, he was undoubtedly shown to be a man of most unusual and diverse talent and of unsullied patriotism.

Despite all his recent troubles as a state official, the former governor viewed his Commonwealth with deep pride. Marbois had not asked him to begin with geography, but as the son of a map maker it was eminently appropriate that he should. The vast domain which Virginia had long claimed was shrinking. That very year (1781) the State offered to the Union the territory north and west of the Ohio, though Jefferson himself was back in Congress before the cession became an accomplished fact. The region he described consisted of the present State, along with West Virginia and Kentucky. It was a roughly triangular area, about one third larger than Great Britain and Ireland, as he estimated somewhat too generously. If not quite so large as he believed, it contained more than 100,000 square miles and was considerably larger than any commonwealth east of the Mississippi at the present time. This was an empire state, before and beyond all others. The military impotence of his last year as governor was now forgotten. He was a citizen of no mean country; in population it stood first in the American Confederation, and if its potentialities were not limitless they were immense.

From Monticello he could look into ten or a dozen counties, but some of his countrymen had seen more of Virginia's imperial domain than he had — George Rogers Clark, Dr. Thomas Walker, and George Washington, for example. The only mountain barrier that he had penetrated was the Blue Ridge; beyond the Shenandoah Valley he had not been and never went. He had seen Natural Bridge on his own property. He described this as the most sublime of nature's works, and before he put his Notes into print he had viewed the passage of the Potomac through the Blue Ridge at Harper's Ferry, which he regarded as a "stupendous scene." [8] But he never blazed trails in the wilderness as his

[8] To H. G. Spofford, May 14, 1809, saying that he visited Harper's Ferry in October, 1783; L. & B., XII, 280. To Volney, Feb. 8, 1805, saying that he had not

father had. He gained his knowledge of the outlying region from maps, beginning with that of Fry and Jefferson, from occasional printed accounts, and from talks with Indians and explorers.

The great western country was a vivid reality in his mind, nevertheless, and when he started talking he could not hold himself within the boundaries of Virginia. He spoke not merely of the Potomac, the Rappahannock, the York, the James, and the Appomattox, but of the Ohio — "the most beautiful river on earth" — the periodically flooded Mississippi, the muddy Missouri, the gentle Illinois, the lovely Wabash, and a dozen other major or lesser streams of the wild interior. In the light of his later deeds as President, chief interest attaches to what he said about future commerce on the Father of Waters, namely, that it would be of the first importance. But his comments on the Potomac, and by comparison the Hudson, are worthy of passing note. Through one or the other of these waterways, he believed, the interior could be best connected with the Atlantic; and his local feeling disposed him to recognize the natural advantages of the former. It was more direct, less impeded by winter ice, less endangered by Indians. He recognized that there were real difficulties in getting from the headwaters of the Ohio to those of the Potomac, and he afterwards discussed with Washington the necessity of opening the upper stretches of these rivers.[9] In this respect history proved that he was not infallible as a prophet; it gave the verdict to the Hudson gateway and caused New York not Virginia to be the Empire State. In their immediate setting, however, his remarks are significant in revealing his genuine concern for internal commerce, and also in showing his vigorous realism as a local patriot.

He appeared here, however, as far more than a localist. He started with Virginia but proceeded by irresistible impulse into the vastness of the West. He began by describing the flora and fauna of his Commonwealth and drifted into the broader subject of the vegetable and animal life of the North American Continent, which he compared with that of the Old World. If Virginia was his microcosm it was, after all, a large one; and, since his State was so strong relatively, there was no need for him to be envious of others. Through this wide door he could

gone farther west than Staunton, *Ibid.*, XI, 63. In the legend of the map he afterwards published with his *Notes* he said that for the region west of the Alleghenies he relied on the work of Thomas Hutchins, "who went over the principal water courses, with a compass and log-line, correcting his work by observations of latitude," and that he himself made additions "where they could be made on sure ground." He consulted this geographer personally before printing; see letter from Hutchins, Feb. 11, 1784, MHS. For a good discussion of Hutchins, and of Jefferson's reading generally in this connection, see Marie Kimball, p. 267.

[9] For the discussion in the *Notes*, see Ford, III, 98–100; for comments in his letter of Mar. 15, 1784, to Washington, see *Ibid.*, III, 422–424.

survey the whole American scene and the expanding universe of philosophy.

It was in no spirit of narrowness or uncritical pride that he described his "country," developing in detail the broad outline which Marbois had so conveniently provided. He spoke of its topography and minerals, its birds and beasts, trees and vegetables, its military force, its aborigines, its counties and towns, its legal and educational institutions (with *obiter dicta* about architecture), its religion and manners, its manufacturing and commerce, its revenue and expenses, its histories and state papers. Nobody had ever before given such a description of an American state in such a spirit. This work may be properly regarded as the precursor of the vast library of state and federal reports on natural and human resources which has subsequently been assembled, and in terms of influence it may be regarded as the most important scientific work that had yet been compiled in America.[10] No wonder that historians, from that day to this, have been turning to this treasure house of information and this sourcebook of Jefferson's own ideas.

His comments on the political organization of the State which he had so recently ceased to govern deserve first consideration. Together with his remarks about slavery, which have already been referred to, they constituted, in his opinion, the most controversial part of the entire work. To later generations, who are relatively indifferent to the problems of a single commonwealth at the close of the American Revolution, they will appear more interesting because, in certain important respects, they anticipated later attitudes of Jefferson himself to the government of the United States. After three years as a legislator and two as an executive he was even more convinced than he had been in 1776 that the constitution of Virginia did not provide a genuinely representative government. As he had proposed a constitution before he drafted the Declaration of Independence, he drafted another within two years of the time that he answered the questions of Marbois. This draft was afterwards published with the *Notes* as an appendix, and it may be regarded as a constituent part of that work. It was his answer to his own criticisms.[11]

He now proposed to include within the electorate of any county, along with property holders, "all free mail citizens" who had resided there for a year or had been enrolled that long in the militia. He wanted the suffrage to be extended, not restricted, and he strongly urged that

[10] G. Goode, *Beginnings of Natural History in America*, p. 88; see also comments of Merle Curti, *Growth of American Thought*, pp. 149–150.

[11] It can be conveniently consulted in Ford, III, 320–333.

representation be based on the number of qualified electors in any county. He wanted to remove the inequities of the existing county-unit system, which worked to the disadvantage of the more populous districts, and in increasing degree to that of the regions above the fall-line.[12] Thus he again aligned himself with the upland, mountain, and transmontane country, which was under-represented and more democratic than the Tidewater region in its spirit.

If anybody should be disposed to identify democracy with the dominance of the popularly elected legislature, however, Jefferson was definitely opposed to that. To the theoretical objections he had raised in 1776 he added observations based on his own experience. "All the powers of government, legislative, executive, and judiciary, result to the legislative body," he said. "The concentrating these in the same hands is precisely the definition of despotic government. It will be no alleviation that these powers will be exercised by a plurality of hands, and not by a single one. 173 despots will surely be as oppressive as one. . . . As little will it avail us that they are chosen by ourselves. An *elective despotism* was not the government we fought for, but one which should not only be founded on free principles, but in which the powers of government should be so divided and balanced among several bodies of magistracy, as that no one could transcend their legal limits, without being effectually checked and restrained by the others." [13]

For protection against despotism he relied on the separation of departments and on a system of checks and balances. Ideas like these dominated the minds of most of the framers of the federal Constitution a few years later, and received classic expression in Madison's contributions to the *Federalist Papers*. In one of these he quoted Jefferson's very words.[14] The Jefferson of this period was certainly not one to make demagogic appeals to the ignorant multitude, or to tolerate tyranny in democratic any more than in monarchical guise. His major concern was for freedom as it always had been, and he would not leave freedom to chance but would buttress it by law.

It seemed to him that under existing conditions the department of government most likely to be guilty of encroachment was the legislature. On the basis of his own experience he could now say: "The direction of the executive [by the Assembly], during the whole time of their session, is becoming habitual and familiar." This he attributed neither to ill intention nor to corruption. Nor did he say, as he could have, and as Alexander Hamilton probably would have, that meddling

[12] Ford, III, 222–223, 322–323.
[13] *Notes*, Ford, III, 223–224.
[14] P. L. Ford, ed., *Federalist Papers*, no. 48, pp. 331–332.

with the executive contributed to administrative ineffectiveness and thus endangered the security of the State. He was fuller of fears about the future than of regrets about the past, but he was not specially fearful of disorder. He was chiefly disturbed by the dangers to liberty in general which would result from the probable abuse of this unlimited legislative power at a later time. It seemed to him that the whole idea of a representative republic was imperiled whenever any part of the government assumed authority beyond its mandate from the sovereign electorate. This was the main reason why he again objected, and far more strongly than in 1776, to the framing of a constitution by a legislative body, rather than by a specially chosen convention. In his opinion a constitution was superior to ordinary legislation, and provided far greater safeguards. He rang the changes on this argument for years without persuading his countrymen to call a convention and frame a new instrument of government. This conception of a constitution, however, was the one which came to prevail in the United States.

In view of the painful legal limitations to which he had been subjected as governor, particular interest attaches to his specific proposals with respect to the executive.[15] He did not give a precise description of executive functions. Unquestionably he wanted to extend these, but he was more anxious to guard them against encroachment. He would have left with the Assembly the election of the governor, while making him considerably more independent of that body by giving him a term of five years, after which he would be ineligible for re-election. He recommended the continuance of the Council of State, thus showing that he was still opposed to anything approaching autocracy.

One proposal of his would have obviated the embarrassment he had suffered at a time when the conduct of the Assembly deserved investigation quite as much as his. He advocated the creation of a standing court of impeachment, in which all three departments of the government would be represented and before which any member of any department might be brought on charges of misbehavior. It was a well-reasoned proposal, and it would have served as a constant reminder to the legislators that a good rule works both ways. He devised another check on legislative despotism and unwisdom in the form of a council of revision, consisting of the governor, two members of the Council of State, and three judges. This body was to have the veto power, which he lacked as governor, though it could be overridden by a two-thirds vote. It might have served a valuable purpose in connection with the form as well as the substance of legislation.[16]

[15] Ford, III, 325–328.
[16] *Ibid.*, 329–331.

The sort of government he favored would have been more representative, better balanced, and more just than the one that existed, and it might have been considerably more efficient. Under such a system he himself would almost certainly have been a more effective governor, in either war or peace, and it is a pity that apathy prevented his wise recommendations from being seriously considered. He and Madison believed that the chances of calling a constitutional convention, and of gaining desirable results if one were called, would have been greatly enhanced by the removal of Patrick Henry from the scene. Jefferson continued to guard his comments on the most popular political figure in the State; even when talking about him in private letters to Madison, he had recourse to cipher. He never lost his admiration for Henry's pre-Revolutionary services, but he now regarded him as an ambitious politician, and he was probably correct in believing that any new constitution framed for Virginia while the orator still lived would be bad. The presumption is not that Henry would have tried to create the forms of personal dictatorship, as Jefferson still feared. A more likely guess is that he would have wanted to leave power with the legislature, which he generally controlled. As to orderly and well-regulated administration, if Jefferson's interpretation of the habits of the man was approximately correct, Henry had very slight interest in that.[17]

Jefferson himself advocated a calculated dispersal of functions; and, despite his wartime experiences, he still favored a government which was mild as well as reasonable. Incredibly industrious as he was in person, he had not moved far in the direction of an energetic government such as was afterwards advocated by Alexander Hamilton on the larger stage. He made no special provision for the exigencies of war or other dangerous crises, and he was thinking in long-range terms rather than in those of any temporary emergency. He regarded this sort of civil organization as sufficient for a society already practised in local self-government and which he hoped would be blessed with peace.

He had been one of the instigators of rebellion; and, although he had not become a soldier like Hamilton and Marshall and Monroe, he had gone forth to war as truly as any civilian can. He left no possible doubt, however, that he wanted his Commonwealth and the Confederation to follow henceforth the paths of peace, insofar as possible. "Young as we are," he said, "and with such a country before us to fill with people and with happiness, we should point in that direction the whole generative force of nature, wasting none of it in efforts of mutual destruction.

[17] Jefferson to Madison, Dec. 8, 1784, Mar. 18, 1785 (Ford, IV, 16, 35). Henry was again elected governor in November, 1784.

It should be our endeavor to cultivate the peace and friendship of every nation, even of that which has injured us most, when we shall have carried our point against her." [18]

He was speaking of not merely Virginia but the whole Union, and the ideas he expressed on the subjects of commerce, manufacturing, and agriculture must be viewed chiefly, though not wholly, in this larger setting. He believed it was in the American interest to throw open the doors of commerce and to ask European countries to do the same. He set no goal of national self-sufficiency such as Alexander Hamilton and Henry Clay did later. In order to avoid the occasion of future quarrels with European countries he was willing to abandon the ocean, leaving it to others to bring goods in and carry them away. Such a policy would make America independent of the Old World, he thought, and would have the result of turning everybody on his continent to the more salutary occupation of cultivating the soil. Nevertheless, even before he became necessarily concerned with commerce as a federal official, he was convinced that the full abandonment of the sea was but the dream of a philosopher. Americans as individuals would continue to engage in commerce. Since this would involve them in some danger of war, he recognized that some provision for naval defense was necessary.

His enthusiasm, however, was not for swords or ships, and certainly not for looms and spindles. Workshops of the domestic type he liked; in the course of time his servants and employees made carriages, furniture, and even nails at Monticello. But he hoped that shops of the industrial sort would remain in Europe. The industrial revolution was dawning in England but he did not care to live or labor in that light. With freedom of trade (which he hoped for) a country would be free to make the economic arrangements best suited to its circumstances. The young American Republic, richly endowed with land, should be mated with the pure damsel of agriculture; commerce was a vixen and manufacturing a diseased harlot beside her.

As a realistic farmer, who had observed in his own region the soil-exhausting effects of tobacco culture, he looked to the cultivation of grain crops for the diffusion of plenty and happiness.[19] But it was not primarily as an economist nor even as an agronomist that he assessed the merits of agriculture as a way of life. It was as a political scientist (though he did not use the term) and even more as a moralist that he eulogized the husbandman in words bordering on the poetic and revealing his own deep love for nature. Other men should be rooted in

[18] *Notes* in Ford, III, 278–279.
[19] Reply to Query XX, esp. Ford, III, 271.

the soil as he was, and thus be assured of abiding independence, purity, and strength.

> . . . Those who labour in the earth are the chosen people of God, if ever he had a chosen people, whose breasts he has made his peculiar deposit for substantial and genuine virtue. It is the focus in which he keeps alive that sacred fire, which otherwise might escape from the face of the earth. Corruption of morals in the mass of cultivators is a phaenomenon of which no age nor nation has furnished an example. It is the mark set on those, who, not looking up to heaven, to their own soil and industry, as does the husbandman, for their subsistence, depend for it on casualties and caprice of customers. Dependance begets subservience and venality, suffocates the germ of virtue, and prepares fit tools for the designs of ambition. This, the natural progress and consequence of the arts, has sometimes perhaps been retarded by accidental circumstances: but, generally speaking the proportion which the aggregate of the other classes of citizens bears in any state to that of its husbandmen, is the proportion of its unsound to its healthy parts, and is a good enough barometer whereby to measure its degree of corruption. While we have land to labour then, let us never wish to see our citizens occupied at a workbench, or twirling a distaff. Carpenters, masons, smiths, are wanting in husbandry: but, for the general operations of manufacture, let our work-shops remain in Europe. . . . The loss by the transportation of commodities across the Atlantic will be made up in happiness and permanence of government. The mobs of great cities add just so much to the support of pure government, as sores do to the strength of the human body. It is the manners and spirit of a people which preserve a republic in vigour. A degeneracy in these is a canker which soon eats to the heart of its laws and constitution.[20]

Utopia he did not envisage but a vast Arcadia he did. His concern was less for crops than people; less for the rapid multiplication of numbers than for the preservation of distinctive political ideals and institutions. The ruthless exploitation of natural resources and the extraordinarily rapid settlement which occurred in the United States in the two generations after his death might have been expected to displease him. Also, if he had maintained the temper of his post-Revolutionary years, he would have been fearful of the tide of foreign-born which engulfed the land. He always welcomed refugees from despotism, and he favored the speedy granting of citizenship to such foreigners as should come in; but, on political and moral grounds, he now thought it safer to be

[20] Ford, III. 268–269.

patient about future developments and to depend primarily on the natural increase from the existing stock.

> . . . It is for the happiness of those united in society to harmonize as much as possible in matters which they must of necessity transact together [he said]. Civil government being the sole object of forming societies, its administration must be conducted by common consent. Every species of government has its specific principles. Ours perhaps are more peculiar than those of any other in the universe. It is a composition of the freest principles of the English constitution, with others derived from natural right and natural reason. To these nothing can be more opposed than the maxims of absolute monarchies. Yet from such we are to expect the greatest number of emigrants. They will bring with them the principles of the governments they leave, imbibed in their early youth; or, if able to throw them off, it will be in exchange for an unbounded licentiousness, passing, as is usual, from one extreme to another. . . . In proportion to their numbers, they will share with us the legislation. They will infuse into it their spirit, warp and bias its directions and render it a heterogeneous, incoherent, distracted mass. . . . Is it not safer to wait with patience . . . for the attainment of any degree of population desired or expected? May not our government be more homogeneous, more peaceable, more durable? [21]

He did not speak in this way at the end of the century, when his political foes were advocating a policy of exclusion, and such words as these were capable of illiberal misconstruction.[22] But they show anew that he was more concerned and more consistent about ends than means. He often was conservative in his efforts to safeguard the purity of political society, and as a reformer he was in no hurry.

Even more interesting than his incidental remarks on immigrants (or emigrants, as his generation called them) are those he made on the oldest group of native Americans. He listed tribes of Indians with a fullness and precision which were uncommon in his age, and he discussed the characteristics of the savages with an objectivity which was rare among the philosophers and naturalists of other lands. Nevertheless, sentimentalism blurred his scientific vision to some degree, and his enthusiasm for Indian eloquence caused him to repeat a story which got him into considerable trouble in later years. His account of the

[21] Ford, III, 189–190.

[22] See, for example, the way S. F. B. Morse used them in *Imminent Dangers . . . through Foreign Immigration* (1835); quoted in Thorp, Curti, and Baker, *American Issues*, I (1941), 332–333.

murder of the family of a Mingo chief named Logan, who had been conspicuously friendly to the whites, aroused a more lasting controversy than his strictures on the constitution of Virginia. It was not challenged until the last years of the century, however, and the whole matter then became inextricably involved with the virulent partisanship of that time. Our main concern here is with what he wrote in the first place, and his reasons for writing it.

While Lord Dunmore was still governor, Jefferson recorded in his ever-present Account Book the current and accepted story of the murder of Logan's family. This occurred on a creek which emptied into the Ohio near Wheeling, and it was an important incident in the outbreak of what is known historically as Dunmore's War. He could have heard the story in Williamsburg and read it in the *Virginia Gazette*, along with the speech which Logan made afterwards. Both in this speech and the accompanying story the blame for the woes of the Chief was laid on Colonel Michael Cresap, a conspicuous leader on the frontier whose direct responsibility now seems improbable.[23]

The authenticity of Logan's little oration was not then questioned, and it may now be regarded as firmly established. Since Jefferson's main desire was to perpetuate this, he could not have avoided the use of Cresap's name. Condemnation of the cruelty of white men to Indians was quite in his character, but to him Cresap was a symbol rather than a person. The alleged villain of the piece died in 1775 and nobody bothered to defend him publicly until it was possible to make political capital by so doing. In his sympathy for an unfortunate Indian Jefferson unwittingly took the risk of reflecting unjustly on a white border leader; and, without the strict verification required by modern historical scholarship, he repeated a generally believed story. This he did in order to introduce a morsel of native eloquence which, in his opinion, deserved comparison with any single passage in Demosthenes or Cicero. It was not merely as a scientist or historian but also as a man of humane sentiment that he echoed the lament of the once-friendly Indian: "Who is there to mourn for Logan? — Not one." [24]

[23] Account Book, 1775, pp. 5–7. The story was in the *Va. Gazette*, Feb. 4, 1775, the events having occurred in the spring of 1774.

[24] The Logan-Cresap passage as originally published in the *Notes* is practically identical with the one in Jefferson's Account Book. It is given in Ford, III, 155–157, and is followed by editorial notes relating to the later controversy. In 1797–1798, after two American editions of the *Notes* had appeared, Luther Martin of Maryland, son-in-law of Cresap and a vigorous Federalist, took up the latter's defense in the Baltimore newspapers. Jefferson naturally regarded the action at this late date as primarily political and wisely refused to be drawn into public dispute. However, he sought evidence from various people and in 1800 published as an appendix to the *Notes* much of the material he had collected, along with

He had no thought of future American controversy in connection with Logan's speech, except possibly with those who condoned cruelty to the red men; but he was fully aware, by the time he published his book, that he was inviting scientific conflict with naturalists across the sea. In certain passages about the Indians he was directly answering Buffon, and his exaggerated emphasis on Indian eloquence was part of his larger effort to demonstrate the excellence of what was native to America. For just the same reason he wanted to prove that the animals of the New World were big. All of this harmonized with the task he afterwards assumed in France when, besides being a diplomat, he also served as a minister of information. His scientific work was inseparable from his local patriotism, but actually it was less significant in terms of European controversy than in the light of American developments. We are more concerned with the latter than the former at this point. The spirit of scientific curiosity was arising in the United States, and in connection with this he again proved himself a pioneer.

About the time he wrote his *Notes on Virginia,* Jefferson's long association with the American Philosophical Society began. Eventually he belonged to a vast number of scientific and agricultural organizations, lending the weight of his influence and prestige to them in all parts of the United States, but of all these the American Philosophical Society was the most important and his relations with it were the most significant. It had been established in Philadelphia, then the chief intellectual center, for the promotion of useful knowledge. The wise and witty Franklin was still president when Governor Jefferson was elected a

---

a summary of his own. From this it appeared that the original story was incorrect in detail and that Daniel Greathouse rather than Cresap was in command when the most cold-blooded of the killings occurred. Jefferson did not correct the text of his book, however, and made no unequivocal retraction of the charges against Cresap. Undoubtedly, he still regarded the latter as culpable in general and he continued to give his sympathies to Logan. A more serious criticism of Jefferson than the partisan one of Martin was made considerably later by Brantz Mayer, in *Tah-Gah-Jute; or Logan and Cresap* (1867), esp. pp. 149–156. Mayer cited a letter of G. R. Clark to Dr. Samuel Brown, dated June 17, 1798, and sent to Jefferson Sept. 4, 1798. This exculpated Cresap from the specific charge which had been made, while connecting him with previous killings and describing the cruelties as even greater than had been reported. Mayer claimed that Jefferson suppressed this letter. Ford and L. C. Wroth, in the article on Cresap in the *D.A.B.,* follow Mayer, and they both assume an unfavorable attitude toward Jefferson's conduct in the entire controversy. In my opinion they make too much of the alleged suppression of Clark's letter, for this actually added little to what Jefferson did publish and there may have been some other reason why he did not give it out. He undoubtedly manifested greater concern for historical truth in this confused controversy than his political opponents did, and he showed himself to be more humane.

member in the year 1780, along with George Washington, Marbois, the Reverend James Madison, and other men of prominence or scientific worth.[25] Elected a councillor in 1781, he wondered just what was expected of him, and late in the year he asked his fellow councillor Charles Thomson if his replies to Marbois would constitute a suitable offering to the Society. In his mind the thought had dawned that he had not merely supplied factual information about his State which would be useful to the French ally, but that perhaps he had also made a contribution of a sort to natural philosophy.

The Secretary of Congress had not yet seen the replies to the Secretary of the French Legation, but he thought they *would* constitute an acceptable present.[26] In the light of history this remark may be cited as an unintended but classic example of understatement. Any society in any enlightened land would have afterwards prided itself inordinately on receiving a copy of Thomas Jefferson's original manuscript of the *Notes on Virginia*. Thomson himself, who came to know the work better than almost anybody except the author, soon began to wonder if it should not be given a fuller title. During Jefferson's first year in France Thomson termed it "a most excellent natural history not merely of Virginia but of North America and possibly equal if not superior to that of any country yet published." [27] Soon after this the private printing of the book was finished in Paris. Jefferson did not forget his philosophical brethren in Philadelphia, but they had to content themselves with lesser pieces which he presented to them at a later time.

Unwittingly Thomson understated the case before he actually saw Jefferson's first offering to the shrine of useful information, but no one has better expressed the spirit which animated them both as they surveyed the American scene in 1782:

> This country opens to the philosophic view an extensive, rich and unexplored field [he said]. It abounds in roots, plants, trees and minerals, to the virtues and uses of which we are yet strangers. What the soil is capable of producing can only be guessed at and known by experiment. . . . Agriculture is in its infancy. The human mind seems just awakening from a long stupor of many ages to the discovery of useful arts and inventions. Our governments are yet unformed and capable of great improvements in police, finance and commerce. The history, manners and customs

[25] He was elected a member on Jan. 21, 1780, and councillor on Jan. 5, 1781; Gilbert Chinard, "Jefferson and the American Philosophical Society," *Proceedings*, LXXXVII, esp. pp. 264–265 (1943).

[26] Thomson to Jefferson, Mar. 9, 1782, LC, 8:1220, replying to a letter of Dec. 20, 1781.

[27] Thomson to Jefferson, Mar. 6, 1785; LC, 12:1977.

of the Aborigines are but little known. These and a thousand other subjects which will readily suggest themselves open an inexhaustible mine to men of a contemplative and philosophical trend. And therefore, though I regret your retiring from the busy anxious scenes of politics, yet I congratulate posterity on the advantages they may derive from your philosophical researches.[28]

These were words to warm the heart, and when Jefferson read them he could congratulate himself on his strategic situation. The vexations of his governorship were then over; the military battle for political independence had been won and peace was near; in philosophic calm on his little mountain he could survey a vast unexplored country and its developing institutions. But he soon found out that his period of undisturbed reflection was tragically short. He never lost his observing eye, discerning mind, and enthusiastic spirit; but circumstances forced him to remain an incidental scientist and philosopher.

[28] Thomson to Jefferson, Mar. 9, 1782; LC, 8:1220.

[XXVII]

Tragedy and a False Start

1782–1783

JEFFERSON did not yet know all that the war had done to his personal fortunes, for the time had not come to calculate the full effects of the depreciation of the currency. However, he had speedily estimated the damage which Cornwallis had wrought during the ten days that he made headquarters at Elkhill, when, as Jefferson firmly believed, the Earl had acted in the spirit of "total extermination." Said the former Governor: "He destroyed all my growing crops of corn and tobacco, he burned all my barns containing the same articles of the last year, having first taken what he wanted; he used, as was to be expected, all my stocks of cattle, sheep and hogs for the sustenance of his army, and carried off all the horses capable of service: of those too young for service he cut the throats, and he burned all the fences on the plantation, so as to leave it an absolute waste. He carried off also about 30 slaves. Had this been to give them freedom he would have done right, but it was to consign them to inevitable death from the small pox and putrid fever then raging in his camp. This I knew afterwards to have been the fate of 27 of them. I never had any news of the remaining three, but presume they shared the same fate." [1]

Some of his slaves were still wandering in the lower country late in 1781.[2] The permanent losses in this category were chiefly from Elkhill and Cumberland County; but, if the old-age story of one of his bondsmen is believed, the British carried off a number of the house servants

---

[1] To Dr. William Gordon, July 16, 1788 (Ford, V, 39). He viewed the devastation soon after it occurred, and carefully recorded his heavy losses in his Farm Book, listing the slaves by name.
[2] Wythe to Jefferson, Dec. 17, 1781 (LC, 7:1191–1192).

the Governor had had with him in Richmond.[3] His supply of slaves was not seriously depleted, for he still had more than two hundred, and his very special "people" — such as the coachmen Jupiter and John, "King" George and his wife Ursula, the cook Sukey, and the superior Heming family of "bright" mulattoes — were safe at Monticello after the scourge of invasion was removed. Life there resumed its normal character and tempo.

The earliest important description of the mansion and its master by a contemporary dates from the spring of 1782, when the Marquis de Chastellux, a member of the French Academy and a major general in Rochambeau's army, made a memorable visit to the little mountain. Innumerable pilgrims came thither in later years and many left record of their impressions, and at least one of the Hessian officers had commented on the place already, but Chastellux left the best Revolutionary description. Indeed, it is doubtful if any foreign visitor ever described Jefferson and his situation more aptly. No object had escaped this extraordinary man, said the Marquis; "and it seemed as if from his youth he had placed his mind, as he had done his house, on an elevated situation, from which he might contemplate the universe." [4]

The house "in the Italian taste," though not faultless, seemed rather elegant even to a highly cultivated European. Essentially it had assumed the form which it retained until this same architect and builder remodeled it more than ten years later. The pillars of the two porticoes had now been set. Internally, the major features were the lofty "saloon" on the first floor, not yet completely decorated in the "antique style" which was intended, and the library of the same form above it. The wings were small, and this visitor did not talk about bedrooms. His main interest was in the center of social intercourse downstairs and the library where the master's treasured books were, along with the tools he used so ingeniously. Chastellux saw the results rather than the operations. The Lord of the Manor was fully capable of turning out a bookcase, and, as an old servant said, he was "as neat a hand as ever you see to make keys and locks and small chains, iron and brass." [5] He had not entered upon his most fruitful period as a designer of furniture and

[3] Isaac Jefferson said this in his manuscript Life (UVA), connecting the events with Arnold's raid. His memory of dates cannot be relied on, but from his amusing story it appears that he himself as a child was for a time captive at or near Yorktown.

[4] *Travels in North-America, in the Years 1780, 1781, and 1782* (2 vols., Dublin, 1787), II, 46. (Hereafter called *Travels.*) References here are to this edition, II, 40–46, 49–51, although phrases have been drawn from the French ed., *Voyages* (2 vols., Paris, 1786), II, 32–45.

[5] Isaac Jefferson's Life; see also Randall, I, 375.

domestic devices, but he was sufficiently active in the building of his house for Chastellux to report that he was often one of the workmen. He did not actually lay bricks and set timbers, however, so another observation was more significant: "We may safely aver, that Mr. Jefferson is the first American who has consulted the fine arts to know how he should shelter himself from the weather." [6]

It was the host rather than the mansion that Chastellux was most eager to describe. He did not claim that Jefferson was a "perfect whole" like George Washington, and most notable for the proportions of his character, personality, and physique, but this he did say: "Let me describe to you a man, not yet forty, tall, and with a mild and pleasing countenance, but whose mind and understanding are ample substitutes for every exterior grace. An American, who without ever having quitted his own country, is at once a musician, skilled in drawing, a geometrician, an astronomer, a natural philosopher, legislator, and statesman." [7] Supplementary physical details can be added from other sources. The tall frame of this inveterate student was not stooped from study; he was, as a servant said, a "straight-up man." He had a long face and a high nose; he bowed to everybody he met; he talked with his arms folded. [8] To a stranger like Chastellux he seemed serious at first, even cold; but as soon as he discovered kindred tastes he warmed up, established intellectual intimacy, and displayed enthusiasms which might have been regarded as extravagant by those who did not share them.

One joint enthusiasm which he and his guest discovered over the punch bowl one evening when Mrs. Jefferson had retired, and one which could have been easily ridiculed afterward, was for the poems of Ossian, which were not recognized by them as a literary hoax. Some years earlier Jefferson had described this "rude bard of the North" as the greatest poet who had ever existed. [9] With the aid of a book which was brought down and placed near the punch bowl, they now quoted from these "sublime poems" far into the night. [10] Few of Jefferson's favored companions stimulated him as much in the realm of verse as this member of the French Academy. It was to Chastellux, several years

[6] *Travels*, II, 42. For an authoritative interpretation of Chastellux's description of *Monticello*, see F. Kimball, *Jefferson, Architect*, pp. 29–30.

[7] *Ibid.*, II, 42. For comments on Washington, see I, 136.

[8] Details chiefly from Isaac Jefferson.

[9] To Charles McPherson, Feb. 25, 1773 (Ford, I, 413). He was then seeking from James McPherson the originals, which actually existed only in the latter's imagination and naturally were not supplied; Charles McPherson to Jefferson, Aug. 12, 1773 (LC, 1:81).

[10] *Travels*, II, 45.

later, that he addressed his "Thoughts on English Prosody." His own imagination, however, was not of the poetic sort. He was more interested in the rules of accent and measure than in mere felicity of phrase, just as he was more disposed to date the blooming of the narcissus, the feathered hyacinth, and the hollyhocks in his garden than to comment on the beauty of his hillside scene.[11] The observations he made to Chastellux on climate and winds and natural history were more in character than his punch bowl enthusiasm for the language of any writer.

By this time Jefferson had developed his deer park in a lordly style, but his visitor judged him to be no sportsman; on the contrary, he amused himself by feeding the tamed animals from his hand with Indian corn. This was a pleasing picture to transmit to posterity, but the pity is that Chastellux did not give equal space to Mrs. Jefferson and the children. He contented himself with describing her as mild and amiable and them as charming. He reported that she was expected every moment to "lie in," and thus make another addition to the human stock at Monticello.

There were still only two little Jeffersons: Martha or Patsy who was in her tenth year, and Mary or Polly in her fourth. Early in May, after Chastellux had gone off to Natural Bridge, another girl arrived. She was given the same name, Lucy Elizabeth, that had been borne briefly by the daughter who died in Richmond about a year before. Meanwhile, Jefferson had taken his sister Martha, widow of Dabney Carr, and her six children into his family. For upwards of a year he had been teaching the eldest, who came nearer being his son than any other surviving person, and he had been able to give him more attention lately. Peter Carr was reading Virgil and about to start French. Two other boys were coming along, and all of them were of "very hopeful genius," he said. They must not be abandoned to nature. Also, there were three girls who were now regarded as marriageable and were approaching an expensive period. He really had nine children, all told, and he believed that he owed them a great deal of time and attention.[12]

The presence of his sister Carr was doubly welcome at the time of his wife's *accouchement*. He anticipated this with grave forebodings, and it would have been accepted as a sufficient explanation of his refusal at this time to be drawn back into the public service. But he did not

[11] For the "Thoughts on English Prosody," written in France, see L. & B., XVIII, 415–451; for his calendar of the bloom of the flowers in 1782, see *Garden Book*, p. 94.

[12] To Overton Carr, Mar. 16, 1782 (LC, 8:1223–1224).

avail himself of this ready excuse — partly, we may presume, because of his extreme reluctance to air his personal affairs, partly because this might have been regarded as only a temporary disqualification, partly, it may be, because anxiety had already blurred his judgment. Therefore, while his adored wife lay on what proved to be her death bed he was drawn into painful correspondence which should have been avoided.

Two days before his daughter was born he wrote to the Speaker of the House of Delegates, abruptly declining the office of delegate for his County to which he had recently been elected.[13] It may be assumed that he had not been present at the meeting of the freeholders, and that if they were aware of his reluctance to serve they believed that his objections could be eventually overborne. James Monroe, who had just been elected to the same body from another county, was in Richmond, anxiously awaiting his arrival; and, when he did not come, Monroe as a friend informed him of the state of opinion at the capital. It was said that his fellow citizens of Albemarle had elected him previously to gratify him (in order that he might attend the Assembly and defend himself), and that they had now elected him to gratify themselves. One good turn deserved another, and he was accused of showing a selfish spirit in refusing this service to his county and country.[14]

Speaker John Tyler, who had laid Jefferson's letter before the House, also applied polite pressure, reporting that the members did not think the acceptance of the resignation was warranted, and saying that he would be glad to yield his own office to him, since he could fill it with more propriety. "I suppose your [reasons] are weighty," he continued, "yet I would suggest that good and able men had better govern than be governed, since tis possible, indeed highly probable, that if the able and good withdraw themselves from society, the venal and ignorant will succeed. . . . In times of peace men of moderate abilities perhaps might conduct the affairs of the state, but at this time when the Republic wants to be organized and requires but your influence to promote this desirable end, I can not but think the House may insist upon you to give attendance without incurring the censure of being rigid."[15]

Nothing was said here about Mrs. Jefferson's illness. He himself described it to Monroe as dangerous two weeks after he wrote the Speaker. He mentioned it towards the end of a long letter, almost casually, almost as though he hated to admit the fact; but this extraordi-

[13] To the Speaker, May 6, 1782 (LC, 8:1232).

[14] Monroe to Jefferson, May 6, 11, 1782 (Hamilton, I, 15–16).

[15] Tyler to Jefferson, May 16, 1782 (LC, 8:1235–1236).

nary communication cannot be understood except on the background of extreme anxiety. His natural sensitivity had been abnormally heightened, and he explained with painful elaboration the reasons why he was adamant in his determination to retire wholly from public life. Then he drew around himself a mantle of impenetrable silence; so far as is known he wrote no more letters for four months.[16]

"Before I ventured to declare to my countrymen my determination to retire from public employment," he wrote to James Monroe, "I examined well my heart to know whether it were thoroughly cured of every principle of political ambition, whether no lurking particle remained which might leave me uneasy when reduced within the limits of mere private life. I became satisfied that every fibre of that passion was thoroughly eradicated." This is one of the few admissions he ever made that at one time he craved public honor. "I considered," he said, "that I had been thirteen years engaged in public service, that during that time I had so totally abandoned all attention to my private affairs as to permit them to run into great disorder and ruin, that I had now a family advanced in years which require my attention and instruction, that to these were added the hopeful offspring of a deceased friend [Dabney Carr] whose memory must be ever dear to me." All of this was normal and human enough but he began to appear morbid when he referred to the public ingratitude he had experienced. "I had been so far from gaining the affection of my countrymen, which was the only reward I ever asked or could have felt, that I had even lost the small estimation I before possessed." He admitted that the representatives of the people afterwards relieved him of blame; but in the meantime he had "stood arraigned for treason of the heart and not merely weakness of the head"; and these injuries had inflicted a wound on his spirit which only the grave could heal.

Anyone who took his words at their face value would have believed him wholly unforgiving. On the other hand, almost any normal person would have interpreted the present attitude of the legislators — their insistence that he join them again — as a sign that they wanted to forget all the criticisms of him in the past. Nor was there occasion for him to go into legalities, as he proceeded to do, in the effort to determine whether or not the state might *require* public services of its citizens through an indefinite period. There was no reason for him to add, as a bitter afterthought, that he had received a sufficient indication that

[16] To Monroe, May 20, 1782 (Ford, III, 56–60). Randall, I, 381 *n*, says there were no more letters for six months. There was one on Sept. 22, 1782 (see Ford, III, 60) and there may have been others, but to all practical purposes he ceased to write.

he would not be oppressed with perpetual service. It would have been quite enough to say that, having spent the best part of his life in public pursuits, he hoped to pass the rest of it in private quiet.

There is no way of determining just how many of the leaders of the State knew about this bitter letter. Madison, who was in Philadelphia, was imperfectly informed of Jefferson's private situation, but he learned of his general attitude and commented unfavorably on it. "Great as my partiality is to Mr. Jefferson," he said, "the mode in which he seems determined to revenge the wrong received from his country does not appear to me to be dictated either by philosophy or patriotism." [17] Upon the face of the matter the judgment was undeniably just, but Monroe was in better position to serve as an understanding friend. Distressed by the news about Mrs. Jefferson, who had been very kind to him, and by the even more alarming reports of her condition which were now circulating in Richmond, he contented himself with an expression of deep sympathy, leaving the question of his mentor's "retreat" from the public service to the arbitrament of time. Jefferson himself, crazed by anxiety, was wholly unresponsive. Under normal circumstances he would have been much pleased to learn that Monroe had been elected to the Council, but he was in no mood to give the advice requested "on every subject of any consequence." To him nothing mattered but what should occur at home. [18]

It was not until September 6, 1782, that he recorded the saddest of all the items in his incredible Account Book: "My dear wife died this day at 11:45 A.M." He did not gratify the curiosity of posterity by leaving a description of the scene. In the slave quarters it was remembered that the house servants were allowed to file in before the end; and in the family they recalled that Mrs. Eppes was there, along with Mrs. Carr. The recollections of Patsy Jefferson from a time when she was ten constitute the major source of information. She remembered that for four months her father shared with his sister and his sister-in-law the task of nursing, always remaining within call; that he was led from the room almost insensible just before his wife died and that this strong man then fainted; that he kept his own room for three weeks afterwards, Patsy herself being continuously by his side. Then he began to ride incessantly, and by mid-October he emerged from a "stupor of mind" which had rendered him "as dead to the world as she was whose loss occasioned it." [19]

---

[17] Madison to Edmund Randolph, June 11, 1782 (Hunt, *Writings*, I, 207-208).
[18] Monroe to Jefferson, June 28, 1782 (Hamilton, I, 17-19).
[19] The recollections of his daughter are in Randall, I, 382; another story is in

He found an epitaph for her in the Iliad. This he used for other reasons than the display of classical learning; he thereby revealed his devotion to the initiated while veiling it from the vulgar gaze.[20] In the same spirit of jealous delicacy he carefully preserved and deeply cherished small souvenirs of his dead wife, but eventually he also saw to it that none of their letters should ever be open to prying eyes. No one realized more than he that full details of public conduct must be ultimately revealed, but he was determined that the sacred intimacies of a lover and husband should remain inviolate. His wife did not belong to posterity; she belonged to him.

Because of this impenetrable silence on his part, probably we shall never know much about Martha Wayles Jefferson and her life with him. Such contemporary comments by others as have survived leave no doubt that she was musical and a few of them suggest gaiety of spirit, but the last ones refer to her gentleness, even to her saintliness. Normally she was stricter with the children than he was, though she probably grew milder as she weakened. Toward them as they grew older he was rigorous in moral and intellectual matters but otherwise indulgent, and towards her it may be safely assumed that he was always gentle. He was strongly possessive, nevertheless. He had no advanced ideas about women, and something more than jocularity may be perceived in his later remark to his sister-in-law about her woman's "trade."[21] His own wife engaged in it far beyond her strength. She gave him six children in ten years, after having already borne one to her first husband. The effort was out of all proportion to the lasting results, for only two of them attained maturity. Experiences of this sort were common enough among the gentry at that time, but the widower could hardly have avoided the poignant reflection that he had asked far too much of her and that her love for him was her undoing. She had not reached the age of thirty-four. He himself was now only thirty-nine but, much as he craved affection, he never looked for another wife.

Even if he had not suffered this irreparable loss, Jefferson could scarcely have failed to return at some time to the public life he had renounced. But he would hardly have done so just when he did. In

Pierson, *Jefferson at Monticello*, pp. 106–107. The final and now-familiar quotation is from Jefferson's letter to Chastellux, Nov. 26, 1782 (Ford, III, 64), replying to one he received Oct. 17.

[20] The Greek epitaph, with Pope's rendering, is in Randall, I, 383. See also the sensitive comment of Tucker in the note.

[21] To Mrs. Eppes, July 12, 1788 (*Domestic Life*, p. 137).

his mind personal grief quickly swallowed up the pain he had suffered at the hands of his countrymen and made that seem a minor concern. Politicians tried to reopen old wounds at a much later time, but he himself could look back on the years before his wife's death through the haze of sentimental memory and regard them as the most blessed in his life. Thus he wrote to a friend of his youth after he had gone to France: "My history . . . would have been as happy a one as I could have asked, could the subjects of my affection have been immortal. But all the favors of fortune have been embittered by private losses." [22] He rarely mentioned public misfortunes to anybody during the rest of this decade. The public wound had healed and he wasted little time looking at the scar.

Madison took the initiative in getting the once-embittered Governor back into affairs of state, by moving in Congress the renewal of Jefferson's appointment as a member of the commission to negotiate peace. He had been elected to this position a year and a half before, along with Adams, John Jay, Franklin, and Henry Laurens; and in declining it he had expressed deep regret that he could not avail himself of the opportunity to see at close hand the countries of Europe which he had hitherto admired from afar.[23] Even then he felt no such distaste for service abroad as he did for the public business of his Commonwealth; he had had much too large a dose of that.

Although Cornwallis had surrendered since that summer and the war was virtually ended, peace had not yet been declared and negotiations were still going on. Two months after his wife's death it was thought in Congress that the reasons for Jefferson's original appointment still obtained. A prominent consideration in the minds of the Virginians was the protection of Southern interests, and they believed that his presence was the more desirable since Laurens would probably be unable to participate. That commissioner unluckily became a prisoner of war, and, though he was eventually released from the Tower of London and went to Paris, he actually served there for only a couple of days. Other delegates, besides Virginians and Southerners, thought it desirable to send fresh advices by Jefferson's hand, and nobody raised any objection to the renewal of his appointment.[24]

If this action seemed to Congress eminently fitting, it came to Jefferson as a godsend. His cherished plans to seek satisfaction and happiness

[22] To Elizabeth Blair Thompson, Jan. 19, 1787; Bixby, p. 21.
[23] To Lafayette, Aug. 4, 1781 (Ford, III, 48–49).
[24] Madison to Edmund Randolph, Nov. 12, 1782 (Burnett, *Letters*, VI, 539); Madison's "Notes on Debates," Nov. 12, 1782 (Hunt, *Writings*, I, 259–260).

in philosophical activities in the bosom of his family had been shattered; he welcomed for once the chance to get away from Monticello, where he believed he could never be so happy again; and, although Richmond and the Assembly did not allure him, the vaunted scene of Europe did. Toward the end of November, therefore, he accepted the appointment. He thought there was some chance to reach Philadelphia in time to sail on the same boat with Chastellux, with whom he hoped to play chess and talk on elevated themes, and he was sure he could get there within a month.[25]

He was no longer at Monticello, but at Colonel Archibald Cary's Ampthill in Chesterfield County, having his children inoculated against smallpox and serving as their chief nurse. This was a sufficient excuse not to attend the meeting of the Assembly, though his name was still on the roll.[26] His sister-in-law may already have taken the infant daughter to near-by Eppington, and the widower now arranged to leave the baby and little Polly there. He was determined to take Patsy with him wherever he went, and educational arrangements for the young Carrs could wait. He eventually got Madison to aid him in these. Business matters he left in the hands of Francis Eppes of Chesterfield and Nicholas Lewis of Albemarle, and he arrived in Philadelphia late in December, just as he had promised.[27]

It was a year and a half before he left for France, however, and if he had not attained a state of philosophic calm he might have been not only embarrassed but deeply disappointed. The reasons for delay were twofold and little short of contradictory. To begin with, the British had not given him safe conduct across the sea. Congress was reluctant to ask this for fear of a refusal, and the precedent of Henry Laurens was not encouraging. On the other hand, advices from Europe already suggested that his belated crossing might prove unnecessary. The preliminary Anglo-American articles had been signed before he reached Philadelphia and it looked as though he might have nothing to do in Paris but join in the celebration of peace and victory.

Congress still wanted him to go, notwithstanding, and he immediately began to arm himself for negotiation, having no thought of being unprepared. He had plenty of time, for the French vessel which was supposed to take him was not yet ready. Nearly all of the month of January he spent in Philadelphia, associating pleasantly with Madison

[25] To Robert R. Livingston, Nov. 26, 1782 (Ford, III, 61–62); to Chastellux, Nov. 26, 1782 (*Ibid.*, III, 65–66).
[26] *Journal*, Oct. 28, Nov. 6, 1782; Randall, I, 384.
[27] Ford, III, 67; Madison to Edmund Randolph, Dec. 30, 1782, Burnett, *Letters*, VI, 570.

and others who lodged with Mrs. House and her daughter Mrs. Elizabeth Trist. He strengthened his ties with the American Philosophical Society by making a cash contribution; he noted in his Account Book that Dr. Franklin had had another birthday and was now seventy-seven; he bought a chessboard and chessmen, even though he could not sail with Chastellux; he sent messages to the Eppes family and the children he had left behind him; he wrote a little note of appreciation to George Washington, offering to perform personal commissions for the General in the Old World.[28]

Toward the end of the month he spent five days and endured execrable accommodations and society getting to Baltimore, where he had supposed a French vessel was ready to bear him off. He wasted a month in that city, terribly bored as he always was in the absence of employment and interesting amusement. He had expected to sail with the Chevalier de Villebrun, commander of the *Romulus*, who also had the frigate *Guadaloupe* with him, but found that the bad weather had forced the Frenchman to fall down the bay and had cut him off from all communication. About a week later Jefferson managed to get through in a boat, after having been stuck in the ice at the halfway point, but the result of his conference was not encouraging, and he returned to Baltimore. The British, having little else to do on this side of the Atlantic, had concentrated their strength against the little naval force of the French, and it was generally agreed that this was no time to sail. About the middle of February Jefferson got word from Congress that he should not proceed until he received further instructions, and he himself feigned indifference as to whether he went or stayed. Early in March he was back in Philadelphia and there he spent the month. Not until April 1, after he had pressed Congress for a decision one way or the other, was he formally released from his appointment. He then wrote John Jay that he really would not need lodgings in Paris.[29]

His leave-taking in Virginia had been premature, but there was no reason to rush back to Monticello, so he proceeded home by way of Richmond, where he discussed affairs with various leaders. Soon the Assembly elected him a delegate to Congress, to begin service in the fall. The prospect of a state constitutional convention then seemed bright, and one of the first things he did after his return to his lonely mountain in early May was to make the draft, embodying his own ideas, to which we have referred already. This he sent to Madison some

---

[28] Account Book, Jan. 1783; to Eppes, Jan. 14, 1783, Ford, III, 296–297; to Washington, Jan. 22, 1783, *Ibid.*, III, 297–298.

[29] Various letters and documents, Jan. 31–Apr. 11, 1783; Ford, III, 298–316.

six weeks later, authorizing him to use it as occasion offered.[30] The proposed constitution for Virginia showed that the mind of the widower had fully emerged from stupor. He did not let it lie fallow during this relatively inactive period.

In the year 1783 he drew up a catalogue of his library which afterwards became celebrated.[31] Ever since the fire at Shadwell in 1770 he had been assiduously collecting books, and only during his governorship was his pursuit of this favorite avocation seriously interfered with.[32] He maintained contact with booksellers in Williamsburg, made purchases in Annapolis, and established important connections in Philadelphia. We need not linger here to make a detailed inquiry into the books he owned, for they formed part of the developing collection which became a national possession a generation later.[33] We need only note that he had 2640 volumes in the spring of 1783, by his own count, and that he had adopted a scheme of classification by then. This went back to Lord Bacon, and it was continued by the Library of Congress for two generations after he himself was dead.[34]

He was not disposed to leave his books in disorder or to arrange them, as most people then did, primarily by their size. He preferred an arrangement by subject matter rather than one that was strictly alphabetical, for even he could forget an author's name. He found a basis for his system in Lord Bacon's "table of sciences." Following the division of the faculties of the mind into memory, reason, and imagination, he classified his books under the corresponding headings of history, philosophy, and the fine arts. He drew subdivisions under each, making more detailed provisions for works on law, government, and political history than a theologian or physician would have done.

[30] To Madison, June 17, 1783 (Ford, III, 334). He had set out for Monticello from Tuckahoe on May 7. His letter of that date to Madison (Madison Papers, Lib. Cong., 4:17) contains acute comments on various leaders.

[31] The catalogue, in the form of a bound manuscript volume, is in the MHS. It has naturally been dated by the statement in it that on Mar. 6, 1783, he had 2640 volumes. At that time, however, he was in Philadelphia, not at Monticello, and it may have been compiled earlier or later. He probably worked on it at various times, giving considerable attention to the arrangement of his books during the summer of 1783.

[32] This matter is discussed authoritatively by William Peden in his unpublished dissertation, "Thomas Jefferson: Book Collector," ch. 8, which was made available to me through his kindness and that of the University of Virginia. The same author has given a brief account in "Some Notes Concerning Thomas Jefferson's Libraries," *W. & M.*, 3 ser., I, 265–272 (July, 1944).

[33] A comprehensive and highly competent study of his library of 1815 is being made under the auspices of the Library of Congress by Miss E. Millicent Sowerby.

[34] The scheme was discussed by Jefferson himself in letters to George Watterson, May 7, 1815, in W. D. Johnston, *Hist. of Lib. Cong.*, I (1904), 143–145, and Augustus B. Woodward, Mar. 24, 1824 (L. & B., XVI, 17–20).

He wanted a well-rounded collection and listed not merely what he had but also numerous titles he intended to acquire. His library was that of a practising statesman, but he would neglect nothing important in any field.

In later years one of the servants often wondered how his master came to have "such a mighty head." When you asked the master about anything he would go straight to a book and then tell you all about it. He had an abundance of books; sometimes he would have twenty of them on the floor at once; he would "read first one, then tother." [35] We may be sure that the score of friendly volumes on the floor were carefully put back in their appointed places, for Jefferson kept the house of his mind in order. He collected books not merely to own but to use them, and for the same purpose he assiduously assembled ideas and information in his capacious head. He had a rich and ordered storehouse to draw on when, a period of quiet having followed one of sharp tragedy, he turned his attention again to affairs of state. Also, he was thoroughly prepared for the wise men of Europe when, at last, the opportunity for learned conversation with them came.

[35] Life of Isaac Jefferson, UVA.

[XXVIII]

An End and a Beginning

1783–1784

JEFFERSON played his final role in the drama of the American Revolution as a member of the Continental Congress; and his six months' service in that feeble body, ending with his foreign appointment soon after he became forty-one, constituted the closing scene of a notable legislative career. He afterwards presided over the Senate of the United States, but never again was he a member of a representative assembly or any other sort of deliberative body. So far as lawmaking was concerned this was the end. At the last this experienced performer played a stellar part, but the contemporary audience was small and apathetic, the cast as a whole was weak, and the setting was unimpressive in the extreme. During much of the time he operated in a vacuum, for Congress as a working body was often non-existent. At the outset he did not even know where he should go to find it.

When he accepted election as one of Virginia's delegates early in June, 1783, he supposed that in the autumn he would have quarters in Philadelphia, where he could find more kindred philosophical spirits than on any other American spot. He soon learned, however, that the discredited Congress of the Confederation had fled to Princeton, a pleasant but physically inadequate village and not then an intellectual center of wide renown. Nobody knew where the legislature would sit after that. A group of mutinous soldiers who were seeking back pay had precipitated the flight. The authorities of the Commonwealth of Pennsylvania had not provided the necessary safeguards, and there were those who viewed the departure of the delegates without regret. A disgruntled officer said: "The grand Sanhedrin of the Nation, with their solemnity and emptiness, have removed to Princeton, and left a state where their wisdom has long been questioned, their virtue suspected, and their dignity a jest." [1] Even after Congress had been three months gone Dr. Benjamin Rush said that it was "abused, laughed at and cursed in every company." [2] The derided body, being determined to preserve its independence and a modicum of dignity, would not accept the proffers of hospitality which numerous citizens of Philadelphia now held out.

On personal grounds Jefferson would have liked to serve there; he could have lodged pleasantly with Mrs. House and Mrs. Trist, as he had done briefly in the previous winter, and he could have remained near Patsy, whom he had decided to leave in the metropolis in any case. Father and daughter, riding in a two-horse phaeton, reached Philadelphia toward the end of October, and Jefferson went on to Princeton. Congress was still there, but on the day he arrived it adjourned to meet in Annapolis about three weeks later; so, after taking his seat, he came straight back. There was little time for relaxation at Princeton, but he managed to get a shave. [3]

Back in Philadelphia after a meaningless trip, he wrote the Governor of Virginia about the future residence of this wandering Congress. [4] In this matter he was admittedly a localist, though no more so than everybody else. He wanted the permanent seat of Congress to be as near his own State as possible, and he preferred Georgetown to Annapolis, hoping that the commercial benefits would accrue to the Potomac rather than Chesapeake Bay. He went on record at this early date as favoring a Potomac site, and before he ceased being a legislator he analyzed sectional opinions, estimated distances, and considered the whole problem with characteristic thoroughness and realism. [5] He was fully informed on this subject long before he had any occasion to bargain with Alexander Hamilton.

Before leaving Philadelphia for Annapolis the last week in November he made more lasting arrangements for his daughter. It was probably on the suggestion of warm-hearted Elizabeth Trist, who unfortunately

---

[1] Maj. John Armstrong to Gen. Gates, June 26, 1783, quoted in Burnett, *Continental Congress*, pp. 579–580.

[2] Sept. 30, 1783; *Ibid.*, p. 585.

[3] He arrived in Princeton on Nov. 4, 1783; see Account Book, and Dumbauld, p. 230. He voted "no" on the motion that the Commander in Chief be directed to discharge the federal army except for 500 men after the evacuation of New York by the British; *Journals*, XXV, 807.

[4] Nov. 11, 1783 (Ford, III, 340–343).

[5] There are several memoranda on the subject in his papers, as LC, 10:1560–1564, 1600; see the materials printed in Ford, III, 458–463. The precise dates are uncertain but internal evidence indicates the approximate time. These and other related documents for the years 1783–1784 are brought together in *Thomas Jefferson and the National Capital*, ed. by S. K. Padover (Washington, 1946), pp. 1–12.

was soon to leave town herself, that Mrs. Thomas Hopkinson, mother of Francis Hopkinson, took the eleven-year-old girl into her home. She was a widow and rather too old for Martha to regard her as a mother, but this deeply religious lady was obviously of the kindly sort. The circumstances facilitated the friendship of Jefferson with Francis Hopkinson, who was not only a fellow signer of the Declaration but also a musician and author of some note. Separated from her father, Patsy danced out the old year at the home of this gentleman with the young Hopkinsons and the children of David Rittenhouse, whose attainments in astronomy Jefferson so much admired, while her host played on the pianoforte.[6]

This was a circle in which the mathematical and music-loving Virginian would himself have liked to linger, and he took comfort in the thought that Patsy would be more "improved" in it than she could have been at Annapolis with him. He had already planned a serious course of reading for her — not because of any advanced ideas about the education of girls and women generally but because of his anticipation of her future responsibilities. Writing to Marbois, who had kindly undertaken to find a French tutor for her, he said that he had to look forward to the family she would have someday. His comments were not complimentary to his countrymen. "The chance that in marriage she will draw a blockhead I calculate at about fourteen to one, and of course that the education of her family will probably rest on her own ideas and education without assistance. With the best poets and prose-writers I shall therefore combine a certain extent of reading in the graver sciences." The latter would have to wait until she rejoined him, however, and in the meantime he hoped that she would acquire in Philadelphia more taste and proficiency in the arts than she had been able to in the forest of remote Albemarle. Besides English and French, the rigorous schedule he worked out for her after he went to Annapolis called for three hours every day in music, and three every other day in dancing and drawing. However, the Frenchman who had been engaged to teach her drawing, and paid a guinea as a retainer, claimed that she had no capacity for the subject, and he could not be induced to continue. Jefferson insisted that the unwilling tutor keep the guinea for his pains.[7]

He did not reproach Martha but he did continuously exhort her to

[6] G. E. Hastings, *Life and Works of Francis Hopkinson* (Chicago, 1926), pp. 331-335.

[7] To Marbois, Dec. 5, 1783 (Bibliothèque Nationale, courtesy JP); to Martha, Nov. 28, Dec. 11, 22, 1783 (Randall, I, 390-392); Feb. 18, 1784 (*Domestic Life*, p. 72).

strive to be good and accomplished. He insisted on her writing regularly to him and to her aunts, warning her about her spelling — despite the inconsistency of his own. Following a suggestion from Mrs. Trist, he urged her to be specially careful of her personal appearance; he hoped that from the time of rising she would be so neatly dressed that no gentleman could discover a pin amiss. He was a moralistic parent, urging her to obey the inner monitor, the conscience God had implanted in every breast, but Patsy remembered his kindness best. Her father's wanderings were something of a trial to her then and thereafter, but she was happier in Philadelphia than Mrs. Trist had expected. She had inherited his sanguine temperament and she probably concluded that he had made the best arrangements for her a homeless widower could.

Madison, who had now become Jefferson's favorite political companion, journeyed to Annapolis with him but, being no longer a delegate, soon proceeded homeward, stopping on the way at Gunston Hall to find out how George Mason stood on various public questions of the moment. The latter's heterodoxy from the Madisonian and Jeffersonian point of view, which was strongly unionist, lay chiefly in his being "too little impressed with either the necessity or the proper means of preserving the Confederacy." [8] A good many others were now heterodox, judging from the extreme dilatoriness of the delegates in getting to Annapolis. It was more than two weeks beyond the appointed date before enough of them were on hand for a meeting at the State House. Twenty were then present, including four Virginians, but only seven commonwealths had two or more delegates and thus it was impossible to attend to important matters of business, which required the vote of nine states.[9] It was possible, however, to give an audience to the Commander in Chief, who wanted to lay down his sword.

Several weeks earlier Jefferson, who was deeply solicitous for the weary veteran, saw Washington for the first time in seven years, and noted with pleasure that the General had more health in his face than he had ever seen in it before.[10] Jefferson was chairman of the committee that made arrangements for the public audience two days before Christmas, though the report on details of ceremony was largely in the hand of Elbridge Gerry.[11] Congress gave "an elegant public dinner" the day before; some two hundred guests were plentifully supplied

[8] Madison to Jefferson, Dec. 10, 1783 (Hunt, *Writings*, II, 27–28).
[9] Dec. 13, 1783; in *Journals*, XXV, 809–810.
[10] To Gov. of Va., Nov. 11, 1783; see Ford, III, 343.
[11] Ford, III, 363–364; *Journals*, Dec. 22, 1783, XXV, 819–820.

with good food and liquor, thirteen toasts were drunk, and thirteen cannon shots were fired — despite the fact that officially almost half the states were absent. Jefferson may not have been at the ball that evening in the State House, but he was at the audience there next day with the other delegates and numerous spectators. It is said that all of the latter wept when Washington solemnly resigned his commission, and that most of the congressmen did. Jefferson, with customary restraint, contented himself with saying that Washington's address was worthy of him and that it was an "affecting scene." [12]

No one was more anxious than he to do Washington honor, but he was not feeling very well and was deeply disturbed by the state of public affairs. "I have had very ill health since I have been here and am getting rather lower than otherwise," he wrote to Madison on New Year's Day. [13] The health of the Union was worse; Congress was suffering from anemia at a time when there was at least one supremely important thing to do. The peace treaty had been signed on September 3 and delivered to the President of Congress seven weeks after that. It was then learned that ratifications must be exchanged within six months of the signing, but until nine states were represented Congress could not sign. Soon after the first meeting in Annapolis, when two and a half of the six months had already passed, Jefferson wrote to the Governor of Virginia: "I am sorry to say that I see no immediate prospect of making up nine states, so careless are either the states or their delegates to their particular interests as well as the general good which would require that they be all constantly and fully represented in Congress." A week later he reported that the pending departure of a member would leave only six states represented. There was still a chance that somebody would show up in time to get the ratification to England by March 3, but he saw another alarming possibility: if it did not get there on time the British, of whom he was invariably suspicious, might seize the excuse not to ratify the treaty unless the terms were changed. [14] He bore special responsibilities, for he was chairman of the committee on the treaty.

Some delegates, including Jefferson's colleague Arthur Lee and two members of the committee, took the position that the vote of seven states was sufficient, since the preliminary articles had been accepted by nine and these were practically the same as the final ones; some even

---

[12] To Gov. Va., Dec. 24, 1783 (Ford, III, 364); Burnett, *Letters*, pp. 590–591. Trumbull's painting shows the delegates uncovered, but the committee report indicates that they were covered.

[13] Jan. 1, 1784 (Ford, III, 372).

[14] To Gov. of Va., Dec. 17, 24, 1783 (Ford, III, 350–351, 364–365).

said that the British need never know. Jefferson did not believe that this opinion would have prevailed but as chairman thought himself obligated to take the lead in combatting it. He maintained that ratification by nine states was expressly required by the Articles of Confederation, that the other contracting party might reject anything less than full legal action, and that any deception of the British could be properly regarded as a breach of faith.[15]

He fully recognized the desperateness of the situation, nevertheless, and in the effort to get the requisite number of states he made a proposal which now seems ludicrous. It probably seemed much less so at the time. Since Delegate Beresford of South Carolina was too ill to come to Annapolis, Jefferson suggested that Congress go in a body to his bedside in Philadelphia — that is, if the expected reinforcement of another state should come. But this reinforcement did not come immediately, and all he could be sure of was ratification by seven states. Accordingly, he moved that a resolution approved by that number be sent to the American commissioners abroad, that they should seek an extension of time, and that they be authorized to present this resolution with explanations only if a ratification by nine states had not arrived by the latest necessary date.[16]

By these means he stayed the movement for reckless action until January 14, when the convalescent Beresford and two others appeared in response to frantic calls. Unanimous ratification by twenty-three delegates representing nine states followed immediately. There were mishaps even after this action, and the formal exchange of ratifications took place not in March but May. About that time Congress received from Franklin the opinion that no objections would be raised by the British on the ground of delay. At the very end of his service, therefore, Jefferson had good reason to believe that peace had really come.[17]

There was an anticlimactic quality in the final events; and, more immediately, it looked as though ratification would be followed by the peace of death. Two days after Congress acted, Jefferson outlined to the Governor of Virginia the important subjects then pending.[18] He doubted if a decision on any of these questions could be reached, and he believed that this puny body would shortly be compelled to adjourn.

---

[15] Draft of report, in Ford, III, 365–368; contemporary comments in his letter to Madison, Feb. 20, 1784, in Ford, III, 397 (more authoritatively annotated in Burnett, Letters, VII, 447); much later account by Jefferson, Ford, I, 77–81; admirable discussion of the whole matter in Burnett, Continental Congress, ch. XXIX.

[16] To Madison, Jan. 1, 1784, in Ford, III, 371; motion of Jan. 2, 1784, III, 372–375.

[17] On Franklin's communication, see Burnett, Letters, 416 n.

[18] Jan. 16, 1784; see Ford, III, 379–380.

The trouble was that seven of the states were represented by only two delegates each, and any one of these fourteen men by differing with the others could paralyze proceedings at any time. Things turned out to be even worse than he expected, for the gentlemen immediately began to absent themselves and not until six weeks later, on March 1, were nine states again represented. Meanwhile, he was thrown back into another legislative vacuum.

Among the small body of delegates some were disposed to fill this void with pretentious words and petty bickering. If Jefferson's later comment on this Congress is not already a classic it richly deserves to be. "Our body was little numerous, but very contentious," he said, naming his colleague John Francis Mercer as one who was "afflicted with the morbid rage of debate" and "heard with impatience any logic which was not his own." Mercer, who had had Jefferson's guidance in legal studies several years before but who, unlike Monroe, had not become a disciple, once asked him how he could remain silent in the midst of so much false reasoning which a word would refute. "I observed to him," said Jefferson, "that to refute indeed was easy but to silence impossible. That in measures brought forward by myself, I took the laboring oar, as was incumbent on me; but that in general I was willing to listen." [19] Emulating the examples of Franklin and Washington, he laid his shoulder to the main point, avoiding needless and irritating argument. In this very session he wrote to the General: "An experience of near twenty years has taught me that . . . public assemblies, where every one is free to act and speak, are the most powerful looseners of the bands of private friendship." [20] The error of Congress in 1784, he said, lay precisely where it did a generation later — in too much disputation. But how could it be otherwise, he asked, in a body of lawyers, "whose trade it is to question everything, yield nothing and talk by the hour?" [21]

While Congress was marking time so vociferously Jefferson urged Madison, now back in Virginia, to buy some available land near Monticello, as Monroe and William Short, another protégé of his, were going to do. "With such a society," he said, "I could once more venture home and lay myself up for the residue of life, quitting all its contentions which grow daily more and more insupportable. . . . Life is of no value but as it brings us gratifications. Among the most valuable of these is rational society." [22] He was not finding much of it in

[19] "Autobiography," in Ford, I, 81.
[20] To Washington, Apr. 16, 1784; in Ford, III, 466.
[21] Ford, I, 82.
[22] To Madison, Feb. 20, 1784, in Ford, III, 406.

Annapolis. He cast no aspersions on the charming little capital at the mouth of the River Severn, nor upon the inhabitants who, as certain Northern delegates observed, seemed bent only on pleasure, but he had long ceased to be interested in balls or horseraces and at this time he had little stomach for social gaiety of any sort.[23] He sought a retired existence and kept company chiefly with his young friend Monroe. After a time they rented a place and did joint housekeeping, assisted by a Frenchman who must have been a factotum since he was called Partout.[24]

The only other member of the Virginia delegation Jefferson cared for was Samuel Hardy, whose sole fault in his eyes was his excessive good nature. He was sharply critical of Mercer on other grounds than verbosity, describing him as vain, ambitious, and intriguing.[25] How little compatibility of spirit there was between the former Governor and Arthur Lee is shown by a slight but revealing story he passed on in cipher to Madison. "Lee, finding no faction among the men here, entered into that among the women, which rages to a very high degree. A ball being appointed by the one party on a certain night, he undertook to give one, and fixed it precisely on the same night. This of course has placed him in the midst of the mud." [26]

The quality as well as the quantity of this legislative body was low. Said a foreign visitor that spring: "The members of Congress are no longer, in general, men of merit or of distinguished talents. For Congress is not respected as formerly; indeed its influence is feared. Besides, the state governments and the foreign missions absorb the finest characters of the Union." [27] Jefferson's associates were like the short-growth pines in the wasteland outside Annapolis, while he was a primeval longleaf. It must have seemed that his talents were wasted in this vacuity.

Congressional business was trivial, the punch bowls of Annapolis were unalluring, and at first the returns from correspondence were disappointing. He wrote Edmund Pendleton soon after he reached

[23] Among the comments on Annapolis those of Elbridge Gerry of Massachusetts and Samuel Dick of New Jersey are particularly interesting; see Burnett, Letters, VII, 461, 472.

[24] His account with Monroe, as of May 10, 1784, showed that they rented from a Mr. Dulany, beginning on Feb. 25 (LC, 11:1905). See also Monroe to Jefferson, May 14, 1784; Hamilton, I, 24–26. Previously he had been in lodgings. For details see Edith R. Bevan, "Thomas Jefferson in Annapolis," Md. Hist. Mag., XLI (March, 1946), 115–124; and Dumbauld, pp. 56–57.

[25] Jefferson to Madison, Apr. 25, 1784 (Burnett, Letters, VII, 501).

[26] To Madison, Feb. 20, 1784, deciphered by Burnett, Letters, VII, 448; incompletely deciphered in Ford, III, 399.

[27] G. K. van Hogendorp, quoted in Burnett, Letters, VII, 495 n.

Annapolis: "It is very essential to us to obtain information of facts, of opinions, and of wishes from our own country: with this view I have been writing by every post to acquaintances in the General Assembly but never yet have been able to provoke one scrip of a pen from any person of that honourable body." [28] However, Edmund Randolph, the Attorney General, promised to send him "all the intelligence which the barrenness of this place [Richmond] can supply." [29] Jefferson's chief informants about Virginia affairs in this period were Randolph and Madison, but eventually he got letters from others, such as Pendleton and John Tyler, and his attitude of receptivity must have been widely known.

It was also becoming a matter of wide knowledge that he welcomed interesting information and inquiry of a scientific or philosophical sort. He and President Madison of William and Mary compared notes about the temperature; Jean de Crèvecoeur wrote him from New York to inquire if in remote Virginia or Carolina settlements brandy had actually been distilled from potatoes; a fellow planter gave him information about a "white negro"; Thomas Hutchins the geographer discussed with him the periodical floods on the Western waters; and such soldiers and frontiersmen as George Rogers Clark, John Sullivan, and William Whipple wrote him about various matters of natural history, particularly the dimensions and characteristics of the moose. He was collecting his ammunition to fire a blast at Buffon, who had dared assert that American animals were small.[30]

His main business was supposed to be legislative, however, and he was unceasingly diligent at that. In this petty Congress he served on practically every committee of consequence and drafted, as has been estimated, no fewer than thirty-one papers.[31] By March he was at last able to do something that seemed important. In the middle of the month he wrote to Madison: "I am considerably mended in my health and hope a favorable change in the weather which seems to be taking place will reestablish me." [32] The weather in Congress had also improved. Nine states were represented on March 1 and he had turned immediately to the pressing problem of the western lands.

[28] To Pendleton, Dec. 16, 1783, in Burnett, *Letters*, VII, 390–391.

[29] Jan. 30, 1784 (M. D. Conway, *Edmund Randolph*, pp. 52–54).

[30] From Crèvecoeur, Jan. 23, 1784 (LC, 10:1630); from Charles Carter, Feb. 9, 1784 (LC, 10:1638); from Thomas Hutchins, Feb. 11, 1784 (MHS); from Sullivan, Mar. 12, 1784 (LC, 10:1646); from Whipple, Mar. 15, 1784 (MHS.).

[31] The observation and estimate are those of Ford, I, xxviii–xxix. The Papers of the Continental Congress (LC, reproductions JP) confirm his great activity as a committeeman.

[32] Mar. 16, 1784; Ford, III, 426.

On that date the delegates from Virginia laid before Congress the deed of cession of their territory beyond the Ohio.[33] For more than three years this highly important matter had been pending. The original cession of 1781 had been unsatisfactory to Congress; more than a year after that it was formally rejected; and not until the autumn of 1783 were terms specified by the federal body and complied with by the State. The arrangement was not wholly satisfactory to Virginia, for Congress declined to void certain private claims and to guarantee the rest of the State's western lands. However, Jefferson now thought compliance by Virginia necessary, as Washington did, and immediately after the formal acceptance of this princely gift by Congress, he, as chairman of the committee to prepare a plan of temporary government, brought in a report. This was recommitted, presented by him again in a somewhat revised version, and adopted in late April after amendment. It is known to history as the Ordinance of 1784. Its essential features were incorporated in the more famous Northwest Ordinance of 1787, and by means of it Jefferson again revealed his towering stature as a prophet.[34]

The Ordinance of 1784 is most significant historically because it embodied the principle that new states should be formed from the western region and admitted to the Union on an equal basis with the original commonwealths. This principle, which underlay the whole later development of the continental United States, was generally accepted by this time and cannot be properly credited to any single man. Jefferson had presented precisely this idea to his own State before the Declaration of Independence, however, and if he did not originate it he was certainly one of those who held it first. It had been basic in his own thinking about the future of the Republic throughout the struggle for independence. He had no desire to break from the British Empire only to establish an American — in which the newer region should be subsidiary and tributary to the old. What he dreamed of was an expanding Union of self-governing commonwealths, joined as a group of peers.

One important feature of the plan which he now brought forward, distinguishing it from the more renowned but more limited Ordinance of 1787, was its provision for governments, not merely in the territory

---

[33] Rough draft in Ford, III, 406–407. A deed of cession in Jefferson's hand is in The Papers of the Continental Congress. Expanded, this was spread on the *Journals*, XXVI, 113–161.

[34] For the report of the committee (Jefferson, Chase, Howell) on Mar. 1, 1784, see Ford, III, 407–410; for that of Mar. 22, see *ibid.*, III, 429–432; for the general background and events, see Burnett, *Letters*, pp. 597–600.

northwest of the Ohio, but in all that should afterwards be ceded by individual states. He already wanted his own Commonwealth to permit the formation of a separate Kentucky, and at this time he urged a further cession of territory amounting to somewhat more than the present state of that name. He believed that Virginia should draw her boundary at the meridian of the mouth of the Great Kanawha (that is, its junction with the Ohio). "Further she cannot govern," he wrote George Washington; "so far is necessary for her own well being." [35]

In his first bill this far-seeing man drew boundaries for fourteen new states, even though there were only thirteen in the original Union, and he gave names to ten.[36] He followed his penchant for mathematical exactitude by arranging these in tiers. The whole plan was ingeniously logical — too logical, if anything, for this regular geometrical pattern is not pleasing to the eye. It was never put into effect but the present map of the American West suggests that it was influential. In general he translated Indian names or geographical features into classical form, but his list was not liked then and has often been ridiculed since that time. Cherronesus, Assenisipia, and Pelisipia were well lost. No Metropotamia or Polypotamia came into existence, but there is a Michigan for his Michigania, and for his Illinoia there is Illinois. Of his historical names, Saratoga might well have been preserved, as Washington was. All the names disappeared from his second report, though they may still be seen on old maps, and in 1787 it was decided that his boundaries were too small.

The specific provisions for government were not to become effective until after the lands had been purchased from the Indians and offered for sale; and actually they were superseded by the provisions of the Ordinance of 1787. They were chiefly significant in allowing for successive stages of government, and for self-government at every stage. The most striking feature of the report was the statement of the principles upon which both the temporary and permanent political structures of these states were to be based. That they should be subject to Congress and the Articles of Confederation like their elder sisters, that they should be responsible for their share of the public debt, that the various governments should be republican in form — these requirements might have been expected in any proposal of this sort. Much more notable were the provisions that they should remain forever a part of

[35] Mar. 15, 1784 (Ford, III, 421).

[36] The boundaries as they would have been applied within the whole of the territory are shown on the map of David Hartley, from a manuscript in the William L. Clements Lib., Ann Arbor, Mich., reproduced by their permission as an illustration in this volume, facing this page.

the United States, that they should admit to citizenship no person holding a hereditary title, and that slavery should not exist among them after 1800. Since these provisions applied to the territory ceded and to be ceded — that is, to the region south as well as north of the Ohio — Jefferson's ordinance was designed to prevent the spread of slavery as a legal institution outside of the original states, and it would have made secession impracticable if not impossible. Only in the light of tragic history can the wisdom of his preventive measure be fully appreciated.

But Congress struck out the clauses prohibiting slavery and hereditary titles. Jefferson reported that the former was lost accidentally by a single vote, and believed that the latter was dropped because the prohibition was regarded as unnecessary in that particular region.[37] He was quite sure that sentiment in Congress was against hereditary titles because he had perceived strong dislike there for the military Society of the Cincinnati, which had been initiated the year before and was then designed to be hereditary. There is no better illustration of his own attitude than the contemporary judgment he passed on the Society.

He himself was not eligible to this organization of veterans, and the original list of members contained no close friend of his except Monroe. Opposition to it was greatest among men who had remained civilians in the war, and of these opponents Jefferson has generally been regarded as the strongest and most persistent. His reasons were not those of personal pique, however, as George Washington had good reason to know. The General was president pro tem, and, sensing the opposition, he asked Jefferson's opinion of the organization about this time. The former Governor was temperate and judicious in his reply, but he left no doubt that he disliked and feared the Society and would have preferred that Washington not lend his great prestige to it. Also, in calmly stating the objections that were most frequently voiced against it, he not only gave a classic statement of the civilians' case against the military; he showed at the same time the social convictions which dominated his own mind. He was still in the mood of the Declaration of Independence, after all these years of war, and he now realized even more fully the implications of his own famous words.[38]

[37] Jefferson to Madison, Apr. 25, 1784 (Ford, III, 471). A broadside of the final report, with amendments in Jefferson's hand, is in Ford, III, opp. p. 428. He noted that it was passed Apr. 23, 1784, by a vote of ten states out of eleven present.

[38] The whole matter can be conveniently surveyed by reference to *General Washington's Correspondence Concerning the Society of the Cincinnati* (Baltimore, 1941), ed. by E. E. Hume. This contains Washington's letter to Jefferson, Apr. 8, 1784, and the latter's classic reply of Apr. 16, 1784 (also in Ford, III, 464–470), Washington's suggestions for changes, and other important documents with further references. Jefferson's later accounts of the Annapolis meeting are in the "Anas" (Ford, I, 157), and a letter to Martin Van Buren, June 29, 1824 (Ford,

The deepest objection to the Society of the Cincinnati was that it was contrary to the spirit of American political institutions, for the foundation on which these were built was "the natural equality of man, the denial of every preeminence but that annexed to legal office, and particularly the denial of a preeminence by birth." The danger of oppression by hereditary groups in America he believed to be still remote, but only the moderation of Washington, probably, had prevented this revolution from closing, like most others, in "a subversion of that liberty it was intended to establish." He had found that the organization was opposed with an "anguish of mind" such as he had never observed before, and was certain it would never be approved by Congress. It could be made unobjectionable only if modified almost to the point of annihilation.

It never was rendered unobjectionable to him, but Washington stopped by Annapolis on his way to the general meeting of the Society in New York in May, and discussed the matter with him by the light of candles until after midnight. Furthermore, the modifications which the President soon recommended, including the abolition of the hereditary provision, showed the clear mark of this counselor's ideas. Jefferson's own deep respect for Washington had not wavered, and he retained the conviction that the General would have dropped the organization altogether if circumstances had not forced him to accept it in modified form. At this stage Jefferson viewed it as no partisan. He wrote the General: "I consider the whole matter as between ourselves alone, having determined to take no active part in this or anything else which may lead to altercation, or disturb that quiet and tranquility of mind to which I consign the remaining portion of my life." [39] He was firm in his political faith, he was outdoing himself in the effort to be constructive, and he far outstripped his congressional fellows in the daring of his mind, but his aversion to public controversy had in no way diminished as the quarrelsome session wore on.

He made no public fuss about the changes Congress made in his ordinance, but it is likely that he was more disappointed than he admitted. The unamended report got into one of the Philadelphia papers, and, in a letter to Francis Hopkinson which he tried to make humorous, he termed this a "forgery." Beneath his irony, resentment may be detected. The exclusion of hereditary titles and the abolition of slavery in the West were not within the level of congressional politics, he said;

X, 311-313). These are not contemporary records, and it should also be observed that Jefferson's comments on the Society were much less temperate after he became a more partisan figure, as to Madison, Dec. 28, 1794 (Ford, VI, 517).

[39] Letter of Apr. 16, 1784 (Ford, III, 470).

the delegates had no sympathy with such pettyfogging ideas, and he himself was regarded as a daring innovator.[40] But, behind the scenes, he won something of a victory over hereditary titles, and sentiment afterwards shifted in his direction with respect to slavery. In the Ordinance of 1787 slavery was prohibited, though only in the region northwest of the Ohio. Credit for this historic action has been much disputed, but the date and scope of Jefferson's proposal are open to no question and its later influence may be presumed. He himself laid little stress on it afterwards, and his state of mind in 1784 was certainly not one of self-gratulation. He was operating in an atmosphere of legislative futility and nothing was adopted as he proposed it.

His lengthy report on the mode of locating and disposing of western lands, a companion piece to the ordinance on government, was not debated until after he had left Congress.[41] His proposals were not accepted and if he influenced later action on this question he did so chiefly by advocating orderly survey in advance of sales. He advocated the "geometrical mile," subdivided into 10 furlongs, 100 chains, and 1000 paces, on the decimal principle.[42] He was more successful in his attempt to decimalize the coinage.

This was not the first time he concerned himself with the disorderly monetary situation. In 1776 he drafted a report on the value of the various gold and silver coins current in the states, though this was left lying on the table.[43] The question of coinage came up again, before he returned to Congress, and Robert Morris, the superintendent of finance, made a report. Jefferson could not get hold of this but he did see a sketch of the financier's plan, and he submitted to Morris the notes which he himself threw together. He had no hope of action at this session, but he wanted his recommendations to be available at the next meeting, and he had a sufficiently good opinion of them to print them later on, with explanations which he added after he heard from Morris.[44]

Jefferson's "Notes on the Establishment of a Money Unit, and of a Coinage for the United States" proved exceedingly influential, and

[40] May 3, 1784 (Burnett, *Letters*, VII, 511–512).
[41] Report made Apr. 30, 1784 (Ford, III, 475–483).
[42] To Hopkinson, May 3, 1784 (Burnett, *Letters*, VII, 512). In his draft of an ordinance he specified that the geographical mile should be 6086.4 feet (Ford, III, 476).
[43] Jefferson to Robert Morris, Apr. 26, 1784, in Burnett, *Letters*, VII, 502 and note; various memoranda and drafts preserved in his papers, such as in LC, 2:217–221; Wythe to Jefferson, Nov. 11, 1776, LC, 2:312.
[44] Ford, III, 446–457; Jefferson to Robert Morris, Apr. 26, 1784, in Burnett, *Letters*, VII, 502–503 These notes were printed in Paris in 1785.

despite the technicality of the subject, they make highly interesting reading. The unit proposed by him was the Spanish silver dollar, which was already in wide use and of a convenient size. Morris had proposed a unit which was the largest common divisor of the penny of every state and was calculated as the 1440th part of a dollar. Jefferson regarded this as too minute for practical affairs; he saw no use in valuing a horse worth 80 dollars at 115,200 units. Morris later agreed with him on this point and recommended a new unit which would have the value of 1000 of the first units and $25\frac{5}{36}$ of a dollar, but Jefferson thought the familiar dollar much to be preferred. The exact relation between this and gold he regarded as a technical question, and he pressed no precise ratio.

He did insist on the subdivision of the dollar on the basis of tenths and hundredths. Morris himself had proposed that the coins be in decimal proportion to one another, but Jefferson made the argument overwhelming. "The bulk of mankind are school-boys through life," he said. The perplexities of money-arithmetic are always great to most people, he observed, and even mathematical heads welcome the relief of a simpler process. "Certainly, in all cases where we are free to choose between easy and difficult modes of operation," he continued, "it is most rational to choose the easy." [45] He wanted to get rid of pounds, shillings, pence, and farthings; and at a later time he made vigorous efforts to extend the decimal idea to weights and measures generally. He fully realized the tyranny of habit over the human mind, however, and sought to systematize the coinage in the most practicable way. Thus he not only recommended the adoption of the familiar dollar; he also proposed that the subdivisions would coincide as nearly as possible with other well-known coins. The tenth (dime) which he recommended was comparable with the Spanish bit, the double tenth was like the Spanish pistareen, and the hundredth would be nearly enough like existing coppers. There was no close companion to the half-dollar, but the gold Eagle (ten dollars) was near enough to the half Joe and the double guinea to be quickly estimated. Anyone desiring information about the coins in circulation at that time, or about the value of the pound in the various states, will find plenty of details in the notes of this extraordinarily observant man.

In the end Congress accepted the decimal system of coinage without dispute, adopted the dollar instead of Morris's proposed new unit, and accepted most of Jefferson's suggestions about other coins. The main difference between his proposals and those of Morris lay in their more

[45] Ford, III, 447.

immediate practicability. Here he showed himself to be not merely a prophetic statesman but also in the best sense of the term an opportunist.[46]

There was little or nothing of importance in Congress that he did not concern himself with. For example, he reported on the arrears of interest on the national debt and made proposals for current financial operations; he was no ignoramus on that subject when he confronted Alexander Hamilton at a later time.[47] Nor did he need any reminders from his historic rival about the desirability of preserving the Union and giving it visible reality. No one was more concerned than he, except possibly Secretary Charles Thomson, lest the government go by default during the inevitable recess of Congress, and he was the moving force in setting up a committee of states to preserve a "visible head" when the delegates had scurried home, as they threatened to do at any time. Early in the session he drafted a report, defining in detail the powers to be exercised; and, this proving too elaborate, he presented a briefer one at the end of January.[48] The powers of this interim committee were necessarily slight; and, following the Articles of Confederation, the vote of nine members was required for any action beyond adjournment. The committee of states was a weak instrument but there was doubt in many minds whether there should be any instrument at all. It was not created until after Jefferson had left — and, unhappily, it amounted to nothing, in spite of the efforts of his colleague Samuel Hardy, its chairman. The representatives of nine states could not be kept together and there was much quarreling among those who did attend. Charles Thomson wrote to Jefferson in France that he feared the "invisibility of a federal head" would have bad effects in Europe.[49] Franklin, after hearing of the bickering, told Jefferson a story of factionalism in a lighthouse in the English Channel, which was wholly inaccessible in winter. The two keepers quarreled in the fall, divided into two parties one above and one below, and did not speak till spring.[50]

[46] An excellent summary of later developments is in C. Doris Hellman, "Jefferson's Efforts towards the Decimalization of United States Weights and Measures," *Isis*, Vol. XVI (Nov. 1931), 266–314. Jefferson followed developments in regard to the coinage with keen interest while he was in France. The mint was not established until after he became secretary of state, and it was while he was in that office that he was most active about weights and measures.

[47] Report; Ford, III, 434–442.

[48] For the earlier draft, see Ford, III, 388–392; for the one presented Jan. 30, 1784, see III, 392–393.

[49] To Jefferson, Oct. 1, 1784, in Burnett, *Letters*, VII, 598–599. On the whole matter, see Burnett, *Letters*, pp. 607–611.

[50] Autobiography, Ford, I, 76–77.

It was by joining the inimitable Franklin that Jefferson escaped the petty squabbles of the representatives of the American states. The change in his prospects came suddenly, when on May 7 he was elected minister plenipotentiary to share in the negotiation of treaties of amity and commerce with European nations. Congress had been talking about this subject from the beginning of the session. As long ago as December Jefferson had presented a report on instructions to the ministers, and this formed the basis for the instructions which were adopted on the day of his own appointment.[51] John Adams, Benjamin Franklin, and John Jay were already in Europe, and the southern delegates had been clamoring for the addition to the commission of two ministers who were familiar with the commercial needs of their part of the country. Congress had balked at this but was disposed to add one minister; and it was generally expected that this would be the delegate who had taken the lead in matters relating to the peace treaty and foreign affairs.[52] The whole situation was cleared by the news that John Jay was coming home. Congress immediately elected him to the long-vacant office of secretary of foreign affairs, chose Jefferson to replace him in Europe, and adopted the instructions. Unanimity prevailed in Congress and everybody was pleased. A delegate from New England described Jefferson as a "sensible, judicious man"; and the Virginians, reflecting on the benefits of his appointment to the Union, regarded themselves as compensated for the loss of a very able and amiable colleague. Monroe, who was going to miss him most of all, summed things up by saying that foreign affairs were now on as excellent a basis as anyone could desire.[53]

Not all of the Virginia leaders at home were pleased, however, and John Tyler was one who voiced regrets. His comments are the more pertinent because they show just what sort of public servant Jefferson was thought to be. "If it is your wish to go abroad," wrote Tyler, "to be sure mine would be to gratify you, . . . but I know it will be hard to supply your place; for those gentlemen whose abilities are not despisable, are either too sick and indolent to make any sacrifice for the public or too poor to give up better prospects for supporting their families. . . . God send you safe to the destined port, continue you there in health and happiness, as long as you choose to stay, and waft

[51] Ford, III, 355–363, 489–493; *Journals*, XXVI, 357–362.

[52] Elbridge Gerry to Joseph Reed, May 5, 1784 (Burnett, *Letters*, VII, 515).

[53] *Journals*, XXVI, 355–356. Among various letters referring to the matter the following in particular may be cited: Jonathan Blanchard to Pres. of New Hampshire, May 15, 1784 (Burnett, *Letters*, VII, 529); Va. Delegates to Gov. of Va., May 13, 1784 (*Ibid.*, VII, 525); Monroe to Gov. of Va., May 14, 1784 (*Ibid.*, VII, 527).

you back to your native country, where you will always be acceptable to the good and virtuous." [54] The references to Jefferson's character and his disinterested patriotism were typical; nobody thought of him as one who had a political ax to grind or was in any sense a trouble-maker. "Since your departure we have done nothing," wrote Samuel Hardy afterwards. "Congress have been involved in a scene of confusion greater than you can conceive." [55] There would have been confusion had he remained there, but those who knew him well realized that he lived on a higher plane.

The best description of him at this time came from no colleague but from the young Dutchman, Hogendorp, who had such a low opinion of Congress in general. On his visit to Annapolis he had fallen quite in love with Jefferson. "I very soon observed that your conversation bent on serious objects could be more useful to me than that of any gentlemen in town I had met with," he said. "Your making no hyperfluous compliments, your retired life, made you appear a man of business. Even your cool and reserved behaviour prepossessed me in favour of you. . . . With your writing [a manuscript copy of the *Notes on Virginia*] I went on solitary walks in the wood that looks so beautiful from the little meadow behind your house. At the same time I became acquainted with your state and with yourself. I grew fond of your benevolent character, as much as I admired your extensive learning, your strength of judgment. I pitied your situation, for I thought you unhappy. Why, I did not know; and though you appeared insensible to social enjoyments, yet I was perfectly convinced you could not have been ever so. One evening I talked of love, and then I perceived that you still could feel, and express your feelings." [56]

Jefferson introduced this newly embraced friend to Washington as the best informed man of his age that he had ever seen. He had no liking for bickering politicians but he loved young men who were full of enthusiasm, information, and ideas, and throughout life he exerted on them an irresistible appeal. In another letter this one said: "The esteem of a man of your character is a great reward of my endeavors to deserve it, but his affection makes me happy." After his signature he wrote these words: "K. means Karel, that is Charles, which signature if you will accept of I shall employ in the future." He had occasion to employ it again in later months.[57]

[54] To Jefferson, May 20, 1784 (LC, 10:1706).
[55] To Jefferson, May 21, 1784 (LC, 10:1710).
[56] G. K. van Hogendorp to Jefferson [May 1784] in LC, 11:1908–1909.
[57] To Jefferson, May 22, 1784, in LC, 10:1711. On Hogendorp, see Burnett, *Letters*, VII, 495 *n*.

The new Minister did not have time to return to Virginia to see his two little children. Picking up Patsy in Philadelphia, Jefferson set out for New York and after six days went on to Boston. He carried with him the manuscript of his *Notes on Virginia*, having been disappointed in his hope of getting them printed inexpensively in Philadelphia. He also bore more than a score of commissions authorizing him, Adams, and Franklin to negotiate treaties with as many countries.[58] Since he was to deal mainly with questions of commerce, he wisely sought to familiarize himself with the commercial needs of the different localities as he proceeded through the successive seaport towns.[59] He expected to be far more than a representative of Southern interests, and he made a special point of acquainting himself with the needs of New England, which he had never visited before.

He was treated with the utmost cordiality. Leaving Providence, he was attended for a few miles by some of the "principal inhabitants," and soon after he arrived in Boston the General Court of Massachusetts ordered that a chair be assigned him if he was disposed to attend the meetings of the House. Also, a special committee was appointed to confer with him and give him useful information about the State.[60] His time was not wholly given to business, however; much of it was occupied with the hospitalities and civilities of Boston, which he experienced in the "highest degree." His hospitable reception was partly owing to letters of introduction given him by his recent congressional colleague Elbridge Gerry, and before sailing he left as a present for Gerry what the latter described as "an elegant travelling desk." [61] He went as far north as Portsmouth, New Hampshire; and Patsy congratulated herself on having seen so many states. Her father's score was identical. He had missed only Georgia and the two Carolinas of the thirteen.

Jefferson did not regard himself as merely a commissioner of commerce, and was not so regarded by others. Roger Sherman, delegate to Congress from Connecticut, had given him a letter to President Ezra Stiles of Yale, describing him as a gentleman of much philosophical as well as political knowledge, and predicting that his conversation would

[58] More than twenty are preserved, MHS, under the dates May 12–June 3, 1784. Thomson wrote him about them May 16 (in LC, 10:704).

[59] Details of his itinerary are shown in Account Book. Further information about the journey is given in Dumbauld, pp. 57–59, with excellent notes.

[60] June 21, 30, 1784; *Journal, Mass. House Reps.*, 1784–1785, pp. 77, 103.

[61] Jefferson to Gerry, July 2, 1784; Gerry to Jefferson, Aug. 24, 1784 (J. T. Austin, *Life of Elbridge Gerry*, I, 1828, pp. 452–456). His close personal contacts with New England, through the Adams family and others, will be referred to in the early chapters of the next volume of this work.

prove entertaining. So it did. He told the President of Yale about a new piece of electrical apparatus and about the great bones that had been dug up on the Ohio, these marvels suffering no diminution in the telling. He saw the library and apparatus of the College, talked about the state of academic affairs at William and Mary, and impressed his host as a truly scientific and learned man, excellent in every way.[62] It is not surprising that he and Stiles afterwards exchanged long, philosophical letters; and that, a couple of years later, he was awarded the degree of LL.D. by Yale. This honor anticipated by two years a similar one from Harvard, but he already had the degree of D.C.L. from William and Mary.[63] Unlike Franklin, he was rarely referred to by academic title, but Dr. Jefferson was recognized in New England no less than in Virginia or Philadelphia as a leading literary and scientific light.

He arranged with others besides Ezra Stiles to communicate with him about the wonders of natural history. One of these correspondents, General John Sullivan of New Hampshire, writing him further about the moose, expressed a hope which was in many minds — that his success in his new endeavor might equal the zeal he had always shown in the cause of his country.[64] Jefferson himself was using the latter term in its more provincial sense when, on relinquishing his seat in Congress, he wrote to the Assembly of his own Commonwealth: "I have made the just rights of my country and the cement of that union in which her happiness and security is bound up, the leading objects of my conduct." The statement was correct. He had been a good Virginian and a consistent unionist throughout his public life. He made a further observation in a final letter to Madison: "I find the conviction growing strongly that nothing can preserve our confederacy unless the band of union, their common council, is strengthened." [65]

This serious and highly cultivated gentleman who was so averse to controversy continued to view the young Republic as a whole and to advocate the strengthening of the feeble Union, but actually he left his worst fears of disunion and disorder behind him when he sailed from Boston on the good ship *Ceres* on July 5, 1784, at 4 A.M. The contrast which impressed him first and most in the Old World was not between European order and American anarchy, but between ancient tyrannies

[62] Ezra Stiles, *Literary Diary*, III, 124–126; Stiles to Jefferson, July 7, 1784 (LC, 11:1755).

[63] Stiles to Jefferson, Sept. 13, Dec. 8, 1786 (LC, 24:4177, 26:4487–4488); Jefferson to Stiles, Dec. 24, 1786 (L. & B., VI, 25). The date of the degree from William and Mary was Jan. 1783, MHS. President Willard wrote him about the Harvard degree Sept. 24, 1788; Jefferson to Willard, Mar. 24, 1789 (L. & B., VII, 325).

[64] Sullivan to Jefferson, June 22, 1784 (LC, 11:1751–1752).

[65] Jefferson to Assembly, May 11, 1784 (LC, 10:1720); to Madison, July 1, 1784 (Ford, III, 502).

and the political liberties which his countrymen so generally enjoyed. He remained more than five years on the vaunted scene of Europe, witnessed without alarm the beginnings of a revolution that shook the world, and returned home to be embroiled in more bitter wrangles than he had ever known before. But he did not anticipate this when he embarked on the *Ceres* with his daughter, and sailed pleasantly across calm seas. He was only forty-one years old, but a distinguished career of patriotic service and personal achievement already lay behind him, and he thought this almost if not quite enough. He expected more quiet and greater richness in the new phase which had begun.

Appendices

I Genealogy

   A. The Early Jeffersons

   B. The Randolphs

     1. The Tuckahoe Randolphs

     2. The Line of Isham Randolph

   C. Children of Peter Jefferson and
      Jane Randolph

   D. The Wayles Family

   E. Children of Thomas Jefferson and
      Martha Wayles

II The Jefferson Estate

   A. The Estate of Peter Jefferson

   B. Lands and Slaves of Thomas Jefferson

     1. Patrimony, 1764–1773

     2. Consolidation of the Patrimony,
       1774–1782

     3. The Wayles Inheritance, 1774–1800

     4. Losses from the Enemy, 1781

III The Walker Affair, 1768–1809

⌈APPENDIX I⌉

Genealogy

A. *The Early Jeffersons*

VARIOUS efforts have been made to trace the line beyond the person designated in this work as the first Thomas Jefferson (died 1697). Thus Paul Berghaus has compiled a genealogy (copy at University of Virginia) in which he connects the Virginia Jeffersons with the West Indies and takes the name back, through Jeaffreson, to a remote Norman origin. However, the sources seem too scanty and unauthentic to warrant such conclusions.

The earliest dependable sources are the unpublished records of Henrico County in the Virginia State Library. My attention was first called to these by Miss Maude H. Woodfin of Westhampton College, who generously made available her extensive notes on the early Jeffersons before I had an opportunity to examine the materials in person. I have not succeeded in going beyond her in this field and have been able to use only a small portion of the many items she collected. For helpful clues I am also deeply indebted to Mr. Edgar C. Hickish of Portsmouth, Va., whose unpublished study of Peter Jefferson I was privileged to examine in 1941, along with a valuable map drawn by him which shows land grants. A fresh and painstaking investigation was made by Marie Kimball who utilized her findings in her valuable study, *Jefferson: The Road to Glory* (1943).

The net result of all these inquiries, including my own, is to show that the early Jeffersons were rather more prosperous and prominent than has commonly been supposed. In both the unpublished work of Mr. Hickish and the published study of Mrs. Kimball, however, it seems to me that the reaction has been carried a little too far. The financial status of Thomas Jefferson I was modest, and though there are numerous references to him in the county records these are to minor matters. The most important fresh information is that concerning the official position of Thomas Jefferson II, for this identifies him clearly with the lesser gentry.

The following chart outlines the genealogical story of the early Jeffersons as far as it relates to the subject of this work.

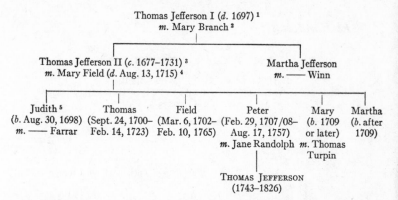

Thomas Jefferson I (*d*. 1697) [1]
m. Mary Branch [2]

Thomas Jefferson II (*c*. 1677–1731) [3]
m. Mary Field (*d*. Aug. 13, 1715) [4]

Martha Jefferson
m. —— Winn

Judith [5]
(*b*. Aug. 30, 1698)
m. —— Farrar

Thomas
(Sept. 24, 1700–
Feb. 14, 1723)

Field
(Mar. 6, 1702–
Feb. 10, 1765)

Peter
(Feb. 29, 1707/08–
Aug. 17, 1757)
m. Jane Randolph

Mary
(*b*. 1709
or later)
m. Thomas
Turpin

Martha
(*b*. after
1709)

THOMAS JEFFERSON
(1743–1826)

[1] Will proved Oct. 1697; Henrico Order Book, 1694–1701, p. 169. Inventory, *Va. Mag.*, I, 208–212.

[2] Afterwards married Joseph Mattocks, Charles City County. Marriage contract, Nov. 16, 1700; license, Nov. 17, 1700; Henrico County Deeds, etc., 1697–1704, p. 213; Stanard, Extracts, p. 185.

[3] Will dated Mar. 15, 1725, proved April, 1731; Henrico County, Miscellaneous Court Records, 1650–1807, p. 849.

[4] Daughter of Major Peter Field and his wife Judith, widow of Henry Randolph and daughter of Henry Soane; *Va. Mag.*, XXIII, 173 *n*. Date of license to marry Thomas Jefferson II, Oct. 20, 1697, date of death from *Tyler's Mag.*, VII, 121. The evidence pointing to the probable remarriage of Thomas Jefferson II is as follows. In 1721, a Thomas Jefferson of Henrico County acknowledged a deed and his wife Ailce (Alice?) relinquished her dower rights to the land conveyed. (Henrico Minutes, 1719–1724, p. 116.) Since there was a similar transaction two years later (*Ibid.*, p. 276), the reference was not to the Captain's son of the same name, who was then dead. No wife is mentioned in Captain Jefferson's will, drawn in 1725. The best guess is that he did remarry between 1715 and 1721 and that he was again a widower in 1725; but we cannot be absolutely sure that there was not still another Thomas Jefferson in Henrico County.

[5] Birth dates for the children, from Judith to Peter from data in an old Bible, *Tyler's Mag.*, VII, 121–122. Mary and Martha are mentioned in their father's will of 1725 as then being under sixteen; the latter, about whom I have no further information, was to be cared for by her aunt, Martha Winn. The name of Mary, who married Thomas Turpin, appears in several places, as in *Two Unpublished Letters from Thomas Jefferson to His Relatives the Turpins*, ed. by Marie Dickore (Oxford, Ohio, 1941).

B. *The Randolphs*[1]

1. THE TUCKAHOE RANDOLPHS[2]

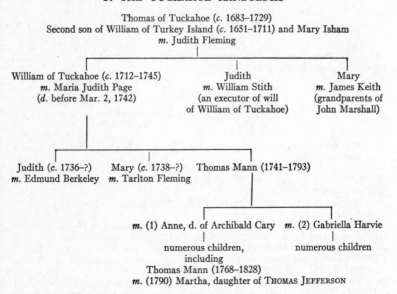

Thomas of Tuckahoe (*c.* 1683–1729)
Second son of William of Turkey Island (*c.* 1651–1711) and Mary Isham
m. Judith Fleming

William of Tuckahoe (*c.* 1712–1745)
m. Maria Judith Page
(*d.* before Mar. 2, 1742)

Judith
m. William Stith
(an executor of will
of William of Tuckahoe)

Mary
m. James Keith
(grandparents of
John Marshall)

Judith (*c.* 1736–?)
m. Edmund Berkeley

Mary (*c.* 1738–?)
m. Tarlton Fleming

Thomas Mann (1741–1793)

m. (1) Anne, d. of Archibald Cary   *m.* (2) Gabriella Harvie

numerous children,
including
Thomas Mann (1768–1828)
m. (1790) Martha, daughter of THOMAS JEFFERSON

numerous children

[1] No attempt is made here to trace the vast ramifications of the genealogy of the Randolphs. On the family in general, see W. C. Bruce, *John Randolph of Roanoke* (1922), I, 9–17; W. G. Stanard in *W. & M.*, 1 ser., VII, 122–124, 195–197; VIII, 119–122; R. I. Randolph, *Randolphs of Virginia* (1931); H. J. Eckenrode, *The Randolphs. The Story of a Virginia Family* (1946).

[2] Chart is based on works cited for the family as a whole, and, in addition: Will of William of Tuckahoe, Goochland County Will & Deed Book, No. 5, p. 73, attested copy UVA; *Va. Mag.*, XXXII, 390–395, containing three photographs of Tuckahoe; J. R. Anderson, *Ibid.*, XLV, 55–86, and *Annual Report of the Monticello Asso., 1936*, pp. 9–35. Further references on Tuckahoe are T. T. Waterman, *Mansions of Virginia* (1945), pp. 85–92; R. A. Lancaster, Jr., *Historic Va. Homes and Churches* (1915), pp. 168–173; Thomas Anburey, *Travels through the Interior Parts of America* (1791), II, 318–319.

2. THE LINE OF ISHAM RANDOLPH

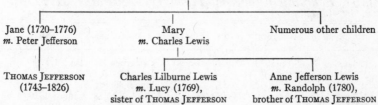

Isham Randolph of Dungeness (*c.* 1685–1742) [1]
Third son of William of Turkey Island (*c.* 1651–1711) and Mary Isham

Jane (1720–1776)	Mary	Numerous other children
m. Peter Jefferson	*m.* Charles Lewis	

THOMAS JEFFERSON	Charles Lilburne Lewis	Anne Jefferson Lewis
(1743–1826)	*m.* Lucy (1769),	*m.* Randolph (1780),
	sister of THOMAS JEFFERSON	brother of THOMAS JEFFERSON

[1] For Isham's inheritance from his father in what afterwards became Goochland County, see Henrico Records, 1710–1714, Pt. I, pp. 215–218. The first grant to him there appears to have been for 1200 acres on May 6, 1730, and the largest, for 3000, on May 4, 1734; see *Council Journals, Colonial Va.*, IV, 218, lv, 323, 349; other grants and patents are on pp. 313, 409. Marie Kimball in *The Road to Glory*, p. 308, note 31, says that between 1730 and 1736 he patented 8800 acres adjoining his original inheritance in Goochland. In my opinion the total of Isham Randolph's holdings in Goochland was smaller than this estimate, but he was unquestionably a large landholder in the county and he received extensive grants elsewhere, whether or not all of these were perfected.

Further details on his service as adjutant general and the surrounding circumstances are as follows: Governor Gooch was present at the meeting of the Council on Aug. 28, 1740, but did not attend again until Oct. 15, 1741. Isham's service as chief military officer, accordingly, occurred between these two dates. On Gooch's participation in the expedition see *W. & M.*, 1 ser., XVI, 18; *Va. Mag.*, XXX, 1–20, 390–391. Capt. Lawrence Washington was the ranking Virginia officer under Gooch, and afterwards named his place Mount Vernon for the commander of the naval forces.

C. *Children of Peter Jefferson (Feb. 29, 1707/08—Aug. 17, 1757) and Jane Randolph (February, 1720—Mar. 31, 1776)*[1]

NAME	BIRTH	PLACE	MARRIAGE	DEATH
1. Jane	June 27, 1740	Fine Creek (?)	Unmarried	Oct. 1, 1765
2. Mary	Oct. 1, 1741	Fine Creek (?)	Jan. 24, 1760, to John Bolling	
3. THOMAS	Apr. 2/13, 1743	Shadwell	Jan. 1, 1772, to Martha Wayles Skelton	July 4, 1826
4. Elizabeth[2]	Nov. 4, 1744	Shadwell	Unmarried	Feb. or Mar., 1774
5. Martha[3]	May 29, 1746	Tuckahoe (?)	July 20, 1765, to Dabney Carr	Sept. 3, 1811
6. Peter Field	Oct. 16, 1748	Tuckahoe	——	Nov. 29, 1748
7. Unnamed Son	Mar. 9, 1750	Tuckahoe	——	Mar. 9, 1750
8. Lucy	Oct. 10, 1752	Shadwell	Sept. 12, 1769, to Charles Lilburne Lewis	
9. Anna Scott	Oct. 1, 1755	Shadwell	Oct. 1788, to Hastings Marks	
10. Randolph[4]	Oct. 1, 1755	Shadwell	July 30, 1780, to Anne Jefferson Lewis	Sept. 15, 1815

[1] Based on entries in Peter Jefferson's prayer book, in handwriting of Thomas Jefferson (reproduced by Randall, I, 17), with supplementary information and minor corrections from other sources. Some of the dates of death are unknown.

[2] The date of the death of Elizabeth Jefferson is taken from Jefferson's Account Book, Mar. 1, 1774, where he says: "My sister Elizabeth was found last Thursday being Feb. 24." The funeral service was performed on Mar. 7. This contemporary record takes precedence over the date, Jan. 1, 1773, based on a later record. Jefferson probably wrote some of the dates in the prayer book from memory, but he was more than a year off in this instance.

[3] Martha's husband, Dabney Carr, died on May 16, 1773. His circumstances appeared modest to Jefferson when he wrote John Page on Feb. 21, 1770 (Ford, I, 373); but according to W. G. Stanard (*Va. Mag.*, II, 22–28) the inventory of his estate showed that he was a prosperous man at the time of his death, when his home appears to have been in Goochland. On Dec. 1 Jefferson paid Dr. Gilmer a substantial bill on account of the estate, to which he was himself indebted because of two substantial loans from his friend. (See account with the estate in his Fee Book.) I have been unable to substantiate the traditional account of the death of Dabney Carr and of subsequent events as given by Randall, I, 83–84. It is entirely possible that the first burial was at Shadwell, and that the remains were reinterred. There is no doubt that the grubbing in the graveyard, described in *Garden Book*, May 22, 1773, was on account of Dabney Carr or that he was the first person buried there. He left six children, three boys and three girls. I know of no precise evidence that they were living at Monticello until somewhat before Mrs. Jefferson's death, and it seems unlikely that room could have been found for them in 1773. The Carrs probably came to live at Monticello by 1781. In a letter to Overton Carr on Mar. 16, 1782 (LC, 8:1223–1224), Jefferson says that he had been teaching Peter for upwards of a twelvemonth. In this letter he also implied that his sister had managed the estate, greatly aided by Sam Carr during his lifetime (see also *Domestic Life*, p. 270). I have found no account of his own as executor. His account with the estate in his Fee Book balanced various payments made by him with his own debt to Carr. In 1782, Jefferson wanted Overton Carr to assume the education of the second son, Sam, and apparently he did. On his own departure for France in 1784, he asked James Madison to serve as Peter's guardian. (See Elizabeth D. Coleman, "Peter Carr of Carr's-Brook, 1770–1815," *Papers Albemarle County Hist. Soc.*, IV (1944), pp. 5–23.)

[4] See *Thomas Jefferson and His Unknown Brother Randolph*, Introduction by Bernard Mayo (Charlottesville, 1942).

D. *The Wayles Family*[1]

John Wayles (Jan. 31, 1715–May 28, 1773), born in Lancaster, England; married on May 3, 1746, Martha Eppes.

Martha Eppes (Apr. 10, 1721–Nov. 5, 1748), born at Bermuda Hundred, was the daughter of Col. Francis Eppes.[2] At the time of her marriage to John Wayles she was a widow. Jefferson gives the name of her first husband as Llewellin Epes, but there is doubt about it and it is unimportant here. She bore John Wayles twins, who did not survive. She then bore Martha, and died very soon thereafter.

Martha Wayles (Oct. 19/30, 1748–Sept. 6, 1782) married, on November 20, 1766, Bathurst Skelton (June, 1744–Sept. 30, 1768), who was the son of James and Jane Meriwether Skelton and the younger brother of Reuben Skelton.[3] She bore him, on November 7, 1767, a son John who died on June 10, 1771, according to Jefferson's memorandum.[4] Martha, on January 1, 1772, married Thomas Jefferson.

John Wayles, after the death of Martha's mother, married as his second wife Miss Cocke, according to Jefferson's memorandum. She bore him one daughter who died and three who survived him: Elizabeth, Tabitha, and Anne.

Elizabeth Wayles (*b.* February 24, 1752) married Francis Eppes, often said to have been the brother of the first wife of John Wayles, but apparently her nephew.[5] This marriage probably preceded that of Jefferson; for the codicil to the will of John Wayles, Feb. 12, 1773, shows that by that date this couple had two children, Richard and John Wayles Eppes (Apr. 1772–Sept. 15, 1823). The latter married Mary or Maria Jefferson on October 13, 1797. Francis and Elizabeth Eppes may have been living at the Forest at the time of Jefferson's marriage, and they almost certainly were for some years after the death of John

[1] This account is based largely on a memorandum of Jefferson, copied in a notebook in the Edgehill Randolph Papers, UVA, which appears to be generally accurate as far as it goes. Supplementary items have been gained from *Tyler's Mag.*, VI, 265–270, containing the will of John Wayles, and from other sources as indicated by the notes. In this connection, Randall, I, 62–63, is rather inaccurate. See also Appendix II, B, 3, on the Wayles Inheritance.

[2] *Va. Mag.*, III, 395; *Burgesses, Journals, 1773–1776*, p. 83.

[3] *W. & M.*, 1 ser., XII, 61–62; 2 ser., IX, 209–213, signature of Bathurst Skelton opp. p. 216.

[4] The day may be inexact. Jefferson was at the Forest on June 9, but not on June 10, and he did not return immediately, as might have been expected. There is no record that the child was ever at Monticello.

[5] *Va. Mag.*, III, 393–396.

Wayles, for Jefferson visited them there. Later they lived at Eppington in Chesterfield County.

Tabitha Wayles (*b.* Nov. 10, 1753) may be presumed to have married Robert Skipwith shortly before Jefferson's marriage. Jefferson,
writing to him on August 3, 1771, referred to "our dear Tibby," and
Skipwith spoke of Martha as "my sister Skelton." [6] In the codicil to
his will, dated Feb. 12, 1773, John Wayles left him £250, but he did not
sign the notices of lands to be sold and does not appear to have been
an executor like the other sons-in-law.

Anne Wayles (*b.* Aug. 26, 1756) married Col. Henry Skipwith of
Cumberland County on July 7, 1773.[7] He was one of the executors,
with Francis Eppes and Jefferson, and engaged in certain land transactions with the latter. Jefferson's relations with him, however, were never
so intimate as with Francis Eppes.

John Wayles, following the death of his second wife, married in January, 1760, Elizabeth Lomax, the widow of Reuben Skelton, elder
brother of Bathurst.[8] She died on Feb. 10, 1761, without issue.

[6] Ford, I, 399; to Jefferson, Sept. 20, 1771, MHS.
[7] *Va. Mag.*, XXIII, 87.
[8] *W. & M.*, 1 ser., IV, 119; 2 ser., VII, 103.

E. *Children of Thomas Jefferson*[1] *and Martha Wayles* (*Oct. 19/30, 1748—Sept. 6, 1782*)

NAME	BIRTH	MARRIAGE	DEATH
1. Martha	Sept. 27, 1772, at 1 A.M. at Monticello	Feb. 23, 1790, to Thomas Mann Randolph, Jr.	1836
2. Jane Randolph [2]	Apr. 3, 1774, at 11 A.M. at Monticello		Sept. 1775
3. Son [3]	May 28, 1777, at 10 P.M.		June 14, 1777, at 10:20 P.M.
4. Mary [4]	Aug. 1, 1778, at 1:30 A.M.	Oct. 13, 1797, to John Wayles Eppes	Apr. 17, 1804, 8–9 A.M.
5. Lucy Elizabeth [5]	Nov. 30, 1780, at 10:45 P.M. in Richmond		Apr. 15, 1781, at 10 A.M.
6. Lucy Elizabeth [6]	May 8, 1782, at 1 A.M.		c. Oct. 13, 1784

[1] This chart is based chiefly on the register in Jefferson's prayer book in his own handwriting, reproduced by Randall, I, 383, and on items in Jefferson's Account Book; see also *Tyler's Mag.*, VI, 267.

[2] From his Account Book, Jefferson is shown to have been at Monticello in September, 1775, until the 25th, when he set out for Philadelphia, but he does not refer to the death of this child.

[3] In his Account Book, Jefferson refers on both Apr. 3 and June 4, 1777, to "our son," but gives the child no name.

[4] Numerous references to Mary Jefferson will be given hereafter.

[5] Name not given in prayer book, but in reference to death; Account Book, Apr. 15, 1781.

[6] Reference to birth in Account Book.

[APPENDIX II]

The Jefferson Estate

A. *The Estate of Peter Jefferson*

IT seems impossible to determine the exact amount of land that Peter Jefferson acquired and held in the Province before his death, and it would certainly be unsafe to add up the acres mentioned in the various grants made to him by the Council. In his case, as in others, there was a considerable degree of overlapping and duplication, and certain of these grants appear never to have been followed by an actual patent. Permission to survey large tracts in outlying districts was often obtained by planters in a spirit of speculation, and in many instances, perhaps in most instances, formal title was never acquired.[1] To cite an example, it is exceedingly doubtful if one of the largest grants to Peter Jefferson of which we have record was ever perfected. This was made to him, William Randolph, and four others for 50,000 acres, "beginning at a place called the Crab Orchard . . . on the head Springs of Sherrando [Shenandoah] River & runing [sic] South Westerly between the Blue Ridge & third Ridge."[2]

The safest procedure is to start, not with the lands granted, but with those known to have been and to have remained in his possession. The latter tracts are not listed specifically in either his will or the inventory afterwards filed with it. The available records of Thomas Jefferson, however, are more detailed. Thus, in his Farm Book he gives his land roll for 1794, with annotations showing the dates of acquisition of the

---

[1] For valuable information about the granting and patenting of lands during this period, I am indebted to Manning C. Voorhis, whose doctoral dissertation at the University of Virginia, "The Land Grant Policy of Colonial Virginia, 1607–1774," I have been privileged to examine, and to Prof. T. P. Abernethy of that institution, under whose direction the study was made. For going over this Appendix, I am indebted to Prof. Edwin M. Betts, who is now editing Thomas Jefferson's Farm Book, and Charles W. Watts, who has made a careful study of lands in colonial Albemarle. My figures tally closely with theirs, and our general conclusions are essentially the same.

[2] Aug. 5, 1737, *Council Journals, Colonial Va.*, IV, 402.

different tracts actually held by him; [3] and in his Fee Book, under the heading "Personal Estate in Account with Real Estate," he records his land transactions, 1764–1779.[4] Since he inherited all of his father's lands in the Rivanna district and appears to have sold none of them, it may be assumed with considerable confidence that his father acquired no tract there, or at least kept none, which he did not list. For supplementary information we can turn to such contemporary records of grants and patents as exist.[5]

On his land roll, Thomas Jefferson shows no tract that was acquired before July 19, 1735, when 1000 acres, including the later Monticello site, were patented.[6] On June 14, 1734, the Council had granted Peter permission "to have three Surveys lying on the North Side of North River" [Rivanna], beginning at the Secretary's Ford and running down the river and back to the Secretary's line.[7] The wording is loose and the acreage is not specified. When he first came into possession, however, Peter did not have enough land *north* of the river for a homesite, and on November 1, 1734, he was authorized to patent 1200 acres, in three surveys, on the *south* side.[8] Presumably, this was the tract that he actually patented on July 19, 1735, despite the slight difference in acreage; and Thomas Jefferson appears to have been correct in his belief that the Monticello tract was the first acquired.

The next transaction was the famous one with William Randolph for 200 acres for a homesite.[9] This was completed on May 16, 1741, by the addition of 200 acres and the payment of £50, current money of Virginia.[10] Meanwhile, Peter had acquired a little tract of 150 acres south of the river known as Portobello.[11] He received other grants elsewhere before his son was born, but the strong presumption is that he had in the Rivanna district in April 1743 only the Monticello, Shadwell, and Portobello tracts, including from 1550 to 1750 acres.

After his return to Shadwell from Tuckahoe Peter rounded out the Rivanna estate which his elder son inherited, and created the comparable estate on the Fluvanna which ultimately went to the younger. In connection with the former, he purchased 650 acres at Pantops, north of the river, and patented 150 at Tufton, south of it.[12] He also acquired

---

[3] MHS, photostat UVA; reproduced in Randall, II, 237–238.

[4] HEH, photostat UVA.

[5] Marie Kimball, *Road to Glory*, pp. 309–311, gives a documented list of entries, prepared after painstaking investigation of many sources. This is most helpful, though it gives the impression that Peter held more land than, in my opinion, he actually did hold.

[6] The date checks precisely with Va. State Land Office Patents, 16, 1735.

[7] *Council Journals, Colonial Va.*, IV, 330.

[8] *Ibid.*, IV, 340.

[9] May 18, 1736, *W. & M.*, 1 ser., V, 112.

[10] Goochland County Deed Book, No. 3, Pt. 2, p. 535. The original deed has generally been described without reference to its sequel.

[11] Patented Sept. 16, 1740; Farm Book.

[12] Farm Book. Pantops transaction undated; Tufton patented Sept. 10, 1755.

a tract which was identified on his son's land roll as "Pouncey's" and which, even at a much later time, was valued mostly for its timber. Peter devised 100 acres of this, on Carrol's Creek, to James Spears (Speirs, according to Thomas), but his son afterwards repurchased this. Thus the Rivanna estate included the following tracts:

Monticello	1000 acres	
Shadwell	400 "	(Life interest to Jane Randolph Jefferson)
Portobello	150 "	
Pantops	650 "	
Tufton	150 "	
Pouncey's	300 "	(as inherited)
	2650 "	

The Fluvanna estate may not have been quite as large as this, though it was doubtless equally or more productive. In 1754 Peter procured south of the river (still in Albemarle County) a tract of 2050 acres, 500 by purchase and the rest by virtue of an order of Council.[13] With this he devised in his will a small body of land on the Hardware River called Limestone, but in the course of time this came into the possession of Thomas, rather than Randolph, under unknown circumstances. The disposition of the houses opposite the courthouse near the ferry landing which Peter owned and rented to Richard Murray, ordinary keeper, is uncertain.[14] At all events, the Snowden tract of 2050 acres represented the bulk of the Fluvanna estate.

Judging from the records of Thomas's land transactions and his later land rolls, the bulk of his additional landed inheritance as residuary legatee was also in Albemarle, as constituted at the time of his father's death. The Fine Creek property, which was in Cumberland County by 1764, appears to have gone to him, for an incomplete entry of that year suggests that he expected to sell it, though apparently he did not. He also inherited land in Bedford County, for he sold some of it, but the description of the important holdings that he had afterwards at Poplar Forest tallies, not with his inheritance, but with his wife's. The best guess is that the residual estate amounted to approximately as many acres as the Rivanna holdings; and that, apart from speculative claims of which no advantage seems to have been taken, Peter Jefferson at the time of his death held approximately 7500 acres of land, much the larger part of which was in Albemarle.[15] Such holdings as he had elsewhere turned out afterwards to be unimportant.

A few details follow about the executors of Peter Jefferson's will and the administration of his estate.

[13] Albemarle County, Surveyor's Book No. 1, sect. 1, p. 293; undated, but flanked by entries for that year. See also his will.
[14] John Harvie's Account Book, HEH, pp. 12, 40.
[15] In 1757, John Harvie as executor paid quitrents on 4375 acres in the County, but the total holdings appear to have been considerably larger.

John Harvie of Belmont, the active executor until Thomas Jefferson attained his majority, died in 1767.[16] Colonel Peter Randolph, who had been associated with Peter Jefferson as an executor of William Randolph, was a member of the Council. Thomas consulted him before going to William and Mary; he also died in 1767. Thomas Turpin, husband of Mary Jefferson, and brother-in-law of Peter, had engaged with the latter in surveying in Albemarle and elsewhere, and in various land transactions. He was one of the first magistrates of Cumberland County.[17] John Nicholas, brother of Robert Carter Nicholas, married the daughter of Joshua Fry. He was the clerk of Albemarle, 1750–1792, and was succeeded by his son John.[18]

The surviving accounts of John Harvie are in three supplementary segments which overlap to some degree. They can be consulted conveniently at the University of Virginia, where copies or photostats of all of them have been assembled.

"1760, *Dr.* The Estate of Colo. Peter Jefferson deced in acco. with John Harvie one of the Executors & a Guardian of the orphans." [19] This contains the best summary to its date.

"The Estate of Peter Jefferson to John Harvie as Settled with the Court" [20] (Albemarle County, 1760).

"Account Book of John Harvie as executor of Peter Jefferson, 1757–1765" [21] (Albemarle County). This has the largest number of individual accounts and the fullest details.

From these records we learn that in 1759 there were three overseers: Martin Dawson (Snowden), Joseph Dawson, and Fred Gilliam. The last of these produced only *c.* 5000 lbs. of tobacco, but he appears to have been at Shadwell, where much corn was grown. There was also a steward, John Moore, 1758–1760 and possibly longer, who was paid at the rate of £20 a year. The profit from the water-mill in 1758 was £41, and from the tobacco crop in 1759 was £188. The credit balance at the end of three years was over £300. The names of other overseers are given at one time or another, but they appear never to have numbered more than three, while there were only two in some years. The best guess is that there were three farms. The account of the surveyor's office is rendered in detail.

The accounts of Dr. Thomas Walker with the estate, chiefly 1757–1765, are in the papers of the former, W. C. Rives Collection, Library of Congress (permission of Mrs. Philip M. Rhinelander, Washington, D. C.). These are most interesting as showing visits to Peter Jefferson

[16] Woods, *Albemarle*, p. 224; *Va. Mag.*, XXVI, 318.

[17] Alexander Brown, *The Cabells and Their Kin* (1895), p. 50.

[18] Woods, *Albemarle*, p. 289; on the latter, who became a bitter Federalist, see M. J. Dauer, "The Two John Nicholases," *Am. Hist. Rev.*, Jan. 1940, pp. 338–353.

[19] Will Book No. 2, Albemarle County, pp. 83–87, typewritten copy, UVA.

[20] MHS, photostat UVA.

[21] HEH, photostat UVA.

during his last illness, and payments made on Thomas Jefferson's account at William and Mary.

B. *Lands and Slaves of Thomas Jefferson*

1. PATRIMONY, 1764–1773

As shown in the previous section, Thomas Jefferson inherited from his father some 2650 acres of land on the Rivanna, and approximately as many more elsewhere.[22] He did not come into legal possession of the Shadwell tract until after his mother's death in 1776, but from 1765 he farmed it, renting from her certain slaves (five, to begin with) at a specified rate and crediting her at a given rate with the board of the children.[23] He inherited the water-mill immediately that he came of age, and this probably continued to be profitable until 1771, when it was swept away in the "great fresh." His later efforts to rebuild it caused him great trouble and expense but these need not concern us here.[24]

Except for his assumption of responsibility for the Shadwell farm, his land transactions prior to his marriage on January 1, 1772, were on the negative side, for he divested himself of more acres than he acquired. Probably because he needed cash, he sold 700 acres of land in Amherst County in the year that he became twenty-one, receiving a total of £190 in two transactions.[25] Apparently he did not sell to John Scott the Fine Creek property, for he left both the acreage and the selling price blank in his entry, and he sent his family there at least once during the Revolution, but he did not list it on later land rolls. In September, 1771, he sold and bought lands in Bedford County, one transaction balancing the other from the monetary point of view. From this time forward, his interests centered in Monticello, and not until his wife came into her inheritance in 1774 did he make any important deals in land. He did some buying in 1773, acquiring a lot in Richmond and 300 acres in Bedford, but the latter he did not long keep. During this year, also, he was granted leave to survey 1000 acres in the Southwest Mountains.[26] Judging from the description, this land adjoined his own and that of Thomas Mann Randolph north of the Rivanna, but it corresponds to nothing on his later land roll except possibly an unnamed tract of 730 acres, most of which was surveyed for him at a date not given. Presumably it was woodland that ran up the mountain-side. Later in 1773 he entered into a deal with Augustine Claiborne, whereby

[22] This total considerably exceeds the estimate of T. J. Randolph that his grandfather got 1900 acres; Randall, III, 675.

[23] Account with Jane Randolph Jefferson, Fee Book, HEH, photostat UVA.

[24] The fullest account of the mill that I have seen is in LC, 232:42029, "Grounds for Estimating the Value of the Shadwell Mills," etc. Another good reference is LC, 211:37573, dated Aug. 17, 1817.

[25] "Personal Estate in Account with Real Estate," 1764–1779, in Fee Book.

[26] Mar. 11, 1773, Council Journals, Colonial Va. (Photostat, UVA).

he was to have a share, estimated by him as at least 10,000 acres, of a tract on Little River in Augusta County which had been granted in 1750; but I have found no record of this beyond a statement in his Account Book on October 29, 1773.

By his father's will, Thomas inherited at least twenty slaves. His transactions in slaves he recorded in his personal account with real estate in his Fee Book, but prior to his marriage these were unimportant. He continued to hire from his mother certain slaves who worked on the Shadwell lands, and on September 29, 1773, she conveyed these to him along with others of whom she retained the use during her lifetime. They came to eleven altogether, and the transfer was made because of large sums of money which he had advanced and she had no means of repaying.[27] Earlier in the same year, and almost exactly a year after his marriage he had purchased three slaves from the executor of James Skelton. In effect the deal was made on behalf of his wife.

Jefferson's first entry about his "proper" slaves in his Farm Book (January 14, 1774) shows that he then had forty-one, plus eleven he had title to from his mother. Of these, twenty were laborers in the ground and four were discharged from labor because of age or infirmity.

2. CONSOLIDATION OF THE PATRIMONY, 1774–1782

So far as his own lands were concerned, as distinguished from those he acquired on behalf of his wife, Jefferson's transactions during the Revolution consisted of ridding himself of more distant properties and consolidating his holdings in Albemarle. In the years 1775 and 1776 he sold approximately 1300 acres, 400 on Bold Branch in Albemarle and nearly 900 on Tomahawk and Rockcastle Creeks in Bedford and Amherst. The latter property included the lands bought in Bedford in 1771 and 1773 and, judging by the selling price, it was valuable. Outside of Albemarle, he made one acquisition of interest. On July 5, 1774, he patented 157 acres in Rockbridge County which included Natural Bridge.[28]

His purchases in the home neighborhood aggregated about 1500 acres. In 1774 or 1775 he acquired the tract of 819 acres which he afterwards described as Lego.[29] In 1777 he bought 169¼ acres at a high price and added them to the farm at Pantops, also north of the river.[30] In the same year he acquired from his neighbor, Colonel Edward Carter, nearly 500 acres on High Mountain (Montalto), adjoining Monticello.

[27] Photostat of indenture at UVA; references also in Farm Book.

[28] Land Roll of 1794 in Farm Book, Randall, II, 238. Plat of survey MHS, I, 30; photostat UVA.

[29] In his Fee Book he dates the purchase "Jan. 1775," but in his Farm Book he assigns four slaves to Lego in 1774. His own survey of the fields there, made in 1794, is reproduced in *Garden Book*, Plate XV.

[30] Fee Book, Aug. 7, 1777. The price was £1254.

This he doubtless intended to leave in its wooded state. In 1782 he was assessed for 4125 acres in Albemarle, and probably had somewhat more. By 1794, when he gave the first full land roll that I have seen, he had added about 150 acres to the Monticello and Montalto properties, but he regarded only 500–600 acres as arable.[81]

He began his Farm Book in 1774, and odd items about crops and overseers appear in his personal records even earlier.[32] But his interest in agriculture was greatest after his retirement in 1794, and long after that he denied ever having given minute attention to farming.[33] His occupations forbade it, he said. We may assume, therefore, that he was unable to give to his properties very close personal attention at this time.

He was not the largest landowner in Albemarle. In 1782, Edward Carter was assessed for 9700 acres. He was followed by the estate of Robert Carter Nicholas with 7500 acres, Thomas Walker with 6050, and John Coles with 5000. Jefferson stood fifth on the list, but he was above John Walker, who was assessed for 3000 acres.[34] His patrimony, which he had maintained in effect though not precisely in its original form, made him a substantial landowner but not a great one by Virginia standards. However, the lands which his wife inherited and which lay outside of Albemarle doubled his holdings, as he said. Through this inheritance he became, relatively, an even larger owner of slaves. In his own county in 1782, only Edward Carter had more than he.

3. THE WAYLES INHERITANCE, 1774–1800

John Wayles died on May 28, 1773, and his large estate was divided early in 1774. Jefferson was one of the executors.[35] It is not clear on just what basis the division was made. So far as Jefferson's wife was concerned, matters were complicated by the fact that a settlement with respect to her had been made previously by her father and mother; and all of the heirs were affected by the fact that John Wayles also transmitted a heavy debt. We need not go into all the ramifications of complicated transactions, however, in order to ascertain approximately what Jefferson acquired on behalf of Martha. Altogether, her inheritance consisted of 135 slaves and more than 11,000 acres of land, along with her share of the debt. In order to cover the latter, Jefferson shortly sold approximately half of the land, retaining Poplar Forest, Elk Island,

---

[81] To Samuel Biddle, Dec. 12, 1792, *Papers*, MHS, pp. 43–45.

[32] Such, for example, as an estimate of the tobacco crop at Monticello, July 31, 1769, cited in *Garden Book*, p. 17; and "Hints for Contracts with Overseers," Account Book, 1773, entry following that of Aug. 4.

[33] To T. M. Randolph, Jan. 31, 1809, *Papers*, MHS, p. 134.

[34] Land Tax Book, Albemarle, 1782–1799, Auditor's Office of Va., X, at Va. State Lib.

[35] For the will, see *Tyler's Mag.*, VI, 268–270; for advertisements of land to be sold, July 15, Sept. 16, 1773, see Ford, I, 417.

and Elkhill.[36] As we shall see, however, he afterwards had to provide for the debt all over again.

Elk Island in the James (330 acres), which Thomas and Martha acquired, was connected with the estate of Bathurst Skelton and appears not to have entered into the division.[37] Jefferson wanted to join this as a plantation unit with Elkhill (266 acres) on the mainland; and to effect this purpose he made what amounted to a swap of certain lands in Cumberland for Elkhill.[38] He also sold most of the other inherited lands of hers in the latter county. These Cumberland lands, however, had belonged originally to Martha's grandfather, Francis Eppes, and were entailed. Accordingly, Thomas Jefferson and Martha his wife petitioned the House of Burgesses to dock the entail on 2400 acres in Cumberland and to settle lands of the same value in Goochland, and this request was granted.[39] Here is one instance of personal difficulties which Jefferson faced in connection with entailed property, before he himself effected a revision of the law.

According to one of his estimates, the Poplar Forest property in Bedford consisted of 4819 acres when John Wayles died. As listed in his own land roll in 1794, it comprised about 200 acres less, though all of his lands in Bedford and Campbell counties then added up to about 5100 acres. Despite the fact that his father had once had lands in the Poplar Forest neighborhood, this favorite property of his must be credited to the Wayles inheritance. He made a trip there on September 8, 1773, which appears to have been his first.[40]

Apart from the swap by which he gained Elkhill, Jefferson's early sales from the Wayles lands were as follows:

1774, Jan. 26.	To Henry Skipwith, 1200 acres, Cumberland	£2000
1775, Sept. 29.	To James Gatewood, 2000 acres, Bedford (possibly a part in Amherst)	£1000
1778, June.	To James and —— Gatewood, 1850 acres on Fluvanna and Judith's Creek	£2836 +
	5050 acres	£5836 +

These sales were made despite his characteristic reluctance to part with land. "Of all things it is that of which I am most tenacious," he said later.[41] By that time he knew that he had gained nothing by parting with these acres.

Most if not all of the Wayles debt which Jefferson assumed was to

---

[36] His transactions to 1779 are recorded in his Fee Book, under "Personal Estate in Account with Real Estate"; several estimates about the Wayles lands are in his Account Book, 1773; and the slaves are listed in his Farm Book, in the year 1774.

[37] Fee Book, Account with the Estate of Bathurst Skelton; will of Skelton, *Tyler's Mag.*, VI, 268; Jefferson's Account Book, 1773.

[38] Transactions of Jan. 14, 26, 1774, with Henry Skipwith.

[39] *Burgesses, Journals, 1773–1776*, pp. 83–84, May 9, 20, 1774.

[40] *Garden Book*, p. 42.

[41] To Col. Harvie, Feb. 22, 1796, MHS.

William Jones (later Farrell & Jones) of Bristol. Writing Jones a decade after he made these sales, Jefferson said: "I offered the bonds of the purchasers to your agent Mr. Evans, if he would acquit me, and accept of the purchasers as debtors in my place. . . . These debts, being turned over to you, would have been saved to you by the treaty of peace, but he declined it." [42] Failing in this effort to relieve himself of Mr. Jones, he made another. When he himself was paid in paper money two or three years after the lands were sold, he deposited "the identical money" in the treasury of the State, which then stood engaged, by the loan-office provisions of the bill he himself had drawn, to pay the British creditors after the war. This money was used in the conduct of the war, he said; he might have said that it went down the rathole.[43] It became all too clear that the State could not meet these obligations in hard money, and he recognized that his personal obligation was still binding. Before he went to France and while he was there he arranged that all of the proceeds of his own farms should go to his creditors, and he then thought the matter was honorably settled.[44]

His grandson said that his share of the Wayles debt was £3749. The Farrell & Jones account probably approached this amount in the first place; as entered in his own Balance Account in the spring of 1794 it was for more than £4544, but more than a third of this was for accumulated interest. He was also involved in a considerable debt to Henderson, McCaul & Company, which amounted in the spring of 1794 to more than £2000, and if this was not originally a part of the Wayles debt it doubtless resulted from it indirectly. While "scuffling to pay what I could of that," he said, "I suffered my own accounts to accumulate." Alexander McCaul was a good friend of his, however, and he had his greatest difficulties with the other firm.[45]

In the late eighties and the nineties a plaintive note appeared in many of his letters. "I am miserable till I shall owe not a shilling," he wrote from Paris to Nicholas Lewis, who was managing his local affairs: "the moment that shall be the case I shall feel at liberty to do something for the comfort of my slaves." He had been forced to sell some of them, and at least to talk of hiring out some of the others. Several years later, saying that the necessity of paying the Wayles debt all over again had compelled him to mortgage all his tobacco, as it were, to that purpose,

[42] To Jones, Jan. 5, 1787; Ford, IV, 354. He told essentially the same story in other letters.

[43] Ford, IV, 355; II, 200. Account Book entries of May 21, 1779, when he deposited £1000, and Feb. 2, 1780, when he paid in slightly more than £1666. There may have been other payments.

[44] His general attitude toward the American debt question is well expressed in his letter of Apr. 19, 1786, to Alexander McCaul; Ford, IV, 201–205. He demurred about interest during the war years, but, so far as Farrell & Jones were concerned, apparently he did not escape it.

[45] Randall, III, 676; Balance Account in Fee Book; Jefferson to Col. Robert Lewis, Oct. 5, 1791, MHS.

he added: "It consequently cripples all my wishes & endeavors to be useful to others, and obliges me to carry on everything starvingly." [46] In a business letter of January 1, 1792, he said that for seven years he had not drawn for his own use one shilling from the profits from his lands, and that, finding these measures still insufficient, he had again sold enough property to pay the whole debt. "Not having the power of creating money, I know not what more I could have done." [47]

In 1791, he had sold the last of his Cumberland lands, but Richard Hanson, representing Jones, preferred Jefferson's bonds to those of the purchaser.[48] Previously, he had rented Elkhill but collections fell in arrears, and early in 1793 he completed the sale of that place.[49] This was not the end, however. In 1795, a suit was brought by Hanson against the Wayles executors as security for the late Richard Randolph, under circumstances which seemed to Jefferson as a lawyer not sufficient to cause them to be liable. Nonetheless, judgment went against them and, expecting his portion to be £700-£800, he thought of selling Pouncey's in Albemarle.[50] Apparently his part of this debt, including interest, turned out to be nearly £1000.[51] Under these circumstances, desiring to protect Henderson, McCaul & Co., he conveyed to them fifty-two slaves.[52] By that time he was paying off one by one a series of personal bonds to Farrell & Jones, payable 1791–1797, which were covered by bonds due him from various individuals. He devoted himself to this troublesome business during the period of his retirement, 1794–1797. In 1800, he expressed the hope that he might soon close the "last remnant of Mr. Wayles's debts," which he had been "working off ever since the peace." [53] A monograph on his financial history could be written, but the general state of his affairs has been described with sufficient fullness for present purposes.[54]

Of all the land gained from the Wayles inheritance, in the end Jefferson retained only Poplar Forest. Some of the 135 slaves that he acquired he also had to sell, and before those sales were made he had lost about thirty in the Revolution, besides suffering other heavy losses

[46] To Lewis, Dec. 19, 1786, Ford, IV, 343; to Mr. Carr, May 8, 1791, MHS.

[47] To J. Dodson, Jan. 1, 1792; MHS.

[48] Apr. 5, 30, 1791; MHS.

[49] Jefferson to Daniel L. Hylton, Jan. 20, 1793, MHS; see also Ford, V, 281.

[50] To James Lyle, May 12, 1795; to Col. Harvie, Feb. 22, 1796, MHS. A fairly full account of this case, which led to political rumors, is in a letter of S. T. Mason to D. C. Brent, Oct. 25, 1796, LC, 100:17236–17237.

[51] John Wickham to Jefferson, Dec. 8, 1796, MHS. The debt was then to Cary & Welch and troublesome Hanson was out of the picture, but Eppes and Skipwith were involved and it appears to have been the same matter.

[52] May 12, 1796, Indenture, MHS; he had paid off numerous bonds to them previously.

[53] To L. W. Tazewell, Mar. 17, 1800, MHS.

[54] His papers in the MHS are full of letters and memoranda dealing with finance.

at Elkhill.[55] Between 1783 and 1794 the number of his slaves decreased from 204 to 155, presumably by sale, and had not again reached the higher figure by 1810.

His own statement that the ease of his circumstances was doubled by the Wayles inheritance was conservative, so far as the immediate effects were concerned. At no time in his entire life did he appear to be as prosperous as he was from 1774 until depreciation ensued toward the end of the American Revolution; and never was he so warranted in living in the grand manner as during the period of his married life. It is by no means impossible that the financial difficulties into which he fell as the Revolution neared its close contributed to his willingness to return to public life after his wife's death. During his stay in France he tried to live on his salary, while continuing to play the part of a fine gentleman. The troubles which he faced thereafter may have had a good deal to do with his later adoption of a simpler form of life. The references to his simplicity in dress are from the later, not the earlier, period.

His unfortunate experiences after the Revolution, when he was involved in debts not of his own making and could not collect from people who owed him, also left a mark on his own thinking. It was probably because of them that he became so painfully aware of the extravagance of his countrymen in Virginia. Furthermore, his own difficulties illustrated the relentlessness of creditors in England, and they could hardly have endeared the British to him. Here also is the personal background for the philosophy of economy and hostility to debt which he voiced in public life, both as Secretary of State and President. The whole of his later life was colored by the fateful Wayles inheritance, which first enriched and then impoverished him.

4. LOSSES FROM THE ENEMY, 1781

In a letter to Dr. William Gordon, who was preparing a history of the American Revolution, Jefferson described his personal losses from Cornwallis at Elkhill. Since the most important part of this letter is quoted in the text of Chapter XXVII, it need not be repeated here.[56] These losses he listed at the time, or soon after the event, in his Farm Book.[57] He gave by name the thirty slaves who fled to the enemy and died from smallpox and camp fever. They were chiefly from Elkhill and Cumberland, though there were two runaways from Shadwell and one from Monticello who returned and died. He also listed his other losses. These included 9 horses and colts, 59 cattle, 30 sheep, and 60 hogs, along with quantities of corn, wheat, tobacco, hemp, flax, cotton,

[55] Farm Book, p. 29.
[56] July 16, 1788, Ford, V, 38–40
[57] Page 29.

and barley, either stored or growing, and 1000 barrels of flour. Of additional monetary expenses which resulted he gave items amounting to more than £100. He afterwards said that the total loss to him was more than equivalent to his entire debt to Farrell & Jones.[58] For Virginia he estimated, in his letter to Gordon, that it was about three millions sterling.

[58] To William Jones, Jan. 5, 1787; Ford, IV, 354.

⌈ APPENDIX III ⌉

The Walker Affair

1768–1809

THE Walker affair appears not to have come into the open until Jefferson's presidency, when it became a public scandal. Historically, it is inseparable from the campaign of abuse which was waged against him at the height of his political career; and our scanty knowledge of what actually took place between Jefferson and Mrs. Walker in his young manhood is derived, not from records contemporary with the events, but from documents dated a generation later. In order to arrive at the unvarnished truth it is necessary to divest these of their political coloration, while allowing also for the inaccuracy of memory. This is an exceedingly difficult task.

According to the statement of John Walker, made a generation later, the chronological outline of the affair was as follows: it began in 1768, before Jefferson was married; it continued until 1779, some years after he was married; and it did not become known to Walker himself until after Jefferson had gone to France in 1784 and the lady had given her husband the full story. From other evidence it cannot be doubted that Jefferson and Walker maintained the most amicable of relations throughout the Revolution; and occasional remarks in Jefferson's own letters while he was in France lead to the supposition that he then regarded their old friendship as unmarred.

The beginnings of political divergence, after his return to America, may have been connected with the election of his protégé, James Monroe, to the United States Senate in 1790 over Walker.[1] Information about his personal association with his old friend in that decade is scanty, but there is evidence that cordial relations with other members of the Walker connection continued. It was in 1793, however, that Henry or Light-Horse Harry Lee married Ann Hill Carter,

---

[1] Monroe to Jefferson, Oct. 20, 1790, Hamilton, *Writings*, I, 217–218 and note.

justly renowned as the mother of General Robert E. Lee. She was the niece of Mrs. John Walker. Henry Lee was distrusted by Jefferson and became his implacable political foe, and it was he who later served as mediator between Jefferson and Walker.[2] There is little reason to doubt that Lee's major role was that of troublemaker.

By 1802, there was an open personal breach between Jefferson and Walker. In that year the notorious scandalmonger, James Thomson Callender, gave wide currency to the story about Mrs. Walker, along with a much more unsavory one about one of Jefferson's slaves.[3] The Walker story had probably been bandied about somewhat earlier and had led to some correspondence which Callender had seen or heard about and which he threatened to publish. Walker said that he "constantly wrote" to Jefferson, without saying when. Apparently these letters have not been preserved, but the presumption is that they were not written before Jefferson's presidency. Whatever may have passed between the alienated friends, the ugly story continued to go the rounds. It was published, with others that reflected on Jefferson's morals, in the *New-England Palladium* on Jan. 18, 1805, and entered into a debate in the House of Representatives of Massachusetts.[4] Goaded by all these circumstances, Walker demanded further satisfaction from Jefferson, Henry Lee serving as his intermediary.[5]

This was in the spring of 1805. In the summer Jefferson communicated the matter to particular friends because he wished "to stand with them on the ground of truth," and to one of them, speaking of the attacks of his enemies, he said: "You will perceive that I plead guilty to one of their charges, that when young and single I offered love to a handsome lady. I acknolege its incorrectness [that is, the incorrectness of his own conduct]. It is the only one founded in truth among all their allegations against me."[6] The kernel of indubitable truth is that he made improper advances to his friend's wife before he himself was married. Added to this is the virtual certainty that he gave to Walker a statement wholly exculpating the lady from blame.[7] As a gentleman he could do no less, but it certainly need not be assumed that he placed the stamp of truth on the whole of Walker's *ex parte* account of the events and circumstances.

Walker's statement, as preserved in the handwriting of General Lee, was as follows:

[2] *Va. Mag.*, XXV, 436; D. S. Freeman, *R. E. Lee*, I (1934), 7, 8.

[3] Especially in Richmond *Recorder*, Oct. 27, 1802; on Callender see article in *D. A. B.*

[4] Especially Jan. 25, 31, 1805; *Defense of Young and Minns, Printers to the State* (Boston, March, 1805).

[5] Walker to Lee, Mar. 28, 1805; LC, 148:25833.

[6] To Robert Smith, Sec. of the Navy, July 1, 1805, Bixby, p. 115. The enclosed copy of a letter to Mr. Lincoln which apparently contained a fuller statement has not been found.

[7] Henry Lee to Jefferson, Sept. 8, 1806; LC, 161:28252–28253.

I was married at Chelsea the seat of my wifes father on *6th* [5th?] of June 64. I was educated at Wm & Mary where was also educated Mr J.

We had previously grown up together at a private school & our boys acquaintance was strengthened at college. We loved (at least I did sincerely) each other.

My father was one of his fathers exr & his own guardian & advanced money for his education. . . .

I took Mr J. with me the friend of my heart to my wedding. He was one of my bridemen.

This as I said above took place in 64.

In 68 I was called to Fort Stanwix being secretary or clerk to the Virginia commission at the treaty with the Indians there held by Sir W Johnson which was composed of Gen'l A Lewis & my father.

I left my wife & infant daughter at home, relying on Mr Jefferson as my neighbor & fast friend having in my will made before my departure, named him first among my executors.

I returned in Novr. having been absent more than 4 months.

During my absence Mr J conduct to *Mrs* W was improper so much so as to have laid the foundation of her constant objection to my leaving Mr J my exct telling me that she wondered why I could place such confidence in him.

At Shadwell his own house in 69 or 70 on a visit common to us being neighbors & as I felt true frds. he renewed his caresses placed in *Mrs* W! gown sleeve cuff a paper tending to convince her of the innocence of promiscuous love.

This Mrs W on the first glance tore to pieces.

After this we went on a visit to Col. Coles a mutual acquaintance & distant neighbor. Mr Jefferson was there. On the ladys retiring to bed he pretended to be sick, complained of a headache & left the gentlemen among whom I was.

Instead of going to bed as his sickness authorized a belief he stole into my room where my wife was undressing or in bed.

He was repulsed with indignation & menaces of alarm & ran off.

In 71 Mr J was married and yet continued his efforts to destroy my peace until the latter end of the year 79.

One particular instance I remember.

My old house had a passage upstairs with a room on each side & opposite doors.

Mr J and wife slept in one. I & my wife in the other.

At one end of the passage was a small room used by my wife as her private apartment.

She visited it early & late. On this morning Mr J' knowing her custom was found in his shirt ready to seize her on her way from her chamber — indecent in manner.

In 83 Mr J went to France his wife died previously.

From 79 Mr J desisted in his attempts on my peace.

All this time I believed him to be my best *frd* & so felt & acted toward him.

All this time I held him first named in my will, as exct. ignorant of every thing which had passed.

Soon after his sailing for France was known *Mrs* W then recurred to my will & being as before asked her objections, she related to me these base transactions apologizing for her past silence from her fear of its consequence which might have been fatal to me.

I constantly wrote to him. You have our correspondence & you go now to Mr. J. My injury is before you. Let my redress be commensurate. It cannot be complete & therefore ought to be as full as possible.[8]

In the light of our knowledge of Jefferson's temperament and personality and of the surrounding circumstances, only the part of the statement referring to the year 1768 is wholly convincing; and this part of it is quite in line with his own admission. The alleged advances of 1769 and 1770 are not in conflict with that admission, since he was still unmarried, but such gaucherie, and such personal aggressiveness in the face of rebuffs, were not characteristic of him as a man. He was more sensitive than the average and appears to have been diffident toward women until after he had acquired a wife and family of his own. Such comments of his on love and marriage as remain show that in these respects his standards were thoroughly, if not excessively conventional. It is hard to believe that under these discouraging circumstances his lapses were several times repeated.

That he should have continued to make advances to his friend's wife after his own marriage is little short of inconceivable, in view of his single-minded devotion to his wife and the degree of happiness he enjoyed with her. One of his friends afterwards said that there was no whisper in the neighborhood at the time, and there is no evidence that there was.[9] It is equally difficult to believe that he could have carried on an affair over a period of eleven years, during which time the husband remained in complete ignorance and the lady constantly repulsed him. The only sensible procedure seems to be to disregard the details of these "base transactions" as reported at secondhand long afterwards and to leave the matter just where he left it. As has been said, he was guilty of "an unmoral, not an immoral act."[10] But for political rancor and the activities of scandalmongers, it would have been left in that oblivion where it long rested and where it should have remained.

Inviting John Page to spend a summer holiday with him at Monticello in 1803, Jefferson said: "You have another old friend too [John Walker] in the neighborhood to attract you: and tho' he & I have unhappily fallen out by the way, yet both cherish your friendship, and neither says with Achilles 'my friend must hate the man who injures

[8] LC, 155:27117–27121, corrected only by insertion of periods at end of sentences. The original of this statement was probably enclosed in Walker's letter of Mar. 28, 1805, to Lee; LC, 148:25833. Certain of the details were known to Callender in 1802, but he may have received them orally. These documents are not a constituent part of the Jefferson Papers as he left them. They were acquired later by the Library of Congress and incorporated in them, with doubtful propriety.

[9] Richmond *Enquirer*, Sept. 27, 1805.

[10] W. C. Ford; Bixby, p. xiv.

me.' " [11] In reply, among other things, Page said this: "Curses on the Tongue of Slander! Perdition seize the wretches who would open the scars of wounded Friendship, to gratify private resentment & party spirit." [12]

Even Henry Lee recognized Jefferson's desire to make amends. Said he: "I repeated [to Walker] my conviction of yr. sincere desire to do every thing which truth & honor would warrant to give peace to his mind & oblivion to the cause of his disquietude." [13] Also, he reported the mutual hope that old friendship might be restored. To some extent it was, when John Walker lay dying and his wife also was feeble and low. After Jefferson had retired from the presidency his neighbor, James Monroe, passed on to him the suggestion that a visit to his old friend at Belvoir would be considered as an act of great kindness and be received with much sensibility. Presumably he did not go, but he dispatched a gift of fruit which was gratefully acknowledged.[14] In the end perhaps John Walker concluded that Jefferson, as well as he, had received undeserved injury.

[11] March 18, 1803; LC, 130:22504–22505.

[12] Apr. 25, 1803; LC, 131:22632–22633.

[13] To Jefferson, Sept. 8, 1806; LC, 161:28252.

[14] Monroe to Jefferson, Sept. 4, 1809; Hugh Nelson to Jefferson, Sept. 4, 1809, both writing from Albemarle County; LC 188:33464–33465. The editor of Monroe's *Writings*, V, 102, says his letter was endorsed "not sent." It was endorsed by Jefferson, however, as received on Sept. 4.

Acknowledgments

FULL acknowledgment of the innumerable services and kindnesses done me while preparing this book is impossible. I have made specific reference to a great many of them at appropriate points in the notes, appendices, bibliography, and elsewhere, but my indebtedness to certain institutions and individuals is so great as to require special mention.

The first word of special thanks must go to the University of Virginia, not only because this project was conceived there years ago, but also because the concentrated work on this volume was begun and for nearly two years was centered there. The choice of locality was natural and appropriate, for no other place except Monticello itself is so hallowed by memories of Jefferson, and nowhere else can his beginnings and local setting be studied so advantageously. I was received as an old friend, with more than traditional hospitality, and the rich resources of the Alderman Library were at my entire disposal. My old colleague Harry Clemons, the librarian, and his associates — especially Jack Dalton, Miss Louise Savage, and, after they got back from the war, John C. Wyllie, Jr. and Francis L. Berkeley, Jr. — gave me the fullest possible co-operation. As one example of their continuing interest, Messrs. Clemons, Wyllie, and Berkeley read the chapter on the *Notes on Virginia* in galley proof and gave me the benefit of their comments. Of the many other people at the University who helped me with materials and suggestions mention should be made of Professors Thomas Perkins Abernethy (who kindly read several chapters), Edwin M. Betts, then working on his edition of the *Garden Book*, and James Southall Wilson. Miss Mary Topping did a vast amount of typing with a speed and accuracy which I have found difficulty in matching elsewhere.

Some months after I began to give my major attention to this work, a grant in support of it was made by the Rockefeller Foundation. Without this generous financial aid the continuance of the undertaking on its projected scale would have been impossible. For the arrangement which enabled me to continue it I am particularly indebted on the one hand to David H. Stevens, who sympathetically comprehended the requirements of the task from the beginning, and on the other to President John Lloyd Newcomb of the University of Virginia, who assumed the necessary institutional sponsorship of the grant. This volume was not completed until after I had taken up residence in Columbia University — where again I received whole-hearted co-operation — but it remains predominantly Virginian. The responsibility and faults of execution are wholly mine, but whatever credit may accrue to the book I want to share chiefly with the University where I did most of the work and the Foundation which so greatly aided it.

Obviously, the resources and facilities of the Library of Congress have been indispensable. I was permitted to go through the appropriate volumes of the Jefferson Papers there at the only time they were available during the abnormalities of the war period — when they were out of storage temporarily for purposes of cataloguing and microfilming. Mrs. Helen Duprey Bullock, who was indexing all of them while I was going through only a part, made invaluable suggestions as she went along, besides passing on many bits of information from her great store of knowledge about colonial Virginia and Jefferson's musical interests. Since the end of the war I have been able to work under highly favorable conditions in the Division of Manuscripts, receiving countless kindnesses from St. George L. Sioussat, Thomas P. Martin, and others; but most of the research work on this volume was done in the abnormal period. Among the many other persons in the Library of Congress who have helped me, special mention should be made of Miss E. Millicent Sowerby, who is making a thoroughgoing study of Jefferson's library of 1815, and who generously placed at my disposal far more of her extensive information about his books than I have yet been able to use.

As is stated more fully in the Bibliography, Julian P. Boyd greatly facilitated my work by permitting me to check my materials against the comprehensive files he has assembled at Princeton in the course of preparing a genuinely comprehensive edition of Jefferson's Papers. He and his associates, Lyman H. Butterfield and Mrs. Mina R. Bryan, were to the highest degree co-operative, as I tried to be in turn with them, and I shall always be grateful for their sympathy and understanding.

My use of the Jefferson materials in other repositories is sufficiently described in the Bibliography, but at least a word of appreciation should be spoken here. Since I enjoyed the hospitality of the Massachusetts Historical Society in the earliest stages of my detailed study of Jefferson, my debt to them is of long standing, and at all times they have been generous in granting permission to reproduce their unique materials. For similar courtesies I am indebted to the Huntington Library, and particularly to Miss Norma Cuthbert. The William L. Clements Library has no specialized Jefferson collection, but Randolph G. Adams informed me about rare documents and an interesting map, and granted permission to reproduce or use them.

In Virginia I am particularly indebted to the Virginia State Library (especially to William J. Van Schreeven), Colonial Williamsburg, Inc., the College of William and Mary, the Valentine Museum, Richmond (especially to Mrs. Louise T. Catterall), and the offices of the Clerks of Albemarle and Goochland Counties.

To Yale University I return belated thanks for the grant of a Sterling Senior Fellowship years ago. This enabled me to follow Jefferson to France, which I cannot do in this volume, but it also started me on my detailed research in his career. For this generosity Yale has received very slight return up to this time.

Despite the references in the notes, certain persons besides those already mentioned should be thanked individually:

Professor Verner W. Crane of the University of Michigan, for materials from England and suggestions about the reception of Jefferson's *Summary View* there;

Edward Dumbauld, Department of Justice, Washington, for personal comments supplementing his admirable *Thomas Jefferson, American Tourist*, and for reading the chapters on Jefferson's legal education and law practice;

Miss Adrienne Koch of Newcomb College, for reading chapters dealing with Jefferson's thought and making valuable comments on them;

Anthony Marc Lewis of Washington, for letting me see in advance of publication two admirable articles (listed in Bibliography);

William H. Peden, then at the University of Virginia, for materials and suggestions about Jefferson's books;

Charles W. Watts, then at the University of Virginia, for the privilege of examining his excellent unpublished study of Colonial Albemarle, and for valuable corroborative judgments on land holdings;

Miss Maude H. Woodfin of Westhampton College, for the use of her extensive notes on the early Jeffersons, and for many valuable comments on Virginia history.

Finally, I want to thank Douglas Southall Freeman of Richmond for his unfailing interest in this project and for invaluable suggestions about procedure — of which I fear I have availed myself most imperfectly; I want to express my appreciation of the patience and wise counsel of my publishers, Little, Brown and Company, who have gone far beyond the line of duty; and I want to express sympathy for my long-suffering wife in having a scholar and writer in the family who may be properly fastidious but who must often have seemed painfully slow.

List of Symbols and Short Titles[1]
Most Frequently Used in Footnotes

Account Book	Jefferson's informal account books, in various repositories. Cited by date only.
A.H.R.	*American Historical Review.*
Burgesses, Journals	*Journals of the House of Burgesses of Virginia.*
Burnett, *Letters*	*Letters of Members of the Continental Congress,* ed. by E. C. Burnett.
Commonplace Book	*Commonplace Book of Thomas Jefferson,* ed. by Gilbert Chinard.
Council Journals, Colonial Va.	*Executive Journals of the Council of Colonial Virginia.*
D.A.B.	*Dictionary of American Biography.*
Delegates, Journal	*Journal of the House of Delegates of Virginia.*
Domestic Life	*Domestic Life of Thomas Jefferson,* by Sarah N. Randolph.
Fitzpatrick	*Writings of George Washington,* ed. by J. C. Fitzpatrick.
Force	*American Archives,* ed. by Peter Force.
Ford	*Writings of Thomas Jefferson,* ed. by P. L. Ford.
Garden Book	*Thomas Jefferson's Garden Book,* annotated by E. M. Betts.
Hamilton	*Writings of James Monroe,* ed. by S. M. Hamilton.
HEH	Henry E. Huntington Library, San Marino, California. Unless otherwise indicated, references are to the Jefferson manuscripts.

[1] Repositories are designated by Roman capitals run together, the names of editors and authors are in Roman type, and the abbreviated titles of printed works are in italics. To avoid excess of italics, however, in the Bibliography which follows, long titles are in Roman. Further details about these works, and about others frequently used but more easily identified from the references in the notes, are in the Select Critical Bibliography which follows.

Hening	*The Statutes at Large: Being a Collection of All the Laws of Virginia*, ed. by W. W. Hening.
Hunt	*Writings of James Madison*, ed. by Gaillard Hunt.
JP	Papers of Thomas Jefferson, Princeton University; files for edition by J. P. Boyd. Citations include specific references to the sources made available through their courtesy.
L. & B.	*Writings of Thomas Jefferson*, ed. by A. A. Lipscomb and A. E. Bergh.
LC	Library of Congress. Unless otherwise indicated the references are to the Jefferson Papers.
Literary Bible	*Literary Bible of Thomas Jefferson*, ed. by Gilbert Chinard.
MHS	Massachusetts Historical Society. Unless otherwise indicated the references are to the Jefferson Papers.
O. L.	*Official Letters of the Governors of the State of Virginia*.
Papers, MHS	*Jefferson Papers, Collections Massachusetts Historical Society*, 7 ser., I.
Randall	*Life of Thomas Jefferson*, by H. S. Randall.
Tyler's Mag.	*Tyler's Quarterly Historical Magazine*.
UVA	Alderman Library, University of Virginia. Unless otherwise indicated the references are to the Jefferson manuscripts.
Va. Council Journals, State	*Journals of the Council of the State of Virginia*.
VHS	Virginia Historical Society.
VSL	Virginia State Library.
Va. Mag.	*Virginia Magazine of History and Biography*.
W. & M.	*William and Mary Quarterly Historical Magazine*.

Select Critical Bibliography

A. *Manuscripts*

THE most important collections of Jefferson's papers bearing on this period of his life are in the following repositories:

Library of Congress, Washington (LC)
Massachusetts Historical Society, Boston (MHS)
Alderman Library, University of Virginia, Charlottesville (UVA)
Virginia State Library, Richmond (VSL)
Henry E. Huntington Library, San Marino, California (HEH)

In the notes I have indicated the location of the manuscripts referred to, whether the latter are in these major collections or elsewhere.

The materials assembled at Princeton University, for the edition of the Papers of Thomas Jefferson that is being prepared there, comprehend all the manuscript collections along with items drawn from many other quarters. I have been privileged to check my own findings with these inclusive files, and thus to supplement them, although my procedure has necessarily been selective.

In the final volume of this work I will publish a detailed account of the manuscript sources for Jefferson's life as a whole, unless the publication of the Papers by Princeton is then so far advanced that such an account would be superfluous. Meanwhile, recourse may be had to the excellent survey by HELEN D. BULLOCK, "The Papers of Thomas Jefferson," *American Archivist*, IV (1941), 238–249. Also, I can repeat the observation already made by me in the Introduction that the personal sources before Jefferson became an important public figure are scanty in comparison with those for all the rest of his life.

The letters in the Library of Congress (LC) dating from the period 1743–1784 are chiefly to be found in the first eleven volumes of his Papers, in the Manuscript Division, though numerous items bearing on this period are in later volumes. (The documents are not all arranged chronologically, as is shown by the fact that I used an important one for the year 1779 from Volume 232. The explorer is now greatly aided, however, by the full index which is available.) To most students the value and fascination of these manuscripts lies less in the formal documents, the most important of which were long ago selected from the mass for printing, than in the letters. Through no other means can one gain such intimate acquaintance with Jefferson as by reading his letters just as he wrote them, and the investigator is likely to find more clues to the causes and meaning of events in such informal sources than in formal papers. I myself have found the letters to Jefferson even more illuminating than those from him, chiefly because fewer of the former have been printed and many of the latter repeat what is already well known. In my citations I have given names, dates, and volume and folio numbers, but I have distinguished between autograph letters, press copies, and drafts only when there was reason for doing so. Specific reference is also made in the notes to other collections in the Library of Congress which I have used. For this period the Papers of James Madison, Vols. I–V, and the Papers of the Continental Congress are the most important.

The Jefferson Papers in the Massachusetts Historical Society (MHS), which I began to go through many years ago, I have cited merely by names and dates. The originals of the Garden Book and Farm Book, of a number of the Account Books, and of many architectural drawings are in this collection, which is second in size only to that of the Library of Congress. In general it is more personal and less public, but there is overlapping all along the line.

The manuscripts at the University of Virginia (UVA), which are specially rich for family connections and local associations, fall into several categories besides the Jefferson Papers themselves — such as the Edgehill Randolph Papers, the Carr and Cary Papers, and the Maury Deposit of related materials — and some of them are the particular property of the McGregor Library of that institution, though all are housed together. I have tried to make proper acknowledgment in all citations. The checklist at the University of Virginia, which represented the first significant attempt to cover all the Jefferson materials everywhere, proved invaluable. The Alderman Library also has an important collection of photostats and microfilm, and I used this extensively. There are few other places where Jefferson can be studied so conveniently.

The materials in the Virginia State Library (VSL) bear chiefly on Jefferson's ancestors, land grants, patents, tax rolls, and the like (see details in Appendices I and II), and on his services as legislator and governor. Manuscript items dealing with the latter I saw chiefly in the reproductions at Princeton.

For this volume the materials at the Henry E. Huntington Library (HEH) are most valuable for the accounts and estate of Peter Jefferson and for Thomas Jefferson's legal career (see especially Appendix II and the notes on Chapter IX), and I used them mainly in photostatic form at the University of Virginia.

Other items were secured from the clerks' offices of Albemarle and Goochland Counties, Virginia; from Colonial Williamsburg, Inc.; from the William L. Clements Library, and elsewhere — as is shown sufficiently in the notes and Bibliography.

A further word should be said about the Account Books, which are cited only by date in this work and will probably not be published until late in the course of the Princeton project. Complete photostatic sets are at the University of Virginia, where I used them most, and in the Library of Congress. The location of the originals, for this period, is as follows:

1767–1770	LC	(Property of Gen. J. R. Kean)
1771	MHS	
1772	MHS	
1773	LC	
1774	MHS	
1775	HEH	
1776–1778	MHS	
1779–1782	LC	
1783–1784	MHS	

Partly because of physical difficulties these have not been used extensively by writers until relatively recent years (except by Randall, before they were scattered). By means of them it is possible to follow Jefferson's movements almost, if not quite, day by day, as Edward Dumbauld has done for the period of travel in *Thomas Jefferson, American Tourist*. The Account Books contain many items besides the financial, but unfortunately they do not often reveal what Jefferson was thinking about.

B. *Jefferson's Published Writings*

When the Papers now being edited at Princeton by Julian P. Boyd are published they will inevitably supersede all other printed collections. The chronological form of citation which I have followed will facilitate reference to that edition when it appears, for the arrangement there will be largely chronological. In the meantime, my page and volume references to existing printed collections, while not essential in all cases, will be useful. A good account of these existing collections is given by Helen D. Bullock in the article already cited. Using the other large ones only for purposes of supplementation, I have drawn chiefly on the two following:

The Writings of Thomas Jefferson, ed. by Paul Leicester Ford (10 vols., New York, G. P. Putnam's Sons, 1892–1899). This edition is well annotated, though with a slight bias against Jefferson; it is limited in scope, especially in non-political matters, but is generally reliable as to form; and I have cited it whenever possible.

The Writings of Thomas Jefferson, ed. by A. A. Lipscomb and A. E. Bergh (20 vols., Washington, 1903). Often referred to as the Memorial Edition, this is the most extensive collection and the easiest to acquire. It is practically without annotation and cannot be relied on for exact transcription; also, the arrangement is confusing and individual items are often hard to locate.

The following smaller collections are generally reliable:

The Jefferson Papers, Collections Massachusetts Historical Society, 7 ser., I (Boston, 1900).

Thomas Jefferson Correspondence. Printed from the Originals in the Collection of William K. Bixby. With notes by W. C. Ford (Boston, 1916). Very little of this volume falls in the period 1743–1784.

Official Letters of the Governors of the State of Virginia. Vol. II: The Letters of Thomas Jefferson. H. R. McIlwaine, gen. ed. (VSL, 1928). This preserves Jefferson's idiosyncrasies of capitalization and spelling and has useful notes. It is invaluable for the governorship.

The Letters of Lafayette and Jefferson. Introduction and notes by Gilbert Chinard (Baltimore, Johns Hopkins Press, 1929). Excellent within its limits.

Some Jefferson Correspondence, 1775–1787, ed. by W. C. Ford. (Reprinted from New-England Historical and Genealogical Register, 1901–1902). Letters to Jefferson.

Because of the letters and documents it contains, H. S. Randall's Life is to a considerable extent a sourcebook, and this is true to a lesser degree of Sarah N. Randolph's Domestic Life. Occasional letters from this period are in print elsewhere, but, having explored the main collections and the manuscripts, I have not always cited minor printed sources.

Although the references in the notes to particular writings of Jefferson may be deemed sufficient, the following separate publications deserve special mention:

The Commonplace Book of Thomas Jefferson. A Repertory of His Ideas on Government. With an Introduction and notes by Gilbert Chinard (Baltimore, Johns Hopkins Press, 1926). Invaluable for the period before the Declaration of Independence.

The Literary Bible of Thomas Jefferson. His Commonplace Book of Philosophers and Poets. With an introduction by Gilbert Chinard (Baltimore, Johns Hopkins Press, 1928). Important in showing the scope of Jefferson's early interests.

Thomas Jefferson's Garden Book, 1766–1824. Annotated by Edwin M. Betts (Philadelphia, American Philosophical Society, 1944). The painstaking notes extend to Jefferson's agricultural as well as horticultural interests.

Reports of Cases Determined in the General Court of Virginia. From 1730 to 1740, and from 1768 to 1772 (Charlottesville, published by the legatee of Jefferson's manuscript papers, 1829). This work contains a few of his own cases.

A Summary View of the Rights of British America. With an introducduction and a bibliographical note by Thomas P. Abernethy (New York, Scholars' Facsimiles & Reprints, 1943). Despite the excellence of this edition, I have cited the text in Ford, I, 421–447, for convenience of reference.

The Declaration of Independence. The Evolution of the Text as Shown in Facsimiles of Various Drafts by its Author, Thomas Jefferson. By Julian P. Boyd (revised edn., Princeton, Princeton University Press, 1945). Invaluable for the expert appraisal, as well as the documents.

Report of the Committee of Revisors [Jefferson, George Wythe, and Edmund Pendleton] Appointed by the General Assembly of Virginia in 1776 (Richmond, 1784).

Notes on the State of Virginia. This famous work appeared in many editions, but since it was not published until after Jefferson went to France its literary history does not greatly concern us here. For convenience of reference I have cited the text in Ford, III, 68–295.

C. *Official and Semiofficial Collections*

PROVINCE AND STATE OF VIRGINIA

Executive Journals of the Council of Colonial Virginia (5 vols., VSL, 1930–1945). The fifth volume ends with May 7, 1754.

Virginia Journals of Council reproduced from the Public Record Office of England. (Photostats UVA.) Cover the years 1726–1774.

Journals of the House of Burgesses of Virginia (6 vols., VSL, 1905–1906).

Calendar of Virginia State Papers and Other Manuscripts, 1652–1781, ed. by W. P. Palmer (Vol. I, Richmond, 1875).

The Statutes at Large, Being a Collection of All the Laws of Virginia, ed. by W. W. Hening (13 vols., Richmond, 1809–1823).

Journal of the House of Delegates of Virginia. Various volumes covering the years 1776–1785 (Richmond, 1827–1828).

Journals of the Council of State of Virginia, 1776–1781, ed. by H. R. McIlwaine (2 vols., VSL, 1931–1932). Unfortunately, the record for most of Jefferson's governorship is missing.

A Register of the General Assembly of Virginia, 1776–1918, and of the Constitutional Conventions, by E. G. Swem and J. W. Williams (Richmond, 1918).

BRITISH PARLIAMENT

Parliamentary History of England, Vol. XVI, 1765–1771; Vol. XVIII, 1774–1777 (T. C. Hansard, London, 1813). This and the following are of interest because of the comments on the affairs of America and Virginia.

SIR HENRY CAVENDISH. Debates of the House of Commons, 1768–1771 (2 vols., London, 1841).

UNITED STATES

Journals of the Continental Congress (34 vols., Washington, 1904–1936). The most important years for Jefferson are 1775–1776, 1783–1784.

PETER FORCE. American Archives (Washington, 9 vols., 1837–1853). Contains documents not readily accessible elsewhere.

Revolutionary Diplomatic Correspondence of the United States, ed. by Francis Wharton (6 vols., Washington, 1889).

CHURCH AND SCHOOL

WILLIAM S. PERRY, ed. Historical Collections Relating to the American Colonial Church. Vol. I, Virginia (Hartford, 1870).

"Journal of the Meetings of the President and Masters of William and Mary College" (1758–1764), in *W. & M.*, 1 ser., III, 62–64, 128–132, 195–197, 262–265; IV, 43–46, 130–132, 187–192; V, 224–229. Strictly speaking, not a collection, but cited here because of its value.

D. *Contemporary Writings* [1]

1. CORRESPONDENCE AND DIARIES

ADAMS, JOHN. Works, ed. by C. F. Adams (10 vols., Boston, 1856). Of value in this period, but of more later.

AMBLER FAMILY. "An Old Virginia Correspondence," *Atlantic Monthly*, Vol. 84 (July–December 1899), 535–549. Slight but illuminating bits about the British invasion.

---

[1] At various points in the footnotes, contemporary books and pamphlets known or supposed to have influenced Jefferson are referred to, but it has not seemed desirable to list them here.

BLAND, THEODORICK, JR. The Bland Papers, ed. by Charles Campbell (2 vols., Petersburg, 1840–1843). Several revealing letters.

BURNETT, E. C., ed. Letters of Members of the Continental Congress (8 vols., Washington, Carnegie Institution, 1921–1936). This important work gives some of the best clues to contemporary opinion.

BYRD, WILLIAM. The Secret Diary of William Byrd of Westover, 1709–1712. Ed. by Louis B. Wright and Marion Tinling (Richmond, Dietz Press, 1941). This and the following contain items about Jefferson's ancestors.

——. Another Secret Diary of William Byrd of Westover, 1739–1741. Ed. by Maude H. Woodfin, tr. and coll. by Marion Tinling (Richmond, Dietz Press, 1942).

CARTER, LANDON. Letter to George Washington (in Force, 5 ser., II, 1306). A direct attack on the repeal of entails.

CLARK, GEORGE ROGERS. "George Rogers Clark Papers"; Collections Illinois State Historical Library, VIII (1912). Valuable for Western developments in Jefferson's governorship and shortly before.

FITHIAN, PHILIP VICKERS. Journal and Letters, 1767–1774. Ed. by J. R. Williams (Princeton, Princeton University Library, 1900). This has no direct bearing on Jefferson but is probably the best social source-book for Virginia in its period. Cited by dates.

GILMER, GEORGE. "Papers, Military and Political, 1775–1778"; Collections Virginia Historical Society, n. s., Vol. VI (1887), 71–140. Gilmer was an intimate friend of Jefferson's.

JONES, JOSEPH. Letters of Joseph Jones of Virginia, 1777–1787. Ed. by W. C. Ford (New York, Historical Printing Club, 1889). Jones was the uncle of James Monroe.

LAFAYETTE, MARQUIS DE. Writings in:
CHINARD, GILBERT. Lafayette in Virginia: Unpublished Letters (Baltimore, Johns Hopkins Press, 1928).
GOTTSCHALK, LOUIS. Letters of Lafayette and Washington (New York, 1944).

LEE, RICHARD HENRY. Letters. Ed. by J. C. Ballagh (2 vols., New York, Macmillan, 1911–1914).

LEWIS, THOMAS. The Fairfax Line: Thomas Lewis's Journal of 1746. Footnotes and index by J. W. Wayland (New Market, Virginia, 1925). Of special interest for Peter Jefferson.

MADISON, JAMES. Writings. Ed. by Gaillard Hunt (9 vols., New York, G. P. Putnam's Sons, 1900–1910). Obviously an important supplement to Jefferson's own writings.

MAURY, JAMES. "A Dissertation on Education in the Form of a Letter from James Maury to Robert Jackson, July 17, 1762," ed. by Helen D. Bullock; Papers Albemarle County Hist. Soc., II (1941–1942), 36–60. Casts fresh light on Jefferson's first important teacher.

MONROE, JAMES. Writings. Ed. by S. M. Hamilton (7 vols., New York, G. P. Putnam's Sons, 1898–1903). Valuable for Jefferson at an even earlier date than the writings of Madison.

RIEDESEL, Mrs. General. Letters and Journals Relating to the War of the American Revolution. Trans. by W. L. Stone (Albany, 1867).

STILES, EZRA. Literary Diary of Ezra Stiles, ed. by F. B. Dexter (3 vols., New York, Charles Scribner's Sons, 1901).

WASHINGTON, GEORGE. Writings. Ed. by J. C. Fitzpatrick (33 vols., Washington, 1931–1941). Of special importance during Jefferson's governorship.

2. TRAVELS AND MEMOIRS

ANBUREY, THOMAS. Travels through the Interior Parts of America (2 vols., Boston and New York, 1923). Virginia part in Vol. II, covering the years 1779–1780.

BACON, EDMUND. See PIERSON, HAMILTON W.

BURNABY, ANDREW. Travels through North America. Reprinted from the 3d and enlarged edn. of 1798, ed. by R. R. Wilson (New York, Wessels & Bissell Co., 1904). The travels occurred in 1759–1760, and the 1st edn. was in 1775.

CHASTELLUX, MARQUIS DE. Travels in North America, in the Years 1780, 1781, and 1782 (2 vols., Dublin, 1787). Contains one of earliest descriptions of Jefferson and Monticello.

DARLINGTON, WILLIAM. Memorials of John Bartram and Humphrey Marshall (Philadelphia, 1849). Bartram visited Isham Randolph.

MAZZEI, PHILIP. Memoirs . . . 1730–1816. Trans. by Howard R. Marraro (New York, Columbia University Press, 1942). Unreliable for factual details but good for atmosphere.

PAGE, JOHN. "Autobiography," in Virginia Historical Register, III (Richmond, 1850), 142–151. A valuable bit from an old friend.

PIERSON, HAMILTON W. Jefferson at Monticello (New York, 1862). Reminiscences of Edmund Bacon, chief overseer and business manager of Jefferson's estate. Most valuable for a later period.

RANDOLPH, EDMUND. "Essay on the Revolutionary History of Virginia, 1774–1782," Va. Mag., XLIII–XLV. An approach to a contemporary judgment, though written after the events described.

RIEDESEL, MAJOR GENERAL. Memoirs, and Letters and Journals, during his Residence in America. Trans. by W. L. Stone (2 vols., Albany, 1868).

SCHOEPF, JOHANN DAVID. Travels in the Confederation. Trans. and ed. by A. J. Morrison (2 vols., Philadelphia, 1911). Covers the years 1783–1784.

SMYTH, J. F. D. A Tour in the United States of America (2 vols., London, 1784).

TARLETON, LIEUTENANT COLONEL. A History of the Campaigns of 1780 and 1781, in the Southern Provinces of North America (London and Dublin, 1787).

E. *Newspapers and Periodicals*

Newspapers are relatively unimportant for this phase of Jefferson's career, though the *Virginia Gazette*, Williamsburg, contains some details of information. There were concurrent papers of that title and publishers changed. My citations include the name of publishers, as well as dates.

The materials in the following historical periodicals, made accessible by E. G. Swem's indispensable *Virginia Historical Index* (2 vols., 4 parts, Roanoke, 1934) are of uneven quality but very considerable value, especially for the early chapters.

Tyler's Quarterly Historical Magazine (*Tyler's Mag.*).
Virginia Magazine of History and Biography (*Va. Mag.*).
William and Mary College Quarterly (*W. & M.*).

F. *Secondary Works and Articles*[2]

ABERNETHY, THOMAS PERKINS. Western Lands and the American Revolution (New York, 1937). Valuable for political alignments in Virginia as well as the land question.

——. Three Virginia Frontiers (Louisiana State Univ., 1940).

ANDERSON, DICE R. "Jefferson and the Virginia Constitution," *American Historical Review* (*A.H.R.*), XXXI, 750–754 (July 1916). An admirable brief study.

BECKER, CARL. The Declaration of Independence (New York, Peter Smith, 1940).

BEVERIDGE, ALBERT J. Life of John Marshall (4 vols., Boston, Houghton Mifflin Co., 1916–1919).

BLANTON, W. B. Medicine in Virginia in the Eighteenth Century (Richmond, 1931).

BOWERS, CLAUDE G. The Young Jefferson, 1743–1789 (Boston, Houghton Mifflin Co., 1945).

BOYD, JULIAN P. The Declaration of Independence. The Evolution of the Text (revised edn., Princeton, Princeton University Press, 1945). Already described in B, above.

[2] This very select list contains the titles of indispensable works and others to which I personally am most deeply indebted.

BRANT, IRVING. James Madison, the Virginia Revolutionist (Indianapolis and New York, Bobbs-Merrill Co., 1941).

BRIDENBAUGH, CARL AND JESSICA. Rebels and Gentlemen (New York, 1942).

BULLOCK, HELEN D. My Head and My Heart (New York, G. P. Putnam's Sons, 1945).

BURK, JOHN DALY. History of Virginia (4 vols., 1804–1816).

CHINARD, GILBERT. Thomas Jefferson, the Apostle of Americanism (Boston, Little, Brown and Co., 1939).

CRESSON, W. P. James Monroe (Chapel Hill, University of North Carolina Press, 1946).

CURTI, MERLE. Growth of American Thought (New York, Harper, 1943).

DAVIS, R. B. Francis Walker Gilmer (Richmond, Dietz Press, 1939).

DICKORE, M., ed. Two Unpublished Letters from Thomas Jefferson to His Relatives the Turpins (Oxford, Ohio, 1941).

DISBROW, NATALIE J. "Thomas Walker of Albemarle," Papers Albemarle County Historical Society, Vol. I (Charlottesville, 1941).

DORFMAN, JOSEPH. "Thomas Jefferson: Commercial Agrarian Democrat," in The Economic Mind in American Civilization (New York, The Macmillan Co., 1946), I, 433–447.

DUMBAULD, EDWARD. Thomas Jefferson: American Tourist (Norman, Okla., University of Oklahoma Press, 1946). Useful for this period, but much more for the next.

ECKENRODE, H. J. The Randolphs: The Story of a Virginia Family (Indianapolis and New York, Bobbs-Merrill Co., 1946).

——. The Revolution in Virginia (Boston, Houghton Mifflin Co., 1916). Best for the period before Jefferson's governorship. Sources now available for the latter change the picture considerably.

——. Separation of Church and State in Virginia (VSL, Richmond, 1910).

FITZPATRICK, JOHN C. The Spirit of the Revolution (Boston and New York, Houghton Mifflin Co., 1923).

FLIPPIN, P. S. The Royal Government in Virginia (New York, Columbia University Press, 1919).

GARLICK, R. C., JR. Philip Mazzei, Friend of Jefferson (Baltimore, Johns Hopkins Press, 1933).

GILMAN, DANIEL COIT. James Monroe (Boston and New York, Houghton Mifflin Co., 1911).

GOODWIN, EDWARD LEWIS. The Colonial Church in Virginia (Milwaukee and London, Morehouse Publishing Co. and A. R. Mowbray and Co., 1927).

GOODWIN, RUTHERFOORD. A Brief and True Report concerning Williamsburg in Virginia (3 ed., Williamsburg and Richmond, Colonial Williamsburg and Dietz Press, 1941). Because of the quotations, practically a sourcebook.

GOTTSCHALK, LOUIS. Lafayette and the Close of the American Revolution (Chicago, University of Chicago Press, 1942).

GRIGSBY, HUGH BLAIR. The Virginia Convention of 1776 (1855). Contains interesting sketches of Jefferson's contemporaries, as does the following.

——. History of the Virginia Federal Convention of 1788 (2 vols., 1890–1891).

HARRELL, I. S. Loyalism in Virginia (Durham, Duke University Press, 1926).

HARRISON, FAIRFAX. "The Northern Neck Maps of 1737–1747," W. & M., 2 ser., IV, 1–15 (January, 1924).

——. "A Portrait of Governor Fauquier," Fauquier County Historical Society Bulletin, No. 4 (1924), pp. 323–340.

HASTINGS, G. E. Life and Works of Francis Hopkinson (Chicago, University of Chicago Press, 1926).

HAZELTON, JOHN H. The Declaration of Independence: Its History (New York, 1906). Contains many documents.

HEMPHILL, W. E. George Wythe the Colonial Briton: A Biographical Study of the Pre-Revolutionary Era in Virginia (Doctoral Dissertation, UVA, 1937).

HENDERSON, ARCHIBALD. "Dr. Thomas Walker and the Loyal Company of Virginia," Proceedings American Antiquarian Society, n.s., XLI (Worcester, 1932), 77–178.

HENLINE, RUTH. "A Study of the Notes on the State of Virginia as an Evidence of Jefferson's Reaction against the Theories of the French Naturalists," Va. Mag., LV, 233–246 (July, 1947).

HENRY, WILLIAM WIRT. Patrick Henry. Life, Correspondence and Speeches (3 vols., New York, Charles Scribner's Sons, 1891). Too favorable but contains numerous letters and is thus an important source.

HILLDRUP, ROBERT L. Life and Times of Edmund Pendleton (Chapel Hill, University of North Carolina Press, 1939). Gives valuable clues to his relationship with Jefferson.

HONEYWELL, ROY J. The Educational Work of Thomas Jefferson (Cambridge, Massachusetts, Harvard University Press, 1931). An admirable monograph.

JENSEN, MERRILL. The Articles of Confederation (Madison, Wisconsin, University of Wisconsin Press, 1940).

468   SELECT CRITICAL BIBLIOGRAPHY

KEAN, JEFFERSON RANDOLPH. "Origin of the Monticello Graveyard"; "Genealogy of the Jefferson Eppes"; "Genealogy of the Jefferson Randolphs"; in *Ann. Report of the Monticello Asso.*, 1922, pp. 9–20; 1925, pp. 11–14; 1929, pp. 9–11, and thereafter.

KEIM, CLARENCE R. "Influence of Primogeniture and Entail in the Development of Virginia," in *University of Chicago Abstracts of Theses*, Humanistic Series, V, 289–292. Brief but important.

KIMBALL, FISKE. "In Search of Jefferson's Birthplace," *Va. Mag.*, LI (October 1943), 313–325. The best study of Shadwell.

———. "Jefferson and the Arts," *Proceedings American Philosophical Society* (hereafter abbreviated), CXXXVII (1943).

———. Thomas Jefferson, Architect (Boston, 1916). The classic work on the subject.

KIMBALL, MARIE. Jefferson: The Road to Glory, 1743 to 1776 (New York, Coward-McCann, Inc., 1943).

———. Jefferson, War and Peace, 1776 to 1784 (New York, Coward-McCann, Inc., 1947).

KIRKPATRICK, JOHN E. "The Constitutional Development of the College of William and Mary," *W. & M.*, 2 ser., VI, 95–108.

KOCH, ADRIENNE. The Philosophy of Thomas Jefferson (New York, Columbia University Press, 1943).

LEWIS, ANTHONY M. "Jefferson's *Summary View* as a Chart of Political Union, Its Place among Contemporary Tracts on the Connection with Britain." Article accepted by *William and Mary Quarterly*. Seen in advance by me through the courtesy of the author and editors.

———. "Jefferson and the Kentucky Pioneers, 1774–1781." Article accepted by the *Mississippi Valley Historical Review*. Seen in advance by me through the courtesy of the author and editors.

LINGLEY, CHARLES R. The Transition in Virginia from Colony to Commonwealth (New York, Columbia University Press, 1910). Still the best work on the subject.

MACMILLAN, MARGARET B. The War Governors in the American Revolution (New York, Columbia University Press, 1943). This monograph shows what other governors besides Jefferson faced.

MAURY, ANN. Memoirs of a Huguenot Family (New York, 1872).

MAURY, ANNE FONTAINE. Intimate Virginiana, A Century of Maury Travels by Land and Sea (Richmond, Dietz Press, 1941).

MEAD, EDWARD C. Historic Homes of the South-west Mountains, Virginia (Philadelphia, 1899).

MEADE, WILLIAM. Old Churches, Ministers and Families of Virginia (2 vols., Philadelphia, J. B. Lippincott Co., 1857).

MORRIS, ROLAND S. "Jefferson as a Lawyer," *Procs. Am. Philos. Soc.*, LXXXVII (1943), 211–215.

MORTON, LOUIS. Robert Carter of Nomini Hall (Williamsburg, Colonial Williamsburg, Inc., 1941).

NOCK, ALBERT JAY. Jefferson (Harcourt, Brace & Co., 1926).

PALMER, JOHN McAULEY. General Von Steuben (New Haven, Yale University Press, 1937). Distinctly anti-Jefferson but with some reason.

PEDEN, WILLIAM. "Some Notes concerning Thomas Jefferson's Libraries," W. & M., 3 ser., I, 265–274 (July 1944).
———. Thomas Jefferson: Book Collector (Doctoral Dissertation UVA, 1942). Very helpful for Jefferson's libraries.

PERRY, RALPH BARTON. Puritanism and Democracy (New York, Vanguard Press, 1944). Particularly valuable here for the treatment of the Declaration of Independence.

RANDALL, HENRY S. The Life of Thomas Jefferson (3 vols., New York, 1858). The most extensive of the biographies.

RANDOLPH, ROBERT ISHAM. The Randolphs of Virginia (Chicago, 1936).

RANDOLPH, SARAH N. The Domestic Life of Thomas Jefferson (New York, Harper and Bros., 1871). A 3d edn. by Mary R. N. McAdie (Cambridge, Massachusetts, 1939) does not follow the original pagination.

RAWLINGS, MARY. The Albemarle of Other Days (Charlottesville, Michie Co., 1925).

ROWLAND, KATE MASON. The Life of George Mason, 1725–1792, including his Speeches, Public Papers, and Correspondence (2 vols., New York, 1892). Practically a sourcebook.

SLAUGHTER, PHILIP. Memoir of Col. Joshua Fry (1880).

SMITH, GLENN CURTIS. "Parson's Cause," Tyler's Mag., XXI, 140–171, 193–306 (1939).

SMITH, PRESERVED. History of Modern Culture (New York, Henry Holt and Co., 1934).

STEVENS, B. F., ed., The Campaign in Virginia: An Exact Reprint of Six Rare Pamphlets on the Clinton-Cornwallis Controversy (2 vols., London, 1888).

SWEM, EARL G. "Maps Relating to Virginia," Bulletin VSL, VII (Richmond, 1914).

TRENT, WILLIAM P. "The Case of Josiah Philips," A.H.R., I, 444–454 (1896). Jefferson was involved in this.

TYLER, LYON G. Letters and Times of the Tylers (2 vols., Richmond, 1884–1885).

TYLER, MOSES COIT. Patrick Henry (Boston, Houghton Mifflin Co., 1887).

VOORHIS, MANNING C. The Land Grant Policy of Colonial Virginia, 1607–1774 (Doctoral Dissertation UVA, 1940).

WARREN, CHARLES. A History of the American Bar (Boston, Little, Brown and Co., 1913).

WATERMAN, THOMAS T. The Mansions of Virginia, 1706–1776 (Chapel Hill, University of North Carolina Press, 1945). Has much to say about Jefferson's architecture.

WERTENBAKER, T. J. The Old South (New York, Charles Scribner's Sons, 1942).

WILLIAM AND MARY. The History of the College of William and Mary from its Foundation, 1660, to 1874 (Richmond, 1874).

——. "Notes Relating to Some of the Students who Attended the College of William and Mary, 1753–1770," W. & M., 2 ser., I, 27–42.

——. A Provisional List of Alumni, Grammar School Students, Members of the Faculty, and Members of the Board of Visitors of the College of William and Mary in Virginia, from 1693 to 1888 (Richmond, 1941).

WIRT, WILLIAM. Sketches of the Life and Character of Patrick Henry (Philadelphia, 1817). Based in part on materials provided by Jefferson.

WOODFIN, MAUDE H. "Contemporary Opinion in Virginia of Thomas Jefferson," in Essays in Honor of William E. Dodd, ed. by Avery Craven (Chicago, University of Chicago Press, 1935), pp. 30–85. Gives the best clues I have found to local attitudes.

WOODS, EDGAR. History of Albemarle County, Virginia (Charlottesville, 1901).

WRIGHT, LOUIS B. The First Gentlemen of Virginia (San Marino, California, publication HEH, 1940).

——. "Thomas Jefferson and the Classics," in Procs. Amer. Philos. Soc., LXXXVIII (1943), 223–233.

Index

Index

Theater, attended by TJ in Williamsburg, 64, 125, 156

Thomson, Charles, secretary of Congress, 229; on *Notes on Virginia*, 375, 388; on scientific opportunities in America, 388–89; and committee of states, 418

Tocqueville, Alexis de, on laws of inheritance, 254; on slavery, 268

Townshend duties, opposed in Virginia, 135–37

Trade, Board of, in Virginia, 307, 322

Trist, Mrs. Elizabeth, TJ lodges with, 400; befriends Patsy, 404, 406

Tuckahoe, 4, 12; services of Peter Jefferson there, 19–20; description, 21–2

Tufton, 28, 436–37

Turpin, Thomas, executor of Peter Jefferson, 32, 438; letter of TJ to, 67; TJ occupies his house as governor, 302

Tyler, John, 98, 365, 411; student friend of TJ, 59, 64; hears Patrick Henry, 92; flees to Staunton, 359; on TJ's retirement (1782), 394; on TJ's foreign mission, 419–20

UNGER, JOHN LEWIS DE, Hessian admirer of TJ, 295–96

VINCENNES, 309

Virginia, Province, TJ's relation to its society, xiii–xv; Fry & Jefferson map, 25–6; social life and manners, 78, 86–7; political organization, 88; political alignments after 1765, 95–6; "burgessing," 129; House of Burgesses (1769), 131–38; Assembly prorogued by Dunmore, 169–70; Burgesses create committee of correspondence (1773), 170–71; fast resolutions (1774), 172–73; Convention (Aug. 1774), 180, 181; enforcement of Association, 192–93; Convention (Mar. 1775), 193–96; Assembly (June, 1775), 198–201; Convention (July–Aug. 1775), 208–09

Virginia, Commonwealth, constitution of 1776, 217, 235–40; designs for seal, 242–43; land question, 251–59; disestablishment of Church, 274–79; failure of TJ's educational proposals, 283–84; political organization, 238–40, 304–07, 379–82; collapse of government (1781), 352, 354–55; cession of Northwestern territory to U.S., 377, 412

WALKER, JOHN, friend of TJ from boyhood, 42, 57, 59, 153–54; in Burgesses with TJ, 142, 172, 180; on Albemarle committee, 192; on Council of State, 306; quarrel with TJ, 154–55, 447–48, 450–51; letter to Henry Lee, making charges against TJ, 449–50

Walker, Mrs. John (Elizabeth Moore), TJ's affair with, 153–55; 447–51

Walker, Dr. Thomas, 115, 252, 365, 377; neighbor and executor of Peter Jefferson, 28, 30, 32, 154, 438; in House of Burgesses, 129, 154; letter to, about *Notes on Virginia*, 376

War, Board of, in Virginia, 307, 321–22

Washington, George, 177, 203, 254–55, 306, 400; in House of Burgesses (1769), 134, 137; political standing (1774), 181; in Virginia convention (March, 1775), 195; as commander in chief, sets out for New England (1775), 202; urges better men in Congress, 290; on case of Henry Hamilton, 310–12; letters to, 321–24; receives report of Leslie's raid, 331–32; consulted about expedition against Detroit, 334–35; and Arnold's raid, 336–37, 339, 341–42; appealed to by TJ (1781), 353–54; thanks TJ for support, 354; talked of, as dictator, 361; congratulated by TJ, 365; described by Chastellux, 392; resigns commission, 406–07; discusses Society of Cincinnati with TJ, 413–15; compared with TJ, viii

Wayles, John (father-in-law of TJ), 156–57, 432; death and estate, 161–63; history of inheritance from him, 441–46

Wayles, Martha (wife of TJ), 294, 301; marries Bathurst Skelton, 156; marries TJ, 153, 159–60; description, 156–59, 397; children, 160, 165, 287, 349, 393, 434; inheritance, 162–63, 441–46; bad health, 214, 241, 245–46; last illness and death, 393–96; genealogy, 432

Weather, observations on, 77, 229, 288

Weedon, General George, of Virginia militia, 347

Whipple, William, writes TJ about natural history, 411

William and Mary, College of, account of in TJ's student days, 50–53, 59–60; TJ attempts to transform, 284–85; gives D.C.L. degree to TJ, 422

Williamsburg, description in TJ's stu-